REINVENTING THE MUSEUM

REINVENTING THE MUSEUM

The Evolving Conversation on the Paradigm Shift

Second Edition

EDITED BY GAIL ANDERSON

ALTAMIRA PRESS
A Division of Rowman & Littlefield Publishers, Inc.
Lanham • New York • Toronto • Plymouth, UK

Published by AltaMira Press
A division of Rowman & Littlefield Publishers, Inc.
A wholly owned subsidary of The Rowman & Littlefield Publishing Group, Inc.
4501 Forbes Boulevard, Suite 200, Lanham, Maryland 20706
http://www.altamirapress.com

10 Thornbury, Plymouth PL6 7PP, United Kingdom

British Library Cataloguing in Publication Information Available

Library of Congress Cataloging-in-Publication Data

Reinventing the museum : the evolving conversation on the paradigm shift / edited by Gail
Anderson. -- 2nd ed.
     p. cm.
 Includes bibliographical references and index.
 ISBN 978-0-7591-1964-2 (cloth : alk. paper) — ISBN 978-0-7591-1965-9 (pbk. : alk. paper)
 1. Museums—Philosophy. 2. Museums—Social aspects. 3. Museums—Historiography. 4.
Cultural property—Protection. I. Anderson, Gail, 1954- II. Title.
 AM7.R435 2012
 069.01—dc23
                                                                                    2011034126

Printed in the United States of America

Lovingly dedicated to my parents
Barbara and Fred

With gratitude for a lifetime of love and encouragement

CONTENTS

Part II: The Emerging 21st-Century Ideology   191

Part III: Perspectives on Meaningful Public Engagement   287

---

* Indicates chapters pubished in the first edition.

Preface

REINVENTING THE MUSEUM: The Evolving *Conversation on the Paradigm Shift* is the second edition of the 2004 publication *Reinventing the Museum: Historical and Contemporary Perspectives on the Paradigm Shift*. This volume continues the conversation begun in the first edition by capturing the current and ongoing dialogue about the reinvention of museums. Containing forty-four thought-provoking essays by a diverse selection of authors from within the museum field and beyond, this book celebrates multiple perspectives and new frameworks that remind us where we come from and challenge the thinking that will move us forward.

Organization

Like the first edition, this anthology is organized into five topic areas that capture the key shifts in thinking about the role of museums and the complexity of their operations. The structure of this second edition mirrors the shift toward integrative thinking that has been occurring in the field. The framework that follows sets the stage for the book with a discussion about the broad concept of reinventing the museum, the philosophical framework for this book, and illustrated in The Reinventing Tool. The Reinventing Tool has been revised significantly to more fully reflect contemporary thinking and trends. The five distinctive sections are referred to as parts that create the structure of the book. The selected chapters or writings that are featured are referred to as chapters. The five parts highlight hallmarks of the changing paradigm for museums: Part I: Pivotal Moments in the 20th-Century Dialogue; Part II: The Emerging 21st Century Ideology; Part III: Perspectives on Meaningful Public Engagement; Part IV: Shifting Frameworks and Infrastructures; and, Part V: Strategic Implications for Leadership. Each part has an introduction that relates the discussion to the reinvention concept and frames the chapters that follow with a brief statement about each author and the focus and emphasis of their writing.

Part I features seminal moments that embrace different aspects of the evolving role of museums in the 20th century. The first few chapters are from the first half of the century while most chapters date from the last three decades. The heavy representation from this period is in part due to the proliferation of writing during that period and due to the fact that each chapter represents a depth and sophistication of discourse that captured the tenor of thinking at the close of the 20th century. The goal of this anthology is to present the best thinking in the field on the evolving role of the museum and contemporary museum practice.

The chapters featured in the remaining parts date from 2000 forward. Part II continues the discussion about the evolving ideology of museums in the early part of the 21st century, revealing how the issues continue to be redefined and refined. Part III focuses on the conversation around meaningful public engagement and all of its implications on an institution wide level. Part IV features chapters that connect the ideology to emerging frameworks supporting the more integrative approach to operating museums. Part V outlines implications for trustee and staff pointing to the fact that leadership is the key to the reinvention process.

Essay Selection

The selected works address the paradigm shift in museums from a field-wide perspective. Exemplary works were culled from a broad review of the literature in a process that unfolded over a year-long period. Many articles and books were reviewed and considered. One goal was to select an array of perspectives that represented the best thinking on issues and concepts that museums are addressing in contemporary times. A second goal was to select works that captured the essence of the dialogue from a philosophical or issue-based perspective rather than from a how-to perspective. Thankfully, an excellent array of resources is available from professional associations, conference proceedings, and various print and on-line sources to fill that important need.

Each selected chapter demonstrates clear writing and sound reasoning, and references the evolution and issues of the museum profession. Some provide a helpful historical sketch surrounding a topic, still others feature international examples, and many have excellent bibliographies. A deliberate effort was made to include international authors when possible, although overall there is a predominantly American focus. In an effort to show the broadest representation of writers, most authors are represented only once, with the exception of prolific author and contemporary museum critic, the late Stephen Weil; educator, theorist, and researcher John Falk; and well-known speaker, writer, and provocateur, Elaine Heumann Gurian. A balance of male and female perspectives, and diversity in background and expertise, was also sought. The represented authors are committed to the vitality of museums as cultural and educational institutions in society and in many cases are lobbying for substantial change, as the reader will discover.

The chapters transcend variations in museum type, size, and location. An early decision was made not to select essays with a heavy emphasis on any particular type of museum or one highlighting a single institution. Likewise, trying to cover the content issues represented in the diverse museum community was deemed unrealistic and outside the scope and goals of this publication. Although some of the featured chapters reveal leanings toward one area of specialization or another, the overriding qualities of the piece merited inclusion in the book. The editor's interest in leadership, cultural history, and anthropology may be evident to the reader, yet the goal was to be as evenhanded as possible in selecting a range of perspectives.

In the end, the overarching goal was to build a book that was balanced in content and useful to trustees, volunteers, museum students, and professionals—whether seasoned, midcareer, or newcomer.

Recommendations for the Reader

Reinventing the Museum: The Evolving Conversation on the Paradigm Shift has many intended uses that include:

- *outlining the evolution and dialogue about the museum* as an institution in order to understand the roots of contemporary issues and the future of museums;
- *highlighting museum leaders* in the field who have made and continue to make significant contributions to our understanding and thinking about museums;
- *providing inspiration for discussion and dialogue* among staff members, trustees, and students about the issues affecting museums to influence practice and instigate meaningful change;
- *offering a basic review of the literature* for students and professors of museum studies while stimulating dialogue about the evolving issues in the field;
- *encouraging* students, colleagues, and trustees to continue the dialogue in the field, to contribute to the literature on museums, and to challenge the museum community to keep the conversation fresh and moving forward.

In recognition of the many excellent essays that could not be included in this anthology, the reader is encouraged to seek out other related books and articles. It is also recommended that references about museum techniques be consulted to complement the philosophical ideologies presented in this volume. At the end of the book is a select bibliography representing additional recommended reading. Finally, as the title suggests, this is an evolving conversation and those committed to a viable future for museums have an obligation to continue the discussion.

Acknowledgments

IT IS ONLY FITTING TO BEGIN MY ACKNOWLEDGMENTS by extending my profound gratitude and respect to all the museum professionals represented in this volume. Their thoughtful writing and perspectives have been instrumental in shaping the current thinking about museums. I am inspired by their eloquence, courage, and tenacity to push the field forward.

Several colleagues played a key role in reviewing the book at different stages in its development, providing guidance as the book took shape, suggesting chapters for consideration, and challenging my own perspective and thinking. My deep indebtedness goes to colleagues who provided invaluable support and ideas including Leslie Bedford, Jane Clark Chermayeff, Dr. Selma Holo, Dr. Robert Janes, Margaret Kadayama, Wendy Luke, Adrienne McGraw, Kathleen McLean, Marjorie Schwarzer, Marsha Semmel, Susan Spero, Wendy Meluch, and numerous others. Elaine Heumann Gurian, early on, provided a thorough critique of the last edition, along with insight about the direction for this volume. To my long-time friend, colleague, and mentor to many, I extend my respect and gratitude to Stephen Weil, who encouraged many museum professionals to find their voice and speak out about the issues facing museums. While he is no longer with us, his support of my work on the first volume was significant and remained a source of inspiration for the work for this edition. His contribution to the field remains indelible and profound.

Cheryl Kessler and Aubrey Wilder, who volunteered for the creation of the first volume, had the courage to look at the framework of the second one and provide useful insights. I am very indebted to Georgianna La Goria and Aubrey Wilder who read my writing near the end of the production of this book, providing candid feedback and pushing me to achieve greater clarity. Rachel Faust contributed valuable research in the area of collection-related issues.

Seair Lorentz, the Research Associate and Project Manager for this project, dedicated hundreds of hours to helping build this second edition. Thank you for your tireless effort in conducting research, maintaining project records, attending numerous work sessions, reading endlessly, and participating in the ongoing review and critique of chapters for inclusion. I extend my deep gratitude for withstanding the thankless job of securing copyright permissions. Simply put, this book would not have happened without your most significant contribution.

And to my family, John and Maya, your patience, love, and support has made undertaking this project possible. Maya, thank you for giving up some of our time together so that I could work on this book, and for making me laugh when I needed to lighten up. John, thank you for your support throughout the long process of creating this book, and for challenging my thinking and reminding me to stick to my convictions.

A Framework
Reinventing the Museum

THROUGHOUT THE HISTORY OF MUSEUMS, museum leaders have been grappling with the evolving transformation of the museum and its role in society. During the 20th century and into the beginning of the 21st, every aspect of museum operations has at one point or another been placed under the microscope and examined for its clarity of focus and function relative to furthering the role of the museum as a cultural and educational institution. Like most institutions, museums are not immune to local or world events, issues, and trends—or an increasingly discriminating and discerning public. Survival for museums today requires understanding the external forces that impact museums coupled with institutional reflection to define a strategic direction. Institutional reflection must include the examination of values and assumptions, the refinement of the mission and the vision to assure relevancy, and an assessment of institutional capacity in order to refine institutional effectiveness and public impact.

Thus, the challenge for museums to remain relevant in society is an ongoing process of assessment that is both external and internal—that is, given the contemporary environment and emergent issues (external) and the museum's capabilities and available resources (internal): What role should the museum assume? What services can the museum offer that will be meaningful for the public in a complex and ever changing world? What defines relevancy for each museum in their unique setting? The interplay of these complex issues creates a distinct reality for each museum, but the path that is ultimately chosen rests with the leadership of the governing board and staff who must balance the choices carefully. Visionary and astute leaders have developed the ability to juggle a changing backdrop of challenges with their institution's ability to do strategic and meaningful work that is relevant to its public and constituents.

The change museums are confronting in the twenty-first century is complex: the explosion of technological innovations has expanded the way ideas and information are generated, exchanged, and accessed; social media allows people to connect whenever and wherever they like about topics of their choice; new regulations about nonprofit accountability heightens public scrutiny; the inter-connectedness between people and communities across continents has shifted the sense of belonging and the place of museums on the world's cultural stage; limited and diminishing natural resources impacts sustainability; global economic volatility translates to financial unpredictability; and political unrest often leads to redefined national agendas and deposed dictators. All of these are reminders that the events or trends experienced in one nation can be felt on the other side of the globe almost instantaneously. Such sweeping changes abroad and closer to home challenge long-held assumptions prompting new innovations, triggering the creation of different models of operation, and causing a fundamental shift in the role of museums in today's world.

Reinventing the museum is not just adding a program, reinstalling a gallery, or increasing financial reserves—it is a systemic shift in attitude, purpose, alignment, and execution. Many museums are repositioning themselves to be central players in their communities, while others are merging or creating alliances to increase capac-ity and survive. Other museums are tackling the challenging work of reorganizing into a more integrated, holistic, and less compartmentalized structure—better able to respond with agility, greater efficiency, and higher levels of productivity. Some museum leaders have shifted to a collaborative spirit and a shared commitment to fulfilling a greater public service mission.

The Reinventing the Museum Tool, shown on pages 3 and 4, captures the essence of the trends in the paradigm shift and provides the underpinnings of the structure and concepts presented in this volume. The parallel lists of terms were developed over more than three decades of working with museum leaders and listening to conversations about the changing role of museums. The terms on the left depict the assumptions and values that reflect the stance of the traditional mu-seums. The terms on the right illustrate the characteristics typical of the reinvented museum. Please note that the term *traditional* is not intended to be pejorative but is rather a term for reference in this particular dialogue to illustrate one viewpoint around the museum as institution and concept.

Within an institution, an illuminating dialogue can unfold using the Reinvent-ing the Museum Tool to discuss where a museum currently stands in the con-tinuum between the traditional museum and the reinvented museum and where it wishes to be. Issues about relevancy, institutional vitality, and alignment with con-temporary museum practice can be discussed relative to a specific institution. Such a dialogue may point to a need to revisit the mission or shape a new vision in order to embrace the institution's greatest potential within today's complex environment. In the process of self-examination, the reinvented museum is likely to modify some traditions and retire others. In its most dramatic iteration, the conversation may cause a museum to overhaul the institution systematically at all levels of operation, including organizational restructuring. Each museum will determine which aspects of its operation to retain and which new strategies to adopt, while charting a path that is realistic and appropriate for its capacity, location, and focus. Further, some

Reinventing the Museum Tool

Traditional Museum	*Reinvented Museum*
Institutional Values	
Values as ancillary	Values as core tenets
Institutional viewpoint	Global perspective
Insular society	Civic engagement
Social activity	Social responsibility
Collection driven	Audience focused
Limited representation	Broad representation
Internal perspective	Community participant
Business as usual	Reflective practice
Accepted realities	Culture of inquiry
Voice of authority	Multiple viewpoints
Information provider	Knowledge facilitator
Individual roles	Collective accountability
Focused on past	Relevant and forward-looking
Reserved	Compassionate
Governance	
Mission as document	Mission driven
Exclusive	Inclusive
Reactive	Proactive
Ethnocentric	Multicultural
Internal focus	Expansive perspective
Individual vision	Institutional vision
Single visionary leader	Shared leadership
Obligatory oversight	Inspired investment
Assumed value	Earned value
Good intentions	Public accountability
Private	Transparent
Venerability	Humility
Caretaker	Steward
Managing	Governing
Stability	Sustainability

Reinventing the Museum Tool

Traditional Museum	Reinvented Museum
Management Strategies	
Inwardly driven	Responsive to stakeholders
Various activities	Strategic priorities
Selling	Marketing
Assumptions about audiences	Knowledge about audiences
Hierarchical structure	Learning organization
Unilateral decision-making	Collective decision-making
Limited access	Open access
Segregated functions	Integrated operations
Compartmentalized goals	Holistic, shared goals
Status quo	Informed risk-taking
Fund development	Entrepreneurial
Individual work	Collaboration
Static role	Strategic positioning
Communication Ideology	
Privileged information	Accessible information
Suppressed differences	Welcomed differences
Debate/discussion	Dialogue
Enforced directives	Interactive choices
One-way communication	Two-way communication
Keeper of knowledge	Exchange of knowledge
Presenting	Facilitating
Two-dimensional	Multi-dimensional
Analog	Virtual
Protective	Welcoming

Note: This chart was originally presented in *Museum Mission Statements: Building a Distinct Identity,* edited and written by Gail Anderson and published by the American Association of Museums Technical Information Service in 1998. It was featured in the 2004 edition of *Reinventing the Museum* and has been significantly updated for this edition.

institutions may decide that their desired position on the continuum is mid-way or at a place that represents compromise. Regardless of the position, the point is to be deliberate, honest, and clear.

At the onset of tackling any level of reinvention or transformation is the need to engage diverse stakeholders in the conversation that a fundamental shift needs to take place. Writings and reflections about change, the topic of many management and leadership experts, reveal one overriding constant: change is complex and takes a unique shape depending on the individuals involved, the history of the institution, and the capacity of leadership to bring along the key players in a sustained process. Acceptance of the need for change may well be the biggest barrier to overcome. It is equally important to understand that an institutional reinvention tends to unfold in phases that can span years. Perseverance is needed at many levels for a new institutional paradigm to fully take hold and be internalized and sustained over time.

To be blunt, significant change or reinvention will not happen without a united, enlightened board in partnership with a visionary director who can coalesce the staff and volunteer corps to embrace a new reality and new ways of being. Together, this leadership team must build consensus with stakeholders about a shared vision for the future while inspiring board, staff, and volunteers to work together to undertake transformation. The director must work in a healthy partnership with trustees to foster optimal functioning of the board in their governance capacity while nurturing and growing the talents of staff and incorporating the contributions of volunteers in meaningful ways. The immediacy of change requires a deft juggling act of building resources and capacity while adjusting the museum's public persona and offerings.

What does the reinvented museum look like? The following brief discussions illustrate some of the characteristics of the reinvented museum as listed in the above table.

Institutional Values

Institutional values embody the underlying beliefs and tenets of a museum that reveal its core essence. Values should permeate the organization and be embraced by the people who work on its behalf—trustees, staff, and volunteers—365 days a year. The reinvented museum views values as guideposts for operating responsibly and as tools for communicating what matters to stakeholders and constituents. Values complement the mission, the reason the institution exists, and the vision, the strategic target of accomplishment set in the future. The centrality of the public, learning, and civic engagement embody some of the most significant shifts in institutional values for museums. Collections—historically viewed as the center of museum activities—have moved to a supporting role that advances the educational impact of the museum. The collection holdings are no longer viewed as the sole measure of value for a museum; rather, the relevant and effective role of the museum in service to its public has become the central measure of value.

With values as a touchstone, museum leaders ensure that the organizational culture embodies those values, translating them into practice internally while trustees, staff, and volunteers are held accountable for upholding them. Institutional values naturally influence priorities and the nature of work within the museum while informing the manner in which the museum engages with its public and communities. Values translate into behavior at the organizational level and within the board, staff, and volunteers as they interact with others in their efforts to build visibility and an institutional presence, create meaningful opportunities for public participation, and raise financial support.

At the core, public and civic engagement continues to have a central role on museum operations. With increased frequency, the public and members of communities are invited into the conversation about the future of museums providing useful perspectives about the content of relevant exhibitions, programs, and collections. The visitor/user is regarded as both customer and guest, to be served with the goal of achieving satisfaction and building a broader constituency, and in many cases long-lasting relationships. Thus, offering effective visitor services and focusing on the visitor experience have become integral to daily operations. Today, enlightened museum leaders know that this shift in values translates to a shift in operations, necessitating a multilayered approach that calls on market and audience research, trend tracking and analysis, and new criteria and processes for decision-making and priority-setting. The reinvented museum shifts the focus from internal to global, singular voice to multiple perspectives, and focused on the past to forward-looking.

Each museum must define their core values and understand fully how those values translate into reality, action, and meaning for the people and communities that the museum serves. Values are not just words—they are principles that guide the institution on all levels—the people, nature of communications, sense of place, and reason for being.

Governance

The governing body of a museum, the board of trustees, provides strategic direction, fiduciary oversight, and leadership for the proper and ethical care of a museum's resources in support of fulfilling its public service mission, while assuring long-term vitality and sustainability. The role of the governing body is critical: an effective board of trustees can enable a museum to move forward and fulfill its role in the community, or an ineffectual board may impede the growth of a museum, cause it to function at a level far below its full potential, or even jeopardize its future. Leaving behind the elitist club image of boards, the reinvented board strives to diversify its membership in order to serve its community and fulfill its mission more effectively. An enlightened board of trustees uses the mission and vision statements as essential management tools for making decisions and guiding the work of the museum. The role of a trustee is clear and focused on shaping policies to guide the museum's work; upholding legal, ethical, and professional standards; and ensuring prudent financial management and adequate resources to support the museum. Boards require committed individuals who understand not only the range of issues and complexities unique to museum governance in contemporary times but also the difference between their role and the role of implementation that is delegated to staff.

The reinvented board understands that it is accountable to the public and has a social responsibility to further the work of the museum in the public interest. The reinvented board builds consensus and takes actions in service to the museum and its community—actions that increase the value of the museum for the public. A culture of inquiry, strategic thinking, and accountability are pillars of the reinvented board. Finally, the board and staff understand that earning public trust is an ongoing endeavor and goal of the entire museum.

Management Strategies

Inspired management strategies are a blend of innovative approaches balanced with a realistic view of institutional capacity and resources. Solid strategies reflect and foster clarity and flexibility and build institutional robustness. Some core management tools include clear roles and responsibilities for trustees, staff, and volunteers; a well-defined and relevant mission, values, and vision; and a strategic plan that is responsive, holistic, and integrated. Some management practices such as knowledge of market trends, once the purview of the corporate world, are now understood to be essential ingredients for enabling the museum to survive and achieve its mission. In the reinvented museum, philosophy translates into practice, and practice reflects philosophy, values, and mission.

In the reinvented museum, assumptions are scrutinized and questioned as a matter of course. Regular evaluation of museum operations and public services provides ongoing feedback that keeps the museum on track and responsive to the shifts in public attitudes. Staff understands how their role advances the mission and adds value to the work of the museum. Clear delineated decision-making processes reflect institutional values with an understood accountability for actions taken. A museum's participation in the cultural life of the community is not taken for granted. Understanding the challenges of the marketplace and dynamism of communities is viewed as an essential ingredient for informed decision-making. There are no isolated silos of operation. Instead, a holistic and interrelated mode of operations is fostered, supported by a deliberate and healthy organizational culture and reinvented institutional structure that fosters innovation, individual successes, and informed risk-taking. All aspects of museum operations support each other and contribute to the advancement of the mission. Thus, the reinvented museum is responsive, exudes a clear identity and public image, and is able to implement the appropriate strategies to ensure a healthy and viable institution.

Communication Ideology

Effective communication and mutual respect among trustees, staff, and volunteers are critical to a museum's ability to be effective, especially the individuals who are in contact with the public. Key stakeholders need to understand all parts of the whole and how each individual, no matter his or her role, enables the institution to move forward. Further, the responsibilities of trustees, staff, and volunteers are to be regarded with the highest ethical integrity given the institution's public service mission.

Sharing information openly within the organization is fundamental for staff and volunteers to understand and support institutional decisions and to participate with appropriate responses to pressing problems such as financial shortfalls. In order to achieve this, an organizational culture that welcomes diverse points of view and fosters respectful dialogue is essential to staff so they feel safe to voice their opinions and share constructive ideas. Acceptance, trust, mutual respect, and accountability are at the heart of the reinvented museum's organizational culture and communication philosophy.

Internal communication is only part of the equation given the fundamental importance of museums interacting with the public. The traditional communication ideology of the museum has been to see the museum as the holder of knowledge and truth with a responsibility to exercise one-way communication *to* the public. In the reinvented museum, communication *between* museum and public is exemplified by a mutually respectful relationship; the ideology of two-way communication *with* the public creates a more responsive interchange of ideas and shared understandings supplanting the more traditional, paternal approach.

The meshing of internal and external communication in the reinvented museum can spawn creative problem solving and team building. Exhibition development has often been the exemplar of this kind of thinking with teams of audience advocates, community members, facilitators, interpreters, designers, and people with other expertise coming together to fulfill the goal of the exhibit and to grasp the needs of the exhibit's target audience. These cross-functional and diverse groups help facilitate a dialogue that merges concerns and messages into a product that is more effective as a result of shared responsibility, planning, and blend of diverse perspectives. This co-created style of working needs to resonate in many other aspects of museum operations to build more robust, integrated and resilient institutions. This particular example reflects many elements of the reinvented museum—integrated management, collaboration, social responsibility, and healthy communication, to name a few.

Conclusion

The central underpinnings of the Reinventing the Museum Tool and the philosophy of this book are rooted in convictions about museums as cultural institutions that have the power to make a difference. At the heart of this conviction is a belief that *a fundamental shift in ideology and practice is essential for museums to remain relevant and integral in a twenty-first-century world*. Thus, the core beliefs evident throughout this volume are:

- A global world of interconnectedness requires a shift to a more expansive and inspired thinking of museums as integral players in contributing to meaningful change for the future.

- Museums are central to the vitality and health of towns, cities, and regions and can serve as gathering places for building community and dialogue around contemporary issues.
- Meaningful public engagement and financial sustainability go hand in hand and are the business and responsibility of all trustees and staff. Every action and decision made impacts the museum's long-term vitality on behalf of its public.
- The fulfillment of the social contract with the public necessitates serving, engaging, and reflecting diverse people and communities in equitable institutional practice and openness to multiple perspectives.
- Collections, a distinguishing characteristic of museums, can illustrate and illuminate stories, aspects of contemporary life, people, and the natural world in ways we are just beginning to explore.
- Public engagement is on site, off site and online, and is defined and created where people decide to make it happen.
- Informed, humble, passionate, and enlightened leadership must be present at all levels in order to further the work of museums in a responsible, meaningful, and relevant way.
- The contemporary museum management toolkit ensures a relevant mission, vision, and values on behalf of the public emboldened by strategies that foster responsiveness, flexibility, innovation, and informed risk-taking.

The dialogue in the museum community will continue in the years ahead as new external pressures and new challenges stir museum leaders to reflect on and reassess their work. Keeping the dialogue alive on the local, regional, national, and international stage keeps the ongoing process of revitalization alive and helps avoid stagnation. The reinvented museum is not formulaic, nor is it one size fits all. The reinvented museum is a living organization that will continue to evolve in the years ahead.

The discourse that unfolds in *Reinventing the Museum: The Evolving Conversation on the Paradigm Shift* reveals the diverse levels and foci of the evolution of the museum over the past century from the perspective of some of its most vocal and gifted leaders. When considering the relevance of John Cotton Dana's "The Gloom of the Museum," written almost a century ago, it becomes clear how long it has taken for some of his ideas and challenges to be embraced. In today's museum community, some museums are exercising extraordinary courage and leadership to embrace fundamental change, yet for too many it takes a financial crisis and the threat of going out of business to spur a call to action. This is a time of unprecedented change—the rules of the game have changed. The creative ideas and new frameworks presented by the authors in this collection of essays provide a springboard for inspiration, innovation, and revitalization—fuel for the ongoing conversation on the paradigm shift—and a challenge to courageous and visionary leaders to maximize the potential of museums in contemporary society.

PIVOTAL MOMENTS IN THE 20TH-CENTURY DIALOGUE

I

THE LAST CENTURY OF SELF-REFLECTION—the beginning of the reinvention of the museum—was initiated by the general movement of dismantling the museum as an ivory tower of exclusivity and toward the construction of a more socially responsive cultural institution in service to the public. While the seeds of change were sown by forward-looking thinkers, like John Cotton Dana in the early 1900s, it has taken almost a century of debate and discussion for the museum profession to embrace some of the core tenets espoused by Dana and other leading thinkers. The evolving dialogue and general acceptance of the new ideology within a much broader segment of the museum profession indicates that the paradigm shift from collection-driven institutions to visitor-centered, community-responsive museums has largely taken root. Policy statements and program initiatives advanced by museum associations reinforce this, while some innovative leaders introduce new practices to challenge established thinking. But, as with any shift or realignment, each museum and museum professional interprets and applies new perspectives in ways unique to their specific institution and to the extent leadership capacity can initiate and sustain the momentum required for institutional transformation. At the heart of the reinvention of the museum is the imperative that museums have the unique opportunity to contribute good in society.

The chapters in this part capture the evolution of the role of museums over the past hundred years. Presented chronologically, these chapters convey some of the milestones in the dialogue about museums and their role in society. Some of the articles enumerate a shift in thinking while others capture a pivotal moment triggering significant change in field-wide practice. This carefully selected set of articles documents the unfolding thinking of the last century. Today's museum professionals stand on the shoulders of these inspiring writers, and leaders who challenged the field to think anew.

It is appropriate that John Cotton Dana, the innovative director of The Newark Museum in the early 1900s, introduces this part. Dana, recognized by museum professionals as a museum pioneer, has been heralded by generations of museum professionals for his conviction to publicly challenge museums about their then-current practices of serving an elite group of patrons and not the broader public. In one of his most noteworthy articles, "The Gloom of the Museum," written in 1917 and a part of his *The New Museum Series,* Dana encouraged museum leaders to take their message to the greater community and to establish new methods for reaching a broader public, including dismantling an exclusive attitude about who should benefit from museums. He was a revolutionary spokesperson in his own right, and today he is still regarded as one of the most visionary museum leaders in American museum history.

Theodore Low, a museum educator at the Metropolitan Museum of Art and another widely acknowledged contributor to the national discourse, was commissioned by the American Association of Museums (AAM) to write about museums. In his seminal piece "What Is the Museum?" written in 1942 while the world was at war, Low makes the case that the primary role of museums is as an educational institution contributing to society. He launched a discussion that has dominated professional discourse for decades in which he argues for recognizing the museum as a vital educational resource along with schools and universities.

On the heels of the civil rights movement of the 1960s, the protests against the Vietnam War, and the growing role of television and the media, new voices were being heard in fundamental opposition to the establishment. Just a few years later, Watergate pushed open the door of public scrutiny and accountability, alerting civic leaders that actions taken must be carefully measured in anticipation of public review and comment. This reality has remained a part of the fabric of American life and for museums as well. The remaining chapters in this part depict and outline some of the heated debates and issues that surfaced in the final decades of the 20th century.

In 1970, the birth of the American Association of Museums Accreditation Program launched a new chapter in the development of industry standards on a national level. Simultaneous with the introduction of national standards, numerous professional museum training programs were launched in recognition of the need to produce qualified museum professionals able to guide their institutions toward achieving standards. Given the social tenor of this period, it is not surprising that in "The Museum, a Temple or the Forum," written in 1971, by the late Duncan Cameron, the former director emeritus of the Glenbow-Alberta Institute, he poses a defining question: Are museums to be places for reverence and worship of the object or places where the public gathers to debate, to consider issues of the day and the consequences of human actions? At the time, many museum leaders felt they had to choose. Today, many museums elect to embrace both.

By the 1990s, museum professionals began to publish articles and books at a more substantial rate than in decades past. This proliferation of writing aligned with the confluence of several key historic moments in the world of museums. In the early 1990s there was a collection of seminal writings that addressed the growing litigious nature of museum work and the impending complexities of caring for collections responsibly on behalf of the public. In 1991, Willard L. Boyd, law professor and the former longtime director of the Field Museum, wrote "Museum Accountability: Laws, Rules, Ethics, and Accreditation," an eloquent clarification of the distinction among each of these formal guidelines for museums and captured the ever-increasing levels of parameters of operation for directors and museum professionals to uphold and advance.

Written in the same year, "Deft Deliberations" explains one of the most significant pieces of legislation to affect museums in the United States in recent times: the Native American Graves Protection and Repatriation Act (NAGPRA) of 1990. Authors Dan Monroe, the executive director and CEO of Peabody Essex Museum, and Walter Echo-Hawk, then staff attorney for the Native American Rights Fund in Boulder, Colorado, document the historic legislation between U.S. museums and Native American tribal leaders devoted to the respectful care and stewardship of Native American religious artifacts and burial remains. NAGPRA requires museums to return human remains and sacred objects adhering to a deliberate, and measured process to be jointly followed by museums and tribal leaders and representatives.

Another 1991 article, "Deaccessioning: The American Perspective" by Marie Malaro, professor emeritus and former director of the Museum Studies Program at George Washington University, and author of *A Legal Primer on Managing Museum Collections,* discusses the process of honing collection holdings through deaccessioning—the legal removal of an object from a museum collection. Handled with forethought and sensitivity to donors and the public, deaccessioning can be an effective management strategy for strengthening the focus and depth of collection holdings for museums, but the need to exercise care, prudence, and deliberation cannot be stressed enough. It is important to note the dominant presence of clear guidelines around ethical and legal standards for collection management as defined by national and international museum associations. These standards remain some of the most rigorous guidelines that museums must uphold.

The late Michael Ames, a well-known anthropologist, museologist, and a former director and professor at the Museum of Anthropology, University of British Columbia, examines museums from an anthropological point of view—studying the often-peculiar habits and assumptions made by museums. In his 1992 article "Museums in the Age of Deconstruction," Ames adeptly analyzes the actions and attitudes of museums to illustrate how museums have approached the interpretation and voices of other cultures in museums. Ames enumerates how museums use and impose museological and anthropological practices when interpreting and exhibiting cultures past and present, frequently resulting in culture clashes between museums and their respective publics and communities.

While the civil rights movement figured prominently in the national media in the 1960s, racism and equity did not enter the national dialogue in the museum community more fully until the late 1980s. Amalia Mesa-Bains, a MacArthur Foundation Fellow, professor, and champion of the Chicano artist movement, eloquently unveils the impact of a colonial paradigm in a world of multiple voices and diverse communities—a world in which most of those communities are not represented in museums. In her 1992 article "The Real Multiculturalism: A Struggle for Authority and Power," Mesa-Bains highlights how racial and societal inequities have played out within the walls of museums.

Although not reprinted here, readers should keep in mind that at the same time the Mesa-Bains article was published, the American Association of Museums formally adopted the policy paper *Excellence and Equity: Museums and the Public Dimension*. This policy paper was created under the leadership of the late Joel Bloom, then president of AAM who launched the initiative, and Bonnie Pitman, the founder of EdCom, a standing professional committee on education for AAM, and former executive director of the Dallas Museum of Art, who chaired the committee of museum professionals that shaped this policy. This document, a clarion call to the profession, emphasized the necessity for equity in all aspects of museum operations and heralded the primary role of museums as educational institutions.

Lisa Corrin's article, "Mining the Museum: An Installation Confronting History," documents one of the most revolutionary museum exhibit installations of the 20th century, *Mining the Museum,* which was conceived and installed by the artist Fred Wilson. Given the opportunity to interpret the collections and mount an exhibit at the Maryland Historical Society in Baltimore (April 1992–February 1993), Wilson took ordinary objects and juxtaposed them with unlikely partners to make poignant visual statements about prejudices and racial inequities in the world and the traditional biases of many museum displays.

George Hein, one of many addressing the complexities of learning in the museum environment, lays out his convictions in "The Constructivist Museum." Hein discusses the tensions between theories of learning and theories of knowledge making the argument that museums as educational institutions must elucidate a philosophical framework upon which to base decisions that influence the visitor's experience. He advocates for the constructivist ideology that integrates how people learn, and the beliefs around how knowledge is acquired yielding an approach that creates an educational framework from the perspective of the learner.

The late Stephen Weil's 1999 essay "Creampuffs or Hardball: Are You Really Worth What You Cost or Just Merely Worthwhile?" is a challenge to museum leaders to question the validity of their institutions and their actions as leaders. Fearless and direct, Weil lays out the facts about survival for museums today, suggesting that museum leaders abandon long-held assumptions about what is adequate and appropriate, and move toward developing meaningful measurements of value.

Elaine Heumann Gurian, a widely respected thought leader and prolific writer, makes a passionate case for museums to rethink how they approach engaging the public in "Savings Banks for the Soul." Gurian makes the case that the museum can play a dynamic and deeply personal role for individuals, recognizing that museums can become places for self-reflection and public engagement, Gurian maintains that the challenges facing today's communities provide an unparalleled opportunity for museums to facilitate safe and open environments for building community connections and thus a sense of belonging.

Lisa Roberts, a consummate museum educator, wrote the book *Knowledge to Narrative: Educators and the Changing Museum* in 1997. In "Changing Practices of Interpretation," an excerpt featured in that book, she traces the evolution of educational offerings in museums, illuminating the changing definition of interpretation to accommodate today's understanding of museums as educational institutions. She presents a historical perspective on this evolution while highlighting the impact of contemporary issues as instigators of change in museum interpretation.

Reflecting the evolution of consumer tastes, the concept of "The Experience Economy," was introduced by two renowned experts from outside the museum industry, B. Joseph Pine II and James H. Gilmore. They encourage museums to become rightful leaders in the marketplace of delivering cultural experiences. Museums, they argue, have the unique ability to create multidimensional experiences, tapping into the senses, past experiences, and personal dimensions of the people who visit and engage with museums.

Closing out Part I is the oft-quoted, seminal article, "From Being about Something to Being for Somebody" written by Stephen Weil in 1999. This piece succinctly captures the shift of thinking away from the collection-dominated focus of museums of previous decades and toward a realigned purpose of creating meaningful public connections using collections as a means to that end.

The Gloom of the Museum

1

JOHN COTTON DANA

Prologue

TODAY, MUSEUMS OF ART ARE BUILT to keep objects of art, and objects of art are bought to be kept in museums. As the objects seem to do their work if they are safely kept, and as museums seem to serve their purpose if they safely keep the objects, the whole thing is as useful in the splendid isolation of a distant park as in the center of the life of the community which possesses it.

Tomorrow, objects of art will be bought to give pleasure, to make manners seem more important, to promote skill, to exalt handwork, and to increase the zest of life by adding to it new interests; and these objects being bought for use will be put where the most people can most handily use them: in a museum planned for making the best use of all it contains, and placed where a majority of its community can quickly and easily visit it.

Part I: How the Arts Have Been Induced to Flourish

The story of an art epoch in the life history of a people seems to resolve itself into something like this:

Character and circumstances lead the people into conquest. It may sound better, though it means the same, to say that character and circumstances bring out a few men of genius who lead and rule the people and take them on to conquest. The conquest means wealth, and this is true whether the conquest be of other peoples by leadership and force of arms, or of the land's natural resources and of methods of producing and using power.

John Cotton Dana (1856–1929), a prolific writer and librarian, was the founding director of The Newark Museum in Newark, New Jersey, and widely recognized as one of the pioneer museum thinkers of the last century. "The Gloom of the Museum" written by Dana in 1917 was part of *The New Museum Series*, a series of small booklets that addressed issues pertinent to museums. It is reprinted here by permission of The Newark Museum Association/The American Association of Museums.

Always a few gain most of the wealth and hold most of the power. The conquest being somewhat well assured, these few have leisure. They search for occupations and things and indulgences which may give them pleasure. Whatever else these occupations, objects, and indulgences may be, they must be such as the common people cannot have; for the rich and ruling class must always keep itself distinct from the lower classes in its pleasures and pastimes, just as it always did in its leadership in war and government. These distinctive recreations and diversions and admired objects of the powerful and rich have always been of about the same character. War is first choice; if not war of the higher kind in which is involved the existence of the tribe, family, city, dukedom, principality, kingdom, or nation over which the rich and powerful in question rule, then a war of petty conquest, mean in itself, but permitting some braggadocio, keeping up the clan spirit and exalting the ruling class. Lacking a vigorous and dangerous war on battlefields to engage all their activities, the rulers have often turned to hunting—to hunting in a form which nature, or special laws, or the rules of the game make somewhat dangerous; for if it does not at least seem dangerous, those who engage in it will not appear brave to the lower classes. The form of hunting chosen is usually one which is quite inaccessible to the poor and weak. Big game near home, and better still at a good distance; falconry, the right to use falcons being easily restricted to the few; fox hunting on horseback; dangerous athletic sports; and latterly automobiling, ballooning, and flying—these have all had or shall have their vogue.

Another obvious method of distinguishing their life from that of the common people has been the possession of distinctive residences beyond all need in size, number, cost, and adornment. It is through these residences that the rich and powerful have chiefly been led to become patrons of the arts. The wish to make full use of the religious habits of the ruled has often led the rich to build and adorn churches; and always, of course, the need of expensive and peculiar dress has been an occasion for calling in the aid of artisans of certain kinds. The study of literature, language, history, and the fine arts has also often been a recreating of the rich, though usually these studies have been pursued by proxy. As unusual native ability has almost always been one of the essentials to success in acquiring wealth and power, it is not strange that an occasional member of the class of the ruling rich has shown marked ability in letters and the arts, or at least in appreciation of them. But pursuit of art and letters has usually ended with little more than such a patronage of them as would bring in return ample adulation, a reputation for learning, and glorification in history.

Comparative security, then, after a series of profitable wars, finds the rich and powerful compelled to engage in expensive sports, to build large and expensive residences, and to decorate them and to adorn elaborately their own persons that there may be no lack of distinctions between themselves and the common people. The demand for architects, painters, sculptors, gold and silversmiths, ironworkers, and artisans of all kinds thus at once arises; and a demand also for teachers, poets, orators, and historians to make a pretense of love of learning.

It is worth noting here that in former days these workers produced without the intervention of machinery; that the rich have usually been ready to adopt the older methods in art productions if for any reason they were inaccessible to the poor; and that today admiration for the handmade is largely born of a desire to have something which, being unique in its kind, will impart a little of the old leisure-class exclusiveness to its owner.

The patronage of the arts, with the consequent development thereof, has varied in extent in the rise to wealth and leisure of the leaders among different peoples, as circumstances dictated, but its origin seems always to have been about the same. Whenever this patronage has appeared—whenever, that is, the demand for objects of art has arisen—the supply has been forthcoming.

Fashion among the rich has sometimes prevented the results of this patronage of art from showing themselves very plainly in the country of the rich. In our day, for example, the fashion is to import from abroad and to say that good artwork cannot be produced at home; so we have a Barbizon painting factory in Paris, makers of antiques in Italy, and a digging up of gone-by utensils and furniture in all European and Asiatic countries. These old things cost more in the first place, the tariff makes them more expensive still, and their ownership gives considerable of the ruling-class distinction. Were it to become the fashion to patronize American designers and craftsmen in all lines and to give artists and architects a free hand instead of insisting on conformity to the ancient ways as interpreted by the ignorant rich, we would have a larger art demand in America; the supply would raise prices and wages; art study would be encouraged; more men of genius, skill, and training would come here from abroad; and we would begin our own renaissance.

Those who know Mr. Veblen's delightful book, *The Theory of the Leisure Class*, will see that I have borrowed from him in my statement about the character of the diversions and the conspicuous waste of the rich.

But our renaissance does not come. We have an aristocracy based on wealth, with accompanying power. This aristocracy feels the same need that aristocracies have always felt of acquiring ancient, rare, and costly objects that the possession of them may mark them as superior to the poor and weak. They find that the easiest way to acquire such objects is not to cause them to be produced by artists and artisans of their own country—America—but, as already noted, to purchase them in older countries. What had already given distinction to their owners in France, Italy, England, and Germany is seen at once to be peculiarly well fitted to give a like distinction here. Hence the products of our own people are definitely held in no esteem as honorific possessions. Art in America does not flourish.

I have used the foregoing remarks, taken from a paper published in the Independent seven years ago, as a preface to the essay which follows on the gloom of the museum in the hope that they will make still more self-evident the statements in the latter concerning the origin of American museums of art. The kinds of objects—ancient, costly, and imported—that the rich feel they must buy to give themselves a desired distinction are inevitably the kinds that they, as patrons and directors of museums, cause those museums to acquire. Veritably, most of our great museums look with open scorn on the products of American artists and artisans.

The peculiar sanctity of oil paint on canvas has been graciously extended in some small degree to New World products, and our great museums occasionally buy, more often receive as gifts, and still more often receive as loans for exhibition the works of American painters. But most of our richer museums of art, that in Chicago being a notable exception, follow the dictates of the rich. They very evidently do not think it is the proper function of a museum of art to promote, foster, or patronize American talent.

The new museum, for the development of which this series is designed, will hold that its first duty is to discover talent and encourage its development here at home.

The rich and powerful collect foreign things and insist that foreign things only shall be enshrined in the museum they patronize. The poor follow the rich in this thinking. The attempt to modify this state of affairs is not one that is full of hope. But the growing habit of cities to maintain their own museums will surely tend to democratize them; and if, in the beginnings of the museums that are now coming into existence, the suggestions for making them immediately and definitely useful to their founders and patrons—the public—which we find today so widely approved among museum workers are quite generally adopted, the day will soon come when many public museums will look upon the promotion of American art as one of their most important functions.

Part II: The Gloom of the Museum, with Suggestions for Removing It

Prefatory Note

The art of museum construction, acquisition, and management is in its infancy. No one can say with authority how that art will be developed in the next few years. But on this much at least the public may congratulate itself: that museum authorities now feel that their respective establishments should be, above all things, attractive in a sane and homely way to the public which owns them.

Art museums of necessity have the faults of their ancestry, and these faults are so obvious that even a layman like myself may see them, and the plain statement of such of them as a layman dares to say he sees may help to move the intelligent part of the public to set to work to correct them.

Throughout this discussion I have art museums almost solely in mind.

How Museums Came to Be So Gloomily Beautiful

One need visit only a few of the older museums of art and archaeology in Europe to understand why most American museums of the same subjects are so ineffective.

In Europe, these older museums have objects of great importance to students of art, of history in general, of the history of art, of social development, and of the history of invention and discovery. Large groups of these objects were first collected many years ago by wealthy and powerful individuals: princes, kings, emperors, and members of the nobility. These collectors were usually entirely selfish in their acquisition, rarely looking beyond their own personal pleasure or the aggrandizement of their immediate families. They collected that they might possess, not that they might use, or that others might use, the things collected for the pleasure and advancement of the world at large.

As the idea of general welfare crept into and modified the government of any given country, the ruling powers of that country in many cases confiscated or purchased these collected treasures, added other purchases and gifts to them, made them so-called public collections, and deposited them for safekeeping in national and municipal buildings. These buildings were for the most part erected for other purposes than the reception and proper display of works of art and archaeology. This fact usually made it possible to install collections in them only under such conditions of space and light as prevented either logical or artistic arrangement and made both casual observation and careful study of most of the objects a burden instead of pleasure.

As the collections were of very great value—consisting usually of originals which no money could replace, which should therefore be guarded with the utmost care—the first thought in regard to them was their preservation; their utilization being a secondary and rather remote affair.

Why Museum Buildings Are Temples and Palaces

The character of the buildings which, as time went on, were here and there erected to house these collections of priceless originals, was determined by several factors. As most of the collections had found their first homes in the palaces of rulers or members of the nobility, it was quite naturally concluded that their new homes should also be in the style of the local palace or royal residences. As the things collected were objects of art, it seemed obvious that they should be housed in artistic buildings, and as for several centuries it has been difficult for architects or those having power over art collections to conceive of an artistic building save in terms of Greek or Renaissance architecture, nearly all special museum buildings imitated either the Greek temple or the Italian palace.

In Europe, therefore, we find museums to be either old buildings of the royal palace type or later constructions copying the palace or the Greek temple; containing priceless originals in all lines of art, craftsmanship, and archaeology; arranged as the characters of the several buildings compel; guarded with extreme care; dutifully visited by serious-minded tourists; and used sparingly by a small number of special students.

New America Copies the Old Europe, of Course

This, roughly speaking, was the museum idea as it embodied itself in Europe when the subject of museums began a few decades ago to be taken up seriously in America. It was inevitable that the first wish of all our museum enthusiasts should be to produce imitations of the European institutions. Those institutions were, in most cases, long established and greatly admired, and they furnished the only illustrations of the museum idea.

Moreover, collections more or less well suited to form the beginnings of art museums had been made here, after the European manner, by a few of the rich; some of these had fallen by gift or will to public use, accompanied not infrequently by the requirement that they be permanently housed in art buildings which were inevitably fashioned after the European type.

The promoters of art museums in America had no choice in the matter. The approved examples of Europe, the precedents already established in America in accordance with those examples, the unanimous votes of architects and trustees on what it is that makes a building a fit home for works of art, and the voice of so much of the general public as had ever seen or heard of European museums—all these factors united to complete the erection here of the kind of museum building which now oppresses us.

Why Museums Are Way Off in the Woods

The prevalence of the European idea of a museum determined not only the character of our museum buildings but also their location. As they must be works of art, and as temples and palaces need open space about them to display their excellences, and as space in the centers of towns is quite expensive, donors, architects, trustees, and city fathers all agreed that the art museum building should be set apart from the city proper, preferably in a park with open space about it. Distance from the center of population and the difficulty most citizens would encounter did they attempt to see the museum's contents were given no weight in comparison with the obvious advantages of display of the building's outer charms.

The Museum of Religious Gloom

A city may with perfect propriety set itself to the task of making a collection of rare and ancient original products of man's craftsmanship, spending, for example, $10,000 for a piece of tapestry, $100,000 for a painting, $30,000 for a marble statue, $20,000 for a piece of porcelain, and so on; it may add to these by gift and may place them all in a one-story, poorly lighted, marble, fireproof building set in a park remote from the city's center. But it ought to do this with a full comprehension of the fact that, while it is in so doing establishing a "Museum of Art" in the sense in which that phrase is most often used today, it is not forming an institution which will either entertain or instruct the community to an extent at all commensurate with its cost. In such an establishment the city will have an "art museum" of the kind which the citizen points out with pride to visiting friends; which appears in the advertising pamphlets of the local boards of trade; which is the recipient of an occasional painting or other work of art from a local art patron; which some strangers and a few resident women and children occasionally use to produce in themselves the maximum of fatigue with the minimum of pleasure; which will offer through the opening of loan collections a few opportunities each winter for society to display itself and demonstrate its keen aesthetic interests.

Rarity and High Price Make Things More Beautiful

The European examples which were so disastrous in their effect on the character and location of our museum buildings had an unfortunate influence also on the character and arrangement of their contents.

In the order of events in Europe, as already noted, one country after another and one city after another came into the possession of treasures of art and archaeology—priceless originals—which it was the duty of the authorities to preserve with the utmost care. Our own art museum enthusiasts, imitating their predecessors, sought also to form collections of unique and costly objects. A delusion like that which everywhere possesses the art novice as to the relative value of real oil paintings, however atrocious, and colored lithographic reproductions of paintings, however excellent, possessed those who made private art collections and those who selected and purchased objects for our museums. Art museum objects were not chosen for their beauty or for the help they might give in developing good taste in the community, but for their rarity, their likeness to objects found in European museums, and for their cost.

The older collections on the continent are naturally largely historical and archaeological. This seemed sufficient reason for making our collections of the same kind.

The wish to form collections which should illustrate the development of this or that special form of art also influenced greatly the character of our early museums.

But the wish to make them, like their European models, include a large number of things peculiar, unique, not copies, not obtainable by others, and costly, was probably the chief factor in making our museums mausoleums of curios.

The objects acquired being rare and costly, it was inevitable that they should be very carefully safeguarded, placed where they could be seen only (and that not very adequately), and never handled and examined closely.

American Museums Today

That this rough outline of recent museum history in America is fairly correct is amply demonstrated by present-day American museums themselves. They are usually housed in buildings fashioned to look like Greek temples or Renaissance palaces, which are very poorly adapted to the proper installation of collections and very rarely well planned for growth. These buildings are set apart from the city whose citizens they are built to serve, often in remote parks. The objects in them are very largely second-rate original artworks, usually with large additions of things historical or archaeological of little art value. Many of the buildings are so expensive to administer and to light and to heat that the managers can keep them open to the public only a small part of the hours when the public can best visit them. They are visited by few, that few being made up largely of strangers passing through the city; and the objects displayed are used for practical, everyday purposes and are looked to for suggestions applying to daily life by a very small number of persons, and by them very rarely.

Museum Failures Are Not Chargeable to Specific Persons

It may be said that if this development of American art museums into remote palaces and temples—filled with objects not closely associated with the life of the people who are asked to get pleasure and profit from them, and so arranged and administered as to make them seem still more remote—it may be said that if this development has been as natural and inevitable as has been suggested, then no one can be charged with responsibility for the fact, and not much can be done to correct the error.

It would indeed be difficult to lay the burden of this unfortunate line of development on the shoulders of any persons who may be specifically named. It would be difficult also to correct the mistake already made. No one, for example, would quite dare to suggest (taking up the point only of location) to the citizens of Boston, New York, Buffalo, and Cincinnati that they can much better afford, in the long run, to move their museums into the centers of daily movement of population and thereby secure a tenfold enlargement of their use and influence, than they can to go on paying large sums for their maintenance in relative idleness where they are now.

And it would be idle to attempt to persuade architects and trustees and a public, bound to accept the architectural conventions of their time, that when they use the outward presentations of one-story buildings designed for housing gods in a perpetual twilight as the peripheries of well-lighted and convenient and easily warmed and controlled spaces for the display of precious objects to thousands of visitors, they show a certain magnificent courage, but not good architectural traits, not originality, and not common sense.

But, in spite of the depressing influence of fashion and of the architectural paralysis induced by the classic burden in these matters, one may hope that all museums hereafter built need not conform to the old ideas, and that some of the museums already in existence can be so modified as to be far more useful and influential than they are today.

The Art of Museum Making in Its Infancy

The art of making museums which will be largely used by those who pay for them and will please and profit all who visit them is in its infancy. No one ventures to describe definitely the ideal American art museum. A few suggestions may at least provoke helpful discussion.

Museums Should Be Central

An art museum should be so located that it may be reached by a maximum number of persons with a minimum expenditure of time and money. It should be near the center of the city which maintains it—not its population center but its rapid transit center—and as near as possible also to its more important railway stations that strangers may visit it quickly and cheaply.

It may be said that a collection of art objects properly housed in a beautiful building gains somewhat in dignity and importance and in its power to influence beneficially those who visit it if it is set apart a little from the city's center of strenuous commercial and material life; holds itself somewhat aloof, as it were; detaches itself from the crowd; and seems to care to speak only to those whose desire for its teachings is strong enough to lead them to make some sacrifice of time and money to enjoy them.

The suggestion is a specious one. This theory of the fitness of remoteness is born of pride and satisfaction in the location and character of museums as they are. The buildings are remote and are religious or autocratic or aristocratic in style; their administrators, perhaps in part because of this very aloofness and sacrosanct environment, are inclined to look upon themselves as high priests of a peculiar cult, who may treat the casual visitor with tolerance only when he comes to worship rather than to look with open eyes and to criticize freely; and the trustees are prone to think more of their view of the proper museum atmosphere than of museum patronage, more of preservation than of utilization.

This same theory as to the preciosity which remoteness may confer, applied to art in general and carried to its logical conclusions, would forbid the expenditure of public funds or private gifts on the beautifying of streets or bridges or public buildings. Under its application, one might say that a commercial city should be built in the coldest, baldest possible style, and that beautiful façades of homes, office buildings, and factories should be erected as façades only in remote parks and boulevards, there to be solemnly visited and viewed by those who truly care to exalt their souls and purify their intellects.

The Museum Building: Some of Its Obvious Qualities

The museum building located in the city's center should satisfy the fundamental conditions of all good architecture: It should be large enough for its purpose; it should be constructed of the materials, proper in its day, which are best adapted to its form and size; it should be in harmony with its surroundings; and it should be as beautiful as the highest technique and the best taste of the time can make it.

A building of steel and concrete in a modern American city is not made an appropriate home of the fine arts by placing on its front the façade of one or the façades of half a dozen Greek temples or of 15th-century Italian palaces. It is impossible to believe that the best Greek architects, if they were the masters in good taste we suppose them to have been, would have continued to make their buildings look as though they were built of columns of stone, with huge girders and crossbeams of the same material, long after they had learned to use steel and concrete in construction.

In time we shall learn to insist that great public buildings like libraries and museums be erected as such and not as imitations of structures developed for quite other purposes, in other cities, in other times, and under limitations as to material and method by which we are no longer bound.

A modern museum building for an American city is a distinct problem in arrangement and a difficult one not to be solved by the adoption for its exterior of a type, however beautiful, which in origin and development never bore the slightest relation to the subject of museums.

It may be said that the contents of art museums are in part priceless, cannot be replaced, must be so housed as to make their destruction by fire impossible, and that, therefore, the only safe location for a museum is in a park, far from all other buildings. In reply it may be said that the high value put on many of the objects in art museums is largely fictitious, born of the rivalry of rich collectors and even of rich museums in their search for objects of honorable uniqueness; that a few students could truly feel their loss; but that as instruments of human enlightenment and happiness they are by no means priceless. Next, it may be noted that it is doubtful if any art museum authorities have yet erected a remote building on the contents of which they can get fire insurance rates as low as they could get them on the same contents housed in a fireproof building in the center of their city. There are risks in remoteness as well as safeguards. It should also be said that if a city wants a warehouse for the storage of art treasures, build it by all means; but do not encumber it with the fine, open spaces of a public park. But if it wants an institution of the newer museum type, something from which can be derived pleasure, surely, and profit if the gods permit, then let that be built where it can be easily made use of, in the city's center.

In a great city the museum building could properly be several, perhaps many, stories high, and if open space about it were quite impossible for financial reasons, light could be had from courts. Nearly all rooms would then be lighted from one side, as nearly all exhibition, study, and lecture rooms should be.

The Vast Extent of Museum Collections Leads to Obscurity

The objects gathered in art museums will continue to include the works of men's hands in all materials, for all purposes, of all countries, and for all time. Students of every form of art will continue to ask that museums include not only the products of that art when it was at the highest point of its development, but also its products in every stage of its growth and of its decline. Museums—that is, some of the large museums at least—must continue to be not only museums of many arts, but also of the histories of those arts, and therefore of archaeology and of ethnology.

But as time goes on, many collections, thus expanding naturally into other fields than that of art, will become unwieldy, overloaded with objects of interest only to the very special student, mere confusing masses of seemingly unrelated objects to the ordinary visitor. They will lose all effectiveness in what should be their special field—that of suggesting to the observer that a certain refinement of daily life is worth all it costs—and, to the would-be promoter of this refinement, that certain special methods in this, that, and the other field have been successful once and may be successful again. That is to say, art museum collections continually tend to lose the power of doing that which they were designed to do, which is to say to us that manners and feelings are important parts of life. For the objects which have to do with age-long gropings after good things will always tend to become so numerous as to hide the good things themselves.

The Undue Reverence for Oil Paint

The extreme veneration now paid by museum authorities to great paintings will surely become weaker as the possibilities of a museum's influence become better understood. Painting in oil upon canvas is not a craft that makes a strong appeal to the average man, save through the stories it tells. Its value, after all, is almost entirely pictorial. As mere pictures—which is all that they are to the average observer of ordinary intelligence, plus the interest born of their age, their history, and their cost—they each year suffer more and more from the competition of other pictures not done in oil on canvas, found in posters, in journals and newspapers, and in the cinema. In due course the oil painting will take its place in museums with other products of men's hands simply as one of the many things of high beauty and great suggestiveness produced in perfection only by men of special talent who have been able to master a difficult technique.

This fact will in time be recognized and acted upon: that the oil painting has no such close relation to the development of good taste and refinement as have countless objects of daily use. The genius and skill which have gone into the adornment and perfecting of familiar household objects will then receive the same recognition as do now the genius and skill of the painter in oils. Paintings will no longer be given an undue share of space, and on them will be expended no undue share of the museum's annual income. It is doubtful if any single change in the general principles of art museum management will do as much to enhance museum influence as will this placing of the oil painting in its proper relation with other objects.

The Subordination of Painting and the Promotion of Applied Art

If oil paintings are put in the subordinate place in which they belong, the average art museum will have much more room for the display of objects which have quite a direct bearing on the daily life of those who support it, visit either the main buildings or its branches, and make use of its collections. One need not be specific; the museum will show by originals or replicas what has been done by other people to make more convenient and attractive all the things that we use and wear and see day by day, from shoes to signposts and from table knives to hat pins. As the museum gives more space and more attention to these things, it will quite inevitably also display the objects in which its own city is particularly interested. It will have no absurd fear that it will be commercialized and debased if it shows what is being done today in the field of applied art in its own city and in other parts of the world. It will take no shame from the fact that it is handling and installing and displaying articles made by machinery for actual daily use by mere living people. One of the grotesqueries of expertness in museum work today is the reverential attention paid to products of craftsmanship which are (1) old, (2) rare, (3) high in price, (4) a little different from all others, and (5) illustrate a change in method of work or in the fashion of their time. Still more depressing is this reverence when it is accompanied, as it often is, with indifference, or scorn, or fear of commercial taint, toward products of craftsmanship which are (1) modern, (2) common, (3) not high in price, (4) a copy of the old, rare, and priceless.

What could be more ludicrous than the sight of those who, openly devoted to the worship of beauty, treat with scorn modern reproductions of old things which they have pronounced beautiful, even if they copy the old so well that only labels and microscopes can distinguish one from the other, or even if, not professing to be exact reproductions, they show originality and high skill in design, are technically quite perfect, and either disclose the taste of the time or are factors in the betterment of that taste.

Surely a function of a public art museum is the making of life more interesting, joyful, and wholesome; and surely a museum cannot very well exercise that function unless it relates itself quite closely to the life it should be influencing; and surely it cannot thus relate itself unless it comes in close contact with the material adornment of that life—its applied arts.

The necklace found on an Egyptian mummy is unique, old, and costly. But even if presented to a museum by someone of wealth and influence, it still may be hideous and it may have no suggestion whatever for the modern designer. If it has certain suggestive value in this line, it thereby becomes just as well worthy of its place in the museum as is a necklace made yesterday in a neighboring city. Being unique, it should be kept. Its origin gives it an archaeological value. But if it is admitted to a museum of art, it need not stand in the way of the display in the same museum of modern necklaces which may interest many and may give suggestion and stimulus to modern designers.

Of course, it is not the Egyptian mummy's necklace which stands in the way of the display of modern necklaces, but the spirit of curators, experts, directors, and trustees. They become enamored of rarity, of history, and, in this specific instance, of necklaces as indicative of steps in civilization. They become lost in their specialties and forget their museum. They become lost in their idea of a museum and forget its purpose. They become lost in working out their idea of a museum and forget their public. And soon, not being brought constantly in touch with the life of their community through handling and displaying that community's output in one or scores of lines, they become entirely separated from it and go on making beautifully complete and very expensive collections, but never construct a living, active, and effective institution.

Is the Department Store a Museum?

A great city department store of the first class is perhaps more like a good museum of art than are any of the museums we have yet established. It is centrally located; it is easily reached; it is open to all at all the hours when patrons wish to visit it; it receives all courteously and gives information freely; it displays its most attractive and interesting objects and shows countless others on request; its collections are classified according to the knowledge and needs of its patrons; it is well lighted; it has convenient and inexpensive rest rooms; it supplies guides free of charge; it advertises itself widely and continuously; and it changes its exhibits to meet daily changes in subjects of interest, changes of taste in art, and the progress of invention and discovery.

A department store is not a good museum, but so far are museums from being the active and influential agencies they might be that they may be compared with department stores and not altogether to their advantage.

The Museum as the Teacher and Advertiser

To make itself alive, a museum must do two things: It must teach and it must advertise. As soon as it begins to teach, it will of necessity begin to form an alliance with present teaching agencies, the public schools, the colleges and universities, and the art institutions of all kinds. It is only by bearing in mind the history of its development and the part that imitation has played in that development that one can understand how American communities have been able to establish, build up, and maintain great collections of works of art, beautifully and expensively housed and administered, which yet have almost no cooperative relations with all the other educational and social-betterment institutions of the same communities. Teaching tends to become dogmatic. Dogmatism in art is injurious, but museum teaching need not be dogmatic. Indeed, museums might well be less dogmatic than they now are. They buy high-priced paintings and spend vast sums for rare brocades, pottery, ancient wood carvings, and whatnot, and then set these (with an ample air of assurance of wisdom which may very well be called dogmatic) before their constituents, saying, "Look, trust the expert, and admire." Far less dogmatic would it be to set side by side in a case ancient and rare modern and commercial pottery, and say, "Here are what some call the fine products of the potter's art when it was at its best in Italy long ago, and here are products of the potters of America today. You will find a comparative study of the two very interesting."

Would there be anything debasing in such an apposition? Would it be less dogmatic than is nearly all museum presentation of itself today?

By no right in reason whatever is a museum a mere collection of things, save by right of precedent. Yet precedent has so ruled in this field that our carefully organized museums have little more power to influence their communities than has a painting which hangs on the wall of some sanctuary, a sanctuary which few visit and they only to wonder as they gaze and to depart with the proud consciousness that they have seen. Some of the best of our museums, spending many thousands per year on administration and many other thousands on acquisitions, are now pluming themselves on the fact that they employ one—only one—person to make their collections more interesting to the thousands who visit them; that they have a hall in which during a winter a few lectures are given; and that they publish a bulletin recording their progress in piling up treasures, and catalogues which are as devoid of human interest as a perfect catalogue can be.

Museums of the future will not only teach at home, they will travel abroad through their photographs, their textbooks, and their periodicals. Books, leaflets, and journals—which will assist and supplement the work of teachers and will accompany, explain, and amplify the exhibits which art museums will send out—will all help to make museum expenditures seem worthwhile.

Why Not Branch Museums?

Museums will soon make themselves more effective through loan exhibits and through branches.

The museum is in most cases so remote from the city's center that even if it were to rival in attractiveness the theater, the cinema, and the department store, the time and money it takes to reach it would bar most from ever paying it a visit. It should establish branches, large and small, as many as funds permit, in which could be seen a few of the best things in one and another field that genius and skill have produced; in which could be seen the products of some of the city's industries, placed beside those of other cities, of other countries, and of other times; in which thousands of the citizens could each day see—at the cost of a few minutes only of their time—a few at least of the precious objects which their money has been used to collect.

Even though the main museum building is centrally situated, the need of branches—in a large city, at least—is quite obvious. The small branch would be more effective in the appeal it could make to many visitors than the main building could ever be. A half hour in the presence of one fine painting, a dozen Greek vases (with perhaps a few of other times and countries for comparison), one great piece of sculpture—each of these with ample descriptive notes and leaflets—would arouse more genuine feeling and a deeper interest than an aimless stroll through rooms full of the world's best art products.

These branches need not be in special buildings. Often, a single room conveniently located would serve as well as, or even better than, an elaborate and forbidding structure. How the idea would be worked out in detail no one can say. Apparently it has never been tried. But there seems to be no reason other than that found in precedent why the art treasures of a city—its own property, bought by itself to illuminate and broaden and make more enjoyable the life of its citizens—should rest always in the splendid isolation of that remote temple or palace erected for them.

Museum Objects May Be Lent

Art museums frequently borrow collections of objects and show them temporarily. Why do they not more often reverse the process?

More than twenty years ago, a self-constituted committee of women established in Massachusetts what was in effect a library art league. With the aid of the libraries which joined the league, they brought together a large number of interesting collections, chiefly of pictures of many kinds and dealing with many subjects, which traveled about and were shown at one library after another. For many years the University of the State of New York has been sending out from Albany collections of pictures to be exhibited in the libraries of the state and in other proper institutions.

Groups of museums, notably the group now operating under the direction of the Federation of Arts, have long been borrowing and successively showing collections of paintings, engravings, pottery, bronzes, and other objects. The Newark Library has prepared or arranged several exhibits of art and handicraft which have been shown in a total of more than 100 American cities. The American Museum of Natural History lends annually thousands of specially prepared exhibits to the schools of New York and vicinity. The Commercial Museums of Philadelphia prepare collections for the schools of the whole state of Pennsylvania. In St. Louis, an educational museum—geographical, scientific, and industrial, maintained by the board of education—lends many thousands of objects and collections each year to the schools of the city. In Germany, there go forth each year from a central bureau in Hagen many carefully prepared exhibitions of objects of art and handicraft gathered from the best workshops in the empire; and the South Kensington museum has been lending objects to towns and cities in Great Britain for many years.

In spite of all these good examples of the possibilities for helpfulness which lie in loan collections shown for brief periods in each of a score of cities or in each of a hundred schools of the same city, the habit of lending subjects from and by museums of art is almost unknown in this country.

Even the youngest and most modest of museums—unless it is of the purely mortuary type, housed in a temple, complete in all its appointments, installed for all time according to the museum laws of its founders and hastening to its destined end of disuse—even such a museum has objects which would find a hitherto useless life crowned with good works were they lent freely to schools, libraries, art schools, civic centers, and whatnot in the town to which they belong.

Museums of science are sending their exhibits to their patrons, old and young. It is quite evident that art museums will soon follow their example.

The art museums are just now greatly concerned over the question of how they shall make themselves of value to the young people of their respective communities. It is plain enough that it is impossible in a large city for the young people to make the journey to the central museum times enough to gain more than the most fleeting of impressions. They have not the money for car fares, they must go in crowds and teachers must accompany the crowds, and school time for this is lacking, and if they were to go times enough to get any enduring lessons from their visits, they would crowd the central building to the doors.

Why not take the museum to the young people? Public branches can serve the adults; and collections, groups, single objects, and photographs and other pictures can easily be placed in school houses, and surely soon will be.

Do We Need Museums at All?

I have ventured to mention the great department stores in the same sentence with museums of art. No sooner is the comparison made than other suggestive comparisons come to mind. The dealer in paintings has his art gallery, always convenient, open to all without charge, with exhibitions constantly changing. Dealers in works of art in general seem to approach even nearer to the museum ideal. Then on the industrial side we find that every factory and workshop is a museum in action, and, if it produces beautiful objects, is a living exhibit of arts and crafts.

Stores are each year more attractive and more informing; each year factories are more humanely and rationally managed, are more inviting and more informing, and are more freely open to interested visitors under reasonable restrictions. Each year the printing press produces better and cheaper illustrations of artworks of every kind, with a descriptive letter press which grows each year not only more ample but also more direct and simple. And each year the cinema reproduces for us more faithfully the activities of men in all lines of work and in all countries and makes it easier for us all to understand what books and journals try to tell us through text and pictures.

This question then arises: Does a world which is supplied by mere trade and industry with convenient storehouses of the world's products old and new, the best as well as the poorest, with industrial exhibits in factories of every kind, and with pictures and texts of amazing beauty and suggestiveness—does a world having all these things need the art museum at all?

The Museum as the Public's Friend and Guide

The question just asked answers itself at once, of course. Save for the very young, the opportunities for self-education offered by the street, the store, the factory, the movie, and the all-pervasive page of print are quite ample. Any boy or girl who will can gain an excellent education without the ministration of the school. But, on the whole, in spite of its manifest deficiencies, it seems wise to maintain the school and promote education through it.

Just so with those refinements of human nature—those betterments of manner and feeling, which I have ventured to name as good things which art museums exist to promote—these refinements may be attained by any, save the very young, who will attend thereto and will diligently use, to that end, the materials always at hand in dress, architecture, shop window, nature, and the ever-present picture and printed page. But in spite of the infinity of ever-present opportunity for everyone's education in the refinement of life and the enrichment of the leisure hour, it has seemed wise to establish and maintain the museum of art.

I have tried to show that this museum has been so absorbed in one aspect of its work that it has left untouched its more important and pressing duties. It has built itself an elaborate and costly home, beautiful after the fashion of its time and the taste of its community. In this home it has gathered the rare, the curious, the beautiful, and always, when possible, the unique and costly. So doing it has paid its debt to history and archaeology, has gained for its city a certain passing and rather meretricious distinction, and has given a select few an opportunity to pursue their study of fashion in taste, in ornament, and in technique.

Now seems to come the demand that the museum serve its people in the task of helping them to appreciate the high importance of manner, to hold by the laws of simplicity and restraint, and to broaden their sympathies and multiply their interests.

What Is a Museum?   2

THEODORE LOW

The Museum and the Present

SLIGHTLY OVER TWO YEARS AGO Francis H. Taylor very emphatically stated the position of the museum in his article, "Museums in a Changing World."[1] In the short time that has elapsed since the appearance of that article, the world has increased its rate of change with alarming rapidity. Museums have not followed suit. To discuss the situation of world affairs is far from the purpose of this report, and yet, it is only in their relationship to the vast changes which are taking place that the museums can find their rightful role.

No one can deny that museums have powers which are of the utmost importance in any war of ideologies. They have the power to make people see the truth, the power to make people recognize the importance of the individual as a member of society, and, of equal importance in combating subversive inroads, the power to keep minds happy and healthy. They have, in short, propaganda powers which should be far more effective in their truth and eternal character than those of the Axis which are based on falsehoods and half-truths. Museums with their potentiality of reaching millions of our citizens must not fail to recognize their responsibility. Adam saw the ability of the museums to carry on this work when he said,

> The antidote to cunning misinformation by emotion-rousing posters and enslaving prejudices is honest science, popular symbolic art, and the growth of independent judgment. Museums are powerful visual instruments to bring these gifts to the public. Their control is no routine or honorary matter but a frontline job in the continuous struggle to preserve social freedom.[2]

That museum leaders are conscious of their part in the war effort is self-evident in the resolution passed on December 21, 1941, by the Association of Art Museum

---

Theodore Low (1915–1987) was a museum educator at the Metropolitan Museum of Art. "What Is a Museum?" written by Low in 1942, was commissioned by the American Association of Museums. It is reprinted from *The Museum as a Social Instrument*, published in 1942 by the Metropolitan Museum of Art for the American Association of Museums.

Directors with the concurrence of the Officers and Council of the American Association of Museums. The four steps in that resolution are as follows:

1. First, that American museums are prepared to do their utmost in the service of the people of this country during the present conflict;
2. Secondly, that they will continue to keep open their doors to all who seek refreshment of spirit;
3. Thirdly, that they will, with the sustained financial help of their communities broaden the scope and variety of their work;
4. Fourthly, that they will be sources of inspiration illuminating the past and vivifying the present; that they will fortify the spirit on which Victory depends.

Nothing but praise can be given to this resolution as it pertains to the war effort. However, the value of the museum in wartime must necessarily be limited to the maintenance of morale. In addition it must be admitted that museums today reach but a minute proportion of the public. Had the museums of yesterday realized the role which they should have had in community life, they would be infinitely better prepared to meet the emergency at hand today. Be that as it may, it is clearly apparent that the present job of museums goes far beyond the normal wartime duties. It is the army and navy which will win the war. The museum's task lies in preparation for the peace to come. It is then, in a world which we hope will be more ready to understand the problems of others, from nations down to individuals, and which will be searching for ways to make "peace" a word having real and lasting meaning, that the museum can assume a leadership befitting its position.

What Are Museums Today?

The word "museum" has little if any meaning the way it is used today. Actually one cannot define it because it has acquired so many different connotations. When a specific museum is mentioned, the scholar thinks of the magnificent collections and perhaps of his favorite objects; the man on the street thinks of a huge pseudo-something-or-other building with pigeons flying above and peanuts on the sidewalk in front. One could find a definition for most museums if one started with "a dynamic force in the cultural life of the community" and went down the list to "a collection of buttons." Most would be nearer the buttons, but in any case such a procedure does not help us. The fact is that a definition must be made for the word out of the actions of the institutions which it denotes.

The answer, then, to our question, "What is a museum?" is not to be found in words but in the nature of the institutions themselves. Many museums, of course, can hardly be called active, and for them the original meaning of the word may still hold. Not, however, for long, let us hope. Naturally it is toward the others which may rightfully be designated as active that this report is directed. That activity takes different forms, and the fact that it does is an added difficulty in discovering what a museum actually is. These different phases of activity, or if preferred, these functions, have been summarized by Paul M. Rea as

> the acquisition and preservation of objects, the advancement of knowledge by the study of objects, and the diffusion of knowledge for the enrichment of the life of the people.[3]

There can be little quarrel with that analysis in simply defining the functions. The trouble is that on paper such a statement makes it appear that the three functions are equal and receive an equal emphasis. Nothing could be farther from the truth. Stress has been and still is laid heavily on the first. Nor does Mr. Rea's statement give any indication of the fact such a thing as harmony does not exist among the three. The first two have forced the last to maintain a subordinate position creating a sharp inner division.

Let us face the issue fairly and squarely. Most museums are erected on the departmental structure. This type of division was started long before museums became aware that public education had any part to play in the life of museums. However, because that division into departments was already in existence, when education finally arrived, it was placed in a similar category and the "Department of Education" was born. The absurdity of giving education a place only equal in power to a single curatorial department was not realized. Often it did not even attain this status since at the beginning and as it too often remains at the present day, it was considered merely as a means to increase attendance. Mr. Taylor neatly phrased it when he said,

> And it has become the hallowed practice among all institutions to permit the educational department to be the legitimate tail to wag the rest of the dog. Thus, having paid a certain half-hearted tribute to the public welfare, they could turn to the more exciting pleasures of collecting and exposition.[4]

What he forgot to add was that it is the custom today among certain breeds to clip the tail to such an extent that it can produce nothing more than a comic wiggle.

Furthermore, in many cases public education has been placed in a moral quarantine by the rest of the staff. They have not only forced its submission but they have set it off as a necessary but isolated evil. This was the result, as we saw earlier, of the emphasis on collecting, the imitating of European museum manners, and the control of administration by men who were scholars and specialists in some curatorial field. Thus it was only natural that the directors should favor the attitudes of the curators from whose ranks they were drawn rather than the newer ideas of the educators. Certainly it is indicative of the American spirit that education forced its way into the museums to the extent that it did. Europe never has had education in our sense in its museums, and it has always been the educational aspects of American museums which have distinguished them from the European ones which they have tried so hard to imitate.

This battle which education has fought in the past to gain entrance into the museum has not been an easy one. Indeed, the odds have been almost overwhelmingly aligned on the opposite side. The opposition to consistent advance in the use of collections has been formed of a block of conservative men which may be divided into three sections. The first and largest are the curators. Since the beginning they have been the custodians and the purchasing agents for museums and in these positions are largely responsible for carrying out the first function as mentioned by Rea. They have also, however, gradually assumed complete control over the second function as well. Thus it has become their responsibility so to arrange the objects in their care that the scholars, students, and only incidentally the general public may see them and study them on their own initiative. This duty has been fulfilled by permanent arrangements, by the erection of study collections, and, most important, by the temporary exhibition. Obviously, this latter is essentially an educational feature of museum work, but, instead of being under the control of the educators, it has become the function of the curator. Once the exhibition has been arranged without consulting the educational staff the curator says, "Here it is. Now you explain it to the public."

The second groups of conservatives have been the directors. Because of tradition they have been much more interested in the building up of collections and in the scholarly prestige of the institution than in making it useful. Unfortunately, this scholastic bias has had the tendency to make most directors shy off from any form of popularization in the fear that it would lower standards. Frankly, there is some justification in this attitude when one sees some of the forms of popularization which have been attempted. On the other hand there is no reason in the world to maintain that popularization cannot be accomplished without loss of standards, and it may, in fact, raise them. In short, and it might as well be admitted, the majority of directors have not been administrators and have approached their task with an outlook and attitude which have prevented them from seeing the museum as something much more than the sum of its collections. More often than not this attitude was not their fault, and many strove to fight against themselves, but that in general what has been said is true must be affirmed when one looks at the present state of museums.

Finally, the third group of this body of loyal opposition consists of the trustees. Of the three there is no question but that the trustees represent the group which alone has the legitimate right to be conservative. Indeed, it is their beholden duty since they serve the cause of moderation. This does not mean that trustees should be adamant and oppose change merely because what is proposed is novel nor does it necessarily mean that a prerequisite for the position of trustee must be gray hair. On the contrary, trustees should be willing to abet and further the progressive ideas which are presented for their consideration, if the ideas represent carefully thought out plans for the future and not mere passing fancies. As representative members of the lay public and of the community, the trustees should remember that part of their responsibility is to see that their community is served as well and as efficiently as possible by their institution. Adam stated this clearly when he said,

> One of the first steps necessary is to clear away the legal fiction that museum trustees are mere guardians of funds and endowments. They are, in fact, active governing bodies in a field of great social movement and should be openly recognized as such by every element in the community.[5]

Another fact which bears mentioning is that the charge of ultra-conservatism which the educators have so often levelled at the trustees, although frequently justified, is not necessarily true in every case. Often they are conservative through no fault of their own since the progressive ideas of the educators fail to reach their ears or, if they do, they are drowned out by the arguments of the curators and directors. From a purely practical point of view this worked out all right as long as the question of public support did not materially affect the financial status of the museum. Recently, however, with a rapid decline in income, museums have been faced with a very acute financial problem which cannot be solved by trustees alone. Thus from a purely mercenary viewpoint the question of increased public support has become extremely important for the future of museums. Candidly, unless it is obtained, museums may soon cease to exist. That this is the wrong way to approach the vital problem of the museum's place in the community cannot be denied. On the other hand the educators should rejoice that the pressing need for financial support has become their ally albeit unwittingly. Because of this need the conservative block is beginning to wonder whether there is not something in this popular education after all. The danger lies in whether, once they realize this, their attitude is going to be one of grudging acceptance or of whole-hearted support. It is up to the educators to show them the way. In fact, before the public will be able to receive what it wants and needs, there must be a determined effort to reorient the ideas and attitudes of the curators, directors and trustees.

If these three groups contain the men who have consistently prevented the museum from taking its rightful course, who are the men who make up the progressive element within museums? They are, of course, as has already been intimated, the various educational staffs. Later, I wish to go into more detail on this subject. For the present, then, it must suffice to say that they are small in number but strong in spirit. Recently they have been able to add to their ranks men from the traditionally conservative groups. This cross-cutting of the opposition is a healthy sign and points to concrete results in the near future. Conversely, however, some of the educational people have been under fire for so long that their initiative and foresight have burned down to the point of extinction and they, too, have become ultra-conservative. Some may well be aroused again, but others must gradually sink from sight. As a group, however, they have the public at heart and are willing to accept new ideas and to fight to make the museum a more valuable institution.

The ultimate result of this conflict between scholarship and popular education is only too evident in the utter confusion as to purpose and function which characterizes museums today. They are little more than masses of conflicting ideas centering around masses of often unrelated objects. Some have gone a long way on the road to securing harmony and to making the museum into a distinctly American institution. Others are still in the state which provoked Dana to write against them. None, however, have been able completely to solve the problem. Until that problem is satisfactorily solved, museums will continue to wander in the darkness, fighting among and within themselves.

The first and foremost task, then, which faces museums is a realization of their potential force for good and the resolution of their internal strife so that they may put that force into action. There can be no doubt that this must be done and done now. The last ten years and the ten years to come will probably prove to be the test period for museums. Barring world conditions over which they have no control, it is possible for museums to make for themselves a permanent, useful place in society. There is a possibility that the turning point is past and that museums are already on the right road. If that is so, it is all to the good; if not, there is still time, albeit precious little. Let us become more specific now and look at what can be done to make the word "museum" actually mean something.

What Can Museums Become?

The first problem as we have seen is to weld the museum into a unit. This can be divided into two aspects. First there is the establishment of a single goal toward which all of the museum's activities are striving. Secondly, there is the discovery of the role which each activity is to play in relation to the others.

Some people might say that acquisition and preservation, scholarly study, and popular education are incompatible. That is far, far from the truth as they are all bound up in the same process and are so interrelated as to make one inseparable from the others. The difficulty is that museums have separated them in an artificial manner and have created jealousies which have resulted in the discord about which we have already spoken. Perhaps the most devastating result of this conflict (and universities are to blame as well as museums) has been that scholars have come to look with disdain on popular education and popular education has, in turn, come to decry the narrow-minded, haughtiness of the scholars. The fact is that both pursuits are just as lofty, just as rewarding, just as difficult and both have distinct functions to perform. Furthermore, in the case of museums both are dependent on the function of acquisition and preservation which supplies them with the objects to be used for their respective ends.

What, then, is this common goal for which all three functions should be striving and in the fulfillment of which they should abet rather than oppose each other? Naturally, it can only be expressed broadly and, that being the case, the simpler the explanation the better. Briefly, the purpose and the only purpose of museums is education in all its varied aspects from the most scholarly research to the simple arousing of curiosity. That education, however, must be active, not passive, and it must always be intimately connected with the life of the people. Each of the three functions must be thought of as existing for the public and not as processes isolated and self-sufficient unto themselves. Finally, to fulfill this purpose, the museum must find its own place in the total process of education, since then and then only can it make its own distinctive contribution to life itself.

The second step if museums are going to become a dynamic force must be the realization that the functions are not static either in their relationship to one another or in their importance. Both aspects change even as do the times. Thus, if the term "museum" is going to mean something in the future, museums of today must be willing to alter and to modify their internal structure and their ideas to fit the changing world conditions and the advances in social thought. Museums have failed to do this and have shown a most extraordinary reluctance to accept new social theories and new social ideas.

If we go back into the recent past, it is possible to illustrate what is meant, function by function. In the early stages of their existence museums found it necessary to place emphasis on the first function, acquisition and preservation. That was logical as we have pointed out. They were building up the collections of basic material for the future. Today in our large museums those collections are formed, and acquisition has become a kind of scholar's jigsaw puzzle where he fits a piece in here and fills a gap in there. Obviously museums will and should continue to make acquisitions but the importance of the role which that process has played must be diminished. The use which is made of objects bought in the past is of much greater significance today than the occasional purchase of additional material. The other aspect of this first function, preservation and all that it implies, need not be elaborated on.

The second or scholarly function grew up along with the first, and its development is best illustrated in the case of the art museum. The art historian is a relatively recent addition to professional ranks, and it is quite safe to say that the American version had his birth in the museum. For a long period the art museum was the natural place to teach art history for the simple reason that courses could not be found elsewhere, and there was a definite need to be filled. This was all very well and necessary at the time, but it had the unfortunate result of increasing the emphasis on the museum as an institute of higher learning reserved for the few and, at the same time, of overshadowing the fact that museums were founded for the benefit of the total population.

Today that emphasis still holds, and museums are still primarily interested in teaching art history when actually that function has been taken over by the colleges and universities. The art historian of today is not born in the museum, but in those colleges and universities, and the courses which he attends and will attend are not those given at the museum. Nor need it be emphasized that aside from the actual objects, the college and university can surpass the average museum in physical teaching equipment. The same holds true for the scholar as well. He will come to the museum to study the objects, but, if he does any teaching, it will be in a college or university. He may agree to give a lecture at a museum which may serve to sustain the museum's intellectual face, but which is usually far above the heads of the audience. If it is not, one may be fairly certain that the audience is composed of university people, and very likely a large portion are the lecturer's own students if he teaches in the same city. It would seem, then, that in trying to carry on in the old tradition museums are needlessly overlapping the functions of other educational organizations. Furthermore, it is likely that the future will bring more extension work on the part of the universities which will increase the duplication. At present the demand for the scholarly type of art lecture is certainly not exorbitant and can be easily handled by the universities, colleges and other organizations.

The point is brought to attention here because it is only too evident that the conception of the museum's duty to scholarship and thus to the performance of the second function must be thrown into a new light. The answer would seem to be to abolish all efforts at scholarly teaching and to substitute that kind of instruction which the museum can offer better than any other institution or organization. The museum will always have a duty toward scholarship as long as it has collections, but there is nothing that demands that that duty remain static.

The situation is, of course, complicated by the fact that as time goes on the overlap of function between the curator and the college or university professor becomes increasingly marked. Needless to say, both are scholars and specialists in the same fields and both write and publish works on the same subjects. Their existence side by side has never really been challenged but the time is not far away when that challenge must inevitably come. Actually the professorial ranks are on the increase both in numbers and proficiency while the curatorial position appears to be undergoing drastic modifications. At present the distinction between the two types of scholar lies in the fact that in putting his knowledge into action the professor teaches while the curator purchases works, cares for them, and arranges them in exhibitions. Were this division of duties to remain static, there would be no cause for confusion, but that is not the case.

One hesitates to make prophecies related to this problem because of the difficulties in determining which way current trends are leading. The common complaint of museum men that the college professor knows more about photographs than he does about objects is hardly tenable when one reviews the roster of the faculties of our large eastern universities. They are still the main sources of future art historians. On the other hand it is unfortunately true that whereas the faculties may have had wide experience with objects the students do get most of their knowledge second hand. Museums complain bitterly about this fact but few have done their share in counteracting the effect.

Actually the problem is far more complicated than it appears on the surface. With the present emphasis on degrees for degrees' sake and the rigidness of academic requirements few students have time to travel to the extent necessary. If by chance they do, they usually lack the money to do it. One suggestion which might help alleviate the difficulty would be for museums to have a type of in-school training which could be credited toward a degree. To draw students, however, the latter qualification is essential.

If, within the next twenty or thirty years, some system is worked out whereby everyone entering museum service will have had experience with objects, one begins to wonder whether or not the curatorial position will undergo some change. In this case the trend definitely points to an affirmative answer. Thus, in the first place, the curatorial function of arranging exhibitions should fall more and more under the aegis of the educational department. They and not the curators are closest to the public pulse. Secondly, the actual work of preservation and care of objects is coming more and more into the hands of scientists trained for the purpose. Particularly in our larger museums that will become a full time job. Finally one wonders whether or not the time now spent by curators in uncovering possible purchases will be decreased because of the simple fact that purchases themselves will be drastically curtailed.

Just how quickly this change in the curatorial position will come is impossible to tell. It is important, however, to face it now and to be considering what path will be followed. What is apparent is that the curator must be made to realize that he is a part of a working organism. At the present time most curators are amenable to limited demands made on their material by the educational departments. On the other hand it is extremely difficult to make many realize that the museum has a much more fundamental and worthwhile purpose than the mere preservation, acquisition, and exhibition of objects. Furthermore, it must be admitted that interdepartmental jealousy which is as needless as it is absurd is a very important factor in the failure of museums to do their duty. For their own sake and particularly in regard to the training of future museum men it is necessary for the curators to study their own situation with an open and critical mind. If they do not, they may well find themselves to be a group isolated from the main museum movement.

Whatever may eventually happen along that line, one thing is certain and that is that museums must shift the emphasis from scholarly work to the third function—popular education. Needless to say the latter may be increased without diminishing the former. On the other hand the curator's control over the use of his material must be modified to fit the interests of greatly extended and far more powerful education departments. In this connection it would be far more to the point to have one or two scholarly exhibitions a year devoted exclusively to the interests of the experts and have the rest of interest to the general public than to travel the present course which museums follow in presenting exhibitions which are neither one nor the other. There is no rule which says exhibitions must be intelligible to one and all. Such a procedure is not followed in other fields and there is no reason for it to be true in museums.

Still, however, with reference to the relation between scholarly work and popular education there is one factor which museums refuse to recognize. Museums are public institutions. Some it is true are semi-public and some private if the classification is made on the basis of finances. Despite that fact the swing of events points to the greater and greater need for public support and even those museums now classed as private may soon feel that need. Regardless of that, all types of museums are public institutions by virtue of the nature of their contents and as such have a distinct moral duty to the community in which they are situated. This being so, they must recognize that that duty automatically includes all types and all classes of people. I want later to discuss the question of the museum's public in greater detail, but it is necessary to bring this point up in this connection because it is a determining one in any discussion of museum purpose.

The fact is that museums have devoted a disproportionate amount of time and energy to the cultivation of the upper circles, both of intelligence and of society. More often than not they have been extremely fearful of getting "the wrong kind of people." It does not take any statistics to prove that the people who now frequent museums form a minute fraction of the total population of any one community. What becomes of the vast majority of the people? Are they not members of the public? Hasn't the museum a definite duty to fulfill toward them?

There is only one answer to the above questions. It is here, in the field of popular education, that the museum belongs today. It is here that the museum can make its own and its greatest contribution to the total cause of education. As we have said, the duty to scholarship remains, but in the light of the vital importance of this other work it must fade into a place in the background of the museum's consciousness. Museums are public institutions. That cannot be forgotten again. No doubt the scholars will verbally object to this altered conception of the museum's purpose and they are doing it already. They have enjoyed the feeling that the museums existed primarily for them, and they have enjoyed the ready-made retreats which were supplied to them. Some will and, it is true, some have already seen the importance of shifting the emphasis to the broader field. To the others it is well to issue one further warning. I know that in times like these it is the scholar's habit to say that only here in America can scholarship survive, and therefore it becomes the duty of every good scholar to bury himself deeper in his work, to maintain or, if possible, to raise standards, and to keep the flag of true scholarship waving in the breeze. The theory seems to be that, come what may, they will grit their teeth, close their eyes and forge ahead. It is a noble thought, but one which has a tendency to cloud the main issue. The fact is that scholarship will never die in a free land, but it is woefully dependent for its lifeblood on the latter condition. The intellectual sterility of the totalitarian countries is not a coincidence but a fundamental necessity for their continued existence. No one of intelligence, moreover, can deny the possibility of something similar happening here from without or, more likely, from within. Thus it would seem that the scholars, admittedly the best minds of the nation, should turn their efforts to the prevention of that possibility. That cannot be accomplished by further entrenchment in their own little corners of intellectual life. It makes little difference whether books on Byzantine ivories, Asiatic sarcophagi, or Borneo bushmen appear this year or next year as long as they eventually appear. The only way to assure that eventuality is to make certain that the social conditions under which they alone may survive are stable and ready to meet the threats which are so forcibly present today. Thus the scholars must be prepared to play their part in the struggle for maintaining that freedom without which scholarship dies, and the least that they can do is to throw their support whole-heartedly behind the movement for popular education.

What, then, is this popular education on which museums must concentrate their attention? To begin with it is not something narrow and clearly defined in the old sense of classes, courses, examinations, grades and degrees. Those words belong to the vocabulary of formal, academic education. Popular education is vastly more comprehensive, is part and parcel of the everyday experiences of life, and more often than not it cannot be recognized as education in the accepted sense of the word. On the one hand it embraces such things as books, the theatre, the movies, sports, radio, in fact, almost every branch of human activity to a greater or less degree depending on the relative power that each has to increase the knowledge, happiness, and experience of the individual. In these it is usually unconscious on the part of the individual. On the other hand it embraces the rapidly growing adult education movement. In this case it is more often a conscious effort on the part of the individual to improve himself in some way or other. Here it differs from formal education despite the organization of classes in that it is always a voluntary act of the individual. The success of the movement has long since proven that there is a demand for education of this sort and that the ability and desire of adults to learn is not a mere matter of wishful thinking on the part of those idealists who are set to remake the world.

To clarify the meaning of popular education still further I would like to quote two paragraphs from an article by C. A. Siepmann on "Can Radio Educate?" It is not a definition. I do not think that a definition is possible of a term which embraces so much. In it, however, one can find the type of spirit which is in back of the movement and which is far more important than any definition could possibly be. He asks why so little use of the radio has been made for purposes with educational significance and answers his own question in the following manner:

> The fault, I think, rests, as I have said, in part with the educators. We keep barking up the wrong tree. What we have failed to realize is that there exists today a new urgency for the wholesale dissemination of education. 'Money is like muck, not good but it be spread.' So with education. Radio disposes of our inability to spread education and offers us techniques peculiarly well suited to the kind of education that is wanted. We have been slow to appreciate the fact, slow to dispense with our own conceptions of what education is. We, as educators, suffer from the limitation of our own experience. Our background of education is that of a formal discipline extending over years, deriving from the teacher, or rather a succession of teachers, and from study, and directed toward the realization of a culture remote from that which can as yet be realized for the masses. We are the products of a selective process, aimed at the development of skills of an intellectual order and associated with cultural notions of taste and discrimination, the refinement and the good manners bred of the arts and of philosophy. We suffer, in fact, from a kind of intellectual

inbreeding that tends to remove us both socially and in terms of experience from the hard facts and circumstances of suffering and strain of ordinary people. The fruits of such education stand unassailable in their own right. But having regard to the urgency of our time and the circumstance and background of the majority of our fellows, they are, for radio, largely irrelevant.

It is for this reason among others that I believe we tend to shirk the adoption of techniques of interpretation which offend our taste and have for us little intellectual appeal. To have read the poets, to have studied art, to have a comprehensive understanding of history, to have shared the thoughts and speculations of the great philosophers is a great privilege, an unforgettable experience. But what highbrows tend to overlook is that in respect of fundamental values, in respect of fellowship, of honesty, the decencies of behavior, and the normal sympathies which make life worth living, there are other and cruder disciplines which approximate a similar achievement. If, without such a background of education, the good life is not possible, then indeed the condition of the world is parlous in the extreme. But that does not happen to be true. Poverty is not a bar to decency, nor is the lack of formal education a fatal obstacle to the appreciation of what citizenship and the practice of Christian virtues mean. Values derive from the heart and not the head. It is at the heart of the people and not at their heads that popular education should aim.[6]

The fact is that this type of education has been going on since time immemorial, but until recently the term education has had such a limited application that the educators never realized the wealth of teaching material which was lying by just waiting to be used. Belatedly leaders in the field have been attempting to bring order out of chaos, to study the ways and means of putting new mediums to good effect rather than to evil, and to reorient and reorganize the forces which can and should guide the movement. This is already being done to a very great extent by the various adult education organizations and in particular by the American Association for Adult Education. These are coordinating agencies and not sources of materials and teachers. They are the guiding lights, but they must be supported by other organizations and by other institutions.

It is here that the museum as an already established institution with vast resources of material of all kinds and description must take its place beside the library as a bulwark of the movement for popular education. These two institutions, one the exponent of the printed page and the other of the visual object, can provide a stability to the movement which it might otherwise lack and at the same time participate whole-heartedly in the drive which is necessary to keep the movement always going forward. Active public libraries and active public museums are an American creation and as such they can play an exceedingly important role in maintaining and strengthening that thing which we like to call "the American Way of Life."

It is, indeed, just this conception of a museum that was held by Choate and later by Dana. The difference between the times in which they spoke and today lies in the urgency of the situation. Two voices have spoken recently from the ranks of the adult educators. In an address delivered by Morse A. Cartwright before the

American Association of Museums on the subject of The Place of the Museum in Adult Education he said,

> I think the museum, too, must realize its responsibility from top to toe as an agency for molding as well as for reflecting public taste and opinion. I think it must move out on its own initiative and that, in addition, it must be ready to serve as auxiliary to other agencies working for adult education in its multifarious forms within the community.[7]

T. R. Adam stated the case a little more fully when he said,

> Viewed in proper perspective, museums can be seen to be powerful instruments of popular education affecting the social history of our people. The need for rapid diffusion of new knowledge is not constant but varies in accordance with the rate of change in the social environment. When society can afford to pursue traditional paths, custom and habit are the best educators; when science or politics or industry suddenly breaks through into new fields, the community stands in danger of chaos until methods of spreading the essential facts of the new outlook have been discovered and perfected. There can be no social stability until a changed environment has been reduced in men's minds to accepted custom based on a common understanding of the forces at work.
>
> It is this element in museums—their use as modern weapons in the struggle for popular enlightenment—that has caused them to flourish so successfully in our times. Separated from its social content a museum is meaningless to anyone but its curators. We are fortunate in possessing in this country a museum movement that is consciously seeking to base its fortunes on the performance of forward-looking tasks rather than on smug memories of the past. A time element exists that gives a dramatic quality to the present situation; cultural upheavals are taking place all around with a rapidity scarcely ever equaled in history. Museums, like all institutions, are slow and cautious in their adaptations. Whether the instruments we need to initiate men in the mysteries of our emergent civilization can be made ready in time, before ignorance and suffering destroy the physical basis of our culture, is a question few would be hardy enough to answer.[8]

Adam wrote those words in 1939 and in the intervening years events have shown that the cultural lag of which he spoke has increased rather than decreased. Museums have remained as part of that lag instead of taking their rightful position in the front rank of those struggling to close the gap. Moreover, that success in combating the evil forces now at work in the world can only come through popular enlightenment is clearly evident. Therefore it seems only logical that museums should turn from passive institutions used only by the scholars and the initiated into active institutions serving the total population of their respective communities.

Notes

1. Taylor, F. H., "Museums in a Changing World," *The Atlantic Monthly*, Vol. 164, No. 6, December 1939, pp. 785–792.

2. Adam, op.cit., p. 28.

3. Rea, P. M., "What Are Museums For?," *Journal of Adult Education*, Vol. II, June 1930, pp. 265–271.

4. Taylor, op.cit.

5. Adam, T. R., op.cit., p. 29.

6. Siepmann, C. A., "Can Radio Educate?," *Journal of Educational Sociology*, Vol. XIV, No. 6, February 1941, pp. 352–353.

7. Cartwright, M. A., "The Place of the Museum in Adult Education," *Museum News*, October 15, 1939.

8. Adam, T. R., op.cit.

The Museum, a Temple or the Forum

3

DUNCAN F. CAMERON

OUR MUSEUMS ARE IN DESPERATE need of psychotherapy. There is abundant evidence of an identity crisis in some of the major institutions, while others are in an advanced state of schizophrenia. These, of course, are relatively new museum ailments, and we still have to live with the more traditional complaints—delusions of grandeur on the one hand and psychotic withdrawal on the other—but the crisis at the moment, put in the simplest possible terms, is that our museums and art galleries seem not to know who or what they are. Our institutions are unable to resolve their problems of role definition.

Having made a statement as damning as that, one is obliged to provide some evidence. Here, in a more or less random way, are a few anecdotes and examples offered in the hope that the gestalt of these will justify the psychiatric diagnosis.

In Toronto the provincial government spent somewhere between thirty-five and fifty million dollars building and putting into operation the Ontario Science Centre. In its earliest days—from 1964 to 1966—this immense new institution was planned as a museum and was staffed by museum professionals with a variety of backgrounds. By the end of 1966, the government and some members of the board had decided that museums were somehow a bad thing. The word museum was unacceptable. A museum with collections and a research program, with a conservation laboratory and a research library—this kind of museum was of no real interest, in their view, to the modern public.

In the course of a few months, all but one of the staff members with any museum background had left. The planning and development of the institution switched to the design group, public service officials, and a staff borrowed from the

Duncan F. Cameron (1930–2006) was a Canadian museologist, former director of The Brooklyn Museum, and director emeritus of the Glenbow-Alberta Institute. His article "The Museum, a Temple or the Forum" appeared in *Curator: The Museum Journal* in 1971 and in UNESCO's *Journal of World History* in 1972. It is reprinted here by permission of UNESCO.

provincial Department of Education. There was an absence of museum expertise and the Centre, as a matter of policy, was not to be a museum.

When the Science Centre opened to the public, with much fanfare, the brochure that was distributed carried this statement on the front cover:

Make a list of everything you've been taught about public places, especially museums. Things like:

don't touch anything
don't get excited
don't take pictures
don't laugh out loud

Got your list? Good.
Now tear it up in little pieces and throw it away.

The Ontario Science Centre is certainly not a museum, although it was originally planned as one. Today it contains a veritable chaos of science exhibits mixed with industrial and technological exhibits sponsored by corporations. There is an infinite number of buttons to push and cranks to turn. Interspersed among all of these are hot-dog stands and purveyors of soft ice cream in a claustrophobic maze of cacophonous noncommunication.

It is an "activity center," as the government promised, but how did a plan for a great museum of science and technology turn into the most expensive funfare in the world?

The Art Gallery of Ontario (AGO), also in Toronto, never had any doubt about its role as a museum of art history and a place for exhibitions of modern art. It was an art gallery, plain and simple. In the last twenty years, the gallery had to make difficult decisions about the exhibitions of local artists' societies. Perhaps the quality of the annual society shows was in question, but there was, quite rightfully, a concern with the maintenance of standards of excellence at the AGO. Then, during the 1960s, the problem of accommodating new contemporary forms, including happenings, electronic environments, and so forth, was faced by this gallery as it was by dozens of others. They did the best they could. Now, in the 1970s, there are plans for a greatly expanded art gallery building, and, at least in one stage of the planning, it was the intention to include large exhibition spaces, or environmental chambers, designed with maximum flexibility, wherein it was said that anything could be tried or made to happen.

The gallery had decided that it was no longer simply a place where proved works of excellence should be exhibited and interpreted to the public. Rather, it was also to be a place where the unknown and the experimental should be given a chance to happen, to become whatever it became, good or bad.

In Washington, D.C., in Anacostia (one of the great black ghettos of that city), there is a museum that has attracted international attention. The Anacostia Neighborhood Museum is sponsored by the Smithsonian Institution. It has an important program, which is defensible in every way. (Some readers may have seen the film about the rats exhibition. The purpose of that project was to examine the rat as an urban problem and especially a slum problem, to come to some understanding of the nature of the beast itself. Museum techniques were used, museum professionals were involved, but, most important of all, there was a remarkable degree of participation by members of the Anacostia community.) Here one must ask whether or not the name *museum* is appropriate to the operation of Anacostia. Is it not a community center serving an important and very necessary function in interpreting the immediate environment and the cultural heritage of that community by means of exhibition techniques but without permanent collections and curatorial functions? Is it not therefore a community exhibition center as distinct from a museum?

And what can be said of the new centers for contemporary art, of Sue Thurman's pioneering efforts in Boston or of Jan Vandermark's work in Chicago? In those instances, surely, the word *center* is more appropriate than the word *museum*. And if that is so, what of the Museum of Modern Art in New York? It is a center that became a great museum.

One can find many examples of the new science centers that hold no collections and do no original research but present a continuing program of science demonstration exhibits. There are many art history museums pushing back yesterday's heritage to make way for today's experiments. And then there are the growing numbers of cultural centers that strive to be all things to all men. Many of these include, somewhere in their complex and often frenetic programs, something called a museum.

Is a museum something that can be housed, with any degree of compatibility, side by side with ballet classes for three-year-olds, amateur arts programs of every variety, and the occasional bingo game benefit for a local charity?

There are institutions such as the Roberson Center for the Arts and Sciences in Binghamton, New York, that would say "yes" in answer to that question. The recent brochure from the Roberson says on the cover, "Roberson—the happening place—it is the center." And, on the back of the same handsomely designed piece, it says, "It is an art museum, a science museum, an historical museum, an arts council, an activity center for art, music, dance, drama—an educational center for all." There is little doubt that the Roberson is relevant, that it is serving its community well, and that the director and his staff are to be commended. But consider the question that is more significant than mere semantics: "Is there really a museum at the Roberson?"

Of course, none of these questions can be answered until it is decided what a museum is. Attempts to define a museum have been made for almost as long as there have been museums, yet there is no definition to my knowledge that meets with everyone's satisfaction. Another attempt is made here to provide a definition of a sort that may at least help to clarify the issue central to this discussion.

In order to approach the problem of definition, it is necessary to repeat some things that I have said elsewhere but which may not be familiar to the reader.

The starting point is the idea of collecting as a universal behavior. It is argued that men, in all times and all places, have collected things and gathered objects around themselves and arranged them and rearranged them in an attempt to come to terms with the reality they perceived. It might be added that men also collect ideas and arrange them and rearrange them, collect words and sounds, have collections of stories and songs, and use these in a similar way. But, at the moment, the concern is with the collecting of objects.

The best evidence I can provide for this universal collecting behavior is not just the fact that collections and the arranging of collections of objects are recorded throughout history and are evidenced by archeological findings, but, more important, that this same behavior continues today on an intimate and individual basis. Here are examples that may strike chords in your own memories or recall earlier observations in a new light.

Consider what happens to a little boy or girl taken from the city into the country on a vacation for the first time. Does the child not bring into the house or the cottage or the hotel an unusual variety of objects that he has gathered from the new environment? Does he not bring in the dead toad and the mushroom and the colored leaves, as well as the pebbles, bits of driftwood, a dead fish, shells, and the jetsam of the seashore, depending upon where he may be? And, characteristically, will he not take these now prized possessions to a corner that he regards as his own (perhaps a window ledge or a table close by his bed)? And does he not arrange them and rearrange them as he examines and studies his new finds?

The child has been busy sampling a new environment, and with his sample he is attempting to structure a model that will help him to understand it. The importance of structuring a model is demonstrated by the child's reaction when a parent or brother or sister disturbs the child's arrangement of his collection. Mother, perhaps, while tidying up takes the childish array and reorganizes it in a neat row along the window ledge. The child is distressed not because his objects, his prizes, have been damaged but because the meaningful relationships he was establishing among them have been destroyed.

Over a period of time, if a child were to remain in that environment and it became familiar to him, he would collect in a somewhat different way. He would then be selecting objects from the environment that were significant or important in that environment—as he had come to understand it. Eventually, at a level of greater sophistication, he would select from the environment and enshrine in his collection those objects that best symbolized the operating values he employed in the environment or, alternately, the accepted values of the society in which he participated.

Isn't this a behavior common to us all in one way or another? Next time you have the opportunity, take a thoughtful look at the objects that are arranged in your own house or in your private room. Take a good look at an executive's desk with its collection of mementos and souvenirs and the so-called office equipment (much of which is not nearly as utilitarian as it first appears). These structured collections will tell you something about the way in which the collector perceives reality.

For a very dramatic demonstration of all of this, watch what happens in the private rooms of young people in their teens and even their early twenties. Their rooms very often appear to be in a state of constant chaos, upheaval, and unreasoned change from the viewpoint of the parent or the adult. In fact, what is happening there is that the young person, trying very hard to find his place in the scheme of things, is collecting, rejecting collections, building new collections, reorganizing them, establishing new relationships, and seeking a nonverbal reality model that will express his dreams and aspirations—the answer to his search for identity.

Another, and last, example of this untested hypothesis about the individual and collecting is that of the houses or rooms inhabited by the aged. In our time, especially, it is very difficult for those who have now lived the better part of their lives to accept the virtually revolutionary changes that continue to take place in society. Thus, in their rooms, we find extensive collections of memorabilia and souvenirs, photographs and keepsakes; they have structured them in their attempt to maintain belief in a reality they once perceived but which is, in fact, long passed. It becomes clear, then, that the collection as a reality model serves the collector first and may aid or deter not only the objective perceptions of the collector but also the perceptions of the visitor.

Until a century ago, or at most two centuries ago, collections were private collections, and public museums did not exist in any contemporary sense. These collections were autistic in that they reflected, in virtually all cases, some individual's private perception of reality and self-image. The collections may have said, "Look how curious I am and how meticulous and how thorough. Here is my scientific collection, which reaffirms my belief in the order of the universe and the laws of nature." The collection may have said, "See how rich I am," or, "Look at this. Look at how I surround myself with beautiful things. See what good taste I have, how civilized and cultivated I am." It may have said, "Oh! I am a man of the world who has traveled much. Look at all the places I have been. Look at all the mysterious things I have brought back from my adventures. Yes! I am an adventurer." And if you or I were invited to view one of these collections, it presented no serious problem. We weren't being told that this was our collection nor that we had to accept the collector's view of the world or of himself. We simply saw his collection and through it, perhaps, saw him more clearly.

Noting the exceptions, it can be said that it was but a century or a little more ago that we began, in western society, to create public museums. In large part, these public museums were private collections opened to the public, and, as long as that was made quite clear, there was, as mentioned earlier, no real problem. The trouble began with the introduction of a new idea: the democratic museum.

The idea was simple enough. It was to assemble collections of many different kinds and interpret them to the general public for the furtherance of its education, for its enlightenment, and for its recreation. In declaring these collections to be public in the sense of being publicly owned, however, it was no longer being said that this was someone else's collection that you, the visitor, could look at. Rather, it was being said that this was your collection and therefore it should be meaningful to you, the visitor.

The public museum was now an institutionalization of the individual collecting behavior. Thus the public had a right to expect that the collections presented and interpreted would in some way be consistent with the values of its society and with its collective perceptions of the environment or, if you wish, of reality. Unfortunately, there were two principal problems in creating such public collections and, it is suggested, these are problems that have not yet been solved in the majority of museums and art galleries.

The first of these was that the collectors and those responsible for organizing and structuring the collections were now the members of an academic, curatorial elite; they were most familiar and most comfortable with the models that were specific to their academic disciplines. Thus the public collections were structured as models that could only be meaningful to those with an education in which they had been introduced to scientific systems of classification, to prevailing theories of history, or to the academic approach to art and art history. One might almost say that the private collectors had been replaced by an exclusive, private club of curators. The public was still being offered private collections but with a new name over the door.

The second and related problem was that the value systems that determined not only the selection of material but also the priorities for its presentation tended to be the value systems of the middle class if not an upper-middle-class elite. This was, of course, most particularly true of museums of art.

We created great science museums that might be described as no more than three-dimensional textbooks. We created great art museums that reflected the heritage of bourgeois and aristocratic culture to the exclusion of popular or folk culture.

But, even given these faults or limitations, those segments of society with the power to do so at least created museums that were the temples within which they enshrined those things they held to be significant and valuable. The public generally accepted the idea that if it was in the museum, it was not only real but represented a standard of excellence. If the museum said that this and that was so, then that was a statement of truth. The museum, at least for a time, was the place where you could go to compare your own private perceptions of reality with the soi-disant objective view of reality that was accepted and approved in your society.

I suspect that it is for this reason that I have said from time to time that the museum, sociologically, is much closer in function to the church than it is to the school. The museum provides opportunity for reaffirmation of the faith; it is a place for private and intimate experience, although it is shared with many others; it is, in concept, the temple of the muses where today's personal experience of life can be viewed in the context of "The Works of God Through All the Ages; the Arts of Man Through All the Years."[2]

It might be inferred from this attempt at a definition that this paper is to be a conservative and reactionary defense of the traditional museum; it may be useful, at this point, to deny the implication. It is argued that the museum as a temple is valid and furthermore that such museums are essential in the life of any society that pretends to civilization. But there will also be an argument for museum reform. That will lead to the question not of reform but forums, which are something else again.

Reference here to the reform of museums does not mean plans to convert them into social clubs or funfairs but reform to make them better and more effective museums in the sense of the museum as a temple. The initial step will be to reestablish the museum's role or, if you wish, its social function. The museum must be steadfast in its insistence on proved excellence, on the highest possible degree of objectivity in selection, organization, and interpretation. There must be a willingness to admit to the things that are not known, are not understood, as well as to argue with confidence for those things that are held to be true and for those things that are the considered judgments of time, if there is to be credibility.

The academic systems of classification, which constitute an undecipherable code for the majority of museum visitors, must either be replaced, or better, be supplemented by interpretation of the collections that is based on the probable experience and awareness of the museum audience. Those collections that are essentially representative of bourgeois and aristocratic cultures of the past must be put into the context of popular culture, folk art, and the life style of the peasant or working classes in the culture from which the collections are derived. Social history and the insights of the anthropologist must be used to develop techniques of interpretation that will put the collections, and especially the museum "treasures," in a more realistic perspective.

A very special task in reform for those museums concerned with alien, exotic, or historic cultures is to relate those collections to contemporary life and society. Most museum directors would be shocked if they knew how their visitors interpret oriental collections or collections from the classical world when they are presented in the traditional fashion. By failing to provide meaningful interpretation of the collections, museums are, by that omission, guilty of misrepresentation, distortion of fact, and the encouragement of attitudes toward cultures other than our own that are dangerous and destructive in what McLuhan has called today's "global village."

In effect, these museum reforms are part of social responsibility in cultural programming. They are necessary to the democratization of culture, or, to use an expression I prefer, to the creation of an equality of cultural opportunity.

These reforms, of which much more could be said, are in no way new suggestions, and they are certainly not original here. Such reforms of museums have been proposed for decades, and a great deal has been said and written about them since the end of World War II. Unfortunately, the majority of the great museums have yet to do very much about it. The time has come, however, when museums must institute these reforms or perish.

Some readers may have heard of the disruption of the meetings of the American Association of Museums in New York City in the spring of 1971. A protest group, composed principally of disenchanted artists in New York City, demanded admission to the meeting. When a representative group was admitted, they disrupted meetings, presented a manifesto, struggled for microphones on the platform, and refused to be silent. The majority of the American museum professionals present were not only shocked but greatly surprised by these developments. They did not expect to find protest against museums and art galleries. Having been in Paris and Brussels at museum meetings only a few months earlier, I was less surprised. The alliance of artists with the intellectuals and with the radical student movements of protest in Europe is a matter of record, and there I had heard much discussion of the antimuseum protest movement.

The argument that there can be no progress in the arts, or in the democratization of the arts, until the Louvre is burned is a cliché in the West European radical art movement. There is protest against the maintenance of great public museums that do nothing more than enshrine the evidence of bourgeois and aristocratic domination of society, and there is protest against arts education in which bourgeois values, exemplified by the Louvre, are imposed on the masses. One may or may not wish to use the vocabulary of radical protest, and I doubt that many in the museum world wish to set fire to the Louvre, but I do feel that it must be conceded that the protest against the museums and art galleries does have a basis in reality and that museum reform is long overdue.

A far more important inference that can be drawn from current protest is that there is something missing in the world of museums and art galleries. What is missing cannot be found through the reform of the museum as a temple. In my view, it is clear that there is a real and urgent need for the reestablishment of the forum as an institution in society. While our bona fide museums seek to become relevant, maintaining their role as temples, there must be concurrent creation of forums for confrontation, experimentation, and debate, where the forums are related but discrete institutions.

In an address to the Canadian Conference of the Arts in September 1970, Dr. Mavor Moore of York University summed up his proposals for democratization and the creation of equality in cultural opportunity, saying that the essence of the problem was, "Will the establishment finance the revolution?" I agree with Dr. Moore that the establishment (and by that is meant the corporations, governments, and private individuals) must, in effect, finance the revolution by creating opportunities for the artists and the critics of society to produce, to be heard, to be seen, and to confront established values and institutions. What they have to say must be subjected to public judgment and to the test of time! These are the functions of the forum.

In practical and specific terms, I am proposing not only exhibition halls and meeting places that are open to all, but also programs and funds for them that accept without reservation the most radical innovations in art forms, the most controversial interpretations of history, of our own society, of the nature of man, or, for that matter, of the nature of our world. It intrigues me and at the same time distresses me that the need for a forum applies primarily to experimentation and new thought in the arts and humanities but not in the sciences. The scientist who wishes to undertake research, even though his results may upset established scientific theory, is provided with laboratories, his work is published, we give him grants. And if he does upset the apple cart, we award him great honors even if the new theories he produces have disturbing effects upon our society and our way of life.

We are quite prepared to debate the virtues or evils of new birth control methods, the fluoridation of water, test-tube babies, or the exploration of space, but it never occurs to us to put in jail the research scientists who created the very thing that we are prepared to argue about and which we oppose. In the arts and humanities this is not the case. The artist or scholar who criticizes our society and offends our sensitivities or our values is, in effect, regarded as an enemy of society even before we have allowed time for his work or his statements to be judged and considered.

At the outset it was suggested that there was schizophrenia and an identity crisis in the world of museums. Perhaps now that can be made more clear. Many institutions cannot decide whether they wish to be a museum, as a temple, or wish to become the public forum. Some have tried to bring the forum inside the temple. That is true of many of the institutions that call themselves museums but now claim to be "the place where it's at, an activity center, an institution swinging with a hip philosophy of social relevance." Unfortunately, the idea of bringing the forum—the place for confrontation and experimentation—inside the temple is to inhibit and, in effect, to castrate the performance in the forum.

Admission to the museum (even a swinging museum) is acceptance by the Establishment. So often the introduction of controversial, experimental, or radical activities into the museum is little more than paternalism. Some museums, I suspect, have decided to incorporate manifestations of the antiestablishment movement within their establishment institutions because they feared protest or perhaps violence and sought to neutralize the enemy. Others, I suspect, have gone this route because they simply wanted to be where the action was. (Surely it must be frustrating to follow the excitement and vitality of the contemporary art scene if you happen to be a curator of modern art, stuck in a museum, and you're not really a part of it.) But, regardless of the motivation, it is argued here that those museums that attempt to integrate these two discrete sociological functions of forum and temple are in error.

The error, as said, is in part that they rob the forum of its vitality and autonomy. There is an even more serious aspect to this error—the acceptance into the museum of the untried and experimental tends to devalue those things that are properly in the museum. Museum collections, as suggested earlier, are based on the careful sampling of reality where both time and expert judgment determine what shall come in and what shall stay out. It has to be understood that the very nature of an object changes when it becomes a museum object. A work of art, an archeological specimen, or an antique is just that and nothing more when it is in the shop or in the street or perhaps in the forum. The moment that it is purchased or accepted by the museum it takes on a new quality. You and I will judge it differently. When the object was not in the museum, we were completely free to decide whether we approved or disapproved, liked it or disliked it. Once it is in the museum, we make our judgment in the knowledge, if not awe, of the fact that the experts have already said, "This is good," or "This is important," or "This is real." The object has been enshrined.

If the museum has opened its doors to all manner of innovation and experimentation, can we go on believing in the value of the museum's other judgments? Or, looking at another possibility, will we begin to accept with little reservation the importance of all innovations and experiments just because they happen to be in the museum?

To underline the point and to summarize for the moment, the forum is where the battles are fought, the temple is where the victors rest. The former is process, the latter is product.

Something must also be said about social responsibilities in museum programming that are somewhat apart from the issue of the museum as a temple or as a forum. It was suggested that protest, confrontation, the experiment, and the innovation were all appropriate to the forum and not to the temple. Some might infer an argument for the museum as a temple being apolitical, sitting on the fence, unconcerned with social issues, and so forth. That is not at all the case.

Years ago I worked in a museum where the natural scientists talked frequently at coffee breaks about problems of the pollution of our lakes and rivers. In the mid-1950s those scientists were deeply concerned with pollution and some of them sat on international commissions that were studying the growing problem. The galleries and special exhibition programs for which those scientists were responsible as curators did not reflect these concerns, however. It is only now, when pollution is a rather popular subject for discussion, that the museum in question is thinking of turning its resources toward the interpretation of the pollution of our environment.

That is a story of social irresponsibility in museum programming. Where museums, be they of art, history, or science, have the knowledge and the resources to interpret matters of public importance, no matter how controversial, they are obliged to do so.

Propaganda has, at no time, any place in the museum. Public education, the interpretation of science and of art, and attempts to explain what little we do know of the nature of man and of human society—these things have a place at all times, assuming objectivity and willingness to tell all sides of the story.

To return to forums and temples, certain organizational and functional relationships are important. It is desirable that each should have its own administration and governing body. Where there is a common administration, it seems far too likely that the forum would become a kind of purgatory and the museum a paradise, with the museum director playing the role of St. Peter at the pearly gates.

A most difficult question, because of the financial crisis in the world of museums and the increase in cost of construction, is whether or not the forum and the museum can be housed within the same structure. Ideally it would be most desirable to establish those manifestations of the forum that require a physical structure apart from the museum, but with a relationship such that they could not only share some common services but also could share the audience. Where both functions must coexist within one structure, then it is necessary to create a visual separation and a psychological distinction of the two by the use of color signs, and interior architectural modifications.

The important thing, and it need hardly be repeated again, is that they be recognized as distinct, one from the other; that each make its own function and its own role clear in the minds of the visitor. The distinction must be equally clear in the minds of the curators, the directors, the trustees, and the funding agencies.

Thought must also be given to the question of potential audience and communication effectiveness, whether we are concerned with the forum or a museum. Although there have been dramatic increases in museum audiences in the last two decades, it can safely be said that the majority of the population are not museum or art gallery goers. There should be great concern about the audience that museums do not have rather than excitement because the members of the present audience come more frequently and pump up the attendance statistics that are so gleefully printed in annual reports.

One of the studies of the use of leisure conducted in metropolitan Toronto[3] convinced me that museum visiting and attendance at spectator sports were very much alike in that they were functions of the characteristic use of leisure time rather than functions of special interests in either museums or baseball. It appears that there are some people who are not mobile in the use of leisure and who tend to rely heavily on television, radio, newspapers, magazines, books, records, and tapes. There are others who are highly mobile and seem to go everywhere to see everything and do everything.

There is evidence of a correlation between high educational achievement levels and the use of art museums and the more traditional performing arts. This does not appear to apply, however, to general museums, museums of history, archeology, or natural science. It can also be hypothesized from the study in question that individuals who have sophisticated or, if you wish, educated tastes in music, literature, and the visual arts may not be museum goers simply because they are not mobile, while others who would appear to be most unsophisticated show a high frequency of visitation.

All of this leads to the conclusion that, whether the concern is for the temple or the forum, the mass media must be used if the total audience which is prepared to listen is to be reached. Museum exhibitions should be designed from the very beginning so that they become the basis for television programs, films, feature articles in magazines, and well-designed, highly readable museum publications. There must also be extension or "outreach" programs that take museum materials into the community, into the inner-city areas of large urban concentrations, and especially into the schools. Similarly, the relatively unprogrammed and often unexpected events in the forum must be transmitted through the mass media. The public forum must be integrated into the circuits of electronic communication networks if it is to be significant in society. It must not be confused with the "forums" created by these networks.

More than half of the potential audience will not come to either the forum or museum. They will have to go to their audience. And even the roughest cost-benefit analysis will show that a telecast, a radio program, or a weekly newspaper column will get more information and experience to more people for fewer dollars than publicity campaigns designed to drive the unwilling in through the front doors.

Museums and art galleries, like the majority of other established cultural institutions, must institute reform and create an equality of cultural opportunity. Society will no longer tolerate institutions that either in fact or in appearance serve a minority audience of the elite. As public funds in support of these institutions increase, the public will demand its right to more than it has now. The public will make its demands known.

It is a difficult and precarious time for museums and art galleries, and those in the museum profession are charged with greater responsibilities than ever before.

Museums must concern themselves with the reform and development of museums as museums. They must meet society's need for that unique institution which fulfills a timeless and universal function—the use of the structured sample of reality, not just as a reference but as an objective model against which to compare individual perceptions. At the same time, and with a sense of urgency, the forums must be created, unfettered by convention and established values. The objective here is neither to neutralize nor to contain that which questions the established order. It is to ensure that the new and challenging perceptions of reality—the new values and their expressions—can be seen and heard by all. To ignore or suppress the innovation or the proposal for change is as mindless as to accept that which is new because it is novel.

In the absence of the forum, the museum as a temple stands alone as an obstacle to change. The temple is destroyed and the weapons of its destruction are venerated in the temple of tomorrow—but yesterday is lost. In the presence of the forum the museum serves as a temple, accepting and incorporating the manifestations of change. From the chaos and conflict of today's forum the museum must build the collections that will tell us tomorrow who we are and how we got there. After all, that's what museums are all about.

Notes

1. This article is derived from the 1971 University of Colorado Museum Lecture. It is prepared for *The Journal of World History* special number, "Museums, Society, Knowledge" (1972), reprinted with the permission of UNESCO.

2. Inscription at the entrance to the Royal Ontario Museum, Toronto, Canada.

3. An unpublished study of leisure and the use of cultural resources conducted for the Royal Ontario Museum by Dr. David S. Abbey and the author, 1961.

Museum Accountability

4

Laws, Rules, Ethics, and Accreditation

WILLARD L. BOYD

Museums . . . hold their possessions in trust for mankind and for the future welfare of the [human] race. Their value is in direct proportion to the service they render the emotional and intellectual life of the people.

—AAM CODE OF ETHICS FOR MUSEUM WORKERS, 1925

THE AMERICAN ASSOCIATION OF MUSEUMS (AAM), as early as 1925, adopted a code of ethics affirming the responsibility of museums to the public. Now AAM has adopted a new Code of Ethics which resolutely confirms "the ethic of public service as the foundation of [museum] actions and their contribution to society."[1]

This commitment to public service and responsibility is remarkable, since most museums in the United States are organized as private not-for-profit corporations. Private museums do not think of themselves as public institutions. In fact, they are quasi-public institutions because, in America, private organizations are used to accomplish public objectives in lieu of governmental agencies. Unlike other countries, we channel a substantial amount of social and economic effort through our private not-for-profit organizations. To encourage private action, nonprofits are given special tax status and frequently receive some governmental funding. The "not-for-profit" sector is a hybrid between private business and government. As a hybrid, it has a quasi-public character. In that sense, every museum has a mission of public service.

Since museums are institutions of public service, it follows that they are accountable to the public. In an era of more public accountability for government and business, there is a rising demand for accountability by nonprofits. Public

Willard L. Boyd is the Rawlings-Miller Professor of Law at the University of Iowa, and President Emeritus of the University of Iowa and the Field Museum of Chicago. "Museum Accountability: Laws, Rules, Ethics, and Accreditation" appeared in *Curator: The Museum Journal* (Vol. 34, No. 3 [July 1991], pp. 165–177). It is reprinted here by permission of John Wiley & Sons. All rights reserved.

accountability is institutionalized through regulations. Accordingly, museums are increasingly subjected to government-imposed, self-imposed, and peer-imposed regulations. While the increase in museum regulations is certain, still not clear are: who is accountable? for what? and to whom?

Who Is Accountable?

Most often, the museum itself is said to be accountable. Yet museums are people and, therefore, individuals are accountable for the actions they take in the museum's name—historically, the board, administration, and curators but increasingly education, library, and collection management staffs. To be a professional in any field is to be accountable for a generally accepted standard of performance.

Accountable for What?

Museums are accountable for the acquisition, conservation, management, and de-accession of collections. Museums are also accountable for the content, nature, and quality of their scholarship, exhibits, and programs.

Museums are accountable for endowment accumulation, preservation—or loss—and expansion of income sources. Museums are accountable, of course, for budget deficits.

In operating its auxiliary enterprises, museums are accountable to ensure that these enterprises are related to the museum's central mission. For example, publications and stores must be educationally oriented, and food services must be aimed at visitors.

Finally, museums are accountable for drafting personnel policies and practices that comply with legal requirements for both paid and volunteer staff. For instance, museums are accountable for implementing safety procedures that comply with state and local legal requirements.

Accountable to Whom?

Museums owe this accountability to the public. The public is comprised of various individuals, groups, and organizations: visitors to the museum; donors; peers; other museums; regulators, including the state attorney general, the legislature, and the IRS; cultural groups; employees; and the community at large.

There must be a generally acceptable standard of conduct for all museums since the actions of a few can affect all. For example, some contend that museums in concert with donors abused the deduction of gifts in kind by overvaluing objects. That abuse was partially responsible for federal restrictions on the deductibility of gifts of appreciated objects, which are the lifeblood of museums. Following a series of articles concerning donor and curatorial activities involving the Smithsonian gem collection, *The Washington Post* on March 30, 1983, editorialized that the tax deduction for gifts of objects should be eliminated to stop this abuse.[2]

Year by year, museums, their boards, and staff members are being subjected to greater accountability. That accountability is emanating from three sources: the public law, the museum's own regulations, and the peer community standards.

Government-Imposed Regulations

Governmental laws and regulations are contained in common law (customary law developed by judicial interpretation) and statutory law. Laws are prescribing more and higher standards of operational conduct for museums.

Statutory Law

All levels of government are regulating not-for-profits. Federal, state, and local governments are enacting laws and promulgating rules to carry out these laws.

The principal form of federal regulation of museums is through taxation. Museums seek income-tax-exempt status that will free their income from taxation and assure tax deductions for their donors. The Internal Revenue Code specifies the basis for exemption and the nature of deductions. In addition, granting agencies such as the National Endowments for the Arts and Humanities, the Institute for Museum Services, and the National Science Foundation (NSF) assure compliance with grant restrictions through financial audits and program reports.

Recent NSF audits of university and research museums concerning indirect and direct costs are vivid examples of government oversight. On January 10, 1990, the Los Angeles Times reported that nineteen museums were being audited by NSF in a rigorous manner comparable to university audits.[3]

Federal regulatory legislation also affects how museums conduct business. The major federal safety, health, and environmental laws apply to museums—the Occupational, Safety and Health Act (OSHA), including the latest Laboratory Standard, and the Resources Conservation and Recovery Act (RCRA) on hazardous waste management. The new Americans with Disabilities Act (ADA) requires reasonable accommodations for disabled employees. In addition, the Civil Rights Act of 1964 (Title VII) and the Americans with Disabilities Act impact on a museum's employment practices.

Local government reporting requirements are increasing for museums receiving local government support—requirements concerning both requests for and administration of funds. In addition, museums and other nonprofits have to be concerned about local property and sales-tax exemptions. In the past, these exemptions have been granted to charities and educational institutions. But as local governments aggressively seek tax revenue, nonprofit local tax exemptions are questioned. In 1983, an unsuccessful attempt was made to withdraw the Asia Society's real-estate tax exemption on the grounds it ". . . failed to meet the definition of an educational institution by the New York state property tax law."[4]

Local governments are also asserting that the mounting "commercial activities" of nonprofits make them ineligible as charities for real-estate and sales-tax exemption.

This is particularly true in the hospital arena, where nonprofit and profit hospitals compete and local real-estate-tax exemptions are being withdrawn to provide a level playing field for all commercial enterprises.[5]

Most museums are organized under state nonprofit laws. They file annual reports with the secretary of state, setting forth their compliance with the laws under which they were created.

The state attorney general monitors the activities of the state's not-for-profit organizations. Museums must file annual reports concerning their conduct in general and, in particular, their solicitation and administration of funds secured from the general public. The National Association of Attorney Generals promotes legislation designed to protect the public from unscrupulous fund-raising practices. For example, there is increasing public concern over telephone solicitations for seemingly worthy causes where most of the funds collected have gone to pay for the soliciting. The approach of the attorney generals is to require solicitors to disclose how much goes to the worthy cause.

Common Law

Under common law, museum accountability traditionally centers on the fiduciary responsibility of its board, principal administrative officers, and curators. Museums, like for-profit corporations, are now also responsible for wrongful acts committed by employees in the course of their duties.[6] Injured parties can seek compensation from those employees, their supervisors, board members, and the museum.

Common and statutory fiduciary duties are divided into two general categories: the duty of loyalty and the duty of care.

THE DUTY OF LOYALTY. The duty of loyalty addresses conflicts of interest—where an individual's interest conflicts with that of the institution, and the possibility exists that the individual will put his or her self-interest ahead of the institution's. The conflicts are of two types:

1. Self-dealing that involves a transaction between the individual and the institution. Self-dealing occurs when a staff or board member sells an object to the museum for its collection or provides legal services for compensation. Self-dealing also occurs in the case of an employee who has a separate business that sells exhibit products or consulting service to the museum.
2. Self-dealing that involves taking an opportunity for individual gain, an opportunity that the individual became aware of because of the museum connection and an opportunity in which the museum also may have an interest. The classic case is the curator or board member who collects in the same general area as the museum and learns about an opportunity through his or her museum association. Without disclosing the opportunity to the museum, the employee or board member acquires the object for his or her individual collection.

Conflicts of interest are not per se improper or prohibited. While avoiding them is preferable, they can—and must—be managed so that they avoid unfairness to the museum. Proper management requires a full disclosure of both the conflict and the opportunity to disinterested museum persons in authority. In addition, the common law ordinarily provides that the person with the conflict cannot be a crucial participant in making the decision affecting the conflict. A board member who wishes to purchase an object from the museum or to sell an object or a service to the museum can be at the board meeting and can be counted in determining a quorum but cannot be counted toward the majority needed for action. The common law does not require the higher standards the public is coming to expect.

With increasing public concern about "conflicts of interest," it is good practice for the board member to be absent from the board meeting and to refrain from discussing the issue with the other members of the board, together or separately. We live in a time when ethics statutes that require disclosure and sometimes avoidance of conflict of interest are being enacted. For example, the 1990 reauthorization legislation for the National Endowment for the Arts prohibits a representative of an applicant from serving on a panel that reviews the application.

In all circumstances, it is good practice to follow the highest conflict-of-interest standards whenever there is dealing between the museum and its board members, officers, and employees. Museums should strive to avoid even the appearance of impropriety. A museum should annually require disclosures from board members, officers, and staff of their potential conflicts of interest with the museum.

THE DUTY OF CARE. The duty of care requires regular and responsible action with respect to the museum's affairs, action which is taken in good faith and which is prudent under the circumstances. "Good faith" means an honest belief that the action is the right thing for the museum. That alone is not enough. The duty is also to exercise sound judgment. The action must be sensible in light of the museum's mission and needs.[7]

Due care as well as good faith must be exercised in the operation of a museum. What do a prudent board and staff do when the museum is operating at a deficit and the building and collection are deteriorating? Do they sell a part of the collection in order to save the museum? It depends on all of the circumstances. There is no simple answer.

The highest fiduciary duties apply to the collections, which are the sine qua non of museums. The collections are intended to be a permanent asset and are not intended to be acquired or disposed of for profit. On the other hand, in the case of the museum store, the purpose is to buy and sell. In between the collections and the store is the endowment. It needs to be conserved, but it needs to be invested so that it will grow to offset inflation. It is not prudent to freeze the endowment principal.[8]

Since the exercise of the duty of care is evaluated after the fact, careful recording of all deliberations of the board, administrators, curators, and staff is imperative.

Board meetings, reflected in the minutes, should focus on the pros and cons of major actions to be taken so that subsequent examination will reveal a reasonable basis for them. Board members must participate and will be considered to have acquiesced in the action unless they registered their dissent.

Assuming that there is a breach of the duty of loyalty or care or both, who can sue and when? Historically, the attorney general of the state in which the museum is incorporated represents the public in bringing actions. The decision to sue or not to sue is discretionary but may be influenced by other issues, such as media pressure. After a series of articles in the Chicago Tribune, the Illinois Attorney General commenced an action against the Harding Museum directors for breach of fiduciary duties resulting from alleged improper deaccessions, investments, self-dealing, salaries, and failure to open the museum to the public after it had moved to new quarters. Although the litigation covered some fifteen years, the appellate opinions on the case did not produce any holdings or dicta that are instructive on the subject of fiduciary duties. However, the public interest aroused by the case led to a report by the Illinois Legislative Investigative Commission causing many Illinois museums to adopt formal deaccession policies.

The major lesson of the Harding case, like other newsworthy cases, is that fiduciary duties of museum board members and staff are fashioned by public inquiries and reports as well as by cases and statutes. On the negative side of public scrutiny is the possible overreaction to isolated cases resulting in unrealistic and unnecessary demands on board members and staff. On the positive side is the impetus for codes of ethics and sound practices and procedures for museums.

It is the primary responsibility of the museum's board to assure that the museum staff and board members discharge their fiduciary duties of loyalty and care. It is possible for board members to bring an action against one or more co-board members. It is also possible for successive board members to sue previous board members.

Unlike board members, founders, donors, visitors, and the public generally have not been permitted to enforce fiduciary duties. This is to prevent undue litigation and harassment of not-for-profit board members.

It is unclear whether museum members can sue. If members have no voting rights and are merely "friends groups," they usually do not have standing to sue.

Recent state and federal legislation provide that Native Americans have the right to request return of human remains and certain other objects where the petitioners have cultural affinity or similar connection with remains or objects claimed.[9] Museums are beginning to adopt formal repatriation policies dealing with Native American remains and objects and, in the case of the Field Museum, other cultural groups as well. Based on internal museum policies, several museums have returned to the Zuni tribe of New Mexico specific "War Gods." In deaccessioning patrimonial collections, museum board members must be mindful of their legal duties under the law of the state in which the museum is incorporated so that the fiduciary duty of care with respect to collections is properly discharged.

Assuming that there is standing to sue, the attorney general and others can bring an action immediately to enjoin a questionable action of the museum. When the act has occurred, the appropriate parties can sue to recover the money damages sustained as a result of the breach of fiduciary duty. If there is no monetary damage, there is no basis for a suit.

In addition to the common law, fiduciary duties are also created by statute. For instance, the Revised Model Nonprofit Corporation Act (Section 8.32) provides: "A corporation may not lend money to or guarantee the obligation of a director or officer of the corporation."

On the other hand, there is a growing statutory movement to protect unpaid nonprofit board members and officers for breach of the duty of care. These volunteers are liable only for willful and wanton conduct. Such volunteer-protection statutes could be argued to relieve volunteer directors of their duty to act prudently if they have acted in good faith.

As an added protection, most nonprofit codes permit the museum to indemnify board members for judgments and legal costs assessed against them where the members acted in good faith and in a manner which was believed by them to be in the best interests of the museum.

Self-Imposed Regulations

Self-imposed museum policies and procedures are expanding because the public, the museum profession, and museum board and staff want them. The museum may adopt regulations affecting its own conduct either because of government mandate or because the peer community deems them appropriate. For instance, a museum might adopt its own affirmative action policy to implement a government policy or adopt its own code of ethics in order to comply with the 1991 [the most recent] AAM Ethics Code.

Museum regulations ordinarily cover the conduct of all members, paid and volunteer. These policies may refer to equal-opportunity employment, termination, sexual harassment, and overtime. Usually initiated by staff, the governing board adopts policies. Administering them is a staff function.

As self-imposed regulations expand, the nature of the staff relationship to the museum may change. Under common law, most staff members are employees at will and serve at the pleasure of the museum's board or administration; they can be terminated immediately with or without cause. However, courts are beginning to hold that some personnel policies and practices may restrict the employer's right to terminate.

Of course, an employer is not free to terminate a person for an illegal cause, such as one involving a discriminatory motive based on an employee's race, age, sex, or religion. In the absence of legislative restrictions, the more specific the promise to an employee by the employer, the more likely it is that a promise or policy may be construed as an implied-in-fact contract of ongoing employment that is not freely terminable. For example, courts have held that specific representations made in employment handbooks and policy manuals may constitute terms of a binding employment contract. Even codes of ethics may soon give rise to rights that are enforceable in the courts by museum staff members. The more that is said about the duty of a museum to staff, the more likely it is that a court may infer the terms of contract of employment.

Generally speaking, self-imposed rules and regulations should apply equally and consistently to all employees. The existence of a well-articulated grievance procedure for registration of staff complaints is good personnel practice. A museum may provide for a grievance committee of staff members to review disciplinary actions and make recommendations to the museum director or president. If the staff member is not satisfied, he or she may have a right to appeal the action externally, first to a governmental agency and then possibly to the courts. The courts will generally be reluctant to interfere if a museum has an established procedure that the courts consider to be binding upon the museum and that appears to have been followed in a consistent and fair manner. Other judicial and administrative forums of redress are also available to employees in disputes involving discrimination, unemployment compensation, and worker's compensation.

Peer-Imposed Regulations

These usually take two forms: codes of professional ethics and institutional accreditation. Ethics codes may apply to individuals or institutions or both. Accreditation is usually institutional. The peer group may be an umbrella group, such as the AAM, or a specialized group, such as the Association of Art Museum Directors and the American Institute for Conservation of Historic and Artistic Works.

Ethical Codes

Ethics are the rules of conduct adopted by a profession for serving its clientele and for regulating relationships among the professionals themselves. First developed in law and medicine, ethics are the means by which self-employed professionals police themselves. Ethics are now also beginning to deal with the relationship of professionals to institutions. Imposed by the profession or by the institution itself, ethics are ordinarily higher than the legal standards of conduct. For example, while a board member with a conflict of interest can legally be present when the board addresses the conflict, the museum's ethical code may prohibit it.

Ethics statements are not always precise. What is ethical is often in the eye of the beholder. Ethics really involve putting the public—the constituency—ahead of the institution, ahead of the profession. Failure to do so has led to national concern about ethical conduct. The country is awash in charges of ethical abuses. Every day, the newspapers carry stories about government officials, business leaders, professionals, and even museums that have taken advantage of the public to further their own objectives.

Ethics courses are springing up in all "professional curricula." Frequently they focus on specific cases—how to shave it closely, as in the case of collecting by museum staff and board members. Seldom is there an emphasis on the underlying thesis of ethics. We need always to remember the fundamental basis for ethics so that we avoid close encounters. Ethics go to the essence of our beliefs and reflect how we feel and care for others. A code of ethics inhibits our freedom to act solely for our own gain and demands a sense of responsibility to others.

In the not-for-profit field, there is a unique condition not found in the for-profit area. A cadre of specialists often controls the central service performed by the nonprofit organization. College and university faculties, hospital medical staff, and museum curatorial staff are accorded great latitude in their performance because they are the most knowledgeable about their subject matter. They have broad discretion and privileges within the institutions, but that broad discretion carries with it professional, and institutional duties and responsibilities. These professionals, recognizing their power, adopt peer ethics codes to assure that their conduct is in the public interest. However, the public is usually not invited to participate in the drafting and enforcing of these professional codes.

According to the 1991 AAM Code: "In submitting to this code, museums assume responsibility for the actions of the members of the governing authority, employees, and volunteers in the performance of museum-related duties." The proposed code affords a broad framework in which each museum can develop its own code. It admonishes the governing authority to ensure the museum's ethical conduct—and properly so because legally the governing board is the museum and is ultimately responsible for the adoption and enforcement of an ethics code. Although the Museum Trustee Association understandably felt left out of drafting the 1991 code, museums now look to their trustees to take the initiative with their museum administrations to enlist staffs to draft individual museum codes based on public service. The time has come for our trustees and museum staffs to set aside their differences in favor of the public interest.

Accreditation

Institutional evaluation is designed for public protection. The public needs this protection because it cannot determine the quality of the museum's services as easily as it can judge that of consumer goods. Accreditation is a means by which a group of similar institutions seeks to standardize institutional quality without casting all institutions into the same mold.

The accreditation process is basically a dialogue between peers in and outside the museum. It centers on a self-study designed to encourage systematic planning that leads to clearer goals and more effective action to achieve them. The AAM handbook states that accreditation promotes "the achievement of the highest standards" and "increased awareness of these standards among all museums." The standards are general in order to encourage diversity. The AAM accreditation manual states that there are two questions to be addressed in the process:

1. How well does the museum achieve its stated mission and goals?
2. How well does the museum's performance meet standards and practices as they are generally understood in the museum field at large?[10]

The handbook further states:

> There is no list of the specific requirements for museum accreditation. The entire program is predicated on recognition that standards in museums continually evolve and that the needs and resources of individual museums vary significantly.[11]

This seems almost circular in its logic and elusive in its enforceability. Fortunately, by focusing accreditation on the self-study, the institution sets its own mission and goals and then is judged by its peers as to how well it is achieving those goals.

There is no sanction for failing to be accredited. AAM membership is not predicated on accreditation. Nor does a lack of accreditation preclude a museum from securing federal funds, unlike the case of colleges and universities.

Like other accrediting agencies, AAM states that the data involved and the decisions made are confidential. Among post-secondary educational institutions, there is a trend to disclose information about the accreditation of a particular institution. Journalism schools make all accrediting information available to the public. Nevertheless, there is concern that too much disclosure will inhibit gathering information and making forthright recommendations. Because nonprofit accreditation is based on protecting the public, it can be argued that some accreditation records and proceedings should be open to the public.

The AAM's accreditation program was initiated in 1970 to help the public and various private and public agencies "identify those museums that meet accepted professional standards of cultural and educational service to the public." Presently, there are 685 accredited museums out of a total of 6,500 museums listed in the AAM Official Museum Directory. Museum accreditation is in its early stages compared to that of schools, colleges, and hospitals. Nevertheless, museum accreditation is exceptionally well formulated; and the self-study components such as governance, collections, and exhibitions are clearly articulated.

Conclusion

The 1991 AAM code of ethics rightfully stresses that museums exist to serve the public. As public servants, museums are accountable to the public through government-, self-, and peer-imposed regulations. The more we try to be accountable, the more our constituencies will hold us accountable.

The governing board, as the legal persona of the museum, is responsible for assuring that board and staff members comply with the regulations. The board should not administer, but it must monitor, the museum's compliance with these external and internal regulations. In the final analysis, the board is the body accountable for the museum. To assure this accountability, the board might well establish a regulatory compliance audit committee comparable to, but separate from, the financial audit committee. More and more for-profit organizations are developing compliance mechanisms like this. However structured, the board must assure that its oversight role is regularly and vigorously exercised.

We have moved beyond the rhetoric and have entered the reality of accountability. Museum regulations must be followed every day by everyone. Self-regulated compliance is the essence of accountability.

Notes

1. American Association of Museums Code of Ethics for Museums (second draft, February 1991) p. 4. In 1978, the AAM adopted a second code of ethics. Museum Ethics, AAM 1978. The AAM has also published elaborations on ethically related issues through seminal monographs such as "Museum Trusteeship" (1981) by Alan and Patricia Ullberg, and "Of Mutual Respect and Other Things" (1989) by Helmuth Naumer.

2. See also "The King of Gems" by Ted Gup. *Washington Post* (3/27–30/83).

3. "U.S. Clamps Down on Museum Grants" by Alan Pericini. *Los Angeles Times* (1/10/90).

4. "Should Museums Be Exempt From Taxes?" by John Russell. *New York Times* (3/20/83).

5. See *Utah County v. Intermountain Health Care*, Inc. 709 P. 2d 265 (Utah, 1985).

6. See, e.g., Brown and Boyd. The Program Fraud Civil Remedies Act: The Administrative Adjudication of Fraud Against the Government, 50 Federal Contracts Report 691, 695–96 (1988).

7. See Marsh, "Governance of Non-Profit Organizations: An Appropriate Standard of Conduct for Trustees and Directors of Museums and Other Cultural Institutions," 85 *Dickinson Law Review* 607 (1981). See also Section 8.30, Revised Model Nonprofit Corporation Act, adopted by The Subcommittee on the Model Nonprofit Corporation Law of the Business Law Section, American Bar Association, Summer, 1987, Prentice Hall Law and Business (1988).

8. See, e.g., *Stern v. Lucy Webb Hayes National Training School for Deaconesses and Missionaries*, 381 F. Supp 1003 (D.D.C. 1974).

9. Native American Graves Protection and Repatriation Act Pub. L. No. 101-601, 14-Stat 3048 (Nov. 16, 1990). See also Boyd, "Disputes Regarding the Possession of Native American Religious and Cultural Objects and Human Remains: A Discussion of the Applicable Law and Proposed Legislation," by Thomas H. Boyd, 55 *Missouri Law Review*, 883, 901–907 (1990).

10. *Museum Accreditation: A Handbook for the Institution*, 1990. Washington, DC: American Association of Museums, p. 25.

11. Ibid.

Deft Deliberations   5

DAN L. MONROE AND WALTER ECHO-HAWK

THE NATIVE AMERICAN GRAVE PROTECTION and Repatriation Act of 1990 might be the most important human rights legislation ever passed by Congress for Native Americans. It also represents landmark legislation for museum people.

Repatriation legislation is important for native people because it provides them equal rights regarding their dead. It recognizes that scientific rights of inquiry do not automatically take precedence over religious and cultural beliefs: it provides a mechanism for return of objects that were not acquired with the consent of rightful owners; and it creates an opportunity for Native Americans and museum people to work in partnership together.

Federal repatriation legislation is important for museums because it establishes a new ethical outlook for them in their relationships not only with native people but with all racial and cultural minorities. Museums are leaders, not followers, in creating a society that respects and celebrates cultural pluralism. The recent legislation creates the basis for a new partnership between museums and native people that may enhance knowledge of collections and create a new and richer form of public education through exhibits, programs, and publications. Rich as these benefits may be, the greatest benefit to museums is likely to be the increased maturity that comes of a commitment to truth and moral courage born out of the repatriation debate.

Museums and Native Americans debated and discussed repatriation for years inside and outside Congress. Museum people were among the first to recognize the value of Native American art and culture. They collected and preserved millions of Native American cultural items to prevent their loss or dispersal. They documented and recorded Native American culture to preserve traditional knowledge for future generations of natives and non-natives alike. And they interpreted and

---

Dan L. Monroe is executive director and CEO of the Peabody Essex Museum in Salem, Massachusetts. Walter Echo-Hawk is a Native American attorney, tribal judge, author, activist, law professor, and counsel to Crowe & Dunlev's Indian Law and Gaming Practice Group. "Deft Deliberations" is reprinted here with permission from *Museum News*, July/August 1991. Copyright 1991, the American Association of Museums. All rights reserved.

presented Native American culture to millions of people worldwide in a substantial education effort.

Yet when Native Americans first asked museums to return Native American dead or sacred objects, many museum people felt threatened: What would happen to museum collections if objects were repatriated? Who would assure preservation of repatriated objects? How would museums carry out their educational or scientific missions if collections were gutted through repatriation claims?

Before detailing some of the ramifications of the new federal legislation established to address these questions, it is useful to review the debate that preceded Congressional action.

Violation of Rights

From the point of view of Native Americans, one of the many "trails of tears" in American Indian history is the fact that U.S. museums and universities hold staggering numbers of dead native people who provide mute testimony to the pervasive violation of Native American rights.

Respect for the dead is deeply ingrained in U.S. society and jurisprudence. Yet legal safeguards taken for granted by most citizens did not protect the graves and dead of Native Americans. American law and social policy wholly failed to protect the sanctity of the Native American dead (as Chief Seattle said in 1855, "To us, the ashes of our ancestors are sacred, and their resting place is hallowed ground") or the sensibilities of the living. As a result, tribal communities suffered painful human rights violations. Repatriation is one means of redress.

Historians documented the troubling means by which many of the dead were collected. Samuel Morton, an early American physical anthropologist, collected large numbers of Indian crania in the 1840s. His "finding" that native people were racially inferior to white people and therefore bound for extinction provided ample "scientific" justification for taking land from Indians, relocating them, and committing cultural genocide through government policies. In 1868, the U.S. Surgeon General issued an order directing Army personnel to obtain as many Indian crania as possible; thus those killed in battles were decapitated and their heads sent East for scientific study.

The policy of treating Native American dead unlike white Americans was translated into law in 1906 when Congress passed the Antiquities Act. This law, intended to protect archaeological resources, defined dead Indians located on federal lands as archaeological resources and converted them to federal property. Consequently, governments—and many museums and universities—treated dead Native Americans not as human beings but as "historical property," "pathological materials," "scientific data," or "scientific specimens."

This treatment stemmed, in part, from lack of access to U.S. courts by native people. Disputes between Native Americans and U.S. citizens usually were settled on the battlefield, not in courtrooms. Even when Indians managed to get into the courts, they had little hope of a fair hearing given the prevailing racial views of most white Americans. It was not until 1879 that federal courts recognized an Indian as a person within the meaning of law; citizenship was granted by Congress in 1924.

Thus state and federal law failed to recognize native American burial practices and religious beliefs. No consideration was given during the development of U.S. common law to the effect of forced displacement of native people from their homelands and traditional burial grounds.

The Power of Social Myth

Social myths shaped the views of most U.S. citizens—including museum people—in their interactions with Native Americans. Until recently, U.S. schools taught that Europeans "discovered" America. Students learned that their ancestors came seeking religious and political freedom: they brought law, order, and civilization to a great and untamed wilderness; and they created a new nation dedicated to liberty and freedom for all. No mention was made of the facts that early settlers took land from Native Americans by force and chicanery; that they dismembered native cultures; and that surviving natives subsequently were placed on reservations considered unfit for any other purpose. It was within this context that museums collected cultural materials and Native American dead.

Acting on the assumption that native people were destined for extinction or cultural assimilation, museums began collecting Native American materials in an effort to preserve them before they disappeared. And competition was keen to build collections, especially between 1875 and 1929. Some museum people robbed graves or participated in other forms of theft or deceit to acquire objects, although it also is true that the majority of acquisitions were made legally and ethically.

In retrospect, museum collecting continued long after the initial rationale had disappeared, and Native American material by the 1940s was upgraded to the status of art. Collecting gathered momentum, and museums acquired objects for their own purposes—sometimes including objects needed to continue traditional Native American religious practices or tribal or clan identities. The greatest jeopardy many objects faced was the potential of acquisition by other collectors. Museum interest in collecting sometimes superseded the needs and interests of the people who made the objects or their culture.

Museums, however, used their collections to create a new and widespread awareness of Native American people and culture in the United States and abroad. Since 1960, museums have produced a host of exceptional traveling exhibitions on Native American art and culture seen by millions of people: museums also produced high-quality publications. This increased visibility has helped native people advance many causes, including repatriation.

The Repatriation Law

Following intense negotiations, the Native American Grave Protection and Repatriation Act was signed on November 23, 1990, and codified as 25 USC 3001.

This law and its accompanying legislative history—which further clarifies its provisions—should be studied closely both by museums and Indian tribes. We believe that implementation will be easier and more harmonious when all parties are fully informed about the duties and opportunities afforded by the law.

The law does four things:

1. It increases protection for Native American graves located on federal and tribal lands and provides for disposition of cultural items found there in the future.
2. It prohibits traffic in Native American human remains.
3. It requires federal agencies and federally funded museums to inventory their collections of Native American human remains and associated funerary objects in five years and repatriate them, if requested, to culturally affiliated tribes or native groups.
4. It requires federal agencies and federally funded museums to summarize their collections of Native American sacred objects, objects of cultural patrimony, and unassociated funerary objects in three years and repatriate items to specified native claimants when the agency or museum does not have a right of possession.

Many sections of the law spell out definitions, standards, and procedures for accomplishing these objectives. Separate procedures are given for the treatment of human remains and associated funerary objects and all other cultural items covered by the law (sacred objects, objects of cultural patrimony, and unassociated funerary objects). Each of these items is defined in the law, and the legislative history gives more clarification.

Human Remains and Associated Funerary Objects

Museums must inventory these in five years. The inventory must be done in consultation with tribal government and Native American religious leaders. The required inventory must be a simple itemized list; new studies and research are not required. If necessary, museums may request an extension from the Secretary of the Interior.

If culturally affiliated tribes request return of human remains or associated funerary objects, museums are required to comply with the request expeditiously. There is a provision for delay if a scientific study of national importance is being conducted on the remains or objects, in which case return must be accomplished 90 days after completion of the study.

Cultural Items

Museums are required to summarize their Native American cultural items and notify appropriate tribes within three years. The procedure for handling requests for return of sacred objects, objects of cultural patrimony, or unassociated funerary objects involves a four-step process. Native people must show that the requested items fall within the definitions given for sacred objects, objects of cultural patrimony, or unassociated funerary objects. Native people must next establish their cultural affiliation to the object in question or show prior ownership.

If the foregoing steps are met, then native people must present a prima facie case showing the federal agency or museum does not have a right of possession to the item. The law spells out the criteria for a right of possession based on relevant common and property laws and principles. The federal agency or museum then may present its case for right of possession. Finally, the institution must make a decision, based on the preponderance of the evidence, regarding disposition of the object.

If Native Americans are unsatisfied with the decision, they may submit the matter to a Federal Review Committee comprised of Native American and museum representatives. The review committee may issue findings that are not judicially binding but may help resolve the matter. The issue may also be submitted to a court of competent jurisdiction for resolution.

The relationship between museums and Native Americans has been complex and impossible to characterize as good or bad. The passage of the Native American Grave Protection and Repatriation Act of 1990 recognizes the necessity for change, and the change in attitudes, values, and mutual understanding that underlie the new law create an opportunity for museums and native people to work together.

As the result of input from AAM and its new repatriation task force, we are confident that museums and native people will succeed in resolving questions regarding collections and enriching the interpretation of Native American life and culture. We also look forward to seeing tribes and museums move into the future as partners.

Here Are Answers to Common Questions about the Congressional Action

Many museum professionals have questions about the new Native American Grave Protection and Repatriation Act of 1990. Here are answers to some of the most common:

1. How will museum and Native American costs be met? The act authorizes Congress to appropriate funds for implementation. AAM and native groups are pressing Congress for such appropriations: Museum and federal responsibilities for compliance, however, must be met with or without federal appropriations.
2. How can museums satisfy requirements to consult with native people? Consultation with native leaders is desirable. Tribal governments are easy to locate and contact. AAM is establishing a special task force consisting of native and museum representatives to assist museums in this and other aspects of the new law.
3. Should museums expect large numbers of repatriation requests for cultural items? The repatriation process for cultural items requires careful research

and preparation. Requests, then, are likely to focus on a comparatively small number of objects of paramount importance to native people.

4. What happens if museums fail to comply with the law? Monetary civil penalties can be assessed against museums by the Secretary of the Interior. In addition, federal courts can hear actions brought by parties claiming a violation of the law.

5. How will museums know what objects are sacred objects or objects of cultural patrimony? In many cases, museums will not know. The purpose of the notification of tribes and the narrative summary of a museum's collections is to establish the basis for dialogue regarding a museum's collections.

6. What should a museum do if it questions the integrity of a repatriation request? The law emphasizes the importance of working with tribal governments and traditional Native American leaders. It is in the best interest of the museum and native people to ascertain together that repatriation requests have merit.

7. How can museums obtain further clarification of key definitions of the new law? House and Senate reports and floor statements elaborate on the definitions, so consult these sources first; AAM can help museums obtain these reports (contact the Government Affairs department, AAM, 1225 Eye St. N.W., Suite 200, Washington, D.C. 20005, (202) 289-9125). The Secretary of the Interior will issue regulations to carry out parts of the law. Tribal groups and traditional Native American religious leaders will be able to assist, and the AAM task force might also be of assistance. Finally, consult with legal counsel as necessary.

Deaccessioning   6
The American Perspective

MARIE C. MALARO

PERHAPS I SHOULD BEGIN BY POINTING OUT that I have never been able to find the word *deaccession* in my dictionary. The fact that those who bless new words have never seen fit to recognize the term does not seem to bother many in the United States. We have been engaged in "deaccessioning" for years, and if there has been debate—and there has been—it has not been over terminology but over the practice which the term describes.[1]

First, let me define what I mean by deaccessioning: "It is the permanent removal of an object that was once accessioned into museum collection." Accordingly, the term does not apply when an object is placed on loan by a museum (there is no permanent removal) nor does it apply if the object in question was never accessioned. For example, if a museum acquires an object but never accessions it because it is not deemed of collection quality, the disposal of that object is not a deaccession. There was never an intellectual judgment made that the object in question was worthy of indefinite preservation and therefore, the removal of that object raises less formidable hurdles. Also, I use the term "deaccession" to cover the entire process of removal. In other words, for me, deaccessioning encompasses two major questions:

- Should this object be removed?
- If so, what is the appropriate method of disposal?

I make this clarification merely because some limit the term to just the first issue— the decision to remove—and consider the method of disposal an administrative detail. From my experience it is more prudent to consider all aspects of a proposed removal before any decisions are made. Sometimes the method of disposal can raise more difficult questions than the issue of whether the object should go.

Marie C. Malaro is professor emerita and former director of the Museum Studies Program at George Washington University. "Deaccessioning: The American Perspective" originally appeared in *Museum Management and Curatorship* (Vol. 10, No. 3, 1991, pp. 273–279) published by Taylor & Francis. It is reprinted here with permission of the publisher. All rights reserved.

One more prefatory comment is in order. When discussing deaccessioning we must bear in mind both legal and ethical standards.

- Legal standard—What I can and cannot do.
- Ethical standard—What I should or should not do.

It is important to understand the difference because each standard serves a specific purpose, and when we confuse the two, intelligent discourse is all but impossible. The law sets the lower standard. It tells us how we must act if we want to avoid civil or criminal liability. We find the law in statutes or by reading decided cases—what the lawyer calls precedent. The law is not designed to make us honorable—only bearable—and therefore we often can engage in some highly questionable conduct and yet stay within the law. The law, however does have clout. If you are found guilty of violating the law you must pay fines or you may go to jail.

Ethics are a different matter. A code of ethics sets forth conduct deemed necessary by a profession to uphold the integrity of the profession. It sets a higher standard because it is based on principles of personal accountability and service to others. A code of ethics, however, frequently has no enforcement power. It is effective only if there is personal commitment and informed peer pressure. This distinction between law and ethics is very important to bear in mind when we look at the history of deaccessioning in the United States. We have very little law in the United States that inhibits deaccessioning, and we have a tremendous variety of museums that are governed mainly by independent boards composed of private citizens. Accordingly, we have had all sorts of museums experimenting with deaccessioning under a wide variety of circumstances. And we have everyone commenting on the ethics of each particular situation with little law defining what is actually enforceable. You name it, we have probably done it in the United States, so it is worthwhile to take a closer look at how we have fared.

Most museums in the United States are not controlled by the government. They are what we call nonprofit organizations—organizations incorporated to serve a public purpose but run by boards of private citizens. Support comes through private donations, grants, and some revenue-producing activities. It is estimated that well over 90 percent of the objects in United States museums have been donated. The nonprofit sector is deeply rooted in the American tradition, and one of the reasons we sustain this sector is to provide diversity. Anyone in the United States can start a museum for any purpose as long as the purpose falls within our broad definition of "service to the public." We have museums in this nonprofit sector of every size and shape. For example, the Smithsonian Institution is not a government agency. It owes its existence to the bequest of an Englishman, James Smithson, who left his fortune to start, in the United States, an institution "for the increase and diffusion of knowledge." The Smithsonian is chartered as a nonprofit organization and is governed by an independent board of regents. The Metropolitan Museum in New York is an independently managed nonprofit organization, as are the majority of the almost 7,000 museums listed in our professional directory.

Under our laws a nonprofit organization has a broad range of powers, and one of them is the ability to dispose of its assets under the supervision of its governing board. Thus any museum organized as a nonprofit has an inherent right to deaccession material unless its charter specifically limits this right. It is possible for the creator of a museum to restrict the ability to remove objects as, for example, the Freer Gallery of Art in Washington or the Gardner Museum in Boston. Here under the terms of the donors' gifts no objects can be removed from those collections, but these instructions reflect the wishes of private parties, they do not reflect public policy. What all this means is that whether a museum in the United States engages in deaccessioning is pretty much left to its governing board, acting in light of its own particular circumstances.

Added to this is the factor that the United States, with very limited exception, has never seen fit to restrict the movement of cultural objects located within its borders.[2] In fact, cultural objects can leave the country more freely than they can enter. What we have then is no centralized policy regarding collecting our collections and a government that plays no discernible role in shaping a national cultural policy. What is collected and what is disposed of is usually left in the hands of those who are interested in a particular museum. But all is not laissez-faire. Perhaps to fill a void, the museum profession in the United States talks a lot about ethics and public accountability. Several of our major professional organizations promulgate codes of ethics and each code has something to say about deaccessioning. The codes recognize deaccessioning as a valid practice, but set down guidelines for implementation. For example, the code promulgated by the American Association of Museums makes the following points:

1. Every museum should have a public statement regarding its policy on deaccessioning.
2. When considering disposal, the museum must weigh carefully the interests of the public that it serves.
3. When disposing of an object due consideration should be given to the museum community in general as well as the wishes and financial needs of the institution itself.
4. While the governing board bears the ultimate responsibility for a deaccession decision, great weight should be given to the recommendation of the curatorial staff regarding the pertinence of the object to the mission of the museum.[3]

The code promulgated by the Association of Art Museum Directors stresses the following points:

1. Deaccessioning should be related to policy not to the exigencies of the moment.
2. Procedures for deaccessioning should be at least as rigorous as for the purchase of major works of art.

3. While final decisions rest with the governing board of the museum, full justification for a disposal should be provided by the director and the responsible curator.

4. Funds obtained through disposal must be used to replenish the collection.[4]

A careful reading of each code shows that both professional organizations require a museum to have a policy regarding deaccessioning, both place final decision-making responsibility with the governing board (as the case law in the United States requires) and both require that the board pay attention to curatorial opinion, but in other respects there are different emphases. The Association of Art Museum Directors addresses the use of proceeds from deaccessions and insists that these proceeds be used to replenish the collections. The American Association of Museums, which represents all types of museums, has (at the time of writing) nothing in its code about use of proceeds from deaccessions. Instead, it speaks of considering the needs of the museums community generally when one is contemplating deaccessioning. In other words, there is less focus on dollar return, with more emphasis on trying to place the unwanted object with another collecting organization. These differences in the codes of ethics themselves highlight the fact that even in a country where deaccessioning is generally accepted there are differing views on its implementation, and differences frequently can be associated with discipline. For example, art museums are quite comfortable with sales in the marketplace but there is great pressure to require that sale proceeds be used only to replenish the collections. History museums seemed more concerned with finding an appropriate new home for a piece, and less stress is put on the matter of what is done with any proceeds that may accrue. Anthropology museums and natural science museums tend to favor only exchanges with other collecting organizations. These differences can be explained in part by the fact that up until recently only art brought substantial prices in the marketplace. With this factor changing, because now there seems to be a market for almost anything, and with the very high sale prices we have seen over the last few years, history museums as well as natural science museums are being forced to grapple with the lure of the marketplace.

If I were listing recent developments in the United States that are affecting deaccessioning this might be the first one:

Development 1. The very active and lucrative market for not only art but other collectibles has put added pressure not only on art museums but on all types of museums.

There are other developments that have been equally if not more responsible for renewed attention to deaccessioning. One is the fact that in 1986 a new tax reform act was passed in the United States, which makes it less attractive at times for individuals to donate objects to museum collections. As I mentioned earlier, museums in the United States depend almost exclusively on donations to form their collections. With donations down this means that collections will not grow unless museums can buy in the marketplace—buy, in many cases, the very works that would-be donors are now selling. But where is the money to come from, especially with prices escalating? A logical solution for many is to look for objects to deaccession and sell in order to raise purchase money.

The second development then is:

Development 2. The change in the United States tax law that discourages donations of objects to museums and forces museums to consider buying.

But there have been more profound and pervasive developments. Over the last decade or so the museum community in the United States has begun to examine itself more carefully, and this has been brought about by several factors. One is that there is more public interest in museums. As people become more educated and more affluent they are demanding more from museums and they are questioning the quality of governance in museums. At the same time we are seeing more professionally trained people attracted to museum work. In an effort to respond to the greater demands on museums these people are examining in a comprehensive way how their museums operate. Too often what they find are: disorganized collections, poor documentation, and horrendous storage conditions. A natural response is to re-examine the collecting practices of a museum so that there is some assurance the museum will collect wisely and that objects, once acquired, can be maintained, conserved, and used effectively. Accordingly we have a growing number of museums in the United States that have refocused their collecting activity and are seriously concerned about proper maintenance and conservation of their collections. Because of this, I can add to my list two other developments that are affecting deaccession activity. These are developments not usually highlighted by the press when a deaccession story makes the newspapers, but they are of fundamental importance.

Development 3. Many museums have more carefully focused their collecting and now find themselves with objects that are extraneous to their missions.

Development 4. Because of heightened concern for quality storage and conservation, museums are questioning the validity of retaining objects that are not clearly furthering the goals of their museums.

Because of all the above-described developments we are seeing more deaccessioning activity in the United States and, as might be expected, renewed debate concerning the practice. Most of the newspaper stories and magazine articles feature major art museum deaccessions because these are always more dramatic and often involve the disposal of a work or works in order to acquire immediately a preferred replacement. This allows everyone the opportunity to play critic on the merits of the particular exchange and some, in their zeal, call for the outlawing of all deaccessioning. I do not believe it likely that the United States in the foreseeable future will consider seriously any legislation that would ban deaccessioning. Such a move would be at odds with our concept of a museum and with our whole tradition of leaving cultural development in the hands of the people rather than the government.

On the first point—our concept of a museum—we view museums essentially as educational organizations with responsibilities to collect wisely, maintain prudently and encourage public use and enjoyment. Collecting in an educational organization is not a mechanical process. It is a combination of intelligent selection and periodic re-evaluation. What serious educator would ever take the position that what is deemed "right" today should never be subject to review? But this attitude is inherent in a general prohibition against deaccessioning. How can a museum present itself as an educational organization and yet relinquish a continuing responsibility to review critically its progress in achieving its particular goals? Accordingly, in the United States, the prevailing view is that if museums want to be considered educational organizations they must be free to deaccession.

The second reason for arguing that the United States would never seriously consider outlawing deaccessioning is our tradition of leaving cultural development in the hands of the people—as evidenced by our nonprofit sector. This system, which encourages great diversity, has served us rather well. We have museums that never dispose of anything, others that are free-wheeling, and every shade in between. Each can survive as long as enough people are willing to support it. By encouraging diversity we encourage the direct participation of many in shaping a cultural heritage. A ban on deaccessioning, which would seriously inhibit the present system, just does not make sense.

While I would argue that the last thing the United States needs or wants is any legislation inhibiting deaccessioning, I will readily admit that our museum community is not without fault in this area. The weak spot is not the general rules we have developed for deaccessioning, it is a failure to promulgate these rules as aggressively as we should. If more time and effort were to be spent educating the profession with regard to these general rules, the few problems we have with deaccessioning would probably disappear.

Our general rules are all drawn from our major codes of ethics, and they reflect our very American view that each museum is responsible for its own destiny. Our rules give wide discretion to those in authority within a museum, but they also require that those in authority answer directly to the people they serve and on whom they depend for support. The general rules on deaccessioning are essentially these:

1. Deaccessioning should never be addressed in isolation. It is dependent on a clear articulation of a museum's collecting goals and prudent acquisition procedures. In other words, deaccessioning is not a method for curing sloppiness in accessioning. A first consideration, therefore, is to have strict acquisition guidelines in place.

2. Collections should be reviewed periodically for relevance, condition and quality. When this is done routinely more objective opinions result, and with no urgency to remove, there is time to reflect on initial judgments.

3. There should be written policies and procedures on deaccessioning. These should stress thoughtful review, clear delegation of responsibility, careful

record-keeping and public disclosure. The policies and procedures should address:

a. reasons that may justify removal;
b. the importance of clarifying the museum's unrestricted title to an object before it is considered for removal;
c. the role of professional staff in the process;
d. when outside opinions are to be sought;
e. appropriate methods of disposal that may be considered;
f. who has final responsibility for deciding whether an object is to be removed;
g. who has final responsibility for deciding the method of disposal;
h. who is responsible for keeping records of the process;
i. who is responsible for providing information to the public on a planned disposal;
j. when and how notification of deaccessioning is given to donors of objects;
k. the importance of avoiding even apparent conflicts of interest in the deaccessioning process.

A museum that has such written policies and procedures—and follows them carefully when deaccession situations arise—will probably make sound decisions and will maintain public confidence. This is so because in the very process of preparing its deaccession policies and procedures the museum will have re-examined its mission, clarified its collecting goals and pondered the long-term effects of its actions. Also, it will be acutely aware that the burden of justifying deaccessioning decisions rests with it. After all this preparation, the museum is truly ready to take on individual cases, and as decisions are made the museum will be able to convey a sense of purpose and thoughtful adherence to previously articulated goals. This is the essence of good governance.

However, I must mention that I am always rather perplexed by the amount of controversy we see on the subject of deaccessioning as compared with the general apathy concerning the issues of mindless collecting or collecting with negligible documentation. Is the public better served by an undisciplined or poorly documented collection? I would suggest that if there is persistent agonizing over deaccessioning the museum profession should look more deeply. Those who cannot come to terms with deaccessioning may be avoiding taking decisions in other areas of collections management. When you look at the total collection management picture within a museum, and demand that all facets be reviewed and controlled in light of the museum's mission, the matter of deaccessioning falls into perspective. It becomes a small part of an integrated plan and, as such, it can be handled with confidence and in a way that inspires confidence.

In conclusion, if there are lessons to be learned from studying deaccessioning in the United States they are these:

1. In order to justify deaccessioning you must first be able to demonstrate that the museum has control over its collections. Control means that there is a collecting plan which is in accord with the mission of the museum, and the plan is religiously followed.
2. You must be able to demonstrate that your collections are periodically and objectively reviewed for adherence to collecting goals.
3. You must have written procedures for considering proposed deaccessions, and these procedures should stress full discussion, clear delegation of decision-making authority and complete record-keeping.

If these lessons are followed one does not have to worry about deaccessioning being used as a quick and shallow solution to immediate problems. By the time a museum has taken all the required steps and is at a point where deaccessioning can be considered it will have educated itself. What decisions are then made should be relatively thoughtful, supported by clearly articulated policies. This approach offers the public the greatest protection because it demands that the museum profession understand and practice the full scope of its responsibilities.

Notes

1. Some claim the word merely demonstrates ignorance of Latin. *Ad cedere* is the Latin for "to cede to" or "accession." *Decedere* is the Latin for "to cede from" or, logically, "decession." Somehow we "deaccession" or "cede from to."
2. The exceptions are mainly archaeological objects removed from federal or Indian lands. Federal statutes control the use of these objects. States may have similar statutes regarding such materials found on state property.
3. *Museum Ethics* (American Association of Museums, 1978).
4. *Professional Practices in Art Museums* (Association of Art Museum Directors, 1981).

Museums in the Age of Deconstruction

7

MICHAEL M. AMES

The "Ethnic Question" in the Age of Deconstruction

PROBLEMS RELATING TO ETHNICITY APPEAR to be occupying an increasing part of public discourse.[1] The 9 April 1990 issue of Time, for example, refers to the "Browning of America," suggesting that if present trends continue the average U.S. resident will be non-European by the middle of the 21st century (Henry III 1990). White pupils are already a minority in California schools. Independence, "ethno-nationalist," or "ethno-cultural" movements among indigenous and minority communities around the world receive regular media attention and scholarly debate. Under the circumstances it is hardly surprising that anthropologists also direct attention to ethnic phenomena, asking how ritual and aesthetic expressions, cultural performances, and political activities contribute to group identity formation, economic adaptation without cultural assimilation, and political separatism. As Williams (1989:401) notes in his review of ethnic studies: "The concept of ethnicity has become a lightning rod for anthropologists trying to redefine their theoretical and methodological approaches and for lay persons trying to redefine the bases on which they might construct a sense of social and moral worth."

My interests are not in ethnicity per se, but in the social anthropology of cultural institutions, such as museums and art galleries, and in the anthropology of public culture. Obviously, these institutions are involved in ethnicity, whether by default or by intent. Instead of looking at how such public forums help manifest ethnicity, I want to turn the question around: what is the impact of ethnicity on those institutions and on the public expressions of anthropology? Might we expect to see a gradual "browning of anthropology"? At the very least visible and

Michael M. Ames (1933–2006) was the director of the Museum of Anthropology and professor in the Department of Anthropology at the University of British Columbia. This excerpt is reprinted with permission of the publisher from *Cannibal Tours and Glass Boxes: The Anthropology of Museums* by Michael M. Ames. Copyright University of British Columbia Press 1992, pp. 151–168. All rights reserved by the publisher.

other "minorities" or underrepresented populations are demanding more space or "voice" in the mainstream institutions.

The public concern with ethnicity seems like a natural outgrowth of our current disputatious times, which might be described as an "Age of Deconstruction." I do not know whether French philosopher Jacques Derrida invented or borrowed that term, nor do I know what he meant by it (he was not inclined to define it, and the term itself may soon go out of fashion after a brief run through literary circles). It nevertheless sounds like an apt term to summarize the past decade or so in the world of cultural affairs. Traditional standards of literacy were attacked for ethnocentric bias; traditional modes of scholarship in the social sciences and humanities were placed under siege by radical and feminist critiques from both the left and the right; the authority of cultural and educational institutions was questioned; and the traditional canon was criticized for its Eurocentric and male-oriented biases.

Not only did the Berlin Wall and the Soviet Union start to crumble in the early 1990s but so did the barriers between disciplines and around public institutions. The past few years have seemed like an age of deconstruction, reconstruction, and self-construction, where everything is questioned and almost anything goes, at least for awhile. Someone coined the term "postmodern" to refer to such adventures, though the terms "deconstructing" and "reconstructing" come closer to describing what actually has been happening.

How have these issues of voice and self-representation impinged upon public museums and art galleries? Cultural institutions frequently serve as playing fields upon which the major social, political, and moral issues of the day are contested. Not only are the definitions of truth and beauty subject to debate, as one might expect, but so are other thorny issues, such as what constitutes public taste and who has the right to determine it, what kind of knowledge is deemed to be useful—indeed, even what constitutes proper knowledge, and who has the right to control its production and dissemination. Lying behind the rhetoric of these debates and controversies are larger questions about what kind of society we want to live in, how much social and cultural diversity we can tolerate, and how we wish to represent ourselves and others.

Thus, the activities and institutions dealing with "art and culture"—subjects often considered secondary to the important things in life, such as earning a living—are, to the contrary, deeply implicated in the major issues confronting contemporary society. Museums also strongly affect the public understanding of anthropology, another reason to pay attention to what they are doing and what is being done to them. Public response to museums helps to redefine those disciplines they represent.

I will briefly review some of the controversies surrounding displays in public places to see what wider lessons can be learned. (Collecting controversies is a hobby of mine.) Cultural institutions certainly play paradoxical roles, sometimes reflecting popular opinion and at other times guiding it, sometimes reaffirming dominant ideas and at other times opposing them. In the cases to be considered here, and in all others I know about, one constant or recurring factor is the embeddedness of cultural affairs in political relationships, that is, relationships involving status and power. Art, artefacts, and their institutions have politics, including the politics of representation (the "ethnic question" again). Other common threads may emerge as we proceed through the review.

Public Art: "The First Great Canadian"

Stationed on a hillock overlooking the Ottawa River that runs between Ottawa, Ontario, and Hull, Quebec, and commanding a majestic view of five important Canadian landmarks—the Canadian Museum of Civilization, the National Gallery of Canada, the Parliament Buildings, the National Archives of Canada, and the classic Chateau Laurier Hotel—stands an equally majestic bronze statue of Samuel de Champlain, described on the accompanying bronze plaque as "The first great Canadian."

Who is publicly proclaimed to be "The first great Canadian" says much about who is considered a part of history and who is not. Crouching below the feet of de Champlain, who holds aloft an astrolabe as if to signal his territorial ambitions, is a scantily clad Indian, one-third the size of de Champlain, and presumably a representative of the peoples whose land de Champlain has claimed.

Ironically the Indian looks towards the new Canadian Museum of Civilization and has turned his back on the equally new National Gallery. This is an unintentional, but dramatic statement about the relations between indigenous peoples and white society and about how museums and art galleries deal with indigenous peoples' culture—by dividing and separating it into art and artefact, the separate and jealously guarded realms of art historians and anthropologists, each armed with their own particular "astrolabes" of theory, method, and language. This division is contested by many indigenous peoples. From an academic point of view it is simply a matter of how to order the works of others through classification. From an indigenous perspective, it is a problem of how cultural patterns, which they view holistically, are being divided and segregated according to alien systems of conceptual domination.

Indigenous artists ask why their art is not collected and displayed in the National Gallery and other art museums and is always subjected to artificial contextualization by anthropologists. "Free us from our ethnological fate," they say.

What is to be done with the contemporary arts of indigenous peoples has become increasingly problematic (Duffek 1989; R. Phillips 1988). Anthropologists query whether it is really authentically indigenous, since it does not always look like earlier material, and art historians wonder whether it is authentically art since it does not always correspond to what white artists do, either. Probably most art curators and art historians still practise what Canadian art critic John Bentley Mays advocates: define what is art in terms of post-Renaissance Western experience.

As Mays (1990b) suggested in his review of an exhibition of Inuit carvings at To-ronto's Art Gallery of Ontario:

> If it is to be useful, the word sculpture will surely be kept as an historical term ap-plied restrictively to products of a certain practice, namely, the Western inquiry into plasticity, volume and visual meaning that has descended from the Greeks, through Rodin, to Duchamp and Carl Andre and beyond. Applied like a kind of honorary title to whatever we happen to like or think beautiful, the word sculpture is merely a grunt of approval, not a description of a class of related objects.

In contrast, the indigenous peoples view their creative works, contemporary and earlier alike, as neither art nor artefact but both or, even more likely, more than both. Deciding what is "art" is not only a matter of academic tradition, semantics, or personal preference, it is also a political act. The label determines what is to be admitted into that inner sanctum of the cultural establishment, the prestigious gallery of art. To deny serious consideration of the art of indigenous peoples, that is, to exclude it from mainstream institutions, a reader (Millard 1990) wrote in response to Mays's newspaper review of the Inuit exhibition, is "to collaborate in the suppression of their identity and in their continuing exclusion from the full life of this country." There is always an "on the other hand" to these issues, of course. As Susan Sontag remarked during the 1986 International PEN conference (Ozick 1989:125), "Genius is not an equal-opportunity employer." That is to say, there may be standards that transcend ethnicity, in which case works would be included or excluded according to merit rather than ethnic origin. But how then is genius defined?

Some major art galleries and museums in North America, Australia, and New Zealand have begun to recognize contemporary indigenous arts. They are follow-ing the lead of smaller institutions and commercial galleries, however, and the great divide between art and artefact continues to be a part of mainstream thinking and institutional practice in universities as well as in museums.

To make it more complicated, consider women's works. They are usually as-signed to the lower status categories of "craft" and "decorative arts." One example is Haida artist Dorothy Grant's "Feastwear," designer clothes for special occasions. If it is fashion, can it be art? And if it is not traditional, how can it be Haida? How-ever, Haida art has always been usable and adaptable. Adapting Robert Davidson's Haida graphics to her elegant clothing allows Grant another way to express her creativity while also taking her culture into a broader arena (Fried 1990:10).

Beyond the question of where does one put it is the problem of how to inter-pret it. Do non-Natives any longer have the right to interpret Native creativity? And even if they do have a right, will they get it right? Will they have sufficient inside knowledge of, or intimacy with, the culture in question?

There is an "irony," noted First Nations writer Kerrie Charnley (1990:16), "about people who claim to want to get to know who we are through the stereo-types they themselves have created about us rather than being receptive to who we are in the way that we express ourselves today." Once scholars begin to debate their own social constructions of other peoples' lives, as they are prone to do, the people themselves are gradually dropped from sight. They become the "disappeared" of the scholarly world.

The debate goes beyond cultural institutions and the question of ethnographic authority, of course, for it affects all systems of representation. This was illustrated by the controversy over W. P. Kinsella's "humourous" stories about fictional residents of the real community of Hobbema, home of four Cree bands seventy kilometres south of Edmonton, Alberta (Lacey 1989). Some Hobbema residents objected to Kinsella's use of their community's name. Authors have the right to appropriate stories from another culture, Kinsella replied (Canadian Press 1989a): "If minorities were doing an adequate job [of telling their stories], they wouldn't need to complain."

Ojibway writer and storyteller Lenore Keeshig-Tobias also criticized Kinsella's appropriation. "When someone else is telling your stories," she said (Greer 1989:14), "in effect what they're doing is defining to the world who you are, what you are, and what they think you are and what they think you should be."

Do artists, scholars, or curators any longer have the right to claim free access to the world of knowledge, or should there be some limits to cultural trespassing? Shirley Thomson, director of the National Gallery of Canada, has said (Bennett 1990:12): "Ideas don't recognize geographical boundaries. Why should the professionals who work in the institutions that house them?" York University (Toronto) professor of literature Terry Goldie offers the other view. We have hit an evolutionary moment, he says (Drainie 1989), at which it is no longer good enough for white writers to claim a spiritual kinship with Natives: "Their culture is one of the only valuable commodities natives own in this country, and for white writers to keep telling their stories is inevitably appropriation." People like Kinsella, writing stories about fictional Indians in a non-fictional Hobbema, are committing "cultural theft, the theft of voice," according to Keeshig-Tobias (Greer, ibid.). Stories are not just entertainment, "stories are power." They reflect and transmit cultural values. When non-Natives appropriate Native symbolism and monopolize the media, she continues, the Native voice is marginalized, or it has to be redefined to fit the format established by others: "They are trivializing our gods" (Vincent 1990).

The National Gallery: "Fire the Curators"

The National Gallery of Canada faces other challenges to its curatorial prerogatives besides those presented by indigenous artists, and though they may not involve ethnic or minority issues, they still involve contests over the rights of representation. For example, the gallery's 1989 purchase of Barnett Newman's abstract Voice of Fire for $1.8 million (Canadian Museums Association 1990:1–2) was denounced. A National Gallery spokesperson (Hunter 1990) described the painting as an "electrifying . . . 18-foot punch." Director Shirley Thomson said, "We need something to take us away from the devastating cares of everyday life," reminding us, as Toronto art critic John Bentley Mays noted (1990a), that art museums "exist to serve the life of the mind."

Those explanations were not enough to persuade everyone. "Well, I'm not exactly impressed," was the response from Manitoba Member of Parliament the Honourable Felix Holtmann (Canadian Press 1990a), who also chaired the House of Commons culture committee and was promising a committee inquiry into the purchase. "It looks like two cans of paint and two rollers and about ten minutes would do the trick." Others complained that public funds were being used to purchase a work from a deceased foreign (U.S.) artist rather than to support living Canadian artists. They should fire "the irresponsible curators," Canadian poet and editor John Robert Colombo (1990) wrote to a Toronto newspaper, for paying such a hefty amount for the work of a foreign artist who is "a spent force."

Perhaps what the National Gallery needed was to explain its purchase of an abstract painting in language ordinary citizens could understand and appreciate—but that is not what cultural experts are well trained to do.

Into the Heart of Africa?

The theft of cultural or ethnic copyright or cultural trespassing is also what Afro-Canadians in Toronto accused the Royal Ontario Museum of committing in its 1989 exhibition, "Into the Heart of Africa" (Da Breo 1989–90; Drainie 1990). This exhibition, curated by anthropologist Jeanne Cannizzo (1989), is an example of good intentions gone wrong or being misconstrued.

Cannizzo's mission was to show the origins of the ROM's African collection within the context of white Canadian imperialist history. It was first an exhibition of 19th-century Canadians in Africa and Canadian attitudes towards Africans. What may have been for some a passing comment on the questionable adventures of an earlier generation became for others a painful reminder of a history of oppression. Some Afro-Canadians picketed the ROM in protest, claiming that it was extolling colonialism when it should have recorded the great achievements of Africa. But how can an imperialist society talk about its own history without using imperialist emblems?

The protestors may have misread the intent of the exhibition, and/or it was too subtly stated. In any case, they found parts of it a painful, therefore offensive, reminder of colonial subjugation. Those picketing the ROM asked that the exhibition text be changed or the exhibition be closed. The ROM did neither, referring to the judgements of critics and the response of museum visitors who thought the exhibition provided a useful insight into Canada's imperialist past (Blizzard 1990; Freedman 1989). One is left to ponder how offensive it is permissible to be in the exercise of free speech and scholarly interest; if it matters who is offended; how offensive may the offended be in their protest; and whether a curator's good intentions count for anything any more. (The exhibition ran its course at the ROM, but its projected North American tour was cancelled when those museums scheduled to receive the exhibition bowed to protests by Afro-Canadians. Museums do not want to be offensive.)

The Question of Authenticity:
The Canadian Museum of Civilization

When the new Canadian Museum of Civilization opened in June 1989 it was immediately and widely criticized for costing too much and for showing too little too poorly. The CMC was obliged by government decree to open before construction was completed. It did cost more than originally estimated (so far, about C$256 million), with a cost overrun of about C$9 to $12 million. Less than half the exhibition space was finished (at a cost of C$35 million), and it has been estimated that many millions more will be needed to complete the museum as planned (Jennings 1990). It probably will become, if it is not already, the most expensive public building in Canada and the largest museum in the world. But is it any good?

The CMC was accused of substituting Disneyland–style pyrotechnics for educational substance and for presenting, not artefacts, but contemporary reconstructions smelling like a lumberyard—"Disneyland on the Ottawa, with the emphasis on illusion rather than on the real artifact" (Canadian Press 1990b). Even the design by Alberta architect Douglas J. Cardinal did not escape criticism, being described by another architect as "prairie gopher baroque."

The illuminated Parliament Buildings in the background of the cover photo of MacDonald and Alsford's (1989), *A Museum for the Global Village: The Canadian Museum of Civilization*, fills in quite nicely for Fantasyland Castle. It was also appropriate, even if unintentional, that during the same week in 1987 when the then U.S. vice-president, George Bush, visited Prime Minister Brian Mulroney, someone dressed as Mickey Mouse visited Speaker of the House John Fraser and made him an honorary citizen of Walt Disney World (Canadian Press 1987:A5).

In the debate about cost overruns and the Disneyland–Global Village references by CMC director George MacDonald, what has tended to get lost are his and his staff's attempts to restructure the very nature of the museum enterprise. For example, they systematically integrate theatre and art gallery functions and associated disciplines with anthropology and history displays; consult with indigenous peoples and others on how they are to be represented; increase access to information about collections through electronic technology; develop marketing plans based on the concept of cultural tourism; borrow management and display techniques from theme parks; and substitute the authenticity of the visitor experience for the authenticity of the "real" object.

The way the CMC is redefining the traditional concept of authenticity is particularly significant. Museums pride themselves on being the last refuge for the "real thing," the "authentic object," MacDonald has said, but they fail to portray the real cultures from which those real objects derive. North American curators, MacDonald notes (1988:29),

> are 98 per cent white Euro-Americans whose knowledge of North or South American Indian, African, Japanese or Chinese culture is definitely second-hand. Most curators, even in anthropology, spend at most a few years in the cultural milieu of their "specialty." In fact, they have the cultural credibility and often linguistic

competence of a four-year-old child from that culture . . . They have never been
cultural participants and will never have the credibility of "the real thing."

Collections become an expensive burden to museums because of the mandate to
preserve and exhibit them even though so little is known about them that it is difficult to present them authentically:

> Most museum directors now feel like directors of geriatric hospitals whose budgets
> are devastated by patients whose survival for another day depends on expensive,
> high technology support systems. Conservators in museums are like a host of rela-
> tives who guard the wall plug of the life-support machines. Sixty per cent of most
> museum budgets are spent on life-support systems for the "reserve" collections,
> and conservators constantly battle to increase that amount. There is no apparent
> solution to this dilemma. The museum is the final repository of "the real thing."
> (MacDonald 1987:213–14)

According to MacDonald museums should give more attention to presenting real
experiences with the assistance of people from those cultures being represented, and
redistributing reserve collections to regional museums. The authenticity of the experience, rather than the authenticity of the object, becomes the objective, and the
use of replicas, simulations, performances, and electronic media intertwined with
real objects—techniques in which theme parks excel—help recreate, reconstruct,
or rerepresent near-authentic experiences (MacDonald 1988). The "real thing" is
the experience of the visitor, not the object or its interpretation by a curator.

One reason why proposals like MacDonald's are controversial within the museum community (Ames 1988b) is their implied shift of power and status away
from curator, registrar, and conservator towards those more directly involved in
public programming, performance, promotion, marketing, other public services,
and revenue generation. These changes respond to growing pressures on museums to generate more of their own operating costs. The curatorial professions are,
in a sense, coming under siege, their prerogatives increasingly encroached upon,
even though they have been actively professionalizing or upgrading their own
standards of work over the past decade. Unfortunately, this professionalization
has been mostly oriented to behind-the-scenes collections management and has
become costly. Registration, cataloguing, condition reporting, insurance reports,
conserving and caring for the object, and so on, are all labour-intensive activities.
Further professionalization, as presently envisaged, typically calls for even more
labour. Museums are heading for a crunch. Curatorial staff want more support for
backstage object-centred work while their programming colleagues try to expand
frontstage activities to enlist more public support. Traditional museological notions
about object care are being increasingly confronted by the seemingly more "commercial" values of public service and cost-effectiveness. The bottom line is coming
to the top of the agenda, making many uncomfortable.

If museums do not become more commercial and popular they may not survive
in any useful form. Yet people continue to criticize museums like the CMC for

sacrificing integrity and authenticity on the alter of populism (see Gray 1988; Thorsell 1989). But how is integrity to be judged? The answer from MacDonald and the Canadian government is straightforward: if about 80 percent of the population rarely visit museums, new approaches must be tried to attract them; entertainment seems to be the way to do it. The fact that half a million people visited the CMC during the first few months, the then secretary-general of the National Museums, John Edwards (1989), said, demonstrates that they must be doing something right, despite what the critics are saying. The Canadian Museum of Civilization turned one year old Friday and its director says it's on its way to becoming the popular people's museum it was meant to be, reported the Canadian Press (1990b) on the CMC's first anniversary. Integrity, from this point of view, means serving the public first, not the objects (or the curatorial professions).

The Politics of Art: "The Spirit Songs" and the Lubicon Boycott

The Glenbow Museum's 1988 exhibition "The Spirit Sings: Artistic Traditions of Canada's First Peoples," like "Into the Heart of Africa," also caused protest over messages stated, implied, and presumed—another example of good intentions leading to mixed results (Harrison 1988; Harrison et al., 1987; Harrison, Trigger, and Ames 1988; Trigger 1989; Ames 1989).

The Glenbow's six curators wanted to demonstrate the richness, diversity, and adaptability of indigenous peoples during the first years of contact with Europeans, but their exhibition got caught in the crossfire of a political campaign to support a land claim by the Lubicon Lake Cree in northern Alberta. The Lubicon called for a boycott of the 1988 Calgary Winter Olympics to draw attention to their fifty-year dispute with the Canadian government over land claims. Attention gradually shifted from the Olympics (and to some extent from the land dispute) to the Glenbow and its right to mount an exhibition of Native arts during the Olympics over the objections of a Native group not represented in the exhibition. Probably many would have agreed with Alberta Native artist Joane Cardinal-Schubert (Patterson 1988:8) who found the Glenbow exhibition "so offensive": "It shows 300–year-old stuff, which only serves to reinforce the lack of attention paid to the contemporary problems of tribes such as the Lubicon. Not only that, but the work itself, all taken from the Indian, is removed from its life involvement."

The museological defence that some works displayed were gifted or sold by indigenous peoples rather than "taken"; that museums have always been expected to preserve and represent the past (otherwise who would?); and that most of the 300-year-old materials probably only survived because they were removed from "life involvement" sounds self-serving when placed against the poverty of these peoples whose lands have been expropriated and lifestyles almost destroyed. Whether they like it or not, museums have become a part of the discourse about endangered peoples. The question is whether they will have anything useful to say or do about the matter. Can museological principles be bent towards worldly concerns?

The strategy of those who proposed a boycott of the Glenbow was to disseminate criticisms of it and the proposed exhibition, effectively turning a debate about land claims into a moral critique of museological prerogatives. As Robert Paine (1985:190) noted about other indigenous protests: "Much of Fourth World politics is about turning physical powerlessness into moral power and then putting that to good political account." The "politics of morality" become "a politics of embarrassment" (ibid.:214) directed against the authorities and their sometimes hapless wards. The campaign against "The Spirit Sings" received widespread attention and sympathy, including the support of many Canadian anthropologists (though it did not resolve the land claims dispute). We see again how the authority of cultural experts and cultural institutions is contested. The Glenbow Museum was challenged on a number of points that have wider implications, including its right to:

1. borrow or exhibit Native artefacts without their permission, even though those artefacts are legally owned by other museums;
2. use money from corporations involved in public disputes (the exhibit was sponsored by Shell Oil, which was drilling on land claimed by the Lubicon);
3. ignore contemporary political issues, such as land claims, even when presenting an exhibition of the history of indigenous peoples;
4. employ non-Natives to curate an exhibition about Native culture; and
5. claim neutrality in public disputes.

The broader issues underlying these challenges affect more than just the privileges of anthropology. Who should decide what constitutes knowledge about a people's history—scholars or the living descendants of those studied? When should moral and political claims outrank legal obligations (such as the Glenbow's agreements with donors and lenders)? And what should be the costs of public association with those accused? Some Lubicon supporters wanted "The Spirit Sings" closed down because Glenbow curators did not change the exhibition text and because it was sponsored by Shell Oil and the federal government. (Interestingly, there was no attempt to boycott Shell products or government agencies. Perhaps the Glenbow offered a better opportunity to define the issues in moral terms and was thought to be more easily embarrassed.) The "fire the curators" syndrome, adding punishment to criticism, appears again. Lubicon supporters made a claim for the higher ground by redefining an academic museum exhibition as a morality play between good and evil. Once evil is identified, it has to be exorcised if goodness is to triumph.

The Politics of Public Taste: Pornography and Blasphemy

Possibly the biggest single debate in the arts community in North America in 1989 and extending into the 1990s, was over the question of who has the right to decide public taste. What sparked the debate were two controversial exhibitions, one of the works of photographer Robert Mapplethorpe, some of whose photos were said to be pornographic and homophobic; and the other by photographer Andres Serrano, whose photos, especially his Piss Christ, were called blasphemous trash.

"Fine Art or Foul?" read the headline to a *Newsweek* cover article (Mathews 1990:46). United States Congress representatives and senators threatened to cut the budget allocation to the National Endowment for the Arts for financing such "shocking" and "abhorrent" materials in the name of "art" and to deny future funding to those galleries that displayed "obscene" works (Alaton 1990; American Association for State and Local History 1990:1). Senator Jesse Helms told the U.S. Senate (Vance 1989:39): "I do not know Mr. Andres Serrano, and I hope I never meet him, because he is not an artist, he is a jerk. Let him be a jerk on his own time and with his own resources. Do not dishonor our Lord." The Mapplethorpe exhibit continued to circulate through U.S. art galleries and got into trouble again in March 1990 in Cincinnati, Ohio, where the director of the Centre for the Contemporary Arts was charged with obscenity for showing the exhibit.

Earlier in 1990 the Mendel Gallery in Saskatoon, Saskatchewan, was also temporarily besieged by the Saskatoon City Council and others for housing the National Photography Gallery's travelling exhibition "Evergon," which also included sexually explicit imagery (Lacey and Vincent 1990; Milrod 1990). "We have laws to clean up pollution in our rivers," one city councillor was quoted as saying, "so we should have laws to ban filth like this." He was perhaps repeating *Washington Times* columnist Patrick Buchanan's metaphor (cited in Vance 1989:41): "As with our rivers and lakes, we need to clean up our culture: for it is a well from which we must all drink. Just as a poisoned land will yield up poisonous fruits, so a polluted culture, left to fester and stink, can destroy a nation's soul."

People called for Mendel director Linda Milrod to be fired and the gallery's budget to be cut. (After weeks of debate, in council and through the local media, city council voted to continue normal funding for the gallery. Milrod subsequently resigned but for reasons unrelated to this controversy.) When Andres Serrano attended the "Art and Outrage" conference on art and censorship at the Winnipeg Art Gallery on 31 March 1990, a Winnipeg councillor described him as "a lunatic who should be in an asylum, not in the Winnipeg Art Gallery." Anthropologist Carol Vance suggested at the same Winnipeg conference that the good people of Saskatoon and Winnipeg were experiencing a "sex panic," projecting upon people like Serrano, Evergon, and Mapplethorpe their anxieties about changes in family and gender relations, abortion, child abuse, and so on. (The Winnipeg conference was reported by Enright 1990. See also Vance 1989, 1990; Wallis 1990.)

Whatever the reasons, it is interesting to note that arguments which first seemed to centre around pornography, blasphemy, artistic freedom, and censorship, gradually began to encompass broader issues (see Robertson 1990) such as what is art, who is it for, who pays for it, and who calls the tune? We have returned to the politics of representation and the question of voice:

a. What is art? Counterbalanced are two views about the purpose of art (and of exhibits, and even of anthropology, one might add): to be inspirational and supportive of mainstream values or to be critical, oppositional, or even sometimes offensive.

b. Who is it for, the elites or everyone?

c. Who pays for it? The debate here is over how much governments should support art or exhibitions that do not support the state or are not supported by the public "in the marketplace."

d. Who calls the tune? Who should decide how taxpayers' dollars are used— legislators, panels of experts, peer review, or special-interest groups through public protest?

Without the freedom to offend, British author Salman Rushdie once said (Findley 1990), there is no freedom of expression: "Without the freedom to challenge, even to satirize all orthodoxies, including religious orthodoxies, it ceases to exist. Language and the imagination cannot be imprisoned, or art dies, and with it, a little of what makes us human" (Rushdie 1990:6).

"It is perhaps in the nature of modern art to be offensive," American writer John Updike (1989:12) wrote in response to the Mapplethorpe controversy. "It wishes to astonish us and invites a revision of our prejudices." What is more (1989:13): "if we are not willing to risk giving offense, we have no claim to the title of artists, and if we are not willing to face the possibility of being ourselves revised, offended, and changed by a work of art, we should leave the book unopened, the picture unviewed, and the symphony unheard." (Might one make the same claim for anthropologists that he makes for artists?)

On the other side—and there is always that other side in these matters (and usually more than one)—is the question of setting limits out of respect for community standards or the sensitivities of others. At some point it is necessary to stop and think about the people who might be offended. U.S. Senator Jesse Helms has frequently spoken out against the use of tax dollars for art he considered offensive. Let people be offensive at their own expense, he says. "Should public standards of decency and civility be observed in determining which works of art or art events are to be selected for the government's support?" asked the *New York Observer* art critic Hilton Kramer (1989:1). Or, stating the issue another way, he continues, "is everything and anything to be permitted in the name of art? Or, to state the issue in still another way, is art now to be considered such an absolute value that no other standard—no standard of taste, no social or moral standard—is to be allowed to play any role in determining what sort of art it is appropriate for the government to support?"

Canada's revenue minister, Otto Jelinek, referring to a Canada Council grant to a theatre that produced a play about homosexuals, remarked (Dafoe 1989) that "some of these ridiculous grants are enough to make me bring up" and that his government should review the arms-length status of the Council.

We have returned to the marketplace as an arbiter of public taste. Public appeal is the test of virtue. As Senator Helms said in reference to the Mapplethorpe/Serrano controversies (Parachini 1989:3): "I have fundamental questions about why the federal government is involved in supporting artists the taxpayers have refused to support in the marketplace." Thus, the debate about the purpose of art becomes a language for examining broader questions about what constitutes a proper society, including the contest between the moral visions of the conservatives and liberals (Alaton 1990; Vance 1990). "The fundamentalist attack on images and the art world," Vance (1989:43) argues, "must be recognized not as an improbable and silly outburst of Yahoo-ism, but as a systematic part of a right-wing political program to restore traditional social arrangements and reduce diversity."

Conclusion: Some Common Threads

If we examined each case in detail we would find many differences and some similarities. I want to focus on the similarities here, especially those that lie behind the differences.

One pattern extends beyond these cases: the widespread inclination to question the authority of cultural agencies, such as museums and universities, and their professional representatives, to make decisions that go against those moral standards that are claimed by some to represent either the public's interest or the concerns of under-represented populations.

This is not new. Sociologist Alvin Gouldner, in his 1970 *The Coming Crisis of Western Sociology* (1970:115–16, passim), noted a long, continuous series of "revolts" against the idea of applying empiricist methodologies to the study of society and its expressions. In his classic 1947 paper, "The Expansion of the Scope of Science," Leslie White suggested that the scientific or naturalistic perspective would appear latest, mature slowest, and receive the most opposition in the psychological, social, and cultural areas of our experience "where the most intimate and powerful determinants of our behavior are found." There have been renewed assaults on the notion of a scientific study of society during the past several decades, from within the disciplines as well as from outside, identifying the limitations, fallacies, and male-centric orientation of the naturalistic approaches. Some, perhaps buoyed along by a postmodernist enthusiasm, reject the possibility of any objective knowledge about society, opting for the equality of insider perspectives. Everyone is his or her own authority, just as the customer is always right. Consumerism and postmodernism, it would seem, share similar ideological foundations. The possibility of positive knowledge cannot be totally extinguished, however, no matter how often attacked by those claiming higher moral grounds.

Resistance and rebellion against naturalistic or empirical interpretations might be seen as recurring features of intellectual history, though their labels change from one age to the next—"postmodernism" being one of the more recent—and though intellectual discourse never totally succumbs to those onslaughts. Other features in our cases seem to be more emergent than repetitive.

One emergent feature concerns the type of morality that appears to be gaining ascendency—or, to use another trendy word, gaining "hegemony"—in contemporary society. It is that populist/postmodernist/consumer ideological orientation referred to earlier and includes, in one form or another, the radical democratic idea that in the marketplace of ideas, customs, and morals, as in the marketplace of products, the customer is always right. As the Member of Parliament the Honourable Felix Holtmann noted in an interview (Godfrey 1990): "I basically believe the people are always right. The customer is king."

Another illustration of this view is Canadian economist Steven Globerman's (1983:37) argument that claims for government subsidy by the cultural sector based on the assumption that some tastes are better than others "is an unacceptable basis for government action in a democratic society." Good taste is popular taste. Or consider British Columbia's former premier Bill Vander Zalm's response (Moore 1987) to those concerned about the impact of free trade with United States on Canadian culture: "What is culture? I'm not sure Canadians are all that concerned by what is traded away in culture . . . I don't think there's much wrong with the marketplace determining what people want in culture."

There are other examples one could cite, but these will do for now. In the broader philosophy (Marchak 1988), of which these are individual expressions, there is a tendency to view citizens as consumers, to redefine cultures as commodities, to measure value by public opinion polls, referenda, head counts, and sales receipts, and to believe that justice is probably best determined by the play of so-called free market forces. In fact, the marketplace is typically represented as an ideal paradigm for organizing social as well as economic relations.

The second emerging feature, ambiguously related to the first, is the increasing public recognition of social and cultural pluralism. Contemporary society is not composed of an anonymous mass of consumers but rather—to borrow from the language of consumerism—of various "market segments," each with its special tastes and vested interests. What is significant about this pluralization or taste segmentation of society is not its existence, which is not new, but its growing visibility and acceptance, even if that growth is slow, frequently petulant, agonizing, and uneven. The implication for cultural institutions, such as museums and universities, is that they are increasingly being expected to meet the multiple demands of ethnically and socially diverse publics. In this new world order the minorities expect the same rights and privileges as the majority. For anthropologists that especially means giving consideration to the interests of Third World peoples and visible minorities. The introduction of third and fourth voices (worlds)—the traditional subjects of anthropological research—has been unnerving for anthropologists, who find themselves being publicly criticized and rejected by the very people they have tried to represent!

Fueling the assertion of minority rights is the idea of equality, which must be one of the most revolutionary ideas in all history. It is difficult to think of any other single principle that has had such an impact on social arrangements and personality formation, that throughout history has been as oppositional, confrontational, or destructive of traditional relations, and as transforming, emancipating, or liberating for individuals and groups. The belief that one has a natural right to be the equal of others is surely one of the most powerful of beliefs. Perhaps its most radical version is the assertion of collective (ethnic) rights over those of the individual and, thus, the right to be different as equal to the right of everyone to be the same.

The growth of cultural and ethnic pluralism and ideas about the equality of groups as well as of individuals in a consumer-oriented, postmodernist, deconstructing society raises several questions about the status of the anthropological perspective. First is the question of voice. In a plurality of tongues what happens to scholarly speech? Naturalistic interpretation, rooted in empiricism, has traditionally claimed cognitive superiority over those based on moral, communal, or popular considerations. But who can claim superiority in an equalitarian society? Is anthropology only to be regarded as one more voice among many, perhaps even inferior to the self-interpretations of underrepresented peoples? Has anthropology become just another story, yet another mythic "discourse," now that its colonial and sexist origins have been fully exposed? It is not just museum exhibits that are being criticized here, by the way—it is the very idea of studying others, never mind representing them, that is challenged. The contest is over the essence of anthropology. How, then, is anthropology to be reconstituted during this age of populist deconstruction?

The second question is about action. How will anthropologists and other cultural workers help people come to terms with the growing multicultural and multivocal realities—discordant realities, one might even say—of contemporary society? Will anthropologists in museums and elsewhere have the authority and public respect, not to mention the courage, to speak out? Or will they be lost in the cacophony of voices, reduced by public criticism, populist sentiments, funding restrictions, and the forces of the marketplace to bland pronouncements and tangled rhetoric?

Notes

Note below is from the article as it appeared in *Cannibal Tours and Glass Boxes: The Anthropology of Museums.*

1. Earlier versions of this chapter were presented to the Plenary Session "Recent Developments in Canadian Anthropology" at the seventeenth annual meeting of the Canadian Anthropology Society, Calgary, Alberta, May 2, 1990, and to the University of Washington "Seminar on Ethnicity, Nationality, and the Arts," coordinated by Professor Simon Ottenberg, May 8, 1990. I am thankful for those opportunities. I am also indebted to Dr. Jeanne Cannizzo, research consultant of the Royal Ontario Museum, Lina Jabra, then director of the Burnaby Art Gallery, and Dr. Judith Mastai, director of Public Programmes at the Vancouver Art Gallery, for supplying information on a number of the case studies discussed here. This chapter is also to be published in a series edited by Professor Ottenberg. Materials from this chapter were included in a report to the Taonga Maori Conference, New Zealand, November 20, 1990, entitled "Biculturalism in Exhibits" to be published by the government of New Zealand, also published in *Museum Anthropology* 15(1991)2.

References

Alaton, Salem. "Liberals and conservatives in row over U.S. arts body." *Globe and Mail* (June 9, 1990): D3.

American Association for State and Local History. "Reauthorization critical for NEH." *History News Dispatch* 5, No. 6 (1990): 1.

Ames, Michael M. "Daring to be different: an alternative." *Muse, Journal of the Canadian Museums Association* 6, No. 1 (1988b): 38–47.

———. "The liberation of anthropology: A rejoinder to professor trigger's 'a present of their past?'" *Culture, Journal of the Canadian Anthropology Society* 8, No. 1 (1989): 81–85.

Bennett, Julia. "High flyers: national gallery's Shirley Thomson masters the modern art world." *Privilege* 2, No. 1 (1990): 11–12.

Blizzard, Christina. "Exhibit mirrors history." *Toronto Sun* (May 8, 1990): 29.

Canadian Museums Association. "MP's try to intervene on gallery's purchase." *Museogramme, Newsletter of the Canadian Museums Association* 18, No. 3 (1990): 1–2.

Canadian Press. "Goodwill ambassador [photograph]." *Globe and Mail* (January 22, 1987): A5.

———. "Kinsella 'ripping off' Indians." *Globe and Mail* (December 8, 1989a): C10.

———. "Gallery purchase raises questions." *Globe and Mail* (March 10, 1990a): C6.

———. Civilization museum seeks popularity: a million visitors logged in first year." *Vancouver Sun* (July 2, 1990b): B3.

Cannizzo, Jeanne. Into the heart of Africa. Royal Ontario Museum, 1989.

Charnley, Kerrie. "Neo-nativists: days without singing. *Front, Newsletter of the Western Front Society*, Vancouver (January 1990): 15–17.

Colombo, John Robert. "Fire the curators." Letter to *Globe and Mail* (March 17, 1990): D7.

Da Breo, Hazel A. "Royal spoils: the museum confronts its colonial past." *Fuse* (Winter 1989–90): 28–37.

Dafoe, Chris. "Jelinek angers arts groups with remarks on grants." *Globe and Mail* (December 21, 1989): C2.

Drainie, Bronwyn. "Minorities go toe to toe with majority." *Globe and Mail* (September 30, 1989): C1–2.

———. "Black groups protest African show at 'racist Ontario Museum.'" *Globe and Mail* (March 24, 1990): C1.

Duffek, Karen. "Exhibitions of contemporary native art." *Muse, Journal of the Canadian Museums Association* 7, No. 3 (1989): 26–28.

Edwards, John. "Novel approaches." Letter to *Globe and Mail* (October 21, 1989): D7.

Enright, Robert. "Notes on 'the arts tonight.'" Canadian Broadcasting Corporation FM program, April 2 and 5, 1990.

Findley, Timothy. "The man who kissed books and bread out of respect." *Globe and Mail* (June 16, 1990): C1.

Freedman, Adele. "A revealing journey through time and space." *Globe and Mail* (November 17, 1989): C11.

Fried, Nicky. "Fashion by Dorothy Grant." *Design Vancouver* (1990): 9–10.

Globerman, Steven. *Cultural Regulation in Canada*. Montreal: Institute of Public Policy, 1983.

Godfrey, Stephen. "Foe of elitism has had his say on arts." *Globe and Mail* (pril 9, 1990): A17.

Gouldner, Alvin A. *The Coming Crisis of Western Sociology*. New York: Avon Books, 1970.

Gray, Charlotte. "Museum pieces." *Saturday Night* 103, No. 9. (1988): 11–17.

Greer, Sandy. "Ojibway storyteller speaks out against film." *Kainai News* (November 9, 1989): 14–15.

Harrison, Julia D. "'The spirit sings' and the future of anthropology." *Anthropology Today* 4, No. 6. (1988): 6–9.

Harrison, Julia D., et al. *The Spirit Sings: Artistic Traditions of Canada's First Peoples*. Toronto: McClelland & Steward and Glenbow Museum, 1987.

Harrison, Julia D., Bruce Trigger, and Michael M. Ames. "Point/counterpoint: 'the spirit sings' and the Lubicon Boycott." *Muse, Journal of the Canadian Museums Association* 6, No. 3. (1988): 12–25.

Henry III, William A. "Cover stories: beyond the melting pot." *Time* 135, No. 15. (1990): 38–41.

Hunter, Don. "The $1.8-million stripe." *Province* (March 18, 1990): 37.

Jennings, Sarah. "Museum's costs questioned." *Globe and Mail* (May 16, 1990): A14.

Kramer, Hilton. "Is art above the laws of decency?" *New York Times* (July 2, 1989): Section 2, 1, 7.

Lacey, Liam. "Colleague's attack only serves to motivate iconoclastic author." *Globe and Mail* (December 21, 1989): A14.

Lacey, Liam, and Isabel Vincent. "Saskatoon Gallery under fire for 'offensive' exhibition.'" *Globe and Mail* (March 23, 1990): A13.

MacDonald, George F. "The future of museums in the global village." *Museum* 39, No. 3 (1987): 209–216.

———. "Epcot Center in museological perspective." *Muse, Journal of the Canadian Museums Association* 6, No. 1 (1988): 27–37.

MacDonald, George F., and Stephen Alsford. *A Museum for the Global Village: the Canadian Museum of Civilization*. Hull, Quebec: Canadian Museum of Civilization, 1989.

Marchak, Patricia M. *Ideological Perspectives on Canada*. 3rd ed. Toronto: McGraw-Hill Ryerson, 1988.

Mathews, Tom. "Fine art or foul?" *Newsweek* 116, No. 1 (1990): 46–52.

Mays, John Bentley. "National gallery should tune out static over painting." *Globe and Mail* (March 14, 1990a): A11.

———. "Carving or sculpture?" *Globe and Mail* (June 16, 1990b): C4.

Millard, Peter. "Art of the Inuit." Letter to Globe and Mail (June 26, 1990): A18.

Milrod, Linda. "Message from the director" *Folio, Newsletter of the Mendel Art Gallery* (February/March 1990): 4.

Moore, Mavor. "Canada's cultural road takes a disturbing turn." *Globe and Mail* (June 27, 1987): C2.

Ozick, Cynthia. "A critic at large (T.S. Eliot)." *New Yorker* 65, No. 4 (1989): 119–154.

Paine, Robert. "Ethnodrama and the 'fourth world': the Saami Action Group in Norway, 1979–1981. In Noel Dyck, ed., *Indigenous Peoples and the Nation-State: 'Fourth World' Politics in Canada, Australia and Norway*. Social and Economic Papers No. 14. St. John's Newfoundland: Institute of Social and Economic Research, Memorial University of Newfoundland, 1985.

Parachini, Allan. "The national endowment for the arts: arts agency—living up to its billing?" *Western Museums Conference Newsletter* (Fall 1989): 1, 3–5.

Patterson, Pam. "Doreen Jensen and Joane Cardinal-Schubert: two native women artists tackle issues through their art." *Gallerie: Women's Art* 1, No. 2 (1988): 4–8.

Phillips, Ruth. "Indian art: where do you put it?" *Muse, Journal of the Canadian Museums Association* 6, No. 3 (1988): 64–71.

Robertson, Art. "Art gets much-needed publicity." *Saskatoon Sun* (March 31, 1990).

Rushdie, Salman. *In Good Faith*. London: Granta, 1990.

Thorsell, William. "A spectacular disregard for cultural integrity" *Globe and Mail* (October 21, 1989): D6.

Trigger, Bruce. "A present of their past? Anthropologists, native people, and their heritage." *Culture, Journal of the Canadian Anthropology Society* 8, No. 1 (1989): 71–79.

Updike, John. "Modern art: always offensive to orthodoxy." *Western Museums Conference Newsletter* (Fall 1989): 12–13.

Vance, Carol. "The war on culture." *Art in American* (September 1989): 39–43.

———. "Misunderstanding obscenity." *Art in America* (May 1990): 49–55.

Vincent, Isabel. "Minority artists assail the mainstream: delegates to conference accuse arts councils of racism." *Globe and Mail* (June 25, 1990): A9.

Wallis, Brian. "Vice cops bust Mapplethorpe show for obscenity." *Art in America* (May 1990): 41–42.

Williams, B. "A class act: Anthropology and the race to nation across ethnic terrain." In Bernard J. Siegel, ed, *Annual Review of Anthropology* 18 (1989): 401–444.

The Real Multiculturalism

A Struggle for Authority and Power

AMALIA MESA-BAINS

FOR THE PAST SIX OR SO YEARS A NUMBER OF US have been involved in conferences in the United States and abroad, talking about everything from the politics of culture to the center and margin, and I'm almost exhausted with the term *multicultural*. So I'm going to try to part the veil a little bit.

I grew up in the sixties, first in the black-power movement with my husband, then in the Chicano movement, and later, as an educator in that golden era of multicultural education in the public schools; so I've heard a lot of jargon come and go. *Multiculturalism* seems to be a term that we are comfortable with at present, possibly because of its euphemistic nature. It allows us to acknowledge our own ethnicity, but not the categorical differences in race, class, and gender that are below the surface and need to be addressed in order to deal in an appropriate and responsive way with the diversity we're talking about.

What we're really talking about is a kind of postcolonial diaspora. Much of art history and our ideas about art, the museum, and collecting have come out of the colonial ages. We are now dealing with the generations descendant from those colonial experiences and occupations, but they have come home to the colonies. In the case of indigenous Mesoamericans, these communities represent an experience of internal colonization. You are now meeting their grandchildren, dealing with those of us and our children who come from that experience of the postcolonial age.

Consequently, all of the institutional and theoretical developments from which your institutions spring conflict with what we, as people of color, represent. The contemporary expressions of individuals and communities who live between tradition and innovation simply don't fit Western categories. Multiculturalism has

Amalia Mesa-Bains, artist, activist, and author, is the codirector of the Department of Visual and Public Art at California State University, Monterey Bay. "The Real Multiculturalism: A Struggle for Authority and Power" was written for *Different Voices: A Social, Cultural, and Historical Framework for Change in the American Art Museum* published in 1992 by the Association of Art Museum Directors (AAMD). It is reprinted here by permission of the AAMD.

allowed the mainstream arts community to grow somewhat complacent. It has drawn a little closer perhaps, but on some levels still maintains a distance—a distance from the issues of racism and linguistics.

In this postcolonial, post-civil rights era we are faced, in many ways for the first time, not simply with issues of quantification, affirmative action, quotas, parity, access, and representation, but with the qualitative aspects of the diverse experiences of uniqueness, the polysemic voice that we speak of so often. These are the issues that I believe on some level have penetrated your institutions and with which you are struggling. Concepts like patrimony. Whose is it? Stewards of a commonwealth. Whose wealth? How was it gained?

We often speak of style, cultural style. I saw a photograph in which a young blond white boy was wearing dreadlocks; I also saw a full-page ad in Glamour showing a light-skinned black woman wearing blue lenses. Style has always been style, but the issues of real cross-cultural or transcultural exchange and, more important, the culturally specific values that people bring to those transcultural encounters are what we have had the most difficulty facing.

Cultural Patrimony

I come from a family that immigrated from Mexico, and I grew up in a community with other undocumented families. I'm the first in my family to receive a higher education and, to some degree, the first to encounter a larger institutional life; consequently, my family values have been put into question time and time again. This goes beyond code switching—learning what kind of clothes to wear or what voice to speak in—to fundamental questions of relationship.

It is in the areas of patrimony, cultural values, and something that Carlos More calls "interethnic intimacy" that we are presently struggling. By interethnic, or interracial, intimacy, we are not talking about that fearful thing called sex, which seemingly is one of the driving forces in racism. We're speaking of something much more intimate than that; that is respect, understanding, and exchange.

In many respects, patrimonial values and interethnic intimacy constitute the battleground in which we will work out the 21st century; and in this large-scale redefinition of aesthetic and cultural identity, there is on the most profound level a call to the institutions that broker learning, thinking, culture, and expressiveness. The Association of Art Museum Directors can play a major role here.

In order to push aside the veil of multiculturalism in its euphemistic sense and conquer the mystifications that come with it, we—as a transitional generation with an inherited view of patrimony, values, and interethnic intimacy—are called upon to assume another kind of moral leadership in what may be a very difficult time. It means we have to deal with some of the very issues that we brought up earlier: issues of power, authority, and privilege.

I define power as the ability to create self-definitions upon which one can act. Action is clearly the issue at hand. Dialogue has been going on for quite a long time. From your point of view, the questions may now be: How should we do this, and what will happen if we do? How far do we have to go with it? Must I give up the type of stewardship my institution represents? What happens when people from multiracial and multicultural communities come into the museum—when we begin to change our curatorial focus and to develop other kinds of exhibition and acquisition policies?

The ability to self-define—a complex task in a postcolonial age—is at the heart of the struggle. I am a Chicana, which means that my parents were born in Mexico. I was born in the United States, and I came to my own sense of power—self-definition followed by action—during the civil rights movement. The Chicano movement was pivotal to me and my self-definition. Chicana, after all these years, is an identity based on the ability to act upon a sense of who I am and what I come from. Even within my own community I have been guided by that sense of identity. But we're talking about something probably even more complex than that because it involves many identities and many struggles.

I would like to share with you a quote from Trinh T. Minh-Ha, whom many of you may know as an artist, critic, and filmmaker. She says: "You who understand the dehumanization of forced removal-relocation-reeducation-redefinition, the humiliation of having to falsify your reality, your voice—you know. And often you cannot say it. You try to keep on to unsay it, but please—we must say it. You try and keep on trying to unsay it, for if you don't, they will not fail to fill in the blanks on your behalf, and you will be said."[1] I believe Trinh is speaking of the very issue we are concerned with today, which is, How do we reflect previous history? It may seem that the art historical situation is set apart from such other contexts, but no art is beyond its social, political, and historical context. How do these issues of power, cultural democracy, and self-definition pertain to exhibitions, audiences, and resources?

Our institutions are ensconced in concepts of history based, as I stated earlier, in a colonial age. Anthropology, psychology, and archaeology originated in those times. The first typologies, which measured the distance between people's eyes to determine their intellectual capacities, included terms like *phlegmatic*, *choleric*, and *melancholic*. Those were the beginnings of psychology. Such colonial-age tools have set the stage for the historical understanding with which the paradigms of art history have been placed.

I was overjoyed to hear Irene Winter refer to James Clifford, because Clifford's work is very significant in helping us to understand why we find ourselves in confusion and disorder over the arts and culture of people of color. I can't refer to them as a minority, because numerically they're not. I could more accurately call them a distinct majority, or multiracial communities. We are talking primarily about issues of race. To some degree, race is also a euphemism of the colonial age, one that was designed to divide resources from linguistic groups. Nonetheless, we deal with these notions of race, and it is Clifford and others like him who compel us to question these original paradigms.

When Clifford talks about the way in which collecting has grown out of colonial-age acquisitions, he emphasizes how this chaotic collecting resulted in an order based on a kind of Western subjectivity. From this early date the cultural expressions of the non-Western world were reordered and misapprehended.

What Clifford points out is that we have devised a dual system in which Western art, construed within the parameters of the museum as masterpieces created by individual artists, is posed against ethnography, that is, the hall of man, the artifact, the culture in which it was created, the anonymous artisan.

Our dilemma is that after years of such a dichotomy, there have emerged in works by artists of color representations that blur and erase such categories as folk art and fine art. In many respects, this blurring allows us to see the contradiction between the dual standards of a Western subjectivity and those standards assigned to otherness. Only now are museums attempting to deal with the misunderstandings and misrepresentations of the post-colonial age.

Resources, Audiences, and Exhibitions

During the course of the day we have talked about the notion that art should be transcendent, apart from the body politic and certainly apart from economic relations (power and race relations). But, we also know that we're in a marketplace dilemma with regard to those very same pieces of art and that the artifact has joined the masterpiece in that marketplace. So, to some degree, the confusion over categories is an economic circumstance as well.

If the European masters are priced out, if Christie's and Sotheby's find that the Latin American market is financially more accessible with those masters of Latin America, such as Rivera, Kahlo, Matta, and Lam, having these familiar cousins in America (Arnaldo Roche, Carlos Almaraz, and Luis Cruz Azaceta to name but a few), then we must begin to deal with their work as well. Hence, the confusion, ambiguity, and disorder over resources, audience, and exhibitions.

To talk about the work, one must talk about the experience; so I'm going to talk first about resources. It is precisely because we often focus first on exhibitions, rather than resources, that we have had confounding experiences. We try to determine the art without understanding the cultural expressiveness of particular groups.

I don't have to say much about the exhibition *Hispanic Art in the United States: Thirty Contemporary Painters and Sculptors*, as I'm sure many of you are familiar with the controversy surrounding it. That was an instance where to some degree the curatorial perspectives started with traditional approaches to exhibitions, rather than an understanding of the resources of the Latino community. When I talk about resources, I am referring to those aspects that are within the worldview of the diverse cultures we are beginning to serve and respond to—their patrimony, values, and sense of an interethnic or interracial intimacy. As a psychologist I have to think first of the resource of cultural memory, because it is memory that allows us to assert our sense of continuity against all odds. Cultural memory allows spiritual and familial practices to be maintained, often through oral traditions. Many of the working-class people of color have not always had access to a formal education;

yet learning is passed from generation to generation in other ways. It is from that cultural memory that much of the work of contemporary artists of color springs.

Resources: Historical Responsibility

The historical responsibility that is an element in those resources is a responsibility for both the past and the present, one that must be shared by cultural leaders. Historical responsibility involves the kind of history that critic Walter Benjamin speaks of: "Only that historian will have the gift of fanning the spark of hope in the past who is firmly convinced that even the dead will not be safe from the enemy if he wins."[2] This quote has to do with the concept of origin and the redemption of the past.

What we see in the African American, Latino, and certainly Asian American and Native American communities is a moving back toward the memory of origin. The African scholarship of people like Dr. Ben Yusef and Dr. Asa Hilliard, who question the relationship of Kehmt, or black Egypt, to the Greco-Roman world, of books such as Martin Bernal's *Black Athena*, and even such works as Cornel West's *Prophetic Fragments*—all are beginning to question the Eurocentric myth of origin.

It was with an awareness of historical responsibility that books like George James's *Stolen Legacy* (1954) and Chancellor Williams's The *Destruction of the Black Civilization* (1974) were written, years before they were accessible except in the most clandestine ways. The decentering of the humanities relies, to some degree, not just on cultural memory passed through communities, but on the historical responsibility of scholars, critics, artists, and institutional leaders who see themselves in this transitional generation as ready and able to move into another system of knowledge and thought.

Resources: Community Practices

Community practices are also part of the resources of the community. Such practices have greatly influenced the development of aesthetic forms. For instance, the preponderance of the ceremonial and the spiritual in particular communities is an aspect of the collective history of religion, spirituality, and spectacle. Other practices reflect the dynamic and interactive processes of exchange and learning, the relationship between tradition and innovation, and the layering of experience that creates new measures of meaning.

At the core of many of the aesthetic representations that are a part of the contemporary school is ancestral legacy. In *The Decade Show: Frameworks of Identity in the 1980s*, concepts of historical responsibility and ancestral legacy are reflected in many of the artworks. Ancestral legacy allows us to consider more than one view of the upcoming quincentennial. For many of us, the ancestral legacy surrounding the quincentennial is not a five-hundred-year phenomenon, not a tabula rasa, or a fertile ground where culture was dropped. The ancestral legacy of which we speak—a splendor of thirty centuries even in Mesoamerica, which is only one part of this continent—is a very, very long one. It certainly outmarks a half a century.

If we are to understand ancestral legacy, we have to look at the forms in which we find it in our own institutions. The quincentenary celebration, which emphasizes historical and cultural Euro-Spanish developments, has to be questioned not only by those within the native communities, but also by the larger institutions that will determine the exhibitions, the outreach, and the activities related to that very market. For our native brothers and sisters, the quincentennial is a marking of genocide, hardly something that should be called a celebration. Nonetheless, it is one aspect of ancestral legacy.

Audiences: Aesthetic Sensibility

An extension of ancestral legacy is reflected in family values and a worldview, even in the cultural styles of the audience. These issues are rarely addressed in major institutions. I've participated in several outreach panels in California and in a number of other places; so I've seen the proposals submitted by major institutions that are trying to outreach, or reach out.

One reason that outreach has not been more successful is the lack of recognition of community resources. Even the composition of the audiences themselves is an issue. I don't have to cite the demographic information. Most of you know that the major cities in America are increasingly made up of people of color. In California, for instance, by the year 2010 people of color will make up 50 percent of the state. These people are distinct, they are unique, and they have historical differences; but they also share certain aspects of a cultural worldview, and these have to be addressed in the audiences that we develop. So, composition reflects diversity in aesthetic perception and valuing. The programming of our institutions has to consider this diversity of aesthetic perceptions and valuing in deeper educational approaches.

A number of you are familiar with the Getty model, the discipline-based approach to education. Those of us in educational institutions, particularly public education in the primary grades, have really begun to question these models and examine how we can expand their limited vocabulary. Simply putting Marianne Anderson on the cover of your booklet and listing a number of artists of color as examples of those categories is not enough. Unless you actually deal with aesthetic perception and values as being as diverse as the experiences from which they spring, you will find yourself going in circles.

The Latino or Chicano sensibility is a perfect example of diversity, with its combination of the colonial baroque age and the dominance of the indigenous. The mixture of the Mexican healing worldview, *rasquachismo* (the aesthetics of the downtrodden), and popular barrio styles is characteristic of this bicultural sensibility. Ceremonial practices that have been anchored and maintained in home altars and healing rituals constitute an aesthetic domain in which we perceive and value those things around us. Beauty and power are concepts that are embedded in cultural experiences. They cannot be reduced to a single set of formal elements across all groups.

Aesthetic value and perception have a great deal to do with socioeconomic class. I lived in a rural valley and did not enter a museum until I was twenty years old. My parents didn't have access to those experiences. I was an artist, and they supported me in the forms that were endemic to my community. My uncles were carvers and welders and made things with their hands. I was privileged from the first day I showed my aptitude because I was marked with a spirit that was valued by everyone in my community and my neighborhood. From the age of six or seven I was referred to as "the artist" and given a kind of passport to experience.

Within the reality of what my family could provide for me, my artistry was singularly important to them and valued, yet access to the institutions of Western artistry was not available. Consequently, my only experiences of masterwork in the Western tradition were within the Catholic church. The tremendous influence of bricolage, display, and abundance is clearly marked in the work of many Latino artists and comes, to some degree, from the Catholic experience and liturgical spectacle.

When we talk about an aesthetic perception or value, we are not talking about superficial categories. We are talking about experience layered through time and aesthetic categories that are deep in their meaning and rooted in regional, topographical, and material realities. For example, what about the Japanese American sensibility, which springs from the insular island culture of Japan. What do such origins imply about the way one looks at things? What do they imply about the preference for a dominance of units, significance of nature, and spirituality in design? The Kimono Mind is a term that refers to the many Japanese American Women who still walk as though their bodies were wrapped in that garment. An aesthetic mentality is certainly part of one's culture. The many histories of a cultural aesthetic are the inheritances that we bring to a national patrimony. The capacity to respond to a diverse national patrimony is both an opportunity and a responsibility for our major institutions.

Audiences: Communication Style and Learning Style

When we talk about audiences, we have to talk about communication styles and language. Surely we know multilingualism is an issue in signage, tours, docents, volunteers, catalogues, and brochures. To deal with this, we have to cultivate the resources of multilingual communities.

Communication style is another area that must be considered in audience development. The communication styles of Latin Americans, African Americans, and Asian Americans, just to name three, are very distinct. Cornel West calls the African American style "kinetic orality," or the movement of the body with language in a very specific way. Innovation in language reflects an African ancestry within African American speech.

The linguistic traditions of African American speech have survived the tremendous influences of mass media and education. African based, the language is one with its own rules for plurals, possessives, tenses, word endings, and colloquialisms. That does not mean that "standard" English should not be learned, but we have to recognize that our children come to us language-rich. If we are not capable of interacting with them, understanding them, and communicating with them, it is our problem, not theirs.

We should bring to the issue of audience, then, a greater understanding of communication style and cultural style. One aspect of cultural style that we have begun to look at is the way in which people interact even in something as simple as closure, the act of ending something. I often give the following example. Shortly after I married my husband, who by the way is African American, we were going to my mother's house for dinner. I said to him, "Now look, when we leave, pull the car out slowly and keep the windows down." He said, "Is something going to happen?" And I answered, "No, they just like to say goodbye for a while!" My husband soon learned that closure in a community that values relationships is not always desirable. All the nuances and manifestations of the highly prized communication is around extending the relationship, not around the end product. In such a value system, closure may often be in conflict with the American preference for closure. Attitudes towards closure must be taken into account when greeting and closing with an audience.

We have much to learn about the ways in which communication and cultural style affect cognition, apprehension, and learning, all of which are intertwined. Culture is a window on the world, and our processes of receiving, distributing, and processing information must pass through that window. The degree to which we Westerners don't understand this relates directly to the degree to which we have not been successful in our mainstream institutions, even those that deal specifically with education.

Differences in time and space, physicality, language, and communication affect the way people enter our institutions, the way they are received in our institutions, and the way in which they learn in our institutions. How we receive diverse communities and how we learn from them are elements we have largely ignored because we have come to think of audience as a problem, not as a resource.

Exhibitions

My experience with exhibitions is both as an artist and a curator. I organized a show called *Ceremony of Memory*, which has been touring the United States. I did that show to put the ceremonial work of Chicano/Latino and Caribbean people in the same place at the same time so we could consider aspects of memory, spirituality, temporality, and spatiality. I wanted to look at what these elements mean and how they are similar or distinct as used by contemporary artists.

It's important to remember that we are the first generation to have had ethnic-studies departments on university campuses. We are therefore both artists and activists. We developed in many ways rather rapidly, not unlike the kind of fast-forward photography in which you see a little plant grow very quickly. Beginning with the seed, the bean goes up, the little leaves come out, and then there's a flower. In many ways, that's what happened to us. Many of us were raised in rural communities or newly urban communities; we had home practices of alternative spirituality and traditions of healing; we had folk tales and *corridos*, or ballads; we had ways of knowing the world that were from another generation, another time, and another culture.

We moved rapidly through the canon and through the academy, and that produced in us a very dense layering: For example, I was raised with Walt Disney and *norteno* music, with the concept of the Mayan ruins and black rhythm and blues. This is typical of the interpenetrations and fusions that characterize the not-so-easy-to-categorize work of artists of my generation, particularly those of color. It is the inability to distinguish folk from fine art, the canon from the other, that has confounded the development of particular exhibition practices among mainstream institutions.

In many ways, we are still struggling with the notion of quality or standards. As I've said before, quality is a euphemism for the familiar. It is a family of artists and ideas to which many have grown quite accustomed; but we are a new extended family. We are new artists, with new ideas that you have not had as much experience with.

The question is not simply one of criteria or standards: these can be amended or expanded. We have only to look at the history of scientific research in this country to understand that anything can be adjusted to encompass those things that we choose to prize. As curators in this transitional time our work is partly to make ourselves familiar with the new American canon.

In many ways, what we've come to understand about exhibitions is that it isn't enough for us to get into the museums; many of us have been in. Access is not the only issue. Interpretation is the new forefront. Sometimes very simple things like the translations of the signage can affect the understanding of the art. One example has to do with the exhibition *Hispanic Art in the United States: Thirty Contemporary Painters and Sculptors*. Included was Cesar Martinez's painting of a very large man with a tattoo of the Virgin de Guadalupe and tattoos of a good woman and a bad woman on his shoulders. The painting is called *El hombre que gusta mujeres* (The Man Who Likes Women). The title was translated as *The Womanizer*, but that is not what it means! This is a man who *loves* women, a man to whom women are so central that he marks his body with them. The profound meaning of this work is reduced, limited, mystified, and misappropriated when a simple thing like a translation cannot be done with understanding, knowledge, and respect.

We've also been into museums where the sheer placement of our work—near lobbies or bathrooms, in rotundas or small rooms—has indicated the inferior value the institution attaches to the work. So access is not the only issue.

Exhibitions have to be formulated with expertise, and that has to be shared. Power—the ability to self-define in a way upon which we can act—must entail shared decision-making, leadership, empowerment, scholarship, and curatorial expertise between the diverse communities and mainstream institutions.

The expanded sense of an American aesthetic is an important part of what we are all struggling with. In many ways the dialogue is best understood when we look at the artists of this generation and the kinds of work they do: emblematic mythology in the hands of people like Lilianna Porter, Roberto Gil de Montes, Carlos Almaraz, Cecilia Vecuna; the indictment of social issues by artists such as Rupert Garcia, Ester Hernandez, Juan Sanchez, David Avalos, Ismael Frigerio, Daniel Martinez, Catalina Parra, and Judite Dos Santos. If we think of the ceremonial, the ways in which sacred space, memory, spirit, and time are located in a contemporary form, we think of Juan Boza, Pepon Osorio, Angel Suarez, George Crespo, and Peter Rodriguez. When we think about the issues pertinent to the environment— nature and spirit, the rain forest—we think about people like Regina Vater, Jonas Dos Santos, and Rimer Cardillo.

If we look at diversity while acknowledging the difficulties of racism and the limits of our own institutional knowledge, we can move toward those audiences with a recognition of their ways of knowing and being. If we use that cultural information to create programming, exhibitions, and educational outreach, we can share leadership and curatorial expertise and develop alliances and partnerships that are based on interethnic intimacy—not appropriation, nor co-optation, nor a good funding proposal, or even a way to get guilt off your back. If we do, then this transitional age is not so hopeless after all.

We must remember that the dialogue about the center/margin politics of culture finally and definitively demands action because to repeatedly speak to audiences (and this is a very personal statement from me) about things that matter so much, that are tied so much to the politics and economics of this country, as well as to your own institution, with no response, makes me feel as though the discourse is mere entertainment.

The definitive question becomes What changes should be instituted in acquisitions, programs, educational models, curatorial expertise, staffing, publications, and criticism within the mainstream institutions in order to respond more effectively to diverse cultures? Change has already begun in many of our institutions, but there is much much more to do. I like to refer to Rex Nettleford, who reminds us that there is such a thing as a "kingdom of the mind,"[3] a passionate creativity, and an emancipatory art that will set us free to understand the world relations of which we are a part.

Notes

1. Trinh T. Minh-Ha. *Woman, Native, Other: Writing Postcoloniality and Feminism.* Indianapolis: Indiana University Press, 1989, 80.

2. Walter Benjamin, "Theses on the philosophy of history," in *Illuminations*, edited with an introduction by Hannah Arendt. New York: Schocken Books, 1989, 255.

3. Rex Nettleford, unpublished remarks at "Cultural Diversity Through Cultural Grounding," conference sponsored by Caribbean Cultural Center, New York City, 1989.

Mining the Museum

An Installation Confronting History

9

LISA G. CORRIN

W HAT IS A MUSEUM ANYWAY? Or a curator for that matter? And what is
an "audience"? Do museums have the corner on historical "Truths"?
Mining the Museum, an installation by Fred Wilson, provided an opportunity to reflect on these questions. Presented from April 2, 1992, to February
28, 1993, Wilson's installation was made possible through a unique collaboration
between The Contemporary and the Maryland Historical Society (MHS), two
Baltimore-based museums.

Founded in 1989, The Contemporary's mission is to explore the connections
between the art of our time and the world we live in. The museum encourages
interaction between artists and audiences and directly involves communities in the
development, implementation, and evaluation of its programs. The Contemporary
works out of a permanent administrative facility but presents exhibitions in temporary locations; its concept of a "collection" consists of placing art in community
settings on long-term loan.

The MHS is a 150-year-old institution with an important collection housed
in a permanent museum. Its fifty-plus staff members oversee many thousands of
objects ranging from decorative arts, paintings, and sculpture to extensive archives
and a library of Maryland history. It is in many ways typical of large, established
state historical museums across the country.

In May 1991, The Contemporary opened its first international exhibition in the
former Greyhound Service Terminal, located near the MHS. George Ciscle, The
Contemporary's director, and I paid a social call on the society's director, Charles
Lyle, to introduce ourselves. We talked at length about the differences between
the ways our respective institutions operate. Lyle expressed his desire to have his

Lisa G. Corrin, former director of the Williams College Museum of Art in Williamstown, Massachusetts, is
a Clark Fellow at the Sterling and Francine Clark Art Institute and a visiting scholar in museum studies at New
York University. "Mining the Museum: An Installation Confronting History" appeared in *Curator: The Museum
Journal* (Vol. 36, No. 4 [October 1993], pp. 302–331). It is reprinted here by permission of John Wiley & Sons.
All rights reserved

institution deal with current concerns and public interests and to develop an audience more representative of the community's cultural diversity.

Coincidentally, The Contemporary had been considering a project with Fred Wilson and had invited him to Baltimore to visit many of the city's museums to choose a permanent collection he would like to work with. Wilson's first choice was the MHS.

The Contemporary returned to the MHS with a suggestion: a three-way collaboration with Fred Wilson in which he would create an installation artwork during a one-year residency period. Our staffs would use the experience as an opportunity for a self-study to help us identify new approaches to interpreting collections, shaping future acquisition policies and programs, and expanding our audiences. Wilson would have access to the MHS collection as a "gold mine" of ideas and reinstall it from his own point of view. Then Mining the Museum began to take shape. We agreed that whatever objects Wilson chose would be made available to him for use in the installation.

The exhibition was designed to address problems we felt were of concern to many museums, regardless of their discipline. The aim would be to confront the difficulty of putting theories of diversity and historical revisionism into practice and to offer a model for change responsive to our particular community. The directors of the two organizations felt strongly that presenting the exhibition concurrently with the 1992 American Association of Museums annual conference in Baltimore might catalyze provocative dialogue within the profession.

About Wilson's Work

Fred Wilson is an installation artist of African-American and Carib descent. His entry into the museum world began with freelance assignments in the education departments of a number of museums, including the American Museum of Natural History, The Metropolitan Museum of Art, the Whitney Museum of American Art, and the American Crafts Museum. More recently, he has been involved with arts organizations as a museum educator, a gallery director, and a practicing artist.

Until Mining the Museum, Wilson's installations had used reproductions and fabricated artifacts in "mock museums" that had drawn attention to the ways in which curatorial practices affect our interpretation and understanding of museum collections. Wilson's "museums" underscored the fact that history is an act of interpretation and that contemporary events are part of its flux. His work has provided a savvy and thought-provoking critique of the museum environment.

His insights first surfaced in Rooms with a View: The Struggle Between Culture, Content and Context in Art, a project he curated for the Bronx Council of the Arts in 1987. Three distinct spaces simulated different display environments: ethnographic and Victorian museums and a contemporary gallery. In each room, Wilson placed different works of art by thirty artists, surrounded by the accouterments appropriate to the space. The ethnography museum grouped objects according to type, with vague labels identifying the artistic medium but not the maker.

The Victorian museum gave the objects a rarefied disposition, suggesting precious antique objets d'art through selective lighting and ornate pedestals. The "white cube" gallery gave the works the necessary cutting-edge mystique to certify them as works of contemporary art.

The new contexts so thoroughly transformed the audience perceptions of the artworks that Wilson decided to take on "the museum." Describing his reasons, Wilson said, "It is there that those of us who work toward alternative visions . . . get hot under the collar and decide to do something about it."

Visitors to The Colonial Collection (1991) at the Gracie Mansion Gallery (no longer in existence) viewed African masks blindfolded with the flags of their French and British colonizers and others labeled "Stolen from the Zonga tribe," highlighting how museum euphemisms whitewash the acquisition of such objects. These "spoils" were displayed in dramatically-colored spaces with theatrical lighting, sometimes animated with the addition of video special effects. This, according to Wilson, illustrated how a museum display "anesthetizes their historic importance . . . [it] certainly covers up the colonial history."

The proposed collaboration offered Wilson an opportunity to work with real museum objects and occupy the curatorial "hot seat," putting his theories into practice in the environment curators operate in every day and with similar limitations.

Developing the Exhibition

Principals on the project from the two collaborating institutions were the directors, the chief curator and the director of education at the MHS, and the curator/educator and an intern at The Contemporary. The Contemporary raised the necessary funds ($25,000) and managed the budget. Public programming, public relations, and development of educational materials were implemented cooperatively. The Contemporary provided orientation to the topic of installation art and the process of creating it for MHS staff and docents.

Wilson made all artistic decisions and set the project's philosophical, aesthetic, and historical trajectory. He participated in all aspects of the project's development and implementation, including education. He visited the society frequently over a one-year period, and for two months prior to the opening, he remained on site. He came to know the collections and other resources as well as the society's curatorial, registrarial, educational, and governance practices.

Mining the Museum was not the first museum collaboration or the first time an artist "curated" a collection or created a museum-critical work for a specific institution. But a self-study process implicit in the installation made the project not only different as an exhibition but an intervention. Throughout the project, an ongoing evaluation of the collaborative process and the impact of the installation was carried on. It examined commonly-held definitions of "museum," "history," "exhibition," "curator," "artist," "audience," "community," and "collaboration." The curators created a "think sheet," a series of topics developed to measure changes in the way individuals saw themselves, the artist, and their institutions during the development of the installation. Wilson was assisted in his research by independent volunteers who had expertise in African-American local and state history, astronomy, and museum history. The curators gave Wilson entry into the less-well-known parts of the museum and shared historical information about the objects.

A Walk Through the Exhibition

The exhibition investigated both the African-American and Native-American experiences in Maryland, using art and artifacts from the MHS collection that either had never been seen before or had never been viewed in this context.

Personal history forms the basis of Wilson's engagement with the past. Objects, he believes, become "generic and lifeless" outside the context of personal experience. "I look at the relationship between what is on view and what is not on view." Wilson's fear of imposing a personal morality on others led him to use the questioning process as the organizing principle of his work.

To encourage visitors to begin questioning immediately, the curators created a handout that was posted in the elevator. It read:

What is it?
Where is it? Why?
What is it saying?
How is it used?
For whom was it created?
For whom does it exist?
Who is represented?
How are they represented?
Who is doing the telling? The hearing?
What do you see?
What do you hear?
What can you touch?
What do you feel?
What do you think?
Where are you?

Mining the Museum employed display techniques that are second nature to most curators: artifacts, labels, selective lighting, slide projections, and sound effects. But they were used to explore our "reading" of historical truth through sometimes startling juxtapositions of objects representing vastly different historical "facts," revealing stereotypes and contrasting power and powerlessness. (Highlights from the installation follow.)

The installation opened with the silver and gold "Truth Trophy Awarded Until 1922 for Truth in Advertising," surrounded by three white pedestals bearing white marble busts of historic personages and three empty black pedestals. It encapsulated the issues at the heart of the exhibition. Whose truth is on exhibit? Whose history is being told? Wilson thus established that Mining the Museum would explore not what objects mean but how meaning is made when they are "framed" by the museum environment and museum practices.

Those left out of the museum's historical narrative were literally given voice in a room where 19th-century paintings were on display. When a viewer stepped toward the dimly lit works of art, spotlights and hidden sound effects were triggered to highlight the African-American children represented. A boy asked, "Am I your brother?" "Am I your friend?" And, alluding to his metal collar, "Am I your pet?" The names of slaves depicted in a rare painting of workers in the fields were added to the label after the plantation owner's inventory book listing them along with other household items and animals was found in the archives.

Examples of how the museum classification system inadvertently represses the layered and complex history behind objects was illustrated in "Modes of Transport," "Metalwork," and "Cabinet-making, 1820–1960." The first of these examined who traveled in colonial Maryland—why and how. A model of a slave ship was shown alongside a once-elegant sedan chair; a painting depicting a similar chair highlighted who carried whom. A Ku Klux Klan hood replaced the customary linens in an antique pram; nearby was a photograph of black "nannies" pushing similar carriages. The suggestion that children absorb their parents' racial stereotypes early on was clear. Disproportionate sizes of objects displayed together conveyed a sense of power or the lack of it. On display in a space focusing on runaway slaves were decoy ducks and a toy figure of a running black soldier "targeted" by a large punt gun used in hunting the birds in Chesapeake Bay. In "the rebellion room," Wilson inverted this relationship. Miniature white figures in a doll house were dwarfed by a black doll dominating them. A diary on display revealed panic on the part of white landowners of a "Negro uprising," reflecting the source of this nightmarish vision.

Some objects were brought into the light here for the first time. A rocking chair, a basket, and a jug made by enslaved African Americans were displayed along with objects made by Africans in the colony for freed slaves in Liberia. Only the jug, made by "Melinda," had been exhibited; few had seen the Liberian objects. Found in storage, a wooden tourist box with its ticket of passage to Africa led to the identification of the "new" objects. The box had been given to the MHS in the mid-19th century by a member of the Colonization Society. At the end of the corridor hung a painting, *Maryland in Liberia*, by John H. B. Latrobe, founder of the MHS and an active member of the Colonization Society.

The final section focused on the aspirations, dreams, and achievements of African Americans. The focal point was a journal kept by the astronomer and mathematician Benjamin Banneker (1731–1806). Software that could generate images of the night sky as Banneker saw it was loaded into an IBM computer. (The computer was labeled.) Drawings from the journal were projected on the wall. Banneker was hired by Thomas Jefferson to help survey the area that became Washington, DC, and the two men corresponded. The journal contains an article that Banneker sent to Jefferson urging him to abolish slavery and saying: "Sir I freely and Chearfully acknowledge that I am of the African race." The book tells the story of a free black who was no less immune to the oppression of the slavery system than his enslaved brothers and sisters.

The installation ended with a globe used in Banneker's time; by formally and metaphorically echoing the opening Truth Trophy, the installation came full circle.

Educational Programs and Outreach

The museum educators reconsidered their usual approaches to interpretation and public programming. Their aim would be to stimulate debate and encourage active audience engagement with the material.

An educational handout was produced after the exhibition opened. "Do you have questions about Mining the Museum?" was based on questions most frequently asked of and reported by guards, docents, receptionists, and gallery-store staff. Visitors received it at the end of the installation, so that the active questioning process of their experience would not be lost. It provided background information on such topics as the lives of historical personages, information about some of the objects, and an explanation of installation art.

Programs for the public took place at the MHS. Open studio visits were held weekly just prior to the opening so that the public could gain first-hand experience of Wilson's working process and have a chance to speak with him. Workshops for the docents on contemporary art focused on the installation medium and how artists today often address social and political issues in their work. They also included tours of the MHS with the artist. Discussions about the exhibition as a work of contemporary art were conducted by nine area artist/docents each Saturday. Other public lectures included: "Contemporary Artists and Cultural Identity," "African-American Women in Maryland 1750–1860," and "Free at Last," a dramatic reading of primary documents related to slavery and abolition in Maryland.

"Exhibiting Cultures," a continuing studies course at the Johns Hopkins University, was based on the book *Exhibiting Cultures: The Poetics and Politics of Museum Display* (Karp and Lavine, 1991). Lectures took a critical look at the challenges curators of all disciplines face when exhibiting artifacts from cultures other than (and including) their own. The final class brought together scholars in the fields of art history, anthropology, and African-American history, including Ivan Karp, to present papers on the issues raised by the installation. The artist/docents were given scholarships to attend the course.

Audience Response

A community exhibit, on view for the final month of the exhibition, chronicled audience participation in the project, including drawings, essays, creative writing by children and art students as well as responses to a questionnaire asking for reactions. Visitors had been requested to hang them on the bulletin board to create a dialogue among members of the audience.

Almost every evaluation received remarked on the emotional impact of the installation. The subtleties of Wilson's work were not lost on the young.

> When I go to a museum, I hope to say "Wow" but today I was thinking "Wow!" in a different way.
>
> I like that he asks questions and doesn't answer them.

And from adults:

> You always have to question information presented because even if presented as "truth" it is always from a specific cultural point of view. (attorney)
>
> It interested me in seeing Maryland History in terms of an African American although I am white. I've never been interested in seeing this museum before this show.
>
> I want a sense of understanding history as good or bad in order to repeat it or to discard it so as not to repeat it. (retired police officer)
>
> I found my history in this exhibition. My ancestors were never slave owners . . . but as a Caucasian American, I share some responsibility for the continuing state of racial strife today. (immigrant economist)
>
> Can you force all of Baltimore to see this? (Unemployed white male)
>
> Never have I witnessed any form of artwork that has had such an emotional effect on me. (college student)

Not all responses were positive.

> Mining the Museum has the ability to promote racism and hate in young Blacks and was offensive to me. (retired dentist)
>
> I found Mining the Museum "artsy" and pretentious. It was a waste of space that could be used to better purpose. A museum should answer questions not raise questions unrelated to the subject. (engineer)
>
> It snookered me.
>
> I liked the pedestals without statues least because they were visually boring and emptiness is decidedly uninteresting, period. (curator)

Discussion and Conclusion

Mining the Museum examined how the MHS had defined itself and how this self-definition determines whose history has been included or excluded. It also spoke to how those excluded have come to see the museum. It was about the power of objects to speak when museum practices are expanded and the artificial boundaries museums build are removed. It was about how deconstructing the museum apparatus can transform the museum into a space for ongoing cultural debate.

It stimulated so much enthusiasm within the profession that children's museums, natural history museums, science centers, and art museums suddenly wanted

"Fred Wilsons" of their own; they were encouraged to look at their own collections with a renewed sense of purpose and possibility. Two Wilson installations based on permanent collections have taken place since the installation at the MHS: The Spiral of Art History at the Indianapolis Museum of Art and Museums: Mixed Metaphors at the Seattle Art Museum. A condensed version of Mining the Museum is currently being developed as a permanent display at the MHS, using objects from the original installation.

Throughout the course of the collaboration, both institutions and the artist have had to deal with problems that arose because of assumptions we had about one another and our expectations for the project. One of the greatest difficulties for the participants was learning to adapt to one another's working style. As one staff member stated, "We occasionally speak a somewhat different language." Gradually, staff and docents began to realize that the way their jobs had been previously defined did not always apply to the role they had to assume for the installation. Wrote one staff member, "The insistence on secrecy and preserving the mystery of the work of art until the last possible moment made it difficult to plan and, indeed, to schedule normal pre-exhibition activities, such as the movement of artworks from storage to the installation space. It took a great leap of faith."

All project evaluations are being utilized to generate short- and long-term goals concerning policies, practices, and future programming at both The Contemporary and the MHS. We continue to reflect on our respective missions and on the role a museum can play in a rapidly changing world. The project offered our staffs a practical way to explore different methodologies and professional points of view and to exchange ideas valuable for future collaborations. The docents are considering how their experiences might become useful in giving tours in other parts of the museum. Mining the Museum also generated a critical exchange of ideas between local artists, area cultural institutions, and our community.

Finally, Wilson's installation demonstrated dramatically that current issues are as legitimate a concern for history museums as the distant past. Our audiences told us that they want to be challenged and feel it is appropriate that cultural institutions provide a forum to discuss issues of a controversial nature. Moreover, they cautioned us that if museums are to be truly diverse, they must allow for questioning and be responsive to the questions they hear. Most important, we realized that the project would have been impossible without Fred Wilson's residency. For, as one educator stated, "only with the perspective and creative resources of an outsider could . . . [any museum] undertake as self-critical and creative a project as Mining the Museum."

Acknowledgments

Thanks for the support of the project go to the Andy Warhol Foundation for the Visual Arts, the Maryland Humanities Council, the Maryland State Arts Council, and the Puffin Foundation and the Mid-Atlantic Arts Foundation (M-AAF). Parts of this report are adapted from Arts Ink, the M-AAF journal (Fall 1992). Thanks also go to the volunteers and docents who were largely responsible for the successful interpretation of the installation, and to the directors, George Ciscle and Charles Lyle, to Jennifer Goldsborough, chief curator at the MHS, and Judy Van Dyke, director of education at the MHS. For further information about the project, see Corrin, Lisa G. (Ed.) (in press). Mining the Museum. Baltimore, MD: New Press. The book includes contributions by Lisa G. Corrin, Ira Berlin, Fred Wilson, and Leslie King-Hammond.

Reference

Karp, Ivan, and Lavine, Stephen D., eds. *Exhibiting Cultures: The Poetics and Politics of Museum Display*. Washington, DC: Smithsonian Institution Press, 1991.

The Constructivist Museum

10

GEORGE E. HEIN

Introduction

CURRENT EDUCATION LITERATURE is dominated by discussions of constructivism.[1] This new name for a set of old ideas has major implications for how museums address learning. Constructivism is particularly appropriate as a basis for museum education if we consider the wide age range of museum visitors. How can we accommodate this diverse audience and facilitate their learning from our objects on their voluntary, short visits?

The Elements of Any Theory of Education

In order to understand constructivism, it is useful to consider the nature of any theory of education. As two articles in last year's *Journal of Education in Museums* point out,[2] an educational theory consists of two major components: a theory of knowledge and a theory of learning. In order to consider how a museum is organised to facilitate learning, we need to address both *what* is to be learned and *how* it is to be learned.

Our beliefs about the nature of knowledge, our *epistemology*, profoundly influence our approach to education. It makes a difference whether we believe that knowledge exists independently of the learner, as an absolute, or whether we subscribe to the view that knowledge consists only of ideas constructed in the mind. Plato believed in the existence of ideal forms, independent of the learner. Thus, for him, learning consisted of arriving at knowledge through an intellectual process. Conversely, Berkeley believed that knowledge existed only in the mind of the knower. Thus, he answered in the negative the hypothetical question about the sound of a tree falling in the forest when no one is there to hear it. We can

George E. Hein is professor emeritus in the Graduate School of Arts and Social Sciences and senior research associate at the Program Evaluation and Research Group at Lesley University in Cambridge, Massachusetts. "The Constructivist Museum" is reproduced with permission from the *Journal of Education in Museums* (Vol. 16, 21–23). Copyright GEM 1995. All rights reserved.

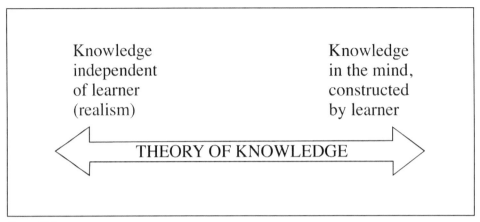

Figure 10.1.

represent this epistemological dichotomy as a continuum, with the extreme positions at each end, as illustrated in Figure 10.1.

The second component of an educational theory encompasses our beliefs about how people learn, our *psychology of learning*. As was the case for the epistemological domain, two extreme positions are possible. One assumes that learning consists of the incremental assimilation of information, facts and experiences, until knowledge results. This view leads to a behaviourist position; to the conclusion that learning consists of the addition of a myriad number of simple associations (responses to stimuli) and that the resultant "knowing" is simply the aggregate of these small steps. Usually associated with this view is the belief that the original condition of the mind is a tabula rasa, and that all that is known has been acquired through experience. Locke is the best known proponent of this view. A diametrically opposed view of learning postulates that the mind constructs schemas and that learning consists of selecting and organising from the wealth of sensations that surround us. This synthetic view of learning is exemplified by Piaget's work. Proponents of this view also usually take the position that certain structures, such as learning language, are part of the anatomy with which we are born.[3]

This second dimension of educational theory can also be represented by a continuum along the dimension of the process of learning as shown in Figure 10.2.

These two dimensions of any educational theory can be combined to produce a diagram that describes four possible combinations of learning theory and epistemology. Figure 10.3 illustrates this combination. Each of the quadrants represents a different approach to education. One familiar position is represented by the top-left quadrant, which I have labelled traditional lecture and text. Within this traditional view of education, the teacher has two responsibilities. First, s/he must understand the structure of the subject, the knowledge that is to be taught. This structure, the logical organisation of the material, is dictated by the content that is to be learned. Much of the intellectual work of the Western world since the Renaissance was devoted to elaborating systematic domains of knowledge with the assumption that

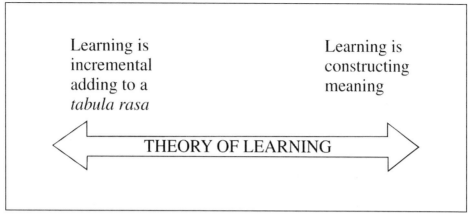

Figure 10.2.

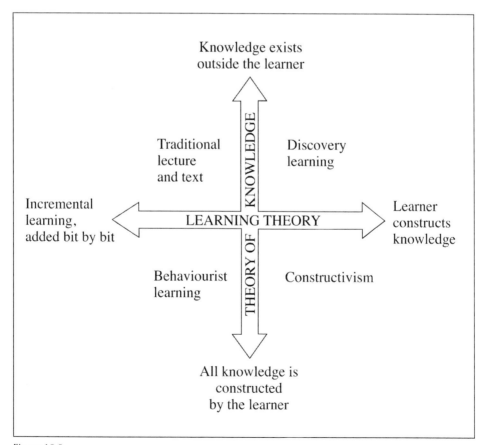

Figure 10.3.

the resulting schemas referred to something that existed independently of the minds that organised it. This intellectual work attempted to develop laws governing the movement of the solar system, classifications of plants and animals, or rules for the organisation of societies that would be true under all conditions, independent of the humans that developed them.

The second responsibility of the traditional teacher is to present the domain of knowledge to be taught appropriately so that the student can learn. Thus, there is a logical order of teaching dictated by the subject to be taught that would make it easiest to learn. The concept of a linear textbook, a great 19th century invention, is predicated on this view of learning. The author presents material in a logical sequence, starting with the simplest elements of the subject and moving on to more complex, until the entire field is covered.[4] This approach to education can lead to "the plain, monotonous vault of a school room," containing "the little vessels then and there arranged in order, ready to have imperial gallons of facts poured into them until they were full to the brim."[5]

A second educational position represented on the top-right quadrant of Figure 10.3 is discovery learning. It subscribes to the same positivist belief about knowledge as the previous one, but it takes a dramatically different view about how this knowledge is acquired. Proponents of this position argue that people construct knowledge themselves, they come to realise concepts and ideas as they build them up using personal, mental constructions. Thus, they also can acquire misconceptions. Proponents of discovery learning believe that in order to learn, students need to have experience; they need to do and see rather than to be told. Rather than organise the subject matter based on its logical structure, from the simplest to the more complex, the teacher organises it so that it can be experienced. Pedagogic simplicity takes on a practical aspect rather than an intellectual one. But the purpose of this hands-on approach is still for the student to comprehend ideas and concepts that are independent of the learner. Through experience, misconceptions will be replaced by correct conceptions.

Constructivism, the bottom-right-hand comer, represents still another quadrant of the diagram. Constructivism argues that both knowledge and the way it is obtained are dependent on the mind of the learner. This view, based on idealist epistemology as well as developmental psychology, and in recent years supported by research in cognitive psychology, comes as a shock to those who wish to preserve the idea of knowledge independent of individual learners or communities of learners. It has been called *radical* constructivism.[6] Proponents of constructivism argue that learners construct knowledge as they learn; they don't simply add new facts to what is known, but constantly reorganise and create both understanding and the ability to learn as they interact with the world. Further, the knowledge that is constructed through this process is individual or social, but has no ontological status outside the mind of the knower.

There is, of course, a fourth position illustrated in Figure 10.3, based on the belief that knowledge is gained incrementally but it need not have existence outside the learner. Simple behaviourism fits into this quadrant, since behaviourism was originally a psychological learning theory and made no claims about the status of the knowledge gained from responses to stimuli.

The Constructivist Museum

The educational positions outlined above can be applied to museums. For any consideration of learning in museums, we can ask an epistemological question, What is the theory of knowledge applied to the content of the exhibitions? We also need to ask a question about learning theory: How do we believe that people learn? These two components of our museum educational theory will lead to a set of four positions, similar to the ones described above, each of which represents a different kind of museum.

The systematic museum, represented in the upper left quadrant in Figure 10.4 is one based on the belief that

1. The content of the museum should be exhibited so that it reflects the "true" structure of the subject matter.
2. The content should be presented to the visitor in a manner that makes it easiest to comprehend.

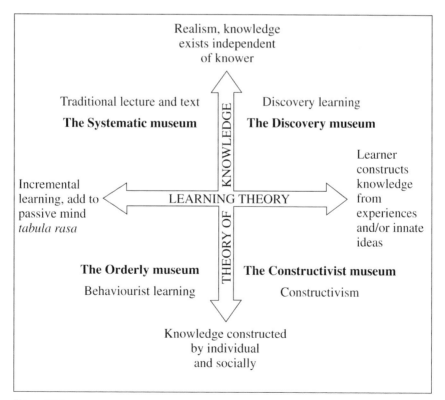

Figure 10.4.

Examples of museums organised around systematic principles are common. The Deutsches Museum in Munich was intended to illustrate the structure of the sciences. Similarly, the Harvard Museum of Comparative Zoology was designed by Louis Agassiz to refute Darwin by illustrating the "true" classification of animals. The National Portrait Gallery, for the most part, hangs its paintings chronologically on the assumption that this order will make most sense to its visitors. Similarly, it is common for exhibits to present material in a single, orderly manner deemed by the exhibit designers to be best suited for visitors to learn the message of the exhibit. In contrast, proponents of the constructivist museum would argue that:

1. The viewer constructs personal knowledge from the exhibit.
2. The process of gaining knowledge is itself a constructive act.[7]

Examples of constructivist museums are harder to find, but exhibits that allow visitors to draw their own conclusions about the meaning of the exhibition are based on this constructivist principle. There is also an increasing number of exhibitions that are designed so that multiple paths are possible through the exhibit and the learner (visitor) is provided with a range of modalities to acquire information.[8]

Within this alternative and diametrically opposed educational view, the logical structure for any subject matter and the way it is presented to the viewer depend not on the characteristics of the subject nor on the properties of the objects on display, but on the educational needs of the visitor. In such a museum, it is not assumed that the subject matter has an intrinsic order independent of the visitor, nor that there is a single way for the visitor best to learn the material. Constructivist museum exhibits have no fixed entry and exit points, allow the visitor to make his or her own connections with the material and encourage diverse ways to learn.[9]

The Characteristics of the Constructivist Museum

What does a constructivist museum look like? The lack of predetermined sequence has already been mentioned, as has the use of multiple learning modalities. Howard Gardner had the constructivist museum in mind when he used the museum as a model for education.[10] Another component of the constructivist museum would be the opportunity for the visitor to make connections with familiar concepts and objects. In order to make meaning of our experience, we need to be able to connect it with what we already know. Constructivist exhibits would encourage comparisons between the unfamiliar and new. Inviting South Asian immigrant women into the V&A to design and make their own embroidered tent hangings[11] can achieve the aim of making the museum more accessible to the community. Inviting hundreds of youngsters from diverse countries to make exhibits about their local rivers and to share them in a grand festival[12] can help them all learn about each other's cultures.

Conclusion

Constructivist educational theory argues that in any discussion of teaching and learning the focus needs to be on the learner, not on the subject to be learned. For museums, this translates into the dictum that we need to focus on the visitor, not the content of the museum.

Museums are remarkable sites for learning. Their power and influence for people is attested to by the amazing learning associated with them. Individuals can recount instances of epiphany-like experiences in all types of museums.[13] Yet, the museum experience, on the whole, is fleeting and elusive.

By considering both the epistemological basis for our organisation of exhibitions and the psychological basis for our theory of learning, we can develop museums that can respond to the dispositions of our visitors and maximise the potential for learning. The constructivist museum acknowledges that knowledge is created in the mind of the learner using personal learning methods. It allows us to accommodate all ages of learning.

Notes

1. J. G. Brooks and M. G. Brooks. *The Case for Constructivist Classrooms*, Alexandria, VA: Association for Supervision and Curriculum Development, 1993; L. P. Steffe and J. Gale, eds, *Constructivism in Education*. Hillsdale, NJ: Lawrence Erlbaum Associates, 1994.

2. R. Jackson and K. Hann. "Learning through the science museum," *Journal of Education in Museums* 15, 1994: 11–13; and T. Russell, "The enquiring visitor: usable learning theory for museum contexts," *Journal of Education in Museums* 15,1994: 19–21.

3. In this brief discussion I am leaving out the social component of learning. Although crucial for understanding education, it is beyond the scope of this classification scheme (see L. S. Vigotsky, *Thought and Language*. Cambridge, MA: The MIT Press, 1962).

4. "Simplest" may refer to either the nature of the subject, or the nature of learning. Some textbook writers (in some subjects) start with the fundamental aspects of what they wish to teach, others start with what is considered easiest to learn. But in either case, the reference point is the perceived logical structure of the material to be learned.

5. C. Dickens, *Hard Times*.

6. E. von Glaserfeld, "An exposition of constructivism: why some like it radical," in R. B. Davis, C. A. Maher, and N. Noddings, *Constructivist Views of the Teaching and Learning of Mathematics*, Washington, DC: National Council of Teachers of Mathematics, 1991.

7. G. E. Hein, "The significance of constructivism for museum education," in *Museums and the Needs of the People*, Jerusalem: Israel ICOM Committee, 1993.

8. B. Davidson et al., "Increased exhibit accessibility through multisensory interaction," *Curator* 34/4, 1991, 273–290.

9. The two additional educational views also have their parallel in museums, leading to the Orderly Museum and the Discovery Museum. Examples exist, but are beyond the scope of this discussion.

10. H. Gardner, *The Unschooled Mind*, New York: Basic Books, 1991.

11. S. Akbar, "The Nehru Gallery national textile project," *Museums for Integration in a Multicultural Society, Proceedings of the Annual CECA Conference*. ICOM-Asia-Pacific Organization, 1993, 88.

12. S. Rozé, L'Europe des fleuves, N. Gesche, ed., *European Museum Communication*, ICOM-CECA Regional meeting. Brussels, ICOM-CECA, Brussels, 1993.

13. J. Falk and L. Dierking, eds., *Public Institutions for Personal Learning; Understanding the Long Term Impact of Museums*, Washington, DC: American Association of Museums, 1995.

Creampuffs and Hardball

Are You Really Worth What You Cost or Just Merely Worthwhile?

STEPHEN E. WEIL

11

T HE QUESTIONS ABOUT THEIR FIELD THAT MUSEUM WORKERS serve up to one another at their periodic gatherings (national, regional, and local) are generally creampuffs. Although shaped and flavored in a variety of ways, these questions can almost invariably be reduced to the single one of whether the museum, in essence, is truly a worthwhile institution. With almost equal invariability, those attending these gatherings conclude that it is. To those who work in them, it appears all but self-evident that, notwithstanding their temporary shortcomings, museums do make an important contribution to society. They preserve and transmit our natural and cultural heritage, they add to the world's store of knowledge, and they provide their publics with expanded opportunities for learning, personal growth, and enjoyment.

As crunch time approaches, however, and as the demands that are made on the public and private resources available to the nonprofit sector continue to grow at a faster rate than those resources themselves, virtually every museum may find itself faced with several much tougher questions—not creampuffs this time but hardball. Without disputing the museum's claim to worthiness, what these questions will address instead is its relative worthiness. Is what the museum contributes to society really commensurate with the annual cost of its operation? Could some other organization (not necessarily a museum) make a similar or even greater contribution at a lesser cost? What would be the consequence—how much lost? how much gained?—if the same expenditure were to be devoted to some other activity entirely? We currently spend billions of dollars each year on the operation of our museums. We have yet to determine, however, in what measure that expenditure represents a wise and informed public policy choice and in what measure it may simply be the hangover of some old and still-to-be-fully-examined habit.

Stephen E. Weil (1928–2005), prolific author, provocateur, and museum philosopher, was a senior scholar emeritus at the Center of Museum Studies, Smithsonian Institution. "Creampuffs and Hardball: Are You Really Worth What You Cost or Just Merely Worthwhile?" is reprinted here with permission from *Museum News*, September/October 1994. Copyright 1994, the American Association of Museums. All rights reserved.

Underpinning these hardball questions is a profound and ongoing shift in the way that nonprofit organizations are being evaluated by those who provide them with resources. This shift, which appears to have started with social service and health care agencies and worked its way through higher education, can now be sensed as spreading across the entire nonprofit sector. It involves a newly heightened concentration on "outcomes" rather than either "inputs" or "outputs" as the principal basis on which to judge a charitable organization's public programs.

Little more than a generation ago, a museum was still measured largely by the resources (i.e., the inputs) that it had available: How good was its collection? How well trained and respected was its staff? How adequate and in what condition were its facilities? How solid was its attendance? How large was its endowment? Good numbers equated with a good museum.

In the years that followed—in the 1970s and well into the 1980s—the principal focus shifted from inputs to outputs. No longer judged so much by the measurable resources that they had available, museums tended to be judged instead by the programmatic use to which they put those resources. "Better utilization of collections" was a key phrase, and peer review became a principal means of evaluation. Who better could judge the skill with which a museum staff deployed the limited resources at its disposal than its colleagues in other museums who daily faced the same challenge? Output analysis goes still a step farther. It examines the impact of those programs rather than simply their quality.

In the United Kingdom, a remarkably direct phrase has emerged to describe the expectation of those responsible for providing public funds. What they expect is "value for money." Typical of its use are recent remarks by the Right Honorable Peter Brooke, who, as the United Kingdom's Secretary of State for National Heritage, oversees the funding of the United Kingdom's major museums. Noting that publicly supported cultural organizations will be expected to carry out their day-to-day operations "within an overall framework of priorities and public policies determined by Government," Brooke emphasized that they must also "assure value for money for the taxpayer in pursuit of those aims."

What this all involves in essence is a new accountability in which organizations will be required to demonstrate not only (a) that they can account for the resources entrusted to them and (b) that they used those resources efficiently but, above all, (c) that they also used those resources effectively—that they used them to produce a positive outcome in the community intended to be served. The museum that seeks to meet the standards of this new accountability must be prepared to show in what positive ways its target community has benefited from its programs. This need not be a narrow constraint. That the museum continues to preserve a community's otherwise endangered heritage might certainly be one such beneficial outcome. Other beneficial outcomes might relate to the transmission of knowledge and/or skills, to the modification of behavior, or simply to the provision of enjoyment or recreation. The only required constant is that the benefits described be in response to what some have called the ultimate "so what?" questions. So what difference did it make that your museum was there? So what would have been the difference had it not been?

Implicit also in this new accountability is the question of limits. How are those allocating funds to determine the boundaries of an applicant's need? Is the outcome that an organization seeks infinite in scope (with the inference that the organization's need for additional resources will consequently be insatiable) or is there a point at which the organization may be considered as accomplishing its goals? Is there such a thing as an adequately funded museum, or is nothing ever enough? Richard F. Larkin, the Technical Director for the Not-for-Profit Industry Services Group at Price Waterhouse, has observed that this is a problem endemic to almost all charitable organizations. Their goals are generally formulated in open-ended terms ("to encourage an understanding and appreciation of contemporary art" or "to improve the health services available to the indigent members of our community") with little to indicate what would constitute actual success or assist an observer seeking to determine whether it was being achieved. This is in sharp contrast to the for-profit organization in which success or failure can be determined by comparing some bottom line "outcome" figure with one or another of the organization's inputs.

Without a definition of success, of course, museums also lack a definition of failure. Might this be the reason that so few museums ever seem to fail? Dance companies dissolve, symphony orchestras collapse, and literary magazines disappear with regularity. Most museums, though—held in place perhaps by their collections—seem to survive indefinitely. They may shrink, they may lose or fail to earn accreditation, but rarely do they expire. Short of outright insolvency, the museum field seems to have few ways to identify those institutions whose chronic inability to achieve any demonstrably beneficial outcome cannot possibly justify the ongoing expense of their maintenance.

The museum seeking to articulate the ways in which it intends to have an effect on its target community would be wise to observe one caution: that it concentrate on those object-related outcomes that are most distinct to museums and not inadvertently undermine its unique importance by describing outcomes that might as easily be achieved by some other organization. Put another way, a museum may only be considered essential so long as its impact is perceived to be both valuable and incomparable. Consider, to use a wicked example, the museum improvident enough to base its case for public support on an economic impact study that quantifies its value to the community in terms of tourism, jobs, and purchasing power. What will justify the continuing public investment in such an institution when some other entity (a sports team, a theme park, a rock concert amphitheater) can demonstrate that—for a similar public investment—an even greater economic impact might be achieved? If museums cannot assert their importance as museums, then museums may not be perceived to be important at all.

More troubling in this respect is the extent to which some museums have begun to stress general educational objectives as the principal outcome for which they ought be valued. By doing so, they may ultimately leave themselves vulnerable to the claims of more traditional educational institutions that these latter could, with a only little inexpensive tinkering, deliver a comparable value at a fraction of the cost. The recent emergence of so-called single-subject museums—story-centered rather than object-centered and relying on what the designer Ralph Applebaum (a leading practitioner of the form) describes as "theatrical constructs" instead of what he calls a "giant cabinet-of-curiosities approach"—may pose a similar problem. The experiential outcome at which these museums aim may eventually (as soon, perhaps, as the widespread advent of virtual reality) be accomplishable by other and, again, less costly means. When incomparability is no longer an issue, then such cost comparisons may validly become the single criterion by which an institution is judged. The museum that casts its aspirations in such nontraditional terms cannot complain of "apples and oranges" when it finds itself unexpectedly measured against organizations of other kinds that can provide a comparable value at a far lower cost.

Beyond making the case for continued support, the ability of a preponderance of museums to define their intended outcomes and to specify what they would consider a successful level of achievement might have an important side effect. It could help lay to rest the perception that museums sometimes operate as what Philip M. Nowlen, Director of the Museum Management Institute, has called "federations of self-interest." In a field so largely self-initiated, the images that Nowlen conjures are all too familiar: the museum whose governing board believes—notwithstanding the clear language of its charter or its current mission statement—that organizational survival is the institution's driving and highest purpose, the museum in which the staff channels a disproportionate effort into its own professional development, the museum summoned into being for no better reason than to house a privately gathered collection that might otherwise have had to be dispersed, the museum that survives primarily to serve as a social focus for those who support and take turns governing it. Future funding prospects may be dimmest for those museums that appear to be little more than sites for self-indulgence, brightest for those that can most adequately answer the question "To what ongoing public need is this institution a response?"

It will be argued by those who resist these impending hardball questions—those who find them crude, insensitive to cultural values, too money-minded, or too result-oriented—that they constitute nothing more than an inappropriate effort to apply a clumsy cost-benefit analysis to an activity that belongs in some different sphere altogether. Although there may certainly be institutions (e.g., the family, public schools, religious orders) as to which such a cost-benefit analysis seems inappropriate, nowhere is it written (nor may it be any more than wishful thinking) that museums necessarily will or ought be exempt from such scrutiny. That museums were once described as "temples of the human spirit" is no guarantee that they will be forever considered sacred. Nor is the fact that they have been well supported in the past a guarantee that they will always be thought to have such an entitlement.

If this analysis still seems far-fetched, consider health care. The time is fast approaching when, in allocating health care resources, public policy–based decisions will have to be made about the value of providing care to one patient in comparison to another, about the value of, literally, saving one life rather than another. That the lives involved may all be worthwhile will be beside the point. Not every human being can be saved, and hateful as we may find the thought, medical care must ultimately be rationed by public decision, just as it has hitherto been rationed by the less visible forces of the marketplace. Might one reasonably expect something more clement for museums?

In summary, when (not if, but only when) the anticipated crunch in public and private funding materializes, worthiness alone may not justify the continued support of every museum or similar institution. The question that each museum may have to answer are just these hardball ones: Are you really worth what you cost or just merely worthwhile? Could somebody else do as much or more than you do for less? Are you truly able to accomplish anything that makes a difference, or are you simply an old habit, or possibly even a kind of indulgence? Beyond doubt, the great majority of museums will be able to develop positive and solidly convincing responses to these indisputably difficult questions. It is by no means too soon, however, for a museum's governing authority and senior staff to begin to consider just how that might best be done. Hardball is nigh.

Savings Bank for the Soul

About Institutions of Memory and Congregant Spaces

ELAINE HEUMANN GURIAN

> *If, disregarding conduct that is entirely private, we consider only that special form of conduct which involves direct relations with other persons; and if under the name government we include all control of such conduct, however arising; then we must say that the earliest kind of government, the most general kind of government, and the government which is ever spontaneously recommencing, is the government of ceremonial observance. More may be said. This kind of government, besides preceding other kinds, and besides having in all places and times approached nearer to universality of influence, has ever had, and continues to have, the largest share in regulating men's lives.*
>
> —HERBERT SPENCER, 1897

WITHIN WIDELY DIVERGENT PARTS of our society a feeling is growing that we must balance individualism with group adherence and independence with compliance. In order for civility to prevail—and it must—we must celebrate diligence and discipline just as we celebrate spontaneity and individual creativity. We must not allow repression, but neither can we condone chaos. We must ascribe to some core orderliness in our families, our cities, and our society.

Excessive individualism is a danger for the society as a whole and for each of us within it. We seem to have upset an important balance that safe society needs, one that celebrates the contribution and creativity of the individual while remaining respectful of the past and the customs that provide necessary anchor and stability. The loss of respect for authority and for adherence to expected norms, within some

Elaine Heumann Gurian is a senior museum consultant specializing in international museum projects and former deputy director for the United States Holocaust Memorial Museum in Washington, D.C. and former Deputy Assistant Secretary for Museums, Smithsonian Institution. "Savings Bank for the Soul" is an excerpt from *Civilizing the Museum: the Collected Writings of Elaine Heumann Gurian*, 2006, p.88–96. It is reprinted here by permission of the author. All rights reserved.

degree of deviation, leads individuals to act on whim with no attendant responsibility for the consequences of their actions.

In response, many of us are regarding with appreciating value the collective in all its forms—organizations, families, neighborhoods, and even ad hoc groups. While not always benign (such groups can, by repression, coercion, or fear, cause violence and destruction), they nonetheless shape our lives and our society.

Institutions of Memory

Some institutions, by their very existence, add to the stability of our society. The ones that store, collect, house, and pass along our past I call "institutions of memory." They include libraries, archives, religious organizations, sacred places, elders (especially in societies that value the passing of information in oral form), schools of all kinds, guilds and societies, courts and systems of law, historic houses, and museums.

Institutions of memory do not necessarily resemble one another in kind, history, structure, or use. What they have in common is that they represent or store the collective holdings of the past. They do so either for select groups or for society as a whole. Neither the method of storage nor the material stored (objects, buildings, words, sounds, music, places, images, and so forth) is their common denominator. What unites these organizations is the responsibility to care for the memories of the past and make them available for present and future use.

Evidence indicates that we do not need to use the organization in question to value its existence and wish for its continuity. We believe, for example, that any church is an important institution even if we are nonbelievers or lapsed attendees. While not blind to their imperfections, we want them around and in good working order so that we can call upon them when we are in need. You might think of institutions of memory as savings banks for our souls.

Disturbing incidents exemplify the importance people ascribe to repositories of history. Why did the Muslims and the Croats, with their limited resources, choose to destroy historic places of their enemies? Surely these sites were not military targets. Why did we force native children to separate from their families and give up their cultural traditions in language, dress, and ceremony in the boarding schools of the early 20th century?[2]

More positive circumstances also reveal the value we place on these institutions. Why do some native communities use drumming circles in conjunction with alcohol rehabilitation? Why does a majority of United States voters approve of funding for the arts and humanities despite being upset by specific examples of artistic excess? Why does a current survey of the Detroit metropolitan community show that the public approves of the Museum of African American History and believes it should receive municipal funding when, at the same time, most respondents say that they are unlikely to visit? Why does a recent survey show that minority tourist travelers in this country chose historic venues as a highly valued destination even when the places visited do not relate specifically to their history (Sharp 1995, Klemm 2002)?

These examples tell us, implicitly, that we regard institutions of memory as important to our collective well-being. Accordingly, we must begin to discuss the preservation of these organizations not because they add to the quality of life, or to lifelong learning opportunities, or to informal education venues (though they do all that), but because without them, we come apart.

Congregant Behavior

Simply ensuring the continuity of our institutions of memory by strengthening their core functions of preservation and education is not enough to maintain civility or collective safety. These enterprises can also purposefully create safe spaces for congregating and, by encouraging the active use of such spaces, foster the rebuilding of community.

We human beings like to be, and even need to be, in the presence of others. This does nor mean we have to know the other people or interact directly with them. Just being in their proximity gives us comfort and something to watch. Further, we will travel to places where other people gather. Being with others is an antidote to loneliness. Human beings get lonely. Many other animals do too. I call this going-to-be-with-others activity congregant behavior.[3]

Consider the group activities we participate in. At some, individual actions are coordinated and synchronous, such as at pep and political rallies, athletic and music events, religious observances, performances, and movies. At others, we expect the people we encounter to be mostly autonomous, peaceable strangers. The actions of these participants are uncoordinated and independent. Occasions like visiting museums, shopping and browsing at shopping malls, markets, carnivals, and fairs fall into this category. In each case, however, the simple expectation that others will be present contributes to the pleasurable anticipation.

While some congregant behavior is mild mannered and peaceable, some can lead to violence. People in crowds can egg each other on. Crowd behavior can be more dramatic and more volatile than the individuals within it might wish. Inherent in group activity is the risk that it might devolve into violence, riots, or stampedes.

Current American society evidences a residual sense of responsibility toward the collective whole and toward individual strangers. Witness how we continue to respond to emergencies and tragedies, where most of the time strangers help each other. Think also of line or queue etiquette in America, where strangers hold each other's place.

Reclaiming Community

Encouraging peaceful congregant behavior is one of the essential elements of reestablishing community.[4] Various trends point to a growing public interest in the reestablishment of functioning communities that include opportunities for enhanced congregant behavior:

- Real estate developers are building planned communities that encourage foot traffic and resemble the villages of our memories.
- Front porches are being brought back, and many neighborhoods are adding them to existing homes.

- Shopping malls have (both intentionally and inadvertently) been adding physical amenities such as play spaces, stages, and "outdoor" cafes. Moms go to malls in the winter to let their homebound children run around. Heart patients walk to improve their cardiovascular activity, health and voter organizations set up information booths, and local arts groups perform.
- It is increasingly common for eating establishments to attract customers by putting porch furniture on the sidewalk (even in unlikely and unattractive locations) during good weather.
- Bars have been upgraded from less savory institutions to havens for everyone, drinkers or not. Television series have memorialized them to underscore their neighborliness.
- Coffee bars have appeared in the midst of every social gathering place. They serve as an anchor for new mega-bookstores, transforming the activity of book-buying into a new way to interact with friends, family, and strangers.
- Towns and cities are holding annual invented happenings that take on new public celebratory dimensions. For example, many cities and towns are replicating Boston's First Night—a series of free events in the city's core that provides multigenerational groups a safe and entertaining New Year's Eve.

At the same time that new opportunities for congregant activity are being created, isolation and a feeling of personal danger are increasing:

- The gulf between rich and poor is growing in the United States. The poor are less able to survive unaided, and evidence of their poverty (homelessness and begging) is more apparent for all to see.
- The rise of technological systems (the virtual world) is making it possible for more and more people to work by themselves, connected to others only electronically.
- The population of the country is getting older, and the elderly are becoming more isolated.
- Chain stores are homogenizing most retail experiences, with a loss of local or regional particularity.
- Loyalty to one's employees and employers is eroding, and people are changing jobs more frequently than before.
- Certain areas of our cities are unsafe for everyone, especially their inhabitants.
- News distributors focus on sensational, pessimistic, disillusioning, or tragic matters over which the individual has no personal power. As a result, we feel less in control of our lives than ever.

In revaluing community, we seek environments that we can personally affect. We wish to be known to our neighbors and service providers. We wish to be free from personal danger, and during some of our time we wish to be in the safe company of others.

Many people are choosing to move their offices and homes to smaller communities because, with technological advances, they can do their work anywhere. So many workers are moving that they are affecting secondary markets: the rise of mail order, the decline of the clothing industry, the creation of specialized magazines, and changing real estate values.

The Internet hosts many interest-based bulletin boards that function as a new virtual community with an emphasis on helpfulness. These new communities are created technologically by distant members who sit home alone working.

In 1969, Alistair Cooke said in a radio broadcast:

> Middle-class standards, as they were planted and have grown everywhere in this country, are the ones that have kept America a going concern. It is time to grit the teeth slightly, prepare for a shower of eggs, and say what those standards are: Fair wages for good work. Concern for the family and its good name. A distrust of extremes and often, perhaps, a lazy willingness to compromise. The hope of owning your own house and improving it. The belief that the mother and father are the bosses, however easygoing, of the household and not simply pals. A pride in the whole country, often as canting and unreasonable as such patriotism can be. Vague but stubborn ideas about decency. An equally vague but untroubled belief in God. A natural sense of neighborliness, fed by the assumption that your neighbor is much like you and is willing to share the same laws . . . or lend you a mower, a hammer, or a bottle of milk. (Cooke 1979)

Cooke may have been talking about middle-class values, or, as I suspect, he may have been speaking about a core set of American values that many aspired to regardless of economic status. In any case, I think the reassertion of these values, with all their imperfections, is emerging nationwide again.

Possible Next Steps

Now what does all of this have to do with institutions of memory? If we believe that congregant behavior is a human need and also that all civic locations offer opportunities for people to be with and see other people, then why not challenge institutions not previously interested in communal activity to build programs specifically to encourage more civil interaction.

Museums can aspire to become one of the community's few safe and neutral congregant spaces. If we do our work well, all members of society—no matter what ethnic, racial, or economic group they belong to—could be made to feel welcome. In order to create such safe environments we must look at the most subtle aspects of our presentations. Do the building guards think all people are equally welcome? Does the signage use words that require a certain education level or specialized knowledge? Can a non-English speaker decode the message? Are staff members sufficiently representative so the public has a sense that everyone is not only welcome but potentially understood? Are employees sensitized to the many acceptable, though culturally specific, ways of acting when in a public space?

Many churches, museums, schools, and libraries serve as forums for debate that foster balanced conversations on issues of the day. Sometimes the debate takes up physical form on bulletin boards or exhibition; sometimes it is transient and oral. The programs stem from a belief that "town hall" is an appropriate role for these institutions of memory.

We could, if we wished, offer programs that turn strangers into acquaintances. Robert D. Putnam, in his book *Bowling Alone*, tells us that today more people than ever go to bowling alleys but fewer go as members of bowling teams (Putnam 2000). Putnam cites this example to maintain that people today choose individualism over group camaraderie. Using his analogy, could we redefine the meaning of "group" to include all who go to the bowling alley at any particular time? Then we could begin to program activities for transient and even unintentional aggregations, but groups nevertheless. What if the bowling alley owner encouraged group cohesion by setting up teams for an evening, giving out team clothing, giving all players name tags, and changing playing partners every once in a while? (He might even find his business's bottom line enhanced.)

What if our organizations intentionally enhanced the formation of group cohesion and responsibility? Docent-led groups in historic houses could begin by having individuals introduce themselves to each other. We could locate our cafes in the heart of the functioning institution rather than on the periphery. The Walker Art Center in Minneapolis, for example, embedded a period cafe within an exhibition and found that strangers began to discuss the exhibition.[5] In all our eating establishments we could set up tables reserved for single strangers to share a meal, as they do in private clubs.

We can make museums one of the few safe and neutral congregant spaces in our communities. If we do our work well, we could help all members of society—no matter what ethnic, racial, or economic group they belong to—feel welcome. To create such safe environments, we must look at all aspects of our presentations and adjust these to enhance interactive opportunities. Is information about neighborhood amenities, like restaurants and other attractions, available in the lobby?[6] Do we invite the museum's neighbors in to see our work and be seen by our visitors? Can we help visitors enter and leave the building without feeling intimidated by the surrounding neighborhood?

Those museums that see themselves as forums for balanced conversations on issues of the day regard their visitors in the transformed role of participants. These museums are also experimenting with programs that invite colloquy. They are using their lecture halls as umbrellas for debate and the airing of ideas.[7] Such programs stem from the belief that serving as a "town square" is an appropriate role for a museum and, conversely, that the museum is a fitting safe place for the discussion of unsafe ideas.[8]

Let us also examine our company culture—the internal climate of our public enterprise—as we build recognizably safer spaces for the public. It is likely that the public can intuit an organization's internal climate. Simplistically, if the staff cares for each other, visitors will feel the staff will be kind to them. If the internal administrative process is arbitrary and biased, if respect for the value of each employee is not the norm, if the internal discourse is allowed to be abusive, then no matter what we do with our programs, I suspect the public will remain cynical and on edge.

The converse is also true. If our program is a little ragged but our spirit is enthusiastic, if we are really happy to see our visitors, they will forgive us our frayed edges and get on with the business at hand, exuding a palpable sense of well-being.

Summary

Most institutions of memory will have to change a great deal in order to be truly welcoming to all. Yet, change or not, they all have a core purpose inherently important to our joint survival: we all need to be rooted in our collective past in order to face our collective future.

In addition, these institutions can significantly enhance their role in the community. They can, if they wish, foster and celebrate congregant behavior within their walls. In so doing, they will encourage civility more generally. Institutions of memory, in making a safe space for all who enter, can add to the safety of the entire community.

Afterword

This paper was originally written prior to the terrorist attacks of September 11, 2001. Thereafter, the preoccupying concern of social conservatives (who held the levers of much of the political power in the United States) moved from excessive individualism to a kind of fearful patriotism that allowed for very little deviation from compliance and conformity. Four years later there is a tentative but uneasy oppositional voice to be heard speaking up for opinions different from the mainstream.

The essay, as written, is a plea for museums to become more civically responsible by encouraging the use of their safe spaces for strangers to congregate. We need such spaces now more than ever but for a different reason than the one that originally motivated this essay. Rereading it reminds me how quickly societies become intolerant of activity outside the norm and how one should not take group acquiescence, or silence through trepidation, for evidence of collective well-being.

When citizens feel threatened by terrorists (real or imagined), it becomes ever more important to find places and activities where groups can cross their own boundaries and recombine with others with some ease. In this context, all sides must see museums as fair and balanced venues. Museums have many assets to work from. Most people perceive them as trustworthy and educative. They fall in the category of important civic venues, yet, I would contend, they have far to go to realize their civic potential.

They are not universally seen as welcoming or useful in the ordinary sense. Many, most especially art museums, are seen as elitist. Many are difficult to navigate

for the novice. A study to determine what minority visitors thought of museums was commissioned by the Museum and Galleries Commission of the United Kingdom in 1997. The groups interviewed were half nonvisitors and half museum users.
Their opinions were similar, irrespective of ethnicity:

> "The Museum" is still the way that museums are perceived; an old building with an imposing appearance, like the British Museum. Typical contents include "Kings and Queens, crowns, suits of amour, weapons, and 'broken pots and rocks'." The atmosphere was described as quiet, reverential and un-welcoming to children. Not surprisingly, this rather unpleasant place was felt to be for intellectuals, and posh people. Art galleries were perceived as even more distant and elitist. There was a real fear that the displays would be too difficult to understand. (Hooper-Greenhill 1998)

Yet when the program appeals diversely to the visitor, when outside leadership declares the museum to be welcoming, when one finds the outing supportive at enlightening to one's family, when museums raise to accept the challenge of sustaining the community through unexpected catastrophes, the museum can, if it wants to fulfill its broadest mission as a useful and engaging savings bank for the soul.

Notes

1. This chapter was originally prepared as a keynote speech at the Museums Australia 1996 Conference, Thursday, October 30, 1996. It was subsequently published in two differed versions (Gurian 1995, 1996). This chapter is a mixture of both those published paper with an after word to comment on the issues from a more current perspective.

2. For further discussion on objects as important to the "soul" of a people see (Gurian 1999).

3. I understand that "congregant space" or "congregant behavior" is an unorthodox use of the term congregant, which has a dictionary meaning of "one who congregates, especial a member of a group of people gathered for religious worship." I use it as a form of congregating which means "to bring or come together in a group, crowd, or assembly without the religious connotations." I continue to use the term throughout many of my papers.

4. For further explication of the many spaces that fit within the category of "congregant space see (Gurian 2005).

5. There have been a number of successful experiments with placing food venues within visual sight of exhibition material. One such venue is the new Walker Art Center building and program whose slogan is "where art meets life." Another is to be (found on the mezzanine Te Papa, the National Museum of New Zealand in Wellington. And increasingly, museums are displaying objects in sealed cases used within food service venues. While they might serve merely as decoration, they might also prompt conversation.

6. The Mexican Fine Arts Center Museum in Chicago has intentionally decided not to have in-house food service so that people will patronize local eateries. Visitors find out where go by speaking to someone at the front desk. While this practice reduces potential income (the museum has no admission fee), it makes the museum a very good neighbor and

is prized by local establishments, since it is an attraction that brings people to the neighborhood for the first time (Torturer 2004).

7. The Newsome in Washington, D.C., has regularly scheduled programs that are broadcast throughout the country. The audience is invited to participate. Similarly, the National Museum of Australia, in Canberra, has a professional broadcast studio where students question important officials on the air.

8. For example, the mission of the Association of Children's Museums (ACM) is: The Association of Children's Museums builds the capacity of children's museums to serve as town squares for children and families where play inspires creativity and lifelong learning.

Bibliography

Cooke, A. "Eternal Vigilance by Whom?" in A. Cooke, ed. *The Americans*, New York: Berkeley Books, 1979.

Gurian, E. H. "Offering Safer Public Spaces," *Journal of Museum Education* 20, No. 3 (1995): 14–16.

———. "A Savings Bank for the Soul," *Rainmakers in the Arts Reader*, 7, No. 2 (1996): 6–9.

———. "What Is the Object of This Exercise? A Meandering Exploration of the Many Meanings of Objects in Museums," in *Daedalus*, 128, No. 3 (1996), 163–183.

———. "Threshold Fear," in S. Macleod, S., ed. *Reshaping Museum Space: Architecture, Design, Exhibitions*. London: Rutledge, 2005.

Hooper-Greenhill, E. "Cultural Diversity, Attitudes of Ethnic Minority Populations Towards Museums and Galleries," *GEM News*, 69 (Spring) (1998): 10–11.

Klemm, M. S. "Tourism and Ethnic Minorities in Bradford: The Invisible Segment," *Journal of Travel Research*, 41, No. 1 (2002), 85–91.

Putnam, R. D. *Bowling Alone: The Collapse and Revival of American Community*. New York: Simon & Schuster, 2000.

Sharp, D. "Welcoming Minorities in Cities Coast to Coast," *USA Today*, September 19, 1995, p. 8D.

Spencer, H. "The Principles of Sociology," in E. Goffman, ed. *Relations in Public*. New York: Basic Books, Inc., 1897 (1971).

Torturer, C., executive director, the Mexican Fine Arts Center Museum, personal communication, 2004.

Changing Practices of Interpretation

13

LISA C. ROBERTS

THE USE OF INTERPRETATION WAS INAUGURATED early in museum history by curators, particularly those devoted to the public welfare.[1] Employed sporadically throughout the 19th century, interpretive devices like labels, brochures, and lectures became a permanent fixture in museum halls by World War I. Initially, their content was largely information-based: dates, places, and facts were the norm. Some curators, however, began experimenting with new ways of presenting collections that, they hoped, would more effectively reach visitors. The most innovative of these figures was John Cotton Dana, director of the Newark Museum. Contemptuous of what he called "gazing museums," Dana hesitated to call the Newark a "museum," preferring instead "institute of visual instruction."[2] His many special exhibitions stretched the boundaries of conventional display by featuring, for example, applied and industrial arts, textile and clay products manufactured by local firms, immigrants' handicrafts, and "inexpensive articles of good design." Dana hoped that these exhibits would draw new visitors like housewives, workers, immigrants, and others who might have a natural interest in the objects on display.

More important to Dana than what was displayed, however, was how it was used. He established many now common practices to increase the museum's usefulness: for example, loaning objects to school classrooms, shops, and hospitals; creating a teacher-training course at local colleges; opening a "junior museum" for children only; establishing branch museums in local libraries.

Dana was not the only such innovator. Others came, interestingly enough, from the art-museum establishment, which then even as now had a strong conservative strain. Many art museum officials were moved by wider social failings that they hoped their institutions might help to redress. Others, concerned about America's

Lisa C. Roberts is an independent consultant for museums, gardens, and parks and former director of conservatories for the Chicago Park District. "Changing Practices of Interpretation" is an excerpt from her 1997 book *From Knowledge to Narrative: Educators and the Changing Museum*. It is reprinted here by permission of the Smithsonian Institution Press. Copyright 1997.

weakness in design, felt that museums could have a hand in elevating patrons' taste, thereby educating not only the producers of fine and applied arts but also their consumers, thus creating a demand and model for quality work.

Not lost on museum officials was the more subtle character-building that exposure to good art could induce. Historian Terry Zeller has cited numerous examples of ways museums sought to refine citizens and to raise their standards of beauty and taste.[3] The Toledo Museum of Art, for example, was an early pioneer, engineering a number of civic improvement projects and preaching "the gospel of simplicity and truth." The museum exhibited model homes and landscaping scenes and mounted two period rooms, one "furnished inexpensively and in good taste," and "the other room exhibiting as many as possible of the most common offenses against the laws of truth and beauty."[4] Other museums involved in the beautification movement included the Art Institute of Chicago, through the Better Homes Institute of its Extension Department; the Boston Museum of Fine Arts; and the Milwaukee Art Institute.

Other innovators included the Rochester Museum of Arts and Sciences' Arthur Parker, who labored to make museums active service centers in their communities. Like Dana, Parker mounted exhibits with broad popular appeal and initiated services intended to break down museums' psychological and intellectual barriers. To him, the measure of museums was not their wealth and collections but the values they disseminated. Activities like loaning materials to schools, sponsoring programs for the unemployed, and offering programs to promote patriotism during World War II were just a few of the ways Parker sought to expand museums' community-service role.

In sum, many genuine efforts were made to make collections accessible to viewers before the arrival of professional educators.[5] Most of those efforts, however, whatever their express motives, sought to inculcate the public with specific aesthetic values. Naturally, they were the values of the propertied class who chose and controlled the culture enshrined in museums. Ideology, then, was as much a part of the mission as cultural uplift. As T. J. Jackson Lears has observed,

> Many middle- and upper-class Americans felt that if only the proper educational balance could be struck, immigrants could be assimilated, angry workers calmed, and an incipient leisure class returned to productive life.[6]

Like the museum proprietors of the founding republic, then, many early twentieth-century curators saw in museums the possibility of achieving social and cultural uplift for their public. They, too, were guided by specific, usually middle- to upper-class, ideas of what was good and what was beautiful.

As innovative and successful as some of these early approaches to reaching visitors appeared to be, they were not the norm; most occurred in small pockets throughout the nation, usually in metropolitan museums. Many innovators still faced resistance from colleagues who had differing philosophies about museums' public role, and few were furthering their cause in a broader, professional sense. As Paul Rea noted in his study on the problems and needs of U.S. museums:

> [While] a great diversity of educational methods has been developed and a high order of results has been achieved . . . few methods of juvenile museum education have become universal. There seems to be more interest in devising new small-scale experiments than in the more prosaic work of extending to the whole field such methods as have been found most generally effective.[7]

Still, the foundation was clearly laid for museums' involvement in a variety of public activities. The next stage would be ushered in with the newly emerging museum educators.

As museum education evolved into an autonomous profession, what affect did educators have on the interpretation of collections? Insofar as educators have lobbied for visitors' interests in practically everything museums do, including—and especially—interpretation, their influence has been substantial. It has been most significant in three areas: first, in the mere presence of interpretation; second, in the language used to interpret; and third, in the content of the messages. Educators' impact in these three areas occurred roughly chronologically, although there was considerable overlap.

The first issue—advocating the presence of interpretation—has been an ongoing cause for educators. Providing interpretation was the single most important thing museums could do to engage visitors with their collections. Of course, by the time educators came onto the scene in the 1930s and 1940s, many museums had interpretive and educational programs in place. Many more, however, remained underdeveloped with respect to their public functions; and even those with established programs were subjected to the backlash of conflicting professional opinion.

Art museums, for example, may have been the seat of many innovative programs, but not everyone supported their innovations. Many curators opposed educational activities that appeared to interfere with the direct contemplation of the object. In their eyes, interpretation demeaned art by turning it from an aesthetic phenomenon into a social or historical construct. The following statement by John Walker of the National Gallery of Art exemplifies this position:

> A work of art is not a specimen, not primarily an historical document, but a source of pleasure, analogous to, say, a musical composition. The major purpose of the National Gallery is to allow each painting, piece of sculpture, or other object of art to communicate to the spectator, with as little interference as possible, the enjoyment it was designed to give.[8]

While critiques such as this did not oppose the educational value of art collections, they did oppose the provision of aids to that education. It was precisely this sort of attitude that educators sought to change. In his study about the educational values to be derived from museums, T. R. Adam observed:

> To someone outside the world of art criticism, there must seem an element of almost mystic faith in this belief in the power of great paintings to communicate

abstract ideas of beauty to the uninformed spectator. . . . When background is lacking—where there is no knowledge of what the artist is attempting to say in terms of time, place, or social meaning—the resulting impression is confused and is likely to be painful as pleasurable.[9]

Despite such views, many art museum staff have persisted to advocate unadulterated contemplation as the proper means to understanding. Anything else alters, simplifies, and trivializes not only the art on view but also the experience of looking. Such sentiments were given eloquent voice by Walter Pach. In *The American Art Museum*, he argued that museums could not (and therefore should not) reach the public without lowering their standards:

> In the confusion of values amid which the world is struggling, the man in the street may be so misled by the blare of loud-speakers and the dazzle of fierce lights that his chances of achieving good judgment and good taste are progressively endangered. Much of what he gets over the radio, at the movie house, and from posters, magazine covers, and the like is making his "street" always more unhealthy. In that case, the museum cannot go halfway in meeting him.[10]

In other museums, the issue of scholarship continued to be raised periodically as the proper and primary focus of museum activities. In his 1932 study, Paul Rea admitted that "except in a few more favored or braver museums, scholarship has probably suffered from the public museum movement."[11] Additionally, Herbert J. Spinden in a 1940 *Museum News* article, "The Curators in the New Public Museum," observed:

> It seems that in some institutions curators have little to say about new specimens and little opportunity to develop their scholarship. The great American enigma is why men who have achieved a reputation in some special field are hired because of that reputation and then given no opportunity to do the kind of work for which they are best fitted.[12]

Despite such opposition, educators continued to press forward. Grace Fisher Ramsey's 1938 study of educational work in museums recorded dozens of examples of educational activity in museums nationwide: gallery talks, discussion groups, teacher training, school visits, museum clubs for children, extension work, and programs for disabled people.[13] In 1942 the AAM appointed a Committee on Education to review the social and educational problems facing museums; the result was *The Museum as a Social Instrument*.[14] While Ramsey's and the AAM's studies clearly supported museums' educational potential, they cautioned readers against jumping to conclusions about the effectiveness of museum education.[15] A 1952 study conducted at Chicago's Museum of Science and Industry echoed their concerns: just because visitors look does not mean that they learn.[16]

Still, educational activity in museums proceeded unabated. By 1960, 79 percent of museums were reportedly offering some kind of organized educational program (up from 15 percent in 1932;[7]), and from 1952 to 1962 the gross attendance to museums more than doubled.[18] While impossible to establish a direct association between the expansion of educational offerings and the growth in attendance owing to the former, it is not a far stretch to suppose the two may be linked.

It would seem that museum education had finally taken root in the institution. Yet, despite the widespread allocation of staff and budgets to educational services, education remained a minor institutional mission. Throughout the 1960s and well into the 1970s, educators worked with minuscule budgets in substandard office space; they were rarely involved in exhibit development, and they had little or no voice in museum affairs. Curators still reigned supreme; they kept alive old concerns about the treatment of collections, while educators continued to advocate the inclusion of interpretation that was directed toward visitors, not scholars. In the early 1960s, for example, curator Wilcomb Washburn of the Smithsonian Institution lamented the changes wrought by

> professional educationists, who consider education a professional skill too abstruse to be left in the hands of the scholars, and who, typically, substituted functions and techniques for purpose and content.[19]

Echoing his concerns, Daniel Catton Rich, director of the Worcester Art Museum, exhorted:

> Though from time to time we will be advised to arrange our collections by the latest department store techniques, we must resist. The Kress stores and the Kress collections are quite separate things. Never must we be persuaded to become the supermarkets of culture.[20]

Keeping the debate alive during his tenure at Cleveland's Museum of Art, the irascible director Sherman Lee declared in 1971: "I part company with the concept of a museum as an instrument of mass education."[21] Meanwhile, director Thomas Leavitt of the Museum of American Textile History pushed for the placement of educators under curatorial supervision: "Left to its own devices, a museum education department is like a nervous system detached from the cerebrum, like the chicken's conduct after its head has been cut off."[22]

Fortunately for educators, the AAM did not share these views. In 1973 it approved the creation of a standing professional committee on education to serve as the profession's mouthpiece and advocate. By the end of the decade, educators finally began to achieve parity within the museum institution. Pressure was mounting on museums to address a variety of public issues, such as assisting ailing school systems, diversifying audiences, undertaking community outreach, and increasing attendance to generate revenue and to demonstrate public service. These factors, combined with the growing professionalization of museum education practice, began to make educators more valuable to administrators. Consequently, many began participating on exhibit-development and marketing teams. A few managed to break the glass ceiling with appointments to senior administrative positions.

As educators became more involved in decision- and policy-making, different issues came to the fore. No longer was it the case that they had to push for the inclusion of interpretation. With the possible exception of art museums, where "unadulterated contemplation" remained in high favor, by the 1980s interpretation was an accepted institutional function. However, the nature of that interpretation became a contested issue. Hence, the second area in which educators affected interpretation was language.

If interpretation was to be effective, it had to be expressed in a manner that was both comprehensible and engaging. More often than not, it was neither. Interpretive writing was typically the purview of curators who had the expertise to know what to say but whose ability to say it often left something to be desired. As a result, labels and other interpretive materials often bore a voice that was technical, verbose, and eminently curatorial. "Rules" for effective labels had been put forth ever since Goode's time.[23] But it was the rare curator who practiced what the rules preached. Not surprisingly, few visitors had the wherewithal to absorb label text.

It was not until visitor-studies procedures became a more regular museum practice and interpretation was subject to evaluation that it became clear just how ineffective exhibit labels had often been. Some suffered the pitfalls of poor writing or design; others failed on the grounds of being simply uninteresting.[24] It is probably no coincidence that the bulk of these studies began to appear when the climate in museums was becoming more friendly toward educators and their interests. Museum officials were finally beginning to get the message: interpretation was about communication; and effective communication required bridging the world of the expert and the world of the layperson with language that was intelligible to the latter without being a misrepresentation of the former.

Achieving this balance between accuracy and intelligibility resulted in the development of new writing styles, many of which were reinventions of old rules. Many museums, for example, began to adopt a prose style that was short, simple, and direct. Others, notably the Monterey Bay Aquarium, began experimenting with the organization of information, producing a label hierarchy that distinguished between general and specialized messages. Label writer Judy Rand set a new standard and form of speech at the aquarium through the use of humor, colloquialism, questions, and second-person voice.[25] While many museum professionals balked at the sacrifice or oversimplification of information, evaluations of these new labels showed visitors engaging in such behaviors as reading aloud, pointing to objects, and sharing information. More importantly, visitors understood and were able to reiterate exhibit messages.[26]

Elsewhere, visitor researchers studied various narrative strategies that contributed to label effectiveness. At the Brookfield Zoo, for example, Beverly Serrell found that labels which included explicit visual references to what was on display held attention longer than labels lacking such references.[27] Steve Bitgood, while working at the Anniston Museum of Natural History, found that dividing a single label's text into several discrete chunks of information increased reading time significantly.[28] Separate studies conducted by Bitgood and other researchers confirmed that the inclusion of questions and directives in labels helped to focus visitors' attention and to increase their time spent reading.[29]

Of course, communication extends beyond the words on the wall. Messages are equally borne by the visual presentation, from interpretive graphics to display elements. With the growing acceptance of educative ways of thinking, researchers were conducting more studies on how the design of interpretive devices could improve visitor learning. With the incorporation of interactive elements into labels, along with improvements in legibility and attractiveness, exhibit halls began to receive a long-needed facelift. Standards and guidelines were established regarding type size, placement, figure-to-background contrast, and other design issues. Consequently, interpretive graphics were employed more boldly—both to illustrate messages and to provide atmosphere. Artifacts increasingly shared the stage with elaborate set dressings designed to establish a broader interpretive context. Significantly, these activities marked the growing participation of education and design personnel in exhibit development decisions.

Not everyone welcomed these changes. Critics raised anew questions about the proper treatment and selection of artifacts. When the Field Museum appointed "exhibit developers" from outside the curatorial division to head its exhibit teams, anthropology curator John Terrell had this response:

> [B]ecause curators can't remember how little museum visitors know—and so expect much more from visitors than they reasonably should—from now on, museum educators are to be the "choosers," the lucky ones to decide what visitors may and may not see in museums.
>
> What? The powers-that-be honestly believe exhibitions can be mounted without curators? Preposterous. But, sadly, we have no ruby slippers in our collections at Field Museum to tap together to return to better times.[30]

Terrell is not alone in his views. As educators have become more involved in exhibit and interpretive functions, once the domain of curators, more curators have begun to speak out against what some have called the "Disney-fication" of museum halls.[31]

Educators, however, were to leave their most radical mark in their third area of influence—the content of messages. No matter how engaging the interpretation of, for example, a Cambrian fossil, the question remained: Do visitors even care that another set of creatures once roamed the earth? Indeed, why should they care? The issue of language in museum exhibit text has to do with not just presentation but also context, which has as much to do with the visitors as with the object. In other words, visitors' interest and attention is determined not by an object's inherent appeal but its relevance to their own framework of knowledge and experience. It was but a small step from visitor-centered language to visitor-centered content, and label writers experimented accordingly.

The Denver Art Museum, for example, proposed for labels a new "experience-driven paradigm" in contrast to the traditional information-driven paradigm. Based on their research about how novices view art, the new labels focused on what the visitors wanted to derive from the art instead of what the museum wanted to impart to visitors.[32] Making a human connection, for example, was found to be important to art novices. "Human-connection labels" focused on people—artists, patrons, users, and viewers—and employed such strategies as relaying first-person testimony and referring to the viewers' cultural context.[33]

Other museums also began employing front-end evaluation as a part of exhibit planning to determine visitors' interests in and knowledge about a particular topic. For example, when Minda Borun was education director at the Franklin Institute of Science, she conducted extensive interviews with visitors about their notions of gravity. Visitors' input helped exhibit developers to frame the subject in a way that was sensitive to visitors' preconceptions.[34]

As the climate in museums warmed to visitor input and feedback, exhibit developers also began to seek advice on exhibit content from outside advisory groups that represented various communities—for example, cultural groups, neighborhood residents, and teachers. This cooperative spirit marked an important step in making the production of knowledge and exhibits a shared process, open to everyone who might have a stake.

Finally, a handful of curators who were sensitive to the changing academic tide began to incorporate overlooked perspectives into museum exhibitions. Historians, for example, changed the face of Colonial Williamsburg by bringing to public view interpretations that deal with slavery and the African American experience that had previously been excluded. More exhibits began to consider long-neglected versions of history and culture, thereby giving voice to the perspectives of laborers,[35] women,[36] and other underrepresented groups.[37]

Exhibit content would receive its greatest makeover, however, with the entry of other noncuratorial, nonscientific meanings into the interpretive domain. As studies continued to reveal the vast range of interests, expectations, and experiences that visitors brought to museums, the question of relevance took on new dimensions: for example, who was to say that what was significant about an object to a visitor was any less valid or significant than what was significant to a curator? If a visitor was moved by a crystal decanter that reminded her of a family heirloom, did it matter that she did not learn something further about the Waterford line that had produced it?[38] Museum educator Patterson Williams explained:

> I would argue that the essence of a museum's public function is to enable the visitor to use museum objects to his own greatest advantage. To call for museum literacy, therefore, is to call for a theory of instruction focused on teaching visitors how to have personally significant experiences with objects. . . . The goal [of such a theory of instruction] must be an experience on the part of the visitor which the visitor values; therefore the significance, if any, of the encounter will be determined by the visitor's value system, not by our own.[39]

It became clear that the task of interpretation was first and foremost a task of connection: getting visitors to connect to what they see, on whatever terms that might be. At issue was the legitimization of personal experience as a source of meaning different from but no less valid than curatorial knowledge. Advocates of this view began experimenting with interpretation that encouraged visitors to look inside themselves.

Characteristic of this approach was a shift in focus from the object to the process of looking at it. For some, the goal was to impart not facts, but tools—skills of perception and interpretation. At the Brooklyn Children's Museum, for example, an exhibit entitled "The Mystery of Things" introduces children to the process by which identifications and meanings are assigned to objects. Based on Csikszentmihalyi's work on the meaning of things,[40] the exhibit presents dozens of unfamiliar objects from around the world; interpretation guides visitors to use their senses and make associations to identify the objects. Of special interest is the fact that the exhibit is self-reflective, so that its messages also apply to museums and how they look at and decipher objects.[41]

Other museums have experimented with ways of evoking and validating visitors' personal responses to museum pieces. The Denver Art Museum, for example, developed a two-columned label for some of their paintings that reads on one side, "If you like this painting, is it because . . . ", and on the other, "If you don't like this painting, is it because . . . ." A series of statements on each side helped visitors sort out their reactions to the paintings.

Similarly, in one of the earliest of such examples, the "Game Room" at the Fine Arts Museums of San Francisco made important use of the idea of visitor-centered meanings. Designed as the art world's answer to the participatory earning stations so popular at science museums, the room actually achieved a far more radical result. Its four "games" elicited visitors' personal judgments and opinions by challenging one of curators' most sacred cows: the idea of the masterpiece. In "Guess the Masterpiece," for example, visitors chose their favorite painting and played a computer program that helped them to characterize what they found appealing about it. "The Masterpiece Comparison Game" allowed visitors to compare their assessments of various masterpieces with that of curators.[42]

Another example of museums' experimenting with visitors' responses can be found at the Art Gallery of Ontario, where Doug Worts has been experimenting with different ways of stimulating visitors' personal responses to paintings. For example, "Share Your Reaction" cards, dispensed in some two dozen locations throughout the museum, have encouraged visitors to reflect upon their experiences with the art through writing or drawing. "Explore a Painting in Depth" uses audio to model different ways of engaging with an artwork. Most unusual is a reflective imaging exercise that has guided visitors into a reverie with a particular painting and has helped them to explore the personal reactions, feelings, and memories that it evokes. Both of these methods have elicited some rather dramatic and moving responses.[43]

Again, the significance of these approaches does not lie exclusively in their novelty, because no one denies the power of art to trigger an emotional response. But explanations of art's meaning and significance have always rested on external historical and aesthetic standards. The significance of these experimental approaches for eliciting visitors' response lies precisely in their insistence on internal, personal standards of meaning that are legitimate and that can stand on equal footing with traditional external standards.

Over the course of a few years, educators' interpretive role has thus shifted dramatically from representing the curatorial view to experimenting with new languages and methods for representing that view, and finally to authorizing alternative views altogether. Educators' immediate goal may have been to develop innovative ways of making collections intelligible and interesting; but in so doing they found themselves challenging not only traditional ways of speaking about objects but also the very basis and authority for speaking about them at all. At stake was nothing less than the conditions for knowledge by which museums have traditionally abided. Exactly what that means—for museums, for exhibitions, and for the nature of the interpretive task—is the subject of the next section.

Implications for Museums' Interpretive Role

By promoting interpretations that reflect visitors' worlds and experiences, museum educators have brought the debate about canon into the institution. Questions about what collections represent and who controls their representation parallel closely wider disputes over how knowledge should be defined. As advocates for visitors and their perspectives, museum educators have served as the catalysts of the wider shift to a more context-based definition of knowledge. If museums today are more attentive to displayed objects' contexts, and if they employ advisory groups and other mechanisms to solicit input from those with a special relationship to or knowledge about their collections, then it is largely because educative modes of thinking have pervaded the way exhibits are conceived and developed.

Although educators did not generate the new scholarship and interpretations that have allowed them to make exhibits more inclusive, they are to be credited with taking an activist role in insisting that such interpretations be considered. Their efforts, as a result, go beyond the educational task of imparting understanding, and have had far-reaching political and epistemological ramifications. Three of these ramifications are examined below.

First, the inclusion of alternative ways of interpreting museum collections is open acknowledgment that there is more than one way of knowing. What is so revolutionary, however, is not the fact itself but the legitimacy conferred on those new knowledges by their mere presence in the museum. Ironically, it is that very authority to legitimate that their presence stands to challenge. Museums have traditionally been tremendously authoritative institutions. The history of their development, the architecture of their presence, and the gravity of their responsibility as stewards over the nation's cultural heritage have all bestowed on the institution authority over matters of knowledge. Inherent to this authority is the long scholarly legacy out of which museums grew.

So to permit, even to encourage, the inclusion of alternative interpretations is to acknowledge other modes of knowledge besides that on which museums were built. While practices such as the use of popular linguistic forms and nonscholarly contexts of meaning were promoted as aids to understanding, in fact they achieved a far more radical result. As the literary critics have so ably demonstrated, meaning is intimately connected to both the context in which it arises and the language with which it is crafted. To refer to an object in a different manner is to present not just an alternative way of communicating about it but also an alternative way of conceiving its meaning. The difference may seem insignificant, but it can have tremendous impact. For example, compare these three ways of labeling a gorilla specimen, all of which—until a 1992 renovation—could be found in different exhibits at Chicago's Field Museum of Natural History: "Western Lowland Gorilla"; "Man-like Ape"; and "'Bushman' lived in Chicago most of his life." The first presents viewers with a biological specimen; the second, with an animal depicted in anthropocentric terms; and the third, with an individual who has not only a name but also a history.

Second, curators no longer wield the same authority over museums' interpretive function. Educators now have a hand in that function, although their role is still often confined to presentation: making interpretation available and intelligible. Presentation, however, has turned out be more than mere window dressing. As the above example shows, the manner of presentation affects not just the effectiveness of the communication but also the particular meaning it bears. Furthermore, as educators have become more knowledgeable about visitors' interests and needs, they have campaigned more strongly for interpretations whose content is more reflective of visitors' worlds.

Although curators might hold authority over interpretations stemming from their technical and scholarly knowledge, that does not necessarily qualify them to speak to meanings that are based on nonscholarly criteria of knowing. As visitors' representatives, educators are better versed in the diversity of languages and backgrounds that define visitors' ways of knowing. As a result, they are also more sensitive to the multifaceted nature of the interpretive enterprise. After all, there is no one "visitor-centered" way of interpreting something because museums do not have a single, homogenous audience. One of educators' biggest challenges has been to deal with the fact that even visitor-friendly interpretations only reach those visitors to whom those interpretations are indeed friendly. One solution to reaching a diverse population has been to hand the interpretive process itself over to visitors, so that they may discover for themselves the meanings that speak to them. By providing guides to questioning and looking, visitors are empowered to look for themselves from their own particular vantage point.[44]

Just as the work of white, Euro-American men may not be representative of other Americans' experience, so too may the specialized perspectives of curators never hold meaning for many visitors. By acknowledging such disjunctions and promoting alternative interpretations, educators have begun to shift the balance of power. On the surface, this shift might appear to be primarily territorial: educators now share some of the same interpretive functions that were once the domain of the curators. But it runs far deeper, touching basic assumptions about what museums are and do by authorizing other criteria of knowing and legitimizing other knowledge producers. Not just educators but also visitors themselves may now have a hand in the meaning-making process.

Third, the very nature of museums' exhibit function has been altered. Once a seemingly straightforward matter of displaying collections, exhibition can now be viewed as an eminently interpretive endeavor: not just that the information exhibits present is subject to multiple interpretations, but the very act of presentation is fundamentally interpretive.

As a practice, exhibits were first developed for the sole purpose of presenting collections to public view. Over time, they were embellished in ways that were thought to improve that view: draped fabrics, painted backdrops, illustrative props and graphics were incorporated into exhibits. Such elements served to frame an object, providing not only the intended ambience but also shaping the object's apparent meaning. Literary critics have shown how messages may be borne by nonverbal texts. The props surrounding an object may thus carry a message in their own right by creating a visual context that shapes the way an object is seen and thus comprehended.[45]

Exhibits then are not simply displays; exhibits are systems of signs in and of themselves. They express messages about objects and the worlds from which they came, as well as about the institutions from which those messages emanate. The interpretive act does not end with a decision about what an object shall say, because the arrival at that very decision entails a translation of particular objects and their contexts into language and hence meaning.

The very act of creating an exhibit is thus subject to the same conditions and limitations that apply to the production of knowledge. The function of exhibits is, therefore, no longer driven strictly by the collections they exist to showcase so much as by what is done with them. In other words, many exhibits are now driven by messages for which the collections, when they exist, serve as a vehicle, since an object's presented meaning is ultimately shaped by decisions about its interpretation and display. Once again, it is the literary critics who have demonstrated how signs shape that to which they point. Messages no longer emerge from an object's "inherent" meaning. Messages express meanings that people create.

The exhibition enterprise may be fundamentally interpretive; but museums have been slow to share that fact with the viewing public. Despite the gains that have been made in making collections more accessible, few museums share the decision-making process through which their interpretations are derived. Even though curators may acknowledge the interpretive basis of their work, they generally continue to present those interpretations authoritatively and anonymously. Visitors, as a result, remain uninformed about even the most basic assumptions and rationales behind the messages they are given.

From an educational standpoint, this is the worst kind of teaching: spoon-feeding information without the learner's involvement. More seriously, it preserves the institution's authority to dictate "truth" by denying visitors access to the assumptions and logic on which their messages stand. What is problematic is not that those messages are invalid, but that without an awareness of either the factors or the fact of knowledge production, visitors lack the tools to engage in even the most rudimentary critique of what they are being told. Museums may present various views and knowledges; but their role in doing so remains invisible and thus protected.

A few art exhibits, however, have tackled the issue of how display is an eminently interpretive act. For art curators, exhibition is a primary medium of scholarship. Since debates about quality and value (the art "canon," as it were) are quite lively in the art world, it is to be expected that one should find exhibitions created to address them.[46] Some of the most provocative of such exhibitions have been mounted at the Center for African Art (now the Museum for African Art) in New York. "Art/artifact," for example, displayed a series of African artifacts in four different settings: a 19th-century curiosity cabinet, a "typical" art museum, a natural history diorama, and a contemporary gallery. This extraordinary exhibit thus sought to demonstrate how objects' meanings are linked to what we do with them, and thus to how we choose to see them.[47] "Perspectives: Angles on African Art" interpreted African ritual objects through labels written by a variety of individuals both inside and outside of the museum profession. Each person wrote about the feelings and thoughts that some piece evoked in him or her. This manner of interpretation introduced visitors not only to the variety of meanings these objects might hold but also to the idea that the "knowledge" presented about them consisted of an interpretation.[48] Other art exhibits designed to reflect upon themselves have appeared at such esteemed institutions as the Whitney Museum of American Art, Downtown, and the Parrish Art Museum.[49]

Since exhibition is an integral part of the history and nature of Western art, it is not surprising that art itself has also been created to explore the nature of museums and exhibitions. Furthermore, artwork, unlike other museum objects, can and has expressed a relentless self-consciousness about what it is and how it is experienced. Much 20th-century artwork, in particular, addresses its own institutionalization by dealers, historians, and curators. Some of this work deals specifically with what it means to be enclosed by a museum, by challenging either the museum's scripture (what artwork goes in), its audience (the elitist knowledge they require), or its edge (that there is an inner and an outer that are different).[50] A handful of artists have tackled the issue head-on by creating fictionalized museums and museum exhibits whose very fabrication points out the myriad ways that museums shape objects' meaning through the imposition of such elements as frame, story, and context.[51] Some artists have been so fortunate, and some museums so bold, as to curate an exhibition using an institution's permanent collection to critique conventional notions of interpretation and display.[52]

Outside the art world, however, there are few examples of exhibits that address the basis for their own messages.[53] Without good models of what such interpretations might even look like, it is not surprising that exhibit developers have been slow to incorporate messages that reflect upon themselves.

One of the few noteworthy non-art examples appeared in the late 1980s at Chicago's Field Museum of Natural History in response to protests about a particular interpretation. Tucked away in one of the Native American galleries, a diorama of the Pawnee Morning Star ceremony showed a young woman about to be sacrificed. Naked and bound, she was surrounded by men, one with arrow poised, ready to shoot. On a bulletin board next to the exhibit, a letter was posted from a visitor protesting the depiction of images of violence against women in a respectable, public institution. Also posted was a response from the Pawnee Tribal Council defending the museum's decision not to hide history from public view, however unpleasant it may be. Visitors were invited to comment, and they did— in profusion. The bulletin board was dotted with index cards on which people scribbled their thoughts about everything from women's rights to the historical enterprise to the nature of museums' responsibilities.[54]

Implicit in this approach was an effort to involve visitors in the decision-making process. As visitors learned basic information about how the Pawnee practiced this ceremony, they were also given the means to consider the wider context in which this information is represented and to judge it for themselves. For art museum educator Danielle Rice, this is not just good pedagogy; it is an ethical responsibility:

> [The educator's task is] to bridge the gaps between the value systems of the scholars who collect and exhibit art and those of the individual visitors who come to the museum to look at, and perhaps to learn about art. . . . It is the educator's ethical responsibility to represent, from within the institution, the position that art is only valuable because of ideas conceived by human beings about what constitutes value. . . . In showing that it is people who structure and control institutions, rather than the other way around, and in helping people to analyze the decisions by which aesthetic and other value judgments are made, we empower people to act with greater awareness.[55]

Likewise, it is the educator's ethical responsibility to ensure that history, anthropology, and even science are presented in a manner that reflects people's ideas about what constitutes history, anthropology, and science.

How do we really know what we know? The question is readily addressed by scholars. We would do well to apply it to museums, for museums present not just straight information, but information that is interpreted and communicated in a particular manner based on particular assumptions and decisions.

By omitting any mention about the decisions behind the determination of an object's meaning, museums exclude visitors not only from an awareness that knowledge is something that is produced but also from the possibility that they themselves may participate in its production. Inasmuch as museum educators represent visitors' perspectives, they have paved the way for interpretations that both address alternative contexts of meaning and reflect upon publicly—to visitors—the basis for and decisions behind selecting those contexts. Thus stated, the work of interpretation becomes an act of empowerment, because it provides visitors with both the knowledge and the consent to engage in critical dialogue about the messages museums present.

Notes

The notes in this article vary from the original in that they have been renumbered sequentially beginning at one. In the original they begin at 13 and run through 67.

1. So short has been their existence that when museums educators looked back for evidence of museum education, they found that early efforts were carried out by the then dominant personnel: curators and directors. As a result, many of the profession's founding fathers such as Dana and Goode were, in fact, curators by profession.

2. John Cotton Dana, *The New Museum*, Vol. I. Woodstock, VT: Elm Tree Press, 1917, 19.

3. Terry Zeller, "The Historical and Philosophical Foundations of Art Museum Education in American," *Museum Education: History, Theory, and Practice*, ed. Nancy Berry and Susan Mayer. Reston, VA: National Art Education Association, 1989, 10–89.

4. "The City Beautiful Campaign," *Museum News* 22 (October 1914), quoted in Zeller, "Art Museum Education," 21.

5. For a more complete sense of the scope and nature of these efforts, see John Cotton Dana's list of fifty-one "Helpful Museums" (for reference by those who may be starting a museum), many of which include educational activities. Dana, *New Museum*, 42–47.

6. T. J. Jackson Lears, *No Place of Grace: Antimodernism and the Transformation of American Culture, 1880–1920*. New York: Pantheon Books, 1981, 78.

7. Paul Marshall Rea, *The Museum and the Community with a Chapter on the Library and the Community: A Study of Social Laws and Consequences*. Lancaster, PA: Science Press, 1932, 31.

8. John Walker, "The Genesis of the National Gallery of Art," *Art in America* 32, No. 4 (1944), 167.

9. T. R. Adam, *The Civic Value of Museums*. New York: American Association for Adult Education, 1937, 26.

10. Walter Pach, *The American Art Museum*. New York: Pantheon Books, 1948, 229–230.

11. Rea, *The Museum and the Community*, 29–30.

12. Herbert J. Spinden, "The Curators in the New Public Museum," *Museum News* 18, No. 6 (1940), 7.

13. Grace Fisher Ramsey, *Educational Work in Museums of the United States: Development, Methods, and Trends*. New York: H. W. Wilson Company, 1938.

14. Theodore Low, *The Museum as a Social Instrument: A Study Undertaken for the Committee on Education of the American Association of Museums*. New York: Metropolitan Museum of Art, 1942.

15. Ramsey, *Educational Work in Museums of the United States*, 43, 217, 252–254; Low, *The Museum as a Social Instrument*, 30.

16. Lucy Nielsen Nedzel, "The Motivation and Education of the General Public through Museum Experiences." Ph.D. dissertation, University of Chicago, 1952.

17. Joseph Allen Patterson, "Points of View," *Museum News* 40, No. 1 (1961), 3.

18. American Association of Museums, *A Statistical Survey of Museums in the United States and Canada.* Washington, D.C.: American Association of Museums, 1965, 16.

19. Wilcomb Washburn, "Scholarship and the Museum," *Museum News* 40, No. 2 (1961), 17–18.

20. Daniel Catton Rich, "Museums at the Crossroads," *Museum News* 39, No. 6 (1961), 81.

21. Grace Glueck, "The Ivory Tower versus the Discotheque," *Art in America* 59 (1971), 81.

22. Thomas W. Leavitt and Dennis O'Toole, "Two Views on Museum Education," *Museum News* 64, No. 2 (1985), 27.

23. George Brown Goode, "Museum-History and Museums of History," *Papers of the American Historical Association* 3, ed. Herbert Baxter Adams. New York: G. P. Putnam's Sons, 1888, 262–264; Louise Connolly, *The Educational Value of Museums.* Newark, NJ: Newark Museum Association, 1914, 34–36; William L. Bryant, "Experiments with Museum Labels," *Museum Work* 6, No. 4 (1923), 114–120; Charles H. Blake, "Sizes of Type for Museum Labels," *Museum News* 22, No. 15 (1945), 8; George Weiner, "Why Johnny Can't Read Labels," *Curator* No. 2 (1963), 143–156; Beverly Serrell, *Making Exhibit Labels: A Step-by-Step Guide.* Nashville, TN: American Association for State and Local History, 1983; and Beverly Serrell, *Exhibit Labels: An Interpretative Approach.* Walnut Creek: CA: AltaMira Press, 1996.

24. See, for example, Chandler Screven, "The Effectiveness of Guidance Devices on Visitor Learning," *Curator* 18, No. 3 (1975), 219–243; Minda Borun and Maryanne Miller, *What's in a Name? A Study of the Effectiveness of Explanatory Labels in a Science Museum.* Philadelphia, PA: Franklin Institute, 1980; and Beverly Serrell, "Zoo Label Study at Brookfield Zoo," *International Zoo Yearbook* 21 (1981), 54–61. For a summary of the results of some two dozen studies on the effects of label length, placement, type size, and graphics, see *Visitor Behavior* 4, No. 3 (1989), 8–13.

25. Examples of her approach and a statement of the philosophy behind it can be found in Judy Rand, "Fish Stories That Hook Readers: Interpretive Graphics at the Monterey Bay Aquarium," in *American Association of Zoological Parks and Aquaria 1985 Annual Conference Proceedings.* Columbus, OH: American Association of Zoological Parks and Aquaria, 1985, 404–413.

26. Judy Rand, personal communication, October 6, 1995.

27. Beverly Serrell, "Zoo Label Study."

28. Stephen Bitgood et al., *Effect of Label Characteristics on Visitor Behavior*, technical report no. 86–55. Jacksonville, AL: Center for Social Design, 1986.

29. Steve Bitgood et al., *The Effects of Instructional Signs on Museum Visitors*, technical report no. 86–70. Jacksonville, AL: Center for Social Design, 1986; K. D. Hirschi and Chandler Screven, "Effects of Questions on Visitor Reading Behavior," *ILVS Review* 1 (1988): 50–61; Robert Farrington et al., "Tyrannosaurus Label Study," in *Current Trends in Audience Research and Evaluation.* Washington, DC: American Association of Museums Evaluation and Research Committee, 1989, 6–12.

30. John Terrell, "Disneyland and the Future of Museum Anthropology," *American Anthropologist* 93, No. 1 (1991), 149.

31. Peter Cannon-Brookes and Caroline Cannon-Brookes, eds., "Editorial: False Gods," *International Journal of Museum Management and Curatorship* 8, No. 1 (1989), 5–9; Lynda Murdin, "'Director's Gone Disney' Claims South Kensington Union," *Museums*

Journal 90, No. 6 (1990): 8–9; and "Editorial: A Major Museum Goes 'Populist,'" *Nature* 345 (1990), 1–2.

32. Marlene Chambers, "Improving the Esthetic Experience for Art Novices: A New Paradigm for Interpretive Labels," *Program Sourcebook*. Washington, DC: American Association of Museums, 1988, 213–227.

33. Patterson B. Williams, "Making the Human Connection: A Label Experiment," *The Sourcebook*. Washington, DC: American Association of Museums, 1989, 177–191.

34. Minda Borun, "Naive Notions and the Design of Science Museum Exhibits," *Proceedings of the 1989 Visitor Studies Conference,* ed. Stephen Bitgood et al. Jacksonville, AL: Center for Social Design, 1989, 158–162. Results of the complete "Naive Knowledge" study appear in Borun et al., "Naive Knowledge and the Design of Science Museum Exhibits," *Curator* 36, No. 3 (1993), 201–219.

35. "The Way We Worked: Baltimore's People, Port, and Industries," Baltimore Museum of Industry, Baltimore, MD, 1980; "Worker's World," Hagley Museum, Wilmington, DE, 1981; "Homestead," Historical Society of Western Pennsylvania, Pittsburgh, PA, 1989; "By Hammer and Hand," South Street Seaport Museum, New York, 1990.

36. "Dress for Greater Freedom," Oakland Museum, Oakland, CA, 1972; "Eleanor Roosevelt: First Person Singular," Smithsonian Institution Traveling Exhibition Service, Washington, DC, 1984; and "Men and Women: A History of Costume, Gender, and Power," National Museum of American History, Washington, DC, 1989.

37. "Pawnee Earth Lodge," Field Museum of Natural History, Chicago, 1977; "Essence of Indian Art," Asian Art Museum of San Francisco, San Francisco, 1984; "The Way to Independence: Memories of a Hidatsa Indian Family, 1840–1920," Minnesota Historical Society, St. Paul, 1987; "Field to Factory: Afro-American Migration, 1915–1940," National Museum of American History, Washington, DC, 1989; and "Chiefly Feasts: The Enduring Kwakiutl Potlach," American Museum of National History, New York, 1991–1992.

38. In his study of visitors to the Steinhart Aquarium in San Francisco, Sam Taylor found that the exhibits were frequently used for discussion of past experiences and memories. In fact, reinforcement of previously held knowledge or experience was found to be a more frequent use of exhibits than the acquisition of new knowledge. Samuel M. Taylor, "Understanding Processes of Informal Education: A Naturalistic Study of Visitors to a Public Aquarium," Ph.D. dissertation, University of California, Berkeley, 1986.

39. Patterson Williams, "Object Contemplation: Theory into Practice," *Journal of Museum Education* 9, No. 1 (1984), 10–14, 22.

40. Mihaly Csikszentmihalyi and Eugene Rochberg-Halton, *The Meaning of Things: Domestic Symbols and the Self*. Cambridge, UK: Cambridge University Press, 1981.

41. "The Mystery of Things," Brooklyn Children's Museum, 1988. For more on fostering looking skills, see Danielle Rice, "Making Sense of Art," *Journal of the Washington Academy of Science* 76, No. 2 (1986), 106–114.

42. For a more complete description of the Game Room, see Kathleen Berrin, "Activating the Art Museum Experience," *Museums News* 56, No. 4 (1978), 42–45.

43. Douglas Worts, "Extending the Frame: Forging a New Partnership with the Public," *Art in Museums 5, New Research in Museum Studies, An International Series,* ed. Susan Pearce. Atlantic Highlands, NJ: Athlone, 1995, 164–191.

44. Of course, even guides to questioning carry an implicit perspective by attempting to elicit another perspective—that of the visitor.

45. It is not just the inclusion of props that makes an exhibit "interpretive." Their exclusion itself constitutes a statement and a context that shapes the way an object is seen. When the Art Institute of Chicago places a kachina doll on a bare white pedestal under a Plexiglas cube, the viewer's eye is drawn to formal characteristics like color and shape. This is a different sight from that at the Field Museum of Natural History, where kachina dolls are placed in a diorama that depicts a Hopi apartment. Hanging on either side of a hearth in which a woman is baking cornbread, the kachinas prompt viewers to consider their purpose and use.

46. It is worth remembering that the revolutionary director John Cotton Dana himself raised these questions about seventy years ago. Dana proposed displaying an ordinary drinking glass half filled with water and labeled thus:

> Is it a work of art? The glass surely is; the water is a natural product, like a landscape; look carefully at line and mass, at the gleams and reflections on the glass, on the water within, on the water's surface, on the color gathered from the textile—and perhaps what you are looking at will cease, for a moment, to be merely water in a cheap tumbler, and will come to be an exquisitely beautiful thing. If you thus see it, is it then a work of art?

John Cotton Dana, "In a Changing World Should Museums Change?" *Papers and Reports Read at the Twenty-first Annual Meeting of the American Association of Museums.* Washington, DC: American Association of Museums, 1926, 21.

47. "Art/artifact," Center for African Art, New York, 1988.

48. "Perspectives: Angles on African Art," Center for African Art, New York, 1987.

49. "The Desire of the Museum," Whitney Museum of American Art, New York, 1989; "A Museum Looks at Itself: Mapping Past and Present at the Parrish Art Museum, 1897–1992," Parrish Art Museum, Southampton, NY, 1992.

50. Examples include Marcel Duchamp, Claes Oldenburg, George Segal, Robert Smithson, and Andy Warhol. Forms such as earthworks, graffiti, and performance art seek to challenge traditional definitions of art and proper modes of viewing it.

51. Marcel Duchamp, "Boîte-en-valise," portable museum, 1936; Robert Fillliou, "La Galerie Légitime," gallery in a hat, Paris, 1961; Marcel Broodthaers, "Musée d'Art Moderne," artist's home, Brussels, 1968; "Museum," Städtische Kunsthalle Düsseldorf, Düsseldorf, 1972; "Décors," several versions mounted in major European cities, 1974–1975; Claes Oldenburg, "Mouse Museum," Neue Galerie, Kassel, 1972; Jean-François Lyotard, "Les Immatériaux," Beaubourg, Paris, 1985; David Wilson, "The Museum of Jurassic Technology," Los Angeles, 1988; various artists, "Theatergarden Bestiarium," Institute for Contemporary Art, P. S. 1 Museum, Long Island City, NY, 1989; Fred Wilson, "The Other Museum," White Columns, New York City, 1990; Danny Tisdale, "The Black Museum," INTAR Gallery, New York City, 1990; and Guillermo-Gómaz Peña and Coco Fusco, "The Year of the White Bear," Mexican Fine Arts Center Museum, Field Museum of Natural History, Chicago, 1993.

52. Simon Grennan and Christopher Sperandio, "At Home with the Collection," Lakeview Museum of Art, Peoria, Ill., 1992; Joseph Kosuth, "The Brooklyn Museum Collection: The Play of the Unmentionable," Brooklyn Museum, Brooklyn, 1990; Fred Wilson, "Mining the Museum: An Installation by Fred Wilson," The Contemporary and the Maryland Historical Society, Baltimore, 1992–1993; and Wilson, "The Museum: Mixed Metaphors," Seattle Art Museum, Seattle, 1993.

53. Again, for every generalization, there exist exceptions. For a more complete overview of self-reflective exhibitions and artworks, see Lisa G. Corrin, "Mining the Museum: Artists Look at Museums, Museums Look at Themselves," in *Mining the Museum: An Installation by Fred Wilson,* ed. Lisa G. Corrin. New York: New Press, Baltimore: Contemporary, 1994.

54. At the end of 1990, the Field Museum renovated the exhibit, correcting some of its inaccuracies (for example, making the sacrificial victim a thirteen-year-old girl instead of a mature woman) and adding more background information. The bulletin board was removed and new labels that explained the controversy were installed. A few of the visitor comments have since been printed and are available at the museum's Native American Resource Center.

55. Danielle Rice, "On the Ethics of Museum Education," *Museum News* 65, No. 5 (1987), 17–19.

The Experience Economy

14

B. JOSEPH PINE II AND JAMES H. GILMORE

E XPERIENCES ARE A NEW, distinct economic offering, as distinct from services as services are from goods, but one that until now went largely unrecognized. They have always been around, but consumers, businesses, and
economists lumped them into the service sector. When a person buys a service, he
purchases a set of intangible activities carried out on his behalf. But when he buys
an experience, he pays to spend time enjoying a series of memorable events that a
company stages—as in a theatrical play-to-engage him in a personal way.

Experiences have always been at the heart of entertainment, from plays, concerts, and museums to movies and TV shows. Over the past few decades, however,
the number of entertainment options has exploded. Today, the universe has expanded to encompass a vast array of new kinds of experiences. Traditional service
industries are becoming more experiential. At theme restaurants such as the Hard
Rock Cafe, Planet Hollywood, Dive!, or the Bubba Gump Shrimp Co., the food
functions as a prop for what's known in the industry as an "entertainment" experience. And stores such as FAO Schwartz, Jordan's Furniture, and Nike-town draw
consumers through fun activities and promotional events (sometimes called "shop-
pertainment" or "entertailing").

Entertainment, however, is only one aspect of an experience. Rather, companies stage an experience whenever they engage customers—connecting with them
in a personal, memorable way. Many dining experiences have less to do with the
entertainment motif or celebrity of the financial backers than the merging of dining
with comedy, art, architecture, history, or nature. In each place, the food service
provides a stage for layering on a larger feast of sensations that enchants customers.

Joseph Pine II and James H. Gilmore are the founders of Strategic Horizons, a studio dedicated to helping
companies create new ways of adding value to their economic offerings. "The Experience Economy" is reprinted
here by permission of *Museum News* (March/April 1999). Copyright 1999, the American Association of Museums.
All rights reserved.

But don't assume that experiences apply only to consumers. Individuals comprise all businesses, and business-to-business settings also present stages for experiences. A computer installation and repair firm in Minneapolis dubs itself the Geek Squad. Its "special agents" costume themselves in white shirts with thin black ties and pocket protectors, carry badges, and drive around in old cars, turning a normally humdrum activity into a memorable encounter. Similarly, many companies hire theater troupes to turn otherwise ordinary meetings into improvisational events. And business-to-business marketers increasingly orchestrate elaborate venues for selling. In June 1996 Silicon Graphics, for example, opened the Visionarium Reality Center at its corporate headquarters in Mountain View, California, to bring its customers and engineers together in an environment where they could interact with real-time, three-dimensional product visualizations. They can view, hear, and touch as well as drive, walk, or fly through myriad possibilities of what the customer's products could be. As former chairman and CEO Edward R. McCracken related at the time of Visionarium's opening, "This is experiential computing at its ultimate, where our customers can know what their products will look like, sound like, feel like before manufacturing."

These examples—from consumer to business customers, from themed restaurants to computer repair companies—only begin to reveal the newfound promise of experiences within the United States economy and, increasingly, that of other developed nations as well. These forerunners are but a few of the experiential offerings that herald the emerging Experience Economy.

Experiences

Experiences are memorable events, revealed over time, that engage individuals in an inherently personal way. They occur whenever a company intentionally uses services as the stage and goods as props to engage an individual. While commodities are fungible, goods tangible, and services intangible, experiences are memorable. Experience buyers—or guests—value being engaged by what the company reveals over time. Just as people cut back on goods in order to spend their money on services, now they also scrutinize services in order to spend their time on memorable—and more highly valued—experiences.

The company—we'll call it an experience stager—no longer offers the goods or services alone, but the resulting experience, rich with sensations, created within its customers. All prior economic offerings remain at arms length, outside the buyer, while experiences are inherently personal. They actually occur within any individual who has been engaged on an emotional, physical, intellectual, or even spiritual level. The result? No two people can have the same experience—period. Each experience derives from the interaction between the staged event and the individual's prior state of mind and being.

Enriching the Experience

Because so many examples of staged experiences come from what the popular press loosely calls the entertainment industry, many people conclude that shifting up the Progression of Economic Value to stage experiences simply means adding entertainment to existing offerings. That would be a gross understatement. Remember that staging experiences is not about entertaining customers; it's about engaging them.

An experience may engage guests in any number of dimensions. Consider two of the most important. The first, guest participation, has two components. At one end of the spectrum lies passive participation, where customers do not directly affect or influence the performance. Such participants include symphony-goers, for example, who experience the event as pure observers or listeners. At the other end of the spectrum lies active participation, in which customers personally affect the performance or event that yields the experience. The participants include skiers who actively participate in creating their own experience. But even people who turn out to watch a ski race are not completely passive; simply by being there, they contribute to the visual and aural event that others experience.

The second dimension of experience is the kind of connection, or environmental relationship, that unites customers with the event or performance. At one end of this spectrum lies absorption; at the other end, immersion. People viewing the Kentucky Derby from the grandstand absorb the event taking place beneath and in front of them; meanwhile, people standing in the infield are immersed in the sights, sounds, and smells of the race itself as well as the activities of the other revelers surrounding them.

The coupling of these dimensions thus defines four "realms" of an experience—entertainment, education, escapist, and esthetic. These mutually compatible domains often co-mingle to form uniquely personal encounters. To design a rich, compelling, and engaging experience, don't just automatically choose one realm but instead creatively explore how aspects of each realm might enhance the particular experience you wish to stage. Ask yourself such questions as:

- In what kind of environment should guests be immersed? How should it affect their senses? What could we add (or take away) that would encourage guests to just want to be there?
- What would make the learning experience more active? What should guests do while they learn?
- What information or activities would engage your guests in the exploration of knowledge or skills? What should guests learn while experiencing what you have to offer?
- How can we incorporate elements of fun, spontaneity, and surprise? What would make your guests' stay more fun and enjoyable?

Addressing these design issues sets the stage for service providers to begin competing on the basis of an experience. Those that have already forayed into the world of experiences also will gain from further enriching their experience offerings in light of these four realms.

The sweet spot for any compelling experience is a mnemonic place, a tool aiding in the creation of memories, separate and special from the normally uneventful world of goods and services. Its very design invites you to enter, and to return again and again. Its space is layered with amenities—props—that correspond to how the space is used, and is rid of any features that do not fit this function.

Five Principles to Creating Experiences

Theme the Experience

Just hear the name of any theme restaurant—Hard Rock Cafe, House of Blues, Dive!, or the Medieval Times, to name a few—and you instantly know what to expect when you enter the place. The proprietors have taken the first, crucial step in staging an experience by envisioning a well-defined theme. One poorly conceived, on the other hand, gives customers nothing around which to organize the impressions they encounter, and the experience yields no lasting memory.

At its best, theming an experience means scripting a story in which guests participate in a narrative that would seem incomplete were they not there.

In his insightful book *The Theming of America,* sociology professor Mark Gottdiener identifies ten themes that often materialize themselves in the "built environments" that he calls staged experiences. These are: status, tropical paradise, the Wild West, classical civilization, nostalgia, Arabian fantasy, urban motif, fortress architecture and surveillance, modernism and progress, and representing the unrepresentable (such as the Vietnam War Memorial in Washington, D.C.). An outstanding list, it helps break the code to enduring themes. Yet manifestations of these themes multiply when particularized to specific settings and contexts—just as the same Shakespeare theme evidences itself differently in *Romeo and Juliet* and *West Side Story.*

Developing lists helps suggest possible themes for new experiences, but there exist lots of lists. Marketing professors Bernd Schmitt and Alex Simonson in their instructive book *The Marketing Aesthetic* offer nine "domains" for finding themes: history, religion, fashion, politics, psychology, philosophy, the physical world, popular culture, and the arts. But the key to successfully theming an experience is determining what will prove to be compelling and captivating. Five principles are paramount in developing such a theme.

First, an engaging theme must alter a guest's sense of reality. Creating a new reality—for doing, learning, staying, and being—other than the everyday underlies any successful theme, and is at the heart of establishing place.

Second, the richest venues possess themes that fully alter one's sense of reality by simultaneously affecting the experience of time, space, and matter—the very stuff reality is made of. Any setting suffices to see this truth in action.

Third, engaging themes integrate space, time, and matter into a cohesive, realistic whole. Great books and good movies engage readers and viewers when they create completely new realities, altering every detail of the reading and cinematic experience.

Fourth, themes are strengthened by creating multiple places within a place. The five biomes of American Wilderness Experience (nature attractions operated by Ogden Corporation that feature live animals, foliage, scents, and climates indigenous to various locales) leverage this principle. The change in scenery—from redwood to high sierra to desert to coast to valley—extends the story introduced by video and simulated ride. It puts the guest in motion in the experience.

Finally, a theme should fit the character of the enterprise staging the experience. Anything less runs the risk of appearing disingenuous and detracting from the encounter.

An effective theme must be concise and compelling. Too much detail clutters its effectiveness in serving as an organizing principle for staging experiences. The theme is not a corporate mission statement or a marketing tag line. It needn't be publicly articulated. The theme must drive all the design elements and staged events of the experience toward a unified story line that wholly captivates the customer. That is the essence of theme; all the rest simply lends support.

Harmonize Impressions with Positive Cues

While the theme forms the foundation, the experience must be rendered with indelible impressions. Impressions are the "takeaways" of the experience; the congruent integration of a number of impressions affect the individual and thereby fulfill the theme.

Words alone are not enough, of course. To create the desired impressions, companies must introduce cues that together affirm the nature of the desired experience to the guest. Each cue must support the theme and none should be inconsistent with it. It is the cues that trigger impressions that fulfill the theme in the customer's mind.

Lewis Carbone, president of the Experience Engineering Company in Bloomington, Minn., developed a methodology for "engineering" preference-creating experiences. He persuasively argues for layering on a limited number of impressions, or "clues" as he calls them, "that are sufficiently remarkable to be registered and remembered for some time, without being abrasive." Carbone divides these into "mechanics" and "humanics," or what might be called the inanimate and the animate. The former are the sights, smells, tastes, sounds, and textures generated by things—for example, landscaping, graphics, scents, recorded music, handrail surfaces, and so on. In contrast, "humanics" clues emanate from people. They are engineered by defining and choreographing the desired behavior of employees involved in the customer encounter.

Eliminate Negative Cues

An experience can be unpleasant merely because some architectural feature has been overlooked, underappreciated, or uncoordinated. Inconsistent visual or aural cues can leave a customer confused or lost. Have you ever been unsure how to find your hotel room, even after the front-desk staff provided detailed directions? Better, clearer cues along the way would have enhanced your experience. Experience stagers must eliminate anything that diminishes, contradicts, or distracts from the theme.

Mix in Memorabilia

People have always purchased certain goods primarily for the memories they convey. Vacationers buy postcards to evoke treasured sights, spouses select greeting cards to celebrate important occasions, teenagers collect t-shirts to remember rock concerts. They purchase such memorabilia as tangible artifacts of the experiences they want to remember. Selling tied-in memorabilia after an experience provides one approach to extending an experience; turning items inherently part of the experience into memorabilia is another. With the proper stage setting, any business can mix memorabilia into their offerings. If service businesses like airlines, banks, grocery stores, and insurance companies find no demand for memorabilia, it's because they do not stage engaging experiences. But should these businesses offer themed experiences layered with positive cues and devoid of negative ones, their guests will want and pay for memorabilia to commemorate their experiences.

Engage the Five Senses

The sensory stimulants that accompany an experience should support and enhance its theme. The more effectively an experience engages the senses, the more memorable it will be. In most any situation, the easiest way to sensorialize a service is to add taste sensations simply by serving food and drink. Barnes & Noble found its cafes a wonderful addition to its superstores, encouraging people to spend more time in their stores and thereby increasing the likelihood they'll buy books, and more of them. Services turn into engaging experiences when layered with sensory phenomena.

Some cues heighten an experience through a single sense affected through striking simplicity. The Cleveland Bicentennial Commission spent $4 million to illuminate eight automobile and railroad bridges over the Cuyahoga River near a nightspot called The Flats. No one pays a toll to view or even cross these illuminated bridges, but the dramatically lighted structures are a prop that city managers hope will help attract tourist dollars by making a trip to downtown Cleveland a more memorable nighttime experience.

Companies that wish to stage compelling experiences should begin with the principles outlined above to explore the possibilities that lie in front of them. They must determine the experience's theme as well as the impressions that convey that theme to guests. Most experience stagers actually start by developing a list of impressions they wish guests to take away, and then creatively think about different themes or story lines that effectively bring together the impressions in one cohesive narrative. Then they winnow the impressions down to a manageable number— only and exactly those that truly denote the cogent theme. They next focus on the animate and inanimate cues that could connote each impression, following the simple guideline to accentuate the positive and eliminate the negative. How each cue affects the five senses must then be meticulously mapped out, with care taken not to overwhelm guests with too much sensory input. Finally they add memorabilia to the total mix, extending the experience in the customer's mind over time.

Of course, embracing these principles remains, for now, an art form. But those companies that figure out how to design experiences that are compelling, engaging, memorable, and rich will be leading the way into the emerging Experience Economy.

From Being *About* Something to Being *For* Somebody

15

The Ongoing Transformation of the American Museum[1]

STEPHEN E. WEIL

A T THE END OF WORLD WAR II, the American museum—not withstanding the ringing educational rhetoric with which it was originally established and occasionally maintained—had become primarily engaged in what my Washington colleague Barbara Franco once called the "salvage and warehouse business."[2] It took as its basic tasks to gather, preserve, and study the record of human and natural history. To the extent that some further benefit might be generated by providing the public with physical and intellectual access to the collections and information thus accumulated, that was simply a plus.

Fifty years later, caught up in the confluence of two powerful currents—one flowing throughout the worldwide museum community, the other specific to the United States—the American museum is being substantially reshaped. In place of an establishment-like institution focused primarily inward on the growth, care, and study of its collection, what is emerging instead is a more entrepreneurial institution that—if my own vision of its ultimate form should prove correct—will have shifted its principal focus outward to concentrate on providing a variety of primarily educational services to the public, and will measure its success in that effort by the overarching criterion of whether it is actually able to provide those services in a demonstrably effective way.

This prognostication makes no distinction between museums and museum-like institutions in terms of their funding sources, scale, or discipline. It applies equally to a large statewide historical society, a campus-based natural history museum, and a small private art gallery. The situation of the so-called private museum requires particular mention. Even the most ostensibly private of American museums—

Stephen E. Weil (1928–2005), prolific author, provocateur, and museum philosopher, was a senior scholar emeritus at the Center of Museum Studies, Smithsonian Institution. "From Being About Something to Being For Somebody" appeared in a special issue of *Daedalus, Journal of the American Academy of Arts and Sciences*, from the issue entitled *America's Museums* (Summer 1999, Vol. 128, No. 3).

through the combined effects of its own tax exemption and the charitable contribution deductions claimed by its donors—receives a substantial measure of public
support. Given the nature of that support, such private museums must inevitably be
expected not only to provide a level of public service comparable to that required
of so-called public institutions but also to maintain the standards of accountability
and transparency appropriate to such public institutions.

Among workers in the field, the response to this ongoing change in the museum's focus has been mixed. Some number—a minority, certainly—view it with
distress. They argue that the museum—if not at the height of its salvage and warehouse days, then not long thereafter—was already a mature, fully evolved, and
inherently good organization in no compelling need of further change. Particularly
troublesome, in their view, would be to tamper with the centrality of the collection—even to entertain the notion that the collection might no longer serve as the
museum's raison d'être but merely as one of its resources.

Another and far larger group of museum workers—including several contributors to this issue of *Daedalus*—is sympathetic to the museum's evolution from a
collection-based organization to a more educationally focused one but nevertheless
tends to retreat from making institutional effectiveness so exclusive a test of institutional failure or success. Characterizing the museum as analogous in some measure
to the university, they argue that the traditional museum activities of preservation
(which may include collecting), interpretation (which may include exhibiting),
and, above all, scholarly inquiry are not merely instrumental steps toward an ultimately external outcome but are activities that should also be valued in their own
right—as ends as well as means. From that moderate position, they nevertheless
share with this author the vision of an emerging new museum model—a transformed and redirected institution that can, through its public service orientation,
use its very special competencies in dealing with objects to contribute positively
to the quality of individual human lives and to enhance the well-being of human
communities. Acknowledgedly vague as those purposes may at first appear, so multifarious are the potential outcomes of which this emerging museum is capable that
to be any more specific than "quality of life" or "communal well-being" would be
unnecessarily exclusive.

Finally, at the other extreme, are those museum workers who question whether
the museum truly is an inherently good organization (or whether it has any inherent qualities at all) and whether the traditional museum activities of preservation,
interpretation, and scholarship have any real value in a museum context apart from
their capacity to contribute to an outcome external to the museum itself. Rejecting any analogy with a university, they argue that museum work might better be
understood instead as a basically value-neutral technology and the museum itself as
neither more nor less than a highly adaptable instrument that can be employed for
a wide range of purposes.

This essay considers the American museum from this last point of view, both
examining the currents that now press against it as well as suggesting several pos-

sibly unanticipated consequences that may well follow in the wake of those currents. It is based on the twin premises that, first, those pressures now reshaping the museum will continue unabated for the foreseeable future, and, second, that in yielding to those pressures nothing innate or vital to the museum will be lost or even compromised. As Adele Z. Silver of the Cleveland Museum of Art wisely observed some twenty years ago: "museums are inventions of men [*sic*], not inevitable, eternal, ideal, nor divine. They exist for the things we put in them, and they change as each generation chooses how to see and use those things."[3]

Part I

In a Reflection on the Recent History of Museums Written for the Fiftieth-Anniversary Issue of the UNESCO Magazine *Museum* International, Kenneth Hudson—perhaps the museum community's most astute observer—wrote:

> the most fundamental change that has affected museums during the [past] half-century . . . is the now almost universal conviction that they exist in order to serve the public. The old-style museum felt itself under no such obligation. It existed, it had a building, it had collections and a staff to look after them. It was reasonably adequately financed, and its visitors, usually not numerous, came to look, to wonder and to admire what was set before them. They were in no sense partners in the enterprise. The museum's prime responsibility was to its collections, not its visitors.[4]

Among the several factors to which Hudson points in seeking to account for this change is the enormous increase during the postwar period in both the number and the magnitude of museums. By his count, at least three-quarters of the world's currently active museums were established after 1945. In no way has the level of direct governmental assistance to these museums kept pace with that growth. In some countries it has remained stagnant; in others—the United States, for one—its vigorous growth in the 1960s and 1970s has been followed by an actual decline. The result, almost worldwide, has been the same: to change the mix in the sources of support for museums with a decrease in the proportion coming directly from governmental sources and a corresponding increase in the proportion that must be found elsewhere.

It seems clear, at the most elementary level, that the greater the degree to which a museum must rely for some portion of its support on "box office"—not merely entrance fees but also the related income streams to be derived from shop sales and other auxiliary activities—the greater will be its focus on making itself attractive to visitors. Likewise, the greater the extent to which a museum might seek corporate funding—most particularly funding for its program activities—the more important it will be that the museum can assure prospective sponsors that its programs will attract a wide audience. Under such circumstances, it should hardly be surprising that museums are increasingly conscious of what might be of interest to the public. The consequence is that museums almost everywhere have, in essence, shifted from a "selling" mode to a "marketing" one. In the selling mode, their efforts had been concentrated on convincing the public to "buy" their traditional offerings. In the marketing mode, their starting point instead is the public's own needs and interests, and their efforts are concentrated on first trying to discover and then attempting to satisfy those public needs and interests.

Hudson argues, however—and correctly, I think—that something more profound than mere box-office appeal is involved in this change of focus. He suggests that the museum's growing preoccupation with its audience may be attributable as well to the tremendous increase of professionalism within the museum community during the postwar years. The impact of that development—and, as a principal consequence, the equally tremendous growth in the scale and influence of a great variety of professional associations—should not be underestimated. The policy positions taken by those professional associations—and the insistent repetition of those policies over time—have played a particularly compelling part in shaping the mind-set and expectations of both new practitioners in the field and the larger public beyond. As the sociologists Walter W. Powell and Rebecca Friedkin point out in their analysis of the sources of change in public service organizations, beyond such changes in focus as may be attributable to changes in the sources of an organization's support, for museums, the box-office factor institutional change may frequently represent "a response to shifts in the ideology, professional standards, and cultural norms of the field or sector in which an organization is situated."[5]

That would appear to be the case for the museum. A broad range of national and local professional organizations have played important ideological roles in reshaping the American museum. Earliest among these was the Washington-based American Association of Museums (AAM), founded in 1906 as something of a parallel to the United Kingdom's Museums Association, which dates back to 1889. Narrower in focus but also with considerable impact have been the more recently established Association of Science-Technology Centers (ASTC) and the Association of Youth Museums (AYM). Of perhaps lesser consequence for the American museum—but of enormous influence elsewhere—has been the International Council of Museums (ICOM). More or less descended from the International Museums Office founded under the auspices of the League of Nations in 1927, ICOM was established in 1946 as a UNESCO- affiliated nongovernmental organization and is headquartered in Paris.

The publications and program activities of these associations amply document the degree to which, over the past several decades, they have changed their emphasis from collections and collections' care to public service. Within the AAM, for example, that shift can be directly attributed to the growing influence that museum educators have exercised over the association's public policy positions. That influence can be traced on an ascending curve beginning in June of 1973 when a group of prominent museum educators threatened to secede from the organization. In June of 1976—as a gesture of conciliation—a change in the AAM's constitution granted a committee of educators together with other disciplinary groups a role in the association's governance. With the publication of *Museums for a New Century* in 1984, education was declared to be a "primary" purpose of museums.[6] This upward curve reached its zenith in May of 1991 when the association's governing board adopted the educator-prepared position paper *Excellence and Equity* as an official statement of the association's policy.[7] Woven throughout *Excellence and Equity* are the linked propositions that a commitment to public service is "central to every museum's activities" and that "education-in the broadest sense of that word-[is] at the heart of their public service role."[8]

A similar shift of focus can be traced in the AAM's program of institutional accreditation, which was first proposed in 1968 and which became operational in 1971. In its earliest phase, accreditation was primarily concerned with how an institution cared for its collection and maintained its facilities. With the passage of time, the scope of accreditation has steadily broadened to consider not only the institutional care of collections but also, as importantly, the programmatic use of those collections. Consider the contrast between the types of concern expressed in the AAM's first accreditation handbook of 1970 and in its most recent one, published in 1997. In the 1970 publication, among the positive traits that might support a museum's accreditation were the avoidance of "crude or amateurish" exhibits, evidence that exhibit cases were dust—and vermin—proof, and a showing that the exhibits themselves were "selected to serve [some] purpose and not just [as] 'visible storage.'"[9] Regarding special exhibitions, it suggested that the better practice was to offer exhibitions that appealed to the interest of the general public and not simply to that of an "antiquarian or dilettante" audience. In the AAM's 1997 publication, the emphasis shifted entirely. Suggested areas of inquiry include whether the "museum effectively involves its audiences in developing public programs and exhibitions," whether it "effectively identifies and knows the characteristics of its existing and potential audiences," and whether it "effectively evaluates its programs and exhibitions" in terms of their audience impact.[10]

Contrasting quotations from two other AAM publications may suggest how far the rhetoric—if not yet all of the operational practices—of the museum community has evolved during this period. Those responsible for the 1968 Belmont Report—a mostly forgotten document that was once thought (wrongly, in the event) to offer an irrefutable argument for the increased federal funding of American museums—were certainly aware that "education" would prove the most likely heading under which such increased funding could be justified.[11] They nevertheless seemed reluctant to relinquish entirely the kind of old fashioned satisfaction ("pleasure and delight") that museum collections were traditionally thought to provide. "Art museums," they explained,

> aim to provide the esthetic [*sic*] and emotional pleasure which great works of art offer. This is a primary purpose of an art museum. It is assumed that a majority of the people who come regularly to art museums come to be delighted, not to be taught, or preached at, or "improved" except by the works of art themselves. An art museum, especially, is—or ought to be—a place where one goes to get refreshed.[12]

Never adequately explained in the Belmont Report was why so much re-freshment (particularly in the case of the art museum where that refreshment was disproportionately consumed by the more affluent members of society) should properly be provided at public rather than private expense.

The escalation in rhetoric is suggestive. Over three decades, what the museum might be envisioned as offering to the public has grown from mere refreshment (the museum as carbonated beverage) to education (the museum as a site for in-formal learning) to nothing short of communal empowerment (the museum as an instrument for social change). Describing the growth of museums in rural Brazilian communities seeking to discover their roots and preserve a unique history, Maria de Lourdes Horta wrote in a 1997 AAM publication:

> A museum without walls and without objects, a true virtual museum, is being born in some of those communities, which look in wonder to their own process of self-discovery and recognition. . . . For the moment, in my country, [museums] are being used in a new way, as tools for self-expression, self-recognition, and rep-resentation; as spaces of power negotiation among social forces; and as strategies for empowering people so that they are more able to decide their own destiny.[13]

ICOM, like the AAM, has put an increasing emphasis on the active public service role of museums. Going still further, however, it has advanced toward a view—similar to that from Brazil—that museums can play a particularly powerful role in bringing about social change. To some extent, that conviction has grown al-most in tandem with the number of developing countries included within its mem-bership base. Given that fact, as well as its ongoing relationship with UNESCO, ICOM's current emphasis on social activism must be understood as more than simply a passing phase. It clearly permeates virtually every aspect of ICOM, begin-ning even with its membership requirements. Unlike the AAM, which continues to use a more traditional approach that defines museums primarily in terms of their activities—to present essentially educational programs that use and interpret objects for the public—ICOM's statutes were amended in 1974 to redefine eligible mu-seums as those that have among their characteristics the purpose of serving (in an earlier iteration) "the community" or (in ICOM's current definition) "society and . . . its development."[14]

Among the clearest articulations of ICOM's evolving position was a resolu-tion adopted by the membership at its ninth General Conference in 1971. Re-jecting as "questionable" what it called the "traditional concept of the museum" with its emphasis "merely" on the possession of objects of cultural and natural heritage, the conference urged museums to undertake a complete reassessment of the needs of their publics in order that they, the museums, could "more firmly establish their educational and cultural role in the service of mankind." Rather than prescribing any monolithic approach to this task, individual museums were urged to develop programs that addressed the "particular social environment[s] in which they operated."[15]

At a meeting held in San Jose, Costa Rica, in April of 1998, organized by the AAM in collaboration with a number of ICOM's national and other commit-tees—what is referred to as the first summit of the museums of the Americas—the proposition that museums might play a useful role in social development was taken still a step further. By way of a three-tiered finding that amounted, in effect, to a syllogism, the 150 delegates representing 33 Western countries took the position that the museum was not merely a potential or desirable instrument for sustainable social advancement but, in effect, an essential one. The logic of that position went as follows:

> First, sustainable development is a process for improving the quality of life in the present and the future, promoting a balance between environment, economic growth, equity and cultural diversity, and requires the participation and empower-ment of all individuals; second, culture is the basis of sustainable development; and third (and, in effect, ergo), museums are essential in the protection and diffusion of our cultural and natural heritage.[16]

This is the first of the two currents that are today pushing the American mu-seum out of the salvage, warehouse, and soda-pop business and toward a new line of work. It is powered both by economic necessity—the box-office factor—and by the museum field's changing ideology as transmitted not only through such ma-jor professional associations as the AAM, ASTC, AYM , and ICOM but through countless smaller ones as well. It is coupled with the reality that for many of the more recently founded museums in newly populous parts of this country it will never be possible—whether because of scarcity-driven market prices, international treaties and export/import controls, or endangered species and similar legislation—to amass the kinds of in-depth and universal collections that were built many years ago by the longer-established institutions. For those older museums, public service may nevertheless be their more viable future. For younger ones, though, with neither important collections now nor any great prospect of ever acquiring these, public service may be their only future.

Part II

The second current pushing against the American museum is a local one. Its source is in the not-for-profit or so-called third sector of this country's economy, the organizational domain to which a majority of its museums belong and by which all of them are profoundly influenced. Comprised of well over one million organizations—museums account for less than 1 percent of these—and generally estimated to include something on the order of 7 percent of the nation's wealth, jobs, and economic activity, the third sector itself is in the midst of a profound change as to how it evaluates the relative funding worthiness of its constituent organizations. Increasingly, the principal emphasis of such evaluations is being put on organizational performance, on the kinds of results that an organization can actually achieve.

The genesis of this change may be found in the long-simmering sense that the managers of both governmental agencies and third-sector organizations—lacking in common the reality checks of a competitive marketplace as well as the operational discipline required to demonstrate consistent profitability—have rarely been required to apply their resources with the same effectiveness and efficiency that would be demanded of them in a for-profit context.[17] In the case of federal government agencies, the Congress's desire to assure greater effectiveness has now culminated in the Government Performance and Results Act (GPRA), which was passed with strong bipartisan support in 1993 and which will become fully effective in 2000. GPRA requires every federal agency to establish—preferably in objective, quantifiable, and measurable terms—specific performance goals for each of its programs and then to report annually to the Congress on its success in meeting those goals. For the third sector, where nothing so draconian as GPRA has yet to be proposed, this new emphasis on organizational performance nevertheless constitutes a sharp break with past practice.

Two recent events can be singled out as having further accelerated this growing emphasis on performance. One was the development of the "social enterprise" model of third-sector organizations by Professor J. Gregory Dees at Harvard Business School.[18] The other was the development and advocacy by the United Way of outcome-based evaluation as the appropriate means by which to evaluate the effectiveness of the health and human service agencies to which it provides funds.[19]

The impact of Dees's social enterprise model can best be understood by considering some of the ways in which third-sector organizations have previously been viewed. As recently as the end of World War I—a time when museums were still in their establishment stage and when survival (as contrasted with accomplishment) was widely accepted as a perfectly reasonable indicator of institutional success—the three adjectives most commonly used to describe such organizations were "philanthropic," "benevolent," and "charitable." Remarkably, none of these referred either to what those organizations actually did or to what impact they might hope or expect to make on some target audience. Their reference instead was to the high-minded motives of the individuals responsible for their establishment and support: philanthropic (from the Greek for a lover of humankind), benevolent (from the Latin for somebody wishing to do well), and charitable (from the Latin also: caritas, or with loving care). In the years since, those adjectives have largely been replaced by the terms "nonprofit" and "not-for-profit," notwithstanding the repeated criticism that the third sector is far too large and its work far too important to define it so negatively in terms of what it is not instead of positively in terms of what it is.[20]

What is particularly striking about Dees's social enterprise model is the way in which it cuts through earlier approaches to the evaluation of these third-sector institutions to concentrate directly on what might variously be called organizational outcomes, impacts, or results. In the long run, says Dees, it is those outcomes that matter—not good-will, not an accumulation of resources, not good process, and not even highly acclaimed programs, but actual outcomes, impacts, and results. In essence, those are the organization's bottom line. Thus envisioned, the social enterprise can be seen as at least partially parallel to the commercial enterprise—like it in having the achievement of a bottom line as its ultimate operational objective, yet nevertheless wholly different from it because of the way in which that bottom line is defined. The commercial enterprise pursues a quantifiable economic outcome; the social enterprise pursues a social outcome that may or may not be quantifiable but that, in any event, must certainly be ascertainable.

Dees points to a second important difference between the commercial enterprise and the social enterprise. He calls this the "social method." Whereas the commercial enterprise must rely on "explicit economic exchange relationships, contracts, and arm's-length bargains" in order to obtain resources and to distribute its product, the social enterprise operates in a different environment. At the input end, it may, to some degree, rely on the voluntary contribution of funds, goods, and/or labor. At the output end, it typically provides its services to the public either without any charge or at a price below the actual cost of producing those services. Those differences aside, however, in the social enterprise model—just as in the commercial enterprise one—the ability to achieve an intended bottom line is what distinguishes organizational success from organizational failure.

For the American museum, this is a fresh challenge. To the extent that it has ever accepted that its performance might be legitimately subject to some overall and even possibly comparative evaluation, its "worst case" scenario was that such an evaluation would, like the AAM's accreditation program, be wholly internal. What constitutes a good museum? At one time, it might have been defined in terms of the loyalty and generosity of its benefactors. At some later date, "good" might have referred to the magnitude of its resources and the excellence of its staff: a fine collection, a highly regarded and well-credentialed group of curators, an appropriately large endowment, and a substantial building. Among government-related museums, a good museum might be one that adhered to the best practices and highest professional standards in the field, one that did things "by the book." Or, and this was particularly the case during the heyday of the National Endowments for the Arts and the Humanities with their emphasis on program funding, it might be a museum whose exhibition and other programs were considered exemplary by knowledgeable colleagues who worked in peer organizations. What now seems so extraordinary—at least in retrospect—is that not one of those approaches took into the slightest account the museum's external impact on either its visitors or its community.

Curiously, a rigorous bottom-line evaluation with its primary weight on just such considerations would not really eliminate any of those other inner-directed approaches. It would simply incorporate and supersede them. For a museum to achieve a solid bottom-line result on any consistent basis, it would still need the ongoing support of generous donors; it would still need a solid spectrum of tangible and intangible resources; it would still need to establish and adhere to sound working practices; and it would still need to produce high-quality programming.

In the social enterprise model, those are all necessary but not—either in themselves or in combination—sufficient. The museum that aspires to be successful must still manage to combine those elements with whatever else may be necessary in order to render the specific public service that it itself has identified (both for itself and its supporters) as its own particular bottom line. And what, for museums, might such a bottom line be? Here, I think, the museum community can find useful guidance in the evaluation model that the United Way of America formally adopted in June of 1995. Prior to that time, the United Way had centered its evaluation process around the programs of its applicant health and human service agencies. What it determined in 1995 was that it would henceforth concentrate instead on the results of those programs, i.e., on the identifiable outcomes or impacts that those agencies were actually able to achieve through those programs.

The key concept in the United Way's newly adopted approach is "difference." To qualify for funding, the United Way's applicant agencies are called upon to demonstrate their ability to make a positive difference in the quality of individual or communal lives. A 1996 United Way program manual spells out what some of those differences might be. They are benefits or changes for individuals or populations that may be attributable to their participation in a program.

> [They] may relate to behavior, skills, knowledge, attitudes, values, condition, status, or other attributes. They are what participants know, think, or can do; or how they behave; or what their condition is, that is different following the program.[21]

There are, I think, few people working in the museum field today who doubt for a moment that museums can meet just such a standard. Museums are quintessentially places that have the potency to change what people may know or think or feel, to affect what attitudes they may adopt or display, to influence what values they form. As Harold Skramstad, president emeritus of Henry Ford Museum & Greenfield Village and an author in this issue of *Daedalus*, asked in 1996 at the Smithsonian's 150th Anniversary Symposium in Washington, unless museums can do those things—unless museums can and do play some role relative to the real problems of real people's lives—then what is the point?

In a sense, given the considerable funding that they receive both directly and indirectly from a variety of public sources, American museums have no other choice but to embrace such a role. To repeat an observation I made during a 1997 conference:

> If our museums are *not* being operated with the ultimate goal of improving the quality of people's lives, on what [other] basis might we possibly ask for public support? Not, certainly, on the grounds that we need museums in order that museum professionals might have an opportunity to develop their skills and advance their careers, or so that those of us who enjoy museum work will have a place in which to do it. Not certainly on the grounds that they provide elegant venues for openings, receptions and other glamorous social events. Nor is it likely that we could successfully argue that museums . . . deserve to be supported simply as an

established tradition, as a kind of ongoing habit, long after any good reasons to do so have ceased to be relevant or have long been forgotten.[22]

With the ongoing spread of outcome-based evaluation, however, two cautions seem in order. First, museums need to observe a certain modesty as they identify their bottom lines, lest they overstate what they can actually accomplish. Grand proclamations such as those made at the first summit of the museums of America may be important in highlighting the museum field's overall capability to contribute importantly toward social development. Nevertheless, the individual museum that declares "denting the universe" to be its bottom line may only be setting itself up for failure unless and until it can produce a perceptibly dented universe to demonstrate its accomplishment. Museum workers need to remind themselves more forcefully than they generally do that museums can wonderfully enhance and enrich individual lives, even change them, and make communities better places in which to live. Only rarely, however—and, even then, more often than not in synergy with other institutions—do they truly dent the universe.

The second caution is that museums must take care to assure that the need to assess the effectiveness of their public programs does not distort or dumb down the contents of those programs to include only what may have a verifiable or demonstrable outcome and exclude everything else. The problem is parallel to that faced by the nation's school systems with respect to nationally standardized tests. For all its promise, outcome-based evaluation—like any system—requires a wise and moderate application. Taken to an extreme, it can damage the very institutions that it was designed to benefit.

As part of the worldwide museum community, the American museum is under pressure to make public service its principal concern. Because it is also part of the American not-for-profit sector, the nature of the public service it will be expected to provide can be defined in more specific terms—it is to be through demonstrably effective programs that make a positive difference in the quality of individual and communal lives. Recast in marketing terms, the demand is that the American museum provide some verifiable added value to the lives of those it serves in exchange for their continued support. Recast in blunter terms, the museum is being told that to earn its keep requires that it be something more important than just an orderly warehouse or popular soda fountain.

Part III

Traditional wisdom holds that an organization can never change just one thing. So finely balanced are most organizations that change to any one element will ultimately require compensating and sometimes wholly unanticipated changes to many others. As the focus of the worldwide museum community continues to shift from the care and study of collections to the delivery of a public service, I want to examine at least two other aspects of American museums that may be considered ripe for compensating changes. One is the way that they are divided along disciplinary lines by the types of collections they hold—most typically art, history, and science. The other is the way they are staffed and how museum workers are trained. In both these respects, the overwhelming majority of American museums and museum training programs continue to operate as if World War II had only just ended and as if collections were still at the center of the museum's concerns.

With regard to the division of museums by discipline, let me start with an anecdote. During a visit to British Columbia in 1997, I learned of an exhibition mounted earlier that year by the Nanaimo District Museum on Vancouver Island. Entitled *Gone to the Dogs*, the exhibition not only traced the history of dogs in the community back to its pre-European roots but also took into account the various ways in which dogs—as companions and coworkers—continued to relate to the community today: from tracking predators for the Royal Canadian Mounted Police to acting as "seeing eyes" for the visually handicapped to serving as pets. In a Doggy Hall of Fame, local residents were invited to post photographs of favorite dogs together with brief typed statements as to why they thought them special. A free film series—*Dog Day Afternoons*—presented feature films about dogs. Supplementary programs addressed local dog-related businesses such as pet grooming and veterinary services and highlighted the work of the SPCA.[23] By all accounts, the exhibition was an enormous success. It brought many first-time visitors to the museum, its popularity required the museum to transfer the exhibition to another local venue and extend the closing date, and, above all, it appeared to have left behind the palpable sense of a public enriched by its recognition of a common bond. In the end, the exhibition proved not to have been so much about dogs as it was about the shared concerns and interconnectedness of a community.

Almost as striking as the novelty of that exhibition, however, was the recognition of how few communities in the United States might ever hope—notwithstanding the ease with which it might be replicated—to see a similar exhibition in their own local museums. The mission of the Nanaimo District Museum is defined by geography, not by discipline. It was established to serve the City of Nanaimo and its surrounding district. In seeking to illuminate that region's cultural heritage and link that heritage to its present-day development, no restrictions limit the range of materials that the museum can employ to illustrate such links. In the United States, the overwhelming number of museums are confined to specific disciplines. In the 1989 National Museum Survey—the most recent broad-based statistical information available—only 8.6 percent of American museums classified themselves as general museums not tied to a particular discipline.[24] If children's museums—which are generally multidisciplinary—are counted as well, the total is still barely above 15 percent.

For the remaining 85 percent of American museums, to present an exhibition such as *Gone to the Dogs* would generally be out of the question as beyond their disciplinary boundaries. When collections were at the center of a museum's focus, that kind of disciplinary exclusivity might have made a certain sense. From a managerial perspective, at least, it limited the number of such narrowly trained specialists as discipline-specific curators and conservators who had to be kept on staff. With the refocus of the museum on its public service function, however, strong arguments can be advanced for releasing the museum from this disciplinary straightjacket—most particularly in communities that have only a single museum or, at best, two. Why should those museums not try to broaden their disciplinary scope? Whatever staffing problems that might entail could readily be dealt with through collaboration with local colleges, universities, and research institutions, by outsourcing, or through the use of consultants. In the words by which James Smithson described his expectations of the institution that was to bear his name—that it be for "the increase and diffusion of knowledge"[25]—the public service-oriented museum might well conclude that, rather than pursue both these goals with equal vigor, it would make better sense to emphasize "diffusion" where the museum's unique competencies lie—and to leave the "increase" part to possibly more competent academic institutions with which it could closely collaborate.

Easing the disciplinary boundaries of museums would not be as radical a step as it might first appear. A separation into disciplines was never inherent to the museum as an institutional form. In tracing its origin back to those 16th- and 17th-century cabinets of curiosities from which it sprang, it seems clear that such a separation was a later development. The Tradescant collection, for example—ultimately to become the founding collection for the Ashmolean Museum at Oxford—comfortably combined both natural history specimens and what its first catalog of 1656 called "Artificialls"—objects that ranged from works of art, weapons, and coins to ethnographic materials and Egyptian and Roman antiquities.[26] Many continental European *wunderkammers* were similar. In the United States, the first museums—such as the one Charles Willson Peale opened in Philadelphia in 1786—held equally eclectic collections. Peale's Museum included not only portraits of American Revolutionary War military heroes but also fossils, shells, models of machinery, and wax figures of North American natives.[27] Throughout this century, the case for multidisciplinary museums has been advanced by museum practitioners as diverse in their views as John Cotton Dana in the first quarter of this century and by the proponents of the ecomuseum in more recent years.[28]

There is, moreover, ample room within contemporary museum practice to envision museums organized along other than disciplinary lines. One immediate example, of course, is the children's museum. In her 1992 survey of children's museums across the United States, Joanne Cleaver credits Michael Spock and his staff—with their revivification of the Boston Children's Museum starting in 1961—for having pioneered the idea that "the museum was for somebody rather than about something."[29] An alternative institutional form—a museum that *is* about something, but nevertheless is nondisciplinary—is the community or neighborhood museum. One well-established type is the *heimat*—or "homeland"—museum, a local institution that first began to appear throughout Germany during the latter part of the 19th century and which, after some twists and turns, still survives today.[30]

Although *heimat* museums were intended originally to document rural life and popular culture, particularly in their preindustrialized forms, the potential role of these museums in education and community development was recognized by the turn of the century. Thereafter, under the Nazi regime, it was only a short step from education to propaganda. The *heimat* museums were employed to disseminate a pseudoscientifically based message of Aryan superiority and to preach a nationalist gospel of blood and soil. Notwithstanding that dark episode, there is nevertheless something remarkably prescient of current museological thinking in these 1936 observations by a German curator writing about a *heimat*-like museum in Cologne:

> The *heimatmuseum* must not be a kingdom of the dead, a cemetery. It is made for the living; it is to the living that it must belong, and they must feel at ease there. . . . [T]he museum must help them to see the present in the mirror of the past, and the past in the mirror of the present . . . and, if it fails in that task, it becomes no more than a lifeless collection of objects.[31]

In the contrasting attitudes that German museum workers take toward its postwar continuation, the *heimat* museum can be seen as providing a litmus test by which to separate those who still believe in the primacy of collections from those who now see the museum primarily in terms of public service. Some German colleagues dismiss the contemporary *heimat* museum as beyond the boundaries of the field because, in addition to holding objects, it also serves as an active cultural and social center. For exactly that same reason, other German colleagues consider it to be an especially valuable and viable kind of museum. Outside of Germany, the *heimat* concept has taken on a life of its own. With its emphasis on everyday life and ordinary objects, for example, the Museum of London—which opened in 1976, and which Kenneth Hudson has acknowledged to be "one of the finest city-biography museums in the world"[32]—might simply be seen as the *heimat* museum writ large.

With regard to neighborhood museums, perhaps the best-known model in the United States is the Anacostia Neighborhood Museum, opened by the Smithsonian Institution in 1967. As an institutional type, the neighborhood museum was described by the late John R. Kinard, Anacostia's founding director:

> [It] encompasses the life of the people of the neighborhood—people who are vitally concerned about who they are, where they came from, what they have accomplished, their values and their most pressing needs. Through the various media of its exhibits the museum reflects the priorities already determined by neighborhood people and other community agencies and is, thereby, able to present the issues that demand attention.[33]

Just as few American museums might have had the flexibility to mount the Nanaimo Museum's *Gone to the Dogs*, few might have had the inclination to undertake

so bold and neighborhood specific an exhibition as The Rat: Man's Invited Afflic-
tion—an early Anacostia project generated by local children and the concern they
expressed about the problem of rat infestation in their neighborhood.

Kinard later wrote that it was the *Rat* exhibition that convinced him and his
staff that the museum could no longer afford to deal only with life in the past. Its
exhibitions, he said, "must have relevance to present-day problems that affect the
quality of life here and now. . . . "[34] That conviction notwithstanding, the museum's focus on its immediate neighborhood was eventually to change. Scarcely
more than a decade after the founding of the museum, Anacostia's Board of Trustees adopted a new mission statement pursuant to which it was to offer a more
generalized—but still multidisciplinary program dealing with African American
history, art, and culture.[35] In essence, it was now to be a community rather than
a neighborhood museum with the understanding that the community it served
was to be a national one. In 1987, two years before Kinard's death, the Anacostia
Museum officially dropped the description "neighborhood" from its name and
moved from its first site in a converted movie theater to a new purpose-built facility in a nearby park. In recent years, with additional space at its disposal, its name
was changed again—this time to the Anacostia Museum and Center for African
American History and Culture.

In general, neighborhood museums—following the original Anacostia Model—
have primarily been considered in connection with economically depressed inner-
city or similar locations. There appears to be no reason, though, why their use
should be so limited. One possible sign of the wider application of the neighborhood museum concept—particularly in its concentration on contemporary issues
of genuine concern to its constituents—is the remarkable metamorphosis that has
occurred over the past several years at the Strong Museum in Rochester, New
York. Founded as a salvage and warehouse museum almost by default—Margaret
Woodbury Strong, its patroness, left it more than three hundred thousand objects
after her death in 1969, nearly twenty-seven thousand of them dolls—the museum,
several decades into its life and after extensive and even painful consultation with
its community, determined to change its original focus and to become instead a
museum that had special appeal to local families.

From its previous emphasis on life in the northeast prior to 1940—a concentration supported well by Mrs. Strong's collection—it has turned instead to what
its director calls "history that informs civic discourse about contemporary issues."
Since 1992, the topics examined by its exhibition program have included the Cold
War, AIDS, bereavement, racism, drug abuse, and health care. Most recently, it
has entered into joint ventures with the Children's Television Workshop for an
exhibition built around *Sesame Street*[36] and with the Rochester public library system
to integrate a branch library into the museum.

Some observers argue that museums can only achieve this kind of organizational
breadth through the sacrifice of the depth with which they were previously able to
address a narrower range of subjects. Others—my Smithsonian colleague Robert

D. Sullivan, for one—respond that, whether or not museums are or ever were the most appropriate places for learning in depth, the reality is that an emerging electronic information environment is rapidly reshaping how information is distributed and that breadth-based learning, as typified by the Internet's capacity to provide infinitely branched linkages, will be its hallmark. "In the same way," Sullivan says,

> that the printed word as a medium of diffusion encouraged linear, sequential, and vertical ways of thinking, the Internet encourages non-linear, non-sequential, horizontal ways of thinking and connecting knowledge. The instantaneous horizontal connectivity of the Internet collapses time and space and evaporates and/or challenges all efforts by information and knowledge rich institutions to remain isolated, fragmented, walled chambers.[37]

The abandonment by the American museum—certainly a "knowledge-rich" institution—of its old scavenger/warehouse business would seem fully synchronous with such a change. All the same, though, many in the American museum community—and not merely the moderates of whom I spoke earlier would be very reluctant to see museums lose their capacity to deal with knowledge in depth as well as breadth.

Part IV

The second unintended consequence of the American museum's shift in its central focus away from the care and study of its collections involves the way museums are staffed and how museum workers are trained. Here, we enter uncharted territory. One thing, however, seems clear: tomorrow's museums cannot be operated with yesterday's skills. While museums will still require the expertise of the discipline-centered specialists who today hold many of their senior positions, the successful operation of public service museums will require that those specialists at least share these positions with museum workers of a very different orientation and expertise, museum workers who will bring to their institutions a new combination of skills and attitudes.

Along these lines, Leslie Bedford—for many years with the Boston Children's Museum and more recently associated with the Museum Leadership Education Program at the Bank Street School in New York—has recently proposed the establishment of a training institute that would prepare museum workers for careers in public programming.[38] A thoroughly trained public programmer would, in her view, be a "creative generalist" who combines a variety of specialties now found scattered both inside and outside the museum. These would include an ability to work directly with community members to assess the ways in which the museum might appropriately meet their needs, a practical knowledge of how to establish productive collaborations with other community organizations, both for-profit and not-for-profit, a solid understanding of how best to use all the myriad means—exhibitions, lectures, films, concerts, programs of formal education, and more—through which the museum may interact with the community, and a thorough knowledge of how to make appropriate use of audience research and various forms of program evaluation.

Going beyond Bedford's proposal, the fourth of these skills—knowing how to make appropriate use of audience research and various forms of program evaluation—ought to be in the curricula of museum training programs at every level. In some instances, its current neglect—particularly in the case of management training—may in part be due to the tangency of such programs with graduate schools of business. In the for-profit sphere, where at least short-term success or failure can be determined from financial and other periodic reports, evaluation simply does not perform the same critical function of measuring effectiveness and distinguishing success from failure that it does among governmental agencies and not-for-profit organizations.

Critical to understand here is the changing standard of not-for-profit accountability. As effectiveness becomes more firmly established throughout the third sector as the overarching criterion of institutional success, accountability will eventually boil down to a single hard-nosed question: is this institution demonstrably using the resources entrusted to it to achieve what it said it intended to achieve when it requested and was given those resources? In contradistinction to what he calls "negative accountability"—being able to show that no financial improprieties have occurred and that all of an institution's funds can properly be accounted for—Peter Swords of the Nonprofit Coordinating Committee of New York has referred to this enhanced standard as "positive accountability": being able to show that the resources entrusted to an institution were in demonstrable fact used to accomplish its intended purpose.[39] In such an environment, an organization without the capacity to monitor its outcomes on a regular and credible basis—unable, that is, to render a positive account of its activities—may no longer be fundable. Nor will meeting such a requirement simply be a matter of appropriate staffing. It will also be a matter of budget. Monitoring program impacts is costly, but it will no more be a dispensable frill tomorrow than filing tax returns or tending to workplace safety are today.

For museums particularly, the work that needs to be done here is daunting. In many instances it may start with something so basic as getting a museum's leadership to articulate just what it is that it hopes or expects its institution to accomplish. That so many museums continue today to be so unfocused about their purpose—avoiding any reference to outcomes at all and/or mistakenly defining them in terms of organizationally controllable outputs—is only the beginning of the problem. Compounding it further is, first, that the range of potential museum outcomes—educational, experiential, recreational, and social—is so extraordinarily wide and, second, that the achievement of those outcomes may be far more difficult to ascertain than are the frequently quantifiable results that can be achieved by health and human-service agencies.

On occasion, museums may provide anecdotally recoverable and even life-transforming "Oh Wow!!" experiences.[40] Most often, however, the impact of museums on their communities—on their visitors and nonvisitors alike—is subtle, indirect, frequently cumulative over time, and often intertwined with the impact of such other sources of formal and informal educational experiences as schools, religious bodies, and various social and affinity groups. Museums must not only educate themselves as to how their impact can be captured and described; they must also educate those to whom they are accountable as to what may and may not be possible in rendering their accounts. In no way, however, do these complexities make evaluation any less essential. On the contrary; because the value that the museum can add to a community's well-being may not be nearly so self-evident as that provided by an emergency room or a children's shelter, credible evaluation will be all the more critical to the museum's survival.

At the level of institutional leadership, the most important new skill of all will be the ability to envision how the community's ongoing and/or emerging needs in all their dimensions—physical, psychological, economic, and social—might potentially be served by the museum's very particular competencies. Given its tremendous technical facility in assembling, displaying, and interpreting objects—and given moreover the enormous power that the well-interpreted display of those objects may have to affect what and how people think or know or feel—what can the museum contribute? Can it be a successful advocate for environmentally sound public policies? In what ways might it help the community to achieve or maintain social stability? In what ways might it energize and release the imaginative power of its individual citizens? Can it serve as a site for strengthening family and/or other personal ties? Can it trigger the desire of individuals for further education or training? Inspire them toward proficiency in the creative arts or the sciences? For the newly reshaped American museum fully to achieve its public service objectives, though, even those new skills may not be sufficient. Needed as well may be some attitudinal changes—two in particular. First, museum workers generally must learn to relax their expectations as to why the public visits their institutions and what it may take away from those visits. Exhibition curators, for example, may sometimes imagine a far greater congruence than is really the case between the intensity with which they have prepared an exhibition and the interest that the general public may take in the educational content of that exhibition. The public is not a monolith. It comes to museums for many different reasons and it gets many different things out of that experience.

In *Speak to My Heart*, an exhibition opened by the Anacostia Museum and Center for African American History and Culture in 1998, a label text described the community role of the contemporary African American church as being, among other things, "A safe place to be . . . a haven from the stressful workaday world, a place for personal growth and community nurture, and an outlet for the development and use of natural talents." How pertinent might such a description be to the museum? Is the museum only important as a place in which to receive the authorized curatorial word, or might it have some other legitimate uses as well? [41] That so many different visitors may choose to use the museum in so many different ways should not matter. That it is so potentially open-textured as a destination, so adaptable to a variety of public uses should not—at least in the emerging and visitor-centered museum—be regarded as a defect. Rather, it should be understood as one of its greater glories.

The other attitude in need of change involves the museum's relationship to the community. The emerging public service oriented museum must see itself not as a cause but as an instrument. In some considerable measure, the cost of maintaining that instrument is paid by the community; by direct community support, by the community's forbearance from collecting real estate, water, sewer, and other local taxes, by the considerable portion of every private tax-deductible contribution that constitutes an indirect public subsidy from the community. For that reason alone, it might be argued, the community is legitimately entitled to have some choice—not the only choice, but some choice—in determining just how that instrument is to be used.

In the emerging museum, responsiveness to the community—not an indiscriminate responsiveness, certainly, but a responsiveness consistent with the museum's public service obligations and with the professional standards of its field—must be understood not as a surrender but, quite literally, as a fulfillment. The opportunity to be of profound service—the opportunity that museums truly have to use their competencies in collecting, preserving, studying, and interpreting objects to enrich the quality of individual lives and to enhance their community's well-being—must certainly out dazzle any satisfactions that the old salvage, warehouse, or soda-pop business could ever have possibly offered.

Notes

1. Notwithstanding that museums throughout all of the Americas might appropriately be so designated, the phrases "American museum" and "American museums" as used in this essay are intended to refer solely to museums in the United States.

2. Barbara Franco is director of The Historical Society of Washington, D.C. Her observation was made in conversation with the author, June 1998.

3. Barbara Y. Newsom and Adele Z. Silver, eds., *The Art Museum as Educator: A Collection of Studies as Guides to Practice and Policy.* (Berkeley: University of California Press, 1978, 13).

4. Kenneth Hudson, "The Museum Refuses to Stand Still," *Museum International* 197 (1998): 43.

5. Walter W. Powell and Rebecca Friedkin, "Organizational Change in Nonprofit Organizations," in Walter W. Powell, ed., *The Nonprofit Sector: A Research Handbook.* (New Haven, CT.: Yale University Press, 1987, 181).

6. American Association of Museums, *Museums for a New Century: A Report of the Commission on Museums for a New Century.* (Washington, DC: American Association of Museums, 1984).

7. American Association of Museums, *Excellence and Equity: Education and the Public Dimension of Museums.* (Washington, DC: American Association of Museums, 1992).

8. Ibid., 7.

9. American Association of Museums, *Museum Accreditation: A Report to the Profession.* (Washington, DC: American Association of Museums, 1970).

10. American Association of Museums, *A Higher Standard: The Museum Accreditation Handbook.* (Washington, DC: American Association of Museums, 1997).

11. American Association of Museums, *America's Museums: The Belmont Report.* (Washington, DC: American Association of Museums, 1968).

12. Ibid, 2.

13. From a presentation made during the Smithsonian Institution's 150th anniversary symposium, Washington, D.C., September 5–7, 1996. The full text appears in *Museums for the New Millennium: A Symposium for the Museum Community.* (Washington, DC: Center for Museum Studies, Smithsonian Institution, and American Association of Museums, 1997). The quoted passage is reprinted in Ibid., 107–108.

14. ICOM Statutes, sec. II, art. 3.

15. *ICOM News* 71 (September 1971): 47.

16. Taken from the May 1998 interim report to the American Association of Museums' Board of Directors and the International Council of Museums' Executive Committee on the summit meeting of the museums of the Americas on the theme "Museums and Sustainable Communities," San Jose, Costa Rica, April 18, 1998.

17. See, for example, Judge Richard A. Posner's observation in *United Cancer Council vs. Commissioner of Internal Revenue,* 165 F3d 1173 (7th Cir 1999): "Charitable organizations are plagued by incentive problems. Nobody owns the rights to the profits and therefore no one has the spur to efficient performance that the lure of profits creates."

18. J. Gregory Dees's views can be found in two published Harvard Business School "notes": *Social Enterprise: Private Initiatives for the Common Good,* N9-395-116 (30 November 1994) and *Structuring Social-Purpose Ventures: From Philanthropy to Commerce,* N9-396-343 (15 April 1996).

19. For a basic description of the United Way's approach, see *Measuring Program Outcomes: A Practical Approach.* (Arlington, VA: United Way of America, 1996.)

20. Nancy R Axlerod, the former president of the National Center for Nonprofit Boards, suggested that these negative descriptions of third-sector organizations were no less inappropriate than that offered by the father who, on being asked the gender of his three children, responded that "two were boys and one was not."

21. United Way, *Measuring Program Outcomes: A Practical Approach,* 2.

22. Stephen E. Weil, keynote address to the annual meeting of the Mid-Atlantic Association of Museums, Rochester, N.Y., 13 November 1997.

23. Information about *Gone to the Dogs* and about the Nanaimo District Museum generally was kindly supplied by Debra Bodner, the museum's director/curator.

24. All figures are from the Data Report for the 1989 National Museum Survey, American Association of Museums, Washington, DC, 1992.

25. In his 1826 will through which the Smithsonian Institution was ultimately to be established, Smithson specifically mandated that it be ". . . for the increase and diffusion of knowledge among men."

26. Arthur MacGregor, "The Cabinet of Curiosities in Seventeenth-Century Britain," in Oliver Impey and Arthur MacGregor, eds., *The Origins of Museums: The Cabinet of Curiosities in Sixteenth- and Seventeenth-Century Europe.* (Oxford: Oxford University Press, 1985), 147–158.

27. Germain Bazin, *The Museum Age.* (New York: Universe Books), 1967, 242.

28. The writings of Dana (1856–1929)—beyond question this country's most original thinker about museums—have long been largely out of print. That situation should be remedied in October of 1999, when a generous selection of those writings is scheduled to be published jointly by the Newark Museum and the American Association of Museums. For a brief overview of his life, see the chapter "John Cotton Dana and The Newark Museum: The Museum of Community Service," in Edward P. Alexander, *Museum Masters: Their Museums and their Influence.* (Nashville, TN: The American Association for State and Local History, 1983). A selected bibliography of Dana's museum-related writings was published in *The Newark Museum Quarterly* (Spring/Summer 1979): 58. For a description of the ecomuseum movement, see Nancy J. Fuller, "The Museum as a Vehicle for Community Empowerment: The Ak-Chin Indian Community Ecomuseum Project," in Ivan Karp, Christine Mullin Kreamer, and Steven D. Lavine, eds., *Museums and Community: The Politics of Public Culture.* (Washington, DC: Smithsonian Institution Press, 1992), 327–365.

29. Joanne Cleaver, *Doing Children's Museums.* (Charlotte, VT: Williamson Publishing, 1992), 9.

30. For a brief history, see Andrea Hauenschild, "'*Heimatmuseen*' and New Museology," a paper delivered at the Third International Workshop on New Museology, Toten, Norway, September 14–19, 1986.

31. Quoted in Alfredo Crus-Ramirez, "The *Heimat* Museum: A Perverted Forerunner," *Museum* 48 (1985): 242–244.

32. Kenneth Hudson, *The Good Museums Guide: The Best Museums and Art Galleries in the British Isles.* (London: The Macmillan Press, 1980), 102–103.

33. John R. Kinard and Esther Nighbert, "The Anacostia Neighborhood Museum, Smithsonian Institution, Washington, D.C.," *Museum* XXIV (2) (1972): 203.

34. Ibid., 105.

35. Zora Martin-Felton and Gail S. Lowe, *A Different Drummer: John Kinard and the Anacostia Museum 1967-1989.* (Washington, DC: The Anacostia Museum, 1993), 37.

36. Scott G. Eberle and G. Rollie Adams, "Making Room for Big Bird," *History News* 51 (4) (Autumn 1996): 23–26.

37. Robert D. Sullivan is the associate director for public programs at the Smithsonian's National Museum of Natural History. The quoted language comes from "The Object in Question: Museums Caught in the Net," an unpublished essay presented at the annual meeting of the Visitor Studies Association, Washington, DC, August 7, 1998.

38. Letter to the author, December 14, 1997.

39. Peter Swords discusses this in "Form 990 as a Tool for Nonprofit Accountability," delivered at the "Governance of Nonprofit Organizations: Standards and Enforcement" conference, New York University School of Law, National Center on Philanthropy and the Law, 30-31 October 1997.

40. For a report of one such experience together with an argument that such experiences should be given greater weight in visitor studies, see Anna Kindler, "Aesthetic Development and Learning in Art Museums: A Challenge to Enjoy," *Journal of Museum Education* 22 (2 and 3) (1998): 12–15.

41. I am grateful to Camilla Boodle, a London-based museum consultant, for her suggestion that visitors may find a museum rewarding without necessarily accepting its authority. Conversation with the author, August 1998.

THE EMERGING 21ST-CENTURY IDEOLOGY

II

FUNDAMENTAL SHIFTS OCCURRING in the external and social environment will continue to impact how museum professionals think, act, and lead. The first decade of this century has already introduced unprecedented change marked by events such as 9/11, the election of the first African American president of the United States, and the severe economic downturn. The realities of issues, global interdependence, economic volatility and environmental sustainability, the explosion of social media, and demographic shifts have impacted institutions in previously unimagined ways. Add local community dynamics to this mix and every institution must balance regional and global issues, employ new thinking, and gain new skills in order to navigate successfully in these times of constant change.

Challenging existing beliefs and philosophies is essential to being able to begin the process of reenvisioning, redefining, and reinventing the museum for future survival in a way that is relevant to an evolving environment and changing population. The articles featured in this section advance the dialogue of the past century into the present with discourse on relevancy in a contemporary world, civil engagement, social responsibility, and holistic, integrated operations.

"Change and Complexity in the 21st-Century Museum," written by Lois Silverman, a museum interpretation and research consultant based in the United States, and Mark O'Neill, based in Glasgow, Scotland, adeptly outline the challenges museums must overcome to move ahead and stay relevant in contemporary times. Many of the shifts highlighted in the Reinventing the Museum Tool are referenced in this piece.

Emlyn Koster, long time president of the Liberty Science Center in Jersey City, New Jersey, and newly appointed director of the Institute of Learning Innovation, argues that museums are well suited to facilitate proactive conversations with the public that speak to contemporary events, issues, and trends in order to achieve a museum's relevancy and sustainability. In "The Relevant Museum: A Reflection on Sustainability," he introduces "relevancy progress indicators" a framework of probing questions designed to help museums increase their impact as institutions working within the parameters of their missions to engage with the public on the issues of the day.

Research and evaluation consultant, Randi Korn, eloquently conveys a new model for leaders in "A Case for Holistic Intentionality." Korn argues for the need for museums to be deliberate in clarifying an institutional philosophy, mission, and vision: thus establishing management guideposts that translate into institutional action. Korn suggests that ongoing learning and a culture of inquiry are essential ingredients in developing a relevant institution for the 21st century.

"Museum Collections, Documentation, and Shifting Knowledge Paradigms" written by Fiona Cameron, a museum professional based in Sydney, Australia, de-constructs the concept of knowledge as the new denominator of thinking around collections. Cameron unveils new models of knowledge management as a con-temporary framework for thinking about the potential of museum collections. She challenges the field to think afresh about using, accessing, and building knowledge systems for collections in the era of Wikipedia, Open Source, and social media recognizing the power of contexts for the interpretation for collections.

Jerry Podany, Senior Conservator of Antiquities at the J. Paul Getty Museum, takes the philosophy of collection stewardship to the next level in "Sustainable Stewardship: Preventive Conservation in a Changing World." Podany posits that conservation must be defined relative to contemporary issues such as climate change, the global economy, and ever increasing energy costs. He advocates that conservators embrace the responsibility of stewardship as members of an inter-related global community, addressing ever more complex issues about preserving heritage for tomorrow.

Douglas Worts, a Toronto-based museum professional, played an instrumental role in founding Leadership for Environment and Development (LEAD Canada). In "Culture and Museums in the Winds of Change: The Need for Cultural Indica-tors," Worts presents the thinking, models and methods generated by The Work-ing Group on Museums and Sustainable Communities in Canada tying cultural and institutional viability to sustainability. The Critical Assessment Framework presented at the end of the article is the tool developed for measuring the effec-tiveness of programs and activities in contributing to more sustainable and vibrant communities.

Closing out this section is the piece, "Embedding Civil Engagement" written by Graham Black, who is based at Nottingham Trent University in the United Kingdom. Of note is the fact that Black distinguishes "civil" over civic to con-note the broadest public for meaningful engagement. He advocates that museums have an obligation to empower communities and to address contemporary issues together that make a difference in the lives of its citizens.

Change and Complexity in the 21st-Century Museum

The Real Relics in Our Museums May Be the Ways We Think and Work

LOIS H. SILVERMAN AND MARK O'NEILL

16

S INCE THE 19TH CENTURY, the museum world has been characterized by simplistic oppositions in which everything is either one thing or another—a masterpiece or a minor work, an original or a reproduction, a great artist or an apprentice, this species or that. Such shorthand, colored by the tasks of taxonomy, made the world manageable 100 years ago. But while in the 20th century many fields moved from classification to analysis, museums remain dominated by 19th-century concepts of human nature.

For example, the Victorian theory that human beings are born "blank slates" on which the world imprints its meanings is the basis for many views of communication in museums, though that approach underestimates the complexity of human psychology and genetics. It isn't difficult to understand why this is so. After all, a reduction to the fundamental is handy; a sense of control of the complex is empowering. Yet it also is easy to see that this long-time approach no longer applies in the contemporary world. Professions that aim to benefit society must take the complexity of people and experience into account.

Like other fields, the museum profession seeks graspable explanations and clear theories to support and guide its practice. Over the years, many of us have flocked to lectures by such museum-friendly scholars as Howard Gardner, Mihaly Csikzentmihalyi, Bernice McCarthy, and others for useful typologies and concepts. While the work of these writers has enlightened and informed museum practice, our demanding daily schedules leave little time for deep, critical, and sustained discussion and analysis of theory. All too often, we quickly adopt a seemingly useful academic concept, bringing about minor adaptation that avoids significant change. Those professionals whose responsibilities include evaluation are able to gather

Lois H. Silverman, former professor at Indiana University Bloomington, is a scholar and museum consultant to social agencies and museums internationally. Mark O'Neill is head of museums and galleries, Glasgow City Council, Scotland. "Change and Complexity in the 21st-Century Museum" is reprinted here with permission from *Museum News*, November/December 2004. Copyright 2004, the American Association of Museums. All rights reserved.

informative data from and about visitors. But for most museum staff, the workday holds little opportunity for engaging in the development of a deeper and more complex understanding of the museum experience.

Small steps are taken in our yearly conferences, special projects, and other professional development forums; in the uncommon workplace that commits time for reading and discussion groups; and through the growing number of people writing for the professional literature. Yet despite many museum workers' enthusiastic reception of education scholar Donald Schoen's "reflective practitioner" concept—introduced and advocated in the United States in the 1980s by Mary Ellen Munley—too many museums remain noticeably uncommitted to the development of a deeper understanding of the field as a cornerstone of practice.

The stresses of sustaining a fantasy of simplicity in the 21st century have led to a rigidity in museums. Despite great strides by some institutions, much of the field still operates amid simplistic oppositions that seem more reflective of a fear of change than of a faith in tradition. In each case, two valid concepts are pitted against each other, which both denies the complexity of the underlying issue and stalls real progress. Though this approach seems to provide safety and an illusion of control, in reality the divisions it creates help foster an inaccurate, unproductive, and stifling atmosphere.

We do not advocate complexity for its own sake, but in the belief that embracing complexity might allow museums to do their best possible work. We also do not claim to know the best way to richer, deeper, more accurate understandings—that project will require the engagement of many. We do hope that spotlighting the simplistic oppositions that persist in some institutions will be a useful step toward transcending them and embracing complexity in the 21st-century museum.

Our Messages versus Their Meanings

Just as other fields struggle to understand human behavior, museums seek to explain how and why visitors experience our institutions the way they do. The key to this understanding—and to developing the most effective exhibits and programs—may well be the concept of "visitor" in the minds of those responsible for creating the museum product.

The concept may be simplistic or too subjective. It may narrowly assume that visitors are idealized versions of staff—desiring only an aesthetic experience or to learn a historical narrative. Or museum staff may have a deep intuitive empathy with visitors, which exhibition planners often do. Yet one's own subjective responses are not a reliable yardstick for the responses of all visitors—only, perhaps, those with a similar cultural background, cognitive style, and/or emotional disposition.

Visitor studies provide a perspective that can reveal the blind spots of even the most empathetic staff member. They show that the visitor is a complex being, actively experiencing and seeking a range of meaningful museum experiences. Yet our field continues to divide visitors into two categories: either they are dependent, seeking out meanings and interpretations created by museum staff, or they are autonomous, valuing their own views above all else. In short, we pit our messages against their meanings. The recent popularity of "meaning-making" and the confusion about its application to exhibits indicates that the rift is still alive and well. Accepting the notion that visitors make their own meanings, many museums attempt to link their staff's aims to visitors' experiences or cater to a wider range of cognitive styles. This often leads to a more sophisticated version of the Victorian model, in which the museum transmits and the visitor receives, rather than in any real difference in approach. We fail to account for the depth of visitors' capacities for making meaning or the role that museum objects play in that effort.

Frequently, this is expressed through misunderstandings and conflict between curators and educators. Some of the most public debates in museums have revolved around this issue. Experiments with exhibition teams, audience advocates, and exhibit developers, and the removal of entire cadres of senior curatorial staff all have been attempts to break down this polarization. While there have been some successes, the division still exists, with either curators or educators winning or the two sides maintaining an uneasy truce.

In fact, there are at least two possible outcomes to a visitor's experience—seeing a topic from a new perspective and experiencing something on personal terms. Both are respectable goals for any museum, and they may occur simultaneously or at different times. When we embrace the complexity of visitors as human beings, it soon becomes clear that people can and do welcome both expert interpretation and their own meanings. Insisting that there is a consensus in the field about the best outcome of a museum experience avoids real debate and discounts both human intelligence and the nature of human experience.

Theory versus Practice

Many museum staff are wary of abstract ideas and concepts that appear to threaten institutional traditions. Their hostility is compounded and, in part, justified by the fact that a great deal of theory is jargon-ridden, pretentious, and difficult to understand. On the other hand, some see the museum world as lacking in theoretical underpinning. But what traditionalists see as common sense is, in fact, just old theory that has been fully absorbed. Unfortunately for museums, much of that theory is now static and does not reflect a society that has changed vastly over the last 150 years. As a result, museum leaders sometimes find it difficult to articulate the value of museums or even to explain what museums are.

The museum profession is not the only field that separates theory from practice; journalism, education, and a host of other fields cast their "practitioners" and "scholars" as two distinct groups. Though practitioners often contribute field-changing concepts and scholars develop innovative exhibitions and programs, we still place them in different camps. Usually university and independent researchers develop theory, conduct research, reflect on philosophy—that is the "work" of scholarship. And it is the "work" of museum staff members to collect and preserve artifacts, design exhibitions, develop programs, raise funds, manage personnel and resources, and otherwise operate the institution. Yet adherence to this separation of tasks keeps our knowledge about museums less sophisticated and, ultimately, less useful. No theory will suffice unless it is grounded in practice, and no practice will sustain itself unless it can be understood and explained. The future health of museums requires the continued sharing of knowledge and the bridging of these boundaries.

Museum staff with practical experience and those with scholarship experience must confront each others' stereotypes and insecurities. Training programs, exchange opportunities, and sabbaticals can encourage professional development in both scholarship and practice. Each museum must think about how to become a better institution for the advancement of knowledge about the field—theory, practice, and the connections between the two.

Keepers of Culture versus Makers of Culture

Because most museums collect, preserve, and interpret artifacts, they have long defined themselves as "keepers" of culture. But the decisions museums make over what and how to collect, display, and interpret shape the very culture they profess to guard.

Implied in this opposition between "keeping" and "making" is another pervasive and powerful one: objectivity versus subjectivity. In the "keeping culture" view, museums are seen as objective recorders, gathering accurate and well-researched information and delivering it faithfully. In the "making culture" view, every choice and product made in the museum is a subjective creation of one or more people.

Even in the function of keeping culture, which aims to present only the best research and the verifiable truth, the choices of museum staff alter the product in small or large ways, and the exhibitions that result contribute to the making of culture. Hence, the museum is both a keeper and a maker of culture, a fluid interchange of two crucial purposes. As such, we should strive to recognize the subtle and not-so-subtle implications of our daily decisions; how decisions affect different groups; and what our inclusions, exclusions, and emphases communicate. By blurring the distinction between keeping and making, more compelling questions will arise, such as, why do we select some artifacts for preservation and not others? And how can we use the knowledge we have to help foster a more humane culture? Answers to such questions will make it easier to define and defend museums as cultural institutions.

Depicting Cultures: Art versus Anthropology

Objects from non-Western cultures or minority ethnic groups in Western societies usually are displayed in one of two ways. They are shown either as decontextualized works of art, displayed against as blank a background as possible, or as representative of diverse cultures, visually celebrating the life of a people through photographs and other contextual material. The aesthetic approach assimilates objects to the point of blandness, minimizing the profound differences in cultures in general and in their idea of beauty in particular. And cultural relativism—the practice of not judging other cultures and assuming their values should be respected, no matter what they are—can lead museums to portray cultures as happy families, without conflict or negative heritage.

One of the challenges facing Western museums is to display objects in ways that communicate both their visual power and their meanings to the society that produced them. But if museums move away from aesthetic or ethnographic approaches they will have to become much more critical of both Western and non-Western cultures. As world events challenge us to tackle and interpret the complexities of culture, we must examine societies' positive and negative aspects in museum displays. Such issues as contemporary slavery, female circumcision, infanticide, capital punishment, torture, and the glorification of war—often connected to objects in collections, but seldom discussed—must be addressed. To help museum professionals in this effort, a set of humanistic values should be articulated and maintained by the worldwide museum community. Perhaps the Universal Declaration of Human Rights would be a good place to start. Established after the horrors of World War II, this document—which recognizes "the inherent dignity and the equal and inalienable rights of all members of the human family"—is still a powerful challenge to both intolerance and indifference.

Dealing with the negative aspects of heritage can be dangerous—as the Royal Ontario Museum learned during its 1989 exhibition, Into the Heart of Africa, in which the institution's ironic portrayal of cultural imperialism was read literally. Visitors thought the museum agreed with the imperialistic attitudes discussed in the show. But if museums are serious about promoting the values of "civilized" societies and exploring the issues inherent in their collections—while retaining respect for their authoritative knowledge and serving as safe places for social gathering—they must develop the expertise to manage the risks.

The Collections versus the Public

In the summer 1999 issue of *Daedalus,* Stephen E. Weil characterized a fundamental change in museums since World War II as the shift "from being about something to being for somebody." Many experienced museum staff have gone through this change, often feeling that their institutions were being taken away from them.

Most discussions of the shift from an inward focus on collections to an extroverted focus on the public obscure the very essence of museums: the interaction between people and objects. With doors open, collections out, and interpretation provided, museums are about something and for somebody at the same time. They uniquely provide a variety of spaces and contexts and invite people to encounter and contemplate the tangible artifacts of life. It is from such interactions between people and objects that a multitude of meanings emerge.

The denial of the complex interaction of visitors and objects also can be found in another ongoing and futile opposition between objects speaking for themselves and objects requiring interpretation. Proponents of the former often seem to be unaware that visitors must have a vast cultural background before objects can appear to speak for themselves. On the other hand, museums dominated by graphics, text, and computers can obscure the resonance of objects. There is no easy rule for balancing both sides. If the objects cannot convey a significant part of the exhibition's story, then perhaps the museum is not a suitable medium for the topic. But if the objects can help to tell a story, they should be supported in ways that enable communication with a range of audiences. Every piece of communicative apparatus—from exhibit labels to computer terminals—should foster interaction between people and objects and direct attention to the resonance of the objects.

Learning versus Aesthetic Contemplation

A classic argument in museums often occurs between staff who think visitors want to look at uncluttered objects of beauty and staff who think visitors want to learn and need various kinds of support in that task. In fact, neither side does justice to the variety of experiences museum visitors seek. Increasing numbers of writers are documenting the many other types of visitor experiences and outcomes—such as those that are introspective (Pekarik et al., 1999) or therapeutic (Silverman, 2002)—which don't fit comfortably under the rubric of learning or appreciation. Exploring, understanding, and, above all, facilitating these experiences is vital for the next stage of museum development.

Museums always have served a range of societal and cultural functions, including preservation, collection, interpretation, social bonding, memorializing elite groups, and expressing civic pride. And visitors use museums for a range of purposes, including leisure, education, socializing, relaxation, and renewal. In recent years, museums, in collaboration with other organizations and communities, have realized additional roles for themselves, in such areas as economic regeneration, mediation, civic dialogue, entertainment, and therapy.

There is no consensus about the validity of many of these new roles, even though many have precedents in the missions of early museums. For example, the Victoria and Albert Museum, one of the world's great decorative art museums, was founded to promote design education to help Britain's economy—far from a purely aesthetic aim. It is essential to the future of the field that we clearly articulate, illustrate, and advocate the full spectrum of museum roles to government agencies, potential funders, and diverse publics.

In practical terms, some of these new roles will require radical changes in how museums use objects to present ideas, concepts, and stories. Other roles, such as making it possible for visitors to have a spiritual experience, will require only that that the display allow it to happen. For example, on the surface, the National Gallery in London's Seeing Salvation: Images of Christ in Art (February to May 2000) was thematic art history, but many visitors had a primarily spiritual or emotional experience. Exhibitions and programs often support a multitude of museum roles; how best to do so is a ripe area for further exploration and development.

Traditional Disciplines versus an Interdisciplinary Approach

That 19th-century taxonomic enterprise on which traditional museum categories are based has created boundaries that have little significance in the contemporary world. Yet many museums remain structured around history, archaeology, ethnography, art, and natural history as separate categories. As a result, museums of all types often are subject to what historian David Hackett Fischer calls "the fallacy of tunnel history." Art often is assumed only to be influenced by other art; designed objects are thought to arise only from genetic mutations of earlier objects, untouched by societal changes; and many history and technology museums depict a myth of unrelenting progress. Strict adherence to disciplinary boundaries yields interpretation and exhibitions that are far from multidimensional.

The range of stories told in museums too often is limited to narrow collection categories. For example, even broadly focused museums such as the National Museum of American History and its counterparts in Scotland and Australia do not exhibit the country's greatest art, thus excluding an important form of the nation's creativity from the national repository. Instead, each country has another national museum devoted exclusively to art; the focus, arguably, allows for great depth in interpretation. However, the separateness of these institutions precludes the broader perspectives and holistic understandings that could be gained by combining historical analysis and high aesthetics.

There are certainly technical challenges to creating museum exhibitions that are truly interdisciplinary in nature. Disciplines have noticeable differences in interpretive approach—lengthier labels in history exhibits; "hands-on" activities in children's museums and science centers; an emphasis on aesthetics in art museums. Yet some of the most engaging, refreshing, and educational exhibitions are those that merge and blend disciplinary approaches. Permanent collections such as the Newark Museum's Picturing America, which opened in May 2001, and the Brooklyn Museum's American Identities: A New Look, which opened in September 2001, are intriguing examples, as is Spectrum of Life in the American Museum of Natural History's Hall of Biodiversity—an aesthetically spectacular science display.

Restricting content and interpretive techniques to traditional categories is crippling to museums seeking to facilitate a wide range of possible outcomes. Categories imposed to make phenomena understandable also can compartmentalize and confine experience. By transcending these boundaries, museums will create many more opportunities for engaging visitors, staff, and volunteers with the more complex interconnections of life.

Museums as Learning Institutions: Best Practices versus Innovation

Museums may be sites of expert knowledge, but they often seem to have difficulty adopting new ways of working and communicating. When experts learn, they usually are focused on adding incrementally to their existing stock of knowledge, assimilating changes in matters of detail. An individual expert will not necessarily find learning as a member of an organization easy or even possible. But lest we be a hypocritical profession, museums must be learning institutions— for staff as well as visitors. Learning new ways of thinking is both more difficult and more meaningful than learning information.

All museums have room for improvement. Even major museums sometimes make basic technical errors. (For example, the labels in the Africa galleries in the British Museum fail to meet commonly accepted standards of legibility.) The popularity of "standards" documents in various areas of museum practice and the identification and dissemination of "best practices" are two ways in which the field is responding to its own learning needs. Showcasing effectiveness and establishing standards are clearly hallmarks of professionalization. Knowing what works is essential for success.

At the same time, reliance on best practices alone is not sufficient for a changing world; such models should be considered only steps on the way and must not become the field's new orthodoxies. The potential of museums to develop new means of expression and reach new audiences requires an openness to experimentation and risk taking. The personal and institutional commitment to trying new ideas, innovative approaches, and seemingly risky ventures is as important as the canonization of best practices.

Courage for the Future

Learning new ways of thinking, particularly those that seem to devalue staff members' stock of knowledge, can be very threatening. Preserving hard-won expertise in such circumstances requires a different kind of emotional attachment to knowledge—an ability to reconfigure it creatively and accommodate new perspectives—and doing more than converting the complex and paradoxical into simplistic oppositions. Releasing creativity and energy requires not so much intellect or insight as courage.

References

Fischer, D. H. *Historians' Fallacies: Towards a Logic of Historical Thought.* New York: Harper & Row, 1970.

O'Neill, M. The good enough visitor. In *Museums, Society, and Inequality,* ed. R. Sandell. London: Routledge, 2002.

Pekarik, A., Z. Doering, and D. Karns. Exploring satisfying experiences in museums. *Curator: The Museum Journal* 42 (2), 152–173, 1999.

Silverman, L. Of us and other things: The content and functions of talk by adult visitor pairs in an art and a history museum. Unpublished doctoral dissertation, University of Pennsylvania, Philadelphia, 1990.

———. The therapeutic potential of museums as pathways to inclusion. In *Museums, Society, and Inequality*, ed. R. Sandell. London: Routledge, 2002.

Universal Declaration of Human Rights: www.unhchr.ch/udhr.

Weil, S. "From being about something to being for somebody: the ongoing transformation of the American museum." *Daedalus* 128 (3): 229–258, 1999.

The Relevant Museum

A Reflection on Sustainability

17

EMLYN KOSTER

> *Perhaps the single most difficult task for the field in the 21st century is not to find more money, or more objects, or even more visitors, but to find the courage to embrace complexity in museums.*

— LOIS H. SILVERMAN AND MARK O'NEILL[1]

AS NEWS STORIES UNFOLD and society seeks to understand the nature and significance of events, is the museum field going to adapt to a greater role in exploring the things that profoundly matter in the world?

With its raison d'être traditionally defined by collections, the museum field's principal orientation has been toward the past. Although the number of exhibitions on contemporary subjects is growing,[2] museums would perform a more valuable public service—and uniquely so given their abundance, popularity, trustworthiness and specialized expertise—if they increased attention to the issues that confront their regions and the world, now and into the future.[3] For museums wishing and able to be concertedly relevant in these contexts, there also may well be attractive dividends in terms of institutional sustainability.

Importantly, an external orientation does not necessarily hinge on the results of public opinion surveys. Changes in the outlook of people and institutions, and new paradigms of accountability, have often been spurred by the articulation of a bold vision.

Questions Arising from a Sample of Recent Events

The terrorist attacks in the United States on September 11, 2001, motivated many museums to become community forums for therapeutic conversation, to rethink

Emlyn Koster is president and CEO, Institute for Learning Innovation, and president emeritus of Liberty Science Center in Jersey City, New Jersey. "The Relevant Museum: A Reflection on Sustainability" is excerpted here with permission from *Museum News*, May/June 2006. Copyright 2006, the American Association of Museums. All rights reserved.

their connectedness to diversity in their community, and to start a reference index of local and regional emergency contacts. Have such efforts been sustained?

The intense recent debate on natural versus divine origins of life, and in particular of human life, has been accompanied by a small number of new and touring exhibitions on evolution. Several museums with giant-screen theaters have come under pressure to solicit community input when they select films, possibly compromising the integrity of their missions. Have some filmmakers become irreversibly discouraged from pursuing bold educational goals for museum audiences? Do most museums actively avoid controversial topics?

From news of war-caused damage to cultural treasures to international controversies over the ownership of antiquities, the protocols that govern collections are changing. Through the American Association of Museums (AAM) and the International Council of Museums (ICOM), the United States has recently joined other nations in embracing the international Blue Shield program, which arose from a 1954 convention in The Hague to protect cultural property in the event of armed conflict. Certainly there is new interest in the relative rights of nations, museums and individuals with respect to artifacts. Might recent events also bring about a change in visitor expectations?

The long-term future is often not adequately considered when governments formulate policies. The world faces a daunting array of challenges in school and lifelong education, human health and environmental stewardship. Intercultural tensions are escalating, and there are outbreaks of new infectious diseases. What niche should museums occupy in such matters? Are there compelling reasons for doing less than the maximum possible? Are there differing degrees of practical or desired responses in museums of natural history, human history, art, war, science and technology, and those specifically for children? In comparison with other types of institutions, what are the relative strengths of museums as bridge-builders between various groups and the issues we all face? Do we in the museum field require a major news headline to oblige us to act? In this fast-changing world, is a new type of museum leadership philosophy emerging?

The profound changes that have lately occurred in aquariums and zoos, including an increase in conservation efforts for endangered species, offer an instructive analogue. It is now rare to see primates in small, barred concrete enclosures and fewer mammals are being trained to perform. These trends reflect a heightened sense of responsibility about the physical and mental welfare of animals in captivity. When Bengal tigers and mountain gorillas first appeared in museums, their natural populations were thriving. Today both are close to extinction. What becomes of the interpretational responsibility of museums as the contents of display cases and dioramas outlive the last breathing representatives in the wild?

An Advocacy Seldom Heeded

Ninety years ago at AAM's conference in Washington, D.C., John Cotton Dana presented a paper entitled "Increasing Usefulness of Museums."[4] He elaborated on his prescient views that museums should be "life-enhancing institutions" and that "a museum is good only insofar as it is of use." Another of Dana's unequivocal statements was on the museum's responsibility to fit the needs of its community.

The inward-looking culture that continued to prevail at museums became the focus of an AAM-commissioned critique in 1939.[5] In 1972 in Santiago and in 1989 at The Hague, ICOM declared museums to be "a powerful force for human development" and "places where the public can look for the meaning of the world around them." Looking back, we should see these more as laudable aspirations than reflections of any widespread prevailing reality.[6] The late Stephen Weil's distinguished career was dedicated to making museums matter.[7] He pointed to the attitudinal shifts during the 1970s and 1980s when educators started to gain a foothold in shaping policy and strategy. Already, AAM had posed this evocative question in one of its benchmark publications:

> How can museums—as multidimensional, socially responsible institutions with a tremendous capacity for bringing knowledge to the public and enriching all facets of the human experience—help to nurture a humane citizenry equipped to make informed choices in a democracy and to address the challenges and opportunities of an increasingly global society?[8]

At The Smithsonian Institution's 150th anniversary symposium in 1995,[9] Harold Skramstad issued this strong calling:

> In the world of the future, every institution, including a museum, must be judged on its distinctive ability to provide value to society in a way that builds on unique institutional strengths and senses unique community needs.

Stephen Weil spoke about the "success" or "failure" of museums in terms of mission advancement, not just survivability.[10] He stressed that museums need to distinguish their "outputs" from their "outcomes," defined respectively as productivity versus externally valuable productivity.

From its synthesis of museum trends, Harvard University concluded that "the field has shifted from internally focused and collection-driven organizations to externally driven and market-driven organizations with greatly broadened stakeholders."[11] But is there a significant difference in many museums between their philosophy and their results? AAM's 2002 summary of its Museums & Community Initiative envisioned museums as better citizens, ideally at the center of civic life by leading collaborative dialogues.[12] As others have emphasized,[13] the new task of outreach is not simply a matter of trying to engage the community in what the museum wants to do. Rather the aim is a wholehearted externalization of the museum's purpose and actions. This necessarily includes deeper thinking about audiences—who is visiting and who is not, and why?[14]

Relevancy and Sustainability

Relevancy, although a popular word in discourse about museums, is seldom used with the full force of its definition, which is about relating to the matters at hand.

Relevancy became a buzzword in the 1960s in relation to social concerns such as racial equality and world hunger.[15] Given that museums exist to be places for reflection and inspiration, the field is not justified in using this descriptor unless it is comfortable with and capable of tackling contemporary and consequential subject matter. Relevancy entails a comfort with controversy that, in turn, involves fostering an atmosphere where difficult questions can be broached and a variety of opinions expressed. Preferably, relevant museum experiences go beyond fostering an intellectual appreciation of their subject matter to stimulating new behaviors in their visitors.

At the close of the 20th century, Harold Skramstad expressed this view:

> Now is the time for the next great agenda of museum development in America. This agenda needs to take as its mission nothing less than to engage actively in the design and delivery of experiences that have the power to inspire and change the way people see the world and the possibility of their own lives. . . . This will not be an easy task. It will require changes in focus, organization, staffing, and funding for museums.[16]

The pursuit of relevancy can help museums achieve sustainability. The usual definition of sustainability is behavior that safeguards the well-being of future generations. It is less recognized that sustainability depends on each type of institution in society proactively doing its part now. The survival of a museum is far from guaranteed. A few have closed, many are struggling, and profound changes are afoot in the scale and interests of funding sources.

Relevancy supports sustainability in two major ways. The first is extrinsic to the museum and recognizes that a sustainable world depends upon organizations that exist for the common good. In the 1990s, "doing good and doing well" became a popular corporate phrase. The so-called Gaia philosophy is also pertinent in its contention that all organisms regulate the biosphere to the benefit of the whole. Humanity, as a strongly dominant influence on all other living things, must bear an immense share of the total responsibility.

The more intrinsic second way is articulated by the "triple bottom-line concept." This calls for improving human and environmental conditions while also safeguarding financial health.[17] Public- and private-sector funders of museums are seeking a demonstrable return on their investments. This trend comes with "making a difference" and "value-add" language. It is increasingly common to frame expectations in terms of a particular societal or environmental problem that the proposed activity seeks to alleviate.

Given the increasing demands across society for government assistance, public funding of museums would seem to require obvious benefits. Causes are becoming more numerous and funding is becoming more competitive. In a triple bottom-line context, therefore, a museum's pursuit of relevancy correlates with its eligibility for funding.

The impact that pursuing relevancy has on earned revenues is more of a mixed picture. Teachers look for museum programs to be aligned with the prevailing curriculum standards. What the broader public prefers in a museum's offerings depends on the museum's brand image and regional cultural norms.

Overcoming Inertia

There appear to be several reasons why museums have been slow to embrace John Cotton Dana's pioneering advocacy. These include the traditional focus on collections and the historical subject matter of exhibitions that feature them; a preoccupation with attendance; an aversion to controversy; private support that sustains traditional approaches; and a lack of momentum in the debate about a new paradigm for museums.

Attendance is a pervasive factor because it continues to be the most frequently used measure of a museum's external worth and a principal source of operating revenue. In boardrooms, attendance increases are widely regarded as unquestioned success and respectively decreases as worrisome, and sometimes even as failure. Generally, museums view attendance in the same way the for-profit sector views the stock market: growth builds confidence, a decline erodes confidence.

Our field's desire for record-breaking attendance is illustrated by the buzz over time-limited blockbuster exhibitions and their box-office performance.[18] In the new book *Looking Reality in the Eye: Museums and Social Responsibility*, a blockbuster is likened to an "addictive substance . . . the impact is fast and undeniable, but quickly dissolves in the quest for more, and there is never enough."[19]

Museums should aim for the largest possible audience as the fruit of their labors. The caveat, though, is that the desire to be popular must responsibly be equaled by a determination to be useful.[20] To conceive, design and offer experiences that are both engaging and worthwhile must surely be the museum field's highest aim.

Funding sources and trends are also a strong influence on how a museum thinks and operates. Especially in art and history museums, the generosity of affluent patrons can be a powerful sustaining force. On the other hand, a science center may need to rely on a more varied and entrepreneurial portfolio of earned and contributed revenues. Science centers have also been cautioned that popularity may be insufficient as "a life preserver."[21] For all museum types, government funding is generally on the decline and the increasingly competitive climate of foundation and corporate support comes with rising expectations of substantiated positive outcomes.

Transforming Consciousness

Nowadays, there are calls for community leaders to position themselves as activists, establishing and pursuing the social agenda of their organizations.[22] This parallels the conclusion of recent research into the core purpose of leadership, which incorporates Aristotle's philosophy—namely, that leadership is about the harmonious pursuit of positive consequences in the world.[23] An organization's journey from self-interest to the common good is preferably driven by a persistent desire to be outwardly beneficial. However, adverse publicity or financial pressure can also force the transformation.[24]

These principles of transformation in consciousness apply to museums pursuing increased relevancy. Certain museums, although a very small number, were founded with a socially responsible orientation because they exist on sites where heart-wrenching events occurred.[25] For all other museums, the required journey is a holistic effort that involves values, leadership, mission, positioning, partnerships, approaches, and audience.

It is essential, though, that there be a clear distinction between effectiveness and efficiency. Using the metaphor of a vehicle on a journey, efficiency is about maximizing the miles traveled per gallon without breakdowns. Effectiveness is about the value of the destination. Stephen Covey reminds us that efficiency means "doing things right" and effectiveness means "doing the right things."[26] One can also think in terms of climbing the proverbial ladder of success but the first decision must be which wall to lean the ladder against. Low efficiency undermines effectiveness and, efficient or not, a purposeless organization is inconsequential. An organization's mission, vision and strategy depends on clarity around, respectively, why does it exist?, where is it heading?, and how does it get there? In turn, this effectiveness depends on high efficiency with the organization's fuel—its intellectual, financial and physical resources.

A team at Stanford University has developed a procedural guideline for "social entrepreneurship" with five signal behaviors: (1) adopt a mission to create and sustain social value; (2) recognize and relentlessly pursue opportunities to advance that mission; (3) continuously innovate, adapt, and learn; (4) act boldly without being limited to the resources at hand; and (5) be accountable for constituency outcomes.[27]

Relevancy Progress Indicators

Whether a museum is new, renewing or simply evolving over time, this checklist can be used to monitor progress toward a goal of relevancy.

1. Is your museum's mission statement explicit about the way(s) in which the institution aspires to be of tangible social and/or environmental value?
2. Has your museum conducted market research to benchmark its optimal niche and then used the results to arrive at a distinctive brand promise that informs all of its advertising, communication, sales and development activities?
3. Does your museum periodically assess its mission in relation to changes in the external environment so as to identify better ways to direct its expertise and resources to areas of beneficial learning by the primary audience(s)?

4. Does the demographic composition of your museum's governance, staff and volunteers reflect the surrounding region and the particular nature of your institution's work?

5. Does your museum actively merge its thinking about new exhibitions, programs and outreach with external advice and review the evaluation of their impacts?

6. Does your museum actively research and pursue entrepreneurial opportunities to advance its mission?

7. Does your museum have an accountability framework measuring both internal efficiency and external effectiveness?

8. Does your museum monitor and apply research findings in self-guided and mediated learning styles, and in allied and competitive fields such as formal education and other learning experiences?

9. Are your museum's funding sources diversifying to include an increasing number of long-term, mission-aligned investors and partnerships with both the private and public sectors?

10. Does editorial coverage of your museum comment on its nature and purpose in gradually different ways? Does it perceive the museum as concerned about its usefulness as well as its popularity?

Putting Theory into Action: Museums of Various Types

To further illustrate the relevancy-driven concept, Table 17.1 provides suggestions regarding content for museums of various types. Echoing an earlier caveat, it does not suppose that relevancy-driven thinking is absent from the museum field, either in the United States or around the world. Rather, the intention here is to encourage a broader range of thinking in each museum type.

Conclusion

Each museum has a choice of overall direction and external contexts from an array of possibilities.

It is clear that the world—on local, regional and global scales—has myriad opportunities for improvement as well as challenges to try to overcome. That these correspond to the subject areas of the different types of museums that have evolved over past centuries is also clear.

Each museum can choose the degree to which it will increase its external orientation to address contemporary and future matters, both locally and globally. Museums that become more relevant are likely to attract more robust funding and therefore become more sustainable, valued institutions. There are factors at play that both encourage and discourage this proposition. Greater currency of content raises the possibility of controversy, and controversy could trigger a mood

Table 17.1.   Relevancy Content Suggestions

NATURAL HISTORY MUSEUMS	WAR MUSEUMS	CHILDREN'S MUSEUMS
Evolutionary processes, human evolution and species manipulation. Meaning and extent of human impacts on biodiversity and ecosystems. Time/space distribution of natural hazards in terms of geological process.	Causes and aims of war; what constitutes victories and losses. Postwar viewpoints of national leaders, combatants and enemy victims. Successes and failures with alternatives to armed conflict.	Field excursions to explore the care of local natural environments. Bringing together children from different socio-economic backgrounds. Understanding of body processes, lifestyle choices and peer pressures.
HUMAN HISTORY MUSEUMS	SCIENCE MUSEUMS	AQUARIUMS / ZOOS
Rise and fall of superpowers across history and profiles of their leaders. Causes of divergence of early peoples into rich and poor nations. Motivations, history and results of terrorism and peace movements.	The Industrial Revolution's spread and impact from its beginnings. A critical analysis of the proliferation of information technologies. Consumption of fossil fuels and exploration of renewable energy sources.	Impacts of human activities on habitats, species and future conditions. Exploration of natural and human causes of animal extinction. Lessons from successes and failures in environmental stewardship.
ART MUSEUMS	SCIENCE CENTERS	
Exploration of the circumstances and motivations of artists and sculptors. How art has documented and interpreted significant historical events. Examples and discussions of provenance and value assessment.	Exploration of pressing regional science and technology topics. Learning and teaching partnerships with local school systems. Experimentation with new learner-centered exhibition technologies.	

of retreat. But another, arguably more attractive perspective is that the museum profession can make an increasingly bold and supportable contribution by helping society understand and improve our collective future through different approaches and extensive collaboration. AAM's centennial is an apt moment for museums to reflect upon their choice in such matters.

Notes

1. Lois H. Silverman and Mark O'Neill, "Change and Complexity in the 21st-Century Museum," Washington, DC: Association of Museums, *Museum News,* November/December 2004, 37–43.

2. J. Davis, E. H. Gurian, and E. H. Koster, "Timeliness: A Discussion for Museums," *Curator: The Museum Journal* 2004, 46, No. 4, 353–361.

3. *Scientific American*, special issue "Crossroads for Planet Earth," September 2005, 293, No. 3.

4. William A. Peniston, ed., *The New Museum: Selected Writings by John Cotton Dana*. Washington, DC: American Association of Museums and The Newark Museum, 1999.

5. Laurence Vail Coleman, *The Museum in America: A Critical Study*. Washington, DC: American Association of Museums, 1939, 3 vols.

6. Emlyn H. Koster, "The Evolving Museum and The Human Journey" in Michel Coté and Annette Viel, eds., *Museums: Where Knowledge is Shared*. Société des musées québecois et Musée de la civilisation, 1995, 81–98.

7. Stephen E. Weil, *Making Museums Matter*. Washington, DC: Smithsonian Institution Press, 2002.

8. American Association of Museums, *Excellence and Equity—Education and the Public Dimension of Museums*. Washington, DC: American Association of Museums, 1992.

9. "Changing Public Expectations of Museums in Museums for the New Millennium," symposium for the museum community, Smithsonian Institution and American Association of Museums, Washington, DC, 1997, 33–50.

10. Stephen E. Weil, "A Success/Failure Matrix for Museums," Washington, DC: American Association of Museums, *Museum News* January/February 2005, 36–40.

11. "Museums in the United States at the Turn of the Millennium: An Industry Note," presented at Museum Governance in a New Age, conference of the U.S. Museum Trustee Association, October 4–7, 2001.

12. American Association of Museums. *Mastering Civic Engagement: A Challenge to Museums*. Washington, DC: American Association of Museums, 2002.

13. Stan Carbonne, "The Dialogic Museum," Canadian Museums Association, *Muse* 2003, 36–39.

14. John Falk, "Visitors: Who Does, Who Doesn't and Why?" Washington, DC: American Association of Museums, *Museum News* March/April 1998, 38–41.

15. http://en.wikipedia.org/wiki/Relevance.

16. Harold Skramstad, "An Agenda for American Museums in the Twenty-First Century," *Daedalus* 128, 1999, 109–128.

17. www.sustainability.com/philosophy/triple-bottom/tbl-intro.asp.

18. Robert "Mac" West. "Human Body Exhibits—Unique Educational Experience or Next Silver Bullet? Or Both?" *The Informal Learning Review*, July/August 2005, No. 73, 1–7.

19. Robert R. Janes and Gerald T. Conaty, eds. Introduction to *Looking Reality in the Eye: Museums and Social Responsibility*. Calgary, Alberta, Canada: University of Calgary Press, 2005, 1–17.

20. Peter J. Ames, "Marketing in Museums: Means or Master of the Mission?" *Curator: The Museum Journal* 32, 1989, No. l, 5–15.

21. Victoria Newhouse, "As a Life Preserver, Popularity May Not Be Enough." *New York Times*, March 7, 1999, 43 and 48.

22. Greg Parston, "Producing Social Results" in Frances Hesselbein, Marshall Goldsmith, and Richard Beckhard, eds., *The Organization of the Future*. New York: Jossey-Bass, 1997, 341–348.

23. Richard A. Barker, *On the Nature of Leadership*. Lanham, MD: University Press of America, 2002.

24. Richard Barrett, *Liberating the Corporate Soul: Building a Visionary Organization*. Burlington, MA: Butterworth-Heinemann, 1998.

25. www.sitesofconscience.org.

26. Stephen R. Covey, *The Seven Habits of Highly Effective People*. New York: Simon & Schuster, 1990.

27. J. Gregory Dees, Jed Emerson, and Peter Economy. *Enterprising Nonprofits: A Toolkit for Social Entrepreneurs*. Hoboken, NJ: Wiley, 2001.

The Case for Holistic Intentionality

18

RANDI KORN

Rationale

MANY HAVE OBSERVED AND DISCUSSED how the museum community is experiencing a paradigm shift. A century ago, the constituents of most museums were curators and the educated upper class. Today many museums want to attract a diverse public and are particularly attentive to those who live in the communities where museums reside. Similarly, a century ago the objects were museums' *raison d'être*. Today, museum professionals are writing about museums and social responsibility (Janes and Conaty 2005), museums as centers of their communities (Pitman and Hirzy 2004), and museums and relevancy (Koster 2006). Stephen Weil characterized the shift as "from being about something to being for somebody" (Weil 1999), although Lois Silverman and Mark O'Neill note that "museums are about something and for somebody at the same time" (2004, 41). Sherene Suchy makes a similar point in her book, *Leading with Passion,* where she notes that the shift in focus does not mean devaluing the collection; it means "revaluing the social relationships that are built around the collection" (2004, 101).

Within this slow-motion shift, many museums appear to be searching for themselves, presenting a range of public programs to see which ones might bolster attendance and attract new audiences while also retaining existing ones. Although this program proliferation may be an indication that museums are experimenting and taking risks, actions appear haphazard and unfocused rather than deliberate. It also appears that museums are continually searching for the next blockbuster, trying to boost their attendance in every way possible, as if attendance were the only measure of a museum's success (Janes and Conaty 2005). The problem is that—except for evaluations that examine the effectiveness of individual programs and exhibitions—museum attendance is the only measure of a museum's success, since

Randi Korn is the founding director of Randi Korn & Associates, a consulting firm that specializes in museum planning, evaluation, and research. "A Case for Holistic Intentionality" appeared in *Curator: The Museum Journal* (Vol. 50, No. 2 (April 2007), pp. 255–264). It is reprinted here by permission of John Wiley & Sons. All rights reserved.

most museums are not actively studying the impact of their museum in any other way. Several have noted that museums need new performance measures (Koster 1999; Suchy 2004; Worts 2006; Falk and Sheppard 2006). Clearly, there are economic reasons why museums focus on attendance. But as Robert Janes and Gerald Conaty note: "Attendance flows from significance and significance flows from the provision of meaning and value to one's community" (2005, 9). With so much turmoil inside the museum and so much competition outside, the museum—as institution—appears hesitant, searching for the next trend for short-term gain.

Some museum practitioners are peering beyond their institutions for answers, but to look exclusively outside the museum neglects important museum assets. History and conventional wisdom suggest that looking exclusively inside the museum will not provide answers either, at least not the right kind of answers for today's complicated environment. Museums need to refocus their ideas and balance internal assets with external needs, since the answer likely lies in how the museum builds a relationship with its public and community while at the same time valuing its material and intellectual assets. Some museums appear to be questioning their ideals and shying away from acting deliberately and with conviction. Weil sees such behavior as overwhelming:

> The work that needs to be done is daunting. In many instances it may start with something so basic as getting a museum's leadership to articulate what it hopes or expects its institution to accomplish. That so many museums continue to be so unfocused about their purpose—avoid any reference to outcomes at all. . . —is only the beginning of the problem (2002, 48).

Museums and Missions

Traditionally, a museum's mission statement represents the essence of what a museum does. For many museums, collections, exhibitions, and educational programming are mission-defining characteristics (Koster 1999). The value that museums place on mission statements is reflected in books that discuss how to approach writing such statements (Jones and Kahaner 1995; Anderson 1998). However, not everyone agrees that mission statements serve a purpose. Milton Bloch (2005) notes that mission statements are usually retrofitted to describe functions and rarely play a role in shaping the museum. The mission statement, as a declaration of the purpose of a museum, may not be at fault, but perhaps the mission statement that staff members ultimately envision does not capture the essence they feel their institution embodies. Similarly, if a mission statement does not accentuate the uniqueness of the museum, it may not be an adequate mission statement. Harold Skramstad, in his remarks during the 150th anniversary celebration of the Smithsonian, noted that mission statements do not answer the vital "so what?" question, and thus miss an important point (1996).

Weil does not discuss mission statements per se, but he often discusses institutional purpose in several of his essays published in *Making Museums Matter*. In "Museums: Can and Do They Make a Difference?"—originally written for a 1997 presentation—Weil asks what constitutes a good museum and identifies aspects of a museum that must be present in the good museum, including a clear purpose and a strong leader determined to achieve that purpose (2002). Later in the essay he accentuates Skramstad's point, saying: "The very things that make a museum good are its intent to make a positive difference in the quality of people's lives and, through its skillful use of resources and under determined leadership, its demonstrable ability to do exactly that" (2002, 73-74).

Mission statements should clarify what the museum values, reflecting what staff members feel their museum embodies and describing how they want to affect their public and community. Weil suggests that establishing a clear institutional purpose is the first step to being able to assess an institution's effectiveness, and he is partially correct. However, to begin the difficult task of institutional assessment, a mission statement, no matter how clear, does not suffice. Mission statements need a companion piece that describes, with fundamental clarity, the outcomes the museum envisions (Korn 2004). In other words, if museums' missions are going to be measured, museum leaders and their staff will have to be able to describe what such achievement looks like and what visitors and community members are doing that demonstrates success. To assess effectiveness, museum staff must write intentions that succinctly describe concepts of what they want to achieve; for survival in the 21st century, these intentions must focus on the impact staff envision for the public and the museum's community.

Intentions

Museums that strive for intentionality operate from a set of carefully crafted intentions that are derived from and reinforce the museum's mission; they define and describe what the museum wants to achieve. They reflect and describe the essence of the museum and its unique value and potential impact on its community. Most important, they represent the deepest passions of museum leadership and staff. Passion is tied to internal commitment and builds a sense of responsibility among individuals—essential ingredients for good programs (Friedman, Rothman, and Withers 2006). Intentions are a driving, motivating force throughout the museum; they build a genuine, shared vision held by everyone because they passionately express the impact the museum hopes to attain.

While intentionality may represent an ideal state of being, the Hedgehog Concept for the Social Sectors, developed by Jim Collins, presents a similar framework (2005). The basis of the Hedgehog Concept is the intersection of three interdependent circles—what you are deeply passionate about; what you are the best in the world at; what drives your resource engine—with each circle representing an element that must be realized in a successful non-profit institution. Collins notes that the work of a great organization must reflect staff members' deepest passions, embody the unique value and service the organization offers its community, and it must "attract and channel resources directed solely . . ." to their intentions and "reject resources that drive them away from the center of their three circles" (2005,

23). An institution with this new focus shifts from program proliferation to intentional programming. Weil notes, "The only activities in which the museum can legitimately engage are those intended to further its institutional purpose" (2005, 38). From Collins' perspective, such a museum is a great organization; in the context of this article, it is a museum whose departments are fully integrated and operating holistically and intentionally.

Intentions are similar to program objectives in that they are written in measurable terms. However, intentions are about the whole museum, not an individual program. They are statements that reflect the museum's aspirations as well as its pragmatic realities. The process of identifying intentions is a process of unpacking and analyzing what the mission statement means in measurable terms. In this unpacking, all staff should describe what the words and ideas in the museum's mission mean to them. Developing intentions allows all staff, guided by a strong leader who believes in striving for holistic intentionality, to find their collective conscience and determine which intentions are imperative and which intentions best represent what the museum ideally hopes to accomplish and realistically expects to achieve. Often a museum's mission is a statement describing an institution's purpose; intentions specifically describe the essence of a museum and the relevant, desirable results that a museum seeks to achieve over a period of time.

Philosophers (Crane 2005) and psychologists (May 1965) have written about intentions and intentionality, and their writings are inspirational in the context of this paper and important to cite in order to clarify meanings and to distinguish intentions from missions and objectives. Psychoanalyst Rollo May noted that "intention" has a strong relationship to "meaning," as in the legal phrase "What is the intent of the law?" (1965). The definition for "intend" in Webster's Dictionary—"to direct the mind on" and "signify, mean"—is also useful to discuss, because "to direct the mind on" also describes the philosophical underpinnings of intentionality, as intentionality refers to various mental states (Crane 2005). Tim Crane describes the history of the term in this way:

> The term derives from the Medieval Latin intention, a scholastic term for the ideas or representations of things formed by the mind. The term was revived in 1874 by Franz Brentano for "the direction of the mind on an object." Brentano's idea was that intentionality is the mark of the mental: all and only mental states are intentional. This idea, often known as Brentano's thesis, can be expressed by saying that one cannot believe, wish, or hope without believing or wishing something. Beliefs, wishes, desires, hopes, and the like are therefore often called "intentional states" (2005, 438).

The process inherent in museum staff developing intentions is important, but so are the intentions—as end products. Intentions are serious statements representing commitment and conviction. They "signify, mean." While they exist on paper, these intentions carry a force, a will, a meaning that has life—so much life, urgency, and import for the institution that the leadership and staff must move the intentions forward—with all the fervor humanly possible because the intention is so deeply important. Behind every intention there is the meaning of it and the movement towards it that is the act (May 1965). Staff members' actions become meaningful only when they are expressions of the museum's intentions. Each act tends towards something; that is, there is a deliberate quality behind every action a staff member takes to move them closer to their museum's intentions.

Balancing Internal Desires with External Needs

A museum striving for intentionality knows and respects its institutional self; it knows exactly who it is, who it wants to serve, and how it wants to serve. This museum's knowledge of its institutional self rises from its intellectual assets (staff), its material assets (collections and exhibits), and its staff members' passions. Such a museum also recognizes the audience and community in which it lives as an asset; it respects, values, and knows its audience and community very well because it collects information about visitors' experiences and the community's needs; and it uses that information to inform decisions and direct resources.

A museum striving for intentionality recognizes that it exists in an external environment and that the external environment affects its internal world; thus, such a museum is flexible and it balances internal desires and resources with its community's needs and external forces. Balancing potentially conflicting ideals, though challenging, demonstrates that the museum is true to itself and true to its audience and community. Museums that strive for intentionality embrace and respect their distinctive places in the cultural landscape and help others realize and experience their significance. If all museums were to strive for intentionality, each museum would be different from the next because each museum would clarify and celebrate its unique qualities. These museums would value innovation and responsiveness to their communities and make decisions based on the impact they envision. Museums striving for intentionality align their practices and resources to support to their core purpose, as identified in their mission statement and intentions.

From Philosophy to Practice

The need for museums to strive for intentionality, as an ideal, is grounded in three primary forces: Weil's and others' observation that (1) museums have not clarified what they hope and expect to accomplish; (2) survival in the 21st century will require museums to effectively make a difference in people's lives; and (3) museums must demonstrate their effectiveness (that they have made a difference in people's lives). What would the organizational behavior of a museum striving for intentionality look like in practice?

There are three primary characteristics that constitute intentionality:

1. Intentionality requires that a museum operates holistically and seeks active participation from all museum staff and board. Ideally, everyone's work is

connected to a museum's purpose; therefore everyone is involved in planning and delivering programs that support a museum's intentions and measuring a museum's ability to achieve its intentions. Striving for intentionality also requires a leader to inspire staff to participate in the museum's work and ensure that all the museum's practices, activities, and resources are aligned with supporting the museum's intentions.

2. Intentionality creates a culture of inquiry. A leader who believes in intentionality as an ideal state encourages staff to explore their passions, and thereby the soul of the museum. Clarification during planning is sought by responding to questions, from fellow staff and others outside the museum, that challenge everyone to investigate their own thinking when determining intentions and designing programs that support those intentions. All participants appreciate when someone asks them why their ideas are important, as this kind of systematic inquiry into "why?" allows staff to think through their ideas and in the process discover what they really care about (Friedman, Rothman, and Withers 2006; Preskill and Torres 1999). Such a leader also encourages staff to explore how programs impact the public, to course-correct existing programs, and help plan new ones. Asking questions—whether during the planning phase or evaluation phase— helps the museum maintain a spirit of enduring inquiry, a characteristic of intentionality.

3. Intentionality promotes planning and evaluation because they are interdependent processes. Intentionality allows museums to function within a continuous cycle of planning, action, and evaluation because planning and evaluation are interdependent (Conservation Company 2002; Yankey and McClellan 2003). Conducting audience research is natural to a museum living within the intentionality work cycle because a museum's intentions meld together staff members' hopes and expectations with community needs. If the museum does not regularly collect information from its constituents and examine the effects of its programs, it will never know its public or community, or whether it is achieving its desired intentions. Thus, information collected from visitors and the community serves a dual purpose: (1) in planning, information helps staff think about and write their intentions; and (2) in evaluation, information is used to indicate the degree to which intentions have been achieved. In the cycle of work, such information helps staff continuously refine intentions and subsequent program designs. The cycle of planning, action, and evaluation requires staff to regularly ask themselves: Where are we going? How will we get there? How well are we doing? Such questions build a framework for continuously examining evaluation findings against the museum's intentions and core purpose. Such questions help staff learn how they can improve their practice and their museum.

Intentionality and Learning

A museum that embraces intentionality applies a whole-organization approach to thinking about and ultimately determining its value and the desired effect of that museum on its community. Rooted in intentionality is a process framework for planning, action, and evaluation. The questions embedded in this cycle of work (such as: What do we want this program to achieve? What does success look like?) are the traditional questions that program planners should—but do not always—ask; they are the traditional questions that evaluators always ask when they participate in all phases of program planning and evaluation. That is, they are planning questions *and* evaluation questions. However, if these questions are asked at all, they are usually asked at the program level, not the institutional level. Museum staff who live within the intentionality work cycle will ask and answer questions in all institutional levels.

Museum program evaluation (including exhibitions) has helped and will continue to help practitioners understand their programs in the context of users or visitors. While the number of museums that conduct program evaluations has increased significantly over the last several decades, remarkably few studies have addressed questions about the impact of museums on communities. While program evaluation is useful for understanding the impact of a single program, it does little to inform staff about their organization. It does not help the board, museum director, and staff members understand how museum practices support the museum in achieving its mission. Program evaluation, as a process, is not at fault; its place in the organization, however, may be the source of the problem. As implied above, evaluation in museums lives in the program realm. In a museum that pursues intentionality, evaluation is elevated to the institutional realm so evaluation can serve the whole organization. However, evaluation is one process of many that live within organizations. Raising evaluation to the institutional level will not solve all organizational problems, but because evaluation is a process that involves asking probing questions in search for clarity and meaning, it may help organizations reorganize and refocus their ideas, and ultimately their work, so they revolve around their intentions. The need for museums to demonstrate organizational impact has reached a tipping point; the need for museums to refocus their organizations and work has as well.

Twenty years ago, many in the museum field observed or directly experienced a fairly significant change in how exhibitions were developed. This noteworthy change may serve as an example, albeit on a much smaller scale, of museums learning from practice and reorganizing tasks associated with their most public work: exhibitions. In the late 1980s, exhibition development in many museums changed from being a curatorial project to an interdisciplinary team project (Blackmon, LaMaster, Roberts, and Serrell 1988). For the first time, educators and evaluators, among others, were invited to work with content specialists during exhibition development. As Kathleen McLean notes, however, the team approach was neither the magic bullet nor a guarantee for excellent exhibitions (1993). Even so, exhibition practitioners learned that interdisciplinary teams of dedicated professionals allowed for rich dialogue and deliberation, as teams weighed how to best convey often complex ideas to the public. People who participate in exhibition teams find the process messy and frustrating, but also invigorating and stimulating. Lisa Roberts notes that the team approach "rang of democracy, fellowship and collaboration" (1994,6). The team approach was initiated as a strategy for creating a visitor-centered exhibition, and while no one has conducted a study to determine whether the team approach creates exhibitions that are more visitor-centered than the curator-centered approach, many would agree that interdisciplinary teams contribute to the exhibition development process and product, and many practitioners new to the field clamor to work on such exhibition teams. The team approach is still prominent in many—although not all—museums.

The same type of revolution needs to happen throughout the whole museum organization—so the museum director, educators, marketing staff, designers, curators, evaluators, and development staff can convene to discuss their museum. When discussing institutional intentions, imagine staff from all departments debating the impact they expect and hope their museum to achieve in their community. Perhaps such cross-institutional discussions happen in many museums, but this author has observed otherwise. Staff from one department have been observed confessing that they do not know what their colleagues across the hall are doing; marketing staff have been observed asking educators thoughtful questions about a decade-old program that they were hearing about for the first time; and curatorial staff in some museums (obviously those that have not adopted the team approach) have been overheard saying that they have no idea what museum educators do. Courageous and intentional leaders must dismantle departmental silos and create an integrated, collaborative environment where all staff can work and learn together.

Most practitioners would agree that they value education and learning and believe that public education is at the center of what they do. They may also agree that they desire to create opportunities where visitor learning—however it is defined—can happen. They might also identify themselves as life-long learners. Should not their institutional culture support their natural tendencies as life-long learners? Should not museum directors and all staff create an environment where all staff can learn about themselves, their values, their colleagues, their work, and their organization? Organizational learning, a much talked about idea in museums and other sectors, refers to how organizations learn (Preskill and Torres 1999). As the revolution in exhibition development has shown, interdisciplinary teams allow question-asking and an open, non-threatening dialogue to flourish. Organizational learning is dependent on individuals, as well as teams, sharing their insights, questions, and values in an ongoing systemic way, and there is evidence that the impact of learning is greater when a higher percentage of employees are involved (Preskill and Torres 1999). Peter Senge discusses "real learning" in his important book, *The Fifth Discipline*:

> Real learning gets to the heart of what it means to be human. Through learning we
> re-create ourselves. Through learning we become able to do something we never

were able to do. Through learning we re-perceive the world and our relationship to it. Through learning we extend our capacity to create, to be a part of the generative process of life (1990, 14).

Intentionality, as an ideal to strive for, will appeal to directors and practitioners who care about pursuing "real learning" and excellence in their work. Such museum practitioners will use the continual planning, action, and evaluation processes embedded in the intentionality work cycle to improve themselves as leaders, practitioners, and co-workers. At the same time, they, with their colleagues, will be improving how their organization functions.

Pursuing intentionality promotes staff learning as the museum continually explores its hopes and desires, and collects and integrates visitor experience information into its thinking and practice. In actuality, a museum will never reach its intentionality because as soon as it achieves its intentions, learning ceases. The very state of intentionality allows a museum to continuously alter its intentions to reflect new internal and external realities. Evidence of its intentionality, and thus an intentional museum, is a museum that cycles through planning, action, and evaluation. Weil, too, saw the intentionality of museums:

> If museums are to be accountable—which no longer seems a matter of choice—we will have to work together to clarify and better articulate the long-term impact and importance of the different outcomes that museums produce…. That we must do so against a confusing and constantly shifting background of changing demographic patterns, accelerating technological development, and evolving social structures does not excuse us from that effort. It simply means that we must accept the frustrating reality that what we are finally able to clarify about museums and their contributions today will almost certainly become cloudy again by tomorrow (2002, 97).

Striving for intentionality demonstrates a desire among staff to help their museum refocus its efforts amidst a very competitive external environment. Each museum must reaffirm its passions and unique value and then deliver this value while being sensitive to its visitors and responsive to its community's needs. The intentionality construct imposes a process-oriented infrastructure to help sustain museums into the future: assisting them in envisioning a purposeful mission and writing measurable intentions, and in achieving ongoing measurable impact in their communities by demonstrating the value of museums in people's lives and in communities, while offering continuous learning opportunities for all staff.

References

Anderson, G., ed. *Museum Mission Statements: Building a Distinct Identity*. Professional Practice Series, R. Adams, ed. Washington, DC: American Association of Museums, 1998.

Blackmon, C. P., T. K. LaMaster, L. C. Roberts, and B. Serrell. *Open Conversations: Strategies for Professional Development in Museums*. Chicago: Field Museum of Natural History, 1988.

Bloch, M. J. Forum: Mission as measure: Second thoughts. *Museum News* 84, No.3 (2005) (May/June): 37–41, 78–79.

Collins, J. *Why Business Thinking Is Not the Answer. Good to Great and the Social Sectors. A Monograph to Accompany Good to Great.* Boulder, CO: Jim Collins, 2005.

Conservation Company. Planning and evaluation: A powerful combination. In *Perspectives: A Newsletter for the Clients and Friends of the Conservation Company* (Fall), 2002.

Crane, T. Definition of intentionality. In *The Oxford Companion to Philosophy*, T. Honderich, ed 438. New York: Oxford University Press, 2005.

Falk, J. H., and B. Sheppard. *Thriving in the Knowledge Age: New Business Models for Museums and Other Cultural Institutions.* Lanham, MD: Altamira Press, 2006.

Friedman, V. J., J. Rothman, and W. Withers. The power of why: Engaging the goal paradox in program evaluation. *American Journal of Evaluation* 27, No. 2 (2006): 201–218.

Janes, R. R., and G. T. Conaty. *Looking Reality in the Eye: Museums and Social Responsibility.* Calgary: University of Calgary Press, 2005.

Jones, P., and L. Kahaner. *Say It and Live It: 50 Corporate Mission Statements that Hit the Mark.* New York: Doubleday, 1995.

Korn, R. Self-Portrait: First know thyself, then serve your public. *Museum News* 83, No. 1 (2004) (Jan./Feb.): 32–35, 50–52.

Koster, E. H. In search of relevance: Science centers as innovators in the evolution of museums. *Daedalus. Journal of the American Academy of Arts and Sciences* 128, No. 3 (1999): 277–296.

———. The relevant museum: A reflection on sustainability. *Museum News* (2006) (May/June): 67–70, 85–90.

May, R. Intentionality, the heart of human will. *The Journal of Humanistic Psychology* 5, No. 2 (1965): 202–209.

McLean, K. *Planning for People in Museum Exhibitions.* Washington, DC: Association of Science-Technology Centers, 1993.

Pitman, B., and E. Cochran Hirzy. *New Forums: Art Museums and Communities.* Washington, DC: American Association of Museums, 2004.

Preskill, H. S., and R.T.Torres. *Evaluative Inquiry for Learning in Organizations.* Thousand Oaks, CA: Sage Publications, 1999.

Roberts, L. C. Educators on exhibit teams: A new role, a new era. *Journal of Museum Education* 19, No. 3 (1994): 6–9.

Senge, P. M. *The Fifth Discipline: The Art and Practice of the Learning Organization.* New York: Doubleday/Currency, 1990.

Silverman, L., and M. O'Neil. 2004. Change and complexity in the twenty-first-century museum. *Museum News* 83, No. 6 (2004) (Nov./Dec.): 36–43.

Skramstad, H. Changing public expectations of museums. Paper presented at Museums for the New Millennium: A Symposium for the Museum Community, September 5–7, 1996, Washington, DC.

Suchy, S. *Leading with Passion: Change Management in the Twenty-first Century Museum.* Lanham, MD: AltaMira Press, 2004.

Weil, S. E. From being *about* something to being *for* somebody: The ongoing transformation of the American museum. *Daedalus, Journal of the American Academy of Arts and Sciences* 128, No. 3 (1999): 229–258.

———. *Making Museums Matter.* Washington, DC: Smithsonian Institution Press, 2002.

———. 2005. A success/failure matrix for museums. *Museum News* 84, No. 1 (2005): 36–40.

Worts, D. Measuring museum meaning: A critical assessment framework. *Journal of Museum Education* 31, No. 1 (2006): 41–48.

Yankey, J. A., and A. McClellan. *The Nonprofit Board's Role in Planning and Evaluation.* Washington, DC: BoardSource, 2003.

Museum Collections, Documentation, and Shifting Knowledge Paradigms 19

FIONA CAMERON

Preface

D OCUMENTATION FORMS THE BASIS in which museum collections are ascribed meaning. Practices, many of which are rooted in 19th-century empiricist modes of thinking, have not been revised at the speed that ideological, practical, and technological transformations are taking place in other areas of museum practice. At this point an opportunity exists for radical changes not only in the manner objects that are documented, but also the way they are perceived as forms of evidence. This chapter, drawing on the findings of the *Knowledge Objects* project and the writing of leading museum theorists and historians revisits the acquisition and documentation process. It proposes the incorporation of new principles, practices, and structures that acknowledge objects as polysemic entities—as holding multiple meanings: the meaning of narratives and classificatory systems as projects of cultural, disciplinary, museum, and curatorial opinion and the role of a diverse range of users in the cycle of knowledge making and the responsibilities of curators and collection managers as knowledge experts and brokers.

Introduction

Despite recent technical advances in museum collections access, most notably on the World Wide Web, a number of key issues still remain. One of the most compelling ones first raised by Thomas and Mintz (1998: 2) concerns the question of data quality. The rate that museum data have been brought online has not been reciprocated by the critical evaluation of the actual significance or utility of the data.[1] The incongruence between this current lack and the potential for significant expansion via new technology also has invoked more fundamental questions about the types of information and the epistemological foundations of that knowledge.[2]

Fiona Cameron is the senior research fellow, Museum and Cultural Heritage Studies at the Centre for Cultural Research at the University of Western Sydney. "Museum Collections, Documentation, and Shifting Knowledge Paradigms" appeared in *Collections—A Journal for Museum and Archive Professionals* (Vol. 1, No. 3, pp. 243–259) published by AltaMira Press. It is reprinted here by permission of the publisher. All rights reserved.

Media theorist Marshall McLuhan (1964) and more recently academic Paul Marty (1999) argued that information infrastructures can be viewed as organic, evolving with society or the organization they support, defining it as much as they are defined by it. Transposing this argument more specifically to a collections context and in the framework of the aforementioned issues, one might ask the following questions. How can documentation systems and practices evolve to meet the needs of contemporary knowledge paradigms and users? In what ways might they transform institutions and the way objects are understood and accessed? On the basis of these imperatives, a sustained consideration beyond technological innovation to pragmatic concerns arising from current acquisition and documentation practices and data quality is necessary. Coupled with this, a consolidated response is required to recent poststructuralist, postmodern epistemological, disciplinary, and museological debates about knowledge making and how these shifts relate to current collections documentation.

In this chapter I will draw on research findings from the *Knowledge Objects* project (an Australian Research Council funded Sesqui grant in partnership with the University of Sydney History Department and the Powerhouse Museum) to answer the aforementioned questions. This study offers fresh insights into ways that collections documentation might be reconceptualized to form new knowledge models in line with contemporary theoretical, pedagogic, and public access concerns. The findings were then used to formulate a novel and flexible multidisciplinary knowledge template to give new documentation concepts a sustainable physical form. Our research also pointed to ways these templates might be integrated into existing collections databases as well as key areas for change in museum policy, staff roles, and the tasks of acquisition and documentation.

New Knowledge Models—The Transformative Process

The transformation of databases from documentation tools to effective and sustainable "knowledge environments" starts at the documentation level. Collections management databases are the primary means in which museums document their collections. And more importantly, these tools form the starting point that museums may define and communicate the significance and heritage value of objects.[3] Prominent museological scholar Gaynor Kavanagh (1990: 10) acknowledges that it is at the individual object records that conventional and totalizing practices take root. The manner in which an object is acquired and documented will, to a large extent, determine how current and future generations understand it. Kavanagh (1990: 63) argues albeit in terms of historical research that:

> The museum databank of objects and a range of other visual material and sound records needs to be understood from a different standpoint, as much more than the raw materials of the historian's craft, but as part, a remainder and a reminder, of cultural expression and social signification where material can have multiple layers of meaning.

If Kavanagh's comments, for example, are placed within a wider disciplinary and museum collections documentation context, it becomes necessary to revise current documentation structures in line with new knowledge as well as the attitudes museum staff members hold towards objects as material evidence. Documentation revision also must take account of the way digital technologies are and could potentially promote new knowledge making possibilities (Cameron 2003). Likewise, in the internet era where potential collections information becomes available to a wide range of potential users, their information needs must also form a basis for collections documentation revision.

At this juncture, an opportunity exists to embrace the opportunity for change.[4] Drawing on some preliminary observations from the *Knowledge Objects* project, the following considerations have been enumerated as critical to the transformative process.

1. Types of information required for in-house use and for diverse and targeted user groups and how these can be streamlined into the acquisition and documentation processes.
2. Contemporary knowledge making discourses and the possibilities they offer in meaning making around collections.
3. Current trends in learning theory.
4. New and emerging technologies and tools and the opportunities they have to offer in extending the interpretive potential of collections.
5. Ways existing data and investments in the digitization of materials can be reused and configured into new relationships.
6. A critical analysis of existing acquisition, interpretive, and documentation/classification paradigms, practices, and procedures and ways they can be adapted, modified, and streamlined to meet new information needs.
7. An examination of the broader information resources in museums and how they may contribute to collections data.
8. Ways to reconcile discipline-based documentation and interpretive practices.
9. A consideration of potential returns, such as the promotion of museums and their collections, increased accessibility and visitation to the physical site, and revenue generation.
10. Resource issues.

Technological Considerations

In the digital era, knowledge about museum collections is now taking the form of a database of separate elements including media, images, sound, and texts that can be linked and navigated in a variety of ways. From a purely technological standpoint, the manner databases and narratives can work together and their potential discursive effects such as new relational paradigms enables users to link information in ways previously not possible, hence calling into question existing documentary structures. Additionally, the ability to store vast amounts of data, search, retrieve, and distribute information in space and to traverse trajectories of information in new ways sets the scene for a substantial revision of the way information is documented and linked. Furthermore, the potential to technologically liberate documentation from a standardized linear narrative descriptive format and to incorporate diverse media and create 3-D objects, visualizations, and simulations has major implications for the types of interpretive evidence gathered, recorded, digitized, and created around museum collections.

Museums and providers of collections management databases have responded to the technical possibilities digital technologies have to offer by exploring more effective ways to contextualize collections. The relational capacities of digital technologies have been harnessed in collection automation systems enabling objects to be contextualized with people, places, events, periods, classification, and multimedia content along with additional fields for the administration and description of collections.[5] Most museum websites now provide access to collections information and contextualize collections according to themes in the form of essays, quantitative data, and digital images.[6] Increasingly tools of navigation and searching employ data visualization models where contextual links and relevance relationships are shown between objects, subjects, and themes with text-based interpretive essays about the object's context, primary source materials, and media forms such as images, sound, digital video, 3-D objects, and movies.[7] These solutions, however, focus on context rather than the inherent plural meanings of collections. Information and multimedia, rather than sourced from databases, operate as a selection of items curated as an online exhibition via a web interface.

Therefore, the next challenge is to revisit the current epistemological foundations on which documentation is formulated and to consider how diverse cultural and theoretical ideas such as polysemic interpretive models (ones that recognize the inherent pluralistic meanings of objects) might revise documentation taking account of these technological potentialities.

Impact of Poststructuralist and Postmodern Paradigms

Manual card systems and collections databases have traditionally functioned as internal documents, tailored to the needs of museum registrars and curators. Collections records favor descriptions, measurements, and taxonomies. These practices are rooted in 19th-century empiricist modes of thinking where a definitive meaning of an object was deemed to lie dormant in its physical form exposed through observation, description, and measurement. Once placed in classification sets, an interpretation of an object emerges, usurping other possible meanings. According to this empiricist tradition, documentation as a process and practice is viewed as the collation of self-evident data derived from the object as source rather than a subjective form of interpretation on the part of the curator as might be argued from a postmodernist's position.[8] Underlying this is the view that object descriptive data, the "cold hard facts" such as measurements and visual form, and meaning created through subsequent interpretive text, are two distinct fields.[9] That is, the former is objective and the latter is subjective in nature. It is from these material practices that current documentation procedures derive such as disciplinary classifications, lengthy descriptions of physical attributes, anonymous statements of significance, and provenance rather than so-called interpretive text. While material collections are no longer given privileged standing as definitive sources of knowledge, legacies of older empirical ways of thinking still reside in documentation practices. This, to a degree, determines and limits the possible meanings objects might derive in a contemporary knowledge context.

Contemporary post-structuralist paradigms in knowledge creation and understanding fundamentally challenge and undermine orthodox concepts about the truth value of traditional forms of museum documentation. These approaches signify three broad theoretical positions (Lyotard 1984; Seely Brown and Duguid 2000). These are: the rejection of the existence of an inherent objective truth replaced instead by the belief in the arbitrariness of singular, authoritative interpretations; that any interpretation is seen as a construct by a given theorist/author; and that knowledge is a tradable commodity, that is not fixed or closed but constantly evolving and contextually specific.

The epistemological stance inherent in poststructuralism has important ramifications in the area of museum object documentation. The provision of standard and universal descriptive categories for objects becomes an imposition of an artificial order that fails to acknowledge the polysemy (intrinsic plurality of meaning) of objects. It calls into question the legitimacy of lengthy description as a means of collecting meaningful data about objects and the authority of museums to make statements about its collections. This approach questions the validity of all practices and methodologies that narrow down the frame of reference for object analysis and interpretation. Rather it supports a position that approaches objects from a variety of standpoints and promotes their multiple meanings.

Material culture has the potential to be interpreted in a variety of ways. Museologist Eilean Hooper-Greenhill (1992: 7) draws attention to this when she writes: "a silver teaspoon made in the 18th century in Sheffield would be classified as 'Industrial Art' in Birmingham City Museum, 'Decorative Art' at Stoke-on-Trent, 'Silver' at the Victoria and Albert Museum, and 'Industry' at Kelham Island Museum in Sheffield." An object's meaning and its classification, is not self-evident or singular, but is imposed on the object depending on the position and aims of the museum. By naming objects according to prescribed and standardized descriptive fields, object documentation systems record the induction of objects into the museum contexts and thereby reduce their array of potential meanings down to one notion of significance. The rigid structures of acquisition, documentation practices, and object records currently in place in museums are ill-suited to new ways of seeing objects as polysemic entities. That is, objects subject to perpetual fluctuations of meaning and open to interdisciplinary interpretations.

This "new" discursive position and its potential for the epistemological reworking of the role of objects in a museum documentary context was most graphically illustrated in English historian Alun Munslow's critique of social historian Arthur Marwick's book, *The New Nature of History, Knowledge, Evidence and Language.*[10] Here Munslow rejects what he terms the "reconstructionist" approach to history, whereby historical sources are empirically identified, studied, and assembled to produce an understanding of what "actually" happened in the past.[11] In other words, the reconstructionist position, based on the premise of linear and objective historical knowledge, accepts the possibility that there is some direct correspondence between the "word" of the historian (the historical text) and the world being described.[12] The reconstructionist believes that the meaning of the past lies dormant in the sources, implying also that meaning is fixed, predetermined and once activated by the historian can only manifest itself in a single unalterable form. In the museum context, objects are seen as sources of various kinds of historical information and curators (and others) fill the role of historians. Therefore, the reconstructionist approach is reflected in documentation practices that emphasize physical description and other "verifiable" details such as date, maker, technique, style, and others, and one interpretation of an object presented as a truth statement.[13]

In attempting to reposition the role and uses of historical evidence in a context where historical inquiry no longer yields conclusive knowledge of the past, Munslow advocates the acceptance of an "epistemic relativist" approach to historical sources.[14] Epistemic relativism differs from what Munslow terms "metaphysical relativism." The latter concept, first expressed by French philosopher Jacques Derrida posits that reality exists only in the mind of the individual, or that there is nothing outside the text. Munslow instead argues that epistemic relativism views knowledge of the "real" as derived through our ideas and concepts, including linguistic, spatial, cultural, and ideological compulsions.[15] As Munslow goes on to explain: "In acknowledging the sources and the weight of language as an ideologically drenched discourse, epistemic relativists do not deny there is no proximate truth in history but there is more than one way to get at it and, for that matter, represent it."[16]

Therefore, conclusive statements about objects and their use as objective "evidence" for past events are thrown into doubt. Given that object meanings from a poststructuralist/postmodern theoretical point of view are now seen as contextually specific, an object's assessment and hence its documentation should address questions such as who was involved with the object, how it was collected, who interpreted it and why, where the interpretation took place and so on.[17] Documentation must be viewed in a new way. First, the meaning and significance of an object or its history will always evade the curator to some extent. Second, meaning can never be objectified. And third, documentation must demonstrate a potential to represent a range of object meanings and relationships.[18]

Digital technologies are being harnessed to revise empiricist based forms of documentation through new discursive, relational possibilities, and the ability to store, search, and retrieve vast amounts of data and media. Technically these capabilities have die potential to emancipate museum objects from narrow cultural, disciplinary, and museum-based understandings afforded them through their relegation to particular cultural areas and institutions and to expose the nature of decision-making processes from which their meanings are ascribed. Much is yet to be done to truly engage polysemic models of interpretation. The authoring information for example, needs to engage users more actively in completing the cycle of knowledge making and expose the specific predilections that lie behind interpretive frameworks and texts.

Findings from user research undertaken as part of the *Themescaping Virtual Collections* research (Cameron 2003) supports this and suggests that the majority of user profiles take a position similar to Munslow's epistemic relativist stance. Museum collections are viewed as tools that provide interpretations at various levels and from different contextual points of view (Cameron 2003). Furthermore, users expressed a desire to exercise their democratic right to access information according to their own choices and be offered a range of opinions, explanations, resources and interpretations about museum collections (Cameron 2003). The majority of users interviewed do not accept an inherent inability to explain collections meanings but rather continue to seek authoritative and trustworthy information from museums according to a modernist paradigm albeit in a modified hyperlinked and authored form (Cameron 2003: 28). In other words, not all interpretations are seen as equal by users and museums must continue to provide reliable information based on scholarly research. Nonetheless, postmodernist fragmentation can be enjoyed through technical solutions such as mindmaps.[19] These, however, must be supported by a "knowable" framework such as chronologies and hierarchies of information in which objects can be placed and meanings made easily accessible (Cameron 2003: 26–28). Most users do not want to take full responsibility for the interpretive process.

Incorporating Theoretical Principles in Practices and Procedures

So how do we get collections documentation up to speed with current thinking, bearing in mind the potential digital technologies have to offer? Here museums are confronted with a difficult challenge. They need to provide a conceptual structure and order to disparate collections at a documentation level and acknowledge and utilize previous investments as well as engage with a growing community of users. The larger task is to bridge the gap between documentation practices and information needs that require the inclusion of modernist, poststructural, and postmodernist paradigms, and the particular social and cultural ideas posited by a diverse community of users. They need to provide authoritative information but also acknowledge the fragmentary, arbitrary, and plural nature of object interpretation. This process also needs to recognize shifts in relationships between museums and users and to allow greater interpretive freedom as a documentary practice. Given that potential user profiles are diverse and exhibit common but also divergent themes, should museums target specific audiences in terms of future acquisition and documentary practices? Whether this audience continues to be primarily curators and collection managers or includes the admission through documentation of the information needs of educators and a range of nonspecialist users is a matter for individual consideration. This decision will be dependent on the mission, priorities, and resources individual institutions deem appropriate to bring to collections documentation reform. Herein, however, I will talk in terms of general documentary principles.

Our research identified three discursive principles that need to be built into collections documentation to address current theories around knowledge making and the specific information and interpretive needs of user groups. These include:

1. The role of objects as polysemic, that is, holding plural, cross disciplinary, alternative and sometimes conflicting meanings.
2. An acknowledgment of the meaning of narratives and classifications systems as products of cultural, disciplinary, museum, and curatorial opinion.
3. In the current knowledge context where the belief in institutional authority, disciplinary privilege, and hierarchies becomes less persuasive, documentation also needs to acknowledge the role of users in the cycle of knowledge making.

Maximizing Existing and Enriched Data

At the most basic level in the creation of new "knowledge environments" there needs to be a consideration through documentation of how information such as fielded data can be structured and coded in new ways. Equally important is the manner in which museums can maximize the use of enriched data through cross-linking and filtering to different collection records. This represents a strategy to improve the interpretive potential of collections and hence the creation of polysemic knowledge models and 3-D navigation and information spaces.

Beyond Description

Recent documentation practices have witnessed a trend away from long descriptions to significance statements. Interestingly, the declining interest in description is related to a shift from a predominately empiricist documentation tradition based on the physicality of objects. Originally written to justify acquisitions to management, there needs to be a further consideration of how significance statements can be written in a compelling way for audiences. Curators need to consider the writing of text in the context of constructivist approaches to learning and to engage users in the cycle of knowledge making. This might, for example, include pointers to additional contextual sources, bibliographies, and media.

Addressing the "Concreteness" of Collections

The next task is to address issues around the concreteness of objects and their interpretations. Having said this, our research suggests that collections items and information must be considered as a growing and evolving body of knowledge rather than a definitive or quintessential set of facts. A science and technology curator at the Power house Museum noted this point and stated that "there is the realization that while writing, a curator is creating an 'artifact' of that time, place and social context."[20] So here we need to present collections and information as temporarily situated expert opinions through authoring and dating.

Additionally we also need to instill a reflexive consciousness among curators regarding the limited legitimacy and lifespan of collections information as demonstrated by the apothecary and taxonomic paradigms mentioned in the previous sections.[21] A program of collections information revision and archiving needs to be instituted as part of the documentation process.

Exposing Interpretive Frameworks

A subsequent task is to expose the epistemological/disciplinary frameworks in which objects are interpreted, to explain the fact that object interpretations change and should no longer be presented as definitive accounts carrying the ultimate authority. Our research suggests that these postmodern principles could be shown through disclaimers, authored text, and linked curatorial essays about disciplinary contexts outlining the types of information privileged in each domain and how each contributes to our understanding of collections. Furthermore, exposing the nature of museum significance assessment procedures and links to museum collecting policies acknowledges the institutions' role in knowledge making.

Promoting Plurality of Meaning

Our research also suggests that museums need to capitalize on a plurality of meaning inherent in collection items, rather than favoring one interpretation. So how can these issues and array of influences be acknowledged and dealt with in documentation? Most basically this involves the rethinking of the relationships and meanings of collections in tandem with an understanding of the limitations of current approaches to knowledge making. The specific conceptual and disciplinary frameworks of art history, social history, science, decorative arts, anthropology, and the institutional tradition curators work within, as well as the individual standpoints of museum staff, determine the types of questions asked of objects. These establish the types of information documented and privileged in significance statements and the subsequent values and meanings ascribed to individual collection items, thereby narrowing their potential interpretive possibilities.

For example, a social historian may focus on the use, context, and the personal significance of an object to the owner or user. In contrast, a decorative arts curator may note its form, function, and material, how it fits into a chronological stylistic framework, the artist/maker, and its history of ownership. A technology curator on the other hand could look at the same object in terms of how it is manufactured, its degree of technological innovation, function, and how it works.

Our research also revealed the personal and idiosyncratic predilections, goals, and interests an individual curator may consciously and tacitly bring to bear on the analysis and documentation of objects.[22] Here the task of object interpretation is exposed as a dialogic and organic process where various influences come into play and intermingle.[23] One participant in the decorative arts focus group discussion at the Powerhouse Museum succinctly espoused the feelings of others by stating that "curators cast interpretations from different backgrounds and some objects have more to offer."[24]

Although many curators we interviewed were aware of the current discursive contexts of objects, appreciated the merits of other disciplinary interpretive frameworks, and experimented with integrating themes in exhibitions, this process has been slow to be applied to documentation. So how do we reconcile these information needs, revise the types of questions asked of collections, contribute to their broader understanding, and create a useful resource? These issues could be resolved through collaborations between departments/curators to discuss potential meanings and the significance of selected objects, and writing joint significance statements to expose a range of meanings and opinions across disciplinary areas. In procedural terms this involves pulling frameworks together while expanding the potential meanings of objects.

Our research also raised a very important point about the problem of "conceptual fit" between existing object meanings and classification schemes highlighting the difficulty of prescribing categories that can be applied universally (Cameron 2000). This was particularly obvious when we investigated issues around access to and the documentation of Maori and Aboriginal collections.[25] Currently institutions require the user to accept the institutional way of organizing information and the meanings ascribed to objects. Here is a strong case for the integration into documentation of alternative classification systems that acknowledge indigenous knowledge models.

Enabling a Polysemic and Shared Interpretive Approach

So how can a polysemic and shared interpretive approach be applied in documentation? Here a new polysemic knowledge model invites the opportunity to create categories and associated linkages through documentation that could potentially connect objects with a whole range of cultural, social, historical, technological, artistic, and disciplinary contexts. In conceptual terms, this involves the virtual layering of meanings and contexts of objects that can subsequently be configured and navigated in different ways in a live environment according to the individual interests of users. This could involve presenting information according to user profiles, age groups, and abilities as well as narrative and object-centered histories enabling multiple alternative interpretations (Cameron 2003). Links to related resources such as primary source materials, bibliographies, websites of current exhibitions, and a provision for user interpretations further elucidate knowledge making options. Establishing relationships between objects on the basis of extended fields and additional ontologies could form the basis of retrieval methods. However, developing concepts on how this metadata is to be handled and standardized will continue to be an important issue.

Extending Thesauri, Nomenclatures, and Glossaries

Our research also revealed that problems of conceptual structure and naming within existing thesauri and nomenclatures need to be dealt with for documentation purposes. Furthermore, ensuring greater intellectual access to collections and enriched data means extending existing thesauri, nomenclatures and glossaries to reflect the plural meanings of objects. Most basically, this needs to occur during the documentation process in order to create a greater range of search and naming options thus contributing to and expanding interpretive options.

Use of Non-text-based Information

The need to address the emerging interest in the contextualization of objects and their nontextual representation in supporting a polysemic approach to collections interpretation emerged through both *Themescaping* and *Knowledge Objects* research. Specifically, user research suggests a trend away from detailed descriptions and primary text-based provenanced information to a greater use of non-text-based evidence such as video, audio, and 3-D simulations in supporting cinematic type experiences (Cameron 2003: 24). Here we need to consider how objects can be documented at acquisition, especially those deemed the most significant, in ways that capture a range of information. For example, this could include the digital recording of significance through comments by makers, users, and donors, the documentation and recording of the pre-museum contexts of objects, the digital rendering of objects in 3-D, and object movies.

Drawing on the Wider Information
Assets to Best Advantage

In Kevin Donovan's formative paper on the future of collections databases, he convincingly argued for the building of knowledge bases that draw together the wider information assets of a museum into a centralized resource.[26] Another important task is to consider how existing museum data can be put to more productive ends in the documentation and interpretive process. Research files, documents, recorded interviews, graphics, audio/visuals, publications, inter actives, and educational materials are all currently held in separate files and collections. Furthermore, in the future all these components could be indexed, managed, and delivered by database tools while contributing to polysemic interpretive models such as relational thematic linkages, multimedia presentations, and rich research resources. The challenge of delivering multimedia within the context of constantly evolving digital platforms, however, will continue to have major implications for the ways in which collections information can be preserved, accessed, configured, and interpreted into the future.

Additionally, the emergence of more creative content environments, in particular 3-D visualizations and multimodal sensory experiences to which this material will contribute, are expected to become cheaper and more persuasive. In a collections context, this could potentially lead to the creation of complex cultural interpretations such as highly detailed and dynamic visualizations and navigation environments that have strong popular and pedagogic appeal for educators. As Scali and Tariffi (2001) argued, the rethinking of collection management and multimedia delivery systems to provide effective access to such multimedia content will have major implications on how collections information can be configured and elucidated.[27]

Linking Practice to Contemporary Knowledge Making

A shift from the predominant use of highly prescribed authored information, text-based descriptions, and significance statements to a greater inclusion of interpretive materials around selected significant objects will involve new curatorial roles. Curators may become more involved in bringing together and linking forms of evidence, for example, creating relationships between information and objects similar to an exhibitions paradigm. Likewise, the tasks of collection managers may witness a greater emphasis on creating and linking digital resources. Nonetheless as our research suggests, many users will continue to look to museum curators and collection managers to provide authoritative scholarly information in the form of authored significance statements, narrative-centered histories, and chronological frameworks.

Despite these content specifications, balancing both the need for modernist style texts with more fragmentary/subjective poststructuralist and postmodernist ones will together ensure a more open and inclusive approach to the ways these materials can be interpreted. This will give greater power to the user to create their own knowledge pathways and to make and "put up" their own interpretations in a kind of shared authorship. While this will undoubtedly require greater effort and resources in compiling each individual record, it will simultaneously allow a greater depth to knowledge woven around a given object, thereby maximizing its meaning potential.[28] One answer to the problem of workload is to institute a program of documentation where deemed significant objects get prior standing. Others, however, could be recorded according to a more simplistic polysemic template where hyperlinks in documentation are used as the primary tool in the creation of relationships and to link sources. Such practices correspond and embrace contemporary theoretical premises, that is, the recognition that objects are legitimately interpretable in a variety of ways.[29] This new way of curatorial thinking was aptly expressed by a participant in the science and technology focus group discussion; "as a curator, I would define myself as a 'knowledge broker:' we have to be aware of notions of pluralism and acknowledge the lack of singular authority of the museum or curator."[30]

Conclusion

The discussions in this paper attempt to go some way toward bridging the gap between theoretical deliberations that interpret museums and documentation processes from a distance and the practice and procedural preoccupations required by staff on a day-to-day basis.

The *Themescaping Virtual Collections* and the *Knowledge Objects* projects have revealed some possible directions for the next generation of online collections and documentation. It looks exciting but one of our greatest issues is the tension between the potential richness collections have to offer and museums as the relatively poorly resourced cultural institutions. This issue, first raised at the Digital Libraries Research for Access to Cultural and Scientific Resources meeting in Luxembourg in March 2000 (the 1st European Commission) will continue to be the single biggest defining matter in the future development of digital collections and knowledge environments.

From a broader discursive standpoint, the transformation of databases and documentation practices to meet these new needs and digital potentialities represents part of an ongoing institutional reframing process. Hilde Hein (2000) argues that objective knowledge and museums claims to it have been weakened by challenges to the empirical scientific genre, an epistemological position of which museums form a part. This decline in faith in a singular reality has instead been replaced by subjectivity and the condition of multiple realities (Hein 2000). Museum transformations have been rapid in some areas of operations such as programming through the inclusion of "other" voices in exhibitions and the growth in audience evaluation but documentation has lagged behind. Therefore, the revision of collections information to embrace user needs, current thinking, and the consequent transformation of the object from positively possessing one real meaning to one that is inherently polysemic is integral to the subsequent and on-going reconstruction of institutional identity, and modes of engagement with their constituents. Documentation, new acquisition processes, and digital media have the potential to reconstitute museum collections as sites for experiences, learning, knowledge making, and deconstruction, as well as inventory.

Bearing resources and the larger institutional transformative processes in mind, developing knowledge bases, and other potential futures such as interoperable libraries of collections and collaborative knowledge spaces can be viewed as an incremental process occurring through the establishment of a program of iterative development.[31] One of our most fundamental strategic issues for the future, however, will be convincing management of the epistemological, educational, and marketing value of such initiatives and committing substantial resources to relevant projects.

Acknowledgments

This research was made possible by grants from the Australian Research Council. Special thanks goes to my colleagues, Sarah Kenderdine and Kevin Sumption, Powerhouse Museum and Bil Vernon, Vernon Systems Ltd, partner investigators on the *Themescaping Virtual Collections* project. I would also like to acknowledge Professor Stephen Garton, a fellow chief investigator, who has been a wonderful mentor and supporter. But most importantly I would like to express my gratitude to research assistant Helena Robinson who made an outstanding contribution to the *Knowledge Objects* project.

Notes

1. See H. Robinson and F. Cameron, 2003. "Knowledge objects: Multidisciplinary approaches in museum collections documentation," unpublished manuscript. University of Sydney and Fiona Cameron, 2003. "The next generation: Knowledge environments and digital collections." *Museums and the Web 2003 Conference*, March 19–22, 2003. Charlotte, NC (www.archimuse.com/mw2003/papers/cameron/ cameron.html).

3. Ibid.

4. Robinson and Cameron, "Knowledge Objects," 3.

5. Ibid.

6. Collection management systems that incorporate these features include KE Software, EMu (www.kesoftware.com/emu/index.html), Willoughby Associates (www.willo.com/ mimsy_xg/default.asp), last accessed March 15, 2004. Vernon Systems, Collection (www. vernonsystems.com), last accessed March 15, 2004.

7. D. Peacock, J. Doolan, and D. Ellis. "Searching for Meaning. Not Just Records." *Museums and the Web 2004 Conference,* March 31–April 3, Arlington, VA/Washington DC, 2004. (www.archimuse.com/mw2004/abstracts/prg_2S0000705.html), last accessed August 4, 2004. Examples include the Metropolitan Museum of Art collections (www. metmuseum.org/works_of_Art), last accessed March 15, 2004; J. Paul Getty Museum Collections (www.getty.edu/art/), last accessed March 15, 2004; National Museum of Australia History browser (www.nma.gov.au), last accessed March 15, 2004; Museum of Rural Life (www.ruralhistory.org/index.html), last accessed January 15, 2004. Examples include Revealing Things (www.si.edu/revealingthings), National Museum of American History, last accessed July 15, 2003; Experience Music Project (www.emplive.com), last accessed August 12, 2003; History Wired (http://historywired.si.edu/index.html), National Museum of American History, last accessed July 15, 2003; Powerhouse Museum "Behind the Scenes" website (http://projects.power house museum.com/virtmus/), last accessed August 4, 2004; National Museum of Australia History browser (www.nma.gov.au), last accessed March 15, 2004; Hypermuseum (http://www.HyperMuseum.com), last accessed January 15, 2004.

8. H. Robinson and F. Cameron. "Knowledge Objects," 24.

9. Ibid.

10. A. Munslow, Book Reviews, Institute of Historical Research, Reviews in History link, Discourse section: (www.history.ac.uk/reviews/discourse/index.html), last accessed August 29, 2003.

11. Ibid.

12. Ibid, cited in Robinson and Cameron, 20.

13. Ibid.

14. A. Munslow, Book Reviews

15. Ibid.

16. Ibid.

17. Robinson and Cameron, "Knowledge Objects," 21–23.

18. Ibid.

19. D. Adolsek and M. Freedman "Artifact as Inspiration: Using Existing Collections and Management Systems to Inform and Create New Narrative Structures," *Museums and the Web 2001 Conference,* March 14–17, 2001, Seattle, WA (www.archimuse.com/mw2001/papers/andolsek/undolsek.html), last accessed July 14, 2003. Also see P. Gillard. "Cruising Through History Wired," *Museums and the Web 2002 Conference,* April 14–17 2002, Boston, MA (www.archimuse.com/mw2002/papers/gillard/gillard.html), last accessed September 15, 2004; P. Stuer, R. Meersman, and S. De Bruyne, "The Hyper Museum Theme Generator System: Ontology-based Internet Support for the Actual Use of Digital Museum Data for Teaching and Presentation," *Museums and the Web 2001 Conference*, March 14-17, 2001, Seattle, WA (www.archimuse.com/mw2001/papers/stuer/stuer.html), last accessed January 15, 2003.

20. Robinson and Cameron, "'Knowledge Objects," 26.

21. Ibid, 23

22. Ibid, 19

23. Ibid.

24. Ibid, 36.

25. F. Cameron and S. Kenderdine. "Themescaping Virtual Collections: Accessing and Interpreting Museum Collections Online." Unpublished manuscript, University of Sydney and the Powerhouse Museum, 2001.

26. K. Donovan. "The Best of the Intentions: Public Access, the Web and the Evolution of Museum Automation," *Museums and the Web 1997 Conference,* March 16–19, 1998, Los Angeles, CA (www.archimuse.com/mw97/speak/donovan.htm), last accessed July 15, 2003. Also see L. Sarasan and K. Donovan. "The Next Step in Museum Automation: Staging Encounters with Remarkable Things (the capture, management, distribution and presentation of cultural knowledge on-line)," *Occasional Papers on the Value and Use of Museum Information,* Willoughby Press, 1998 (www.willo.com/text_frames/content/News/newarticles.htm), last accessed July 15, 2003; H. Besser, "Integrating Collections Management Information into Online Exhibits: The World Wide Web as a Facilitator for Linking 2 Separate Processes," *Museums and the Web 1997 Conference,* March 16–19, 1997; H. Besser, Los Angeles, CA (www.archimuse.com/mw97/speak/besser.htm), last accessed July 15, 2003; "The Transformation of the Museum and the Way It's Perceived', in *The Wired Museum Emerging Technology and Changing Paradigms,* ed. K. Garmil-Jones. Washington DC: American Association of Museums, 1998, 153–170.

27. G. Scali and F. Tariff, "Bridging the Collection Management System Multimedia Exhibition Divide: A New Architecture for Modular Museum Systems," *ICHIM Conference,*

Milan, September 3–7, 2001 (www.archimuse.com/ichim2001/abstracts/prg_115000625.html), last accessed July 12, 2003.

28. Cameron and Kenderine, "Themescaping Virtual Collections," 23.

29. Ibid.

30. Robinson and Cameron, "Knowledge Objects," 26.

31. M. Fleischmann, W. Strauss, G. Blome, J. Novak, and S. Paal. "Netzspannung.org—A Collaborative Knowledge Space for Media Art and Technology," *Museums and the Web 2002 Conference,* April 14–17, Boston, MA (www.archimuse.com/mw2002/papers/blome/blome.html), last accessed January 14, 2004.</notes>

References

Cameron, F. R. "Shaping Maori Histories and Identities: Collecting and Exhibiting Maori Material Culture at the Auckland and Canterbury Museums, 1850s to 1920s." Ph.D. thesis, Massey University, New Zealand, 2000.

———. "Wired Collections—The Next Generation." *International Journal of Museum Management and Curatorship* 19, 2002 (3): 309–315.

———. "Digital Futures I: Museum Collections, Digital Technologies, and the Cultural Construction of Knowledge," *Curator* 46(3): 325–339, 2003.

Hein, H. S. *The Museum in Transition: A Philosophical Perspective.* Washington DC: Smithsonian Institution Press, 2000.

Hooper-Greenhill, E. *Museums and the Shaping of Knowledge.* London: Routledge, 1992.

Kavanagh, G. *History Curatorship.* London: Leicester University Press, 1990.

Lyotard, J. F. *The Postmodern Condition: A Report on Knowledge,* trans. Geoff Bennington and Brian Massumi. Minneapolis: University of Minnesota Press, 1984.

Marwick, A. *The New Nature of History, Knowledge, Evidence and Language.* London: Palgrave, 2001.

Manovich, L. *The Language of New Media.* Cambridge, MA: The MIT Press, 2001.

Marty, P. F. "Museum Informatics and Information Infrastructures: Supporting Collaboration across Intra-museum Boundaries," *Archives and Museum Informatics* 13: 169–85, 1999.

McLuhan, M. *Understanding Media—The Extensions of Man.* New York: McGraw-Hill, 1964.

Scali, G., and F. Tariffi. "Bridging the Collection Management System—Multimedia Exhibition Divide: A New Architecture for Modular Museum Systems." In *Proceedings of the International Cultural Heritage Informatics Meeting* 1: 561–71, 2001.

Seely Brown, J., and P. Duguid. *The Social Life of Information.* Boston: Harvard Business School, 2000.

Thomas, S., and A. Mintz. *The Virtual and the Real—Media in Museums.* Washington, DC: American Association of Museums, 1998.

Sustainable Stewardship
Preventive Conservation in a Changing World

20

JERRY PODANY

Introduction

I HAVE BEEN ASKED TO PROVIDE AN OVERVIEW of the development of preventive conservation within the United States and the challenges involved in collections care and management. While I will try to contain my comments accordingly, I hope the reader will allow me this one excursion into the wider world, since it is increasingly difficult to address such broad and important issues on exclusively a national level.

The world is indeed smaller, shrunken, as it were, by developments in technology and communications that have dramatically expanded our assumptions and expectations regarding accessibility to information, products, people, and heritage collections. In this last decade alone a significant desire has appeared, on the part of museums in both economically developed and economically challenged countries, to lend and to borrow increasingly large numbers of works of art and artifacts for exhibition. The world is hungry for direct access; indeed, it demands it.

The coordinated call for such access is clear. At the 2008 Salzburg Global Seminar, Norman Palmer, Professor of Law at Kings College London and chair of the UK Treasure Valuation Committee, continued his support for harmonization of international loan policies and laws. In a session titled "Achieving the Freer Circulation of Cultural Artifacts," he noted in an interview that the law offending should be the same worldwide.[1]

The trend to minimize barriers to the regular exchange and transport of objects is on the rise, as are the attendant problems with the care of these artifacts and works of art as they are moved from place to distant place. This process is attended by all the assumptions regarding each place's willingness and ability to provide the

Jerry Podany is the senior conservator of antiquities at the J. Paul Getty Museum in Los Angeles. "Sustainable Stewardship: Preventative Conservation in a Changing World" is a transcription of a talk given by Jerry Podany in 2008 at Sustainable Cultural Heritage, a conference sponsored jointly by the National Endowment for the Humanities (NEH) and the Consiglio Nazionale delle Richerche (CNR) of Italy. It is reprinted here with permission of the author. All rights reserved.

very best of care for all of the objects and an adherence to the agreed upon "standard" of care.

The international conservation community is faced with a dilemma in considering these assumptions. And it must decide what role it will play in this exchange of property. Will we be a barrier to be overcome? Or a partner in assuring access? Will we be ready with well thought out, proven and coordinated guidance for the care of loaned objects as well as those which remain "at home"? Or will we cling to precepts that reflect another time . . . dogmatic rules that provide insufficient answers to increasingly common questions, while taking little notice of the broader concerns for sustainability in the 21st century and beyond? And perhaps most importantly, are there essential changes and compromises that are both critical and timely; and that we may now be more willing to make?

This complex set of questions is joined by a myriad of others, making any contemporary overview of preventive conservation rather daunting. But perhaps taking the keywords contained in the title of this paper, *Sustainable Stewardship: Preventive Conservation in a Changing World,* and addressing each in turn will provide the needed structure to venture an attempt. Hence a look at Preventive Conservation, the Changing World, and Sustainable Stewardship.

Preventive Conservation

The Oxford English Dictionary, authoritative on matters of clarity and meaning, defines the verb *conservation* as: "*to keep in safety or from harm, decay or loss; to preserve with care; now usually to preserve in its existing state from destruction or change.*"

The definition amply accommodates the adjective *preventive,* and one is left wondering if the couplet, *preventive conservation,* was ever necessary. Is it perhaps a redundant term for a process we should already be undertaking as an essential part of our activity?

Nonetheless the term preventive conservation has existed at least since the early 1970s, though in fact the concept has been with us much longer as related to our desire for maintenance and protection in buildings, monuments, and individual works of art. In 1849, for example, John Ruskin wrote "Take proper care of your monuments and you will not need to restore them."[2]

Preventive conservation has been labeled a conceptual approach as opposed to the more traditional (read: bench oriented) conservation activities, themselves assumed to be a series of specific, often intrusive, treatments aimed at the stabilization of works of art or items of assigned historic or cultural importance. But conservation, as a whole, is no longer a set of dogmatic and standard acts. The entire effort is now more dynamic, responsive, and significantly broader in scope than just a few decades ago. Increasingly it incorporates a more diverse group of disciplines and relies upon a significantly greater number of areas of expertise. Conservation is not, by its very nature, conceived or executed exclusively by conservators. And a more holistic approach to the challenges of preservation is now, more than ever, necessary. How else will we ever address the ongoing and changing preservation needs of collections, monuments, historic buildings, landscapes and even the intangible aspects of past and present cultures? And this names only the major areas of the pursuit.

A full accounting of all details related to the development of preventive conservation is outside the scope of this paper. The task would surely require an entire book. But it is worthwhile noting a few highlights that formed the concept and the label.

What is often cited as the first position for a Collections Care Specialist in Preventive Conservation in the United States began in 1983 at the Smithsonian Institution.[3]

A few years later the Bay Foundation funded the Pilot Program in Collections Care and the National Park Service began offering training to those involved in the aspects of preventive conservation. The NPS also undertook the development of the Conserve-O-Gram series, which continues today.

At this point I must, by necessity, cross several international borders to note perhaps two of the most influential professionals who have contributed to the development of Preventive Conservation, Gäel de Guichen and Stefan Michalski.

Gäel de Guichen has long and tirelessly worked toward the establishment and enactment of preventive conservation principles. In 1999 he defined a comprehensive plan for preventive conservation as "a project encompassing everybody involved with the heritage of a public or private establishment which provides for the concerted implementation of well-defined direct and indirect measures aimed at the natural and human causes of deterioration in order to increase the life expectancy of the collection and guarantee dissemination of the message they carry."[4] As we will see the most operative words include "everybody," "well defined" and "life expectancy."

Stefan Michalski (as well as others) at the Canadian Conservation Institute began his work on Preventive Conservation in the 1980s with the creation of the CCI Notes, the Framework for Preventive Conservation, and the Light Damage Calculator. His research continues to produce comer stones in this area.

Professionals like Carolyn Rose, who worked with Heritage Preservation on the development of the Conservation Assessment Program, clarified the purpose and direct benefits of preventive care. So too did the Getty Conservation Institute (GCI) when it assembled a group of conservators, engineers and architects to develop the curriculum for the course "*Preventive Conservation: Museum Collections and Their Environment*," offered from 1990 to 1995.

Of particular note in the development of preventive conservation was the Dresden ICOM-Triennial Meeting of 1990. It was here that many formative presentations were given, such as Stefan Michalski's "An overall framework for preventive conservation and remedial conservation," which provided a structure for future growth of the concept.[5]

Four years later, the IIC's 1994 international congress was devoted exclusively to preventive conservation and in 1997 the GCI initiated projects to develop strategies for preserving collections in hot and humid climates using more sustainable and affordable approaches.

Perhaps the greatest step forward in recent years has been the Heritage Health Index developed by Heritage Preservation and the Institute of Museum and Library Services in 2005. The Index was the first comprehensive survey of condition and preservation needs of U.S. public collections. Distributed to more than 14,500 collections encompassing all types of collecting in every U.S. state and territory, its very existence reminded us that over 4.8 billion artifacts are cared for nationwide, in collections that are visited 2.5 billion times a year. The scope of the need became public and undeniable.

The Heritage Health Index found that only 11 percent of museums in the United States had adequate storage facilities and that 58 percent of museums believed that some form of damage had occurred because of this lack in appropriate storage.[6] The most urgent preservation need in U.S. collecting institutions was environmental control and it is likely that the situation has, at best, only marginally improved in the five years since the survey.

More recently the field has begun to more actively recognize the issues embedded in sustainability and the changing world climate as rising challenges to effective preventive conservation. And the dialogue is growing regarding what can be done. In 2007 the topic formed the basis for a conference entitled *Gray Areas to Green Areas: Developing Sustainable Practices in Preservation Environments,*[7] as result of a partnership between the School of Architecture, University of Texas at Austin and the Getty Conservation Institute.

One year later, in 2008, the International Institute for Conservation launched the first in a series of public roundtables entitled Dialogues for the New Century, with the event Climate Change and Museum Collections.[8] This first roundtable explored the effects of global climate change on collections in museums and institutions around the world. Later that same year the Getty Conservation Institute hosted a similar panel discussion that brought together, for the first time, those involved with the conservation of cultural property and those working toward the preservation of natural resources. The GCI and the Natural Resources Defense Council examined the potential impacts of global warming and climate change on natural ecosystems, the communities in which we live, and the places that we have assigned value to. The broadening scope of challenges is clear. And the need for an equally broad scope of solutions is upon us.

This brief and surely incomplete list represents an evolution in the field from the myopic concern for simple maintenance toward a broader more encompassing effort leading to preservation. The field now not only looks beyond its confines for resources to achieve its mission but queries the impact its own activities may have on the world at large.

The Changing World

Not only has the scope of heritage conservation expanded but so has its very nature. In the last few decades, indeed in just the last few years, a combination of threats has risen that creates a rather unique and deeply disturbing situation. As a result we must now manage change brought on by a far broader spectrum of agents. The dynamic challenges to our success in such management have expanded to include:

- Climate change
- Higher energy costs
- The global economic downturn
- A greater demand for access
- The growth of nationalism

Let's consider two of these problems which, when combined as they are now, present a formidable challenge to heritage conservation: climate change and economic downturn.

Although a limited number of locations will find climate change favorable for economic growth and sustainable care of heritage, most parts of the world will experience the negative effects of climate variables. And these variables are expected to only increase in the foreseeable future.

In February 2007 the Intergovernmental Panel on Climate Change (IPCC) issued its fourth assessment of the future.[9] The report noted that the link between global climate change and human activity is unequivocal, and it identified several trends:

- An increase of warmer days and nights over most land masses
- A greater frequency of hot days
- More frequent heat waves
- More frequent incidences of heavy rain
- Increased occurrence of drought
- Increase of intense tropical cyclone activity
- Increase of incidences of extreme high sea level

Such a list should no longer hold any surprises for us. Scientists have predicted such scenarios for decades. What has changed is that we are no longer pointing to subtle effects or models; the stark evidence is all around us. The eight warmest years on record (since 1850) in the United States have all occurred since 1998, with the warmest year yet being 2005 (as of this writing). If greenhouse gases continue to increase, and unfortunately it appears they will for at least a number of years into the future, climate models predict that the average rate of warming over each inhabited continent is very likely to be at least twice as large as that experienced during the 20th century.

While it remains difficult to predict which parts of the country will become wetter or drier, there is no doubt that associated difficulties will follow, such as fires, floods and severe weather.

In his studies on climate change Dr. Thomas R. Knutson of the Geophysical Fluid Dynamics Laboratory at Princeton has noted "It is likely that greenhouse warming will cause hurricanes in the coming century to be more intense on average and have higher rainfall rates than present-day hurricanes."[10]

The implication of such studies is that of an increasing risk in the occurrence of highly destructive storms. Recent events on the U.S. Gulf Coast certainly remind us of the immense loss in human and cultural resources that can result. Is environmental management part of preventive conservation? And when we say "environmental" are we, should we, be speaking only of the galleries and storerooms, or should we mean our entire scope of responsibility to heritage and the planet? They are, after all, quite inseparable.

Michael Henry, one of the authors in this publication, has called environmental management the single most important effort in making our efforts of cultural heritage preservation sustainable, because of its "consequences for cultural heritage conservation, energy consumption, and capital as well as operating costs."[11]

We have not always thought so broadly, even though one of the pioneers of collections environmental control, Gary Thompson, was already noting the eventual problem when he insightfully remarked, in the very last paragraph of his seminal book *The Museum Environment*, that: "There is something inelegant about the mass of energy-consuming machinery needed at present to maintain constant RH . . . something inappropriate, in an expense which is beyond most of the world's museums."[12]

It has become clear that the measures we take to control collections environments can no longer be allowed to contribute to the overall problem of our planet's environment. Higher capacity HVAC systems, which consume large amounts of energy to reach and maintain the target environmental parameters for a collection, are no longer a sustainable, or even reasonable, answer to collections care. Seeking better answers brings us to the next key word: sustainability.

Sustainability

While the very word sustainability can raise the current angst over rapid changes to our modern world, it is also a word that is perhaps a bit overused and even teetering on banality. For our purposes in conservation it might be helpful to take just a moment to remind ourselves of its origins and earlier meaning.

Sustainability, as originally defined by the economist James Tobin in 1974, is the ability to maintain balance. He wrote:

> The trustees of endowed institutions are the guardians of the future against the claims of the present. Their task in managing the endowment is to preserve equity among generations.[13]

A simple replacement of a few words with terms more familiar to conservation issues provides a more usable version:

> The conservators caring for a collection assure future access to that collection by managing its use and preservation today.

Tobin also noted that sustainability involves *pillars,* such as environmental, social and economic sectors or contributors, upon which the process depends for effectiveness. Integrating these pillars when developing sustainability policies results in what is known as *intergenerational equity*. This principle cautions that the spending rate must not exceed its compound return, so that investment gains are spent equally on current and future constituents of the endowed assets. Continuing our translation of Tobin's words, what might we see as the pillars for conservation and what form would intergenerational equity take? The sectors that must be involved for successful conservation of cultural heritage have already been discussed. They are continually increasing and no longer are simplistically limited to chemists, art historians and craftsmen. An entire universe of expertise is now called upon to advise, undertake and review conservation efforts. But broader understanding and support for conservation efforts, which are just as essential as technical finesse, require society's familiarity with the purpose and limitations of conservation in order for the profession's efforts to be effective and sustainable. A review, and perhaps an adjustment, of the pillars we depend upon may well be in order.

In such a light *intergenerational equity,* when applied to heritage, cautions that the long term resources committed to the preservation of cultural material must not exceed the benefits to the material (or to those enjoying the results and consuming the material) and its long-:term survival. Those resources should be used while balancing the current and future needs not only of the heritage collections, but of the planet we live on. Both, after all, should be considered "endowed assets" under our care.

It is a fairly straight forward conclusion to make: our conservation efforts as applied to heritage material today should not contribute to global problems that affect the ability of future generations to enjoy the very heritage we are preserving.

In these challenging economic times such a concept is not only responsible, but is necessary. We will no longer have the luxury of ignoring whether conservation practices not only fail to contribute to sustainability but may work against larger preservation needs by contributing to excessive costs and unregulated, wasteful use of natural resources.

There are, of course, any number of new challenges as we begin to adapt to these emerging concerns. And the perception of our mission and how we go about achieving it are significant among these challenges. Conservators and collections managers already have a reputation (perhaps well deserved and perhaps unavoidable) of concentrating on threats and resisting, rather than facilitating, access. As we add sustainability concerns to our discussion we may be seen even more as agents of alarm and doom. We may become yet one more bearer of bad news, adding even greater burden to an otherwise increasingly saturated populace. But we do have an option which is to broaden the appeal of our efforts by broadening their associated scope. When we say "conserve" we should aim at communicating our larger purpose. It is time we join the other preservation and conservation communities (those concerned with communities, species and natural resources for example) who share our goals. Differences abound of course, but what we have in common far outweighs any of them.

What We Might Lose and What We Might Gain

Without care and advocacy for heritage health we will loose our irreplaceable treasures prematurely. Without mitigation and advanced planning for response we will loose our historic buildings and our collections to moments of disaster.

It is no longer sufficient to only raise the alarm; we must respond now with proactive commitment to the larger issues before us. Decades have passed and storerooms have not improved, emergency plans are not in place, and the field remains largely unaware of the direct impact global climate change will have on its mission and how addressing that impact will be made much more difficult by shrinking budgets.

In the past half century expectations of comfort have been upheld by advances in technology and cheap energy. From homes to shopping malls and museums we are rarely too cold and rarely too hot, but kept *just right* by massive and energy-wasteful systems. A full 20 percent of power consumption in the United States is used for air conditioning and much of the energy used to run those systems comes from the consumption of non-renewable and often polluting sources.[14]

Conservation expectations have been built on the same factors, the same expectations, as personal comfort. Museum gallery and storage environmental control is continually being defined and redefined by what degree of control is possible, by what can be measured, not necessarily by what is actually needed.

It is time for us to ask what we really need, what our collections really need, versus what we have come to think is ideal and what we think we can provide . . . or once could provide, seemingly free of consequences and in a world of cheap and ample energy.

It is time for us to be aware of and applaud the recent advances in energy efficiency. Improvements in HVAC systems have made them more energy efficient and there is a growing recognition that proper choices of systems as well as their tuning and maintenance can improve performance significantly.[15] The Environmental Protection Agency continues its work to monitor and regulate potential threats. The Energy Star program has encouraged energy efficient developments but must make greater headway in the museum world. The U.S. Green Building Council with its leadership in Energy and Environmental Design (LEED) programs has made a significant impact on new museum construction. And in 1999 a separate chapter entitled "Museums, Libraries and Archives," published again in 2003 and 2007, was developed for the American Society of Heating Refrigeration and Air Conditioning Engineers (ASHRAE)[16]—a significant advancement.

All of this represents notable gains, but much more is needed. It is time to develop informed decision-making regarding what the material heritage we care for really needs to survive. A review of our present assumptions and guidelines informed by new research, modeling and the gathering and analysis of empirically formed information is paramount if we are to conserve in a sustainable way.

Promising concepts and suggestions are already at hand. Stephen Michalski, for example, has put forward the concept of "proofed fluctuations," essentially observing how objects and collections react to given environments over long periods of time, indeed, the period of observation may be generational.[17]

Such an effort at characterization and reevaluation will require what the ASHRAE team called "common professional knowledge."[18] It turns out that conservators have reported that some collections have survived quite well in conditions less than what has been defined as "ideal." And it has been discussed that museums who have claimed to provide ideal conditions did not always in fact do so.[19] Rather than scorning such information, perhaps we should investigate the lessons it contains. Has the ideal surpassed the achievable, surpassed the necessary, and surpassed the responsible? We have a great deal of work to do to answer those questions.

Conclusion

Chris Caple has noted that, in undertaking preventive conservation, the conservator must by necessity leave the confines of the laboratory (or studio) and enter the broader world of management, venturing as Caple says to "the edge of their territory."[20] But in fact many conservators do this daily; sometimes it's all that can be achieved in any one day. Conservators have already made the shift to expanding their influence and responsibility. The question really is whether they will be able to defend the present practices undertaken in their traditional territory. As we step across boundaries, by desire or necessity, can we be confident that our priorities are, or should be, shared?

There is no doubt that conservation is far more complex than it was just a decade ago and that this complexity is a good thing. The profession has taken on much broader responsibility and enjoys the input of a larger community of expertise. We see perhaps more clearly than ever before our impact upon the appearance, stability and life-span of objects, collections and the information carried by each. We must now add to those concerns our impact on the planet itself and the cost effective, or not, nature of our actions.

Our response should seek a balance that is reasonably weighted and firmly well founded. But our conservation data, as Stephen Michalski points out, consists of unlinked case histories and fragmentary deterioration studies.[21] Small groups convene to explore mutual interests and concerns without sufficient concern for inclusivity and outreach. And our profession remains, as has recently been noted, invisible to the population as a whole.[22]

It is time to change. It is time, as David Stam had encouraged so many years ago,[23] to abandon partitioning in favor of integration to accomplish the museum's mission of preservation. And that integration includes acceptance of broader responsibility and stewardship, not as a unique mantle but as a shared effort.

Samuel Jones and John Holden, the authors of "It's a Material World, Caring for the Public Realm", have stated that, "Conservation refreshes and sustains the values of the past, where we have been, but also reflects values of the present and the future."[24] They imply that conservation reflects the values that are both associated with and are the driving force behind, our journey into the future. If this is the case, and I am sure it is, the inclusive and holistic values of today and tomorrow may well call for more substantiated decisions and broader definitions of what we are stewards of, what we should be conserving . . . and how.

Notes

1. "Achieving the Freer Circulation of Cultural Artifacts" (session 453), Salzburg Global Seminar, Salzburg, Austria, May 9–14, 2008. For the recorded interview with Norman Palmer conducted by Max Anderson: www.salzburgseminar.org/mediafiles/ME-DIA44729.mp3.

2. Ruskin, John. *The Seven Lamps of Architecture*, 5th ed. Kent: George Allan, 1886, p. 196.

3. Jessup, Wendy Claire. "History of preventive conservation". Conservation DistList April 18, 2009; cool-palimpsest.stanford.edu/byform/mailing-lists/cdl/2009/0448.html.

4. De Guichen, Gäel. "Preventive Conservation: A Mere Fad or Far-Reaching Change?" *Museum International* Vol. 51, No 1 (1999): 4–6.

5. Michalski, Stefan. "An Overall Framework for Preventive Conservation and Remedial Conservation," in ICOM-9th Triennial Meeting Dresden, German Democratic Republic, August 26–31, 1990. ICOM Committee for Conservation, Los Angeles, 1990, 589–591.

6. Heritage Preservation. *A Public Trust at Risk: The Heritage Health Index Report on the State of America's Collections*. Heritage Preservation and the Institute for Museum and Library Services, Washington D.C., December 2005.

7. From Gray Areas to Green Areas: Developing Sustainable Practices in Preservation Environments, 2007, Symposium Proceedings. 2008 by The Kilgarlin Center for Preservation of the Cultural Record, School of Information, The University of Texas at Austin. Published online: September 2008, www.ischool.utexas.edu/kilgarlin/gaga/proceedings. html.

8. IIC Roundtable. Climate Change and Museum Collections. September 17, 2008. National Gallery of Art, London, edited transcript published online September 28, 2009: www.iiconservation.org/docs/IICjclimate_change_transcript.pdf.

9. Intergovernmental Panel on Climate Change (IPCC). *Climate Change 2007—The Physical Science Basis: Working Group I Contribution to the Fourth Assessment Report of the IPCC*. Cambridge, UK: Cambridge University Press, 2007; http://ipcc-wgl .ucar.edu/wgl/wgl-report.html, February 2007.

10. Knutson, Dr. Thomas R. *Has Global Warming Affected Atlantic Hurricane Activity?* Geophysical Fluid Dynamics Laboratory/NOAA September 3, 2008; Last revised Oct. 17, 2008 Princeton University. www.gfdl.noaa.gov/global-warming-and-hurricanes.

11. Henry, Michael. "The Heritage Building Envelope as an Active and Passive Climate Moderator: Opportunities and Issues in Reducing Dependency on Air Conditioning." *Contributions to the Expert's Roundtable on Sustainable Climate Management Strategies*. Tenerif, Spain, April 2007, Getty Conservation Institute; www.getty.edu/conservation/science/climate/climate_experts_roundtable.html.

12. Thomson, Gary. *The Museum Environment*. London: Butterworths, 1978.

13. Tobin, James. "What Is Permanent Endowment Income?" *American Economic Review* Vol. 64, No. 2 (May) 1974: 427–432

14. Henry, Michael "The Heritage Building Envelope as an Active and Passive Climate Moderator: Opportunities and Issues in Reducing Dependency on Air Conditioning." *Contributions to the Expert's Roundtable on Sustainable Climate Management Strategies.* Tenerif, Spain, April 2007, Getty Conservation Institute; www.getty.edu/conservation/science/climate/climate experts_roundtable.html.

15. Reilly, James "Specifying Storage Environments in Libraries and Archives." In *From Gray Areas to Green Areas: Developing Sustainable Practices in Preservation Environments.* 2007 Symposium Proceedings, © 2008 by The Kilgarlin Center for Preservation of the Cultural Record, School of Information, The University of Texas at Austin. Published online, September 2008: www.isdiool.utexas.edu/kilgarlin/gaga/proceedings.html.

16. ASHRAE (American Society of Heating, Refrigerating, and Air-Conditioning Engineers). 2003. Museums, Libraries and Archives. Chapter 21 in *2003 ASHRAE Handbook: Heating, Ventilating, and Air-Conditioning Applications, SI Edition,* 21.1–21.23. Atlanta, GA: ASHRAE.

17. Michalski, Stefan. "The Ideal Climate, Risk Management, the ASHARAE Chapter, Proofed Fluctuations, and Toward a Full Risk Analysis Model" in *Contributions to The Expert's Roundtable on Sustainable Climate Management Strategies.* Tenerif, Spain, April 2007, Getty Conservation Institute; www.getty.edu/conservation/science/climate/climate_experts_roundtable.html.

18. ASHRAE (American Society of Heating, Refrigerating, and Air-Conditioning Engineers). 2003. Museums, Libraries and Archives. Chapter 21 in *2003 ASHRAE Handbook: Heating, Ventilating, and Air-Conditioning Applications, SI Edition,* 21.1–21.23. Atlanta, GA: ASHRAE.

19. Ashley-Smith, Jonathan, Nick Umney, and David Ford. "Let's Be Honest—Realistic Environmental Parameters for Loaned Objects" in *Preventive Conservation: Practice, Theory and Research.* Preprints of the Contributions to the Ottawa Congress, September, 12–16, 1994. London: IIC, 1994, pp. 28–31.

20. Chris Caple. "Preventive Conservation Within Conservation Training Programmes" in *Preventive Conservation: Practice, Theory and Research.* Preprints of the Contributions to the Ottawa Congress, September, 12–16, 1994. London: IIC, 1994:, pp. 65–68.

21. Milchalski, Stefan. "Preventive Conservation: Practice, Theory and Research," in *Preventive Conservation: Practice. Theory and Research.* Preprints of the Contributions to the Ottawa Congress, September. 12–16, 1994. International Institute for Conservation of Historic and Artistic Works, London, 1994.

22. Edwards, Charlie and Samuel Jones. *It's a Material World. Caring for the Public Realm.* London: Demos, 2008; www.demos.co.uk/publications/materialworld.

23. Stam, David. "The Implications of the 'New Museology' for Museum Practice" in *Museum Management and Curatorship* 12 (1993): 267–284.

24. Edwards, Charlie and Samuel Jones. *It's a Material World. Caring for the Public Realm.* London: Demos, 2008; www.demos.co.uk/publications/materialworld.

Culture and Museums in the Winds of Change

21

The Need for Cultural Indicators[1]

DOUGLAS WORTS

Introduction

IN THIS DAY AND AGE, one thing seems increasingly clear, at least in industrialized countries. Human beings have created cultures that are unsustainable.[2] From the uncertain implications of climate change, to the realities of a global economic melt-down and the growing gap between rich and poor, there are few indications that a human population of over 6.5 billion can continue to survive, let alone thrive, on planet Earth. As humanity proceeds down the path of globalization, pluralization, and urbanization, there is a niggling question: Can we create a global/local "culture of sustainability"? If so, what might it look like? How do we move toward it? How do we know if we are getting closer, or drifting ever further from this goal?

The Question of Culture

Culture, like *sustainability,* is a term that has come to mean different things to different people.[3] Most would agree that history, art, language, food, music, and clothing are all part of what we mean by the word *culture*—especially when these attributes have a tradition that stretches back through the generations. Certain types of leisure-time organizations (like museums, galleries, theatres, etc.) are commonly thought of as *cultural* because they specialize in selected aspects of human endeavour that are associated with culture (art, artifacts, music, dance, etc.). Further, in our increasingly pluralistic world, culture is often linked to ethnocultural countries of origin. Within all these approaches to culture, there is a tendency to point toward the past and "the other," usually at the expense of seeing that culture envelops each of our communities on a day-to-day basis. Culture may include traditions and the

Douglas Worts is consultant dedicated to advancing creativity, culture, and sustainability in cultural institutions. "Culture and Museums in the Winds of Change: The Need for Cultural Indicators" appeared in *Culture and Local Governance (Culture et gouvernance locale)* (Vol. 3, Issue 1–2, 2010, pp. 117–131) published by the University of Ottawa (Université d'Ottawa). It is reprinted here with permission from the publisher. All rights reserved.

past, and it may even include trips to museums and other leisure-time edutainment organizations; however, first and foremost, culture is the living, changing dynamic of how we live our lives, individually and collectively, locally and globally, consciously and unconsciously.

With a professional background of over thirty years in the museum sector, as well as a recent preoccupation with the intersection between culture and sustainability/unsustainability, my purpose in this paper is twofold: first, to examine some of the larger "cultural" issues related to sustainability in a globalized, pluralized, and urbanized world; and secondly, to explore how museums and other cultural organizations can position themselves to play a more meaningful role in helping to foster a "culture of sustainability."

One of the hallmarks of the modern era has been the fragmenting of the world into areas of specialization. This technique has yielded huge rewards for humanity. Unprecedented advances in knowledge have led to a society of specializations—each one, more often than not, a silo unto itself. Through focused and deep study, engineering, medicine, transportation, finance, and other domains have pushed the limits of what is possible to understand and to do. Yet, something is missing. Humanity lacks a global cultural vision of where it is going as a holistic system within the constraints of the biosphere. Central to grappling with the challenge and the opportunity of global sustainability, is a close look at the term *culture*.

Cultural Insights from a Maori Elder

Since my background is rooted in museums, I will share a short story about how my understanding of the term *culture* was reshaped through an intercultural experience with a Maori elder. In 1993, I was invited to Australia and New Zealand to deliver a series of lectures and workshops on my research into visitor-based creativity at the Art Gallery of Ontario, which focused on the creativity of museum visitors. Through this work, I had begun to think about museums as "places of the muses." Of course the museum was a physical place, but my interest was rooted in a state of mind of visitors that has psychological, social, and even spiritual dimensions. In this place of creativity, a person reflects upon aspects of their lives that they normally do not think much about—opening themselves up to the emergence of new insights. Nurturing creative responses of visitors to artworks frequently generated psychic energy that often surprised and delighted viewers. This research suggested that cultural professionals would benefit from developing an appreciation of visitor-based creativity to complement the work they do on artist-based creativity (see Worts 1995, 2005), and had captured the interest of staff at the Te Papa Museum in Wellington, New Zealand. Two Maori elders, both of whom worked at the museum, attended the workshop I gave, and the time I spent with one of the elders, Bessie Walters, would contribute to fundamentally changing my understanding of culture.

After the workshop, I was invited by "Auntie Bessie" to spend the following morning with her in the Maori gallery. When I walked into the museum to meet her, I did not know exactly what to expect. As I entered the cavernous space at the museum entrance, the magnificent objects before me—including huge ocean-faring canoes, houses, sculptures and more—awed me. Across the room, Bessie waved me over and extended a warm welcome. Then she turned to a life-sized, wooden sculpture and introduced it as an ancestor. My look must have betrayed my confusion as to what to do or say next—how should one respond to being introduced to a wooden carving? There was a twinkle in Bessie's eye as she said, "You can't just stand there, you need to touch him." Confusion turned to nervousness as an inner voice said, "You are a museum professional . . . you know that artifacts are *not* to be touched, at least not without cotton gloves!" With a twinkle in her eye, Bessie took my hands and planted them on the wooden carving, saying that I could not just stand there but had to "caress" the figure. At that point I knew I had begun a cultural experience unlike any I had had before. For the next three hours, Bessie and I explored the museum's extensive collection of Maori *taonga* (treasures)— touching everything as we proceeded. I learned how these objects embodied the living energy of Maori ancestors—not simply representations of people from the past, but the ancestors themselves. Bessie spoke of her relationship to them—that she was part of a continuum. She told me that her ancestors had come to the land, now known as New Zealand, centuries earlier and had killed the original inhabitants of the islands. When she declared that she reflected every day on how the responsibility for her ancestors' actions now rested on her shoulders, I was thunderstruck. At that moment, I gained an insight into the saying that culture involves "standing on the shoulders of ancestors."

It seems increasingly important to recognize how we, as individuals, do not arrive at the lives we live only through our personal experiences and choices. Rather, we are largely defined by the values, attitudes, beliefs, and deeds of those who preceded us. In our contemporary world, especially in the West, individual lives seem so focused on the challenges and opportunities of the present that we think of the past as largely irrelevant. And yet, for much of human history, it has been a combination of wisdom, rooted in the experiences and insights of elders, coupled with the contemporary challenges and connections of the younger generation, that have enabled cultures to grow and change. In contrast, today's society tends to privilege the knowledge associated with expertise more than the wisdom that comes from a lifetime of human experience. The morning I spent with Auntie Bessie has reverberated within my changing perspective of culture for almost twenty years, and will probably continue to do so for years to come.

Redefining Culture

So, what do we mean by the term *culture*? American psychologist Edgar Shein (quoted in Kertzner 2002) has posited that culture is "a basic pattern of assumptions invented, discovered or developed by a given group as it learns to cope with its problems of external adaptation and internal integration" (p. 40). To think about culture as a process of active adaptation and integrated consciousness helps enormously to overcome the limitations of culture being understood as entirely rooted in the past, or being associated with a class of contemporary edutainment/ entertainment that only exists in leisure-time contexts (see UNESCO 1995, Galla 2002, Worts 2006a, Sutter 2006, and Janes 2009). In the light of Shein's definition, all activities of human endeavour, including economic systems, social dynamics, and relationships with the natural environment, become important foundation blocks of our evolving and increasingly globalized culture. This approach leaves us wondering about how the dynamics of culture play themselves out in day-to-day reality, and what the idea of culture as an adaptive process might mean for museums and other cultural organizations. To begin, it is worth examining the dynamics of adaptation.

Adaptive Renewal

The work of C. S. (Buzz) Holling, a biologist and central figure in the study of complex systems, offers a model that may be extremely helpful to those trying to understand culture in our contemporary world. Holling began his work on *adaptive renewal* by studying forest ecosystems over a period of five decades, and saw a predictable pattern emerge that has become known as the *adaptive renewal cycle*. Essentially, there are four parts to the cycle: exploitation, conservation, release, and reorganization (see Figure 21.1). Holling (2004) writes:

> For an ecosystem such as a forest, think of the century- or centuries-long cycle of succession and growth from pioneer species (*r*) to climax species (*K*) followed by

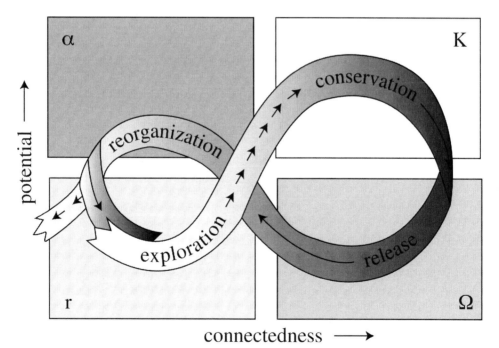

Figure 21.1.   The adaptive renewal cycle. Source: Holling (2004).

major disturbances such as fire, storm, or pest (*fl*). Such disturbances occur as wealth accumulates and the system becomes gradually less resilient, i.e., more vulnerable. As a consequence, a disturbance is created to release accumulated nutrients and biomass and reorganize them into the start of a new cycle (α). That reorganization can then exploit the novelty that accumulates but is resisted or lies latent during the forward loop. (no page)

Adaptive renewal applies to human situations as well as to natural ecosystems. For example, when two compatible people meet through a chance encounter they seize the opportunity and begin to build a relationship—this is the phase in which they explore the potential as a couple *(exploration)*. Tremendous energy is often produced during the early phase of a relationship, not only physically, but also emotionally and psychologically. The second phase *(conservation),* involves the growing complexity of the relationship. Resilience is created to help protect the system from being disrupted or destroyed by external shocks. In an evolving human relationship, domestication and routine often set in during the "mature" phase of the cycle, with all of the complexity that can entail. Throughout this phase, threats and pressures from outside (and inside) the system will try to disrupt the equilibrium. Invariably, the third phase *(release)* will appear. Here, the relationship will be confronted with a variety of crises that lead either to a letting go of certain old attitudes, or to a collapse. In the former, the relationship attempts to creatively adapt, while in the latter, the relationship disappears, leaving both parties free to look opportunistically at the range of options available in the larger social context *(reorganization).*

Other social examples of adaptive renewal can be found in the dynamics of career-development. Here, it is possible for someone to experience many adaptive restructurings of their career over a period of years or decades. In other instances, a career path may be abandoned when external conditions (or the development of a new inner passion) converge which encourages a complete break with one's established career, leaving that person to explore and exploit other options.

One can also see the hallmarks of adaptive renewal at the macro-societal level. An example of this is in the use of energy. When human beings discovered that the power of fire could be harnessed through burning wood, there were countless benefits to be gleaned. However, eventually, energy from burning wood became problematic in a number of ways and societies became open to the opportunities made available by burning coal. This opened the door to the industrial revolution, which had profound impacts on people in every corner of society. Yet problems with pollution and the desire to achieve goals that required liquid fuel soon led to the decline of coal and the ascent of oil and gasoline. As with both wood and coal-based fuels, petroleum fuels enjoyed tremendous opportunistic integration into the fabric of human lifestyles. And after a century of wildly successful exploitation, the pressures of climate change and pollution are conspiring to topple oil from its pre-eminent perch as the fuel of choice.

Culture as an Adaptive Process

If we look at the notion of culture as an adaptive process, then it is critical to pay attention to the ever-changing contexts within which humans live. To this end, our society's dependence on, even addiction to, energy is a defining characteristic of our culture. Similarly, the age we live in, which has facilitated revolutions in transportation, communication, and production technologies, is central to who we are individuals and collectives. The mass migration of huge populations—primarily as seen as movement from the country to the city and/or from one's region of ethno-cultural roots to urban settings in other parts of the world—further defines human culture in the early years of the 21st century. One of the outcomes of this migration has been the pluralization and urbanization of a great many human settlements.

Whereas historically human beings have lived within relatively local precincts, for the past few centuries, the entire planet has increasingly become humanity's frame of reference. Driven by technological advances, as well as the expansion of global markets for goods and services, the very nature of human culture is transforming. It is not that traditional notions of ethno-cultural identity rooted in the heritage of a particular place have become irrelevant, but that identity has become considerably more complex and layered through processes of globalization. Another central aspect of identity today is linked to urbanization and the emergence of a society largely defined by the pragmatic forces of economy and other dimensions of secular life. Whereas traditional cultures spent a great deal of time and energy struggling to relate to the many aspects of life that remain mysterious and unknown (often taking the form of religion), secular society largely ignores what it cannot control through economics, expertise, and brute force. It is in this context that I developed my own definition of *culture* to help clarify the cultural challenges that lie ahead:

> Culture [is] . . . all of the ways in which a people relate to those aspects of life which:
>
> a. they can know and control; as well as,
> b. those they can't fully know or control, but to which they must have a conscious relationship. (Worts 2002)

To suggest that culture is fundamentally a dynamic of relationships is not novel. However, as one lays out the various ways in which humans build their networks of relationships, the challenges of creating a sustainable, globalized culture becomes clearer (see Figure 21.2). Modern societies governed by secular laws, democratic processes, and market-driven frameworks seem to have lost a sense of humility that comes from grappling with the mysterious power of the universe that is beyond human understanding and control. Such humility could help to ensure that the 'precautionary principle' is applied to many aspects of contemporary life where the impacts of actions can reverberate across the planet with barely a flicker of general

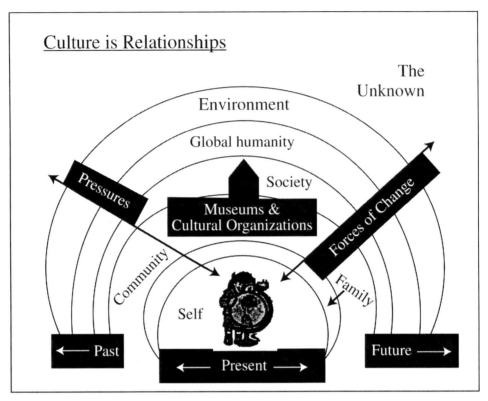

Figure 21.2.   Culture is relationships.

consciousness. For example, in the current phenomenon of climate change—where the burning of extraordinary quantities of fossil fuels has set off a chain of events that is raising the temperature of the planet—many of the impacts or causal relationships are not easy to document, which has been why the International Panel on Climate Change (IPCC) has only recently linked human activity and changing climate. Yet for many the IPCC declarations on climate change are not sufficient to accept the call for fundamental changes to human behavior, especially those related to energy systems and consumption behaviors. I've come to believe that what is needed is a new framework for cultural identities that enables each of us to stretch our individual consciousness to embrace not only personal and local realities, but also the global reality. Globalized economics, systems of product manufacturing, and unfettered mobility are linking each of us to every corner of the planet. Accordingly, there is a need for each of us individually, as well as through our collective systems, to become more conscious of the ramifications of those connections. In turn, it is essential to modify our individual and collective behaviors so that each of us contributes to a sustainable world for all people, within a biosphere that has limitations.

The diagram in Figure 21.2 suggests myriad ways that individuals and collectives are linked to other elements of our world. Some of our relationships exist consciously, while others are unconscious. In a situation where over 6.5 billion people must share the resources of a limited planet, it only seems appropriate that humanity be conscious and responsible in how these relationships are lived.

The argument being put forward here is that *culture* is the foundation of human values, beliefs, attitudes, and behaviors that make up our lived reality (see Figure 21.3). As such, the classic model of sustainable development, which includes three equal, overlapping spheres (environment, society, and economy), can be re-envisioned as showing three differently scaled spheres, resting on the foundation of culture.[4]

Culture and Sustainability

Many people have criticized the classic sustainability model because all human life, including the economy, exists wholly within the biosphere—which is why, in Figure 21.3, it is the largest and all-encompassing sphere. As a subset of the environment, *society* must leave room within the environment for the countless other species that belong to Earth's biosphere. The smallest sphere is set aside for the economy. Represented in this way, the economy is put into a more balanced perspective with society and environment. It is ironic that the economy, which is a tool of society, has for over a century been widely accepted as a more significant indicator of societal well-being than either the general welfare of people or the health of the natural environment. The novel addition here is the placement of the

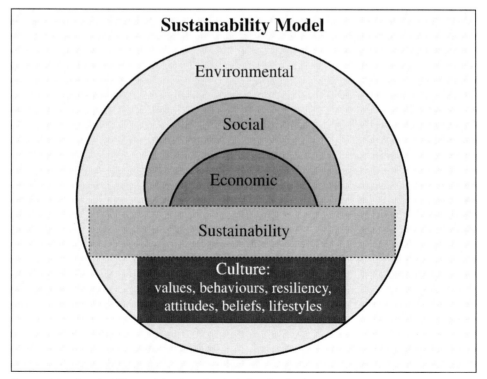

Figure 21.3.   Sustainability model, adapted to include role of culture.

societal and economic spheres on the foundation of culture, within which are the values, attitudes, beliefs, and behaviors that direct human activity.

A natural question emerges: What specifically is contained within the "cultural foundation" in this model?[5] While not an exhaustive list, a "culture of sustainability" could include the following continuously evolving capacities, at individual and collective levels:

- Capacities for reflectiveness
- Capacities for participation/engagement in what is relevant
- Capacities for treating others with equity, trust, and respect
- Capacities for creating a vision of how humans can live sustainably on the Earth
- Capacities for relatedness—compassionate connection to others and to the environment
- Capacities for awareness of histories—and an ability to learn from the past
- Capacities for creativity—to have faith in it personally
- Capacities for conscious systems of knowledge, including values
- Capacities for connection to the symbolic and the spiritual
- Capacities for humility and conscious connection to what cannot be fully understood or controlled
- Capacities for responsible action
- Capacities for ability to embrace change

These are just some of the critical aspects needed to foster a "culture of sustainability" in a world that is facing serious challenges of spiraling population, environmental degradation, and huge social inequities. This list of cultural capacities make the traditional criteria for judging impacts of cultural strategies—where "success" is typically measured in terms of attendance and revenue—seem particularly inadequate.

In fact, contemporary cultures have so far failed to develop effective measures that can identify and address the cultural, social, economic, and environmental needs of a quickly and dramatically changing world. Meanwhile, over the past century or two, globalizing economic, manufacturing, and market systems have dramatically transformed how humans inhabit the world. This has been a work in progress for many centuries—heralded by the adventures of early European traders and explorers. In the 20th century, the military and economic alliances that followed the two World Wars further strengthened the interconnectedness of all humans who share this planet. Yet the resulting social, economic, and cultural elements of globalization have not produced effective feedback loops that could adjust and curtail their most destructive aspects.

Cultural Dimensions of the Economy

Driven by the powerful motivation of maximized economic growth and profit, corporations, governments, and influential individuals have pushed the economy to the forefront of all human considerations. There seems to be little disagreement that our current world is unsustainable, but unless we change the values that guide our economic systems, the future will not be kind—environmentally, socially, economically, or culturally.

There are economists who challenge the dominant growth-based economic approach to human well-being. In Canada, Mark Anielski (2007) and Peter Victor (2008) strongly argue that to focus on simple economic growth is not only destructive for humanity and the planet, but that privileging growth misses the real power of the economy to create a sustainable world. In the United States, Herman Daly (1973, 2008) has been a strong voice for a "steady-state economy" for decades. Daly recently called for a retooling of the global economy:

> The Earth as a whole is approximately a steady state. Neither the surface nor the mass of the earth is growing or shrinking; the inflow of radiant energy to the Earth is equal to the outflow; and material imports from space are roughly equal to exports (both negligible). . . . The most important change in recent times has been the enormous growth of one subsystem of the Earth, namely the economy, relative to the total system, the ecosphere. . . . The closer the economy approaches the scale of the whole Earth the more it will have to conform to the physical behavior mode of the Earth. That behavior mode is a steady state—a system that permits qualitative development but not aggregate quantitative growth. Growth is more of the same stuff; development is the same amount of better stuff (or at least different stuff). The remaining natural world no longer is able to provide the sources and sinks for the metabolic throughput necessary to sustain the existing oversized economy—much less a growing one. . . . Throughput growth means pushing more of the same food through an ever larger digestive tract; development means eating better food and digesting it more thoroughly. Clearly the economy must conform to the rules of a steady state—seek qualitative development, but stop aggregate quantitative growth. (Daly 2008, p.l)

But it is not only economists who are ringing the bell for economic review and change—artists, scientists, theologians, and even some business people are doing so as well.

The Role(s) of Artists in Fostering Cultural Change

In this section, I have chosen to highlight three figures in the art world whose artworks provide compelling feedback loops that are helping to shift aspects of our Western cultural unconscious toward consciousness.

Edward Burtynsky, a Canadian photographer, has produced artwork around the world that brings a magnifying glass to the places where industry, society, economics, and environment intersect. One powerful series of photos depicts the collateral costs of decades of transoceanic shipping of goods. Burtynsky wondered what happened to old freighters after they could no longer sail the seas safely. He found some of them on the beaches of Bangladesh, where local business "entrepreneurs" purchased the vessels for next to nothing. Then hundreds of local people, keen to earn money, would use cutting torches to disassemble the metal hulks. These workers were provided no safely equipment (like goggles or gloves) and frequently worked without shoes. The artist was so horrified by the situation that he purchased 2,000 pairs of safety goggles and gave them to the business owner to distribute to the workers. For anyone who takes for granted the availability of cheap goods, frequently made in developing countries with little or no employment or environmental regulations, seeing one of Burtynsky's images is a wake-up call.[6]

Chris Jordan, a Seattle-based artist, uses computer-manipulated images to make beautiful, but shocking mirrors on product and service consumption in the United States.[7] Swedish artist Jenny Bergstrom has created a compelling artwork for public spaces that is designed to alert commuters to the largely invisible threat of air pollution.[8] Yet the integration of such artistic work into mainstream life in ways that can create meaningful change remains is largely undeveloped. It may be possible for cultural organizations to do more than simply exhibit their work. Perhaps museums could develop strategies to insert the reflective practices and potent feedback of insightful artists into the very decision-making process of government, business, and civil society. Currently, this is undeveloped potential. To move this agenda forward, cultural organizations need to broaden their frame of reference and develop new ways of measuring cultural needs.

Globalized Culture

Globalization is here to stay and now part of humanity's cultural reality. There is little doubt that globalization can deliver many benefits, but there are many hidden aspects of global economics and business that, if allowed to continue unchecked, will prove deleterious to the health of all. Monitoring and feedback systems are needed so that governments, businesses, nonprofit organizations, and individual citizens can monitor how actions at all levels send both positive and negative ripple effects across the planet.

How will the colossal task of forging a global, sustainable culture of humanity be undertaken? Is it possible to stretch human consciousness from the individual scale to the local/regional world of everyday life, and then beyond to the global realities of our contemporary world? Who will be part of the crafting of a global framework for a "culture of sustainability" that not only respects the heritage of each individual, but also brings everyone together in the spirit of peace and happiness for all? I remain optimistic that human ingenuity is capable of rising to meet such challenges head on—although it may well take some significant crisis to precipitate this type of meaningful societal change.

Cultural Feedback Loops and Indicators

If we acknowledge that a successful future for humanity will require fostering "a culture of sustainability," then what roles might we envision for cultural organizations like museums? Such institutions contain a great deal of embedded capital—

not only in their collections and buildings, but also in their staffs and volunteers. Yet few have embraced the cultural challenges of sustainability. Nonetheless, there is a growing movement that is encouraging museums to focus more on the needs of their communities and the issues confronting humanity. The Canadian Working Group on Museums and Sustainable Communities[9] has developed a planning tool to help museums seize the opportunities available to them through embracing the sustainability challenge. The Critical Assessment Framework (Figure 21.4) uses a stratified approach that helps planners develop public engagement strategies designed to address the needs and opportunities related to: individuals, communities, the museum itself, and the global reality (Worts 2006b).

When considering a range of possible public program options, members of a planning team can use the Critical Assessment Framework to ask themselves whether the various strategies under consideration are capable of achieving certain goals. The questions are not intended to be performance indicators, but the questions encourage planners to identify meaningful indicators for each project that will help ensure that multifaceted cultural goals are met. A rating scale is provided in the Critical Assessment Framework, not to record or demonstrate the "objective" strength of any particular strategy, but rather to spotlight how members of the planning team may envision the impacts of a program differently. These variations in perceptions and assumptions become topics of conversation as the team continues its process of clarifying the project and its desired outcomes.

Here is an example of how the Critical Assessment Framework might be applied. If a museum project team decided to develop a project that would address the growing complexity of multicultural realities within an urban setting, they could use the Critical Assessment Framework to assess a variety of strategies. Imagine that one idea is to create an exhibit of materials that is drawn from both the museum's collection as well as from private collections within communities. A second approach is to contract several community-based arts practitioners—each linked to different ethnocultural communities—to generate projects that engage citizens and create something (e.g., public artwork, community performance, etc.) over which citizens feel ownership. In each of these scenarios, the Critical Assessment Framework can be used to examine how well:

1. curiosity, reflection, personalization, intrinsic motivation, civic responsibility are fostered among individuals, etc.;
2. community-based issues are identified; intra- and inter-community dialogues are created; cross-generational dialogue is achieved; new partnerships are forged; etc.;
3. the museum itself builds stronger linkages to diverse community groups; understanding of emerging issues across the community is enhanced; collaborations between existing staffs are optimized; fiscal responsibility is achieved; new skill sets required by the organization is acknowledged and fulfilled; etc.;

Critical Assessment Framework
Douglas Worts & Glenn Sutter – World Views Consulting – Apr/2008

Criteria for assessing initiatives aimed at 4 levels of cultural adaptation

(Rating performance without indicators is subjective. Discussions are useful and will generate criteria.)

When considering a new pubilc program initiative, ask how well the program will:	Poorly 1	2	to 3	4	Well 5	N/A
Personal Level (members of community)						
Contribute and/or generate new insights						
Capture imagination						
Simulate curiosity						
Encourage personal reflection						
Enhance ability to think critically and creatively						
Provide opportunity to examine and clarify values						
Demonstrate relevance and make connection to daily life						
Affirm, challenge, deepen identity						
Help develop a sense of place						
Help deal with complexity and uncertainty						
Increase responsible action						
Stimulate intrinsic motivation						
Community Level						
Address vital and relevant needs / issues / opportunities within community						
Generate information and connection at the personal, community, provincial/territorial, national and global level						
Engage a diverse public						
Provide a voice for diverse groups						
Encourage social interactions and debate						
Act as a catalyst for action						
Stimulate intergenerational interactions						
Link existing community groups to one another						
Initiate or enhance long term collaborative relationships						
Partnerships empower community groups						
Enhance the credibility of all involved						
Result in products and processes that have tangible impact in the community						
Institutional Level						
Challenge personal and institutional assumptions						
Guided by clearly articulated goals, objectives and outcomes						
Use the most effective vehicle for achieving goals						
Create a community of learning within staff						
Integration scientific, local and traditional knowledge						
Act as catalyst for partnering community organizations						
Global Level						
Address issues of global significance – revealing links to local realities						
Foster global ecosystem health						
Reduce global ecological footprint						
Enhance global social justice and equity						
Foster public consciousness of global impacts of local choices						

© The Working Group on Museums and Sustainable Communities – June 2006 (adapted)

For elaboration, see: Worts, Douglas, "Measuring Museum Meanings: A Critical Assessment Framework," *Journal of Museum Education*, vol. 31, #1, Spring 2006, Walnut Creek, California: Left Coast Press, pp. 41–49

Figure 21.4. Critical assessment framework. ©The Working Group on Museums and Sustainable Communities, June 2006 (adapted). For elaboration, see Douglas Worts, 2006. "Measuring Museum Meanings: A Critical Assessment Framework," *Journal of Museum Education*, 31(1):41–49.

4. critical global issues (environmental, social, cultural, economic) are woven into local community dynamics.

Each potential strategy can be discussed within the team and their potentials for impacts can be estimated, questioned, and prioritized.

For most museums, following the framework of the Critical Assessment Framework toward the goal of "a culture of sustainability," the need will likely emerge to reexamine its core values, principal activities, assumed essential skill sets, and performance indicators. This is simply because an organization designed to function within a certain *zeitgeist* will not necessarily be able to shift its focus to address changing cultural needs in subsequent *zeitgeists*. Institutions like museums have been organized around a set of sectoral assumptions, including the importance of:

- Discipline-base, academic specializations (e.g., providing authoritative views of science, art, history, archaeology, etc.);
- Systematic "professional" activities (e.g., collecting, preserving, documenting, etc.);
- A narrow range of public engagement strategies (e.g., exhibits, lectures, collection-based publications, etc.); and
- Corporate performance indicators, such as attendance and revenue, which do not measure *cultural* impacts.

As a result, there is great resistance, both within these organizations and within the bodies that support them (e.g., Ministries of Culture and professional training programs), to embrace the challenges of fostering a "culture of sustainability." This is not difficult to understand: the identity of such organizations and their professional staffs are heavily invested in the institutional status quo. It is not that existing skills are unnecessary, but that there are critical new skills that have to be cultivated in order to foster a "culture of sustainability"—skills such as facilitating personal reflection, encouraging community dialogue, and motivating the public to be involved in creating a sustainable society.

The resistance to change within museums may be considered similar to that found in the world of business. Central assumptions about the purpose, function, and outcomes of many business sectors and organizations are not based on values of contributing to a sustainable society. Instead, corporations have a legal obligation to maximize profit for their shareholders. Organizations do what is necessary to maximize revenues, reduce expenses to the bare minimum, and externalize any costs that they can legally get away with (for example, not taking responsibility for the loss of local ecosystem health damaged by pollution or destroyed during the extraction of resources). If our capitalist economy is to contribute to a sustainable world, all business costs must be fully calculated and properly paid for. However, suggestions that business should become oriented to operating in a *Steady-State* economy and incorporate full-cost accounting are typically viewed as an anathema to, if not an outright assault on, business itself. Similarly, cultural organizations are likely to hold tight to their traditional *modus operandi,* at least until they see that the potential rewards are higher than preserving existing corporate operations.

On the positive side, many cultural organizations are discussing the need for new forms of cultural leadership and public relevance within communities. Some of this discussion is taking the form of a burgeoning interest in the "greening" of museums (e.g., reducing greenhouse gases, achieving energy efficiency, promoting recycling, etc.). This may be a starting point for museums, but much more is required if the cultural challenges that permeate the world are to be addressed.

Conclusion

The world is at a crossroads. Human life, as we have known it on our planet, seems unsustainable. Changes to virtually all aspects of our cultural, social, and economic systems will be required in order to put humanity onto a new, sustainable path. How can our population of almost seven billion people transform itself and strike an enduring, dynamic balance within the biosphere? Human beings have proven themselves to have remarkable ingenuity when forced into a corner. If we look widely across the world, some of the changes that are already afoot in the realms of government, business, economy, culture, cities, and individual lifestyles are inspiring. Moving forward, we will need all of the wisdom and humility that can be mustered in order to construct a viable vision of the future to which everyone can relate. Simultaneously, we will need to have adequate feedback loops that alert us to the benefits and perils of all individual and collective actions. For me, Auntie Bessie provides a good model—always moving forward, always conscious of her past, always humble in the presence of what cannot be fully known or controlled. We can take heart in the fact that, despite the resistance to change that seems hardwired in human beings, there are also "tipping points" which, when reached, can dissolve resistance and precipitate sea-changes capable of transforming the very rules that govern this thing called life.

Notes

1. This article originated as a keynote address at the International Conference of Environmental, Cultural, Economic and Social Sustainability, Ecuador, January 2010 (Worts 2010), and was revised for this issue.

2. Many authors have reflected on this problem, including AtKisson (1999), Hawkes (2001), Jacobs (2004), Wright (2004), Diamond (2005), Homer-Dixon (2005), and Schafer (2008).

3. Over the centuries, many scholars and thinkers have tackled the challenge of defining culture. See, for instance, Hawkes (2001) and Schein (2001).

4. There are numerous instances of recasting the classic sustainability model as embedded spheres.

5. This approach to integrating culture into the sustainability model places culture as a foundation for all other human activity, which differs from Jon Hawkes' use of a "fourth leg" to balance out economy, environment, and society. Positioning culture in a founda-

tional position ensures that it is seen as inextricably bound to all aspects of human life and is not split off as a set of separate concerns.

6. See Edward Burtynsky's work at www.edwardburtynsky.com. Specifically, see "Works: Ships: Ship-Breaking."

7. See artwork by Chris Jordan at www.chrisjordan.com. The section on "Running the Numbers: An American Self-Portrait" is particularly powerful.

8. See Jenny Bergstrom's artwork that addresses the issue of air pollution, at www.jenny bergstrom.com/scripts/Page.asp?id=297.

9. For more information on the Working Group on Museums and Sustainable Communities, see http://worldviewsconsulting.org/?page_id=47.

References

Anielski, M. (2007). *The Economics of Happiness: Building Genuine Wealth.* Gabriola Island, BC: New Society Publishers.

AtKisson, A. (1999). *Believing Cassandra: An Optimist Looks at a Pessimist's World.* White River Junction, VT: Chelsea Green Publishing.

Daly, H. (1973). *Toward a Steady State Economy.* San Francisco, CA: W.H. Freeman and Co.

———. (2008, April 24). *A Steady-State Economy: A Failed Growth Economy and a Steady-State Economy are not the Same Thing; They are the Very Different Alternatives We Face.* London: Sustainable Development Commission UK; www.sd-commission.org.uk/publications. php?id=775.

Diamond, J. (2005). *Collapse: How Societies Choose to Fail or Succeed.* New York: Viking Books.

Galla, A. (2002). Ecomuseology, globalisation and sustainable development: Ha Long Bay, a case study from Vietnam. *Humanities Research Journal,* 1.

Hawkes, J. (2001). *The Fourth Pillar of Sustainability: Culture's Essential Role in Public Planning.* Melbourne, Australia: Common Ground.

———. (2006). Why should I care? *Museums and Social Issues,* 1(2).

Holling, C. S. (2004). From complex regions to complex worlds. *Ecology and Society,* 9(1): 11. www.ecologyandsociety.org/vol9/iss1/art11/.

Homer-Dixon, T. (2005). *The Upside of Down: Catastrophe, Creativity and the Renewal of Civilization.* New York: Viking Books.

Jacobs, J. (2004). *Dark Age Ahead.* New York: Random House.

Janes, R. (2009). *Museums in a Troubled World: Renewal, Irrelevance or Collapse.* New York: Routledge.

Kertzner, D. (2002). The lens of organizational culture. *Mastering Civic Engagement: A Challenge to Museums.* Washington, DC: American Association of Museums.

Schafer, D.P. (2008). *Revolution or Renaissance: Making the Transition from an Economic Age to a Cultural Age.* Ottawa: University of Ottawa Press.

Shein, E. (2001). Organizational culture and leadership. In J. Shafritz and J. Steven Ott, eds., *Classics of Organization Theory.* Fort Worth, TX: Harcourt College Publishers.

Sutter, G. (2006). Thinking like a system: Are museums up to the challenge? *Museums and Social Issues,* 1(2).

UNESCO. (1995). *Our Creative Diversity: Report of the World Commission on Culture and Development.* Paris: UNESCO.

Victor, P. (2008). *Managing Without Growth: Slower by Design not Disaster.* Northampton, MA: Edward Elgar Publishing.

Worts, D. (1995). Extending the frame: Forging a new partnership with the public. In S. Pearce, ed., *New Research in Museum Studies: Art in Museums.* London: Athlone Press.

———. (2002). On the brink of irrelevance? A glimpse into art museums in contemporary society. *ICOM Canada Bulletin,* no. 14. Ottawa: Canadian Heritage Information Network.

———. (2005). The animated muse: An interpretive program for creative viewing. *Curator: The Museum Journal,* 48(3).

———. (2006a). Fostering a culture of sustainability. *Museums and Social issues,* 1(2).

———. (2006b). Measuring museum meanings: A critical assessment framework. *Journal of Museum Education,* 31(1): 41–49.

———. (2010). Culture in the winds of change: Fostering a "culture of sustainability" and making the case for cultural indicators. *International Journal of Environmental, Cultural, Economic & Social Sustainability,* 6(5): 241–254.

Wright, R. (2004). *A Short History of Progress.* Toronto: Anansi Press.

Embedding Civil Engagement in Museums   22

GRAHAM BLACK

Introduction

the majority of museums, as social institutions, have largely eschewed . . .
a broader commitment to the world in which they operate.

(JANES 2009, 13)

ACROSS THE MUSEUM SECTOR, staff and volunteers, governing bodies, academics and politicians are exploring how museums can respond to the "winds of change" (http://douglasworts.org) in wider society, including the responsibility of museums to engage their users in the great issues of the day. This paper focuses on one aspect, namely how museums can actively support community empowerment and civil engagement. It does this through exploring how an urban history museum can move from being a "state space," presenting a single, "official" account of the past to being a shared space representing multiple perspectives, and exploring the relevance of the past to people's lives today and in the future. This is a highly appropriate area for discussion at a time when a raft of master plans for major new city history museums, from Bristol (UK) to Boston (U.S.), and from Stuttgart (Germany) to Taipei (Taiwan), have all placed civil engagement within their core mission.

The "great issue" involved is the growing concern among western governments about the breakdown of community and the wider collapse of public engagement with democracy. Governmental responses have developed from interagency policies designed to combat disadvantage, to strategies that seek to empower communities and develop social capital. As public institutions, museums have sought to respond to these issues. The idea of museums partnering with communities in

Graham Black is a consultant Heritage interpreter, and a reader in public history and heritage management at Nottingham Trent University. "Embedding Civil Engagement in Museums" appeared in Museum Management and Curatorship (Vol. 25, No. 2, pp. 129–146, 2010) published by Taylor & Francis. It is reprinted here with permission of the publisher. All rights reserved.

planning for the future is not new. However, it is only in the last decade that we have seen the active promotion of the museum sector's capacity to empower communities to engage with the great and the local issues of the day.

In the United States, a national "Museums and Community Initiative" promoted from 1998 by the American Association of Museums, following a pilot scheme in Philadelphia, led to the publication of *Mastering Civic Engagement* (AAM 2002). It outlined core principles for museums of greater civic engagement, democracy and community building, and challenged U.S. museums to build and strengthen their community bonds. In Western Europe, where public bodies have traditionally received the bulk of their funding from the public purse, there has been an expectation at both the national and local levels that all such bodies, including museums, will actively support relevant political initiatives. In the UK, regional museums are now receiving funds for the first time from central government, through the *Renaissance in the Regions* scheme, specifically to support community outreach and learning initiatives.

However, in both the United States and Western Europe, the response by museums to the civil engagement agenda has been piecemeal. Conwill and Roosa (2003) suggest this is due to a lack of the necessary:

> organizational capacity to build stronger community partnerships—i.e., adequate time and money, a strong leadership commitment, an organizational culture that embraces change, and staff skilled at listening to community voices and establishing community relationships.

In my view, underpinning these issues is the need for a transformation in museum culture. The purpose of this paper is to inspire such a culture change, support the promotion of best practice and challenge museums to champion civil engagement. If museums are to truly commit to this initiative, we must acknowledge the problems involved. A history museum seeking to achieve a participative relationship with its local communities should be committed to incorporating their voices and life experiences. It should work to connect present and past, enabling people to make fundamental links with the past lives of their own communities and thereby draw out commonalities. It should encourage and support audiences to become actively engaged with displays and programming, and to contribute directly to content. Through enabling communities to discover their area's past, and its relevance to the present, the museum should also reveal to local people and communities the importance of having an active role in decision-making for the future. Therein lies the challenge—can these ambitions be delivered in practice? If they can, it will not be a passive undertaking. Rather, the museum must focus on actively encouraging participation.

Defining Civil Engagement

I have specifically used the term "civil" rather than "civic." In the UK, civic tends to relate to public institutions. My belief is that museums should seek to encourage and support engagement within the wider civil society, not just with public bodies. I adhere to the working definition of civil society put forward by the London School of Economics Centre for Civil Society:

> Civil society refers to the arena of uncoerced collective action around shared interests, purposes and values. In theory, its institutional forms are distinct from those of the state, family and market, though in practice, the boundaries between state, civil society, family and market are often complex, blurred and negotiated. Civil society commonly embraces a diversity of spaces, actors and institutional forms, varying in their degree of formality, autonomy and power. Civil societies are often populated by organisations such as registered charities, development non-governmental organisations, community groups, women's organisations, faith-based organisations, professional associations, trades unions, self-help groups, social movements, business associations, coalitions and advocacy groups. (Centre for Civil Society 2004)

I believe that it is only through more people playing an active role in civil society that we can hope to strengthen our democracy—by empowering individuals and communities to believe they can help to shape their own futures.

The Urban History Museum and Civil Engagement

> Cities are the defining artifacts of civilisation. All the achievements and failings of humanity are here. . . . We shape the city and then it shapes us. (Reader 2004, 1)

Over half the population of the world now lives in an urban environment. While it is in developing countries that the greatest urban growth is occurring, Western towns and cities are also witnessing rapid change physically, in the nature and diversity of their population and in the employment opportunities they offer. It is to neighborhoods within these towns and cities that Western governments most frequently point when speaking of societal breakdown. If museums are to have a meaningful role in civil society in the 21st century, that role will be forged in this urban environment. For urban history museums, that means emerging from the safe environment of an "official" past to explore critically the different perspectives of the communities in their localities. It also means encouraging debate about the impact of the past on the present. It means taking an active role in the present—and "the present is a different challenge in that it is happening now and changing all the time; it is out there in the streets of the city, not inside the museum walls" (Jones 2008, 8). It means using the past and present to support the development of their localities as learning communities, so that people can have an informed involvement in decision making about their futures.

The best museums inspire, excite, empower, give confidence and help individuals and communities to grow. Pilot research at Bristol and the Tyne & Wear museums outlines the positive impact museums can have on individuals (AEA Consulting 2005). Strong institutions like museums and libraries are recognized by many in the communities they serve as essential to community well-being, while the "sense of place" that is conveyed through history museums and historic preservation is a key element in helping a community understand its uniqueness (Wilkening and Chung 2009, 4). Given the difference they can make to people's lives, museums have a duty to the communities they serve, and to those who fund them, to play a civil engagement role. In business terms, this will also prevent the marginalization of museums within their localities, help museums to build sustainable audiences, and prove relevance to funding bodies.

This paper argues that five core principles provide the essential underpinning that would enable urban history museums (and others) to actively support civil engagement:

1. Urban history museums as *memory institutions* can collect, conserve, document and represent the cultures and life experiences of all those who live within their localities, helping to create an inclusive civil environment.
2. Urban history museums as *learning institutions* can help to develop informed individuals and communities who can contribute positively to decision making about their future lives.
3. Urban history museums as *social institutions* can reach out to welcome, support and represent the many voices within the communities they serve—in partnerships of equals.
4. Urban history museums as *democratic institutions* can actively promote civil dialogue and reflective participation in civil society.
5. Urban history museums as *responsive institutions* can work to change their organization and culture to meet the needs of contemporary society.

The first three of these principles are well established across the museum sector, and few museums would be starting from scratch on the journey to support civil engagement. Instead, we can begin by identifying the civil dimensions of our existing work, use that to persuade colleagues and then reach outward with commitment (Thelen 2001).

Museums as Memory Institutions
A museum is the memory of mankind (de Montebello 2008)

There is a long-established association of memory with preservation and storage. It is in this sense that the museum is much more than a typological collection of evidence of past-time frames but is, rather, the storehouse and protector of the memory of humankind—through the objects, including oral histories and sites, held in its collections. Such objects represent the visible, audible and touchable outer world of the memory of past societies—a cultural memory that can last thousands of years but is also relevant to recent times.

In collecting these objects, museums not only store cultural memory, but they are also directly involved in creating and manipulating it:

Preservation in the museum fixes the memory of entire cultures through representative objects by selecting what "deserves" to be kept, remembered, treasured . . . . (Crane 2000, 3)

In the context of civil engagement, it is particularly important to recognise the partial nature and idiosyncrasy of what was deemed worthy of keeping in the past. One can link the gaps in collections to major historical silences, and to past collecting policies relating to the priorities and tastes of the ruling elite within a community—reinforcing the view that museums represent a selective and elitist view of the past. Yet, in recent decades, museum engagement with wider communities and the desire to represent multiple perspectives have been reflected in the revisiting of existing collections to draw out new relevancies, as well as in proactive approaches to contemporary collecting that ensure the representation of previously disenfranchised communities. Civil engagement is underpinned by a sense of inclusion and representation. Museums, through their collection and representation of once excluded communities can play a key role in this:

In this process of transformation from the position of traditional cultural authority to a new role as cultural mediators in a more multicultural environment, museums redefine their strategies of representation of the past and find space for marginalized memories. (Misztal 2003, 20)

Museums as Learning Institutions

> We're talking about building learning communities . . . [it is] essential for a healthy democracy and civic well being to have educated citizens. (Semmel, quoted in Falk et al. 2007, xvi)

There has been a growing acceptance within the museum profession that museums are primarily institutions for public learning. Substantive research has shown that museums are natural locations for what Falk and others have called free-choice learning (Falk and Dierking 2002). The opportunities for museum learning tend to be unpressured and open-ended. Museum display and programming can involve all the senses and create diverse stimuli and responses. This works with a wide variety of audiences, and can reflect a range of opinions, interests, needs and expectations. It involves active engagement of the mind and can be extremely enjoyable.

Developing museums as centers for free-choice learning means comprehensively changing our relationship with visitors—to one of partners on a learning journey where the museum acts as a supporter and facilitator, poses questions, and reflects multiple perspectives from which visitors can construct their own meanings. In this more flexible learning environment, visitors must also play a more active role by taking more control of their own learning, creating personalized learning experiences and potentially contributing to content in a three-way conversation with the museum and other visitors.

All of this provides a framework within which the museum can potentially thrive as a social and democratic institution. The revival of the learning role has transformed the organization and mission of many museums, as well as brought home to museums the importance of partnerships with other agencies and with the communities they serve. The role that museums as learning institutions can play in building stronger communities will be much more effective if carried out in partnership with others.

Museums as Social Institutions

My focus here is on user contributions and the representation of multiple perspectives. Creating a friendly, welcoming external image and museum environment remain central to any ambition to engage communities with museums and this has been written about extensively elsewhere (e.g., Black 2005, 2008; Falk and Dierking 2000; Gurian 2006; Hood 1993), including a recent comment by Falk (2009, 49):

> The number one criteria [sic] of all my subjects—black and white, frequent visitor, occasional visitor, or non-visitor—was feeling comfortable and at ease in one's surroundings . . . and nearly all also valued social interactions.

An urban history museum committed to civil engagement will actively encourage user contributions to content and seek to represent multiple perspectives. History museums have frequently been criticized as institutions that help to create and underpin an authorized collective memory. Their process of selection, documentation and presentation was seen as legitimating a particular construct—rather than representing a multiple past, museums were believed by their critics to present an "official" version. They did this partly through the kinds of narratives and ways of thinking they presented but, perhaps most powerfully, through their silences—"in what it allows to go unnoticed, unrecognized and unacknowledged" (Mezaros 2008, 243). The "new museology" opened the gates to pluralism and multiple perspectives, while the rise of oral history as a discipline also had a profound effect as museums incorporated the lived experiences of ordinary people into display content. Today, many history museums have replaced the single authoritative voice with a representation of many voices and multiple perspectives. They have done so by taking the following steps:

ENSURING CONTENT IS INCLUSIVE
- Researching and integrating diverse aspects of history and heritage into displays and ensuring representative interpretation.
- Involving diverse cultural and community groups in developing displays, resources and interpretation.
- Working with groups and communities to research and celebrate memory.
- Developing imaginative events and activities to highlight the diverse nature of heritage (Wong 2002, 7).

USING A WIDE SPECTRUM OF SOURCES. Incorporating objects, pictures and moving electronic images, written texts, oral narratives, smells, sounds, voices and music are key starting points. These ensure a multisensory approach and provoke a lively and critical historical dialogue about the past.

DEVELOPING USER-GENERATED CONTENT. A museum committed to community participation will actively seek user contributions in its galleries, both in programming within the locality and online, making the museum a public space for opinion and meaning-making, for public discourse and inclusion. Content could include:

- community participation in exhibition development;
- community exhibits incorporated into long-term displays and the museum website;
- incorporating contemporary responses to the collections;
- the voices of users incorporated into displays, for example through comment cards, recorded content and online;
- opportunities to meet with staff and communities;
- seating as a tool to encourage social interaction; and
- opportunities to join interactive discussions on the website.

MOUNTING TEMPORARY EXHIBITIONS. Partnering community groups will encourage ownership of exhibitions and events, ensure changing content in the museum, and add to the provision of multiple perspectives. Some subject matter works better in temporary displays, while on other occasions it can provide an opportunity to experiment before incorporation into permanent content. Temporary exhibitions can also act as a focus for community-led research, while their public display engenders pride and confidence in participants.

BECOMING A MUSEUM WITHOUT WALLS. Urban history museums must go outside their walls and also not be restricted to set opening hours. The museum's most important exhibit is the locality it serves and the museum should both encourage local communities to share their experiences with visitors and encourage users to go out and actively explore the locality—using local voices (live or audio) to reach below the surface patina to develop a real understanding.

New technology is transforming the capacity of the museum to reach outwards and is critical to the museum's role in promoting civil engagement, particularly as it changes from being primarily a source of information to an opportunity for networking. As well as the more traditional roles for the website, many museums are already recognizing the potential to go much further (Samis 2007).

BUILDING STORIES ON WHAT LIFE IS LIKE IN THE LOCALITY NOW. Oral and written testimonies, short films, soundscapes, and images contribute to a wider understanding of a locality's complex culture and history, and could include the recording of personal experiences and life stories as part of the museum's role as a repository of community memory. These could also link to contemporary collecting which would engage with diverse audiences to capture a multitude of connecting narratives. Partnerships with regional and community media, for example, would enable the museum to incorporate up-to-the-minute stories. As previously suggested, town trails developed by individuals and communities would take people outside the museum walls—exploring the area through many eyes.

PEOPLING AND PROGRAMMING IN THE GALLERIES. A key way of including many voices and multiple perspectives in the museum is through people in the galleries—staff and volunteers—and the associated activities ranging from storytelling, to object handling and gallery tours, to the organization of debates. It is essential that spaces are designed for these activities. Staff roles must also be carefully defined and a wide range of community volunteers sought to ensure different voices are heard. Actively seeking community involvement and offering training, including payment where this helps people recognize that their commitment is valued, will be an ongoing task.

In addition to the need to develop new collections discussed above, other problems associated with developing multiple perspectives have yet to be resolved. These include the following.

SHARING AUTHORITY. Raising the issue of shared authority means confronting a primary fear of all professionals (not just museum curators)—the fear of their expertise not being recognized and of losing control. But, if a museum is committed to reflecting the voices of the communities it serves, curators must be willing to share authority for content, and this is best achieved in a partnership of equals. In Leicester, for example, the museum service worked with groups from the local Asian community to create an exhibition and website on their experiences of moving to England. This was part of a national project (www.movinghere.org.uk) which involved over thirty-five archives, museums and libraries and forty-five community groups. For Leicester's museums, projects like this are vital as Leicester will be the first city in the UK where no ethnic group forms a majority of the population.

In projects like Moving Here, individual and community users of the museum bring their ideas, feelings and personal connections with them, while the museum acts as a "mediator of many voices" and provides the context that enables people to reassess these within a "bigger picture" of the past:

> Memories stand on their own; a good history exhibit provides context. We had to somehow join the two. Just as important, from my point of view, we needed to allow thoughtful visitors to reflect on the very nature of memory and history. To allow visitors to understand the value of both approaches to the past would be an important contribution. . . . The way to do this was to share the job of interpretation, of creating meaning with our visitors. (Lubar 1997, 18)

A true sharing of authority with users and communities should allow individuals and communities direct involvement in the selection of which issues to address and in the *production* of historical knowledge. This raises a further issue in that shared authority must always be underpinned by the understanding that with such authority comes trust—the trust of museum users in the content provided. In this situation, one can also see a potential conflict between history and community memory, with popular historical knowledge tending to reflect a highly selective interest in the remains of the past that is permeated with present-day assumptions (Tosh and Lang 2006, 12-13). The issue of the museum retaining editorial control must be addressed early in any potential partnership.

INCORPORATING SELECTIVE PERSPECTIVES. There is a risk that museums incorporate selected perspectives into their content, effectively inviting in some previously marginalized groups to become part of the "authorized version" of the past. Museums must be vigilant in avoiding a tendency to keep working only with those community groups with which they are comfortable. There is an equal risk of giving too much space to those groups which have the strongest sense of community identity and have pushed hardest to have their stories told. Unless museums devise processes to counteract such tendencies, the less organized will remain silent and marginalized.

COMPETING VERSIONS OF THE PAST

> groups of people sharing many of the same experiences and much the same framework for interpreting them - will perfectly rationally be different from one another in the way they see the world. (Goodin 2003, 42)

Seeking to reflect multiple perspectives will not necessarily lead to harmony. There are competing versions of history within and between communities and generations, and differing versions of the past constantly compete for control of the present. For many previously marginalized groups, shared "memories of past injustices are a critical source of empowerment" (Misztal 2003, 18). Not all previously marginalized communities will welcome opportunities for inclusion in existing museums. In fact, there has been a profusion of communities creating their own museums. This is a significant concern as it introduces issues such as who owns the past, or the differing biases in presentation that these museums present. How are we, in these circumstances, to encourage people to reflect on the experiences of others?

Conflicting perspectives on the past represent both a problem and a challenge. There is a need to develop approaches to display that engage people with the points of view of others, as well as to encourage reflection and understanding—the basis of the next core principle.

MUSEUMS AS DEMOCRATIC INSTITUTIONS

> Democratic citizens are supposed to act *reflectively*. . . . Democratic citizens are sup-
> posed to come to some joint determination of what they *collectively* ought to do.
> . . . Democratic citizens are supposed to act *responsively,* taking due account of the
> evidence and experience embodied in the beliefs of others. Democratic citizens are
> supposed to act *responsibly,* taking due account of the impact of their actions and
> choices on all those (here or elsewhere, now or later) who will be affected by them.
> (Goodin 2003, 1)

Goodin sees this discussion of a reflective democracy as representative of ideal standards unlikely to be achieved in the real world. It leads one to question what role
museums can realistically play in supporting engagement and participation in civil
society. What is there that museums do well that will support reflective participation in society?

MUSEUMS AS SOCIAL INSTITUTIONS. Museums have the potential to attract
people who are radically different from each other. Institutions that facilitate social,
cultural and generational mixing are a core underpinning of a civil society. If we
wish to support civil engagement we need to build on these qualities, by reaching
out to wider audiences and, through our approach to display and programming,
encourage conversation between visitors.

MUSEUMS AS INCLUSIVE INSTITUTIONS. Issues of inclusion and exclusion are
central to democracy—who feels a part of civil society, who does not, and why?
Who feels their voice is heard and who does not? Representing diverse communities and their multiple perspectives has been discussed above. But representing
diversity is not enough, as museums must also ensure those representations are
widely communicated. Equally as important, representing the previously silent,
marginalized, spoken for and excluded involves not only minority communities,
but also children, those not yet born, and the non-human inhabitants of the planet.

MUSEUMS AS POTENTIALLY NEUTRAL PLACES CAN OPEN DIALOGUE ON
THE CONTENTIOUS. This sits at the heart of the museum's ability to play an
active role in contemporary society. The museum is an ideal location to act as a
catalyst for unleashing comment, conversation, ideas and emotion from both local
people and users from further afield, particularly about issues of contemporary relevance to a locality. Cameron (2005) explores public attitudes to the presentation
of contentious issues in museums in Australia, noting that "bringing important,
challenging and controversial points of view in a democratic, free-thinking society
was seen as a key role for museums by many." Questions remain, however, about
the extent to which museums can challenge and criticize, as opposed to explore
viewpoints. Cameron's (2003, 2005) research on "Exhibitions as Contested Sites"
is important:

Should they act as provocateurs, leaders of public opinion and offer transformative spaces to challenge and change views? Or are museums to be safe civic places for the exploration of a range of views? Can museums take on a social activism role, to assist in the resolution of issues on a personal or political level or should they be places for non-challenging social experiences? Alternatively can museums be all of these things at once? (Cameron 2003, 4)

Responses to contentious issues are unpredictable and arouse strong opinions and emotions. The museum must, therefore, be very clear on how it both presents the contentious and defines its objectives.

MUSEUMS AS REFLECTIVE INSTITUTIONS

Much of the work of understanding others . . . is done inside your own head, imaginatively projecting yourself into their place. (Goodin 2003, 228)

Communicating and presenting inclusive content, multiple perspectives and contentious issues will only be effective as a tool for civil engagement if it leads to reflection, greater understanding and more informed decision making. Museums must build-in opportunities for users to reflect and review the experiences of their visits, augment their understanding and voice their own theories and opinions:

- Displays could lead with statements and artifacts from a range of viewpoints.
- If relevant, these could be supported with scrapbooks of newspaper articles, flipbooks, and so on. presenting different perspectives, so that users can develop informed opinions.
- Discussion could be encouraged by users posting or recording their comments for others to share. Cooks wrote of this in relation to a travelling exhibition *(What about Aids)* that she helped to organise.

  Our experience dealing with strong feelings around this exhibit made us realize that we needed a place where visitors could safely express their views. . . . We also covered a wall with visitors' positive and negative comments to let people know this was an exhibit that welcomed many different points of view. (Cooks 1999, 19)

- Well-designed seating areas can be central to encouraging discussion and reflection.

The use of interactive technology to encourage reflection, discussion and elicit responses from visitors is only just being recognized. See, for example, the "Room of Opinion" in the *Re-tracing the Past* exhibition at the Hunt Museum, Limerick (Ciolfi, Bannon, and Fernström 2008). Better known is the *Free2Choose* exhibit at the Anne Frank House in Amsterdam, which invites visitors to reflect and then vote on a variety of human rights issues in a way that allows users to compare their own votes with those of others participating at the same time, as well as with all visitors (Simon 2008). In a wider context, outreach projects and the museum web-site play an important role in taking "museum conversations" beyond the museum.

MUSEUMS AS CENTERS FOR DIALOGUE AND DEBATE. Dialogue between a museum and its visitors, and between visitors, can take many forms. The use of visitor contributions within museum exhibitions has been discussed above. But, while exhibitions have a core role to play, museums committed to promoting civil engagement must place much greater emphasis on the role of programming.

McRainey (2008) discusses how the whole approach to programming at the Chicago History Museum was re-planned in the lead-up to the major refurbish-ment completed in 2006, which moved "the interpretive focus in program design away from an exhibition-centered approach to one that is creating new connec-tions between adults, history and the city." The programming includes "panel presentations, forums for debate, seminar discussions and tours" that together "offer participants multiple points for exploration and diverse perspectives for meaning-making." It is the forums that most obviously reflect the new role the museum has taken in supporting civil engagement. These were carefully planned, follow-ing audience studies, to include "diverse perspectives for new insights into topics; primary voices of individuals who have first-hand knowledge; and dialogue among panelists as well as between panelists and participants." There is no opportunity for the museum to rest on its laurels:

> With the recurring monthly schedule, the structure challenges staff to demonstrate their nimbleness and flexibility in program design in timely responses to stories that headline local papers and issues discussed in community centres. (McRainey 2008, 40)

Museums can be effective centers of debate, including dialogue between past, present and future, but this type of initiative is not one to undertake without the appropriate resources. Equally, while it might work with adults who already pos-sess a high level of understanding and experience with debate, a different approach would be required to engage young people or socially disadvantaged communities. Jolly points to the use of "Talking Circles" at an exhibit entitled RACE at the Sci-ence Museum of Minnesota in 2007:

> Talking Circles . . . are facilitated discussions for groups of 20 or less . . . in which all participants are invited to reflect on their experiences in learning about and ex-periencing race as a factor in their lives and communities. More than 4000 people in visiting groups participated, a "valuable, non-confrontational way to explore difficult issues in a safe environment." (Jolly 2009, 90)

The Centre for Cultural Understanding and Change at the Field Museum in Chi-cago established a programme that reflects common concerns across the region defined through over one hundred conversations held with communities and or-ganizations in 2007. The Centre defines its mission on its website:

> The Centre for Cultural Understanding and Change (CCUC) . . . uses problem-solving anthropological research to identify and catalyse strengths and assets of communities in Chicago and beyond. In doing so, CCUC helps communities identify new solutions to critical challenges such as education, housing, health care, environmental conservation and leadership development. Through research, programs and access to collections, CCUC reveals the power of cultural difference to transform social life and promote social change. (www.fieldmuseum.org/ccuc/)

The website, in outlining current projects and programs, illustrates how effectively this works in practice.

In 2004, the Levine Museum of the New South accompanied its Civil Rights exhibition COURAGE: The Carolina Story that Changed America with a civil dialogue component, "Conversations on COURAGE" (Deuel et al. 2007). There was a real concern that the current civic and corporate leadership in Charlotte knew little of the historical background, so the specific aim here was "to use history to help engage current leaders in contemporary issues of race, education and social justice." The ambition was to bring in corporate leaders and their lieutenants to visit the exhibition in teams and then spend an hour in a facilitator-led discussion, making the shared experience into a long-term reference point. The "Conversations" proved highly successful, with 111 teams taking part, from the police chief and his staff to the Bank of America. This proved to be the first of a series of successful projects, with civil dialogue now a standard part of the museum operation and a new phrase to sum up the museum mission, "Using History to Build Community."

However, clearly not all visitors want to actively debate issues. If museums are to become effective centers for civil engagement, it is essential that we have a greater understanding of the differing levels of participation that we offer, the willingness or unwillingness of our users to engage, and the ways in which the environment we create supports or discourages that participation. Simon (2007b) explores differing levels of participation and the barriers between them:

> Level 1: user passively receives. . . . A successful level 1 experience features content that is meaningful and interesting to viewers.
> Level 2: opportunity for user to play with content. The content may be responsive to you, but the interactive experience is non-networked.
> Level 3: individual interaction with content is networked so each individual's interaction is available, in a limited capacity, to the entire group of users (e.g., voting).
> Level 4: individuals still do their interaction with the content singly, but their interactions are available for comment and connection by others. A successful level 4 experience uses social interaction to enhance the individual experience.
> Level 5: the holy grail of social discourse, where people interact directly with each other around content. Healthy level 5 experiences promote respect among users, encourage community development, and support interaction beyond the scope of the content. (Simon 2007b)

Simon believes that if we want to engender debate we must encourage direct interaction. But, as responses to Simon's blog make clear many, perhaps most, visitors prefer the anonymity museums currently offer. It remains questionable whether direct interaction can be a part of a 'normal' gallery visit rather than in a planned forum or debate.

MUSEUMS AS ACTIVE PROMOTERS OF CIVIL PARTICIPATION. In the Power of Children exhibition at the Children's Museum of Indianapolis, children meet the stories of Anne Frank, Ruby Bridges and Ryan White—all of which are used to show that every individual can make a difference. The exhibition culminates at the "Tree of Promise," where:

> children make a promise [that will impact or change the world], which floats up into the tree as a digital leaf. Those promises are then emailed home . . . and families can then elect to join the Tree of Promise social network. . . . If at-home users complete their promises they can return to the museum, where the tree "remembers" and congratulates them. . . . In this way, the "Tree of Promise" takes a quick participatory in-museum experience—writing down a promise—and provides a supportive platform on which users can cultivate and substantiate that action. (Simon 2007a)

Should museums behave in such a specifically social activist way, or is their primary role to encourage reflection?

MUSEUMS AS INSTITUTIONS THAT EVALUATE THEIR OWN ACTIONS. If museums seek to promote civil engagement, they must define outcomes and establish effective ways of evaluating performance. Such evaluation depends vitally on museums acknowledging failure as well as success. The museum must explore the issues that evaluation raises for the whole institution, not just for individual exhibitions or projects. It must focus on the effectiveness of visitor engagement, the contributions they make and the meanings they construct. Sharing experience and expertise is essential to moving forward.

A range of articles provide a starting point for the debate on the evaluation that is required. Douglas Worts has spent more than a decade exploring the opportunities open to museums that seek to serve the cultural needs of individuals and communities, and how museums measure their successes and failures in this field.

His article "Measuring Museum Meaning: A Critical Assessment Framework" (Worts 2006) discusses the development of evaluative approaches and performance indicators, such as the extent to which the museum addresses vital community needs and acts as a catalyst for action. The Inspiring Learning for All (ILFA) initiative in the UK (www.inspiringlearningforall.gov.uk) uses Generic Learning Outcomes (GLOs) and Generic Social Outcomes (GSOs) to evaluate the impact of museum programs on individuals. Economou (2004) outlines the range of evaluation approaches she developed at Kelvingrove Museum and Art Gallery, Glasgow—creating a strategy which she suggests "addressed evaluation holistically, and planned extensively and in-depth how it could be used as a useful tool to support the key activities throughout the organization" (Economou 2004, 31). McLean and Cooke (2003, 161) in their interviews of visitors to the then newly opened Museum of Scotland were able to show that "Rather than reading a one-dimensional static narrative of a nation, the visitors constructed multifarious read-ings that reflected both their individual identities and their collective identities in an imagined community."

MUSEUMS AS RESPONSIVE INSTITUTIONS

> The responsibility of civil society organizations [is] to purposefully craft missions that enable participation in public life . . . .

> (JANES 2009, 21)

If there is to be more than a piecemeal response to the civil engagement agenda, it will only come about if museums and their staff are committed to it. For this to happen, the wider museum culture will have to be transformed.

Museum staffing and organizational structure are rarely designed to reflect com-munity, and achieving the change necessary to drive a civil engagement agenda will require focus on both organizational and individual change. The pressure of day-to-day work, combined with the established culture of an organization, predispose it to remain the same. Unless the organization is supportive, individual staff development is unlikely to happen. There are few published accounts of the change process in museums. Abraham, Griffin and Crawford (1999) provide a stra-tegic overview of the processes used to manage change in twenty-four museums in Australia, Canada, the UK and the United States, concluding that:

> The effective management of change in museums is characterised by patient and considered leadership . . . able to translate external needs to internal vision and then to employee action, integrate tasks, structures, processes and systems at the techni-cal, political and cultural levels and integrate management practices to build internal and external unity. (Griffin and Abraham 2001, 336)

David Fleming, director of National Museums Liverpool, suggests that refocusing a museum service requires root and branch organizational change, including:

- a *new vision* with a focus on audiences and the social role of museums;
- if necessary, a *new senior management* to provide coherent leadership;
- *planning embedded at all levels, from corporate to individual job plans;*
- a *new staff structure* to promote teamwork and cross-departmental working;
- a *new style of involvement* of staff in decision-making;
- greater *political and media awareness;*
- an elevated value for staff *training and development,*
- promotion or recruitment of *"change agents"* within the staff to act as missionaries;
- raised *ambitions;*

- discouragement of factionalism and disrespect for the work of others;
- encouragement of risk-taking and innovation; and
- all of this underpinned by careful financial management. (Fleming 2005)

Fleming, as director of a national museum in the UK, is answerable to an independent Board of Trustees and it is notable that his paper makes no mention of the Board's involvement in such profound change. I cannot imagine this scale of change being achievable in the United States without active Board participation, but most urban history museums in the UK face a different problem. They are funded by and are under the control of elected local authorities. Most museum managers sit low down within departmental hierarchies and must react to agendas imposed from above, rather than having direct access to their governing committees and being able to define agendas. Change in these circumstances is much more difficult—one is fighting against not only the organizational culture of the museum, but also against that of the local authority.

The transformation of wider museum culture is an even greater challenge. A useful parallel is the campaign to re-establish learning as a core function of museums. For example, in the UK this became part of the national political agenda following the election of New Labour in 1997 with Prime Minister Tony Blair's commitment to Education, Education, Education. The publication of David Anderson's *A Common Wealth* (1997) was followed by the ILFA initiative led and funded by the national strategic body—the Museums, Libraries and Archives Council. This campaign brought staff and funding for learning and outreach projects nationwide, a website as a driving mechanism (www.inspiringlearningforall.gov.uk), and the development of an evaluative process. ILFA is ongoing and there is still substantial central government funding supporting it. Yet, the key word here is "re-establish." Museums have always been recognized as learning institutions but during the 20th century this function had been downgraded. Learning is now being restored to its rightful place, but this process still has some way to go.

By comparison, the AAM's *Museums and Community Initiative* has begun the process of establishing core principles related to community empowerment (see above), as well as developing toolkits to support museums and museum personnel along the route. In Western Europe, however, there is as yet little comparable development. Funding and activity continue to focus on the narrower field of audience development, although there is a parallel in UK universities:

> "Engagement" is an important word in modern society. We believe that a closer relationship with Higher Education helps empower people to take an informed part in the democratic process and the decisions affecting their lives. (Alan Thorpe, Chief Executive of the UK Natural Environment Research Council)

UK universities and their various higher education research councils came together in 2008 to establish a pilot initiative, Beacons for Public Engagement, including a National Co-ordinating Centre for Public Engagement (NCCPE) with an initial budget of £9.2 m over four years. Its role is to inspire culture change in how universities engage with the public and to promote best practice (www.publicengagement.ac.uk). As learning institutions and public bodies, British universities are recognizing the role they could and should play in civil society. The scale of this pilot project acknowledges the long road ahead in changing the internal culture of universities. How much longer and more difficult is the road for the museum sector?

Conclusion

Urban history museums can no longer afford to hide behind their walls in the safe confines of the "official" past. As social institutions and public bodies, they have a duty to contribute to the well-being of contemporary society and to work to improve people's lives. Part of this duty involves empowering local people and supporting their engagement with civil society. Many museums are already engaged in this - frequently to a greater extent than they realize—as an evaluation of existing activity based on the principles outlined above will reveal. Based on the work already being done, museums can re-evaluate their organizational culture and refocus their organizations so that they can reach out to wider society with a clear vision of their role and the capacity to achieve it.

No one would claim that this is an easy task that can be achieved rapidly, or that museums can succeed on their own. This paper has, however, sought to lay down core principles for the work ahead and to support individual museums and staff who wish to begin the journey. We are in urgent need of more museums to act as "beacons for public engagement."

Acknowledgments

With thanks to Julie Finch, Director of Bristol Museums, and Kevin Osbon of Focus Consultants for starting me on this journey. Real and email conversations with Katja Mieth, Director of Museum Affairs of the Free State of Saxony, Germany, and Mette Boritz, of the National Museum of Denmark, Copenhagen, added extra dimensions to the article. Carolyn Batstone of the Open University read and raised important issues on the final draft. I owe a particular debt of gratitude to the three anonymous reviewers whose comments made a considerable difference to the final article.

References

AAM. 2002. *Mastering Civic Engagement*. Washington, DC: American Association of Museums.

Abraham, M., D. Griffin, and J. Crawford. 1999. Organisation change and management decision in museums. *Management Decision* 37, no. 10: 736–751.

AEA Consulting. 2005. *Tyne & Wear Museums, Bristol Museums, Galleries and Archives: Social Impact Programme Assessment*. London: AEA Consulting; www.twmuseums. org.uk/about/corporatedocuments/documents/Social_Impact.pdf (accessed March 11, 2008).

Anderson, D. 1997. *A Common Wealth: Museums and Learning in the United Kingdom.* London: Department of National Heritage.

Black, G. 2005. *The Engaging Museum.* London: Routledge.

———. 2008. Creating a museum learning environment. In *Heritage Learning Matters. Museums and Universal Heritage,* ed. H. Kraeutler, 63–76. Vienna: Schlebrügge.

Cameron, F. 2003. Transcending fear—engaging emotions and opinion—a case for museums in the 21st century. *Open Museum Journal* 6: 1–46.

———. 2005. Contentiousness and shifting knowledge paradigms: The roles of history and science museums in contemporary society. *Museum Management and Curatorship* 20, no. 2: 213–233.

Centre for Civil Society, London School of Economics. 2004. *What is Civil Society?* London: Centre for Civil Society, London School of Economics; www.lse.ac.uk/collections/CCS/what_is_civil_society.htm (accessed March 3, 2009).

Ciolfi, L., L. J. Bannon, and M. Fernström. 2008. Including visitor contributions in cultural heritage installations: Designing for participation. *Museum Management and Curatorship* 23, no. 4: 53–65.

Conwill, K. H., and A. M. Roosa. 2003. Cultivating community connections. *Museum News,* May/June 2003. www.aam-us.org/pubs/mm/MN/MJ03_CommConnections.cfm (accessed August 20, 2009).

Cooks, R. 1999. Is there a way to make controversial exhibits that work? *Journal of Museum Education* 23, no. 3: 18–20.

Crane, S. A. 2000. *Museums and Memory.* Stanford, CA: Stanford University Press.

de Montebello, P. 2008. Former director of the metropolitan museum of art, New York, quoted in USA National Public Radio broadcast. *A History of Museums,* November 24.

Deuel, J., J. S. Ramberg, J. Fraser, and T. Hanchett. 2007. Inspiring visitor action in museums: Examining the social diffusion of ideas, COURAGE and time's running out—act now. *The Exhibitionist* 26, no. 2: 20–31.

Economou, M. 2004. Evaluation strategies in the cultural sector: The case of Kelvingrove museum and art gallery. *Museum and Society* 2, no. 1: 30–46.

Falk, J. 2009. *Identity and the Museum Visitor Experience.* Walnut Creek, CA: Left Coast Press.

Falk, J., and L. D. Dierking. 2000. *Learning from Museums.* Lanham, MD: AltaMira Press.

———. 2002. *Lessons Without Limit: How Free-choice Learning is Transforming Education.* Lanham, MD: AltaMira Press.

Falk, J., L. D. Dierking, and S. Foutz, eds., 2007. *In Principle in Practice.* Lanham, MD: AltaMira Press.

Fleming, D. 2005. Managing Change in Museums. Paper presented at the Museums and Change International Conference, November 8–10, in Prague.

Goodin, R. E. 2003. *Reflective Democracy.* Oxford: Oxford University Press.

Griffin, D., and M. Abraham. 2001. The effective management of museums: Cohesive leadership and visitor-focused public programming. *International Journal of Museum Management and Curatorship* 18, no. 4: 335–368.

Gurian, E. H. 2006. Threshold fear. In *Civilizing the Museum,* ed. E. H. Gurian, 115–126. London: Routledge.

Hood, M. G. 1993. After 70 years of audience research, what have we learned? Who comes to museums, who does not, and why? In *Visitor Studies, Theory, Research and Practice.*

5th ed., ed. D. Thompson, A. Benefield, S. Bitgood, H. Shettel, R. Williams, and D. Thompson, 77–87. Jacksonville, FL: Visitor Studies Association.

Janes, R. R. 2009. *Museums in a Troubled World*. London: Routledge.

Jolly, E. J. 2009. Testimony of Dr. Eric J. Jolly, President, Science Museum of Minnesota on "Examining the role of museums and libraries in strengthening communities" before the House Committee of Education and Labor at the Subcommittee on Healthy Families and Communities, September 11, 2008. In *Role of Museums and Libraries in Strengthening Communities*, ed. T. V. Alizar, 87–97. New York: Nova Science.

Jones, I. 2008. Cities and museums about them. In *City Museums and City Development*, ed. I. Jones, R. R. MacDonald, and D. Mclntyre, 1–15. Lanham, MD: AltaMira Press.

Lubar, S. 1997. Exhibiting memories. In *Exhibiting Dilemmas: Issues of Representation at the Smithsonian*, ed. A. Henderson and A. L. Kaeppler, 15–27. Washington, DC: Smithsonian Institution.

McLean, F., and S. Cooke. 2003. Constructing the identity of a nation: The tourist gaze at the museum of Scotland. Tourism. *Culture and Communication* 4: 153–162.

McRainey, D. L. 2008. New directions in adult education. *Journal of Museum Education* 33, no. 1: 33–42.

Mezaros, C. 2008. Un/familiar. *Journal of Museum Education* 33, no. 3: 239–246.

Misztal, B. A. 2003. *Theories of Social Remembering*. Maidenhead, UK: Open University Press.

Reader, J. 2004. *Cities*. London: Heinemann.

Samis, P. 2007. New technologies as part of a comprehensive interpretive plan. In *The Digital Museum: A Think Guide,* ed. H. Din and P. Hecht, 19–34. Washington, DC: American Association of Museums.

Simon, N. 2007a. Beyond hands-on: Web 2.0 and new models for engagement. *Hand to Hand* 21, no. 4; www.museumtwo.com/publications/beyond_hands_on.pdf (accessed January 2009).

———. 2007b. *Museum 2.0 blogspot 20103/2007: Hierarchy of social participation*; museumtwo.blogspot.com/2007/03/hierarchy-of-social-participation.html (accessed January 2009).

———. 2008. *Museum 2.0 blogspot 2011112008: Free2Choose and the social dimension of polling interactives*; museumtwo.blogspot.eom/2008/l 1/free2choose-and-social- dimension-of.html (accessed January 2009).

Thelen, D. 2001. Learning community: Lessons in co-creating the civic museum. *Museum News,* May/June. www.aam-us.org/pubs/mn/MN_MJ01_LearningCommunity.cfm (accessed August 2009).

Tosh, J., and S. Lang. 2006. *The Pursuit of History,* 4th ed. Harlow, UK: Pearson Longman.

Wilkening, S., and J. Chung. 2009. *Life Stages of the Museum Visitor. Building Engagement over a lLfetime*. Washington, DC: American Association of Museums Press.

Wong, J. L. 2002. Who we are. *Interpretation Journal* 7, no. 2: 4–7.

Worts, D. 2006. Measuring museum meaning: A critical assessment framework. *Journal of Museum Education* 31: 41–48.

PERSPECTIVES ON MEANINGFUL PUBLIC ENGAGEMENT

PUBLIC ENGAGEMENT, a more expansive term for audience participation, encompasses activities both on site, off site, and online. The dynamic intersection of communities, technology, and contemporary issues is so multidimensional that where and how the public elects to participate is not confined to activities that occur within the walls of a museum. Public engagement permeates the institutional psyche, merging market research with program development, reflecting the museum's brand with institutional communication strategies, and co-creating community projects and events. Today, the reinvented museum is a facilitator of interchange and discourse: not a purveyor of one truth but a place for many perspectives to be voiced with diverse points of access for dynamic learning and experiences where choice is a given. The public controls and determines the direction of their experience more than ever before.

Today, most museums incorporate the perspective of the public when determining institutional directions and priorities. Examples include involving community representatives in the development of exhibitions and programs, or inviting community members to serve on trustee committees as non-board members providing an important voice. With increasing levels of competition from other leisure and educational providers, museum leaders continue to turn to tactics long familiar in the business world, such as marketing, evaluation, and financial analysis, critical to informed decision making. Today a museum cannot afford to assume it has intrinsic value for the public. Museum staff must continually ask questions that challenge assumptions while factoring in data and research about audiences. Placing the public at the center of a museum's future has resulted in a shift in management practices—in the way exhibitions are developed, in board recruitment strategies, in hiring practices, and in what and how museums collect, if they collect at all. It is a dramatic shift from the days of internally focused decisions made with little regard for public desire or interest. Today's museums know that they cannot survive without ongoing feedback from and involvement with the public. The chapters in this part typify the range of thinking about how museums serve the public including the evolving role of exhibitions, the impact of technology, visitor rights, frameworks about visitor experiences and visitor participation, learning in museums, and architecture and its impact on the visitor experience.

Kathleen McLean, exhibit developer, designer, and author of numerous books and articles on exhibitions and the role of the visitor, looks back at professional discourse about exhibitions fifty years ago, and proposes that little has changed in "Do Museums Have Future?" McLean wonders if museum exhibitions will survive in the future given the unprecedented economic, technological, global pressures, and increasing consumer sophistication.

Peter Samis reveals the evolving impact of technology on museum interpretation in "The Exploded Museum," a chapter featured in *Digital Technologies and the Museum Experience*. Armed with a plethora of technological options from which to choose, museums must consider the learner, the nature of the message, and diverse perspectives before selecting the right technology for the best result.

Judy Rand, an exhibit planner, editor, and writer, outlines a canon for museum professionals in "The Visitors' Bill of Rights." This treatise should be tacked to office doors and posted over desks as a reminder to keep the visitors' perspective and comfort a primary concern in the minds of museum workers.

John Falk, a leading researcher on visitor studies, captures the essence of his publication, *Identity and Museum Visitor Experience* in an article written for the Danish Journal *DREAM* entitled "The Museum Visitor Experience: Who visits, why and to what effect?" Based on extensive research, Falk identifies different types of visitors using motivation as the qualifier for each category. This matrix provides a useful reference for thinking about and planning for more meaningful visitor experiences.

Nina Simon, well-known blogger and provocateur on topics relating to museum participation, outlines her philosophy in *The Participatory Museum*. In the chapter entitled "Principles of Participation" from that volume, Simon explains how to frame participation in light of the fulfillment of the visitor. To illustrate her points she outlines the progressive stages of participant engagement that capture the evolution of the participant from individual consumer to the highest level of social engagement with others.

Anna Cutler reframes learning in museums in "What Is To Be Done, Sandra? Learning in Cultural Institutions of the Twenty-First Century" featured in the Tate Papers published in the United Kingdom. Cutler argues that it is unproductive to apply formal education metrics to the informal learning of the museum setting. Along with her argument to rethink how museums assess effectiveness, she proffers that informal learning, an inherent strength of museums, lends itself to the challenges prevalent in the knowledge age.

One of the most underrecognized aspects of creating dynamic experiences for the public is the role of physical space with its intended public uses. In the final article of this section, Elaine Heumann Gurian discusses the connections between building design and function, and the role of architectural program planning—the process of envisioning what, why, and how a space will be used before architectural designs are created. Aptly titled "Threshold Fear: Architecture Program Planning," Gurian's insights provide wisdom and guidelines for approaching the often daunting world of master planning, building design, and project renovation.

Do Museum Exhibitions Have a Future?   23

KATHLEEN MCLEAN

I WAS ASKED, IN THE FIFTIETH VOLUME of *Curator: The Museum Journal,* to reflect
on the changes in museum exhibitions over the past fifty years and to speculate
about their future In order to ground myself in past practice, I read the entire
first volume of *Curator,* published in 1958, and compared the musings, expectations, and best practices of today with those voiced by our colleagues 200 issues
ago. Then, against this backdrop, I reflected on my increasing concerns about the
future viability of museum exhibitions.

The future is on my mind a lot these days as I ponder a variety of predictions:
fundamentalist movements are dragging us back into the Middle Ages; we are just
starting to simmer in a global warming soup; the U.S. national debt is eroding
world economic stability; and exotic viruses are just waiting for the opportune
moment to infect us. At the same time, across the world, new communities are
forming, woven together by astonishing new technologies and shaped by unprecedented change and complexity. How museums and their exhibitions will fit into
such a chaotic picture is anyone's guess.

Until recently, my response to this uncertain future has been mostly ambiva-
lent. In September 2005, when I was asked to lead a conversation about the future of museums with the Chicago Museum Educators Group, I couldn't decide
whether I was an optimist or a pessimist. In the end, I presented both viewpoints.
Museums might take a leadership role in developing new models for learning and
critical thinking, or they might continue to serve an outdated industrial revolution model of public education. Museums might become centers for inspiration,
reflection, and social interaction, where people connect deeply with their humanity, with beauty, and with the natural world; or they might become more

Kathleen McLean is principal of independent exhibitions, specializing in exhibition development, design, and
planning and is the former director of the Center for Public Exhibition and Public Programs at the Exploratorium
in San Francisco, California. "Do Museum Exhibitions Have a Future?" appeared in *Curator: The Museum Journal*
(Vol. 50, No. 1, January 2007, pp. 109–112). It is reprinted here with permission from John Wiley & Sons. All
rights reserved.

like their amusement park cousins, serving up "fun" determined by a market economy. Museums might open their doors wider to public discourse, becoming physical "Wikipedias" that are created and sustained by the people who use them. Or they might not.

Looking Back

I took the opportunity of this fiftieth anniversary issue of *Curator* to do a bit of backward-looking investigation. My thinking was that if I could connect the historical dots back through time, I might be able to gain some perspective on how far we have come as a profession. And I might be able to plot a more optimistic trajectory going forward.

As I read through the four issues that comprise the first volume of *Curator,* I was reminded that I come from a long lineage of articulate colleagues, passionate and optimistic about the future of museums and eager to experiment with the making of exhibitions. The original editors promised a publication for "the expression of opinion, comment, reflection, experience, criticism, and suggestion on all the activities of museum work" (Editorial Statement 1958, 5–6). I found it interesting that "criticism" was included here, since, in my experience, many museum professionals have an aversion to the notion of criticism. The editors also reminded us that

> The skill and competence now required to organize and administer a modem museum, to plan and prepare exhibits, to serve and deal with the public need for education and knowledge, to use and maintain collections, and to control the manifold interrelations of all these and other things as well, have taken on a highly professional character that reflects both the growing role of the museum in our culture and the high standards of performance that museums have taught the public to expect. (Editorial Statement 1958, 5)

This certainly is true today as well. In fact, I detected a disconcerting similarity between much of what was written those many years ago and what is still being debated today. To test my hunch, I called a respected colleague and read to her quotes from the 1958 articles without disclosing the date or source. She proposed that while the ideas might not be *new,* they are contemporary ideas that generally have not yet been—but *should be*—put into practice.

Every article provided interesting glimpses into the concerns of colleagues across the museum field, but I focused on content specifically related to museum exhibitions and the visitor experience overall. Most of the authors worked at the American Museum of Natural History, which started the journal and published it for nearly forty years. There were also authors associated with the Smithsonian, the Milwaukee Public Museum, university museums, state museums, an art gallery, and a nature center. They came from a variety of backgrounds and disciplines: curators and administrators, designers, educators, and even a "museum television coordinator."

The Visitor Experience

Concerns about and reflections on the quality of the visitor experience were foremost on many of the authors' minds. Some described their own exhibitions and discussed what might be learned going forward; some proposed entirely new ways of thinking about exhibition practice; and two authors even reflected on the implications of what was learned from a visitor survey conducted at their museum (Schaeffer and Patsuris 1958, 25).

I was surprised to see an article on designing for the well-being of museum visitors by providing adequate seating, easily accessible parking, clear wayfinding, and information when and where visitors need it (Reekie 1958). I thought this was a much more current idea, given the lack of such amenities in some museums today.

There was a great deal of discussion about what visitors needed in order to have memorable experiences, acknowledging that their interests and backgrounds are diverse and that they will "pick and choose as the layout designs or objects strike [their] fancy" (Schaeffer and Patsuris 1958, 25). One colleague suggested that we should become much more familiar with the communities in which our museums are situated, and we should work with and speak to those communities in the planning of exhibitions (Beneker 1958, 78). There was even a hint of the notion of museum-as-advocate: "Programs must serve the best interests of our population and stimulate in them the need and desire to form their own opinions, establish their own convictions, and take whatever action is appropriate, whether it be more thought on the subject or a letter to their congressman" (Burns 1958b, 65).

In "Exhibits—Firing Platforms for the Imagination," Katharine Beneker suggested that exhibitions should "enrich and enlarge the life of the person, child or adult, who sees them. Their value lies not within the museum walls, but in how much the visitor takes with him when he leaves. If you have started him on a new thought process, if you have made him curious enough to look more deeply into a subject, if you have changed his point of view, then your exhibition has been successful and your visitor is 'off the ground'" (1958, 81).

Objects and Ideas

Coming out of a tradition of taxonomic display that was the heart and soul of many natural history museums, a number of articles, not surprisingly, focused on the tension between the display of objects and the presentation of ideas. "There is a conspicuous modern trend to attempt, by means of thoughtful arrangement and labeling, to set forth abstract concepts and principles rather than to merely show objects, however intrinsically fine these may be. . . . It seems evident that this shift of emphasis from the particular to the general is a pervasive one found or to be expected in all museums everywhere. Not all of the efforts in this direction have been successful, for much experiment and much testing of results is still essential" (Schmidt 1958, 27-28).

This tension was prompted, in part, by the understanding that object-based exhibits worked well when emphasizing the specificity of the individual object or specimen, but alone they were not adequate for conveying the important, more abstract ideas of the time—related to ecology, biogeography, and evolution—ideas that are even more important today. And the tensions were well articulated: "It is noteworthy that such exhibits demand far closer cooperation between the scientific and the educational staffs than the 'old style,' take it or leave it exhibits. Efforts to transform exhibition halls in this direction are sometimes over-zealous, and there is danger that the museum baby may be thrown out with the bath" (Schmidt 1958, 28).

Out of these discussions of object and idea arose the notion of focusing an exhibition around one main exhibit idea—what museum professionals call "the big idea" today (Serrell 1994). "By far most of the museum visitors are constantly on the move. It would therefore seem a reasonable conclusion that an exhibit should be limited to a single idea or two. . . . This principle of a one-idea exhibit is not new in the field of education. In fact, it is one of the classic rules of teaching. Yet many museums seemed not to have learned it" (Hellman 1958, 75). This notion, put forth by an educator, elicited a curiously familiar response from a curator, who was advocating the value of a primarily aesthetic experience: [He] ". . . states that it is now known that specific 'one-idea' exhibits convey more to the viewer than those giving a general impression. Who, one wonders, found this out? Probably they were educators, who proved it by testing the subjects with small, specific questions" (Amadon 1958).

Interpretation

For me, some of the most relevant and familiar ideas focused on interpretation and learning. Rosenbauer suggested: "Much has been learned in the past fifty years about the nature of the individual, and there is much to be learned. Museums should take advantage of the knowledge that is available and design their activities accordingly. There are also opportunities for research and new knowledge in the field of what is both broadly and loosely called visual education. Museums are the obvious places for such research. This will require some new thinking on the part of curators. Interest must be centered not on things but on the meaning of things to ordinary people with ordinary lives and backgrounds. This would be simple if meanings were fixed and universal—which they are not" (1958, 6).

There were reminders throughout that exhibitions have stories to tell (something I'm hearing a lot these days), and the ways museums tell them should be carefully examined. Robert Dierbeck described how museums might make better use of the medium of television to "speak the language of our time" (1958, 44). Schaeffer and Patsuris referred to "many articles and books on exhibition techniques" that focus on the importance of adequate and well-written labels with clear and understandable language, brevity, and a clear relationship to the objects and ideas being described (Burns 1958a, 32). It would be interesting to compare them to Beverly Serrell's writing on the subject these many years later (1996).

Rosenbauer cautioned us not to focus primarily on facts and information delivery. "Our curiosity, wonder, and delight are the driving forces that keep us constantly seeking knowledge. We should realize that the particular facts we acquire are only important because they fit into and enlarge a total concept. It is awareness of life, not just facts of life, that we must provide." He suggested, "It is essentially a problem of communication. We must first be sure of what we want to say, then find a communicative device that will do what we want. The device will be found to be closer to art than to language" (1958, 9).

Mission and Market

I always assumed that the tensions between mission and market were a relatively recent phenomenon in museums, emerging full-blown in the 1980s with block-buster fever. And yet, to my surprise, I found a number of references to the familiar entertainment-versus-education debate that underlies so many of these tensions: "Trained museum educators must take the responsibility of seeing that museum exhibits are more than a free Sunday afternoon entertainment for the public" (Hellman 1958, 76). "[T]he museum's concern should be less for the number of its visitors than for what it does for them. If it wants to be an educational institution, then it must have an educative philosophy. It must offer the individual visitor something more than the fleeting pleasure of novelty" (Rosenbauer 1958, 7). And in discussing the relationship between museums and commercial television, William Bums noted that "producers and directors on commercial stations worry about ratings even without an agency on their trail, and their shot-in-the-arm for a low audience index harks back to the old-fashioned museum with its bizarre, its mysterious, its largest and its smallest. This is what we have been trying to avoid. . . ." (1958b, 66).

Design and Display

I expected that the more practical and technical aspects of exhibition practice in 1958 would seem quite dated and irrelevant to contemporary museums, but even here I found some unnerving parallels. I was delighted to read about the installation of unprotected chalk murals drawn directly on the walls in the Brontosauer Hall of the American Museum of Natural History (Colbert 1958), not only because they were so elegant and unusual, but because they reminded me of a wall writing and diagramming technique I thought was quite innovative in Bruce Mau's traveling exhibition Massive Change, organized by the Vancouver Art Gallery. The exhibition, which finished its run at the Museum of Contemporary Art in Chicago, looked at design and its potential for improving human welfare.

I found it curious and refreshing that in one issue, six pages were devoted to museum-related photographs of "oddities of institutional sign-posting in New York." In another issue, eight pages focused on a description and critique of Expo '58, including photographs of architecture and exhibit installations—evidence that our colleagues were actively looking outside the museum field for inspiration. Even in the highly technical articles by preparators that Curator was so well known for in the past, I found a contemporary connection. Two different articles described early forms of plastination of biological specimens, one that included a human fetus, and the other a human head (Sills and Couzyn 1958a; 1958b). Here, in plastinated flesh, were the ancestors of Gunther von Hagens's Body World clan.

Foretelling my own concerns about the prescriptive and limiting nature of "best practices," Katharine Beneker declared, "I do not feel that we can establish standards of display, because such standards change with each generation and with each turn of fashion. Our predecessors firmly believed that they were using the latest and most modern display methods when they installed what appear to us to be antiquated exhibits. Today we feel that ours are also the last word. Yet tomorrow or a decade hence, these same exhibits will be just as obsolete. Therefore let our standards be in the field of content—simply, clearly, and accurately defined—and in the richness of our imagination" (1958, 80).

Experimentation

In reflecting upon all the ideas contained in these articles written almost fifty years ago, what I found most surprising was the recurring theme of experimentation, which rarely gets mentioned today, outside the context of prototyping in science museum exhibits. "At the display level, the designers often have to deal with physically small but esthetically subtle and intricate problems that are little appreciated by those not trained to understand them. The problems tend to be unique and therefore not capable of solution by the application of already established principles. Opportunity to experiment is essential" (Parr 1958, 36-37). And ". . . the designer must be allowed to design by trial and error. This may seem extravagant and imply poor planning, but on the contrary, it is a necessary ingredient of all major accomplishments, whether in science, music, or art" (Witteborg 1958, 38).

"In the temporary exhibit we have opportunity to experiment with future forms, without committing ourselves to the results of our experiments, while still being able to expose them to public reaction. Even in the permanent exhibits we work on today we must strive for the forms of tomorrow, if they are not to be 'dated' before the halls are opened. In a natural history museum, it may take five to 15 years to complete a hall. It is logical for us to aim our temporary exhibits not even at the forms of tomorrow, but towards those of the day after tomorrow, so that, in navigator's terms, we can at least get one 'fix' to guide us to the forms of tomorrow in our permanent exhibition halls" (Parr 1958, 40).

Even the way museums conduct fundamental business was grist for experimental ideas: "As for night openings, museums have tried the hours from seven until 10 to give people who work during the day a chance to benefit from their exhibits and programs. What do museums think of staying open 24 hours a day, with film showings at two, four, and five-thirty *in the morning,* with classes in 'Painting for the Amateur' or 'Science for the Layman' at midnight?" (Burns 1958a, 44-45). Two recent examples of presenting programs at unusual hours—both considered quite innovative today—are the Exploratorium's overnight eclipse viewing programs, and the Dallas Museum of Art's centennial celebration, which included staying open for 100 hours. Both were stunningly successful with visitors, and other museums are cautiously considering similar experiments.

And Katharine Beneker reminded us that museum exhibitions exist within a much larger dynamic cultural context, one that we sometimes forget about in our focus on the inner workings of our own field: "For years I have heard that museums are poverty-stricken, but I am inclined to believe that we are stricken with poverty of the mind as well, and this is a more serous drawback than lack of money. An exhibition is a means of communication, and, if we have nothing to say, neither will the exhibit. Too often our lives are confined to four museum walls—fireproof, mothproof, rainproof, and thought-proof. We have not taken the time to broaden our base of understanding by getting out among people to find out how others are thinking, eating, laughing, loving, and hating. Try going to a stock-car race, a 'greasy spoon,' a burlesque show, a rodeo, a revival meeting, an opera, or a ballet, and talk to the people there. By enlarging our experience in all directions, we will bring a freshness and richness to our thinking if not to our pocket books" (1958, 80).

Back to the Present

From today's vantage point, colleagues' 1958 concerns over unprecedented museum growth, hiring people untrained in museum work, and uncoordinated and wasteful museum expansion seem like recurring nightmares. Yet here we are, fifty years later, treading the well-worn path. Is this evidence of professional consistency and a continuing dialectic about museums and society? Or is it a sign that we haven't evolved much over the last fifty years?

Recently, as one of the "silverbacks" in "Silverbacks and Young Bloods Debate the Future of Exhibitions," a panel at the American Association of Museums 2006 Annual Meeting in Boston, I spent a Sunday in Toronto with "young blood" Erika Keissner from the Ontario Science Centre in preparation for the session. We went to three of the city's major museums and compared our experiences. It is not important to know which museums we actually visited or which exhibitions we attended, because, regardless of the specifics, I believe our experiences are indicative of the general visitor experience in many museums today.

There were very few people in the galleries at the first museum we visited, perhaps because it was in the midst of renovation. This museum had excited Erika as a young visitor, and had inspired me as a young exhibit designer, particularly the way the staff had reflected upon their exhibit development processes and evaluated their mission, goals, and galleries. We visited an exhibit that was one of Erika's favorites as a child—an open natural history diorama with labels that encourage visitors to find camouflaged animals in the forest. After ten minutes of searching in vain, we left in frustration. On the way out, a gallery attendant informed us that many of the animals had been removed from the diorama long ago because of deteriorating taxidermy. She blamed visitors who "snuck food into the galleries and attracted pests" to the specimens. Our frustration could have been easily avoided if there had been a sign explaining why the specimens were removed or in some way acknowledged the decrepitude of the exhibit. And the gallery attendant's disdain for visitors could have been tempered, had she been familiar with Gordon Reekie's notion that "as the only personal contact the visitor has during his stay . . . employees represent the museum in a way that is often remembered for a long time" (1958, 94).

We found it curious that several old sporting exhibits were being torn down, while a newer, adjacent case contained the display of a contemporary hockey uniform. We suspected that this might be an attempt to provide objects more "relevant" to the community, but while it's possible to lay your eyes on hockey uniforms almost anywhere in this town, the chance to see these antique sporting artifacts was an opportunity soon to be lost. We reminded ourselves that these were old exhibitions, and that the museum was currently in a major capital transformation. But even the newly opened art galleries, with case upon case of objects without labels laid out like housewares in a high-end department store, seemed a bit behind the times, given that visitor research continues to indicate that people want and need some context and information about objects on display.

Our second destination—a progressive art museum—was only a bit more satisfying, since it, too, was in the middle of renovation, with only a few galleries open for visitors. Over the years, I had read about the museum's innovative interpretive experiments designed to help visitors look deeply at an artwork, and I was interested in experiencing them first-hand (Worts 1990, 1995; Clarkson and Worts 2005). I expected to see several of these exhibit elements on display, since the depth of visitor response and engagement had sounded quite profound. Unfortunately, we were able to find only one small exhibit, and it was suffering from lack of up-keep, with scrunched paper and unsharpened pencils. The artworks in the family center were charming and playful, and the display of architectural models of new buildings around town gave us a different perspective on the city. But there was not much to keep us there for very long.

By the time we reached the third museum, it was three minutes to five and they were locking their doors. Even though Erika knew the guard with the key, he wouldn't let us in for a peek. Too bad they hadn't taken William Burns' advice to stay open during the hours that visitors are actually available (1958a, 44-45). I was never able to see the temporary exhibition that had drawn us to the museum, since I had to leave Toronto early the next morning. Luckily, Erika returned on another day, and it was a satisfying experience for her when she finally saw it. But most general visitors probably would not be that diligent.

After the museums, we unintentionally took Katharine Beneker's suggestion to "get out among people to find out how others are thinking eating, laughing, loving, and hating" (1958, 80). We visited a videogame arcade, where dozens of young people in their teens and early twenties were exhibiting their skills in an electronic dance competition. We then visited a jazz club, where people of all backgrounds, persuasions, and ages—from nineteen to ninety—were thoroughly engaged in keeping the beat with a funky brass band. We ended the evening at a

Chinatown restaurant where dozens of people lined up in the cold to get in for a late-night dinner. In each place, the commingling of a diversity of people, cultures, and social interactions provided us with rich, energetic, and satisfying experiences.

This experiment in museum-going only reinforced a concern I reluctantly have been entertaining these days that museum exhibitions might be an obsolete medium, out on the dying limb of an evolutionary tree, and unless they significantly adapt to their rapidly changing environments in the coming years, they could be headed toward extinction. You might think it unfair to judge those aging museums by their sags and wrinkles. After all, we visited them in the midst of major cosmetic surgery, and soon they would be vibrant once again. Or would they? The nature and scope of the changes—new buildings by celebrity architects, and newly installed galleries with new cases and settings—seem to focus on the bricks and mortar, with no evidence that the exhibitions and programs will be significantly different. And while these museums are undergoing their transformations, they seem to be ignoring the day-to-day visitor experience—evidence, perhaps, of their true affections.

These grand institutions gave little attention to simple things that might have made my experience rewarding, despite the faded carpets or lack of funds. The three venues we visited later in the day—the video arcade, the jazz club, and the Chinatown restaurant—were nothing fancy. The furniture was old and worn, the architecture was less than memorable. But the programs and offerings were compelling, the social energy was uplifting, and the excitement palpable.

Part of the problem comes from a lack of imagination about what exhibitions could be in this new and complex world, and part of the problem comes from the traditional ways in which exhibitions are developed. It may take many years to develop a major exhibition, usually because of museum bureaucracies, fund raising constraints, and the number of people involved. The huge amounts of time and people required means that the exhibitions are very expensive to produce. And the bottom-line reality, combined with increasing marketing pressure to attract millions of visitors, means that much exhibit development time is spent trying to get curators, designers, developers, evaluators, funders, stakeholders, and marketers to agree on what exhibitions should be about. And once built and open to the public, those very same exhibitions are left on their own to deteriorate slowly, forgotten in the rush to create the next new thing.

Certainly, museums and their exhibitions have changed with the times to some extent, reflecting the changing values of the societies of which they are a part. Democratizing influences on authorship and authority, coupled with an increasing reliance on the earned income from admission fees, have pushed museums to diversify their menu of offerings. An increased understanding about how people learn, how they spend their leisure time, and why they attend museums has influenced the goals and features of some exhibitions. And revolutionary advances in new technologies have allowed museum exhibitions to provide a level of dynamism and action that had been much more difficult previously.

But despite these changes, opportunities, and new understandings, exhibition professionals still seem to be saying the same things colleagues were saying fifty years ago, while thinking they are new ideas. And we don't seem to be putting many of these ideas and theories into practice. I find it curious that exhibit professionals today still cite as most innovative the exhibition, Mathematica, created by Charles and Ray Eames in 1961, a couple of years after the first volume of *Curator* was published.

I acknowledge the claims of progress made by museum scholars and historians over the years, yet I see a stultifying sameness in many of the exhibitions being created today. Administrators still think of exhibitions as products; curators, exhibit developers, and designers still think of exhibitions as stages for their own performances; and everyone still uses the phrase "talk about" when describing what an exhibition will do. Most new museum exhibitions today are still primarily populated with glass boxes accompanied by passive labels telling museum peoples' stories. Even when digital media replace the printed label—often at great expense—the experience remains essentially the same, except with talking heads delivering the stories. Most science center exhibits are no exception; instead of glass boxes, just substitute hands-on devices that are the same from one institution to the next. The fundamental changes in most museum exhibitions today seem to reside in the decibel levels of their marketing campaigns, claims of innovation, and ambient sound in the galleries. Most exhibition resources are put into expensive furniture, media, and graphics, and all are designed to last for the next thirty years, which, based on their high costs, will probably be a necessity.

Perhaps this underlying stasis has to do with the nature of museums as civic matriarchs—benign cornerstones of societal infrastructure. Fashions may change, but the general assumption has been that these great cultural storehouses will not be dismantled any time soon. And perhaps this security has created in exhibition professionals a complacency that keeps us predictable, a bit dull, and unaccustomed to imagining how exhibitions could play more engaging roles in this complex and changing world.

Looking Forward

If museum exhibitions continue to cover the same ground, I'm not sure they will have a future, particularly if the future is anything like the predictions looming on the horizon. The James Irvine Foundation, in its new working paper, *Critical Issues Facing the Arts in California,* warns that nonprofit arts and cultural organizations are "facing major, permanent, structural changes brought on by technological advances, globalization and shifting consumer behavior" and "are likely to become increasingly peripheral as the modes of creating, delivering and consuming artistic content and experience are affected by large-scale changes in the broader environment" (2006, 2,1). The report goes on to say:

> [I]ncreasingly audiences expect artistic creators and distributors to be technologically literate; responsive to their personal interests, and constantly generating fresh content. This is a formidable challenge for most nonprofit arts organizations, which

are neither organizationally nor financially structured to allow for rapid innovation or hypersensitivity to consumer expectations. Most cultural organizations are not equipped to "personalize" their audiences' experience in ways that are becoming commonplace in the commercial sector; placing them at a disadvantage in capturing and sustaining customers.

While not all museums are "arts organizations" as described above, I believe they face the same challenges to their future viability. And museum exhibitions—the most prominent and expensive of a museum's offerings—could be the hardest hit. Again, from the Irvine Foundation paper. "The environment for arts and culture in California and the rest of the United States has irreversibly changed, and the nonprofit arts sector has reached a breaking point, where it must adapt to evolving technologies and consumer demand or become increasingly irrelevant. Inaction or business as usual' is not a viable option" (2006, 6).

As our visitors increasingly deal with the effects of religious and cultural conservatism, war and power politics, the effects of global warming and species loss, and deadly new viruses that can spread across the globe in a matter of days, will our exhibitions be enlightening, comforting, or useful to them? As new communities emerge and evolve within the increasingly complex arenas created by new technologies, will our exhibitions have a place on the playing field? Only if, in the words of Thomas Friedman in his bestselling book, *The World Is Flat,* they allow for "multiple forms of collaboration—the sharing of knowledge and work—in real time, without regard to geography, distance, or, in the near future, even language" (2005, 176). And only if, in the words of Katharine Beneker, they "fire the imagination":

> To me an exhibit is a springboard, although I suppose that in this day and age a better comparison would be a satellite-carrying rocket. The rocket gets the satellite off the ground and hurls it into that vast unexplored area, outer space. An exhibit gets the visitor "off the ground" and into an area that is still unknown to him. In both cases, there must be a firing platform, and that, in an exhibition, is the familiar, whether it be an object or an idea. From this platform, you, the exhibitor, can fire the imagination and carry it out into other areas of knowledge, or (and this happens all too often) your exhibit can fizzle and never get the visitor off the ground (1958, 77).

Acknowledgments

I would like to thank Darcie Fohrman, Erika Keissner, Catherine McEver, Wendy Pollock, Beverly Serrell, and Jay Rounds for their thoughtful criticism and suggestions in writing this article

References

Amadon, D. 1958. On first looking into Chapman's new forest. *Curator* 1 (3): 5–7.
Beneker, K. 1958. Exhibits—firing platforms for the imagination. *Curator* 1 (4): 76–81.

Burns, W. 1958a. The challenge of change. *Curator* 1 (1): 42–45.

———.1958b. Should museums try TV? *Curator* 1 (4): 63–68.

Clarkson, A., and D. Worts. 2005. The animated muse: An interpretive program for creative viewing. *Curator. The Museum Journal* 49 (3): 257–280.

Colbert E. 1958. Chalk murals. *Curator* 1 (4): 10–16.

Editorial Statement. 1958. *Curator* 1 (1): 5–6

Friedman, T. 2005. *The World Is Flat*. New York: Farrar, Straus and Giroux.

Hellman, R. 1958. The teaching functions of exhibits. *Curator* 1 (1): 74–76.

James Irvine Foundation and AEA Consulting. 2006. *Critical Issues Facing the Arts in California*. San Francisco: The James Irvine Foundation.

Parr, A. E. 1958. The time and place for experimentation in museum design. *Curator* 1 (4): 36–40.

Reekie G. 1958. Toward well-being for museum visitors. *Curator* 1(1): 91–94.

Rosenbauer, W. 1958. The museum and the individual. *Curator* 1 (4): 5–9.

Schaeffer, B., and M. Patsuris. 1958. Exhibits and ideas. *Curator* 1 (2): 25–33.

Schmidt K. 1958. The nature of the natural history museum. *Curator* 1 (1): 20–28.

Serrell, B. 1994. What's the big idea? *The Exhibitionist* 12 (3): 16.

———. 1996. *Exhibit Labels*. Walnut Creek, CA: AltaMira Press.

Sills, B., and S. Couzyn. 1958a. The embedding of cleared, biologic specimens. *Curator* 1 (2): 87–91.

———. 1958b. Dry preservation of biologic specimens by plastic infiltration. *Curator* 1 (4): 72–75.

Witteborg, L 1958. Design standards in museum exhibits. *Curator* 1 (1): 29–45.

Worts, D. 1990. "Enhancing" exhibition: Experimenting with visitor-centered experiences at the Art Gallery of Ontario. *Visitor Studies: Theory, Research and Practice—Volume* 3. Proceedings of the 1990 Visitor Studies Conference, Jacksonville, Alabama

——— . 1995. Extending the frame: Forging a new partnership with the public In *Art in Museums,* S. Pierce, ed., 165–191. London: Athlone Press.

The Exploded Museum

24

PETER SAMIS

IN A TECHNOLOGICAL WORLD, the museum visit no longer begins when a person enters the building, nor need it end when she or he leaves.[1] The museum's physical space is but one site—albeit a privileged one—in the continuum of the visitor's imaginative universe.

Contemporary artist Olafur Eliasson challenges the traditional model of the museum encounter:

> The very basic belief behind my work is that objecthood, or objects as such, don't have a place in the world if there's no subjectivity, if there's not an individual person making some use of that object. This even goes for gold and diamonds . . . [and] within art, it's even more mystifying, it's more mystical, it's even more alienating. The objecthood is money in the bank, regardless of whether people look at it or use it or have it around them or not. Because this is very counterproductive to what I think is essentially important: namely, that individuality and the nature of individuality . . . has to be reconsidered constantly, as a model, in order to sustain itself in the world today, in order to have an impact on the world today. If the object becomes prescriptive of the individual, of the subject, then we don't integrate time as time passes along. . . .
>
> I think there is a paradox, looking at the history of museums... collecting objects from reality, preserving them in a container somewhat outside of reality.... Museums today, in my view at least, should be a part of the world, a part of the times in which we live. Even if they have historical collections, they still need to emphasize the fact that you are looking at them from where we are today.[2]

Back in 1966, Bob Dylan wrote,

> Inside the museums, Infinity goes up on trial
> Voices echo this is what salvation must be like after a while[3]

Peter Samis is the associate curator of interpretation at the San Francisco Museum of Modern Art. "The Exploded Museum" appeared in *Digital Technologies and the Museum Experience: Handheld Guides and Other Media* (2008), Loïc Tallon and Kevin Walker, eds., pp. 3–17, published by AltaMira Press. It is reprinted here by permission of the publisher. All rights reserved.

Dylan's line was a prescient observation, a precursor to the plethora of publications that, starting in the late 1980s, critiqued the museum field's absolutist stance and protection of Western cultural norms.[4] Indeed, in the intervening decades most museums have continued to rely on the authority of their presentations, as if there were one set of objective truths to be gleaned from the objects in their custody, and the visiting public was an undifferentiated set of empty vessels to be ignored or filled with *la science infuse*.[5]

Meanwhile, some artists, curators, and educators did try to poke at the sacrosanct boundaries of museum practice, from both inside and outside the field. Howard Gardner's "multiple intelligences" theory exploded the "one size fits all" model of education,[6] while constructivist learning models emphasized that no one comes to museums as a clean slate, an empty vessel waiting to be filled. In addition to learning styles and aptitudes, each person brings with them a personal history, a psychobiography, and engages the museum within a social context, visiting alone, with friends or associates, or with family.[7]

Taken together with increasingly granular audience segmentation research, the visitor-studies literature on museums has boomed over the past ten years, and we are coming to know our "guests" in an increasingly sophisticated way.[8] In fact, more and more museums are professing an interest in what that cipher like presence, the once-anonymous visitor, has to say. So while Dylan's next line—"But Mona Lisa must a had the highway blues / You can tell by the way she smiles"— would not have been out of place as a subjective visitor observation in the past, and might have found its way into an inquiry-based docent tour, now it might be published on a museum blog!

Eliasson's emphasis on the perceiving subject echoes the contemporary preoccupation with the varieties of individual experience. The museum as a commodifying factor, a temple on high, is dethroned, and the visitor, with whom all experience must finally succeed or fail, thrive or fall on barren ground, is deemed the final arbiter. The museum is the sum not of the objects it contains but rather of the experiences it triggers. To quote San Francisco Museum of Modern Art (SFMOMA) senior curator of painting and sculpture Madeleine Grynsztejn,

> We don't do our best when we simply instruct. We do our best when we answer questions alongside the visitor, and ask questions alongside the visitor. And when we create a kind of conversation. We don't do our best when we create a one-way dialogue that is assertive and one-dimensional. We do our best when we offer multiple avenues of interpretation, and when we keep a lot of room for audience response.[9]

Exploding Interpretation, in Practice

So how has the use of interpretive technologies paralleled this shift?

We all know: in the beginning was the wall text. And whether it was good or not, it was all visitors had, and we came to depend on it. I use the word "we" advisedly, to include both professional museum staff and our visiting public. The idea of frontloading all the essential concepts for the appreciation of a long and complex exhibition before a visitor has seen a single object is inherently flawed, and yet many museums continue to do so.[10]

Next came extended object labels, in which basic artist/title/date info was augmented by a paragraph of text, and with them an acknowledgment that visitors might require additional information "just-in-time," as they stand in front of an object. (Believe it or not, even today, many exhibitions still do not include them.) Both wall texts and object labels have typically been monovocal, written in an anonymous and authoritative "museum voice."

Corresponding to these typeset texts was the linear audio tour, which had the virtue of channeling the museum voice into your ears as you stood in front of an object, thereby liberating your eyes to actually see it. The "empty vessel" model of knowledge acquisition was alive and well, and our ears were the apertures best fitted for filling.

In the late 1980s to early 1990s, two innovations occurred—one due to a change in the audio tour business, the other to the advent of new technologies. The first innovation was philosophical: the master narrative as promulgated by a single authoritative museum voice gave way to a polyphony of voices, and with them the admission of more than one perspective in evoking the value and meanings of a work of art.[11] The second innovation was digital: the ability to randomly access as much or as little information as you wanted about an object in the gallery, and to pick and choose your way through an exhibition without the museum determining your course. (Exhibitions, of course, remained linear, unfolding in space, but which objects you chose to commune with, and which tour stops to consult, suddenly became your call.)

Taken together, these changes were big: the monopoly of the expert was challenged. Not that people didn't want to hear an expert; by most accounts they do. But the multiplication of points of view pointed to the "many meanings all happening at once" nature of the world, and showed that museum objects are no exception. It meant that multiple entry points could be equally valid for experiencing art and artifacts, meshing with the learning styles and entrance narratives of a variety of visitors.[12] And it turns out that that is one of the things Web 2.0 is all about.

Talking and Tagging

On May 28, 2005, the *New York Times* reported in a front-page story that a professor and his students at Marymount College in Manhattan, dubbing themselves "Art Mobs," had brought their digital recorders into the galleries of New York's Museum of Modern Art (MoMA) and created a set of guerrilla podcasts—alternative audio perspectives on some of the major works in MoMA's permanent collection. These commentaries were available as free downloads on the Web.[13] The news rippled like shock waves from an earth tremor in the museum world. For the first time (or rather the first time again—as artists have a long-standing tradition of undermining museum authority going back at least as far as Marcel Duchamp), someone had publicly usurped the museum voice from an esteemed, authoritative institution and substituted a set of opinionated, perceptive, and irreverent alternatives. Canonical works were no longer hallowed; in fact, some were actively ridiculed. The critics had taken to the airwaves and invited listeners to take their voices along on their next visit to the museum.

MP3 players and the advent of podcasting empowered members of the public to publish their own perspectives and stories on subjects as far flung as anime and politics. Museums were but one of thousands of potential topics, but we weren't used to having anyone else occupy our territory. We weren't used to having to share our space.

MoMA replied by posting their entire audio tour online for free download (in fact, the museum had coincidentally just secured outside funding to make this possible) and by inviting potential visitors to create their own audio programs at home for personal use on their next visit—arguably a rather labor-intensive proposition for a limited audience of one or two. They did not actively solicit public submissions, nor did they exclude the possibility of considering them.[14] But all things considered, their response was rather enlightened: most museums still charge for their audio tours and do not yet post them to their websites. The net effect: free distribution of the master narrative beyond the museum's walls, which, when paired with an increasingly complete online representation of the collection, makes for an informative virtual visit.

Other museums took different approaches with their podcasts. At the San Francisco Museum of Modern Art, we created "SFMOMA Artcasts," an online, illustrated audio zine designed to project a variety of art concepts and voices out into the community, and to invite the community back into the museum.[15]

The voices on the Artcasts include the artists themselves (one of the distinct advantages of being a museum of modern and contemporary art), curators, "Guest Takes" where poets, composers, and musicians are invited to respond in their own art form to works on view, and "Vox Pop," where nonexpert members of the visiting public are asked to reflect on what they're seeing in the galleries. The mix of voices and genres creates a lively dialogue, while our collaboration with Antenna Audio preserved the production values traditionally associated with the museum.

Many other museums now also produce podcasts for various constituencies and with varying degrees of finish. Younger audiences are often targeted, as with Tate Modern's "Raw Canvas" and MoMA's "Red Studio" podcasts, produced by and for teens in collaboration with professional sound designers/engineers. In all cases, the museum retains final editorial control over what it publishes, even as it expands the array of voices and perspectives it presents.[16]

Is there a line museums will not—or should not—cross? How far will we go in accepting visitor contributions to our officially published content? This seems to be the frontier du jour, and it is playing itself out on multiple museum horizons as of this writing. How willing are we to break the proverbial fourth wall and listen in as our visitors describe what they see in our galleries and how they connect art to their lives—or fail to do so? Do we really want to know?

The steve project (www.steve.museum) is one such test case. A research collaboration developed by an alliance of North American museums and funded by the Institute for Museum and Library Services, it aims to test a number of hypotheses about how user-generated tags might aid in the description of—and facilitate access to—museum collections.

An example will suffice to illustrate the discrepancy between official museum cataloging and the cultural literacy of everyday visitors: one of the historical impetuses for the Steve project was the realization that a Web search for "Impressionism" on the Metropolitan Museum of Art's collections site would have omitted most of the institution's holdings. All of the paintings corresponding to that term were listed in the Met's collections management database as "French," "19th century," and "oil on canvas"—but there was no field for "art movement," and hence there were only scattered returns on the word most educated visitors would use to find them. The simple theory behind steve and other efforts at cataloging by crowds is that, if museums use terms submitted by visitors to tag their artworks, other visitors will have an easier time finding them.[17]

Of course, the terms supplied by visitors about an artwork will not all be art related. Many will be subject based, describing the image content of representational artworks, another frequent lacuna in collections management databases. They will be at the intersection of those artworks and the viewers' vision, and inevitably preconditioned by the viewers' lives ("personal context" in Falk & Dierking parlance.) So, among other questions the steve project will address are the following:

- What kinds of terms are useful to others? What kinds of terms are not?
- Useful to whom?
- How will these terms be validated?
- Will statistical agreement among taggers about a given term be enough to ensure its validity? Or does each term need to be reviewed by museum staff?
- Is such a scenario practical or even possible?
- How will subjective responses—for example, to abstract art—be treated?
- Are they helpful to others?

All of these questions and more apply as museums enable tagging or commenting on their exhibitions and collections via mobile devices.

A case in point: at the beginning of this chapter we referred to Olafur Eliasson and his critique of the commodifying aspects of museum experience. Eliasson warns of museums' tendency to "package" their messages in a reductive set of bullets fit for public consumption, preempting the visitors' direct perception of the art. In fact, he takes his argument a step further, emphasizing as key to his project the unique and nonrepeatable nature of each visitor's response, and the lack of any one definitive or authoritative experience of an artwork or exhibition.

> Who has the responsibility for seeing what we see? . . . The qualitative potential,
> let's say, of a work of art lays within the generosity or the sustainability of your
> engagement. . . . Does it have a potential that adds something to you that you could
> use in a different context? . . . I would emphasize the importance of looking at the
> picture as a way of looking at yourself looking at a picture; seeing yourself sensing,
> or seeing yourself seeing, if you want. . . . So it's not, again, about the museum but
> about the spectator. . . . So there's something quite generous here, in my view . .
> . the fact that the museum gives time back to the spectator.[18]

In this context, interpretation can only be an accumulation and juxtaposition of
different experiences, none definitive but each building a case for what is commonly held or individually specific.

Admittedly, Eliasson's project is an extreme example, focused as it is on ensuring that each visitor gain a sense of "criticality"—or perspective—on their own
experience in the galleries. Furthermore, his works themselves are immersive environments—not so much "on view" as "encompassing you." So we may ask: Do
the points Eliasson makes about perception apply equally to paintings hung on a
wall, ancient Egyptian statuary, medieval liturgical censers, and Persian calligraphy?
Is the dose of dialogue between what the museum and visitor bring to bear a constant, or a sliding scale?

What is the proper titration between expert knowledge and visitor inquiry or
response? What is to be gained by facilitating such inquiry, both for the individual
and the museum, which stands to increase its knowledge of its visitors and its
holdings? To take this line of thought one step further, what might be gained by
publishing a range of visitor responses for other visitors, both virtual and physical?
How should such responses be organized, so as not to be overwhelming in an information economy already characterized by infoglut?[19]

Museums are just beginning to explore these questions, which, on one level,
can be seen as taking the informal conversations that have always taken place between visitors to the galleries, and the more structured dialogues that take place on
docent tours, and giving them a published and searchable status on the Web, for
public or private consumption. In this light, as technology evolves, new possibilities emerge. For example, as audio tours are delivered over cell phones, the new
devices offer visitors the chance to both listen and talk back.

In the United States, a number of museums are beginning to avail themselves of
this feature. At the San Jose Museum of Art, visitors were asked to leave comments
about the artworks on view in a "Conversation Gallery." While the responses were
not as numerous or well considered as they had been in their "Collecting Our
Thoughts" exhibition in 2001—where visitors were invited to write wall labels for
the artworks with the promise that the best ones would be posted on the gallery
walls—there was still sufficient feedback to merit redesigning and repeating the
experiment.[20]

It may be that our culture as a whole is becoming more fast paced and oral,
and that part of our task is to encourage visitors to slow down enough to, in Elias-

son's terms, take their own time. Perhaps we will find that the instant dispatches provided by cell phones are antithetical to such consideration.

Making Connections

In 1974, Los Angeles artist John Baldessari famously said that, "for there to be progress in TV, the medium must be as neutral as a pencil. Just one more tool in the artists' toolbox, by which we can implement our ideas, our visions, our concerns."[21] It may be said that with the advent of simple editing tools like iMovie and the phenomenal rise of YouTube and other video-sharing websites, Baldessari's prophecy is finally coming true. However, even before YouTube became a household name, museums such as the American Visionary Art Museum and the Denver Art Museum joined places like Grand Central Station in using video booths and storytelling kiosks where visitors could come in, sit down, comment on exhibitions, or add their own memories to the exhibition content. For the most part, these have so far been used in history, children's, and discovery/science museums, and it is perhaps just a matter of time before such video annotation penetrates more art museums as well.[22] One can imagine digital representations of artworks turned into image maps, which can be tagged by multiple viewer users as a common platform for discussion and experience. Such tags could take text or video form, lead to extended annotations, and even include Web links to other far-flung but related sites. In this way, an artwork (or other museum object) can exist both on its own terms and as a hub or focal point for complex interactions—a veritable knowledge interface enabling visitor explorations, associations, and conversations.

Both Kevin Walker and Rudman et al. describe early work using visitor learning trails and social learning sites such as myartspace.org.uk (now renamed ookl. org.uk). Students visiting museums were given cell phones to photo-document and audio-annotate their personal itinerary through the museum and respond to a structured set of questions. Once they returned to their classroom, they logged onto the My Art Space site, where they were able to retrieve their captured data and reflect more fully on their experience.[23]

A similar experiment was recently conducted at the Centre Pompidou in Paris, where visitors to an exhibition featuring Iranian photographer and filmmaker Abbas Kiarostami and Spanish filmmaker Victor Erice were able to annotate not only their path through the show but also the entire image track of a film, using sophisticated software called Lignes de temps (Timelines).[24]

These efforts to facilitate visitor content creation and publishing represent constructivist learning exercises par excellence. As such, they are probably better suited to the needs and focused time span of a school visit than the harried life of the average museum visitor. Perhaps the "connectivist" paradigm proposed by George Siemens, in which knowing where to find information is as important as having personally made it your own, is more on target for this networked, multiperspectival age in which, in the words of David Weinberger, "Everything is miscellaneous."[25] After all, not everyone is an alpha blogger. In fact, a Forrester Research report suggests that as of April 2007 only 13 percent of those using the Web actively participated by either publishing a blog or a Web page or uploading a video. The vast majority of Web users fall in the less active rungs of this "Hierarchy of Social Participation": 19 percent comment on blogs (the next most active role); 15 percent use Really Simple Syndication (RSS) feeds and tag Web pages; 19 percent use social networking sites; 33 percent read blogs, listen to podcasts, or watch peer-generated video; and 52 percent are listed as "inactives," participating in none of these activities.[26] These figures echo observation of visitor behavior at SFMOMA during the 2006 Matthew Barney: Drawing Restraint exhibition (Table 24.1).

The sweet spot was clearly on the passive, linear media side—not in the interactive zone. That said, appreciation levels rose most dramatically among those who availed themselves of multiple interpretive resources, including the FAQ wall graphics, artist video, digital audio tour, and interactive kiosk/website.[27]

Table 24.1.   Percentage of Barney Exhibition Interpretive Offerings Used by Visitors (n = 251)

Exhibition introduction wall text	78
Exhibition brochure	55
Learning Lounge wall text photos	44
Learning Lounge video	38
Antenna audio guide headset tour	21
Cell phone tour	19
Learning Lounge catalogs	17
Drawing Restraint 9 film	18
Exhibition website	15
Learning Lounge computers	12
Podcast/downloadable tour	7
SFMOMA docent-led public tour	2

Recent research at the Dallas Museum of Art has led to a new model for understanding visitor participation in the art museum. Findings there indicate that, regardless of age, educational level, socioeconomic standing, or ethnic background, visitors fall into one of the following categories:

- Aware: Visitors with little or no experience who are not really comfortable looking at or describing art. They may have been brought to the museum by someone else.
- Curious: Visitors who "like art but are not in love with it." They enjoy the social dimension of museum experience and connections that can be made between art and other parts of their lives.
- Committed: Either educated art consumers who want to be left alone or art enthusiasts who "love art as much as sex and religion" and can't get enough of it, not to mention programs around it.[28]

These levels map nicely to Siemens' first three levels of connectivist engagement:

- Awareness and Receptivity: Learner becomes conscious of new informational nodes/sources of meaning;
- Connection-forming: Learner begins to form connections and uses resources to deepen their knowledge; and
- Contribution and Involvement: Learner contributes to the network, actively gets involved, and becomes visible.[29]

As the visitor progresses in their art experience, the museum promotes personal interpretations over established understandings. In fact, commonly accepted understandings are articulated precisely to open the door to personal responses rather than seal the object in art historical authority.

We are thrown back on the question of the museum-visitor experience and the role of the museum in the visitor's life. Here we are back at Eliasson! We might ask, Is there a continuum of art experience, and where do the museum walls fit within it?

The promise of these new technologies, then, is dual: if they can be made effortless and transparent enough, they can help art ideas to penetrate more effortlessly into visitors' lives, to aid visitors in processing and digesting these ideas and images in their own personal terms. Conversely, new technologies can also open museums to the multiplicity of meanings that our objects trigger in the community of viewers—meanings we haven't yet dreamed of and which stand to be richer and far more diverse than the art historical discourse that is our stock-in-trade.

Notes

1. This essay is dedicated to the memory of Xavier Perrot, friend and museum colleague extraordinaire.

2. Olafur Eliasson, interview with author, Berlin, June 18, 2007.

3. Bob Dylan, "Visions of Johanna," Copyright ©1966; renewed 1994 Dwarf Music. All rights reserved. International Copyright secured. Reprinted by permission.

4. Among them, Ivan Karp and Steven D. Lavine, eds., *Exhibiting Cultures: The Poetics and Politics of Museum Display* (Washington, D.C.: Smithsonian Institution Press, 1991); Eilean Hooper-Greenhill, *Museums and the Shaping of Knowledge* (London: Routledge, 1992); Irit Rogoff, *Museum Culture: Histories, Discourses, Spectacles* (London: Routledge, 1994); Tony Bennett, *The Birth of the Museum: History, Theory, Politics* (London: Routledge, 1995).

5. A French expression connoting inherent—and in some cases inherited— knowledge. See Pierre Bourdieu's sociological studies of the connection between training in the appreciation of the arts and access to elite social status, most notably, *Distinction: A Social Critique of the Judgement of Taste* (Cambridge, Mass.: MIT Press, 1984).

6. Howard Gardner, *Frames of Mind: The Theory of Multiple Intelligences* (New York: Basic Books, 1983).

7. George E. Hein, *Learning in the Museum* (London: Routledge, 1998); John H. Falk and Lynn D. Dierking, *Learning from Museums: Visitor Experiences and the Making of Meaning* (Walnut Creek, Calif.: AltaMira, 2000).

8. An example is Andrew J. Pekarik, Zahava D. Doering, and David A. Karns, "Exploring Satisfying Experiences in Museums," *Curator* 42, no. 2 (1999): 152–173. An archive of visitor studies journals is available at the Visitor Studies Association website: www.visitorstudiesarchives.org/index.php (accessed June 27, 2008).

9. Madeleine Grynsztejn, interview with the author, San Francisco, July 5, 2007. Ms. Grynsztejn has since been appointed Pritzker Director of the Museum of Contemporary Art, Chicago.

10. For more on this point, including statistics from one study on the relative efficacy of introductory wall texts compared to other interpretive resources, see Peter Samis, "Gaining Traction in the Vaseline: Visitor Response to a Multi-track Interpretation Design for Matthew Barney: Drawing Restraint" (paper presented at Museums and the Web, San Francisco, April 2007), at www.archimuse.com/mw2007/papers/samis/samis.html (accessed June 27, 2008).

11. The first multiple-voice museum tour in the United States was produced by Antenna Audio in 1986 for the exhibition "Bronislava Nijinska, A Dancer's Legacy," curated by Nancy Van Norman Baer at the de Young Museum in San Francisco. "Nancy and I went all over the country (mostly New York), interviewing various dancers like Frederick Franklin and Nina Youskevich who danced for Diaghilev in the Ballets Russes and knew Nijinsky very well. It was a great tour. Still one of the best, full of music and wonderful Russian voices telling great stories of the era and all the great choreographers and artists." Chris Tellis, founder, Antenna Audio, personal communication, August 27, 2007.

12. Moreover, recent research has shown that visitors benefit from having multiple complementary interpretive resources at their disposal. Visitors to the 2006 Matthew Barney exhibition at SFMOMA used as many as six different resources, choosing among introductory wall text, audio tour (in three formats), brochure, and a learning lounge that offered an artist video, interactive kiosks, wall graphics, and books to consult. Statistics revealed that among those unfamiliar with the artist, appreciation of the exhibition rose dramatically in proportion to the number of interpretive resources used. See Samis, "Gaining Traction in the Vaseline," and the study it was based on, Randi Korn et al., *Matthew Barney: Drawing Restraint Interactive Educational Technologies and Interpretation Initiative Evaluation* (San Francisco: SFMOMA, 2006), at www.sfmoma.org/whoweare/research_projects/ barney/ RKA_2006_SFMOMA_Barney_distribution.pdf (accessed August 10, 2007).

13. Randy Kennedy, "With Irreverence and an iPod: Recreating the Museum Tour," *New York Times,* May 28, 2005, A1, at www.nytimes.com/2005/05/28/arts/design/ 28podc.html?ex= 12749328008cen=db 1 ced6873dcc4b6&ei=5090&partner=rssuserland &emc=rss%20 (accessed August 6, 2007).

14. The exact language on the Web page was, "If you would like to share your audio guide with MoMA, e-mail us at audio@moma.org. MoMA will review submissions but reserves the right not to post them." In fact, they ended up posting one visitor-submitted set of audio tracks created in response to the 2006 Dada exhibition. The MoMA instructions for creating your own audio program are at www.moma.org/ visit_moma/createyourown. html (accessed September 15, 2007).

15. Visitors showing their MP3 player with an Artcast loaded receive a two dollar discount at the admission booth. The "SFMOMA Artcast" site and archive is at www. sfmoma.org/artcasts. For more on museum podcasting in general and the development of SFMOMA's solution in particular, see Peter Samis and S. Pau, "Artcasting' at SFMOMA: First-Year Lessons, Future Challenges for Museum Podcasters" (paper presented at Muse-

ums and the Web, Albuquerque, N.M., April 2007), at www.archimuse.com/mw2006/papers/samis/samis.html (accessed August 6, 2007).

16. Available at www.tate.org.uk/youngtate/podcast/artlookers and http://redstudio.moma.org/podcasts/2006/index.php, respectively (accessed August 27, 2007).

17. Jennifer Trant, "Exploring the Potential for Social Tagging and Folksonomy in Art Museums: Proof of Concept," *New Review of Hypermedia and Multimedia* [PDF preprint]. For more on steve, see www.steve.museum. Other related initiatives are taking place as of this writing at the Powerhouse Museum in Sydney, Australia, at www.powerhousemuseum.com/collection/database; the Smithsonian Photography Initiative's "Enter the Frame" project, at http://photography.si.edu/; and the Philadelphia Museum of Art, at www.philamuseum.org/collections/socialTagging.html (accessed June 26, 2008).

18. Olafur Eliasson, interview with author, Berlin, June 18, 2007.

19. Thomas H. Davenport and John C. Beck, *The Attention Economy: Understanding the New Currency of Business* (Cambridge, Mass.: Harvard Business School Press, 2001); and Peter J. Denning, "The Profession of IT: Infoglut," *Communications of the ACM* 49, no. 7 (July 2006): 16–19, at http://cs.gmu.edu/cne/pjd/PUBS/CACMcols/cacmjul06.pdf (accessed June 26, 2008).

20. Chris Alexander, SJMA manager of interactive technology, personal communication, August 27, 2007.

21. The statement was made at the Open Circuits conference at the Museum of Modern Art in New York. John Baldessari, "TV (1) Is Like a Pencil and (2) Won't Bite Your Leg," in *The New Television: A Public/Private Art,* ed. Douglas Davis and Allison Simmons (Cambridge, Mass.: MIT Press, 1977), 110. Cited online by Cynthia Chris, "Video Art: Stayin' Alive," *Afterimage* (March 2000), at http://findartides.com/p/articles/mi_m2479/is_5_27/ai_61535391/pg_l (accessed August 6,2007).

22. For more examples of such "storytelling kiosks," see Brad Larson's blog entries at http://weblog.bradlarson.com/storytelling_kiosk/index.html (accessed August 28, 2007). In a recent phone conversation, Larson pointed out that, because children's and discovery museums have traditionally been collection free, they have always focused first and foremost on visitor experience, and have built up an extensive body of research. Art museums may have a lot to learn from them.

23. See Kevin Walker, "Structuring Visitor Participation" and Paul Rudman, Mike Sharples, Peter Lonsdale, Giasemi Vavoula, and Julia Meek, "Cross-Context Learning" in Loic Tallon and Kevin Walker (eds.), *Digital Technologies and the Museum Experience: Handheld Guides and Other Media.* Lanham, MD: AltaMira, 2008, pp. 109–24 and 147–66. See also Kevin Walker, "Visitor-Constructed Personalized Learning Trails," in *Museums and the Web 2007: Proceedings,* ed. Jennifer Trant and David Bearman (Toronto: Archives and Museum Informatics, 2007), at www.archimuse.com/mw2007/papers/walker/walker.html (accessed August 28, 2007).

24. Walker (2008) also discusses *Lignes de Temps.*

25. The seminal article on connectivism is George Siemens, "Connectivism: A Learning Theory for the Digital Age," December 4, 2004, at www.elearnspace.org/ Articles/connectivism.htm (see also the connectivism site, blog, and wiki at www.connectivism.ca/ [accessed August 28, 2007]); David Weinberger, *Everything Is Miscellaneous: The Power of the New Digital Disorder* (New York: Times Books/Henry Holt, 2007). See also the website, at www.everythingismiscellaneous.com/ (accessed August 28, 2007).

26. Clearly, the figures are cumulative and not mutually exclusive: the top 13 percent, the "alpha bloggers," do all of these activities, while levels of engagement fall off after that. See www.powerhousemuseum.com/dmsblog/index.php/2007/04/23/more-on-levels-of-participation-forresters-social-technographics (accessed August 28, 2007). Similar data was reported by the Pew Center for the Study of the Internet and American Life.

27. Samis, "Gaining Traction in the Vaseline"; and Korn et al., *Matthew Barney*.

28. Bonnie Pitman, "Serving Visitors with Choices: How Far Can Art Museums Stretch?" (presentation on a panel at American Association of Museums Annual Meeting, Chicago, May 2007).

29. George Siemens, "Connectivism: Museums as Learning Ecologies" (presentation to the Canadian Heritage Information Network's Roundtable on e-Learning, March 2006), at www.elearnspace.org/media/CHIN/player.html (accessed August 30, 2007).

The Visitors' Bill of Rights

A List of Important Human Needs, Seen From the Visitors' Point of View

25

JUDY RAND

WHEN WE SPEND OUR DAYS SITTING IN MEETINGS, it is easy to stop seeing visitors as real people. In our meeting rooms, we see our own problems, our own needs. In our meeting rooms, the visitors become a bunch of dirty fingerprints, wear and tear on the building, why the carpet needs fixing. How do we get everyone in those meetings back to seeing the visitors as human beings?

That is why I wrote the *Visitors' Bill of Rights: A List of Important Human Needs, Seen From the Visitors' Point of View.*

- **Comfort—***Meet my basic needs.*
  Visitors need fast, easy, obvious access to clean, safe, barrier-free restrooms, fountains, food, baby-changing tables, and plenty of seating. They also need full access to exhibits.
- **Orientation—***Make it easy for me to find my way around.*
  Visitors need to make sense of their surroundings. Clear signs and well-planned spaces help them know what to expect, where to go, how to get there and what it's about.
- **Welcome/belonging—***Make me feel welcome.*
  Friendly, helpful staff ease visitors' anxieties. If they see themselves represented in exhibits and programs and on the staff, they'll feel more like they belong.
- **Enjoyment—***I want to have fun!*
- **Visitors want to have a good time**.
  If they run into barriers (like broken exhibits, activities they can't relate to, intimidating labels) they can get frustrated, bored, confused.

Judy Rand is director of Rand and Associates, an exhibition development consulting firm, and an adjunct faculty member at the University of Washington. "The Visitors' Bill of Rights" first appeared in *Curator: The Museum Journal* (Vol. 44, No. 1, January 2000, pp. 7–14). It is reprinted here by permission of John Wiley & Sons. All rights reserved.

- **Socializing**—*I came to spend time with my family and friends.*
  Visitors come for a social outing with family or friends (or connect with society at large). They expect to talk, interact and share the experience; exhibits can set the stage for this.

- **Respect**—*Accept me for who I am and what I know.*
  Visitors want to be accepted at their own level of knowledge and interest. They don't want exhibits, labels or staff to exclude them, patronize them or make them feel dumb.

- **Communication**—*Help me understand, and let me talk, too.*
  Visitors need accuracy, honesty and clear communication from labels, programs and docents. They want to ask questions, and hear and express differing points of view.

- **Learning**—*I want to learn something new.*
  Visitors come (and bring the kids) "to learn something new," but they learn in different ways. It's important to know how visitors learn, and assess their knowledge and interests. Controlling distractions (like crowds, noise and information overload) helps them, too.

- **Choice and control**—*Let me choose; give me some control.*
  Visitors need some autonomy: freedom to choose, and exert some control, touching and getting close to whatever they can. They need to use their bodies and move around freely.

- **Challenge and confidence**—*Give me a challenge I know I can handle.*
  Visitors want to succeed. A task that's too easy bores them; too hard makes them anxious. Providing a wide variety of experiences will match their wide range of skills.

- **Revitalization**—*Help me leave refreshed, restored.*
  When visitors are focused, fully engaged, and enjoying themselves, time stands still and they feel refreshed: a "flow" experience that exhibits can aim to create.

The Museum Visitor Experience

Who Visits, Why and to What Effect?

26

JOHN FALK

A LTHOUGH IT WAS NOT ALWAYS TRUE, today most museums exist in order to attract and serve visitors—as many as possible. Although arguably museums have long wondered about who visits their museum, why and to what end, understanding something about museum visitors is no longer a nicety, it is a necessity! If we knew the answers to the questions of who goes to museums, what people do once in the museum and what meanings they make from the experience we would gain critical insights into how the public derives value and benefits from museum–going (or not as the case may be) which we could use to make museums better. Better is important as we live in an increasing competitive world where every museum is competing for audiences and resources not only against other museums but against an ever-widening number of other leisure options. And in a world of shrinking government budgets, financial support has become a zero-sum game—resources allocated for one thing (e.g., culture and arts) are resources un-available for other things (e.g., public health or safety). If museums are to maintain their current levels of support and popularity they will need to get measurably bet-ter at understanding and serving their visitors.

Historical Approaches to Answering the Who, Why, and What Questions

For more than a generation, researchers have worked at better describing and un-derstanding the museum visitor experience. I would assert that two major problems limit the validity and reliability of much of this earlier research, including much of my own research. The first of these problems is a spatial and temporal problem. Specifically, virtually all of museum visitor research has been conducted inside the

John Falk is the Sea Grant Professor in Free-Choice Learning at Oregon State University, and president emeri-tus and founder of the Institute for Learning Innovation in Annapolis, Maryland. "The Museum Visitor Experi-ence: Who Visits, Why, and to What Effect?" is reprinted by permission of DREAM: Danish Research Centre on Education and Advanced Media Materials. Copyright 2010. All rights reserved.

museum. Although studying museum visitors exclusively within the "four walls" of the museum superficially seems to make great sense, it also turns out to be highly problematic. This is because only a fraction of the museum experience actually occurs within the four walls of the museum. The whole process of deciding why to go to the museum occurs outside the museum; and this as we'll see has significant impacts on everything that happens afterwards. But even beyond this, research has revealed that what a visitor brings with him/her to the museum experience in the way of prior experience, knowledge, interest and social relationships profoundly influences what s/he actually does and thinks about within the museum (cf., Ellenbogen, Luke, and Dierking, 2007; Falk and Adelman, 2003; Falk and Dierking, 2000; Leinhartd and Knutson, 2004).

The meanings people make about their museum experience also extend beyond the temporal and spatial boundaries of the museum. It is only relatively recently that we have discovered just how long it takes for memories to form in the brain (Baddeley, 1997; McGaugh, 2003). It can take days, sometimes even weeks for a memory to form, and during that time other intervening experiences and events can influence those memories. Ironically then, what happens after a person leaves the museum may be as critical to the nature and durability of that person's museum memories as what actually happened within the museum. Perhaps the most important consequence of this new understanding of the nature of memory is that it raises questions about much of the learning research previously done in museums since virtually all museum learning research has involved data collected within minutes after an experience. This time frame it appears is too short for some kinds of mental processing to occur; so quite literally visitors are incapable of fully describing what they did or did not actually learn. *Accurately understanding the museum visitor experience requires expanding the time frame of investigation so that it includes aspects of the visitor's life both before and after their museum visit.*

The second major problems with most museum research has been the tendency to focus on *permanent* qualities of either the museum, e.g., its content or style of exhibits, or the visitor (demographic characteristics such as age, race/ethnicity, visit frequency or even social arrangement). To many in the museum community the first and most obvious answer to the question of why the public visits museum is that it's all about the content. Visitors come to art museums to see art, history museums to find out about history and science museums to see and learn about science. Although again, superficially this makes perfect sense—since displaying and interpreting subject-specific content is what museums do—it is problematic because it doesn't tell us why, on any given day, someone would visit a museum. Take science museums for example. More than 90 percent of the American public say they find science and technology interesting but nowhere near that number actually visit science and technology museums even occasionally, let alone regularly (National Science Board, 2006, 2008, 2010). Having an interest in the subject matter of the museum is clearly important to determining who will visit, but is not sufficient to explain who does and does not visit. Market researchers tell us that, at least in America, most museum-goers are aware of the content of the museum they visit but rarely is content the most important factor affecting their decision to visit (Adams, 1989, American Association of Museums, 1998).

Certainly content well displayed is what drives a visitor's in-museum experience and determines what they learn and remember, to a degree yes, but only to a degree. The exhibitions and objects within the museum represent a major focus of a visitor's time and attention, but it is not the only thing visitors attend to. According to a major study my colleagues and I did many years ago now, only slightly more than a half of a visitor's attention over the course of a visit was spent looking at exhibits, with the peak amount of content focus being in the first fifteen minutes of a visit (Falk et al., 1985). The other half of the visitor's time was spent engaged in conversations with other members of his/her social group or general observations of the setting. Further research has revealed that there is actually a relatively low correlation between exhibit quality and actual learning (Falk and Storksdieck, 2005). In some cases visitors who saw higher quality exhibitions (defined as those exhibits that most clearly and compellingly communicated their intended content) learned more, but in other cases learning seemed to be totally independent of what exhibits were viewed. In short, the museum experience is influenced by the nature of the museum and its exhibitions, but not exclusively.

Over the past several decades thousands of visitor studies have been conducted in order to better understand who is visiting the museum (though only a tiny fraction have been published). Overwhelmingly, these many efforts to describe museum audiences categorized visitors utilizing traditional demographic categories like age, education, gender and race/ethnicity; qualities of individuals that do not vary from day to day—a white female is always a white female. A predictable outcome of segmenting groups into various measureable categories such as demographics is that patterns emerge, whether those patterns are actually meaningful or not is another question (Desolneux, Moisan, and Morel, 2008). So it is perhaps not surprising that a number of demographic variables have been found to positively correlate with museum-going, for example the finding that museum-goers are likely to be white, well educated and affluent (e.g., Doering and Bickford, 1994). However in an intensive multi-year investigation of the use of museums by African Americans I came to the conclusion that race/ethnicity provided no useful insights into why black Americans did or did not visit museums (Falk, 1993); and subsequent research in Los Angeles has confirmed that race/ethnicity, as well as age and even education and occupation are poor predictors of who does or does not visit museums (Falk and Needham, 2011). *The major conclusion I have reached after studying thousands of visitors over more than three decades is that museum-going is far too complex and ephemeral to be understood merely on the basis of easily measured, concrete variables such as demographics or for that matter tangible qualities like "type of museum" or "exhibition style" (e.g., hands-on, didactic, interactive, etc.).*

Toward a New Model of the Museum Visitor Experience

The museum visitor experience cannot be adequately described by understanding the content of museums, the design of exhibitions, by defining visitors as function of their demographics or even by understanding visit frequency or the social arrangements in which people enter the museum. To get the complete answer to the questions of why people do or do not visit museums, what they do there, and what learning/meaning they derive from the experience, turns out to require a deeper, more synthetic explanation. So despite the considerable time and effort that museum investigators have devoted to framing the museum visitor experience using these common lenses, the results have been depressingly limited. Arguably these perspectives have yielded only the most rudimentary descriptive understandings and none come close to providing a truly predictive model of the museum visitor experience.

Over the past decade I have begun to develop what I think is a more robust way to describe and understand the museum visitors' experience. Undergirding this new approach have been a series of in-depth interviews, now numbering in the hundreds, in which my colleagues and I have talked to individuals about their museum experiences weeks, months and years after their museum visits. Time and time again what leaps out in these interviews is how deeply personal museum visits are, and how deeply tied to each individual's sense of identity. Also striking is how consistently an individual's post-visit narrative relates to their entering narrative. In other words, what typically sticks in a person's mind as important about their visit usually directly relates to the reasons that person stated they went to the museum in the first place; and often they use similar language to describe both pre- and post-visit memories. The ways in which individuals talk about why they went to the museum as well as the ways they talk about what they remember from their experience invariably seem to have a lot to do with what they were seeking to personally accomplish through their visit. Visitors talk about how their personal goals for the visit relate to who they thought they were or wanted to be, and they talk about how the museum itself supported these personal goals and needs. The insights gained from these interviews led me to totally rethink the museum visitor experience; led me to appreciate that building and supporting personal identity was the motivation behind virtually all museum visits (see figure 26.1).

Considerable time and effort has been invested in understanding the motivations of museum visitors. A variety of investigators (see review by Falk, 2009) have sought to describe why people visit museums, resulting in a range of descriptive categorizations. More recently, investigators have begun to document the connections between visitors' entering motivations and their exiting meaning making (e.g., Briseno-Garzon, Anderson, and Anderson, 2007; Doering and Pekarik, 1996; Falk, Moussouri, and Coulson, 1998; Falk and Storksdieck, 2005; Leinhartd and Knutson, 2004; Packer, 2006; Packer and Ballantyne, 2002; Pekarik, Doering, and Karns, 1999). Most visitors appear to enter the museum with a pre-determined

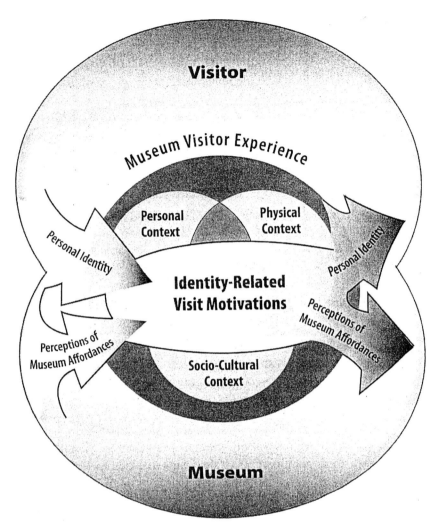

Figure 26.1.   The museum visitor experience and the role of identity-related visit motivations.
Excerpt from *Identity and the Museum Visitor Experience* (2009), p. 161. It is reprinted here
with permission from Left Coast Press. All rights reserved.

reason for visiting. More importantly, these entering motivations appear to be self-reinforcing, directing visitors' learning, behavior and perceptions of satisfaction. What my interviews suggested was that although unique at some level, the ways each of the hundreds of visitor I talked with described why they were motivated to visit a museum converged upon a relatively small subset of categories. These motivational categories, in turn, could best be understood as designed to satisfy one or more personal identity–related need.

Identity has always been a challenging construct to define; and not surprisingly little agreement exists among social scientists as to how to exactly define it. I have ended up subscribing to a view of identity which, like Bronfenbrenner (1979), Holland, Lachicotte, Skinner, and Cain (1998), and Simon (2004) sees identity as the confluence of internal and external social forces—cultural and individual agencies, and, like Bruner and Kalmar (1998) and Neisser (1988) as always influenced, to a greater or lesser extent, by innate and learned perceptions about the physical environment. From this perspective, identity emerges as malleable, continually constructed, and as a quality that is always situated in the realities of the physical and sociocultural world—both the immediate social and physical world an individual may be immersed in as well as the broader social and physical world of an individual's family, culture, and personal history. A key understanding of this view of identity is that each of us has not a single identity but rather maintains numerous identities (cf. Cooper 1999; McAdams, 1990) which are expressed collectively or individually at different times, depending upon need and circumstance. Each of us possesses and acts upon a set of enduring and deep identities (what I call big "I" identities). Examples of "I" identities might be one's sense of gender, nationality, political views or religion; these are identities we carry with us throughout our lives and though they unquestionably evolve, they remain fairly constant across our lives (e.g., most of us do not change our sense of gender or nationality, though our sense of what that gender or nationality means does evolve). These are the types of identity that have been most frequently studied by social scientists and most frequently spring to mind when we think of identity. However, I would argue that much of our lives are spent enacting a series of other, more situated identities that represent responses to the needs and realities of the specific moment and circumstances (what I call little "i" identities). Examples of "i" identities might be the "good niece/nephew" identity we enact when we remember to send a birthday card to our aunt who lives in a different city or the "host/hostess" identity we enact when someone visits our house for the first time. If we were about to get the Nobel prize and someone was interviewing us, these kinds of "i" identities would likely not top our list of characteristics that we would offer as descriptors of "who we are"; but undeniably these types of identities play a critical role in defining who we are and how we behave much of the time. It was my observation that for most people, most of the time, going to a museum tended to elicit predominantly "i" identities. In other words, people went to museums in order to facilitate identity-related needs such as a desire to be a supportive parent or spouse, to indulge ones sense of curiosity or the feeling that it would be good to get away from the rat race of a little while. Nationality, religion, gender or political affiliation did not seem to be the primary motivations behind most peoples' visits to art museums, children's museums, zoos or science centers.

Following on the work of Linville (1985) and Simon (2004), I hypothesized that as active meaning seekers, most museum visitors engaged in a degree of self-reflection and self-interpretation about their visit experience. In other words, within a specific situation, individuals make sense of their actions and roles by ascribing identity-related qualities or descriptions to them. The research of Cantor, Mischel, and Schwarz (1982) and Schutte, Kendrick, and Sadalla (1985) reinforce this model. They found that individuals do indeed construct identity-relevant situational prototypes that served as a working model for the person, telling him or her what to expect and how to behave in situations of a particular type. I believed that this was also quite likely what visitors to museums were doing. People who visit museums typically possess a working model of what going to a museum "affords"; they also have a sense of what benefits will accrue to them by visiting. I hypothesized, and my colleagues and I have now found evidence supporting the proposition, that visitors utilize their pre-visit conceptions of what a museum experience affords to both prospectively justify why they should visit the museum and then again retrospectively to make sense of how and why their visit was worthwhile (Falk, Heimlich, and Bronnenkant, 2008; Falk and Storksdieck, 2005; 2010).

For example, many art museum visitors describe themselves as curious people, generally interested in art. They see art museums as great places for exercising that curiosity and interest. When one particular individual was asked about art museums she responded, "Art museums are great places to visit because they put together exhibitions designed to cultivate people's interests and understandings of art." When asked why she was visiting the art museum today she answered, "I came to see what's new here. I haven't been in a while and I was hoping to see some really new and interesting art." Several months later when I re-contacted this person, she reflected back on her visit and said, "I had a superb time at the art museum. I just wandered around and saw all of the fabulous art; there were some really striking works. I even discovered a few works that I had never seen or known anything about before. That was really wonderful."

The visitor's understanding of their museum visitor experience is invariably self-referential and provides coherence and meaning to the experience. Visitors tend to see their in-museum behavior and post-visit outcomes as consistent with personality traits, attitudes, and/or group affiliations such as the person above who saw the museums as a mechanism for reinforcing her view of herself as a curious person. Other visitors use the museum to satisfy personally relevant roles and values such as being a good parent or an intrepid cultural tourist. Despite the commonalities in these self-aspects across groups of visitors, individual visitors experience these self-aspects as expressions of their own unique personal identity. However, how you see yourself as a museum visitor depends to a large degree upon how you conceptualize the museum. In other words, if you view yourself as a good father and believe that museums are the kind of places to which good fathers bring their children, then you might actively seek out such a place in order to "enact" such an identity. Or, if you think of yourself as the kind of curious person who goes out of your way to discover unusual and interesting facts about the human condition, both in the present and in the past, then you might actively seek out a history museum during your leisure time. I believe that this is what a large percentage of visitors to museums actually do, not just with regards to parenting and curiosity, but as a means for enacting a wide range of identity-related meanings.

As museums have become increasingly popular leisure venues, more and more people have developed working models of what museums are like and how and why they would use them—in other words, what the museum experience affords. These museum "affordances" are then matched up with the public's identity-related needs and desires. Together, these create a very strong, positive feedback loop. The loop begins with the public seeking leisure experiences that meet specific identity-related needs, such as personal fulfillment, parenting, or novelty seeking. As museums are generally perceived as places capable of meeting some (though not all) identity-related needs, the public prospectively justifies reasons for making a museum visit. Overtime, visitors reflect upon their museum visit and determine whether the experience was a good way to fulfill their needs, and, if it was, they tell others about the visit which helps to feed a social understanding that this and other museums like it are good for that purpose. As a consequence, these past visitors and others like them are much more likely to seek out this or another museum in the future should they possess a similar identity-related need.

Over the course of numerous studies, in a variety of museum settings, evidence is beginning to mount supporting the existence of these identity-related feedback loops (Covel, 2009; Falk, Heimlich, and Bronnenkant, 2008; Falk and Storksdieck, 2005; Falk and Storksdieck, 2010; Koke, 2009; Stein, 2007; Storksdieck and Stein, 2007). Although, in theory, museum visitors could posses an infinite number of identity-related visit motivations, this does not appear to be the case. Both the reasons people give for visiting museums and their post-visit descriptions of the experience have tended to cluster around just a few basic categories, which in turn appeared to reflect how the public perceives what a museum visit affords. All the various motivations visitors ascribe to visiting museums tend to cluster into just five distinct, identity-related categories:[1]

- Explorers: Visitors who are curiosity-driven with a generic interest in the content of the museum. They expect to find something that will grab their attention and fuel their learning.

  "I remember thinking I wanted to learn my science basics again, like biology and that stuff. . . . I thought [before coming], you're not going to pick up everything, you know, but you are going to learn some things."

- Facilitators: Visitors who are socially motivated. Their visit is focused on primarily enabling the experience and learning of others in their accompanying social group.

  "[I came] to give [my] kids a chance to see what early life was like . . . it's a good way to spend time with the family in a non-commercial way. They always learn so much."

- Professional/Hobbyists: Visitors who feel a close tie between the museum content and their professional or hobbyist passions. Their visits are typically motivated by a desire to satisfy a specific content-related objective.

  "I'm starting to put together a saltwater reef tank, so I have a lot of interest in marine life. I'm hoping to pick up some ideas [here at the aquarium]."

- Experience Seekers: Visitors who are motivated to visit because they perceive the museum as an important destination. Their satisfaction primarily derives from the mere fact of having "been there and done that."

  "We were visiting from out of town, looking for something fun to do that wouldn't take all day. This seemed like a good idea; after all, we're in Los Angeles and someone told us this place just opened up and it's really neat."

- Rechargers: Visitors who are primarily seeking to have a contemplative, spiritual and/or restorative experience. They see the museum as a refuge from the work-a-day world or as a confirmation of their religious beliefs.

  "I like art museums. They are so very quiet and relaxing, so different than the noise and clutter of the rest of the city."

As predicted, and evidenced in these and many other quotes I could have selected, museum visitors use museums to satisfy identity-related needs—occasionally deeply held "I" identities but more commonly more ephemeral "i" identities. Perhaps most importantly, my research has produced strong evidence that categorizing visitors as a function of these identity-related visit motivations captures important insights into how visitors make sense of their museum experience—both prior to arriving, during the experience and over time as they reflect back upon the visit. In the most detailed study to date, the majority of visitors could not only be categorized as falling into one of these five categories, but individuals within a category behaved and learned in ways that were different from individuals in other categories (Falk, Heimlich, and Bronnenkant, 2008). Specifically, individuals in some of the categories showed significant changes in their understanding and affect, while individuals in other categories did not; for some categories of visitor the museum experience was quite successful, while for others it was only marginally so. Thus, unlike traditional segmentation strategies based upon demographic categories like age, race/ethnicity, gender, or even education, separating visitors according to their entering identity-related motivations resulted in descriptive data predictive of visitors' museum experience. Also unlike demographic categories, these categories are not permanent qualities of the individual. An individual can be motivated to go to a museum today because they want to facilitate their children's learning experience and go to the same or a different tomorrow because it resonates with their own personal interests and curiosities. Because of the differing identity-related needs, the nature and quality of that single individual's museum experience will be quite different on those two days.

Implications for Practice

I believe that this line of research has important implications for practice. Not only is research revealing that the majority of visitors to most types of museums arrive with one of five general motivations for visiting, it appears that these identity-related motivations directly relate to key outcomes in the museum setting, such as how visitors behave and interact with the setting and importantly, how they make meaning of the experience once they leave. In other words, being able to segment visitors this way gives museum practitioners key insights into the needs and interests of their visitors. This is very different than the one-size-fits-all perspective that has historically dominated our interactions with museum visitors. For example, my research has revealed that Explorers are focused on what they see and find interesting, and act out this me-centered agenda regardless of whether they are part of a social group or not. Facilitators are focused on what their significant others see and find interesting, and they act out this agenda by, for example, allowing their significant others to direct the visit and worrying primarily about whether the other person is seeing what they find interesting rather than focusing on their own interests. Experience Seekers are prone to reflect upon the gestalt of the day, particularly how enjoyable the visit is. Professional/Hobbyists tend to enter with very specific, content-oriented interests and use the museum as a vehicle for facilitating those interests (e.g., information that will support their own personal collection or taking photographs). Finally, Rechargers, like Experience Seekers, are more focused on the gestalt of the day. But unlike Experience Seekers, Rechargers are not so much interested in having fun as they are interested in having a peaceful or inspiring experience. By focusing on these needs/interests, museum professionals could begin to customize and personalize the visitor's experience and satisfy more people more of the time.

Using this approach, museums should be able to better satisfy the needs of their regular visitors. Importantly, though, the same model could provide a vehicle for enticing occasional visitors to come more frequently. I also believe that this approach opens the door to new and creative ways to attract audiences who do not visit museums at all. This is because these five basic categories of identity-related needs are not unique to museum-goers. What separates those who go to museums from those who do not, is not whether they possess one of these five basic categories of need but rather whether they perceive museums as places that satisfy those needs. In other words, if we could figure out how to help more people see museums as places that fulfill their needs—and then deliver on this promise—more people would visit.

Fundamentally, research seems to suggest that a large number of visitors arrive at museums with preconceived expectations. They use the museum to satisfy those expectations and then remember the visit as an experience that did just that—satisfied their specific expectations. Therefore, categorizing visitors as a function of the five identity-related motivations yields some measure of predictability about what visitors' experiences will be like as well as qualitatively, what visitors are likely to find memorable. For example, Explorer's are likely to find what they discover memorable while a Facilitator is likely to find what their significant other found interesting memorable. Each visitor's experience is of course unique, as is each museum, but both are likely to be framed within the socially/culturally defined boundaries of how that specific museum visit affords things like exploration, facilitation, experience seeking, professional and hobby support, and spirituality.

The lens of identity-related museum motivations thus provides a unique window through which we can view the nature of the museum experience and potentially can improve it. Although much of what I've discussed here remains a theory, there now appears to be sufficient evidence to justify efforts to use these ideas for improved practice. The hope is that this approach will lead to dramatically better ways to enhance the experience of current museum visitors, improve the likelihood that occasional museum visitors will become regular visitors, and provide new and improved ways to attract groups of individuals who historically have not thought of museums as places that meet their needs. My hope is that this model will enable museum professionals to frame ever better answers to the fundamental questions of who visits museums, for what reasons and to what

References

Adams, G. D. 1989. "The process and effects of word-of-mouth communication at a history museum." Unpublished master's thesis, Boston University, Boston, MA.

American Association of Museums. 1998. *Data Report: From the 1996 National Museum Survey.* Washington, DC: American Association of Museums.

Baddeley, A. 1997. *Human Memory: Theory and Practice, Revised Edition.* Hillsdale, NJ: Erlbaum.

Briseno-Garzon, A., D. Anderson, and A. Anderson. 2007. Entry and emergent agendas of adults visiting an aquarium in family groups. *Visitor Studies,* 10(1), 73–89.

Bronfenbrenner, U. 1979. *The Ecology of Human Development.* Cambridge, MA: Harvard University Press.

Bruner, J., and D. A. Kalmar. 1998. Narrative and metanarrative in the construction of self. In M. Ferrari and R. J. Sternberg (eds.), *Self-Awareness: Its Nature and Development* (pp. 308–331). New York: The Guildford Press.

Cantor, N., W. Mischel, and J. Schwarz. 1982. A prototype analysis of psychological situations. *Cognitive Psychology,* 14, 45–77.

Cooper, C. R. 1999. Multiples selves, multiple worlds: Cultural perspectives on individuality and connectedness in adolescence development. In A. Masten (ed.), *Minnesota Symposium on Child Psychology: Cultural Processes in Development* (pp. 25–57). Mahwah, NJ: Lawrence Erlbaum Associates.

Covel, J. (2009). Guess that quest: Using identity-related motivations to support visitor services at the Monterey Bay Aquarium. Presentation at the American Association of Museums Annual Meeting, Philadelphia, PA, May 4.

Desolneux, A., L. Moisan, and J-M. Morel. 2008. *From Gestalt Theory to Image Analysis: A Probabilistic Approach.* New York: Springer.

Doering, Z. D., and A. Bickford. 1994. *Visits and Visitors to the Smithsonian Institution: A Summary of Studies* (Institutional Studies Report No. 94-1). Washington, DC: Smithsonian Institution.

Doering, Z. D., and A. Pekarik. 1996. Questioning the entrance narrative. *Journal of Museum Education* 21(3): 20–25.

Ellenbogen, K. M. 2003. "From dioramas to the dinner table: An ethnographic case study of the role of science museums in family life." Unpublished doctoral dissertation, Vanderbilt University.

Ellenbogen, K. M., J. J. Luke, and L. D. Dierking. 2007. Family learning research in museums: Perspectives on a decade of research. In J. H. Falk, L. D. Dierking, and S. Foutz (eds.), *In Principle, In Practice: Museums as Learning Institutions*. Lanham, MD: AltaMira Press.

Erikson, E. H. 1968. *Identity: Youth and Crisis*. New York: Norton.

Falk, J. H. 1993. *Factors Influencing Leisure Decisions: The Use of Museums by African Americans*. Washington, DC: American Association of Museums.

———. 2009. *Identity and the Museum Visitor Experience*. Walnut Creek, CA: Left Coast Press.

Falk, J. H., and L. Adelman. 2003. Investigating the impact of prior knowledge, experience and interest on aquarium visitor learning. *Journal of Research in Science Teaching,* 40(2), 163–176.

Falk, J. H., and L. D. Dierking. 2000. *Learning from Museums*. Lanham, MD: AltaMira Press.

Falk, J. H., and M. Needham. 2011. Measuring the impact of a science center on its community. *Journal of Research in Science Teaching* 48(1), 1–12.

Falk, J. H., J. Heimlich, and K. Bronnenkant. 2008. Using identity-related visit motivations as a tool for understanding adult zoo and aquarium visitor's meaning making. *Curator* 51(1), 55–80.

Falk, J. H., J. J. Koran, L. D. Dierking, and L. Dreblow. 1985. Predicting visitor behavior. *Curator* 28(4), 326–332.

Falk, J. H., T. Moussouri, and D. Coulson. 1998. The effect of visitors' agendas on museum learning. *Curator: The Museum Journal* 41(2), 106–120.

Falk, J. H., and M. Storksdieck. 2005. Using the contextual model of learning to understand visitor learning from a science center exhibition. *Science Education*, 89, 744–778.

———. 2010. Science learning in a leisure setting. *Journal of Research in Science Teaching,* 47(2), 194–212.

Holland, D., W. Lachicotte, Jr., D. Skinner, and C. Cain. 1998. *Identity and Agency in Cultural Worlds*. Cambridge, MA: Harvard University Press.

Koke, J. 2009. "Motivational theory as a tool for experience design; The experience of the Art Gallery of Ontario." Presentation at the American Association of Museums Annual Meeting, Philadelphia, PA, May 4.

Leinhartd, G., and K. Knutson. 2004. *Listening In On Museum Conversations*. Lanham, MD: AltaMira Press.

Linville, P. W. 1985. Self-complexity and affective extremity: don't put all your eggs in one cognitive basket. *Social Cognition* 3, 94–120.

McAdams, D. 1990. *The Person: An Introduction to Personality Psychology*. Orlando, FL: Harcourt Brace Jovanovich.

McGaugh, J. L. 2003. *Memory & Emotion: The Making of Lasting Memories*. New York: Columbia University Press.

Moussouri, T. 1997. "Family agendas and family learning in hands-on museums." Unpublished doctoral dissertation, University of Leicester, Leicester, England.

National Science Board. 2006. *Science and Engineering Indicators: 2005*. Washington, DC: U.S. Government Printing Office.

———. 2008. *Science and Engineering Indicators: 2007*. Washington, DC: U.S. Government Printing Office.

———. 2010. *Science and Engineering Indicators: 2009*. Washington, DC: U.S. Government Printing Office.

Neisser, U. 1988. Five kinds of self knowledge. *Philosophical Psychology* 1, 35–59.

Packer, J. 2006. Learning for fun: The unique contribution of educational leisure experiences. *Curator* 49(3): 329–344.

Packer, J., and R. Ballantyne. 2002. Motivational factors and the visitor experience: A comparison of three sites. *Curator* 45: 183–198

Pekarik, A. J., Z. D. Doering, and D. A. Karns. 1999. Exploring satisfying experiences in museums. *Curator* 42, 152–173.

Schutte, N. S., D. T. Kenrick, and E. K. Sadalla. 1985. The search for predictable settings: Situational prototypes, constraint, and behavioral variation. *Journal of Personality and Social Psychology* 51, 459–462.

Simon, B. 2004. *Identity in Modern Society: A Social Psychological Perspective.* Oxford, UK: Blackwell.

Stein, J. 2007. "Adapting the visitor identity-related motivations scale for living history sites." Paper presented at the Visitor Studies Association Annual Meeting, Toronto, CA, July 19.

Storksdieck, M., and J. Stein. 2007. "Using the visitor identity-related motivations scale to improve visitor experiences at the US Botanic Garden." Paper presented at the Visitor Studies Association Annual Meeting, Toronto, CA, July 19.

Note

1. Recently, I added two additional identity-related motivation categories. These categories emerge among those visiting special types of museums such as ethnic or national museums and museums and comparable settings that are designed as memorials to specific historical events.

- Affinity Seekers: Visitors come to the museum because it speaks to their sense heritage and/or personhood.
- Respectful Pilgrims: Visitors come to the museum because they possess a sense of duty or obligation. They see their visit as a way to honor the memory of those represented by the institution/memorial.

Principles of Participation

27

NINA SIMON

Iт's 2004. I'м in Chicago with my family, visiting a museum. We're checking out the final exhibit—a comment station where visitors can make their own videos in response to the exhibition. I'm flipping through videos that visitors have made about freedom, and they are really, really bad. The videos fall into two categories:

1. Person stares at camera and mumbles something incomprehensible.
2. Group of teens, overflowing with enthusiasm, "express themselves" via shout-outs and walk-ons.

This is not the participatory museum experience of my dreams. But I don't blame the participants. I blame the design.

How can cultural institutions use participatory techniques not just to give visitors a voice, but to develop experiences that are more valuable and compelling for everyone? This is not a question of intention or desire; it's a question of design. Whether the goal is to promote dialogue or creative expression, shared learning or co-creative work, the design process starts with a simple question: which tool or technique will produce the desired participatory experience?

Designers have answered versions of this question for many kinds of visitor experiences and goals in cultural institutions. Professionals know how to write labels for different audiences. They know what kinds of physical interactions promote competitive play and which promote contemplative exploration. And while they may not always get it right, they are guided by the expectation that design decisions can help them successfully achieve content and experience goals.

Nina Simon is the executive director of The Museum of Art & History at the McPherson Center in Santa Cruz and Principal of Museum 2.0, a firm dedicated to designing and researching participatory visitor experiences. "Principles of Participation" is an excerpt from *The Participatory Museum* by Nina Simon, published by Museum 2.0 Reprinted here by permission of the publisher. Copyright 2010. All rights reserved.

When it comes to developing participatory experiences in which visitors create, share, and connect with each other around content the same design thinking applies. The chief difference between traditional and participatory design techniques is the way that information flows between institutions and users. In traditional exhibits and programs, the institution provides content for visitors to consume. Designers focus on making the content consistent and high quality, so that every visitor, regardless of her background or interests, receives a reliably good experience.

In contrast, in participatory projects, the institution supports multidirectional content experiences. The institution serves as a "platform" that connects different users who act as content creators, distributors, consumers, critics, and collaborators. This means the institution cannot guarantee the consistency of visitor experiences. Instead, the institution provides opportunities for diverse visitor coproduced experiences.

This may sound messy. It may sound tremendously exciting. The key is to harness the mess in support of the excitement. Being successful with a participatory model means finding ways to design participatory platforms so the content that amateurs create and share is communicated and displayed attractively. This is a fundamental shift; in addition to producing consistent content, participatory institutions must also design opportunities for visitors to share their own content in meaningful and appealing ways. Supporting participation means trusting visitors' abilities as creators, remixers, and redistributors of content. It means being open to

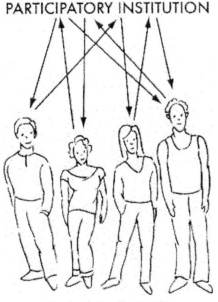

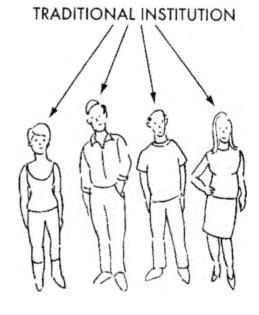

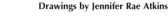

Figure 27.1.   Figure 27.2.

the possibility that a project can grow and change post-launch beyond the institution's original intent. Participatory projects make relationships among staff members, visitors, community participants, and stakeholders more fluid and equitable. They open up new ways for diverse people to express themselves and engage with institutional practice.

Making Participation Physical and Scalable

Most institutions prefer to experiment with participation behind closed doors. Cultural institutions have a long history of prototyping new projects with focus groups. Some museums co-develop exhibitions with community members, whether to represent the unique experience of certain ethnic groups or to showcase works of amateur art. These participatory design processes are often institutionally defined, time-limited, and involve a small number of participants.

The growth of social Web technologies in the mid-2000s transformed participation from something limited and infrequent to something possible anytime, for anyone, anywhere. We entered what MIT researcher Henry Jenkins calls a "convergence culture" in which regular people—not just artists or academics—appropriate cultural artifacts for their own derivative works and discussions.[1] Some cultural institutions responded, as did some music and television studios, by locking down their content so it couldn't be used in this way. But as time has gone on, more and more content providers have opened up their material and have invited people to create, share, and connect around it. Particularly for cultural institutions with a mandate to use their collections for public good, digitization and accessibility of content has become a top priority.

But participating with visitors on the Web is just a start. There are also incredible opportunities for cultural institutions to distinguish themselves by encouraging participation in the physical environments of museums, libraries, and arts centers. These institutions have something few Web companies can offer: physical venues, authentic objects, and experienced real-world designers. By combining professional design skills with the lessons of participation pouring out of the social Web, cultural institutions can become leading participatory venues in our cities, towns, and neighborhoods.

For an institution to manage participation, staff members need to be able to design experiences that invite ongoing audience participation sustainably. Traditional participatory bodies like community advisory boards and prototyping focus groups are important, but those forms of participation are limited by design. Participation has the most impact when designers can scale up collaborative opportunities to all interested visitors. This means offering every visitor a legitimate way to contribute to the institution, share things of interest, connect with other people, and feel like an engaged and respected participant.

This leads to an obvious question: does every visitor really want to participate in this manner in cultural institutions? No. Just as there are visitors who will never pull the lever on an interactive and those who prefer to ignore the labels, there are many visitors who will not choose to share their story, talk with a stranger, or consume visitor-generated content. There will always be visitors who enjoy static exhibitions conferring authoritative knowledge. There will always be visitors who enjoy interactive programs that allow them to test that knowledge for themselves. And there will increasingly be visitors—perhaps new ones—who enjoy the opportunity to add their own voices to ongoing discussions about the knowledge presented.

Many museum professionals argue that there are some visitors for whom participatory experiences might be entirely off-putting. This is true, but the converse is also true. There are many people who engage heavily with social media and are incredibly comfortable using participatory platforms to connect with friends, activity partners, and potential dates. There are people who prefer social and creative recreational activities and avoid museums because they perceive them as non-social, non-dynamic, non-participatory places. Just as interactive exhibits were introduced in museums to accommodate the presumed educational needs and active desires of young audiences, participatory elements may draw in audiences for whom creative activities and social connection are preconditions for cultural engagement.

In 1992, Elaine Heumann Gurian wrote an essay entitled "The Importance of 'And'" to address the need for museum practice to accommodate many different and potentially conflicting goals, including scholarship, education, inclusion, and conservation. She commented that we too often think of different institutional goals as oppositional rather than additive, and that "complex organizations must and should espouse the coexistence of more than one primary mission."[2] While the addition of new pursuits to an institutional plan does force some either/or decisions around policies and resources, it need not inhibit the ability to deliver on multiple promises to multiple audiences.

Participatory techniques are another "and" for the cultural professional's toolbox. They are tools that can be used to address particular institutional aspirations to be relevant, multi-vocal, dynamic, responsive, community spaces. Again, I come back to the analogy with interactive exhibits. Interactive design techniques are additive methods that supplement traditional didactic content presentation. Interactive exhibits, when successfully executed, promote learning experiences that are unique and specific to the two-way nature of their design. And while there are some institutions, notably children's and science museums, that have become primarily associated with interactive exhibits, there are other types of museums, notably art and history museums, in which interactives play a supporting role. The introduction of interactive exhibits does not require an entire institutional shift, and in most cultural institutions, interactive exhibits are just one of many interpretative techniques employed.

I believe the majority of museums will integrate participatory experiences as one of many types of experiences available to visitors in the next twenty years. There may be a few institutions that become wholly participatory and see their entire institutional culture and community image transformed by this adoption.[3] But in most cases, participation is just one design technique among many, one with a particular ability to enhance the social experience of the institution. Implementing participatory techniques requires some changes to institutional perspectives on authority and audience roles, but these changes may be as small or large as a particular organization's commitment.

Participation at Its Best

Whatever role they play in your institution, participatory elements must be well designed to be useful. Poorly designed participatory experiences such as the video comment station mentioned at the beginning of this chapter do little to enhance anyone's experience.

The best participatory projects create new value for the institution, participants, and nonparticipating audience members. When you are driven by the desire to create new value, you end up with products that are transformative, not frivolous. Consider the story of Bibliotheek Haarlem Oost, a branch library in the Netherlands. The library wanted to find a way to invite readers to assign tags to the books they read.[4] By describing books with phrases like "great for kids," "boring," or "funny," readers could contribute knowledge to the institutional catalogue system while also providing recommendations and opinions for future readers. The participatory act of tagging thus would add benefit to institution and audience alike.

The challenge was how to design the tagging activity. The most obvious way would be to ask readers to type the tags into the library's online catalog, either from home or at the library. But the architect designing the library, Jan David Hanrath, knew that very few readers would do that. So Hanrath's team did something very clever: they installed more book drops.

The library created a book drop for each of a set of predefined tags. They also built shelves inside the library for the individual tags. When patrons returned books, they placed them on the shelves or in the drops that appropriately described the books. The tags were electronically connected to the books in the catalog, and the new opinions were made immediately available both to in-person and online visitors.

No patron would call the activity of putting their books in book drops "tagging," and that's a good thing. Participation at Haarlem Oost was made easy and its rewards for the next set of visitors searching for a good book were immediate. There were few barriers to adoption or significant infrastructure or support costs. It worked because it was a clever, simple distillation of the core idea of tagging. That's what I call good design.

Doing a sorting activity is a constrained form of participation, but that doesn't diminish its ability to be useful. When I shared the story of the book drops with Daniel Spock, director of the Minnesota Historical Society's History Center (MHC), he was inspired to adapt their model to his institution. Visitors to the MHC wear buttons in the galleries to show that they have paid admission. On their way out, visitors often throw away the buttons, and some end up littering the exit. Spock's team designed a very simple voting mechanism so that instead of littering visitors could toss their buttons into one of several bins to "vote" for their favorite exhibit they'd seen that day. The simple participatory activity invites people to share their opinions and gives the staff feedback instead of trash. That's what I call value.

What Does Participation Look Like?

Dropping buttons into bins may not sound like substantive participation. Many cultural professionals focus on just one kind of participation: the creation of user-generated content. But people who create content represent a narrow slice of the participatory landscape, which also includes people who consume user-generated content, comment on it, organize it, remix it, and redistribute it to other consumers. In 2008, along with the release of the book *Groundswell: Winning in a World Transformed by Social Technologies,* Forrester Research released a "social technographics" profile tool to help businesses understand the way different audiences engage with social media online. The researchers grouped participatory online audiences into six categories by activity:

1. Creators (24%) who produce content, upload videos, write blogs.
2. Critics (37%) who submit reviews, rate content, and comment on social media sites.
3. Collectors (21%) who organize links and aggregate content for personal or social consumption.
4. Joiners (51%) who maintain accounts on social networking sites like Facebook and LinkedIn.
5. Spectators (73%) who read blogs, watch YouTube videos, visit social sites.
6. Inactives (18%) who don't visit social sites.[5]

These percentages add up to more than one hundred percent because the categorizations are fluid and many people fall into several categories at once. I fall into all of the first five categories. I'm a creator when I blog, a critic when I make comments on others' sites, a collector when I assemble "favorites," a joiner on many social networks, and a spectator when I consume social media. The percentages keep changing (and are different for every country, gender, and age group), but one thing stays constant: creators are a small part of the landscape. You are far more likely to join a social network, watch a video on YouTube, make a collection of things you'd like on a shopping site, or review a book than you are to produce a movie, write a blog, or post photos online.

And while 24 percent of people who engage in the social Web are creators in some capacity, on any given participatory site, the representation of creators is much smaller. Only 0.16 percent of visitors to YouTube will ever upload a video. Only 0.2 percent of visitors to Flickr will ever post a photo.[6] In 2006, researcher Jakob Nielsen wrote a landmark paper on participation inequality, introducing the "90-9-1" principle. This principle states: "In most online communities, 90 percent of users are lurkers who never contribute, 9 percent of users contribute a little, and 1 percent of users account for almost all the action."[7]

Participation inequality isn't limited to the Web. Even the most popular participatory opportunities in cultural institutions attract a small number of people who want to draw a picture, make a comment, or contribute to an exhibition. The surprising thing about participation inequality is not that it exists in the real world but that it exists on the Web. Some people believed that the ease of Web-based publishing tools would turn everyone into a journalist, a musician, or a contributor to a wiki. But that's not the case. There are some people who are drawn to create, but many more prefer to participate in other ways, by critiquing, organizing, and spectating social content. This isn't just a question of making creative tools as easy to use as possible. There are some people who will never choose to upload content to the Web, no matter how easy it is. Fortunately, there are other participatory options for them.

Encouraging Diverse Forms of Participation

When museum professionals express objections to participatory practice, one of the most frequent claims is "we don't want to be like YouTube." While I agree that museums should not focus on showcasing videos of cats doing silly things, as a platform, YouTube is an extraordinary service that carefully and deliberately caters to all kinds of social media participants.

At first glance, YouTube looks like it is made primarily for two audiences: creators, who make and upload videos, and spectators, who watch them. YouTube's tagline—"Broadcast Yourself"—is targeted to the creator audience. Even though only 0.16 percent of visitors to the site will ever upload a video, YouTube's designers know that the participation of these creators drives the content and the experience of everyone else who visits the site. That's why, despite the fact that the vast majority of their audience are spectators, YouTube's tagline is not "watch funny videos of cats."

A deeper look at the YouTube homepage reveals ways that other types of participation are encouraged as well. Prime real estate is devoted not to creators but to other kinds of participants. You can join YouTube and collect favorite videos across the site. You can critique videos by commenting, rating them, and posting follow-up video responses if desired. These ratings are shown on the homepage, which means that critics and their opinions get top billing alongside the video creators themselves. Finally, YouTube displays the number of times every video has been viewed. Your participation as a viewer affects the status of each video in the system. Just by watching, you are an important participant.

While the top navigation bar invites users to upload videos, the majority of the YouTube homepage is geared toward watching and rating videos. The main area displays "featured videos" to watch, not tools to share your own videos.

YouTube provides appealing services to all kinds of participants, but the platform's designers spend more time trying to convert spectators into joiners, collectors, and critics than they do trying to encourage more people to become creators. Why focus on these "intermediate" participatory behaviors? First, these behaviors have relatively low barriers to adoption. It's much easier to rate a video than it is to make one—and so conversion is more likely to be successful. But the other key reason is that the platform's value is more dependent on the number of active critics, collectors, and joiners than the number of creators. YouTube doesn't need 10 percent or even 2 percent of its audience to make and upload videos. The overall YouTube experience would likely be worse for spectators if the service was glutted with millions more low-quality videos. The more content there is, the more content there is. In contrast, the more interpretation, prioritization, and discussion there is around the content, the more people can access the videos (and the conversations) that are most valuable to them.

Despite the diversity and popularity of participatory options, many museums are fixated on creators. I share Forrester's statistics with colleagues, and they say, "Yes, but we really want people to share their own stories about biodiversity," or, "We think our visitors can make amazing videos about justice." Many cultural professionals see open-ended self-expression as the paragon of participatory experiences. Allowing visitors to select their favorite exhibits in a gallery or comment on the content of the labels isn't considered as valuable as inviting them to produce their own content.

This is a problem for two reasons. First, exhibits that invite self-expression appeal to a tiny percentage of museum audiences. Less than 1 percent of the users of most social Web platforms create original content. Would you design an interactive exhibit that only 1 percent of visitors would want to use? Maybe—but only if it was complemented by other exhibits with wider appeal. When I encounter a video talkback kiosk in a museum as a visitor, I never want to make my own video. I don't choose to be a creator in those environments, and thus my only other option is to be a spectator. But I would love to rate the videos on display (as a critic) or group them (as a collector). Unfortunately, those potentially rich participatory experiences—ones which would develop my ability to detect patterns, compare and contrast items, and express my opinion—are not available to me in most museum settings. By making it easy to create content but impossible to sort or prioritize it, many cultural institutions end up with what they fear most: a jumbled mass of low-quality content.

The second problem with focusing on creators is that open-ended self-expression requires self-directed creativity. Much of contemporary learning theory rests on the idea of "instructional scaffolding," by which educators or educational material provides supportive resources, tasks, and guidance upon which learners can build their confidence and abilities.[8] When it comes to participatory activities, many educators feel that they should deliberately remove scaffolding to allow participants to fully control their creative experience. This creates an open-ended environment that can feel daunting to would-be participants. In an open-ended activity, participants have to have an idea of what they'd like to say or make, and then they have to produce it in a way that satisfies their standards of quality. In other words, it's hard, and it's especially hard on the spot in the context of a casual museum visit. What if I walked up to you on the street and asked you to make a video about your ideas of justice in the next three minutes? Does that sound like a fun and rewarding casual activity to you?

The best participatory experiences are not wide open. They are scaffolded to help people feel comfortable engaging in the activity. There are many ways to scaffold experiences without prescribing the result. For example, a comment board that provides ballots for people to vote for favorite objects and explain the reason behind their preferences offers a better-scaffolded experience than an open-ended board with blank cards and a question like "What do you think?" A supportive starting point can help people participate confidently—whether as creators, critics, collectors, joiners, or spectators.

Who's Involved in Participation?

Participatory projects aren't just about empowering visitors. Every participatory project has three core stakeholders: the institution, participants, and the audience. The audience may mean the institution's visitors, but it can also include other constituencies who might have a particular interest in the outcomes of the project—for example, participants' neighbors or associates. For a project to be successful, the project staff should be able to articulate and satisfy the interests of each group.

From the institutional perspective, participatory projects have value when they satisfy aspects of the mission. Institutions do not engage in participatory projects because they are fun or exciting but because they can serve institutional goals.

This is easier said than done. Many cultural professionals are more familiar with providing visitor experiences than thinking about how visitors can usefully contribute to the institution. When designing participatory components to exhibitions, I always ask myself: how can we use this? What can visitors provide that staff can't? How can they do some meaningful work that supports the institution overall? When staff can answer these questions easily and confidently, participation can yield powerful results for institutions and participants alike.

Outcomes for Participants and Audiences

Outcomes of participation may be as diverse as the goals of the institution overall. These outcomes include: to attract new audiences, to collect and preserve visitor-contributed content, to provide educational experiences for visitors, to produce appealing marketing campaigns, to display locally relevant exhibitions, and to become a town square for conversation.

You should be able to define the specific way that a participatory project can benefit your institution and be ready to connect that value to your institution's mission statement. It may be valuable for one museum to receive lots of snail shells collected from visitors, whereas another institution may find value in providing a forum where visitors discuss their opinions on racism. It's also important to clearly state what kinds of participation would *not* be useful. Contributed snail shells that would thrill one institution might be a nuisance for another.

Unfortunately, many cultural professionals settle for an unambitious value of participation that is not compelling to institutional directors nor stakeholders: *visitors will like it.* This is not a robust value. It trivializes the mission-relevance of participatory projects. If you focus solely on participation as a "fun activity," you will do a disservice both to yourself as a professional and to visitors as participants.

Yes, it is fun to help paint a mural or construct a giant model of a molecule. But these activities also promote particular learning skills, create outputs that are usable by others, and promote the institution as a social place. The more you think about which mission-relevant goals you want to support, the more likely you are to design a project that satisfies more than the visitors' desires to be entertained. As Geoff Godbey, professor of leisure studies at Pennsylvania State University, commented in a *Wall Street Journal* article: "To be most satisfying, leisure should resemble the best aspects of work: challenges, skills and important relationships."[11] Participatory projects can accommodate these interests and are often better suited to providing visitors with meaningful work than traditional museum experiences.

Participatory projects suffer when visitors perceive that the staff is pandering to them or wasting their time with trivialities. Participatory activities should never be a "dumping ground" for interactivity or visitor dialogue. In cases where visitors are actually asked to "do work," that work should be useful to the institution. It's fine to design participatory projects in which visitors produce work that could more quickly or accurately be completed by internal staff members; however, the work should still be of value to the institution ultimately.[12] If the museum doesn't care about the outcomes of visitors' participation, why should visitors participate?

Meeting Participants' Needs

In the book *Here Comes Everybody,* technologist Clay Shirky argued that there are three necessary components for a participatory mechanism to be successful: "A plausible promise, an effective tool, and an acceptable bargain with the [participants]."[13] The institution must *promise* an appealing participant experience. The institution must provide *access* to *tools* for participation that are easy to understand and use. And the *bargain* between institution and participants—regarding management of intellectual property, outcomes of the project, and feedback to participants— should accommodate participants' needs. Even if your promise, tools, or bargains have to change over the course of a project, you should always be able to articulate what you offer and expect clearly and openly. Doing so demonstrates your respect for participants' time and abilities.

Note that you can substitute the word *volunteer* for *participant* for a snapshot of the ways an institution's most dedicated supporters would like to be engaged. Volunteers and members are people who express self-motivated commitment and interest to dedicate time and resources to institutions. Too often, staff members struggle to find fulfilling and substantive activities for volunteers to do. But when institutions can clearly convey how participants' actions will contribute positively to the institution and to future audiences, volunteers of all types respond enthusiastically.

When it comes to the promise, staff members need to offer participants something fundamental: personal fulfillment. Institutions have explicit mission-related goals that dictate which activities are valuable to pursue, but individuals don't have mission statements. Instead, participants have a wide range of personal goals and interests that motivate behavior. John Falk's research into visitors and identity-fulfillment indicates that visitors select and enjoy museum experiences based on their perceived ability to reflect and enhance particular self-concepts.[14] If you think of yourself as creative, you will be fulfilled by the opportunity to contribute a self-portrait to a crowdsourced exhibition. If you see yourself as someone with valuable stories to share, you will be fulfilled by the chance to record your own recollections related to content on display. If you perceive yourself as helpful, you will be fulfilled by the opportunity to pitch in on tasks that clearly support a larger goal.

Watching a performance or passively walking through an exhibition does not give people this kind of social, active fulfillment. Especially for adult visitors, museums rarely offer challenges that encourage participants to work hard and demonstrate their creative, physical, or cognitive ability. Games researcher Jane McGonigal has stated that people need four things to be happy: "satisfying work to do, the experience of being good at something, time spent with people we like, and the chance to be part of something bigger."[15] Many people visit museums in social groups to spend time with people they like in the context of something bigger. Creating content can give visitors satisfying work and the experience of being good at something. When you put these together and invite people to participate, the institution can meet all four of these needs.

When presenting participatory opportunities to would-be participants, be explicit about how they can fulfill their own needs and contribute to a project with larger impact. Just as casting activities as being "just for fun" devalues the mission-relevance of participation, it also minimizes visitors' understanding of how they can make a meaningful and exciting contribution to the greater community. If you need participants to make a project successful—whether a research project that requires distributed volunteers, a feedback project that requires diverse opinions, or a creative project that requires many hands on deck—say so. The most compelling promises emerge from genuine needs on the part of the institution.

When it comes to the tool, participants need clear roles and information about how to participate. The tool should also be as flexible as possible. Participants don't need to engage with the same project in a uniform way or at the same level of commitment. You may not want staff members coming in whenever they feel like it, but flexibility is an asset when it comes to participation—you want participants to be able to engage when and how they are most able.

When participants contribute to institutions, they want to see their work integrated in a timely, attractive, respectful way. Too many participatory projects have broken feedback loops, where the ability to see the results of participation are stalled by opaque and slow-moving staff activities like content moderation or editing. In some cases, it is completely acceptable to have a lag between participatory action and outcome for intermediate processing. But if a delay is required, it should be communicated clearly to participants. This can even be turned to the institution's advantage. For example, the museum may send an email to a visitor days or weeks after the visit to inform her that her sculpture is now on display or her story integrated into an audio tour.

Regardless of the timeline, rewarding participants involves three steps that should remain consistent. First, the institution should clearly explain how and when visitors will be rewarded for participating. Second, it should thank visitors immediately upon participating, even if their content will now go into a holding pattern. And third, the staff should develop some workable process to display, integrate, or distribute the participatory content—and ideally, inform participants when their work is shared.

At their best, these three steps are immediate, automatic, and obvious to visitors. Imagine a children's museum that includes an area where visitors can build sculptures or toys out of found objects. Visitors can place their creations on a conveyor belt that moves throughout the museum for all to see. In this case, there are no labels necessary. Visitors see what will happen to their sculptures when they put them on the belt, and they understand of how that might fulfill their self-interest in sharing their work with their community of fellow-visitors.

Providing a good bargain for participation means valuing participants' work. This doesn't require giving every visitor a gold star for participating. It means listening to participants, providing feedback on their efforts, and demonstrating how the institution will use their contributions.

Whether the institution asks for a long commitment or a brief encounter, clarity and honesty are the keys to helping participants feel comfortable contributing. This includes addressing issues of privacy and intellectual property. What happens to the videos that participants record in the gallery? Who owns the ideas they share with the institution? Being clear, specific, and honest about participants' roles in participatory projects helps people know what to expect and evaluate whether an opportunity is right for them.

Lack of clarity erodes trust between institutions and participants and can lead to substandard experiences for both. In August of 2008, I worked with the Chabot Space & Science Center on a participatory design institute in which eleven teenagers designed media pieces for an upcoming Harvard-Smithsonian exhibition on black holes. Unfortunately, while the Harvard-Smithsonian representatives were enthusiastic about encouraging teens to "be creative," they were unable to give the teens any specific information about how their work would be integrated into the final exhibit. There was no initial design, no graphics, and no idea of where the teens' work would fit into the overall website. This lack of clarity made teens suspicious that the client was "hiding" the goals from them and preventing them from meeting the criteria for success. In the end, the teens' work was not in line with the client's final website design, and their work was marginalized rather than being featured in the final product. Lack of clarity at the beginning led to a somewhat frustrating experience for participants and an unsatisfactory product for the institution.

When complete clarity is not possible, honesty suffices. The Chabot project was not a failure. While we could not give the teenagers the answers they wanted, we were direct with them about what we did and didn't know and supported them as best we could. Staff members can change their mind, make mistakes, and evolve with participants if they are honest every step of the way. And the more the staff can express to participants—in actions as well as words—how their work helps the institution or other visitors, the more participants will see themselves as partners and co-owners of the project and the institution by extension.

Creating Quality Outcomes for Audiences

Participatory projects are not solely for institutions and participants. There is another populous constituency: the audience of non-participating visitors. How can a participatory project produce outcomes that are valuable and interesting to the larger institutional audience? Some participatory environments are continually open and evolving, so that any audience member can electively become a participant, but most projects limit participation to a small group. It is simpler to say, "You can submit your idea until the end of the year" or "We will work with twenty teenagers from a local high school to develop this project," than it is to construct a system that can let anyone participate at any time. For many institutions, constraining the scope of participation is an appropriate starting point for collaborative engagement.

No matter how large the participating group, the audience for their work matters. Participants' experiences, no matter how superlative, must be weighed against the experience that others will have with the outcome of their work. A mural isn't just for those who painted it; it must bring pleasure to others as an art object as well. Likewise, exhibits, research, marketing materials, programs, and experiences produced in collaboration with visitors must be compelling outputs in their own right. That is not to say they can't be different from standard institutional programs. Ideally, projects developed using participatory models will have unique value that cannot be achieved by traditional processes.

Audience goals, like participant goals, are based on individuals' diverse and idiosyncratic criteria for fulfillment. You can't please everyone, but staff can decide what kind of experiences they want to offer and design participatory platforms to accommodate those. Some visitors are looking for high-quality consumer experiences and do not care about the process by which those experiences are developed. For those visitors, project staff need to make sure the participatory process can deliver a product at the desired levels of rigor, design, and content. Other visitors want to familiarize themselves with participation from the "safe space" of spectating before jumping in. For those would-be participants, staff members should design in mechanisms that celebrate, encourage, model, and value participants' work. The more specifically you can define the intended audience for a project, the more successful you will be at designing a participatory project that will satisfy their needs.

How Does Participation Work?

There are two counterintuitive design principles at the heart of successful participatory projects. First, participants thrive on constraints, not open-ended opportunities for self-expression. And second, to collaborate confidently with strangers, participants need to engage through personal, not social, entry points. These design principles are both based on the concept of scaffolding. Constraints help scaffold creative experiences. Personal entry points scaffold social experiences. Together, these principles set the stage for visitors to feel confident participating in creative work with strangers.

Participation Thrives on Constraints

If your goal is to invite visitors to share their experiences in a way that celebrates and respects their unique contributions to your institution, you need to design more constraints, not fewer, on visitor self-expression. Consider a mural. If given the chance, very few people would opt to paint a mural on their own. The materials are not the barriers—the ideas and the confidence are. You have to have an idea of what you want to paint and how to do it.

But now imagine being invited to participate in the creation of a mural. You are handed a pre-mixed color and a brush and a set of instructions. You know what you are supposed to do to be successful. You get to contribute to a collaborative project that produces something beautiful. You see the overall value of the project. You can point out your work in the final product with pride. You have been elevated by the opportunity to contribute to the project.

This is a well-scaffolded participatory experience. In successful participatory projects, visitors don't build exhibits from scratch or design their own science experiments. Instead, they participate in larger projects: joining the team, doing their part. Constrained projects often provide opportunities for partial self-expression—a flourishing brush stroke here, a witty sentence there—but the overall expressive element is tightly constrained by the participatory platform at hand. Meaningful constraints motivate and focus participation. As Orson Welles put it, "the enemy of art is the absence of limitations."

The Denver Art Museum (DAM) provided an excellent example of a constrained participatory museum experience in their Side Trip gallery on display in the spring of 2009. Side Trip was an interactive space that accompanied an exhibition of psychedelic rock music posters called The Psychedelic Experience.

In one Side Trip activity, museum educators invited visitors to make their own rock music posters. Rather than giving people blank sheets of paper and markers (and reaching a narrow audience of self-motivated creators), the DAM educators devised an activity that blended collecting, critiquing, and creating. Visitors were offered clipboards with transparencies attached. There were stacks of graphics—cut-out reproductions from the real rock posters on display next door—which visitors could place under the transparencies to rearrange and remix into poster designs of their own choosing. Visitors then used dry-erase markers to trace over the graphics, augment them, and add their own creative flair. When a visitor was satisfied with her recombined poster, she handed it to a staff member, who put it in a color copier to create a completed composite. Each visitor was given a copy of her poster and was given the option to display a copy in the gallery.

Visitors carefully constructed their own rock music posters at the Denver Art Museum by placing graphics under transparencies and drawing additions on top. Side Trip's immersive environment encouraged visitors both to connect to the pscyhedelic era and to behave differently than they would in other galleries.

The results of this physical "remix" activity were beautiful, intricate posters. As a Side Trip visitor, I couldn't easily tell where the remixed artifacts ended and the participants' additions began. 37,000 posters were made over the run of the show, compared to total exhibit attendance of 90,000. The average amount of time spent making a poster was twenty-five minutes. This was a popular activity that visitors took seriously.

The poster-making activity was successful because visitors didn't have to start with a blank slate. Their creativity was scaffolded by graphic cut-outs that also tied their creative experience to the artifacts in the show. The constraints gave participants a comfortable entry point to engagement without limiting their creative potential. It invited visitors who did not think they could make art to engage confidently with a positive result. It created an attractive, high quality body of visitor-generated content for spectators to enjoy.

Why aren't more museums designing highly constrained participatory platforms in which visitors contribute to collaborative projects? The misguided perception is that it's more respectful to allow visitors to do their own thing—that the highest-value participatory experiences will emerge from unfettered self-expression. But that idea reflects a misunderstanding of what motivates participation. Visitors don't want a blank slate for participation. They need well-scaffolded experiences that put their contributions to meaningful use.

Going Social

So far, we've looked at a few techniques for designing experiences that invite diverse participation and produce meaningful work. But another key focus of this book is the design of experiences that encourage people to participate socially with each other. To design successful social experiences, you don't start by designing "for the crowd." Instead, think of yourself as a cocktail party host. Your job is to

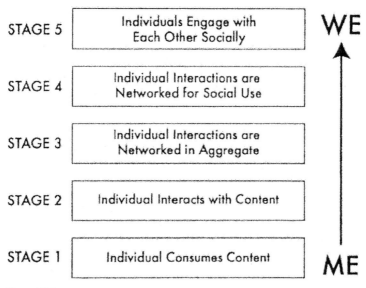

STAGE 5	Individuals Engage with Each Other Socially	**WE**
STAGE 4	Individual Interactions are Networked for Social Use	
STAGE 3	Individual Interactions are Networked in Aggregate	
STAGE 2	Individual Interacts with Content	
STAGE 1	Individual Consumes Content	**ME**

Figure 27.3.

graciously and warmly welcome each individual, and then to connect her with other people whom she might connect with particularly well. When you connect enough individuals to each other, they start feeling like they are part of a communal experience. I call this "me-to-we" design, which builds on individual (me) experiences to support collective (we) engagement.

In other words, you don't start from the top down to design a participatory space. Transforming a cultural institution into a social hub requires engaging individual users and supporting connections among them. While at a party a host might connect people for a variety of reasons—shared professional fields, shared love of basset hounds, common personality traits—in a museum, staff members should connect people through the content on display. By introducing individual visitors through the content they both love, hate, or have a personal connection to, staff can motivate dialogue and relationship building around the core focus of the institution.

This evolution of the visitor experience from personal to communal interactions can be expressed via five stages of interface between institution and visitor. The foundation of all five stages is content. What changes is how visitors interact with content and how the content helps them connect socially with other people.

Each stage has something special to offer visitors. Stage 1 provides visitors with access to the content that they seek. Stage 2 provides an opportunity for inquiry and for visitors to take action and ask questions. Stage 3 lets visitors see where their interests and actions fit in the wider community of visitors to the institution. Stage 4 helps visitors connect with particular people—staff members and other visitors—who share their content and activity interests. Stage 5 makes the entire institution feel like a social place, full of potentially interesting, challenging, enriching encounters with other people.

These stages are progressive in that you cannot consistently design physical environments for a stage 5 experience without providing the groundwork of stages 1 through 4. They are somewhat flexible; there are some highly social people who can easily jump from stage 2 to stage 5, whereas other people may feel most comfortable never moving beyond stage 3. Not all institutional projects should be designed for upper-stage experiences. Each stage affords a different kind of visitor experience, and most visitors experience multiple stages in a given cultural experience.

At present, most institutionally designed experiences are on stages 1 and 2. I do not advocate a re-staging of all visitor experiences but rather the inclusion of a greater diversity of experience types, including some that promote the social over the personal. While many traditional museum visitors may be happy with a blend of stage 1 and 2 experiences, there are other potential visitors for whom the introduction of stage 3, 4, and 5 experiences can make the institution more enticing and meaningful.

Many cultural institutions provide facilitated experiences on all five stages. Tour guides and educators frequently help visitors feel comfortable and confident engaging socially with each other. Facilitated educational programs like camps or reenactments provide stage 5 opportunities to work in a team or group.[16] The problem is that when the facilitator isn't there or the event isn't happening that social engagement ceases to exist. Designing stage 3 and 4 experiences can lay the groundwork to support and encourage unfacilitated social experiences. These frameworks enable visitors to do it for themselves whenever they like.

For example, consider the experience of visiting a historic house on a guided tour. There are many stage one experiences in which visitors can look at things and learn information about the house. There are some stage two opportunities for visitors to touch things, ask questions, and dig into personal interests. Because many visitors tour historic houses in groups with strangers, there is the potential for experiences on stages three to five. Guides can ask individuals to vote for the room they'd most like to live in and see how they compare to others in the group (stage three). Guides can encourage subsets of people who have particular interests, say, in the lives of servants, to spend time in dialogue with each other around artifacts related to that interest (stage four). And the best guides make the group feel like a close-knit team, working together to answer each other's questions and discover new surprises (stage five).

Without a guide, a visit to a historic house is much less social. Visitors look and learn on their own with the companions who accompany them on their visit. The institution makes stage one and two experiences available, but not upper-level social engagement. If visitors engage with strangers, it is based entirely on personal initiative.

How could a historic house encourage visitors to have social experiences with each other outside the guided tour? Stage three and four activities can be designed as unfacilitated experiences. The stage three "vote for your favorite room" mechanism could be a cardboard floor plan on which visitors vote by sticking a pin on their favorite rooms. Visitors could have stage four interactions with other people with similar interests prompted by labels that encourage visitors to share personal memories with strangers through audio-recordings or letter-writing stations.

Designing unfacilitated opportunities for social engagement makes visitors more likely to see each other as potential sources of information and enjoyment in the house. Once this feeling is widespread, the house is ripe for stage five experiences, in which visitors feel comfortable pointing things out to strangers, having brief discussions about their own memories, and so on.

I'm not suggesting that institutions replace educators, front-line staff, or volunteers with exhibitry. Staff interactions provide the most consistent kinds of social experiences, and staff can be an important bridge to support and enhance even the most social exhibit design. Indeed, many of the examples in this book rely on staff or volunteers to work successfully.

But staff cannot be everywhere. Designing physical spaces to support interaction means that it can happen anytime, even when guides or staff members are not available. The goal is not to replace staff but to scale up the opportunity for social engagement. This is what the social Web does so well. It leverages the interests and profiles of individuals to create opportunities for new connections and social experiences.

Let's look at an example of me-to-we design from the corporate world that successfully provides experiences at all stages around a frequently disliked, voluntary activity that takes place all over the world. No, I'm not talking about visiting museums. I'm talking about running, and a platform called Nike Plus.

Case Study: From Me-to-We with Nike Plus

Nike Plus (Nike+) is a combined iPod and shoe sensor product for tracking personal running. It provides real-time data about your progress as you run and stores your data for later review online. You can create goals for yourself and challenge other users (both friends and strangers) to run at your pace or complete a target number of miles. You can also create motivational playlists for the iPod to give you a "power-up" audio boost when you most need it. When you start to lag, your favorite song will get you back on track.

Nike+ uses me-to-we design brilliantly to support a product, an activity, a community, and ultimately, a healthy lifestyle. It offers experiences on all five stages of user engagement.

Each stage has something special to offer visitors. *Stage one* provides visitors with access to the content that they seek. *Stage two* provides an opportunity for inquiry and for visitors to take action and ask questions. *Stage three* lets visitors see where their interests and actions fit in the wider community of visitors to the institution. *Stage four* helps visitors connect with particular people—staff members and other visitors—who share their content and activity interests. *Stage five* makes the entire institution feel like a social place, full of potentially interesting, challenging; enriching encounters with other people.

These stages are progressive in that you cannot consistently design physical environments for a stage five experience without providing the groundwork of stages one through four. They are somewhat flexible; there are some highly social people who can easily jump from stage two to stage five, whereas other people may feel most comfortable never moving beyond stage three. Not all institutional projects should be designed for upper-stage experiences. Each stage affords a different kind of visitor experience, and most visitors experience multiple stages in a given cultural experience.

At present, most institutionally designed experiences are on stages one and two. I do not advocate a re-staging of all visitor experiences but rather the inclusion of a greater diversity of experience types, including some that promote the social over the personal. While many traditional museum visitors may be happy with a blend of stage one and two experiences, there are other potential visitors for whom the introduction of stage three, four, and five experiences can make the institution more enticing and meaningful.

Many cultural institutions provide facilitated experiences on all five stages. Tour experience. When you engage in a collective challenge, you don't just focus on your own running goals or compare yourself to the masses. You have external goals for which you are accountable to virtual teammates. You're motivated to run so you can meet the challenge and contribute to the team. Here's how one enthusiastic blogger, Caleb Sasser, put it:

> And the coolest part about Nike+ running? Like any good online game, you can challenge your friends. First to 100 miles? Fastest 5-mile time? Your call. These challenges wind up being incredibly inspiring—running against good friend and athletic powerhouse J. John Afryl kept me on my toes—and they're also incredibly fun. Logging in after a long run, uploading your data, and seeing where you are in the standings, is a pretty awesome way to wrap up your exercise. And more importantly, sitting around the house, wondering what to do, thinking about jogging, and then realizing that if you don't go jogging tonight you're going to lose points and slip in the standings—now that's true, videogame motivational.[17]

The combination of game mechanics with social challenges makes Nike+ a powerful stage four experience. But what about stage five? One of Nike's goals—and a major component of their online presence—is to encourage people to run together. The company sponsors races and running groups all over the world.

There are many Nike+ online forums and opportunities for meeting up with real people in your real neighborhood to go running. But there are also Nike+ users who have clamored for ways to run with their distant virtual teammates. It's not crazy to imagine a future version of Nike+ that allows you to talk real-time to a running partner halfway around the world as you both navigate the streets.

Think about what a strange feat Nike pulled off with this product. Nike took a non-screen-based, often anti-social, occasionally loathed or feared activity—running—and turned it into a screen-supported social game. It transformed the motivation to run from being about exercise to being about social competition. Nike+ took an uncontrolled venue—the streets and trails used by runners all over the world—and created a compelling experience around it. For its users, Nike+ transforms running into a pervasive, fun, socially driven experience. And if Nike could do it for something as feared and despised as running often is, surely you can do it for your cultural institution.

Notes

1. Learn more about convergence culture and Jenkins' book with that title at www.convergenceculture.org.

2. See pages 14–18 in Elaine Heumann Gurian's book, *Civilizing the Museum* (London: Routledge, 2006).

3. For an example of a radically participatory institution, check out the case study in Chapter 8 of *The Participatory Museum* (Santa Cruz: Museum 2.0, 2010) on the Wing Luke Asian Museum.

4. Tagging is a term that refers to a collecting activity in which people assign descriptive keywords ("tags") to items.

5. The statistics shown here are for adults over 18 in the United States as of August 2009. Up-to-date data for different countries, genders, and ages are available from Forrester Research at www.forrester.com/empowered/tool_consumer.html.

6. These statistics come from the "Principle in Action" page on the 90-9-1 website: www.antseyeview.com/90-9-1-principle/

7. See Jakob Nielsen's October 2006 article, "Participation Inequality: Encouraging More Users to Contribute" at www.useit.com/alertbox/participation_inequality.html

8. Consult the work of Lev Vygotsky for foundational material on instructional scaffolding. For a museum-focused discussion, see George Hein's *Learning in the Museum* (London: Routledge, 1998).

9. See John Warren's October 2008 blog post, Wild Center: Local Leader on Adirondack Climate Change at www.adirondackalmanack.com/2008/10/wild-center-local-leader-on-adirondack.html

10. Explore the full slate of The Wild Center's climate initiatives at www.wildcenter.org/index.php?sub=38

11. See Jared Sandberg's July 2006 Wall Street Journal article on active leisure at http://online.wsj.com/article/SB115317337878109062.html

12. For a longer discussion on the multiple values of participation, see Chapter 5 of *The Participatory Museum*.

13. See Chapter 11 in Clay Shirky's book *Here Comes Everybody: The Power of Organizing without Organizations* (New York: Penguin Press, 2008).

14. See John Falk's book, *Identity and the Museum Visitor Experience* (Walnut Creek: Left Coast Press, 2009).

15. McGonigal shared this list in a cultural context in a December 2008 lecture, "Gaming the Future of Museums." See slide 22 at www.slideshare.net/avantgame/gaming-the-future-of-museums-a-lecture-by-jane-mcgonigal-presentation

16. See page 170 of *The Participatory Museum* for an example of a stage five program at the Conner Prairie historic park called Follow the North Star.

17. See Cabel Sasser's effusive August 2006 blog post, "Multiplayer Game of the Year" at www.cabel.name/2006/08/multiplayer-game-of-year.html

What Is To Be Done, Sandra?

Learning in Cultural Institutions of the 21st Century

ANNA CUTLER

28

1901. VLADIMIR LENIN IS WARMING his samovar and reaching out for his pen, about to embark on writing a political tract that will change the face of history. I am guessing that he did not have to get the kids off to school, put the washing on and respond to sixty emails before he set about this task, but one has to appreciate the quality and pragmatism of the question he asked himself, that is, "What is to be done?"

Of course, this question did not come out of thin air. Lenin was building on the bedrock that was Marxist theory and an ideological imperative for change that was fuelled by inequality and injustice. His plan was about a plan, and that was to put theory into practice to change the face of his society.

2008. The revolution did not turn out quite how Lenin had anticipated. Instead, society has been revolutionised by new technology. Needs are changing, the workforce has diversified, and we are facing a global change in the environment and our relationship to it. We have new and faster access to information than ever before, and there is a shift from industrial economies to those that are knowledge-based. In turn, the production of knowledge through educational practice has been scrutinised, challenged and revisited with new theories and shifts in policy. In the face of all this, I am forced to reflect on my own sector and ask of my colleague, Sandra (with no intended flippancy). "What is to be done?" Are there any theoretical bedrocks for us to draw on and make a plan of our own?

The Idea of Learning

For the past twenty years I have been working in the field of arts, across a range of organised learning environments. I have spent time in what we call formal education (that is, in universities and in schools), as well as in informal learning

Anna Cutler is the director of learning at Tate, England. "What Is To Be Done, Sandra? Learning in Cultural Institutions of the 21st Century" is reprinted here with permission from *Tate Papers*, Spring 2010. Copyright 2010, Tate. All rights reserved.

environments (such as youth groups and cultural settings). What I can say, without hesitation, is that these environments are not the same. A university is *not a* youth club and a school is *not* a gallery. This may appear painfully obvious, but actually sits at the heart of the question of "What is to be done?" because of the different value systems applied to the concepts of the formal and informal, and the questions that lie behind the pragmatism of "what."

These questions are concerned with the choices we make about why we feel it is important for people to learn certain disciplines, traditions and behaviours and not others, and how we go about organising this as a society. Despite the differences inherent in the practices of the formal and informal, what one cannot help but notice is the way in which the organising structures of formal learning are often applied to the informal, such that the concept of departments, sixty-minute transmission models, courses, a teacher imparting information, and a raft of quantitative assessment methods is still apparent. In most of my experiences of the informal sector, my work has been measured against the formal model. My aim, however, has been to explore and generate research about the different ways in which learning takes shape and what the outcomes are for those who participate. My observation, and that of researchers in the field, is that often a *different* kind of experience takes place out of a formal, examined setting and this provides a different set of attitudes and understandings for the individuals involved.

In attempting to unpick the differences between the formal and informal, or rather to explore and explain the similarities and divergences of both, I have come to describe learning and education in more particular terms. There are a variety of ways to explore the idea of learning depending on one's discipline. Neuroscientists describe it as the neurological process of receiving and processing new data. They explain that every human being is wired up the same way to learn. Information from external stimuli is received in the brain where it is filtered through analytical and emotional networks and then stored as memory (or rejected en route). This cognitive process (that is, the mental process through which we acquire and manage information) sorts the wheat from the chaff, and enables us to make decisions as to what to store and what to edit out.[1] They would argue that there is therefore no formal learning and no informal learning to be had. There is only one type (just learning), and it is simply the settings and approaches that differ.

Educational psychologists often describe learning as change through experience. The ways in which this is explored is frequently divided into behavioural, cognitive and constructivist accounts (to name but three). Within these lie a great number of fascinating theories that cannot be explored here, but central to much enquiry is the idea of learning as a process by an individual, whether concerned with observed behaviour, brain processes, or self-constructed ideas and concepts.[2]

Education, on the other hand, might be defined as the structures and systems established to manage and guide learning: *what* we teach/learn; *why* we teach/learn it; and *how* we teach/learn. These are structures based on a set of socially determined values. This means that education is ideologically driven (by ideology I mean the dominant, hegemonically maintained hierarchy of value).[3] Given that our society prioritises formal learning, the informal tends to be labelled as self-improvement or leisure, implying a lack of necessity or seriousness. When measured against the formal system, it often fails to reach the mark. How, given this ideological scenario, could it do anything other?

I have also found it helpful to refer to the two key types of memory at play in our everyday physiological activity; that is declarative and non-declarative (procedural) memory. Declarative memory can broadly be defined as the facts, figures, dates and events that the brain stores, but that you have to call up when needed. Non-declarative memory is that which you do not have to call up and is described as behaviours and habits, such as using a knife and fork, driving, playing an instrument.[4] Importantly, the education system prioritises declarative memory, and this is the feature that is most tested. However, long-term learning, habit and behaviour depend on non-declarative memory, and are what we rely on once our formal learning has finished. After all, how often do most people learn in a group of thirty, seated behind desks, with an instructor present, in their professional lives? Why do we place such high value on the kind of knowledge that trains us for *University Challenge* but that does not enable us to ask better questions?

Current Debates

When looking at the structure of learning systems, four key elements are core to delivery. These are time, space, content and method. The current education system has been devised within the parameters of certain time-slots, and works within a set of spaces (classrooms, lecture theatres and halls). Content has been agreed in terms of a curriculum and in further and higher education as degree courses, units and diplomas in specialised subjects. Methods may differ depending on shifting learning theories, but are currently dominated by information-led, outcome-oriented transmission models, teacher to pupil (although there are clearly changes emerging and there have always been exceptions). These four systematised elements have been challenged by many educationalists and innovators. Charles Leadbeater's paper *What Next? 21 Ideas for 21st Century Learning* (2008) addresses such issues, where it is clear that notions of content and approach, space and time, need some refreshment, not to say rethinking for 21st-century learning.[5]

Over the past ten years a perceptible shift has taken place in education and arts practice at a national and international level. The development of technology and user-generated material, the emergence of the knowledge economy, and the need for creativity (as a means to generate innovation) have meant that models of learning that sought to impart information and prepare and develop a workforce for specific industries (that is, manufacturing or industrialised labour) are no longer sufficient for our societal needs.[6] This shift is reflected within contemporary cultural and education practice as well as in recent research papers. Current users, published governmental and NGO reports, academic articles and artists describe these shifts in practice as follows:

- from the passive to participative: learning that involves participation and hands on activity rather than being a receiver of knowledge.
- from standardised delivery to personalisation: one size does not fit all and different learning programmes are required that can be tailored to an individual's needs.
- from the didactic to co-learning: a shift from the transmission model of learning with a single expert/tutor, to shared learning that is guided in response to the needs of the users and shaped in collaboration *with* them.
- from knowledge acquisition to knowledge application: the movement away from learning information for the sake of doing so, to understanding how to use knowledge across different settings and in original ways for valued outcomes.
- from a single authorial voice to plural voices: the development of collaborative practice and production, giving rise to a wider range of perspectives and opportunity for the student's voice in formalised settings.
- from private knowledge to public access: best exemplified through the world wide web/open source, but relating also to the ways in which the private knowledge of individuals and institutions has been opened up, shifting power relationships away from closed knowledge holders.

Notable commentaries in the UK have come from Tom Bentley[7] and Ken Robinson,[8] for example, and are found in government reports.[9] Indeed, there has been a shift away from the term education towards learning, with the aim of putting the learner more centrally and interrogating what is being learned and why, relative to the organised systems in which learning exists.

What has all this to do with learning in cultural settings? Recent debates about cultural learning have been set up to explore, I assume, exactly the kinds of issues raised here.[10] What marks cultural learning as that which is different from learning in other settings? What is its value and what can we expect to achieve by doing it? Research from Creative Partnerships (now Creativity Culture and Education),[11] engage,[12] the Guggenheim,[13] and research projects at Tate are beginning to reveal the different kinds of learning that take place for people when engaging in cultural activity. For the most part, research projects have been explorations with young people in relation to education in schools (often because of the value this brings). However, there is increasing research into family and adult learning.[14] Findings suggest a range of outcomes from working within different cultural disciplines and with different user groups. This is why comparisons across the arts always seem so difficult to find, as each scenario has a different set of particular inputs. But I would argue that there is also a set of repeated and identifiable similarities that frame cultural learning and that sit to the side of education as described here. For the sake of clarity, let us understand that cultural learning in this instance means learning that takes place beyond the classroom or lecture theatre, within a cultural setting, and that this takes cultural product as its subject matter for direct engagement.[15]

Key findings repeated through the research outlined above can be identified as increased confidence, a shift in attitudes and behaviours, improved motivation and sustained engagement. There is also evidence of an increase in critical thinking applied beyond the learning environment. Interestingly, there is a demonstrable improvement in knowledge of the subject area and skills with which to create a product, but these appear least central within the findings, as though this would be self-evident, the part you had to do, to get the rest.[16] Several of the research documents begin to explore what other associable impacts this learning has across a range of other subject areas in terms of transferable skills and life skills. The particularity of activity and disciplines also has an effect on what is learned. For example, working once a week on a project over twelve months will produce a different outcome from working over just one week, and engaging with dance will give physical skills that visual arts do not. Despite obvious differences such as these, there is a great deal of synthesis to be made of the breadth of data that has been collected over the past five to ten years. Using a form of creative learning (that I defined through working with many groups of learners, teachers and artists), we found that the practice of artists, their own method of approach, encouraged and generated long-term learning.[17] What I would like to draw out here, therefore, is that, as shown by much research in cultural settings, most outcomes are related to non-declarative memory.

So what's going on? The learning that is taking place is affecting attitudes and behaviours. It is also generating critical, reflective thinking and transferable skills, sustained engagement and application across disciplines. I would suggest that cultural learning (or perhaps one should now say cultural creative learning to reflect the point made previously) is helping to form habits of mind, potentially for a lifetime. Its content and its approach differ from the established model of education, as cultural and creative learning seeks to generate sustainable skills that can be applied across subjects and education/personal boundaries. This appears to be a more meta-cognitive approach to learning (that is, being aware of one's own thinking and the strategies one is using).[18]

Example

Using the visual arts as a model for translating these ideas into practice it is possible to see how habits of mind are generated. In a recent talk Shelby Wolf outlined her findings of a project involving young children at Tate Modern called Looking for Change.[19] This is a four-year project that takes place weekly in three London schools and in the galleries. It explores the development of children's visual literacy and focuses on looking, talking and making. This project seeks collaboration with schools to see what can be achieved beyond the gallery walls, thereby maximising the experience when children arrive in the gallery. Wolf suggested that the work being undertaken is shaping the children's memory. She details how, through engaging with art, they are forming habits of mind, building interpretive abilities, forming observational faculties, creating symbolic meaning, developing persistence and moulding a vision of who they might be as adults. This kind of analysis is supported through a publication entitled *Studio Thinking, The Real Benefits of Visual Arts Education*,[20] which moves away from many educational publications seeking to validate or apply the arts in terms of how they can support and improve the "formal" education model and moves, as David Perkins suggests in the preface, "through the looking glass" into long-term impacts of learning, made manifest through applying information directly "or today." Is this the "real benefit" of cultural creative learning: that we generate time to create habits of mind? That we have capacity to do so and that we embody this through direct activity—making the imaginary concrete? And can it be said that gaining cultural skills are only possible over a sustained period of time?

Evidence, and indeed experience, would suggest that sustained contact is crucial in generating long-term learning, and that this not only sets up a series of personal behaviours, but skills and aptitudes. Shirley Brice Heath and Shelby Wolf suggest that in the visual arts:

> Learning to see details also brings the capacity to see the bigger picture—to relate the bits and pieces to what will become a larger whole . . . this fundamental principle applies in the sciences, in everyday problem solving and spatial navigation within the world. Managers and musicians, plumbers and painters, engineers and videographers become successful largely through their ability to see beyond small details into the larger picture.[21]

They also comment:

> seeing details calls for visual focus—sustaining the eyes on a space for more than a few milliseconds. The area of the brain dedicated to visual focus lies at the very centre of the various sections given over to vision. Focus matters, because it allows viewers to look deeply within an object or situation and see detail from line to shape and colour to motion. . . . Hence, as young children work in creating art— regardless of form or medium—they gain practice in holding attention on a sphere of action or range of space. In doing so they take in the fundamental elements or building blocks of the world around them. They gain inner vision.[22]

Clearly, visual learning not only works to develop an understanding of art, but also of a range of much wider and fundamental needs in understanding the visual and spatial world around us. Heath and Wolf also reflect on the importance of guided looking and the advantages of language and metaphor as habits of mind: The first of these advantages comes through the movement of mental processes back and forth from the visual to the verbal.[23]

Certainly within *Looking for Change* we have observed a development in children's oracy and vocabulary together with their interpretation of art works. That is to say, the ways in which they are talking about art involving metaphor and richer description are extending their depth of understanding the art too. Looking and language are here connected. The importance of this, and of the programme more broadly, is that young people build knowledge for themselves through language, looking and discussion; without doing so, they will only ever be able to receive ideas and information filtered by others. Without building one's own knowledge it is impossible to build an understanding for oneself. Real access is about being able to do exactly this, make meaning, transferring relevant ideas from one object to another.

Peppered throughout the research and within accounts from *Inspiring Learning in Galleries: Enquire about Learning in Galleries,* time as an issue is also highlighted.[24] Often it is referred to as an absence—that there isn't *enough* time in a school day to work on cultural or creative programmes. Time also represents motivation, in that the children get so engrossed in the activity that their concentration extends and they are more applied, taking longer over their work, staying late, working through breaks and arriving early at school to achieve more.[25] Becoming skilled requires practice and it is no surprise therefore that the more often the children look, make, and reflect more, the better they are at understanding and analysing.

Working beyond the classroom walls also enables a different experience for the learner, one that is particular to the subject in question and that can use the space appropriately to enable the learner to explore the subject (in this case art) more authentically and directly. Seeing the detail of a real object is quite different from slides, prints or more often photocopies, just as a live performance is different from a video recording of the same event. Generating deeper levels of understanding needs experience of the art form itself and its making, which gives a further dimension and requires materials appropriate to the idea. Working in an environment that has the facilities to enable this to happen challenges us to make, think and talk differently. Space matters because it also disrupts the usual learning experience of sitting down and receiving, opening up the many ways in which we all learn, for example, visually, kinaesthetically and emotionally.

Cultural creative learning, I would claim, has other valuable differences from education as defined here. It necessarily entails engagement with emotions, the realisation of a material product in the real world and the ensuing public engagement that the product demands as it exists within the public realm. These three aspects also develop different abilities from usual learning environments and these are concerned with understanding how to interpret or reflect emotional content, how to apply an idea to its material production, therefore making the abstract concrete, and navigating the public realm in terms of critique. These are important life skills that find little space in the education system and, ultimately, they help form and shape our relationships, to people, to the wider world and to critical reflection.

It is understood that learning without content specificity, facts, figures and subject knowledge is only half a project. One could not learn without declarative memory that constantly informs our behaviours and habits of mind. I am not suggesting, therefore, that we replace detailed content, nor even that we get rid of traditional lectures and information-giving when necessary. But I am arguing that we take the non-declarative more seriously and recognise that without it, we have information but without foundations on which to lay that information, and little understanding of how to *apply* it to different contexts; that is to say, we have knowledge, but potentially not much learning. One habit of mind is to know when you need to input new content information to generate understanding. At present we attempt to learn the other way round; that is, learning how to know rather than knowing how to learn.

Cultural Sites of Learning

What does this mean for 21st-century learning in cultural establishments, institutions and organisations? To focus one minute on the millions of visitors that museums and galleries in particular enjoy each year, many different kinds of publics are formed. Some visitors come as tourists for a few hours, others come for the day. There are those that come once a month or to courses, some with their families ad hoc, and some for sustained periods over years. How do we generate or integrate the best kinds of habits of mind as well as develop knowledge? How do we manage different approaches and audiences as well as take into account the shifts in practice that have taken place globally? This returns us, rather neatly, to the initial and now clearly complex question of "What is to be done?"

"What is to be done" is based on the assumption that something needs to be done—or rather—to be changed. I would argue that learning in cultural institutions does need to transform to meet the requirements of societal changes as outlined in the initial pages here, as well as in cultural and educational practice and production. I would also add that it needs to change its focus to include the development of non-declarative memory such that long-term benefit can be generated. Although it would be wrong to suggest that there is no such work that is taking place (and there are many projects in cultural institutions that are exemplars of such changes), there is nonetheless a sense of uncertainty as to where culture sits and fits in terms of learning and what it can provide beyond education. Part of the problem may also be the potential solution, in that cultural venues have capacity to deliver a range of models for learning—from the lightest of touches to deep long-term projects. I believe that cultural organisations are perfectly placed to model new approaches and work *with* education to reassemble the ways in which we learn across settings. However, learning in cultural organisations may be in a bit of a tangle having been buffeted between intrinsic and extrinsic needs, growing popularity as well as target driven delivery demands. Rather like Christmas lights brought down from the attic each year, the result is a tangle of knots. Some seem to emerge simply from having been left alone, whilst others exist that have been actively tied for good reason—at the time. Perhaps now we can begin to loosen a few of these knots and lay out the lights.

Knot 1: Being Authentic

Cultural institutions are not educational institutions that are required to follow nationally set frameworks for learning. Of course, we all have our own subject/organisation-specific ideological frameworks instead, but there is no imperative to work to exams or any other standardised outputs and we are therefore able to focus on the experience of learning very deeply, should we want to. We need to let go of overwhelming extrinsic demands that pull or shape us in uncomfortable ways. In doing so, we have the opportunity to represent ourselves more authentically, giving us the opportunity to be more diverse, to stretch wider and venture into places and ideas that education (as defined here) may not wish or be able to go. This, I believe, is an exciting prospect, that would enable cultural practitioners to find space (both physically and intellectually) truly to innovate, take risks and be bold about practice. Cultural sites are places where "failing" (and by this perhaps all we mean is trying new things to explore how learning can be developed) can happen safely and be swiftly addressed without damaging any lives, messing up any exams or taking down any institutions. We are cautious of taking risks as we have become more fearful of failure in relation to formal learning and output related requirements. There is, therefore, a bent towards keeping things as they are. But unlike Lenin's plan, this one will never cost lives. What exactly are we frightened of failing about?

Indeed, letting go of the idea of educational *departments* is also necessary, as the idea of departmentalisation has gradually led to learning being perceived as something that only happens within the work of such a department (over there, alongside an organisation's "real" business). We know, however, that learning is generated and takes place throughout organisations and across many teams. At Tate, for example, the act of curating art for exhibition generates its own learning for the professionals involved as well as for the visitors. Courses online, community and regeneration programmes, research projects, archival and library services, conservation and information all offer and generate learning experiences. I am not arguing against having a team of experts working in cultural institutions to develop learning (far from it), but that their purpose, role and value is to use their expertise to construct, draw out and maximise learning opportunities across these many areas and make interventions or animations where needed so that we can more effectively engage with our wide range of publics. Professionals (formerly known as education departments) would therefore shift from being the guardians of learning for an institution and passers—down/on/across of information—to becoming central to the "real" business; facilitators in learning who construct and programme opportunities for the widest range and deepest levels of learning to take place.

Knot 2: Apply Knowledge

Cultural institutions are not working from zero. We need to start using the body of new information, research findings and theory available to us and begin to apply it in our working lives. Of course, changing programmes and systems is always difficult and a bit messy, as it requires letting go of established patterns of working and finding space to take risks and try new things. In large organisations and institutions this is even harder as one has to plan for change with a lot of notice. Purely on a practical level, programmes are set, brochures are designed, and courses are booked often at least a year in advance. We need to begin to form shifts in practice that can take us towards new programmes, new ideas and new ways of thinking. Innovation is not an overnight miracle grown from pixie dust, but a good long-term plan (with the right people involved).

Knot 3: Partnerships

Cultural institutions do not exist in isolation. Art museums typically currently have many partnerships in place and opportunities to work with artists and colleagues within education and beyond, to help us to explore new terrain. Once we understand the boundaries of what we are and how much we can achieve, we can look to others to help us develop and learn more. Recognising that we cannot (and do not need to) do everything ourselves, and that expert knowledge outside the cultural institution is available, means that we can move faster, wider and in ways more tailored to audiences needs. Being able to articulate that we also have something particular and unique to offer others and to work with education more innovatively also means that we can be players in an important and changing landscape of learning. Therefore, partnerships, dialogue and cultural and educational collegiality need to be extended to generate new ideas and learning opportunities together.

Knot 4: Space and Time

Cultural institutions do not have the same time and space limitations that educational institutions have. We already occupy alternative and appropriate spaces for cultural creative learning and for some of us, opportunities to grow more that lend themselves to the global shifts in learning. It is therefore possible to work to the needs of the content rather than of a timetable and we need to let go of feeling the need to replicate educational systems and models, unless they serve the purpose of cultural creative learning.

Knot 5: Quality over Quantity

Quality does not have to be subsumed by quantity nor delivery over what is being delivered. In the McMaster report a clear and strong case is put forward for quality, risk and innovation.[26] The case can be made for depth over breadth and the quality of a learning experience over numbers passing through it. In reality, this is a difficult balance of reaching as many as possible as deeply as possible, but I think it would be fair to say that we may have reached a point in a delivery model that can only just keep up with itself and its audiences, putting an enormous strain on the professionals involved and inhibiting innovation through the need to comply with *known* delivery outcomes. When is it time to take stock and reflect on what we are delivering?

That time is now. But loosening these knots is, of course, easier said than done. However, without doing so, it will be difficult to change practice and move forwards to meet the needs of a changed and changing society. The ability of cultural creative learning to explore, test and model new forms of approach actually place it at the forefront of new practice, should it choose to do so.

Reassemblage

The question of what is to be done regarding learning in cultural institutions comes at a time when fundamental questions are being asked about the ways in which we organise our social learning systems more broadly. I have tried to outline some of the many research papers, books and documents that attempt to offer alternatives, or at least explore the current problems within educational practice needing to be addressed. It is clear, whichever way one looks at learning, that practice is changing, and more value is being given to participative, collaborative learning methods that also enable more flexible methods of generating and applying new knowledge. The move towards creativity in the primary curriculum is one such example of this. I have argued that these changes in practice can be aligned with long-term, non-declarative memory and habits of mind. I have also argued that cultural creative learning gives additional emotional and social value that do not find a place easily within our education system.

Despite cultural creative learning being perceived in our society as having less value than formal and examined learning, I have suggested that the kinds of learning that take place culturally can in fact offer something of benefit to the education system per se and that in art museums we are in a position to trial, test and model learning with our educational colleagues, and, indeed, across disciplines and sectors. In the preface to *Studio Thinking* David Perkins writes, exposing an attitude all too familiar to many of us, "maybe this is the sort of messing around we can afford when we're not dealing with high-stakes core subject matters." He responds to this kind of perspective with, "what if, far from a fantasy world, studio learning turns out to be much more realistic regarding the way learning really works than most typical classroom settings?"[27]

Asking questions about methods of cultural creative learning and habits of mind can, I believe, be significant drivers in the shifts in education we are seeing because they help construct alternative approaches to the norm. Cultural creative learning privileges meta-cognitive processes and long term learning, two important features that are required for a flexible, knowledge-based economy that seeks the application of knowledge in new ways to generate new outcomes for innovation.

Rather than sitting back and waiting for changes and solutions to fall upon us, I am arguing for cultural creative learning to put itself at the heart of change, using its very "otherness" to enable it to take the kinds of risks that education may not be able to take and to do this based on the range of theoretical perspectives borne out of research through practice. I am suggesting the reassembling, not just of the content, methods of approach, time and space, but also of the system and attitude towards learning, an attitude that often manifests itself as a "department" rather than the actual experience.

Within this, there is detail to be had. There is a need to examine the knots of current cultural learning and begin to unpick them whilst trialling new ideas and programmes. These, too, need to be reformulated to reflect the global shifts in learning as outlined above. There is a need to understand that cultural creative learning is more than time spent away from core subjects. We are very far from messing around: we are seeking to find ways of learning that are deep and lasting. Indeed, cultural creative learning can bring a significant range of learning practices and habits of mind to the table. Like Lenin, we need to be considering how to apply theory to practice and this will be complicated given the many complex institutions, extrinsic demands and internal resources that need to be considered. Unlike Lenin, we can do it *with* others rather than in opposition to them. I do not think that anyone has ever deliberately set out to make knots; sometimes they simply appear, sometimes they are tied to respond to a place or context. Reassemblage will be not just possible, but I imagine an exciting episode in the history of cultural creative learning. And with this in mind, Sandra has offered to pop on the samovar and let things simmer for a while. She had not imagined that there was quite so much that *could* be done.

Notes

1. F. Bear, B. W. Connors, and M. A. Paradiso (eds.), *Neuroscience: Exploring the Brain,* second edition. Baltimore, MD: Lippincott Williams & Wilkins, 2001, pp.740–743.

2. C. Griffin, G. Holford, and P. Jarvis, *The Theory and Practice of Learning* (second edition). London: Kogan Page, 2003.

3. It is accepted that some theories bring both the socially determined and the individual's processes together. Clearly both are at play since an individual cannot be separated from his or her social context. It is for the sake of argument here that I have divided the two, to explore how the socially determined values have perhaps overshadowed the individual's learning potential.

4. Bear, Connors and Paradiso, 2001.

5. C. Leadbeater, *What Next? 21 Ideas for 21st Century Learning.* For the Innovations Unit, DCFS, see www.charlesleadbeater.net/home.aspx, 2008.

6. T. Bentley, *Learning Beyond the Classroom: Education for a Changing World.* London: Routledge, 1998, pp. 100–102.

7. Bentley, 1998.

8. K. Robinson, *Out of Our Minds: Learning to be Creative.* Oxford, UK: Capstone Publishing Ltd., 2001.

9. DfES Review Group, *2020 Vision: Report of The Teaching and Learning in 2020 Review Group.* London: DfES, 2006; National College for School Leadership, *Leading Personalised Learning in Schools.* London: NCSL, 2006.

10. J. Holden, *Culture and Learning: Towards a New Agenda.* London: DEMOS, 2008.

11. Creative Partnerships, *This Much We Know.* London: Creative Partnerships, 2007.

12. B. Taylor (ed.), *Inspiring Learning in Galleries: Enquire about Learning in Galleries.* London, 2006. See wwv.en-quire.org/.

13. R. Solomon, *Teaching Literacy Through Art.* New York: Guggenheim Museum, 2007.

14. L. Dierking, D. McCrady, D. Frankel, and L. Adelman, "Facilitating and Documenting Family Learning in the 21st Century." *Current Trends in Audience Research and Evaluation,* vol.15. American Association of Museums, 2002, p. 62.

15. Culture is defined here under the framework of responsibilities for DCMS.

16. Creative Partnerships, 2007.

17. A. Cutler, "Signposting Creative Learning," UNESCO International Arts and Education Conference, Portugal. Conference proceedings at http://portal.unesco.org/culture/, 2005. Key features of creative learning as defined in this chapter include problem identification, divergent thinking, confidence, a balance of skills and challenge, risk-taking, refinement, and the pursuit of a valued goal.

18. See www.standards.dfes.gov.uk/research/themes/early_years/metacognitive/metacog_and literacy. Basic strategies are

- connecting new information to former knowledge;
- deliberately selecting appropriate thinking strategies from a repertoire; and
- planning, monitoring, and evaluating thinking processes.

The study worked on the hypothesis that there are two levels to children's meta-cognition. The first level is the acquisition of meta-cognitive knowledge, the second level is the ability to produce it, which, according to the research, happens over time.

19. This project is supported by UBS.

20. Hetland, E. Winner, K. Veenema and K.M. Sheridan, *Studio Thinking: The Real Benefits of Visual Arts Education.* New York: Teachers College Press, 2007.

21. Heath and S. Wolf, *Visual Learning in the Community School: Art is All About Looking: Drawing and Detail.* London: Arts Council England, 2004, p. 10.

22. Ibid., pp.11–12.

23. Ibid., p. 9.

24. Taylor, 2006.

25. This is supported through the findings as outlined in A. Cutler 2005.

26. Master, B. *Supporting Excellence in the Arts: From Measurement to Judgement.* London: DCMS, 2008.

27. Hetland, Winner, Veenema, and Sheridan, 2008, p. v.

Acknowledgments

A version of this essay first appeared in H. Kunz-Ott, S. Kudorfer, and T. Weber (eds.), *Kulturelle Bildung im Museum: Aneignungsprozesse - Vermittlungsformen – Praxisbeispiele.* Bielfeld, Germany: Verlag, 2009.

Threshold Fear[1]
Architecture Program Planning

29

ELAINE HEUMANN GURIAN

The nature of our buildings and streets affects our behavior, affects the way we feel about ourselves and, importantly, how we get along with others.

—MACDONALD BECKET IN *DESIGNING PLACES FOR PEOPLE, A HANDBOOK FOR ARCHITECTS, DESIGNERS, AND FACILITY MANAGERS* (1985)

At the small museum, there are no inflated expectations, no pretensions, and no awful waits. The exhibitions may be small and somewhat idiosyncratic, but they mirror the small, somewhat idiosyncratic world we know, close to home.

—RON CHEW (2002)

MEMBERS OF OUR MUSEUM COMMUNITY write often about inclusion and of the "new town square" that they wish museums to become. In this chapter, I take the position that for museums to become fully inclusive, they will have to make many and multivaried changes because there are both physical and programmatic barriers that make it difficult for the uninitiated to experience the museum. The term "threshold fear" was once relegated to the field of psychology but is now used in a broader context to mean the constraints people feel that prevent them from participating in activities meant for them.[2] To lower these perceived impediments, the fear-inducing stimulus must be reduced or dissolved. There has been little discussion within the museum field about the aspects of museum spaces that are intentionally welcoming and help to build community. There has been, in fact, a disjuncture between museums' programmatic interest

Elaine Heumann Gurian is a senior museum consultant specializing in international museum projects and former deputy director for the United States Holocaust Memorial Museum in Washington, D.C. Threshold Fear: Architecture Program Planning" is an excerpt from *Civilizing the Museum: The Collected Writings of Elaine Heumann Gurian* (2006), pp. 115–125. It is reprinted here by permission of the author. All rights reserved.

in inclusion and the architectural program of space development—a gap that this essay tries to redress.

Museums clearly have thresholds that rise to the level of impediments, real and imagined, for the sectors of our population who remain infrequent visitors. The thresholds in question may be actual physical barriers—design ingredients that add to resistance—and other more subtle elements such as architectural style and its meaning to the potential visitor, wayfinding language, and complicated and unfamiliar entrance sequences. Further hindrances include the community's attitude toward the institution, the kind and amount of available public transportation, the admission charges and how they are applied, the organization of the front desk, insufficient sensitivity to many different handicapping conditions, the security system upon entering, and staff behavior toward unfamiliar folk. My thesis is that when museum management becomes interested in the identification, isolation, and reduction of each of these thresholds, they will be rewarded over time by an increased and broadened pattern of use, though the reduction of these thresholds is not sufficient by itself.

I started with the assumption that most museums wanted to broaden their audiences, that is, they wanted the profile of visitors to include more people from minority, immigrant, school drop-out, and working-class groups than was currently the case. I further believed that in order to achieve that aim, they would need a multilayered approach that would include less well-known and often untried elements, because many museums had experimented with choice of subject matter alone and had been largely unsuccessful in changing their visitation patterns over the long term. I postulated that if we worked with city planning theories and paid better attention to the aspects of space creation and planning that helped build community, museums might be more successful in their goal of inclusion, especially when they combined this work with the elements they were already using: expanded programming, community liaisons, and targeted free or reduced admissions. Trying all these options together, museums might finally solve the difficult long-standing problem of the narrow demographics of current museum users.

I sought to look at other institutions I believed served a broader audience and, while not in exactly the same business as museums, had sufficient similarities to serve as useful examples: zoos, libraries, for-profit attractions, and shopping malls.

Now, after researching the topic, I am less certain that broadening the audience for museums is achievable in general. Museums of real inclusion may be possible only if the competing traditional object-focused aspirations are reduced or even discarded. On a continuum, individual museums can be positioned from cultural icon to hometown clubhouse, with many stops in between. Cultural icons serve very important purposes, but these, I have reluctantly begun to realize, may be quite different from, and perhaps even mutually exclusive with, museums focused on community well-being. Sadder but wiser, I will argue that there are certain subtle things we can do related to space and city planning that will help museums that are really interested in broadening their visitation. Decisions about space do have a correspondence with mission. That thesis remains intact. However, it is my view that the mission aspired to by many art museums to create a temple of the contemplative, for example, has an easier correlation with both traditional and contemporary architecture than does the mission to create a welcoming, inclusionary museum.

That many museums do not really wish to become more inclusionary institutions is the subject for a different paper. Let me preview that elusive paper as follows. We know a lot about the amalgamated profile of current museum users. The typical visitor is well educated, relatively affluent, and generally has a wage earner who is white collar or professional within the family unit. Many museums, like good commercial product marketers, are programmed to satisfy this niche market—their current users.[3] Many museums, especially the more notable ones, are important elements of the tourism infrastructure in their metropolis, and tourism is primarily a middle- and upper-class activity. These same institutions are often described in the "quality of life" rhetoric that is intended to elicit more managerial-level business relocation, an aspiration intended to enlarge the overall financial base. Finally, and maybe not surprisingly, visitors and nonvisitors alike may not wish museums to change because many citizens separate their belief in the value of museums from their actual use of them.

I have come to believe that to become truly inclusionary, a museum must provide services that the user sees as essential, available on demand, timely, and personally driven. The definition of essential has to do with the personal impulse to transform an internal inquiry into action. Thus going to the library to get a book on how to fix the leaking sink at home makes the library an essential place. To change an institution from "nice to have" to "essential" is difficult. For most museums, concentrating on being the storehouse of the treasures of humanity may seem like virtue enough, regardless of the use visitors make of them. While useful for the overall needs of society, this focus does not make for essentiality.

This essay focuses on some of the space elements that can either help or hinder the mission of the museum, focusing on the elements that foster inclusion—should the museum wish to add space to its programmatic arsenal for just that purpose, understanding now that many may not.

For architects, designing a museum is among the most coveted commissions of the day, and iconic architecture frequently turns out to stimulate increased attendance. The typical affluent educated museum-goer is much impressed with the current architectural emphasis of museum buildings. Thus the creation of new architecture will increase, at least for a limited time, the quantity of users without necessarily changing the demographics.

But when architects do not care about the needs of the visitor (as happens more often than I care to report), especially if visitor needs are seen to interfere with artistic vision, architects create museums that are difficult to use. These inhospitalities reinforce the nonwelcoming nature of museums overall and add to the discouragement of the tentative user. That is a problem both of new buildings and of the augustly overwhelming museums of the past.

If the architect wants to combine a really interesting building with one that is welcoming to the novice user, then, I would contend, he or she must be interested in hospitable and less intimidating spaces, a plethora of easily locatable human amenities, and understandable wayfinding. The grand museums assert monumentality and present themselves as revered but not necessarily comfortable icons. Very few new buildings of note can be seen as friendly and comfortable. There are exceptions of course: the Picasso Museum in a historic building refurbishment in the Marais in Paris and the building I.M. Pei designed for the Herbert F. Johnson Museum of Art at Cornell University are two of them.

With these thoughts in mind, in the following sections I will draw upon a number of architectural planning theories in order to consider some of the spatial and related organizational problems of the museum. Then I will suggest some changes museums might make to become more inclusionary.

Congregant Spaces

The populace needs congregant public spaces and has many at its disposal. Some theorists believe that in order to maintain a peaceful society, people need access to three kinds of spaces: places for family and friends (our most intimate relationships), places for work, and places where it is safe to interact with strangers (Oldenburg 1989). The last category has important meaning beyond the functions these places overtly serve. That they exist and are available to strangers reassures the public that there is order and well-being to be found in populated centers. Whenever these places are considered unsafe for any reason, they are abandoned, sometimes permanently, and society becomes more balkanized.

The congregant places organized for strangers fall into a surprisingly long list. They include (but are not limited to):

- Transportation hubs such as railway stations and airports, and the transportation vehicles themselves.
- Religious gathering places like churches, mosques, and synagogues.
- Places of large and small commercial transactions, such as shopping malls, markets, public streets lined with shops, and the shops themselves.
- Places organized for eating and socializing, such as restaurants, pubs, and cafes.
- Places used for recreation, such as bathing beaches and parks.
- Civic buildings, such as judicial courts and town halls.
- Places that hold access to information and/or present experiences, such as libraries and archives, theaters and concert halls, athletic arenas, schools, and public spaces used for celebrations like parades and pageants.

Museums, historic houses, zoos, botanic gardens, and historic sites belong to this last segment: sites that hold access to information and experiences.

All civic spaces used by strangers have some commonalities, and many kinds of civic spaces have more in common with certain museums than with others. Certain elements of libraries, zoos, shopping malls, attractions, stadiums, and train stations can become models for museums. It is unfortunate that museum personnel have often felt that associating themselves with the kinds of congregant spaces on this list is a disservice to their own uniqueness and status. I would suggest the contrary.

The City Planning Theory of Jane Jacobs and Her Followers

Architectural theorists and city planners refer to physical spaces offering a variety of services often co-located in residential areas as mixed-use space. Mixed-use spaces can be small, found within one strip mall, one city street, and one building, or so large so that they encompass whole sections of cities. These mixed-used spaces particularly interest such theorists as Jane Jacobs (Jacobs 1961). Studies of these spaces have had a profound effect on the development of planned communities and the refurbishment of downtown cities. Theorists have postulated that the broadest array of users inhabit locations that house a multitude of offerings: products selling for a wide range of prices, a combination of useful services (shoe repair, pharmacy, etc.) mixed with more exotic specialties, open hours that are as close to around-the-clock as possible, residential units, public amenities such as seating, and, most important, foot traffic.

They go on to postulate that these mixed-use spaces are perceived as safe to use because they are busy, lighted, and have many people present all the time, including "regulars" and "lurkers" who are vigilant and proprietary but also welcoming, exemplifying a peaceful and even friendly code of behavior that strangers can easily perceive (Gurian 2001).

Since the 1970s, in addition to an explosion of new museum buildings and commissions for high-profile architects, museums have also become keystones to economic revival plans in urban settings recognized as having positive fiscal impacts for the city. A change in the economic base of museums—from philanthropic and governmental support to an emphasis on earned income from retail activities within the building—has profoundly revised the architectural program that museums need and has changed museums (inadvertently) into mixed-use spaces (Gurian 2001).

Museums now offer spaces that provide exhibitions, programs, restaurants and cafes, shopping, and party spaces under one roof. Museums often either incorporate or are adjacent to public transport and to other services (child care, schools, performance spaces, parks, and additional food and shopping opportunities). As they incorporate or align themselves with such services, they become a thoroughfare for a broader population who may have different motivations for entering and different stay-lengths and who use the facility during different times of the day. This quality of mixed use can also be seen in zoos, libraries, and shopping malls.

Architectural Program Planning

There is little understanding within the museum community that creating these varied spaces within one building has yielded a more inclusionary whole. There has been little overt discussion about the spatial considerations that might help provide increased service to a wider community, and there is often a disjuncture between the museums' professed programmatic interest in inclusion and the resulting architectural program of space development. I have often found that prior to embarking on construction of a new expansion or building, senior museum personnel do not understand the architectural process sufficiently, so they do not grasp the relationship between programmatic intention and physical planning. As a result, the museum's strategic direction and its architectural development diverge.

"Architectural writing beginning in the 1960s is full of humanistic philosophy, behavioral design, and a keen interest in the creation and sustainability of livable cities" (Alexander 1964, 1987). Finding this disjuncture between many contemporary museum buildings and the philosophy espoused, I conclude that the people involved (both on the architectural and the museum teams) either did not realize that the new architectural literature could positively affect building plans or were not sympathetic to that notion.

My experience working with architects and museums on architectural program planning is illuminating. First, most museum staff do not know that a process called architectural program planning exists; they think in terms of blueprints and do not know that there is a prerequisite step that focuses on volumes and adjacencies, which is driven by the museum's articulated programmatic needs. They often are not coached by the architect about the process and do not do a thorough job of stating their philosophy, their specific programmatic needs, or their future aspirations. One cannot hope to have a building that corresponds to the philosophic aspirations of the museum leadership without first divining the strategy directions of the museum and translating those into binding architectural terms. Second, some, though certainly not all, architects are happier to gloss over this planning stage because without it the architect is left to design without constraints. Finally, boards of directors, government officials, and directors often wish to build a museum that will enter the world stage by virtue of architectural excellence and novelty. So they come to believe that putting programmatic or even budget restrictions on the architect will only point out their own philistine-like nature. And some architects are happy to capitalize on that fear.

The situations described work against having an architectural program plan of any specificity or rigor. When a museum lacks a specific guiding programmatic document, evaluating the subsequent designs against established criteria becomes difficult. In this regard, it does not matter if we are talking about new buildings, refurbishment of existing structures, or even just rearrangement of the current fit-out. My advice to my clients is that the architectural program plan is the most critical element in the building process.

Location on Neutral Ground

City planners, imbued with the theories of Jane Jacobs and her successors in the livable cities movement, are increasingly interested in enriching the services and liveliness of neighborhoods by enhancing foot traffic, expanding public transport, and creating easily accessible parking in an off-site location. Some institutions are seen to be on neutral ground, equally available to all people, and others seem intentionally isolated and relatively unavailable. Location and placement often create, overtly or inadvertently, turf boundaries where citizens believe that the spaces in question are reserved predominantly for a small segment of society. I am old enough to remember the protests and legal action over the then-legal segregation of swimming pools and playgrounds in my country. Ending legal segregation did not necessarily end *de facto* segregation. Some of these very same swimming pools are still almost exclusively used by either blacks or whites because the area surrounding the pool, while no longer legally segregated, is virtually so. The creation of such nonneutral space can be unintentionally alienating or intentionally off-putting.

Museums must look at their own locations with care. It seems axiomatic that the more accessible its location, the more likely a museum will have a heterogeneous group of users. What constitutes site "ownership" is not always apparent. The regular clientele of one local pub may be a clique established by custom even though there may be many pubs to choose from within a close proximity.

Museums on once-neutral ground can become segregated by changes in resident patterns in the surrounding neighborhood. Similarly, non-neutral space can be turned into more inclusive space by the acceptance and even encouragement of public activities taking place inside and outside the facility that change the perception of use. The Brooklyn Museum of Art, finding its forecourt used by skateboarders, invited them to continue (most building administrators would oust them). Turf ownership, while seemingly entrenched, turns out to be mutable.

Potential visitors' common understanding of how safe or dangerous the surrounding neighborhood will be becomes an important factor in deciding to visit. New Yorkers' perception of the safety of any borough other than middle and lower Manhattan makes visiting museums in the other boroughs adventurous and seemingly fraught with danger for Manhattanites. It was interesting to watch the visitor's hesitation when getting off the subway and trying to locate the Museum of Modern Art in its temporary location in Long Island City, Queens. The reverse is true when a Queens resident decides to visit the Metropolitan Museum of Art. That is also an activity of some adventure. I know; I grew up in Queens.

Learning the Resources before Visiting

Civic sophistication can sometimes be measured by citizens' ease in using unfamiliar available resources. In effect, research management occupies part of everyone's daily transactions. "Which shop will have the specific material we might need?" and "Is the owner reliable?" Much of the most readily available information comes from talking to trusted intimates. Thus word of mouth and street credibility has much to do with use.

In the museum world, we are more reliant on previous satisfied users than we understand. Most new users are people who know and trust someone who has already been there. Spending more time cultivating adventurous pioneers by giving them reliable sources of information, and developing positive street credibility, is an essential task for institutions that want wider attendance. Further, when we diversify our staff, we begin to gain the kind of credibility that pierces many neighborhoods. It is one of the positive outcomes of internalized diversity.

Getting There

In Britain (as in many countries), there is an increased reliance on automobile transportation. A study reports that more than 50 percent of all children's trips involve riding in a car, and there is a much-decreased use of the bicycle.[4] This means that children can go fewer places on their own. For parents it means that things that can be done within walking distance of one parking stop are easier to contemplate than several errands, each needing its own exclusive parking. Hence the growth of the shopping mall and the increase of pedestrian traffic associated with convenient parking.

Here again, museums embedded within public walking thoroughfares can more easily become casual visits and even multiple visits—an ingredient often seen in the more "essential" institutions, such as libraries, which accommodate short, focused, and efficient visitation. The monumentality of the large museum set off by itself, with its need to accommodate patrons' parking or the added cost of a parking garage, militates against casual use.

In the United Kingdom, there are a series of fascinating Web sites that look at social exclusion and its relation to public transportation. One study looks the interconnectedness of public transport availability and the knowledge required for using transport to unfamiliar sites.[5] It seems all too evident that lack of available public transport coupled with inexperience makes it less likely for the nonuser population to visit. However if the motivation is high enough, such as "seeing the doctor" or "going for a job interview," the person will brave the trip if possible.

Visitation becomes a less fearful activity when public transport is in place, experienced users ride along with the inexperienced, and drivers are especially helpful. There is only occasional interest in the museum sector to view public transport as an essential ingredient toward enlarged public use. And rarely are museum personnel involved in lobbying efforts toward improved public transport.

Entering

Once potential visitors have gotten themselves to the front door, it seems easy, on the surface, to enter a museum without the potentially uncomfortable task of revealing too much personal information. Actually, visitors need to reveal quite a lot during the entrance process. They need to show that they can afford the price of admission by paying. If they visit during weekday hours, assumptions will be made that they are on holiday, unemployed, retired, a student, or somehow not in the workforce. Visitors must dress and behave superficially "normal" in order to be allowed to remain in the building. Most of these assessments, and any anxieties they may engender, rest within the potential visitors' minds, of course. But this mental projection is very real to the novice user and impossible to ameliorate except by training museum personnel to become sincere but not effusive welcomers and, most important, to review the entrance sequence to reduce the level of mandatory interaction required.

Much of the initial person-to-person engagement begins at the admissions desk. Since this transaction is directly interpersonal, the collection of charges, I believe, is the single biggest disincentive for entering. Charges make visits to the museum an "outing" rather than a useful casual drop-in errand. A look at the free museums located on pedestrian ways often shows a steady stream of users who are pursuing short-time or casual activities. By eliminating charges, the museum eliminates this scrutiny from the encounter. I contend this change will go a long way toward the reduction of threshold fear.

Unfortunately, eliminating charges itself does not seem to change the demographic make-up of visitors. Many museums in the United Kingdom have gone from free to admission charges and back to free again. In the process, they learned that the total number of visitors falls precipitately when charges are instituted and rise again when they are reversed, but the demographics of their users do not change appreciably.[6]

I would contend that the entrance sequence itself must be rethought so that the novice visitor can become a "lurker," figuring out the process of entering by passive watching from an anonymous location. It helps to have a large lobby available before the entrance sequence or a transparent front wall visible from the outdoors. Large railroad stations allow for such decoding.

More recently, because of perceived security needs in many countries, the encounter that precedes admissions is the most threatening of all: security checking, requiring surveillance by a policelike person. I look forward to the day when museums will eliminate security from their entries. Passing a security checkpoint is a very high threshold for anyone. That is why few libraries and fewer shopping malls use overt security screeners in their entrances. I am convinced that they are just as vulnerable as museums but remain more anxious to serve their public.

Malls and Other Animals

A review of the organization of shopping malls in most countries gives credence to the rightness of Jane Jacobs' philosophy. Shopping mall design intentionally includes the ability to enter anonymously, the possibility of sitting and strolling without committing to organized activity. These amenities allow unfamiliar users to figure out the services and customs required without drawing attention to themselves. Malls offer simple access to easily understood facilities such as toilets, and there are plenty of opportunities to socialize while eating. Finally, they welcome multigenerational groups and increasingly try to understand packs of adolescents who find strolling and meeting in the mall their main avenue of socializing.

Museums, though they currently don't think so, might be lucky if they found themselves with this problem (Kelly et al. 2002). While museums have many of the same amenities as the mall, using them requires passing an entrance sequence.

A museum lobby, like the strolling spaces in malls, can become a meeting place for people who may not intend to visit the exhibitions. What mall designers understand is the notion of impulse buying (Kelly et al. 2002) (if you are there anyway, you might discover you need something). I believe museums must begin to value impulse visiting—that is, savoring a small segment of the museum for a short fragment of time—which will require museums to think of themselves differently.

It is sometimes surprising to find out why some civic spaces are more popular than others. Most zoos provide venues for picnicking with food brought from home. They allow groups (those that have dietary restrictions or do not trust food prepared by strangers) to come to a public place and inadvertently socialize with others. In a community meeting I held in Israel, I learned that being able to picnic using one's own food made the zoo the last remaining neutral public space in Jerusalem used by both Palestinian and Israeli and by both orthodox and nonorthodox Jewish family groups who were otherwise fearful of each other. Upon hearing this, Jerusalem's Bloomfield Science Museum decided that it, too, could arrange for picnic tables and refrigerators, so that in the hopeful future when a more tentative peace might emerge, they could be a location for social interaction among strangers.

Museums have overtly learned from the attractions industry about the importance of customer service. There are now customer-friendly hosts in many museums. These hosts, if they represent the diversity found in the community and are sensitively trained, make the experience more understandable and less alien for the novice. In Jacobs' terms, visitor service personnel act as "regulars" offering reassurance and knowledge on the one hand and demonstrating the behavior norms required on the other.

Malls, zoos, attractions, and libraries suggest other considerations that might increase use by a wider population:

- Create spaces both for small-group interaction and for private contemplation. See that they don't interfere with each other.
- Have help staff available in a physical location that can be easily seen, but do not require interaction from the visitor.
- Train visitor services staff not to be intrusive but still welcoming.
- Hire staff from many different cultural groups and include nonnative speakers.
- Reorient the building toward public transportation and foot traffic.
- Introduce more easily accessible visitor amenities, such as seating, toilets, cafes, and baby spaces.
- Watch for the ways the public actually uses the building, and then formalize these unexpected and even serendipitous uses.
- Revamp systems to focus on avenues of self-directed learning like browsing in the library. This probably means providing visible access to the collections, or at least access to collections information without staff intercession.

- Set the hours of operation to suit the neighborhood rather than the staff.
- Accept behavior, clothing choice, sound level, and interaction styles that are consistent with norms of courtesy of the individuals' community.
- Trust the visitor so that intrusive security can be minimized. Organizing for the best in people is a risk worth taking.
- Last and most important, understand the significance visitors place on seeing the evidence and so encourage interaction with three-dimensional experiences. Museums' special legitimacy remains visual and even tactile access to physical things.

The Repair of the Dead Mall and Other Conclusions

When a mall begins to lose income or even "dies," there is an economic imperative to fix it, tear it down, or repurpose it. A Web site run by Los Angeles Forum held a competition to fix "dead malls."[7] The winning entries offer fascinating glimpses of what architects and merchants think is needed to enhance the usage of moribund shopping centers.

One entrant used the following four categories when contemplating useful spaces: big box cathedral—gathering; global vortex—raving; elastic bazaar—wandering; and smart mobs—swarming. Even the words chosen for the categories intrigue me. Imagine if there were museums that wished for raving and swarming. I think these word choices (and the rest of the Web site) foretell the kinds of spaces needed for increased museum use.

Museums remain one of the important congregant spaces in any community. To encourage use by all citizens we need to be more sensitive to the space requirements that make it clear that the visitor, regardless of previous experience, is welcome. It is my hope that as we readjust the way we build, repair, and reinstall museums we will invite more citizens to join us. I once said I wished museum audiences to be as diverse as those to be found at any given moment in Grand Central Station. Mindful that some do not share my vision, I hope for that more today than ever.

Notes

1. This text was originally delivered as a keynote at the Creative Space conference April 5–7, 2004 at the University of Leicester Department of Museum Studies in Leicester, United Kingdom. A version of this paper was published (Gurian 2005).

2. See for example, *Gypsies and Travelers in Belgium—an Online Interview.* Available at http://home2.pi.be/tmachiel/educati2.htm (accessed August 14, 2004).

3. "Our visitor profile and demographics demonstrate why museum sponsorship is an ideal way to magnify your company's image." Museum of Science, Boston, Web site enticing corporate sponsorship by pointing out that 74 percent of visitors have a college degree or higher and a median annual income of 182,000 (Museum of Science 2005).

4. National statistics of Great Britain. Available at www.statistics.gov.uk/STATBASE/ssdataset.asp?vlnk = 366l (accessed February 25, 2005).

5. Households without a car, in a society in which household car ownership is the norm, are socially excluded within our definition of the term, since they cannot fully participate, that is, behave as the vast majority of society behaves. See "Social exclusion and the provision of public transport, summary report." Available at www.dft.gov.uk/stellent/groups/ dft_mobility/documents/page/dft_mobility_506794-05.hcsp#TopOf Page (accessed February 23, 2005).

6. "Research conducted to determine the impact of free entry to museums and galleries throughout London shows that increase in visitation has been greater among the AB social group. Although free entry was introduced to encourage visitation from all social backgrounds, this has not been reflected in the visitor profile." Maritime Museum UK report, Comparative Visitor Profile 1999–2001. Available at www.nmm.ac.uk/uploads/ pdf/ Comparative_visitor_profile.pdf (accessed January 29, 2005).

7. The Dead Mall Competition Web Page. Available at www.laforum.org/deadmalls/ index.html (accessed December 14, 2004).

Bibliography

Alexander, C. (1964) *Notes on the Synthesis of Form,* Cambridge, MA: Harvard University Press.

———. (1987) *A New Theory of Urban Design*, New York: Oxford University Press.

Chew, R. (2002) "In Praise of the Small Museum," in *Museum News,* March/April, 36–41.

The Dead Mall Competition Web Page. Available at www.laforum.org/deadmalls/index.html (accessed December 14, 2004).

Deasy, C. M. (ed.) (1985) *Designing Places for People, a Handbook for Architects, Designers, and Facility Managers.* New York: Whitney Library of Design.

Gurian, E. H. (2001) "Function Follows Form: How Mixed-Used Spaces in Museums Build Community," in *Curator,* 44:1, 87–113.

———. (2005) "Threshold Fear," in Macleod, S. (ed.) *Reshaping Museum Space: Architecture, Design, Exhibitions.* London: Routledge.

Gypsies and Travelers in Belgium—an Online Interview. Available at http://home2.pi.be/ tmachiel/ educati2.htm (accessed August 14, 2004).

Jacobs, J. (1961) *The Death and Life of Great American Cities.* New York: Random House.

Kelly, L., A. Bartlett, and P. Gordon. (2002) *Indigenous Youth and Museums: A Report on the Indigenous Youth Access Project.* Sydney: Australian Museum.

Museum of Science (2005) *Corporate Sponsorship.* Available at www.mos.org/doc/1026 (accessed March 1, 2005).

Oldenburg, R. (1989) *The Great Good Place.* New York: Paragon House.

SHIFTING FRAMEWORKS AND INFRASTRUCTURES

IV

A S THE PARADIGM SHIFT CONTINUES, more and more museum philosophies and practices have emerged with new structures, frameworks, and parameters for undertaking museum work. Business models, interpretation strategies, and research techniques have emerged in response to new challenges and the pressure to survive. Frameworks help provide guidelines for thinking about complex issues, and opening up internal dialogue in support of sustainable practice and maximizing impact. One common aspect of many of the frameworks, featured in this section, is the integration of thinking and holistic approach to problem solving.

It is important to acknowledge that while new frameworks are being shaped, existing standards, definitions, and guidelines for accepted museum practice in all aspects of operations are also being revisited. There are long established standards for what constitutes an accreditable museum as set forth by the American Association of Museums. Numerous associations affiliated with a specific area of specialization, such as botanical gardens, zoos, and aquaria, also have set standards with which to comply, especially regarding living collections. Balanced against this is the cost of doing business and finding a realistic level of operation that an institution can sustain while fulfilling its mission, upholding standards, and evolving with the times. With the emergence of economic uncertainty, many museums are beginning to think anew about their institutional aspirations and capacity, as well as their priorities and levels of efficiency. The articles presented in this section address business models, evaluation and research techniques, culture experience marketing, legal issues impacting collections, collection planning, and environmental sustainability.

John Falk and Beverly Sheppard initiate this part with "Creating a New Business Model," from *Thriving in the Knowledge Age: New Business Models for Museums and Other Cultural Institutions.* In this chapter, Falk and Sheppard present two contrasting business models of museums: the Industrial Age Business Model, a vertical structure with the driving force being the achievement of extraordinary buildings and collections, with all other aspects of museum operation secondary to that outcome, and the Museum Knowledge Age Business Model, which identifies interrelating components with the public at the center reflecting a more responsive and fluid operation.

In "New Ways of Experiencing Culture: The Role of Museums and Marketing Implications," Neil Kotler, a museum marketing consultant and former staff member of the Smithsonian Institution, argues that the public's increasing demand for participatory cultural experiences should prompt museums to expand audiences by building multidimensional cultural experiences. Kotler provides numerous examples to illustrate different approaches.

"Comprehensive Interpretive Plans: A Framework of Questions," written by audience evaluator Marianna Adams and educator Judy Koke, presents a holistic approach to addressing interpretation within a museum. Their framework of questions ties to six key areas: the unique role of the museum, the public, community needs, relationships, internal alignment, and definition of success. Within each area the authors have included thought-provoking questions and narrative to help an institution delve into the issues that need to be clarified as part of creating an interpretive plan.

"From Knowing to Not Knowing: Moving Beyond Outcomes" written by Andrew Pekarik, challenges the limitations of measuring success with outcome-based evaluation, a form of evaluation that assesses the results of a visitor's experience based on institutional goals tied to an exhibition. Participant-based evaluation, he postulates, provides a broader and more flexible process that incorporates more diverse measurements including revealing why certain results occurred.

The next two articles highlight contemporary complexities of collection management and responsible planning. The care of collections, whether a fine piece of art or a living thing, has evolved into a science of documentation, standards, conservation and preservation, ethics, cultural property rights, and more. As litigious pressures continue to increase in all aspects of museum operations, there is no area more contentious and delicate than collections and the law framed in the international setting of cultural law. Marilyn Phelan in "Legal and Ethical Considerations in Museum Acquisitions," adeptly frames a series of specific laws, implications, and complexities that have emerged in recent years, highlighting the inherent challenges with cultural and art collections.

James Gardner and Elizabeth Merritt, in their article "Collection Planning: Pinning Down a Strategy," emphasize the necessity of collection planning. They argue that such activity is no longer a choice but is necessary to ensure the ongoing, responsible care of the collections in order to make informed decisions for the future development of the collection and its ultimate beneficiary, the public. Succinct and clear, this piece conveys the value of collection planning which becomes ever more critical as the costs of collection care and management continue to increase.

In recent years, the challenge for museums to operate with environmentally sustainable strategies has entered the field-wide dialogue. Environmentally sustainable practice literally touches every aspect of museum operations. Making a daunting topic accessible, Sarah Brophy and Elizabeth Wylie present "It's Easy Being Green," encouraging museum leaders and trustees to amend practices that impact their own institution, while contributing to the larger societal role of environmental responsibility.

Creating a New Business Model **30**

JOHN FALK AND BEVERLY SHEPPARD

I repeat, this is not a test. This is the beginning of a crisis that won't remain quiet for long. And as the Stanford economist Paul Romer so rightly says, "A crisis is a terrible thing to waste."

—THOMAS L. FRIEDMAN

IN A RECENT CONVERSATION, Katherine Lee Reid reflected on her fifteen distinguished years leading two of the largest art museums in the country, including most recently the Cleveland Museum of Art. We specifically asked her to talk about what was different about directing a museum today from the past. Katherine has a particularly unique perspective on this question. Both Katherine and her father, Sherman Lee, directed the same museum, the Cleveland Museum of Art, separated by a period of roughly twenty years.

> The major challenge an art museum director faces today is running a museum in a world that has so many options, a world where people feel less of a connection to the past. Today, a museum must work to bring to life the original works of art because we are surrounded by images and surrogates. We need to figure out how to make art an urgently needed part of people's lives. Although not for everybody, the art museum must become a critical part of the education system.
>
> Today the focus of the museum is on audience and the relationship of art to people. In my father's day, when he ran the museum, the focus was almost exclusively on the idea of art. This is a fundamental shift. We've become very motivated about audience, starting with the person rather than starting with the subject matter.

John Falk is the Sea Grant Professor in Free-Choice Learning at Oregon State University and the president emeritus and founder of the Institute for Learning Innovation in Annapolis, Maryland. Beverly Sheppard is the principal of BKSheppard Consulting, former deputy director of the Institute of Museum & Library Services, and former president and CEO of the Institute for Learning Innovation in Annapolis, Maryland. "Creating a New Business Model" is an excerpt from *Thriving in the Knowledge Age: New Business Models for Museums and Other Cultural Institutions* (2006) by John H. Flak and Beverly Sheppard, published by AltaMira Press. It is reprinted here by permission of the publisher. All rights reserved.

The key thing now is less on acquisition and much more on interpretation. My father's generation was operating on the Victorian model of venerating knowledge, but they were still in the stage of categorizing things. Today we know so much more. Today our goal is to use our knowledge, to interpret what we know so that people can benefit from what we've learned.

Without doubt, the business of running a museum is not only different but arguably a far more difficult task than it was a generation ago. In an interview some years ago, the director of the Metropolitan Museum of Art in New York noted, "All a director needs is administrative ability, knowledge of art, communication skills, international connections, languages, a blue suit and dinner with the trustees."[1] By contrast, today's director experiences complex splits in expectations, balancing new responsibilities for entrepreneurial management, team building, business acumen, vision, and leadership with the traditional requirements for fundraising, subject matter specialty, and a high degree of public visibility. There are now so many more things to deal with, so many more levels of complexity, not the least of which is a rapidly changing world. Steering a fragile ship through reef-filled waters is a lot easier if you not only have a rudder but a chart to show where the reefs lie. Without an overall strategy, without a business model, even if you are the most intrepid of captains, it is hard to get where you are going, or even know where you are going.

Business Model Defined

Business model is a term that emerged rather recently in the business vernacular and is sometimes disparaged because it has often been used in a fast and loose manner. But when defined and used properly, it is a term that can provide valuable insights. Whereas business plans are primarily focused on the overall strategic positioning of a business within the business ecosystem, the term *business model* also includes key structural and operational characteristics of a business. In other words, when used properly, *business model* is a broader description of a business than just its plan or strategy.

In brief, a business model is a description of the operations of a business, including the purpose of the business, components of the business, the functions of the business, the core values of the business, and the revenues and expenses that the business generates. Nonprofits, like museums, have business models just as certainly as do for-profits; it's just that they are not always aware of it. A business model is the mechanism by which a business intends to manage its costs and generate its outcomes—in the case of for-profits, the outcomes are primarily revenues earned, and in the case of nonprofits, the outcome is primarily the public good created. In either case, though, a business model is a summary of how an organization plans to serve the needs of its customers. It involves both strategy and implementation. According to a business encyclopedia,[2] a business model is the totality of how a business:

1. selects its customers
2. defines and differentiates its product offerings
3. creates [benefit] for its customers
4. attracts and keeps customers
5. goes to the market (promotion strategy and distribution strategy)
6. defines the tasks [and services] to be performed
7. configures and optimizes its resources
8. captures profit [or enhances public good]

The business model has accurately been described as the engine of the business, the framework upon which all activities are based. According to businessman and university lecturer Bruce M. Firestone, "If you get the business model right, then the harder you work, the more money you make (Google is an example here). If you get it wrong, then the harder you work, the more money you lose (Napster is an example here)."[3]

Museums seemed to have once live in a rarified world, a world free from the tawdry demands of the marketplace. No longer do museums live in that world. Today, museums must compete for audience, publicity, and resources. Increasingly, museum boards and directors have embraced the language of business. Over the past twenty years museums have created vision and mission statements, strategic plans, and marketing plans. Now we're saying that they have to have a business model. Well, museums have always had business models; every business—large or small, manufacturing or service, for-profit or not- for-profit—operates with a business model. That model can be implicit or explicit, but either way it exists.

A business model requires a well-articulated vision and mission statement, but these are only one piece of a business model. Developing a strategic plan, including setting BHAGs (Big, Hairy, Audacious Goals), is part of the process too. BHAGs is a concept first made popular in the business bestseller *Built to Last: Successful Habits of Visionary Companies* by Jim Collins and Jerry Porras,[4] but as stated above, a business model requires a strategy, but a strategy is not a business model. Every business has products (goods and services for sale), but products are only one of many concrete and visible manifestations of a business model. Every business has assets. An asset management plan is an excellent idea, which should also be part of any good business model. A business model is all of these things. A business model is the theory that undergirds how, why, and in what ways an organization conducts its business. It defines the realities of the environment in which the organization exists and the strategies the organization needs to adopt in order to thrive within that environment.

To be successful, every business must create a business model designed to address and answer four key questions.

1. Why do you exist? Whom are you serving? In the case of museums, who is your public and what specific needs do they have that you are uniquely positioned to satisfy?

2. What assets do you bring to the table? What are the internal assets your institution brings to its business, such as the human resources of staff, board, and supporters; also the assets of collections, building, and brand?
3. How will you forge and maintain partnerships and collaborations with like-minded organizations in the community in order to leverage your impact?
4. How will you support your business? What is your business strategy? What is the unique combination of products and services you can provide in order to satisfy specific public needs and generate sufficient revenues to keep your doors open?

The answers to these four questions cannot be made in a vacuum; the answers must always be situated within the context of the larger world or ecosystem. Each business must understand the realities of the economic, social, and political context in which it operates, both the ever evolving marketplace of the business world but equally the changing values, needs, and desires of the larger society in which the organization exists.

Finally, a business model is a dynamic not a static thing; it must always be evolving and changing because the world in which a business operates is constantly changing. At the heart of any successful business model is a strategy for judging the marketplace, evaluating current successes and failures, and predicting the future so the institution can keep one step ahead of the competition. In today's world the strategy for acquiring this kind of knowledge is research—market research, evaluation research, and basic research. These kinds of research provide data about the internal and external assets and strategies that a business needs in order to sustain itself into the future. Thus it is in the context of all these realities that a business model prescribes how an organization will operate; what its products and services will be; the relationships it will create, both inside and outside of the organization; and finally how it measures success and failure.

Figure 30.1 shows how these elements were traditionally organized by museums into a business model; this is a typical Industrial Age business model. This model is top-down and linear. Ideas flow from the "head" of the organization (director and curators) down to the "consumers" (both general public and scholarly peers). There are essentially no feedback loops from the consumers back to the director and curators. Evidence of success is that people use the products or services; the quantity of units "delivered" (e.g., exhibitions mounted, catalogues printed) are sufficient evidence of success. The most important assets of the organization are tangible resources like collections and buildings. Other assets such as human resources and finances are important but secondary. Importantly, this model suggests that the organization is only tangentially, if at all, dependent upon those outside the organization—collaborators, competitors, economic cycles, and the like. The museum intersects with the outside world through guest curators, fundraising, and marketing. Otherwise it functions essentially as an island separate from the larger world. This is a classic "build it and they will come" approach to doing business.

By contrast we would offer a new model (Figure 30.2). The Knowledge Age business model shows the interaction and interrelationship of all these factors with particular reference to the nonprofit business context of museums. Rather than being *top-down*, the model is *bottom-up*—it emphasizes that the business model must begin with the consumer. Each museum needs to start with figuring how it, given its unique assets, can best understand and meet the needs of the public. Also figuring prominently in this new model is that it is situated within the ecosystem of the larger society. Rather than a linear model, this new model takes a systems approach—all pieces interact and feed back upon each other. When all of these pieces work together and become an integrated whole, then and only then will museums have constructed a business model that will allow them to thrive in the Knowledge Age.

Every nonprofit, every museum, has a business model. As we've pointed out, too often these business models are implicit rather than explicit. As a community, museums have only recently begun to appreciate that they need to be more explicit about their business models, that they need to attend to the details of their business model as much as do businesses in the for-profit world. For just as in the for-profit world, a poor business model for a not-for- profit organization spells troubles.

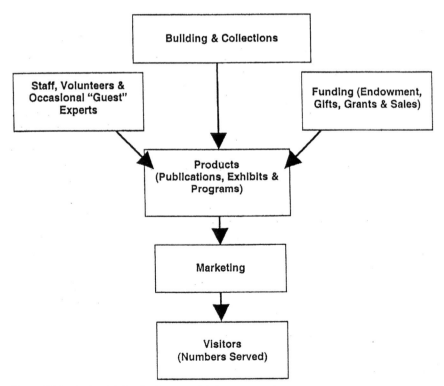

Figure 30.1.   Industrial Age business model (for museums).

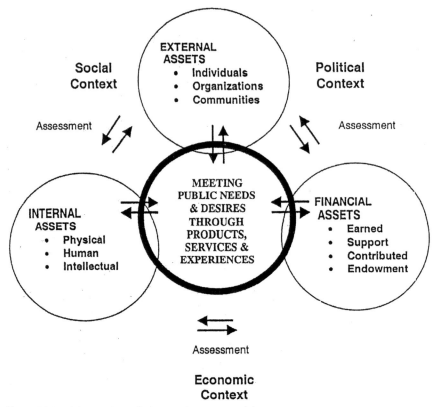

Figure 30.2.   Museum Knowledge Age business model.

Changing Models

As alluded to above, business models do not exist in a vacuum. In fact, the essence of a good business model is that it is a plan for how to succeed within the world, a plan that requires a theory of how the world is. Problems arise when business models do not fully accommodate to the realities of the world—both the internal world of the institution and the external world of the community and larger society. And the world of today is definitely not like the world in which most museums forged their current business models. Most museums today still operate with some variation of the mass-production model forged during the Industrial Age of the 20th century. By contrast, the scenario presented at the beginning of the previous chapter describes a museum with a very different model for how to do business, one utilizing aspects of the new Knowledge Age business model described above.

The old business models of museums worked fabulously during the 20th century, particularly in the last quarter of the century. Yet these old models, like the Industrial Age from which they developed, are increasingly out of step with the realities of the new century. Just as Katharine Lee Reid described how her job at the Cleveland Museum of Art was different from that of her father when he directed the same institution twenty years before, so, too, all of us now live in a world with different needs and expectations.

Change has always been a part of our world. In fact, every generation of Americans has felt that their world was fundamentally different than that of their parents—and by and large they were right. Yet the changes we're seeing today are not evolutionary in nature, they are revolutionary. Everyone seems to agree that we are living through one of the greatest periods of economic and social upheaval in recorded history. Why should we assume that evolutionary changes in the ways we do business are what will be required in these revolutionary times?

In order for museums to become Knowledge Age businesses, they must first abandon the Industrial Age models they currently use. This will not be easy since it will require abandoning many of the attributes that are currently near and dear to many in the museum community. For example, it will probably mean abandoning the paternalistic attitude that the museum can and should be the arbitrator of quality and knowledge. It probably will require abandoning the idea that success can be achieved without knowing anything at all about the publics the museum claims to serve, knowing little or nothing about what they actually want and need. The current business models used by museums dictate that success can be measured by the quantity of individuals served; the greater the attendance, the greater the assumed accomplishment. As was appropriate in the 20th century, the assumption is that high visitor attendance indicates that something good is happening. We believe that museums will ultimately be forced to reject this approach. We suspect that museum professionals will need to radically rethink why museums exist and how they go about meeting their public mandates. For many this will mean redefining the purpose of the museum as a free-choice learning resource rather than as a tourist destination, a place devoted to people rather than things, a place where success is measured in terms of the quality of the transactions that occur rather than in the quantity of people that move through the gates. But we're getting ahead of our story here.

Like any good narrative, the story of business models we're trying to tell here is situated within a context. In order to understand how to build a Knowledge Age business model, museums must understand the context in which they have existed, the context in which they currently exist, and, as much as possible, the context they will soon be existing within. In strategic planning language, this is what is called an Environmental Scan. We would like to provide a business-oriented Environmental Scan for the museum community. We begin this Environmental Scan by taking a journey back in time, back to the golden age of museums as we now know them, back to the 20th century.

Discussion Questions
- Does your organization have an explicit or implicit business model?
- What is your institution's current business model? Is it closer to an Industrial Age or a Knowledge Age model?

- What business are you in? What are your organization's main products and services?

Notes

Epigraph: Thomas L. Friedman, The World Is Flat: A Brief History of the Twenty-First Century (New York: Farrar, Straus & Giroux, 2005), 306.

1. Kent Lydecker, interview with Sherene Suchy, in *Leading With Passion: Change Management in the 21st Century*. Walnut Creek, CA: AltaMira Press, 1996, 75.

2. January 16, 2004, www.en.wikipedia.org, "business model."

3. Bruce M. Firestone, Business Model—A definition, www.dramtispersonae.org/Business Model, 2002, accessed February 20, 2004.

4. Jim Collins and Jerry L. Porras, *Built to Last*. New York: Harper Business, 1994.

New Ways of Experiencing Culture   **31**
The Role of Museums and
Marketing Implications

NEIL KOTLER

Part I

KLAUS MULLER, A DUTCH MUSEUM and cultural scholar, told the story of his frustration in gaining admission to view Leonardo da Vinci's *The Last Supper* in Milan's Convent of Santa Maria. Access was limited by bureaucracy and by conservation concerns, a limitation on visitors, and a short time for visits. Muller had far better access to *The Last Supper* at websites, which subdivide portions of the fresco, enlarge views which show the materials and artistry—perspectives unobtainable at the Convent.

Evelyn Thompson in Chicago creates tours of ethnic neighborhoods that include visits to food markets, bakeries, and delis. During the three-hour tour, visitors learn about cooking, food ingredients, and cuisines and sample foods. Sally Bernstein leads tours on San Francisco's waterfront. Participants meet with wine merchants, visit food stalls, talk with producers, and sample wines and foods, including chocolate. They are given food packages to take home.

Italy offers hundreds of festivals each year for Italians and tourists. Catania, Sicily, as one example, celebrates on February 3–5 a combined spiritual and secular festival, which includes street events, food exhibits and stalls, fireworks, and a procession of a saint's relics. The Cinque Terre region of northwest Italy in late May organizes a popular lemon festival. Siena, Italy, on July 2 and August 16 celebrates the Palio, a medieval tradition of horse racing dating to the thirteenth century. Representing rival neighborhood districts, ten jockeys, riding bareback, race their horses around The Campo, Siena's central square. In the days preceding, medieval jousting and pageantry take place, along with trial races. The Palio has few rules except that one jockey cannot interfere with the reins of another. Bragging,

Neil G. Kotler is the present and founder of Kotler Museum and Cultural Marketing Consultants in Arlington, Virginia, dedicated to assisting museums in developing strategic plans and implementing and monitoring systems. "New Ways of Experiencing Culture: The Role of Museums and Marketing Implications" appeared in *Museum Management and Curatorship* (Vol. 19, no. 4, pp. 417–425, 2001), published by Taylor & Francis. It is reprinted here by permission of the publishers. All rights reserved.

betting, raucous-ness, chicanery, and merriment startle tourists but the Palio is among the most popular Italian national festivals.

Years ago, the author visited Oxford, England. Days were spent walking in the streets, viewing architecture, attending lectures and exploring the interior design of several colleges. The gardens and the Thames River were delights. Sketching the decorated entrance-ways of colleges and the gargoyles was a gratifying experience. A visit to the Ashmolean Museum, with its remarkable collections gathered during the British Empire, was an exceptional experience. Early in the visit, I realized that Oxford, together with its environs, is a museum without walls, a destination with many attractions, especially outdoor vistas, which is filled with beauty and profoundly enriched my knowledge and experience of British culture.

What do these activities have to do with museums, in particular, and formal cultural institutions (theaters, concert halls, archives and libraries) in general? Does the informal, popular culture of festivals, sampling cuisines, neighborhood tours, websites offering superb online exhibitions, influence formal cultural institutions, which, indeed, have become less formal (e.g., following a performance, theater-goers having discussion with actors and directors)? Are the ways of experiencing culture changing? Is there a trend toward experiencing a variety of cultural elements together, formal and informal, rather than pursuing disparate and isolated cultural institutions? Cultural enthusiasts, "cultural creatives," are a group for whom cultural pursuits are a large part of life. Is their style of cultural enjoyment changing? Is cultural experience spreading among the general public?

Museums differ, yet they face common challenges in varying degrees. One observable trend in museums is a growing attention to sociable, recreational and participatory experiences that redirects the traditional and singular focus on collections and exhibitions. A second museum trend is a movement away from museums as walled enclaves toward museums as parts of a cultural mosaic (architecture and design elements, programs outside museums, and a museum's relationship to its community). Interpenetration, if not a fusion, of elements of popular (informal) and elite (formal) culture, form a wide-ranging cultural experience. Consequently, an increasing time is spent exploring contemporary culture rather than the past. Together, these shifts represent the emergence of a new way of experiencing culture, a new cultural paradigm. Museums and other formal cultural institutions are likely to become parts of a cultural itinerary rather than destinations.

Part II

Museums compete in an expanding leisure marketplace. Funding for existing and new programs is a major preoccupation. Small and medium-sized museums face the greatest of hurdles. The idea of experience, which in recent years has captivated the museum world and other formal cultural institutions, is seen as an elixir. Many years ago, a museum visit was prized for aesthetics, visualization, and education. Today, the concept, experience, has several meanings: involving intense sense-perception as well as emotion and intellect; direct, immediate happening; participatory and sociable happenings; situations that evoke strong responses rather than passivity and spectatorship; intense, visceral excitement; one-of-a-kind, memorable happenings. Whatever the implications, tourists and a large number of infrequent visitors expect a "wow" experience.

Participatory experience has become a growing element of cultural experience. In performing arts institutions, symphony orchestras allow members to listen to rehearsals and engage in after-concert discussion with musicians and conductors and listen to contemporary and pop music. Theater-goers can meet with actors and directors. The Smithsonian's Sackler Museum of Asian Art, several years ago, organized a calligraphy exhibition that included a large gallery devoted to teaching visitors calligraphy. Visitors were given calligraphy materials, tables and cushions to work on, and instructors and videos were guides. Children's museums such as the Indianapolis Children's Museum (Indiana) emphasize participatory and learning experiences, as does the Exploratorium [science museum] in San Francisco. Historical museums, increasingly called "centers" (e.g., Minnesota History Center in Minneapolis), focus on "living history," stories, and contemporary events and personalities that are likely to become historically significant. The Missouri Historical Society in St. Louis is known as a "civic museum." A large part of its programming engages audiences in urban and neighborhood issues, conflict resolution, and dialog about urban solutions. Closer to a traditional mission, members in the Historical Society can become urban archeologists, searching for artifacts that reveal the origin and evolution of urban settings. Great natural history museums have sponsored, since their beginnings, significant field research. In addition, they invite members to assist researchers and they explore environmental issues of public concern (New York's American Museum of Natural History). Chicago's Museum of Science and Industry for several years had a large exhibition devoted to HIV, its causes, conditions, and solutions.

Discussion at Colonial Williamsburg of slavery with slave descendants are examples of museum interaction and discourse, a relatively new happening. A digital information gallery, the Micro Gallery at the National Gallery of Art in Washington, DC, represents a movement away from the centrality of tangible objects and the growing role of narrative, interpretative and contextual meaning. The Smithsonian's new National Museum of the American Indian devotes approximately 30 percent of its space to its vast collection and greater space to spiritual strivings, musing, and contemplation. Small and medium-sized museums, lacking in treasured artifacts and icons, face the challenge of creating compelling stories, using narratives, pictures, and copies of treasures, building community support and sociability, and offering first-rate learning experiences.

Sociability is a sought-after experience of visitors and members. Museums have more seating, sociable spaces for members, dining facilities, and even grandparent rooms (the Oregon Museum of Science had game rooms for grandparents while grandchildren romp around museum galleries and spaces). Sociable experience of an intense kind is found in the "young professional" events that usually take place once monthly on Friday evenings. Museums are eager to engage younger people as members and donors and balance the aging population of existing members and donors. These events offer drinks, party foods, usually jazz performances, films, and curator lectures. The Museum of Contemporary Art (Chicago) has a popular, innovative program. The event is accompanied by the opening of a monthly show featuring current Chicago artists. Some young adult groups form committees to raise funds for museums. An additional motivator of participation is networking and the desire to find liaisons.

Besides participation, another significant element of experience is out-of-the-ordinary, enchanting experience, an example of which is a tour of Thomas Jefferson's home, Monticello (Virginia). Visitors are spell-bound in viewing the marked-up books in the library, inventions, collections, architectural designs, gardens and grounds. On a clear day, they can view from the mountain the University of Virginia below, which Jefferson created. Siena, Italy, combines an exceptional urban and rural experience. The medieval walls and beautiful agricultural lands beyond the walls, the baroque churches and renaissance palaces, civic offices and museums filled with frescoes, the shops, cafes, and intimacy of narrow streets filled with people form an unforgettable experience of beauty and enchantment. Matchless museum exhibitions, though fewer today because of the costs of shipping and insurance in an age of terrorism, offer memorable experiences: for example, the Gauguin, Vermeer and Marc Rothko exhibitions at the National Gallery of Art.

Some large, urban museums have expanded and diversified their audiences, increased income, improved accessibility and services, and provided more events, offering visitors a greater variety of experiences. They have expanded their interactive programs for learning and entertainment. Interactive technologies are more widespread, both for learning and entertainment. IMAX theaters are built, whenever funds are available. Story-telling by staff (often in period costumes), audio and video digital guides, extensive text on walls and in brochures, are more widespread and displace the time available for viewing collections. Young visitors manipulate learning blocks, and other innovative learning tools that have entertaining features. Museums have created environments for experiencing situations directly and intensely, similar to Disney World's Epcot (Orlando, Florida). The Museum of New Zealand, Te Papa Tongarewa, has created simulated rides exploring pre-historic New Zealand. The War Museum in Catania, Sicily, offers visitors the experience of being bombed by placing them in a small, dark wartime bunker that vibrates and shakes during bombing raids (parts of Sicily sustained heavy bombing in World War II). The First Infantry Museum at the Robert McCormick Estate in Wheaton, Illinois offers visitors immersion in a World War I battlefield (with sounds, sights, and smells of war); and immersion in a bombed-out French town, re-creating the grimness and horror of civilian casualties and destruction.

Museum members, who represent a large share of earned revenue, expect museums to offer services, diverse programs, exhibition turnover, novelty, and events. Museums have created fancier dining rooms and cuisines (the restaurant at the Boston Museum of Fine Arts is regarded as one of the city's best). New York's

Museum of Modern Art offers a variety of dining places and cuisines tailored to different clientele. Museums have transformed dingy, out-of-the-way shops into carefully designed shops with high-quality merchandise (Smithsonian's National Museum of Natural History). The best museums provide information, guide-books and trained staff who are responsive to visitors' needs (Canadian Museum of Civilization in Hull, Quebec). Visitors and members expect better seating. The Baltimore Museum of Art (Maryland) offers, on request, folding aluminum chairs to use in galleries. Parking spaces are expanded, better lighted, and become more accessible to museum buildings (The Walters Art Gallery in Baltimore).

Museums have created events to satisfy sociable needs. Commemorative and holiday events are widespread, alongside traditional opening-night exhibition events (Connor-Pairie, an historical museum and site in Indiana). Ethnic festivals with food, music, dance, and crafts occur at major museums (The Field Museum in Chicago). Events devoted to evaluating members' art and artifacts are well-received (Minneapolis Institute of Arts). Donors can travel abroad to view great art museums (Art Institute of Chicago). Family programs, usually once a month on Saturdays, allow children to play with artifacts and paints, wear unusual clothes, and listen to riveting stories (Walker Art Center in Minneapolis, Minnesota). Larger, urban museums offer sleepovers for members and their children (Shedd Aquarium in Chicago). Member tours of collections and facilities, behind the scenes, are increas-ingly sought after (Smithsonian Institution). Intern and apprenticeship programs for students and summer camps for children are highly subscribed (Newark Museum in New Jersey). The cost of new, supplementary programs and events represents a growing share of museum budgets.

The attractions of museums (fine restaurants, high-quality shops, films and vid-eos, IMAX theaters), programs, events, and designed experiences ("young profes-sional" nights, family sleepovers), participatory and sociable experiences, are signs that museums are expanding their boundaries, going beyond their walled enclaves. Partnerships formed by a consortium of museums are a benefit for members who gain free entrance at their host museum and at partnering museums. Maps are avail-able to provide itineraries for contiguous museums and extended visits. For tour-ists, museums offering "block-buster" exhibitions often provide discounted hotel, airline, and restaurant services that create a broad experience of culture, commerce, and service—another instance of a museum turning inside out. An example several years ago was the Cezanne exhibition at The Philadelphia Museum of Fine Art. Leasing museum facilities generates income. The Art Institute of Chicago at lunch-time sends educators and slide shows to downtown Chicago firms.

Great museum architecture has motivated museum visits. Some of the greatest architects in the world have been museum builders (Richard Meier's Getty Mu-seum in Brentwood, Los Angeles County; Frank Gehry's Guggenheim Museum in Bilbao, Spain; Renzo Piano's Menil Collection in Houston, among others). Visitors to the Getty Museum take trams up to the hilltop site and spend much of their time enjoying the sun, dining, viewing the panorama of Los Angeles and the ocean, looking down on the homes of movie stars, and strolling the gardens. Many spend little time in the several museum buildings. The Modern Art Museum of Fort Worth (designed by Tadao Ando), surrounded by a pool of water, represents a trend toward museum transparency and demystification. Separate outside entrances to museum restaurants and shops (New York's Museum of Modern Art shop) are signs of museum accessibility and growing prominence of attractions and commerce. Is architecture and design competing with or complementary to museums?

Building well-designed websites is another pathway to museum experiences beyond museum walls. Websites offer practical information about museum hours, fees, and directions and, in addition, market museum products and services. Sophisticated websites offer museum experiences that can be more intense than onsite museum experiences. The website of the Deutsches Museum (Munich, Germany) scans entire galleries, zooms in on particular artifacts, provides videos and stereo sounds, rotates objects for viewing every corner and angle. Extensive information on collections, exhibitions, and artifacts is available. Simulated online museum experiences one day could compete with onsite museum visits.

The addition of recreational activities and a variety of educational and entertaining programs, along with collections and exhibitions, has generated costs, tangible and psychic. Programs and events can cost more than exhibitions. The morale of museum professionals in large, prominent museums can suffer. Curators and educators want to preserve the core function, mission and identity of museums. This has drawn scorn from museum professionals who doubt the ultimate value of crossing the line between entertainment and learning and scholarship. Large museums are burdened by the cost of conserving, maintaining, exhibiting, and interpreting collections. The Smithsonian, with one of the world's largest art and artifact collections, set up a program of loans to "Smithsonian Affiliates," regional museums that need artifacts and, in turn, promote the Smithsonian in local communities. Museum attractions, calculated to draw expanded audience and income, still reach a minority of a given community's population, and fewer ethnic and younger visitors than anticipated.

Part III

Viewing the new challenges and directions affecting museums, particularly, and cultural life in general, leads to certain conclusions. A successful future museum will not be an entertainment center although it will have entertaining elements. It will not be a "cabinet of curiosities," although art and artifacts will be important elements. A future museum will not be exclusively a place supported by collectors, cultural leaders, and elites, although their presence and support will be vital. Nor will it be a place, which caters mainly to adults who can afford membership fees. A future museum will be a place that attracts young people who want to learn and enjoy recreational activities. Museums in the future will be hybrid places, combining recreation and learning, allowing visitors diversions from the intense stimuli of strolling through galleries and viewing multitudinous objects.

Great museums (defined by offerings, not size) always will have a unique role in revealing, interpreting, and celebrating human creativity, beauty, and knowledge. Museums elevate the cultural life of communities and spark cultural pleasures. Science museums offer exceptional learning opportunities that combine theory, practice, and tangible tools, which support school-based science. Yet a great majority of museums are vulnerable. They lack sufficient funds, have not fully connected with audience expectations, have failed to build strong community ties and, as a result, could wither. Art, anthropological, and historical museums are splintering as new ethnic and culturally specialized museums arise. Even great urban museums that organize ethnic exhibitions find that a single ethnic group involved visits its own exhibition and fails to visit other ethnic exhibitions. Even the greatest and largest urban museums, with few exceptions, wrestle with funding, staffing, and complexity of programs. The challenge for museums is articulated in an advertisement for the National Gallery of Victoria in Melbourne:

> NGV Australia is more than a gallery. It's a destination that will inspire at every turn: from the works of art, landscape, architecture, public programs and interactive displays, to the restaurants, cafes, and spaces that all come together to create a great place to be. NGV Victoria is art inside and out.

Part IV

What about new directions in popular culture? Its scope and breadth make popular culture trends more difficult to interpret. However, a few examples of forces propelling popular culture suggest emerging trends. Locals are participating in more festivals, enjoying a medley of restaurants and bars, strolling in neighborhoods, enjoying community and out-door activities. Folk life has gained prominence (Smithsonian Folklife Festival). Participating at cultural festivals, meeting with artists and performers, is more widespread. Neighborhood theaters are spreading faster than formal cultural institutions (Chicago's nearly 100 theaters). Proliferation of cable television stations, specializing in wide-ranging popular culture (food and cooking, home design and restoration, landscape design) is leading to change in cultural interests. Broadcast stations that now present sub-cultures, ethnic life and gay and lesbian life, signify recognition of cultural variation. Public art in large cities is increasingly prevalent, ranging from Chicago's signature "Millennium Park" and public sculptures to Washington, DC's painted fiberglass Pandas placed on most street corners (an outdoor Summer 2004 exhibition called Pandamania, inspired by the National Zoo's pandas). Cultural life in the United States is importing more features of popular culture common in Europe (evening strolling). On the other hand, prices at formal cultural institutions have become steep for many cultural enthusiasts.

Tourists, not bound by itineraries and swift schedules, are discovering cultures on their own, are intent on greater historical depth, language and customary skills, and seek after knowledgeable guides. Tourism is marked increasingly by a variety of cultural experiences, both formal and informal. Cathedrals and religion, popular culture, architecture, rural as well as urban culture, and fresh air, are enjoyed as much as museums and performing arts centers.

Museums and other formal cultural institutions are integral parts of a cultural mosaic that includes popular, informal culture. Museums are part of an evolving, interconnected cultural life that encourages discovery of culture as a whole fabric, in its variety of manifestations. Museums, with some exceptions, are not likely to attract a majority of locals and large numbers of tourists. They are likely to "become . . . less, of a cultural destination and more of a cultural place in an itinerary. Towns, cities, and regions, increasingly, win" become the centers of cultural tourism. At a minimum, for example, Chicago will be viewed as having extraordinary architecture, art and theater, as well as having a variety of rich neighborhood culture.

Part V

What are the marketing implications of these new directions in cultural experience? The first is likely to be greater cultural market trend research that estimates the number of people and the segments most involved in new cultural experiences. Second, examination of the satisfactions and dissatisfactions with hybrid museums and the interpenetration of popular and elite culture; examining reasons that keep individuals from enjoying cultural life. Competitive research will be important, yet a cooperative ethic is likely to arise among cultural organizations. What is the meaning of competition when disparate cultural organizations share audiences and itineraries. What institutions and activities benefit the most and which benefit the least? Planning for communications in a changing cultural landscape is a challenging task. What opportunities and barriers exist in defining value in the new ways of experiencing culture? How will cultural institutions position themselves when a cooperative ethic undermines a competitive one? In what ways will new cultural offerings be communicated?

Management and marketing face a greater complexity of variables in cultural life: for example, visitors negotiating, on their own, cultural places and the mix of popular and formal culture. New cultural models suggest cooperation and coordination among cultural institutions, and this raises the issue of allocating costs and incomes among partners. A significant challenge involves creating complex cultural itineraries, locally and overseas. Will itineraries easily interweave elements of formal culture (museum visits) and elements of popular culture (food sampling and neighborhood trolling)? Who will manage these complex, multi-faceted itineraries? How will they be scheduled and priced for tourists. What is the role of travel agencies, tour operators, mega-travel conglomerates? How will these broader cultural experiences, destinations, ways of experiencing culture, be marketed to a range of target segments? How will marketing work for locals and for tourists with their new cultural agendas? In sum, future marketing is likely to deal with complex cultural itineraries, intricate cultural needs of travelers and locals, a mix of competitive and cooperative forces, a larger array of cultural phenomena, and novel forms

Comprehensive Interpretive Plans   **32**
A Framework of Questions

MARIANNA ADAMS AND JUDY KOKE

T HE 2005 AMERICAN ASSOCIATION OF MUSEUM'S colloquium described a Comprehensive Interpretive Plan (CIP) as a written plan that outlines the messages the museum wants to convey about content, learning, and the role of the museum in its community. Yet, the collected group was unable to articulate the specific components and process of a successful CIP, possibly because the colloquium was somewhat ahead of its time. Although CIPs are still relatively new for museums, interest is growing as evidenced by more conference presentations on the process and benefit of interpretive plans. It stands to reason that over time, as more and more institutions develop CIPs, we will, collectively, create a clearer framework and process. Meanwhile, we are all left with amorphous good intentions, and no straight path. At the moment, we suggest that this path can be illuminated by answering a series of questions—as a small group, as an institution, and/or as an institution in conversation with its communities—in order to articulate the role of your institution in its community's life long learning environment.[1]

Unique Role
What is unique about our institution's mission and collections? What guides our collection policy? What important and relevant ideas and issues are we particularly well positioned to explore and present? What unifies our research, collections and visitor experiences? Why should the public support us?

Marianna Adams is the president of Audience Focus, a firm specializing in the development and evaluation of museum experiences. Judy Koke is the director of education and interpretive programs at the Nelson-Atkins Museum of Art in Kansas City, Missouri. "Comprehensive Interpretive Plans: A Framework of Questions" appeared in *Journal of Museum Education*, Vol. 33, No. 3, Fall 2008, pp. 247–254, published by Museum Education Roundtable. It is reprinted here with permission from Left Coast Press. All rights reserved.

This discussion is obviously cross-functional—integrating all departments and roles. The heart of a CIP is about connecting collections and ideas to audiences and can only be successful if strongly rooted in the collection and organizational mission. At the outset, it is important to be clear and focused on the role of the museum, understanding that how you think about the museum's role should reflect the spirit and passion of the institution. In addition to staff agreement on the museum's role, they should be energized and inspired by the implications that this role will have on their individual practice.

Public

Who is our public? This seemingly simple question encapsulates a broad and frank discussion: Is the museum really everyone? Should it be? Who are we currently serving well? Who doesn't come? Why not? Of the non-visiting public, who do we most want to reach and why?

Again, discussions on this topic need to be iterative and cross-departmental, as individuals with departments often carry surprisingly diverse concepts of who comprises the visiting public and how they benefit from the museum experience.

The process of reaching consensus on this topic affords the museum staff an opportunity to broaden and enrich its perception of current and possible audiences. Typically we think about audiences in demographic terms, particularly the demographics of age (e.g., adults, children), role (e.g., teachers, parents, students), and sometimes race/ethnicity and economic status (e.g., African-American, Hispanic, low-income). Yet, research strongly suggests that demographics explain very little about how and why visitors benefit from museums.[2] Rather, researchers find that psychographic data (e.g., attitudes, interests, prior knowledge and experience, motivations) does a better job of not only explaining differences among visitors, but in informing our decisions about how to create rich and meaningful experiences for them.

For example, the Denver Art Museum studied visitors to better understand their expectations for the visit and the ways that they look at art.[3] They determined two main audiences, Art Novices and Advanced Amateurs. There are clear differences in the expectations between the two groups. For instance, Novices see the social experience as either the focus of their museum visit or the best way to view art. In contrast, Amateurs tend to prefer viewing on their own, even though they might come to the museum with others. Differences in ways of looking between the two groups were equally marked. For example, Novices tend to be more reactive in that they hope art will "knock them out" and they value feelings from a work of art over the intellectual analysis. This group rarely talks about taking an active role in art viewing. Conversely, the Amateur group tends to engage in more focused or discovery looking by comparing and contrasting or looking intensely. While this group values the emotional experience in art looking they are more comfortable with the intellectual analysis of works of art.

The implications of incorporating a psychographic-based approach to audiences means that exhibitions and programs are responsive to the ways different types of visitors approach and make meaning in the museum. For example, family visitors are not a monolithic audience. Families that are frequent visitors to the museum are more comfortable navigating the space and are more willing to explore on their own. On the other hand, families who do not typically visit the museum often or at all, need more advance organizers.

Community Needs

Why do people visit our museum? What needs and interests do our target audiences, current and future, have that we are uniquely in a position to respond to?

Frankly, people can live a full and satisfying life and never set foot in a museum. So why do they come? Jay Rounds suggests that "Visitors come to museums for their own reasons, and those reasons are not necessarily congruent with the goals of the museum."[4] One of their goals is to stabilize and reconfirm a sense of self and the museum is an excellent place to provide a sense of continuity. In addition, museums allow us to explore other ways of being and thinking which often appears as a process of collecting "useless" knowledge, following a relatively random agenda that is driven by what is interesting. This browsing, Rounds claims, serves as an unconscious preparation for the eventuality that we may need to revise or transform our sense of self in the future.

The days of just putting objects on display or creating interactive experiences that teach aspects of science, art, or history, are over. The museum must be more attuned to how communities are shifting and changing. Our cities are experiencing seismic redistributions of populations. For example, 50 percent of Toronto citizens were born in another country. This change has major implications for how a museum becomes meaningful to people.

Relationship

What is our relationship with our community and what new relationships do we wish to develop? How are we relevant to and perceived in our community? Is it in alignment with how we hope to be perceived? What types of changes are necessary, in the public's eyes, to move from current to desired perception? How important is it that our community understands our purpose and mission? Is it realistic to expect that the community see us as we see ourselves?

Related to personal identity work described above is the work that a community does to support itself as a whole. Museums can play an important part in forming community identity. More than repositories of knowledge and objects, museums are shifting to creating an environment where ideas are explored and meaning is made. They are becoming more transparent about their participation as the arbiters of power and value. This can only be done with successful community participation; the community will only participate if they feel the issues and ideas are interesting and relevant to their everyday lives.

For example, the Ogden Museum of Southern Art in New Orleans found itself playing an important role in the community after the devastation of hurricane Katrina.[5] As the only museum that did not suffer substantial damage, it was able to open soon after the storm. The institution served as both a respite from the grim day-to-day realities of rebuilding by offering exhibitions and social events, and a community forum where citizens could formally and informally debate the relative merits of various rebuilding proposals. It was seen as a physically and psychologically safe space.

This kind of discussion is essentially about the "posture" of the institution. Do we perceive ourselves as the expert and disseminator of information? Do we see ourselves as the facilitator of explorations of particular ideas? Is our role to be the facilitator of conversations, which might end in unexpected places? Each of these "postures" necessitates different program designs. For example, round-table discussions versus lectures, exhibitions where the primary gateway to meaning is written text versus opportunities for visitors explore and discover learning on their own through a variety of modalities, and on-site versus outreach programs.

Internal Alignment

How will all areas of the museum (retail, marketing, exhibitions, programs, collections and research) pull in the same direction? How do we align the goals and purposes of various departments into clear, coherent messages for greatest impact? How does this direction or message align with our mission and other policies? How can the Board of Trustees be included in the process to assure their support?

This is perhaps the most challenging part of creating a useful and workable interpretive plan. Yet, without internal alignment the museum will be a wagon pulled in different directions, going nowhere. As people become more and more suspicious of media advertising that pushes empty promises, museums need to focus on how the museum can provide a genuine and personally meaningful experience. As Falk and Sheppard point out, "museums have tried too hard to be all things to all people" and not been successful.[6] In the current economic climate, museums must avoid sending mixed messages and be passionately clear about the value of the museum experience. For example, the marketing focus of the museum shop and the conservation message from the curatorial area must not be at odds.

Definition of Success

What are the criteria for success? How can we tell if we are accomplishing what we set out to do? What are the priority action steps that move the organization towards it goals? What is a reasonable timeline for accomplishing our objectives?

Traditionally, our organizations measure success by attendance and membership numbers, or even in terms of jobs, and impact on tourism and money into community. More recently, the field has come to understand that exhibition and program evaluation needs to assess how visitors benefit from the experience rather than just count admission receipts, attendance figures, or outputs like number of catalogues printed or programs implement Evaluating how well we are doing demands that we listen to visitors and have meaningful conversations with them about their experiences rather than quiz them on the extent to which they ingested specific facts or ideas.

Beyond individual exhibition and program evaluation how will we understand our organization's impact on the community? This most difficult question came into focus for the field with Mark Moore's *Public Value*[7] and has recently been explored in AAM presentations and *Curator* articles by authors such as Korn, Falk, Koster, and others.

Conclusion

In working through these questions, institutions begin the challenging job of clarifying their roles for themselves and their publics. The resulting framework can act as a filter for decision making around public offerings and marketing campaigns, for example, as illustrated in the case studies that follow in this issue. A work-in-progress, the written document will require frequent reassessment and revision, as our roles, audiences, and community needs change and evolve. At all stages of development, museum staff must keep in mind how it wants to use the CIP to inform and guide individual and collective practice. No matter how brilliantly written, unless a CIP is frequently used and revised, it becomes a stale and lifeless piece of paper. Over time, the field will develop a more specific understanding of the content, benefits, and process for developing a CIP. Perhaps we could reconvene in 2015 and finish what AAM started in 2005.

Notes

1. These question topics were originally developed by Scott Eberle, Anil Swarupa, Sonal Bhatt, and Judy Koke for an AAM 2007 Annual Conference presentation. The authors have further developed and added to the original presentation.

2. John Falk, "A Framework for Diversifying Museum Audiences: Putting Heart and Head in the Right Place." *Museum News* 77, no. 5 (September/October 1998): 36–39.

3. M. McDermott-Lewis, "Through their Eyes: Novices and Advanced Amateurs," The Denver Art Museum Interpretive Project (1990): 7–46, www.denverartmuseum.org/discover_the_dam/inuseum_resources.

4. Jay Rounds, "Doing Identity Work in Museums," *Curator* 49, no. 2, (April 2006): 132–150.

5. Presentation by Kate Barron, Education Coordinator, Ogden Museum of Southern Art, at the National Art Education Association Museum Education Pre-Conference (March 2008).

6. John H. Falk and Beverly K. Sheppard, *Thriving in the Knowledge Age*. Lanham, MD: AltaMira Press, 2006.

7. Mark Moore, *Creating Public Value*. Cambridge, MA: Harvard University, 1997.

From Knowing to Not Knowing

Moving Beyond "Outcomes"

ANDREW J. PEKARIK

The ways that museums measure the success of their exhibitions reveal their attitudes and values. Are they striving to control visitors so that people will experience what the museum wants? Or are they working to support visitors, who seek to find their own path? The type of approach known as "outcome-based evaluation" weighs in on the side of control. These outcomes are sometimes codified and limited to some half-dozen or so "learning objectives" or "impact categories." In essence, those who follow this approach are committed to creating exhibitions that will tell visitors what they *must* experience. Yet people come to museums to construct something new and personally meaningful (and perhaps unexpected or unpredictable) *for themselves*. They come for their own reasons, see the world through their own frameworks, and may resist (and even resent) attempts to shape their experience. How can museums design and evaluate exhibitions that seek to support visitors rather than control them? How can museum professionals cultivate "not knowing" as a motivation for improving what they do?

EVERYONE WHO WORKS IN MUSEUMS wants to create exhibitions that are successful. But what exactly is success? How can it be identified? Can the degree of success be measured?

Over the past quarter century, as the field of visitor studies has grown, some museums have come to believe that an exhibition is successful when visitors have the experiences that the museum intended them to have—that is, when outcomes match intentions.

Measuring the extent of the match is known as "outcome-based evaluation" and it has become increasingly popular in recent years. Adherents even see it as the starting point for creating exhibitions—that is, first identify the desired outcome, then select a topic or approach likely to achieve that outcome.

Andrew J. Pekarik is a program analyst in the Office of Policy and Analysis at the Smithsonian Institution. "From Knowing to Not Knowing: Moving Beyond 'Outcomes'" appeared in *Curator: The Museum Journal* (Vol. 53, No. 1 [January 2010], pp. 105–115). It is reprinted here with permission of John Wiley & Sons. All rights reserved.

In this article I will describe why I think outcome-based program management—defined here as planning based on the definition and measurement of objectives—is ill-advised for creating and evaluating museum exhibitions, and I will suggest what a more suitable alternative might be.

The outcome-based approach to evaluation has a long history in America. It is often traced back to the work of Ralph W. Tyler, an educational assessment specialist who was chief evaluator for The Eight-Year Study (1932–1940), a national program that involved thirty high schools in a curriculum experiment that organized material by theme (with input from students) rather than by subject.[1] Tyler emphasized assessment derived from comparing clearly stated objectives with outcomes. The advantage of this method was that it was much simpler than the traditional gold standard for evaluating experiments, namely, comparing treatment groups to control groups. Instead of studying how students who used the experimental curriculum differed from those who used the traditional curriculum, he could simply look for his predefined outcomes. This line of thinking led in the 1950s to Benjamin Bloom's taxonomy, a set of hierarchical categorizations of learning outcomes. In the cognitive domain, these outcomes are: Knowledge, Comprehension, Application, Analysis, Synthesis, and Evaluation; in the affective domain: Receiving, Responding, Valuing, Organizing, and Characterizing (Bloom 1956).[2]

Outcome-based evaluation grew rapidly in the 1970s in connection with the professionalization of evaluation and the need to determine the effectiveness of new, large-scale government programs (for instance, Project Head Start). In particular, the work of Joseph Wholey, an influential public administration scholar, emphasized the use of evaluation for program management. Ultimately, this trend led to the Government Performance and Results Act of 1993 (GPRA), and its emphasis on performance measurement systems and strategic objectives as guides to program decision-making.

In America, within the world of social-service non-profits, the W. K. Kellogg Foundation (1998), the Urban Institute (Hatry 1999), and the United Way (1996) led the call for outcome-based program management in the 1990s. In the realm of museum exhibitions, in response to the GPRA, the Institute of Museum and Library Science (IMLS) has been a leader. According to the IMLS website for grant applicants:

> IMLS defines outcomes as benefits to people: specifically achievements or changes in skill, knowledge, attitude, behavior, condition, or life status for program participants ("visitors will know what architecture contributes to their environments," "participant literacy will improve").[3]

More recently, the National Science Foundation's (NSF) Informal Science Education program developed a Project Monitoring System, a relational database to facilitate the recording of project outcomes for exhibitions. Proposers of projects are required to identify intended outcomes using six "impact categories": Aware-ness, knowledge, or understanding; Engagement or interest; Attitude; Behavior; Skills; and Other.[4]

A similar categorization of outcomes for museums, known as the Generic Learning Outcomes (GLO), was developed in Great Britain. The five categories of GLO are: Knowledge and understanding; Skills; Attitudes and values; Enjoyment, inspiration, and creativity; Action, behavior, and progression.[5]

Among museum evaluators, Chan Screven and Harris Shettel, in particular, have been strong proponents of using objectives and outcomes to determine (and improve) the didactic efficacy of exhibitions since the 1960s. Objections to this approach are also long-standing.[6] The more recent trend has been to expand this method to explicitly include non-conceptual goals, such as inspiration and inter-est; to codify the range of objectives as described by learning-outcome frameworks such as the GLO or the NSF Impact Categories; and to more strictly link evalua-tion to exhibition planning. Despite several compelling factors—the size of the lit-erature surrounding this outcome-based approach to program planning, its history, the clout of its supporters, and its inherently logical character[7]—I am suggesting that this method is not the best direction for planning and evaluating museum ex-hibitions. My argument against the outcome-based approach to exhibition-making and evaluation in museums has three main points:

First, as with all evaluation methods and program management systems, out-come- based evaluation and program management has both *strengths and weaknesses*. Through familiarity with those strengths and weaknesses we can determine where a method is appropriate and where it is not.

Second, outcome-based program management and the use of pre-defined out-come frameworks tend to reinforce conventional wisdom about *museum mission* among exhibition creators; this mode of thinking ultimately limits innovation.

Third, outcome frameworks are very likely to lead—by the coercive rationality of the logic model—to *measurements,* and these measurements, necessarily narrower than the outcomes themselves, further restrict the range of what staff believes ex-hibitions can accomplish.

In place of this, I propose the use of a more recent evaluation approach, *partici-pant- oriented evaluation*, and the adoption of *design experimentation* as the concomi-tant principle to guide exhibition decisions.

Strengths and Weaknesses

The strength of outcome-based evaluation lies in its conceptual simplicity. The advantages include straightforwardness of implementation (provided that objec-tives are dearly defined and outcomes clearly discernible) and ease of presentation (because results are easy to understand). In addition, the approach is well suited to quantitative measurement, since outcomes are precisely definable in terms of the objectives, and thus data needs are relatively easy to predict.

The weakness of outcome-based evaluation and management systems begins with the initial establishment of objectives. It assumes at the outset that the defined objectives are the best expressions of exhibition quality within the context of the museum mission. But who determines objectives for a particular exhibit? On what basis is one objective (or a few) selected over others? Whom does a particular objective best serve? The selection of an outcome is an implicit decision about value. While the choice of objectives may reflect the agendas of program managers and developers, it does not generally take into account the values of all those whom the program purports to benefit.

This weakness can be mitigated when studies in advance of an exhibition (sometimes called "front-end evaluation" or "front-end analysis") obtain input from potential visitors and are used to shape objectives. But even so, the need to specify a limited set of clearly defined objectives tends to limit the range of what is recognized as useful within this data.

For example, outcome-based exhibition development typically favors cognitive objectives, such as increasing visitors' information or knowledge. (It's no accident that outcomes are so often called "learning outcomes.") This traditional preference has its own internal logic: First, the acquisition of a specific idea is easier to define and measure, in comparison to something as vague as inspiration or creativity; second, the method makes sense because exhibitions have been classified as communications media in the minds of many museum people and evaluators. Front-end evaluation that attempts to uncover "what people know" about a subject in order to refine the cognitive message that is to be the exhibition's objective will have trapped itself within the model of outcome-based development, since it is likely to ignore—or not solicit, or not notice—data that points to the value of other, very different visitor goals, including those that are unrelated to ideas.

And even if one were to accept the relevance of pre-packaged sets of outcomes as defined by these external funding entities, how would one decide among competing systems? Although the learning-outcome frameworks such as the GLO or the NSF Impact Categories resemble one another, they are not equivalent, either in their content or in their implicit values. Neither the GLO nor the NSF impacts, for example, give prominence to synthesis, which is the construction (or derivation) of a whole pattern out of diverse parts, even though synthesis stood near the top of Bloom's hierarchical list of cognitive learning outcome categories. In other words, these learning outcome frameworks emphasize the passive acquisition of information and attitudes rather than the active construction of something new and personally meaningful (and perhaps unexpected by the museum).

A second major weakness of outcome-based evaluation lies in its relative neglect of unintended outcomes. Museum audiences are very diverse in terms of their intentions and expectations. The range includes those who are vaguely curious and are visiting perhaps to please a companion, as well as those who are seeking answers to specific technical questions. Much more research, in fact, needs to be done on the motivations (conscious and unconscious) of museum visitors.

Objectives or outcomes are like an arrangement of funnels meant to neatly channel the unruly flow of visitor experiences into bottles for measurement and labeling. But visitors in exhibitions are not under the museum's control. They come for their own reasons, see the world through their own frameworks, and may even actively avoid the attempts of exhibition makers to shape their experience. Objectives-based program development encourages us to undervalue what flows past the funnels in this dynamic stream, and to believe in the illusion of control.

We can be reasonably certain that any choice of one or several outcomes is likely to exclude many in the museum visitor audience who have little or no interest at all in those particular aspects of the museum visit. And despite the focus and efforts of exhibition developers, it is also reasonably certain that—among those who experience that exhibition—there are those who find significant satisfaction and benefit from it in ways that were not predicted by the objectives/outcomes framework.

If such unintended outcomes are captured at all in the evaluation process (and this is unlikely if the evaluation activity is efficient), they will be no more than side-effects with little impact on the comparison of objectives and outcomes that represents the heart of the analysis effort. Repeated iterations of this cycle of evaluation and planning would tend toward ever narrower and sharper objectives directed (inadvertently, perhaps) to ever narrower audiences (in particular, those most receptive to those objectives), since, in the end, the museum shapes its audience by the limitations on what it chooses to offer visitors.

Museum Mission

The valuation and establishment of specific outcomes implies a paternalistic relationship between the organization and its public. It suggests that the task of the organization is to change the visitor in ways that the museum has predetermined are useful and valuable. This attitude is not rare in the history of museums—and it is, of course, an established feature of contemporary schooling—but it is not the only possible way to view the museum's mission.

The deliberate choice to promote museums as primarily educational institutions (a strategy meant to improve the appeal of museums to government funders) has naturally led museums to be seen within the framework of contemporary education and thus closely tied to the kinds of outcomes that are associated with schooling.

In my opinion, the word "education" should be used to mean much more than "schooling" or "training." It should be used to describe something that extends far beyond the acquisition of certain predefined knowledge and abilities. It should describe a type of engagement with reality that leads to independent growth and discovery. Since education, in this sense, is currently treated as a kind of "unintended outcome" of the schooling/training process, its accomplishment is a hit-or-miss affair that is consequently undervalued.

In a comparable way, I see museums as *environments* within which individuals can find opportunities for engagement that can lead to personal growth—intellectually, emotionally, spiritually—in whatever way each individual needs and desires. This is a very different model from the one that sees them as communicators of a limited set of ideas and values.

Metaphorically speaking, the museum is more like Yosemite National Park than it is like Hialeah Race Track. Vast, rugged, wild, and boundary-less (except on maps), Yosemite is a monumental place to wander in. Would you want to see Yosemite re-structured to meet just a few specific, predefined uses? Hialeah is designed for people—racers and bettors alike—who keep an eye on the finish line. How long would it take, how many thousands of studies, to determine all of the ways that individuals of many diverse types find benefit from spending time in Yosemite? Would those experiences be improved if these possibilities were narrowed to the few benefits whose outcomes could be measured? Or should possibilities be continually expanded to meet the needs of an ever-widening circle of users?

To see the museum as a field of potential for human growth is to see it as a place that serves others—rather than as a place that changes people into versions more acceptable to the museum's staff and sponsors (although such changes may indeed happen in some instances). Its task—from this perspective—is to provide a setting that is as rich with opportunities, as alive and intriguing, as is humanly possible. The museum becomes, in a sense, a hyper-reality—a trackless realm to play in, like Yosemite—that offers opportunity for engagement in multiple ways, with the capacity to be intense and powerful.

Now imagine what it is like to create exhibitions from this viewpoint rather than from the mechanical, self-referencing system of objectives and outcomes. Because the field of potential is so vast, one would need to begin by understanding how, where, and for whom this kind of growth is taking place. The construction of any exhibition, in other words, would truly begin with visitors, and would proceed through a process of self-questioning to determine how the museum's resources (contents, facilities, staff, and so on) could be used to expand visitors' experiences, not narrow them down to chosen outcomes.

Measurement

I am arguing for a view of museums that expands outward, rather than one that narrows. The setting of objectives represents a funneling of many possibilities into a select few. Measuring outcomes constricts the funnel even further, since it establishes specific, quantifiable parameters that will then be taken to represent the outcome more broadly.

Outcome-based evaluation requires measurement. It has no meaning if outcomes cannot be measured, since there is then no other way to compare them with objectives in order to prove success. The funders who urge outcome-based evaluation assume that there will be measurement. The NSF impact categories, for example, are each defined as a "measurable demonstration" of its particular type.

The Kellogg Foundation insists that outcomes be SMART, that is: specific, mea-surable, action-oriented, realistic, and timed (W. K. Kellogg Foundation 1998, 17). IMLS defines outcome-based evaluation as "the measurement of results."[8]

In the exhibition setting, however, valid, reliable measures of outcomes are dif-ficult to come by for a number of reasons. First, such measurements are likely to be indirect, subjective, and vague: For example, what about the percentage of visitors who agree that they learned something—even if what they learned was incorrect? Second, thorough testing of visitors is not possible in a museum environment—even if you could test them on a specific idea, how do you account for those who did not learn that idea, but who did learn many others? Third, sample sizes are generally small, either because program audiences are small, or because large-scale studies are too expensive for most museums. Fourth, there is no single ideal time to measure an outcome—should a behavior change be measured immediately upon exit from an exhibition, a short while later, or much later? Fifth, since museum visiting is likely to be only one of a series of inter-related activities that might have a role to play in determining the outcome of a visit how can you control for these confounding variables?

Participant-based Evaluation

Participant-based evaluation originally arose in opposition to outcome-based evaluation. It begins with qualitative inquiry into the experiences of those in-volved in a project, whether as providers or as consumers, or both. Variations on this approach include naturalistic evaluation (Wolf and Tymitz 1978), responsive evaluation (Stake 1984), fourth-generation evaluation (Guba and Lincoln 1989), and collaborative evaluation (Cousins, Donohue, and Bloom 1996). The research aims to discover new dimensions of the situation that have not previously been noted and considered. It is an open-ended inquiry into meaning making that aims to make understanding more complex—rather than to simplify it.

The participant-based approach draws on constructivist thinking and seeks to understand the exhibition and its effectiveness from the point of view of those who experienced it. In place of the single producer-oriented reality represented by objectives and outcomes, this approach admits that each of the participants is constructing his/her own perception of reality. Evaluators seek out the diversity of these perceptions. Because this method is context-sensitive, and represents a process of discovery, it is very sensitive to the variety of participant needs as well as to unexpected outcomes.

Because this kind of evaluation begins as a goal-free, blinder-free search for dis-covery, it provides a view that is more complete and contextualized, more nuanced and complex, and more accepting of multiple viewpoints. Its results address all the elements that impact the experience of visitors—not just outcomes, but processes, settings, needs, issues, values, barriers, and so on. Out of this analysis comes insight that can be used to change the exhibition or to devise new ones.

Another way of putting it is that participant evaluation, unlike outcome evaluation, is not just about what happened but also about *why* it happened. The value of this kind of evaluation far exceeds the simple question of effectiveness of a program. Because it provides insight into the way that diverse participants think and act, it gives exhibition developers a much richer mental model to use in constructing and revising exhibitions. As those exhibitions are studied, in turn, a large, complex body of knowledge is constructed out of the surprises and insights that come from the iterative process of creating programs and studying participants.

In any system of evaluation, one hopes that repeated evaluations will inform the creation and revision of exhibitions. When outcome-based evaluation is employed, the refinement that is achieved over time is movement ever closer to the ideal of a program that will perfectly match objective and outcome (usually achieved most effectively by narrowing the audience). When participant-based evaluation is used, however, the development is an ever richer and deeper understanding of visitors and the confidence to experiment with new ways to respond to those new discoveries about how diverse people engage with the museum.

Of course, there are implications in this alternative model for the way that exhibition development is pursued. While outcome-based evaluation can be handed off to an evaluation specialist or to an outside contractor once objectives are agreed upon, participant-based evaluation—if it is to be used to actively construct programs—needs to be an ongoing activity of the exhibition development team more broadly. Since it aims to capture subtle complexities in the experience of specific individuals, it is most valuable when it is personally experienced. Those who are responsible for making the exhibition need to see and hear first-hand how visitors respond. In this way, their mental models of visitors are consciously *and subconsciously* enhanced. In other words, evaluation becomes everyone's business.

Design Experimentation

In situations where one wishes to understand the workings of a complex, interpenetrating, and overlapping interchange of activities, such as learning in a classroom or visiting an exhibition in a museum, it is very difficult to separate out one strand from the entire system. A learning outcome, isolated from its context, is like a fish taken from the ocean, gasping for air.

In order to understand (and judge) what is happening in complex systems like these, we need to study the system in its totality and examine how the working of that system shifts in response to changes. Just as wind-tunnel testing is used to refine the design of rockets or airplanes, alterations in exhibitions can be studied to determine their impact on participant responses, so that improved versions result. In other words, the exhibition itself can be viewed not as a product to be constructed in its entirety and then judged as successful or not, but as an experiment whose components will be altered. In accordance with those alterations, participants will be studied in an open-ended manner in order to determine what happened, who was affected, and why.

The idea of design experimentation is generally traced to the work of Ann Brown, who said that, "As a design scientist in my field [the study of learning], I attempt to engineer innovative educational environments and simultaneously conduct experimental studies of those innovations" (1992, 141).

The difference between design experimentation and seat-of-the-pants fine-tuning or formative evaluation is that design experiments are done not only to create improvements, but also to construct theory—and not a grand theory like Special Relativity, but a working theory of how content and design choices affect the emergence of particular responses. As Cobb et al. have stated with respect to design experiments in education:

> Design experiments ideally result in greater understanding of a learning ecology—a complex, interacting system involving multiple elements of different types and levels—by designing its elements and by anticipating how these elements function together to support learning. Design experiments therefore constitute a means of addressing the complexity that is a hallmark of educational settings (Cobb et al. 2003, 9).

In my opinion, this is exactly the exhibition development approach that would most benefit museums, because here, too, we are dealing with an extremely complex system of interacting parts and levels. If we organize exhibitions as design experiments, we can begin to define—in a clearer, more thoughtful and accurate way—the ecology of the environment that gives rise to the museum experience. Design experimentation, coupled with participant evaluation, thus can become a powerful engine for change and creativity—one that can respond to changing audiences and media with ease and skill.

Design Experimentation in Practice

I am not aware of an exhibition project that has been or is being consciously developed as a design experiment. (If you have an example, please let me know.) I am involved with several projects that have started to move in this direction, but instead of describing them here, I would like to suggest how I envision this approach being applied in its fullest form.

Instead of thinking of the exhibition as a building that is planned in detail and then built, one would think of it as a living organism. It begins small, perhaps as a few displays set among others. As the exhibition team studies the ways that visitors engage with this embryonic exhibition, the team starts to invent methods for expanding it that seem likely to be fruitful, in view of what team members are learning about visitors and their responses. As the embryonic exhibition is revised and enlarged—perhaps doubled, let's say—it is studied again, and yet again it is changed and built upon. The exhibition, in other words, evolves as the team's understanding evolves in regard to what the visitor experiences and what the exhibition facilitates. Eventually it is declared mature, it stops changing, and, after a decent interval, it begins to the as new growth—new displays, for instance—begin to take away some of its territory.

A living, changing, organic exhibition like this might have some practical benefits in today's museum environment. Obviously this pattern of development is most suitable for the display of permanent collections, not for projects dependent on outside loans. And at a time when museums are turning away from extravagant loan exhibitions towards new ways of using the permanent collection, this practice of experimentation might provide a way to make the display of permanent collections dynamic without radically increasing costs; to incorporate new technologies effectively and efficiently; to increase creativity and experimentation; and to engage new audiences.

Conclusion

If success does not mean that exhibition visitors attain the specific outcomes that the museum intends them to achieve, what, then, does it mean? I am suggesting here that for visitors it means that the experience opens up possibilities in ways they feel are personally meaningful. For museum staff it means that the exhibition provides an opportunity to attain a deeper, richer understanding of the museum experience, one that significantly expands their mental model of visitor response.

In the end, I think, the argument for or against outcome evaluation is a matter of values. What kind of understanding do professionals seek? Is it better to have a solid, established understanding that one can confidently apply in a consistent, objective way? Or is it better to have a fluid, dynamic understanding that is constantly seeking new articulation and is never the same? What is our mission? Is it to disseminate our wisdom? Or is it to help others in their search? What motivates museum professionals? Is it knowing? Or is it not knowing?

Notes

1. The reforms recommended by the study are still considered relevant today. See, for example, Kirdel, Bullough, and Goodlad (2007). For excerpts of the study itself see www.8yearstudy.org/projectintro.html.

2. The taxonomy also identified a psychomotor domain, but did not include subcategories within this domain.

3. See www.imls.gov/applicants/basics.shtm. The page contains a link to the IMLS document *Perspectives on Outcome Based Evaluation for Libraries and Museums*.

4. See Table 3-1, page 21, in Friedman (2008).

5. See wwwjnspiringlearningforall.gov.uk/toolstemplates/genericlearning/index.html.

6. See, for example, the objections to Shettel's approach by Michael Alt (Alt 1977) and Shettel's detailed response (Shettel 1978).

7. The approach is alternatively called "the logic model."

8. See www.imls.gov/applicants/basics.shtm.

References

Alt, M. 1977. Evaluating didactic exhibits: A critical look at Shettel's work. *Curator* 20 (3): 241–258.

Bloom, B. S., ed. 1956. *Taxonomy of Educational Objectives: The Classification of Educational Goals, by a Committee of College and University Examiners.* New York: Longmans, Green.

Brown, A. L. 1992. Design experiments: Theoretical and methodological challenges in creating complex interventions in classroom settings. *Journal of the Learning Sciences* 2 (2): 141–178.

Cobb, P., J. Confrey, A. diSessa, R. Lehrer, and L. Schauble. 2003. Design experiments in educational research. *Educational Researcher* 32 (1): 9–13.

Cousins, J. B., J. J. Donohue, and G. A. Bloom. 1996. Collaborative evaluation in North America: Evaluators' self-reported opinions, practices, and consequences. *Evaluation Practice* 17 (3): 207–226.

Friedman, A., ed. 2008. Framework for evaluating impacts of informal science education projects. National Science Foundation. Accessed Oct. 3, 2009 at www.insci.org /resources/Eval_Framework.pdf.

Guba, E., and Y. Lincoln. 1989. *Fourth Generation Evaluation.* Thousand Oaks, CA: Sage.

Hatry, H. P. 1999. *Performance Measurement: Getting Results.* Washington, DC: The Urban Institute.

Hendricks, M., M. C. Plantz, and K. J. Pritchard. 2008. Measuring outcomes of United Way-funded programs: Expectations and reality. In *Nonprofits and Evaluation: New Directions for Evaluation, No 119,* J. G. Carman and K. A. Fredericks, eds., 13–35. San Francisco: Jossey-Bass.

Kirdel, C. A., R. V. Bullough, and J. I. Goodlad. 2007. *Stories of the Eight-year Study: Reexamining Secondary Education in America.* Albany, NY: State University of New York Press.

Shettel, H. H. 1978. A critical look at a critical look: A response to Alt's critique of Shetters work. *Curator* 21 (4):329–345.

Stake, R. E. 1984. Program evaluation, particularly responsive evaluation. In *Evaluation Models,* G. F. Madaus, M. Scriven, and D. L. Stufflebeam, eds. Boston: Kluwer-Nijhoff.

United Way of America. 1996. *Measuring Program Outcomes: A Practical Approach.* Alexandria, VA: United Way of America.

W. K. Kellogg Foundation. 1998. *W.K. Kellogg Foundation Evaluation Handbook.* Accessed Oct. 3, 2009 at www.wkkforg/Pubs/Tools/Evaluation/Pub770.pdf.

Weil, S., and P. Rudd. 2000. *Perspectives on Outcome-Based Evaluation for Libraries and Museums.* Institute of Museum and Library Services. PDF accessed on Oct. 3, 2009 via link at www.imls.gov/applicants/basics.shtm.

Wolf, R. L., and B. L. Tymitz. 1978. *A Preliminary Guide for Conducting Naturalistic Evaluation in Studying Museum Environments.* Washington, DC: Smithsonian Institution Office of Museum Programs.

Legal and Ethical Considerations in Museum Acquisitions

34

MARILYN PHELAN

I WAS ASKED TO PROVIDE THE PERSPECTIVE OF ONE who views museum philosophy from the "outside" of the profession looking in to answer a specific question: What underlying philosophy/mission should museums pursue in the first half of the 21st century? This was a challenge, but from my perspective, which includes many years of studying laws relating to museums, I must answer this question by focusing on the need for museum professionals to adopt a different philosophy regarding museum acquisitions from that which was prevalent in the 20th century. Although most museums have developed codes of ethics with respect to accessioning and deaccessioning objects in their collections, I have observed that many museum officials tend to apply ethical considerations more readily to deaccessioning their collections than to their acquisition policies. Unfortunately this has led to many museums accessioning cultural treasures without exercising due diligence to review the history of such cultural properties.

In my many years of researching, complying with, and teaching laws relating to museums, I have attempted to relate such laws to ethical principles, particularly with respect to the interplay of legal axioms and ethical theorems regarding the collection and protection of cultural property. One cannot de-emphasize the importance of the law in preserving the archaeological record. We clearly are dependent on the law to protect our cultural heritage, but there are gaps in the law that ethical principles must fill. Countless countries have been stripped of their cultural property through thefts at archaeological sites. Nations, museums, and individuals have lost artworks and other cultural property as a result of pillage during military conflicts. Works of art especially have been part of the spoils of war. In my opinion the greatest challenge to museum officials in the first half of the 21st century is how they will deal with the problem that much of this looted cultural property

Marilyn Phelan was the Paul Whitfield Horn Professor of Law at Texas Tech University School of Law and Professor of Museum Science. "Legal and Ethical Considerations in Museum Acquisitions" appeared in *Museum Philosophy in the Twenty-First Century* (2006), Hugh Genoways (Ed.), pp. 27–46, published by AltaMira Press. It is reprinted here by permission of the publisher. All rights reserved.

has found its way into museum collections. Indeed some museum officials have accepted and even condoned the pillage of the cultural heritage in the interest of enhancing their collections. As the law continues to evolve at both the national and international level, we hopefully can expect that we will acquire sufficient legal means during the 21st century to address and correct the past pillage of archaeological sites and other thefts of cultural property. In the process though, because legal principles are not yet sufficiently adequate to address these issues, ethical principles must provide for needed self-regulation.

I have been interested especially in the interplay between law and ethics with respect to the acquisition and maintenance of museum collections. The Code of Ethics adopted by the International Council of Museums (ICOM) observes that the "illicit trade in objects and specimens encourages the destruction of historic sites" as well as "ethnic cultures," that it "promotes theft at local, national and international levels," and "contravenes the spirit of national and international patrimony."[1] It declares that a museum professional "must warrant that it is highly unethical for a museum to support the illicit market in any way, *directly or indirectly*" (emphasis added).[2] The ICOM Code states:

> A museum should not acquire any object or specimen by purchase, gift, loan, bequest or exchange unless the governing body and responsible officer are satisfied that a valid title to it can be obtained. Every effort must be made to ensure that it has not been illegally acquired in, or exported from, its country of origin or any intermediate country in which it may have been owned legally (including the museum's own country). Due diligence in this regard should establish the full history of the item from discovery or production, before acquisition is considered.
>
> In addition to the safeguards set out above, a museum should not acquire objects by any means where the governing body or responsible officer has reasonable cause to believe that their recovery involved the unauthorised, unscientific or intentional destruction or damage of ancient monuments, archaeological or geological sites, or natural habitats, or involved a failure to disclose the finds to the owner or occupier of the land, or to the proper legal or governmental authorities.

The Code of Ethics adopted in 2000 by the American Association of Museums (AAM) unfortunately is silent with respect to ethical proscriptions regarding a museum's inclusion in its collections of objects that were taken from archaeological sites or were acquired either directly or indirectly through the illicit market. The AAM's policy on collections merely proposes that a museum should ensure its collections are "lawfully held, protected, secure, unencumbered, cared for, and preserved."[3] The code's policy on collections states that a museum must ensure that its "acquisition, disposal, and loan activities are conducted in a manner that respects the protection and preservation of natural and cultural resources and discourages illicit trade in such materials."[4]

The 2000 AAM Code of Ethics does not address the somewhat "problematic" and "questionable" practices on the part of directors of many of the larger and most reputable museums in the United States concerning their amassing of objects from the world's cultural heritage, allegedly for preservation purposes but often simply to enhance their collections.

Despite the fact that archaeologists can construct a history and prehistory for a particular sphere or community through a study of the cultural property of that region, many leading museum officials have been involved, indirectly at least, in the illicit trade in looted antiquities from archaeological sites. A partial justification for this involvement has been the theory that wealthy museums have a better means to curate cultural objects than do source nations with limited resources available for their museums. There still exists a group of theorists who take the position that, because all cultural properties, wherever located, are part of the cultural heritage of humanity, cultural resources should be owned and controlled by those who can best preserve them. Strangely enough, this so-called internationalist theory apparently serves as the justification for many museum directors to maintain within their collections looted, as well as illegally exported, cultural resources.[5] If, in fact, laws have legitimized their methods of collection, they have ignored ethical principles that surely do not.

In December of 2002, officials of eighteen of the leading museums of Europe and North America drafted the "Declaration on the Importance and Value of Universal Museums," wherein they posited a "universality" in their collections.[6] They declared that their museums "provide a valid and valuable context for objects that were long ago displaced from their valuable source" and postulated that calls "to repatriate objects that have belonged to museum collections" must be considered on a case-by-case basis and "judged individually" because "museums serve not just the citizens of one nation but the people of every nation."[7] The directors of these museums have listed "the threat to the integrity of universal collections posed by demands for the restitution of objects to their countries of origin" as one of the most pressing issues facing museums.[8] This indeed is one of the most pressing issues confronting museums, but some members of the museum community view the issue in a different light. Some would contend that directors of the "universal" museums are attempting "to establish a higher degree of immunity from claims for the repatriation of objects" in their collections and would view their "presumption that a museum with universally defined objectives may be considered exempt from such demands" as "specious."[9]

Two recent cases in the United States illustrate the questionable and somewhat alarming position of some members of the AAM regarding the international trade in art and antiquities. The AAM itself openly acquiesced in the view of the internationalists that cultural resources are commodities that should be salable on the international market when it stated its position in the first of these two cases. In *United States v. An Antique Platter of Gold*,[10] the AAM submitted an amicus curiae (friend of the court) brief supporting the actions of an art collector (who also was a benefactor of the New York Metropolitan Museum of Art) in importing into the United States a looted third-century B.C. Phiale.[11] The Phiale was taken from an archaeological site in Sicily, was exported in violation of Italian laws, and was imported into the United States in violation of its customs laws.[12] Pursuant to a 1939 Italian law, an archaeological item is presumed to belong to the state unless its possessor can show private ownership prior to 1902.[13] The Italian government sought the assistance of the U.S. government in investigating the circumstances of the Phiale's exportation and requested that it confiscate the Phiale for return to Italy. The district court ruled that the Phiale must be returned to Italy. On appeal, the AAM filed its amicus brief wherein it urged the appellate court not to give effect to the cultural patrimony laws of other countries. The AAM asserted: "American museums have a deep and longstanding interest in, and commitment to, the responsible collection and exhibition of cultural objects of all countries and civilizations." It declared that "American museums have supported, and will continue to support, all responsible efforts to further the preservation and conservation of cultural objects, and to combat their destruction, looting and theft."[14] However, it then asserted that the decision of the district court (wherein the district court ordered the forfeiture of the Phiale and its return to Italy) "threatens the ability of U.S. museums to collect . . . and make available for public exhibition objects from around the world" that are "the subject of *sweeping* foreign cultural patrimony laws" (emphasis added).[15] It declared that these cultural patrimony laws "are, in significant respects, antithetical to fundamental principles of U.S. law and public policy." It expressed concern that, should the decision of the court below not be reversed, "countless objects" in museum collections would be in peril.[16] The AAM maintained that the decision of the court would "have a profound impact on the law governing all museums and their ability to collect and exhibit cultural objects." It then declared that American museums were "compelled" to urge the court to reverse the decision of the court below.[17] The AAM took the position that the district court committed "fundamental error" in "its automatic enforcement of Italy's patrimony law." The AAM opined that the "unprecedented procedure permitted the U.S. government" by the court made the U.S. government a "surrogate for the Italian government."[18] Curiously, the AAM describe the "efforts of some nations to claim ownership of all objects discovered within their borders" as a "more parochial view of cultural property," one that would "directly challenge the 'common cultural heritage' philosophy" upon which, it stated, "our museums and society are funded."[19] The AAM declared in its amicus brief that "cultural patrimony laws are fundamentally inconsistent with the United States' treatment of its own cultural property and with our underlying system of private property."[20] It further stated that "the effect of the indiscriminate application of these laws will be to jeopardize existing museum collections and the future ability of our museums to continue to collect and exhibit cultural objects for the public."[21] The AAM concluded, in its amicus brief, that, should the decision of the district court (that the Phiale must be returned to Italy) be affirmed, that decision "will amount to a judicial fiat . . . that often will preclude responsible museums from acquiring cultural objects from other countries."[22]

The substance of the AAM's position, as set out in its amicus curiae brief in *Antique Platter of Gold,* is that there should be no limitation on the looting of archeological sites. This astonishing position was reasserted by leading members of the museum community, albeit not by the AAM specifically, in the most recent of the two cases. In *United States v.* Schultz,[23] respectable and prestigious members of the museum community joined in the filing of an amicus curiae brief supporting the activities of a well-known art dealer who was convicted for transporting knowingly stolen Egyptian antiquities. The art dealer, Schultz, was indicted for "conspiring to receive stolen Egyptian antiquities that had been transported in interstate and foreign commerce" in violation of the National Stolen Property Act (NSPA).[24] Schultz contended that the objects he had taken were not stolen within the meaning of the NSPA because, he claimed, they were not owned by anyone and, thus, could not be stolen. The prosecution, on the other hand, showed that the Egyptian government owned the antiquities pursuant to a patrimony law known as "Law 117," which declares that all antiquities found in Egypt after 1983 are the property of the Egyptian government. Evidence in the case showed that an individual (Parry) smuggled an ancient Egyptian sculpture (the head of Pharaoh Amenhotep III) out of Egypt by disguising the figure in plastic and plaster.[25] Schultz later paid Parry a substantial fee to serve as his agent to sell the sculpture. The two men created a false provenance for the sculpture, claiming that it had been brought from Egypt in the 1920s and had been maintained since that time in an English private collection, which they called the "Thomas Alcock Collection." They prepared fake labels for the sculpture, which were designed to appear as if they had been printed in the 1920s. After a jury trial in the U.S. District Court for the Southern District of New York, Schultz was convicted of conspiring to receive stolen property that had been transported in interstate or foreign commerce under the NSPA.[26] The case was appealed to the Court of Appeals for the Second Circuit. Amicus curiae briefs supporting Schultz were filed with the Second Circuit by dealer groups and by a newly formed "Citizens for a Balanced Policy with Regard to the Importation of Cultural Property." The newly formed organization is a group of twenty-seven individuals that includes nine present or former museum curators, members of museum boards, and counsel for museums. The group represented that their interest in the case was their "abiding commitment to the preservation of cultural heritage and the continued existence of a national policy with regard to international trade in cultural property that balances the legitimate but often conflicting interest of archaeologists, art dealers, collectors, museums and our national government."[27] In their brief, the group stated that the indictment of Schultz has "shook the American art world" and, with it, members of their group. The group contended that, if the NSPA covers claims of ownership based on foreign patrimony laws, "our nation's cultural policy is at stake."[28] The Second Circuit Court of Appeals apparently was unimpressed with the group's argument as it affirmed Schultz's conviction.

In 1982, Congress ratified in part the 1970 UNESCO Convention on the Means of Prohibiting and Preventing the Illicit Import, Export and Transfer of

Ownership of Cultural Property by its implementing legislation, the Convention on Cultural Property Implementation Act, which became effective in 1983.[29] At that time, members of Congress noted that the demand for cultural artifacts had resulted in the irremediable destruction of archaeological sites and objects. They expressed concern that this demand was depriving situs countries of their cultural patrimony and the world of important knowledge of the past.[30] Some members of Congress noted that the United States had become a principal market for artifacts of archaeological or ethnological interest and of art objects and that the discovery of stolen or illegally exported artifacts in some instances had strained severely the United States' relations with the countries of origin, some of which were close allies of the United States.[31] The Cultural Property Implementation Act, which was enacted to ratify in part the 1970 United Nations Educational, Scientific and Cultural Organization (UNESCO) Convention, provides that, when a participating nation makes a request to the United States for import restrictions on cultural property from that nation, because the requesting nation contends the cultural patrimony of the nation is in jeopardy from the pillage of its cultural properties, the president may enter into a bilateral agreement with that nation to apply import restrictions.[32]

In 2000, then-Senators Moynihan, Roth, and Shumer introduced a bill[33] that would have amended the Cultural Property Implementation Act to curb the president's ability to comply with the 1970 UNESCO Convention. Sponsors of the bill were concerned that art dealers were not members of the Cultural Property Advisory Committee (CPAC). The CPAC recommends to the president whether import restrictions should be adopted. The bill would have imposed significant administrative burdens on the CPAC, for it would have required input from collectors and traders of cultural property before the president could comply with requests of foreign nations that the United States prevent the importation of their illegally exported cultural treasures. The bill would have required requesting nations to submit evidence to the CPAC reflecting contemporary pillage before import restrictions could be imposed. It would have changed the status of committee members to provide that all would serve in a representative capacity and would not be considered to be special government employees to whom conflict-of-interest provisions apply. Sponsors of the bill wanted the CPAC to consist of eleven members representing four categories of interested parties: museums, archaeologists/anthropologists, dealers, and the public. They wanted a provision that would define a quorum to include at least one member from each category. In addition, they wanted the act to be amended to provide that the president could not act without a recommendation from the committee. Because, to have a quorum, a member from each category would have had to be present, the effect of such a provision would have been that dealer representatives could have prevented the CPAC from acting by refusing to attend meetings of the committee. As the CPAC could not act, so the president could not act. The Metropolitan Museum of Art presented a position statement in which it lent support to the "thrust" of the bill, particularly the provisions that would have required nations seeking import restrictions to provide more information about the material they sought to protect and the provision permitting outside parties an opportunity to provide comments on the findings and recommendations of the committee before the president could act on the committee's recommendations. The museum also supported the provision clarifying that all members of the committee would serve in a representative capacity and would not be considered special government employees. Even though the museum's position paper affirmed its support of principles of the 1970 UNESCO Convention and its deep sympathy "with the problem faced by many countries with regard to the looting of antiquities and destruction of ancient sites," the paper expressed support of administrative restrictions that would have made it impossible to enforce principles of the 1970 UNESCO Convention. Fortunately the Moynihan bill was not enacted. My concern is that the museum community did not come out in force to oppose it and that officials of one of the most prestigious U.S. museums endorsed it.

Members of the CPAC are appointed by the president and serve staggered three-year terms. Curiously, in July 2003, an entirely new committee was established. The eleven appointed members (all appointed in 2003) included three international sales experts and three members of the public.

In 1995, the International Institute for the Unification of Private Law (UNIDROIT) Convention on Stolen or Illegally Exported Cultural Property was adopted in Rome. The convention provides a substantial benefit for owners whose property is stolen by its attempt to tighten the market so as to avoid the present easy passage of stolen goods into the licit market. The United States has not ratified this convention. Among the chief opponents of its adoption in the United States are some leading members of the museum community. The Parliamentary Assembly of the Council of Europe regards the 1995 UNIDROIT Convention as an important contribution to the preservation of cultural heritage of humanity and fully endorses it. It calls upon members of the Assembly to work toward ratification of the convention in their own parliaments.[34]

Cultural patrimony is inalienable, and cultural objects have their greatest value to society when they remain, and can be studied, in their place of origin. All nations, as well as the international museum community, must accept, either based simply on a "moralistic" theory of what is right and justifiable or on the recognition of a crucial necessity to protect and conserve the cultural heritage, that nations, and museums, must join together to help protect and preserve each country's treasures. Such protection and preservation does not translate to a right to take another country's cultural patrimony. It is peculiar indeed that many leading museum officials have not encouraged such a national demeanor and even have condoned, indirectly at least, the trafficking in cultural treasures. Museum officials must begin to follow a stricter code of ethics with regard to their acquisitions. Provisions of the Code of Ethics adopted by the International Council of Museums should provide the example for all museums.

Another example of the failure of many museums to subscribe to and follow ethical principles in their accessioning policies is the past and continuing failure of many leading museum officials to acknowledge that museums should not acquire nor retain Holocaust-looted artworks. It is my opinion that the museum community's tolerance of museums having Holocaust-looted artworks in their collections represents participation in the "crime against humanity" symbolized by the Holocaust. Many leading museum officials continue to refuse to return looted Jewish cultural property that became a part of their collections either as a result of the museums having purchased the property through the international market or having received such property through donations from art collectors who acquired the property in the illicit (or licit?) market.[35] Although many museum officials have begun to recognize a moral obligation to return Holocaust-looted artworks in their museum collections and have offered to open their collections to the Jewish community to determine what works were indeed stolen and, thus, should be restituted, overall the process of returning looted Jewish cultural property has been slow.[36]

Two important recent cases involving rights of possession to Holocaust-looted artworks illustrate the current thinking of courts that society can no longer sanction the use of legal theories to justify the continued possession of property illegally taken by the Third Reich.

In *United States v. Portrait of Wally,*[37] the United States is seeking forfeiture of an Egon Schiele painting, *Portrait of Wally,* which was brought into the United States to be exhibited at the Museum of Modern Art in New York and which was on loan from the Leopold Foundation in Vienna. The facts in the case established that the painting was taken from Lea Bondi Jaray, a Viennese Jew, when Germany annexed Austria in 1938 as part of the "aryanization" of property owned by Austrian Jews.[38] Bondi went to the Belvedere Museum in Vienna after the war and claimed Wally as hers, but received no reply. Dr. Rudolph Leopold, a collector of Schiele paintings, later visited Bondi in London to ask for her help in buying Schiele paintings and mentioned that Wally was hanging in the Belvedere even though it belonged to her. Bondi then asked Dr. Leopold to explain to the Belvedere on her behalf that the painting was her property. Dr. Leopold subsequently acquired *Wally* from the Belvedere and did not tell Bondi. She discovered he had obtained *Wally* in or about 1957 when the painting was featured in a catalogue for an exhibition and Dr. Leopold was listed as the owner. In 1994, Dr. Leopold sold *Wally* to the Leopold Museum of which he is a director.[39] A federal district judge has ruled, in *Portrait of Wally,* that the United States can pursue its claim that the Leopold violated American law by bringing a stolen painting into the United States and, thus, that the painting is subject to civil forfeiture.[40]

In *Republic of Austria v. Altmann,*[41] the Supreme Court recently affirmed a decision of the Ninth Circuit Court of Appeals that a U.S. court has jurisdiction to hear a claim of a victim of the Holocaust as against the Republic of Austria. Maria Altmann brought a claim against the Republic of Austria for the recovery of six

Gustav Klimt paintings the Nazis took from her now-deceased Jewish uncle, Ferdinand Bloch.[42] The Republic of Austria contended it was immune from the jurisdiction of U.S. courts because much of the alleged wrongdoing took place as of 1948, at which time it would have enjoyed absolute sovereign immunity from suit in U.S. courts. It alleged that nothing in the Foreign Sovereign Immunities Act,[43] which was enacted in 1976 and under which Maria Altmann asserted jurisdiction, retroactively divested it of immunity.[44] The Ninth Circuit Court of Appeals had affirmed the decision of the district court that a foreign state is not immune from the jurisdiction of U.S. courts when the issue is whether rights in property were taken in violation of international law. The Ninth Circuit decided that Austria could not expect immunity in light of its complicity in, and perpetuation of, the discriminatory expropriation of the Klimt paintings.[45] It noted that the seizures violated both Austria's and Germany's obligations under the 1907 Hague Convention on the Laws and Customs of War on Land and that Austria's Second Republic officially repudiated all Nazi transactions in 1946. Thus, the Ninth Circuit ruled, and the Supreme Court affirmed, that Austria was not immune from suit in U.S. courts.[46]

There are numerous international agreements in place, some prior to World War II and many others after, that prohibit pillage during military conflicts.[47] Among these are the 1907 Hague Convention on the Laws and Customs of War on Land, which provides that an enemy's property cannot be seized unless the seizure is "imperatively demanded by the necessities of war,"[48] and the 1919 Treaty of Versailles, which required Germany to make restitution of objects taken during the war where it could identify them in territory belonging to Germany or its allies.[49] In addition, in the 1943 London Declaration, the Allies cautioned nations that all transfers of, or dealing with, property taken by the Axis powers could be declared invalid. The Nuremberg Charter included as a war crime the plunder of public or private property during a military conflict. The Nuremberg Tribunal ruled that Germany had engaged in an illegal war of aggression and branded the looting of Jewish property as part of their persecution and, thus, a crime against humanity.[50] The United Nations General Assembly later passed a resolution recognizing the Nuremberg Charter and Judgment as part of the body of general international law that binds all nations.[51]

In 1998, the Washington Conference on Holocaust-Era Assets unanimously adopted principles relating to Nazi-confiscated art wherein the participating nations pledged themselves to identify art that had been confiscated by the Nazis and not restituted and to take steps to achieve a "just and fair solution" with respect to such art. It stated that efforts should be made to establish a central registry of information regarding such art and that alternative dispute resolution mechanisms should be developed to resolve ownership issues. In 1999, the Parliamentary Assembly of the Council of Europe unanimously adopted a resolution that recognized that, while there were moves early after the end of the Second World War to find and return Jewish looted property, much still remains in private and public hands. The Assembly invited the parliaments of all member-states to give immediate consideration to ways in which they could facilitate the return of looted Jewish cultural property. It specifically stated that attention should be given "to the removal of all impediments to identification such as laws, regulations or policies which prevent access to relevant information in government or public archives, and to records of sales and purchases, customs and other import and export records."[52] It provided specifically that entities "in receipt of government funds which find themselves holding Jewish cultural property should return it."[53]

In the Vilnius Forum Declaration, issued at the Council of Europe conference held in Vilnius, Lithuania, in October 2000, governments were asked to undertake every reasonable effort to achieve the restitution of cultural assets looted during the Holocaust era to the original owners or their heirs."[54] It asked governments, museums, the art trade, and other relevant agencies to provide all information necessary to such restitution.

What should be the role of the international museum community? The Parliamentary Assembly of the Council of Europe has urged the advancement of the recovery of looted Jewish cultural property "before the last of those persons from which it was taken has died."[55] The international museum community should recognize its moral obligation to advance the recovery of this looted property and give immediate consideration to a means that will assure the repatriation of all remaining stolen Jewish cultural property in museum collections. The decisions in *Portrait of Wally* and *Altmann* illustrate that courts may no longer countenance the legal arguments museum directors have relied upon to retain in their collections artworks with Holocaust-related gaps in provenance. If widespread litigation eventually will force U.S. and European museums to return Holocaust-looted art, museum officials should take the ethical approach and return these artworks prior to courts forcing them to do so after long, tedious, and expensive litigation.

Current law provides protections for cultural property, but there are impediments to an effective international legal regime for the preservation of the cultural heritage. Some of the problem is that laws in countries that follow the civil law differ from those in common law countries. In addition, while there are international conventions to provide for the protection of cultural property, many countries have not ratified the conventions either in whole or in part.[56]

Common law countries have more effective legal means of preventing the illicit trafficking in cultural property than do civil law countries. The common law, the English *nemo dat* rule, which is codified in the United States in Article 2 of the Uniform Commercial Code,[57] provides that one who purchases property from a thief, no matter how innocently, acquires no title to the property.[58] The title remains with the true owner. One U.S. court commented that this law "stands as a bulwark against the handiwork of evil, to guard to rightful owners the fruits of their labors."[59] The effect of this rule is that purchasers of stolen cultural property potentially are exposed indefinitely in the United States to claims of true owners. This is equally a problem for museums that have looted property in their collections.

The common law rule contrasts with most civil law states where a possessor can obtain title through a limitations period. Countries whose legal systems are based on Roman law generally permit a period of five years after a theft for a legal owner to recover the goods from an innocent purchaser. After that period of time, the purchaser has good title to the property. Still, the person or entity who purchased the property must have been a "good faith" or "innocent" purchaser for the limitations period to begin to run.

In the United States, in all states except New York and California, a purchaser of stolen cultural property also can acquire good title to the stolen property at the expiration of a statute of limitations on the true owner's claim.[60] However, the statute of limitations does not begin to run until the true owner knew or, by the exercise of due diligence, should have known of the possessor's identity.[61] Thus, there can be a cut-off of a victim's title after a certain number of years as is the case in civil law countries if a court decides an owner has not exercised due diligence in pursuing the owner's claim.[62]

In New York, case law has long protected the rights of owners whose property has been stolen, allowing recovery even if it is in the possession of a good faith purchaser. As the court ruled in *Guggenheim Found, v. Lubell,*[63] the statute of limitations does not begin to run against a true owner's claim until the true owner makes demand of a good faith purchaser for return of the property and the possessor refuses to return it. In New York,[64] and in California by statute,[65] limitation on the time during which a rightful owner can bring a claim to recover stolen property does not begin until the rightful owner asserts a claim to the property and the current possessor refuses to return the property. Courts in New York have decided that this rule is preferable to the discovery rule, which is applicable in other states, because it "gives the owner relatively greater protection and places the burden of investigating the provenance of a work of art on the potential purchaser."[66]

Courts in the United States have "balanced the equities" between a victim of a theft and an innocent purchaser of the stolen property, when victims have brought claims for restitution of stolen cultural property. The courts initially tilt the balance in favor of theft victims because the courts have recognized the extraordinary obstacles persons who suffer from art and other cultural property looting confront in locating their property through the "labyrinth of the international art market.[67] When, as between a dispossessed owner and a good faith purchaser of cultural property, equities are balanced in favor of the dispossessed owner, a higher standard of diligence is imposed on the purchaser. Thus, both for legal reasons and ethical concerns, museum officials must exercise due diligence in investigating the provenance or title to a work prior to its acquisition. This due diligence requirement also should extend to a review of the history of works already accessioned.

Laws in the United States have not in the past prevented purchasers from acquiring good title to illegally exported artifacts.[68] A purchaser's possession of an illegally exported artifact generally was not disturbed in the past if the artifact was not stolen.[69] Still, many countries now have patrimony laws that declare state ownership of all property found at their archaeological sites.[70] After a country enacts such a patrimony law, courts can apply the National Stolen Property Act[71] to punish encroachments upon what then becomes legitimate and clear ownership rights to imported artifacts, as noted in *United States v. Schultz*.[72] If a foreign country asserts legal title to artifacts located within its boundaries, courts may apply the NSPA to the illegal importation such artifacts even though agents of that nation may never have physically possessed the artifacts.

While the law is evolving to provide for blanket legal protection for cultural treasures and, as part of this protection, a halt to the illegal trafficking in cultural property, there still are problems. The legal issues relating to claims for restitution of illegally exported cultural property, as well as for Holocaust-looted art, are complex and difficult to administer, principally because of their fragmented nature. There not only are differences in laws in civil law countries from those in common law countries, but there also are differing laws within the civil law and the common law countries. Further, some countries have adopted the international conventions that protect cultural property in whole or in part whereas others have not.[73] When a country or victim brings a claim for restitution of stolen or illegally exported property, legal principles can become barriers to a just and fair solution. An example is the initial, difficult problem of deciding which country's laws apply. To solve this predicament, ethical considerations should predominate and should be applied in the context of a dispute resolution mechanism established by the international museum community to resolve ownership issues relating to artworks and other cultural property in museum collections.

Museums officials must feel an obligation to inform potential claimants of works in their collections that have questionable provenances. They should not employ legal principles, such as burden of proof or statute of limitations defenses, to prevent the true owners the right of redress. If a victim, whether an individual or another nation, can show ownership of a work in a museum's collection, the museum should acknowledge its ethical duty to return the object. Hopefully, in this first half of the 21st century, museum officials will come forward and affirmatively endorse and implement the principles set out in the ICOM Code of Ethics so as to prohibit effectively the direct or indirect illicit trade in cultural properties. All museum officials must recognize an ethical obligation to repatriate those objects in museum collections that have been acquired through questionable, if not illegal, means and, thus, should return such objects to their rightful owners. Once this occurs, museums can step forward to take leadership in a more clearly defined and more effective international effort to protect cultural property. Museums then, but only then, will be the respected voice for the protection of the cultural heritage of humanity.

Notes

1. ICOM Code of Ethics for Museums, 3.2.
2. ICOM Code of Ethics for Museums, 3.2.
3. Code of Ethics for Museums 2000, American Association of Museums, Collections.

4. Code of Ethics for Museums 2000, American Association of Museums, Collections.

5. See Sherry Hutt, "Cultural Property Law Theory: A Comparative Assessment of Contemporary Thought," in *Legal Perspectives on Cultural Resources*, ed. Jennifer R. Richman and Marion P. Forsyth (Walnut Creek, Calif.: AltaMira Press, 2003), wherein Sherry Hutt discusses six theoretical approaches to cultural property law: internationalist, nationalist, moralist, property, scientific, and market.

6. Declaration at www.thebritishmuseum.ac.uk/newsroom/current2003/univer sal-museums.html.

7. Declaration at www.thebritishmuseum.ac.uk/newsroom/current2003/univer sal-museums.html.

8. Declaration at www.thebritishmuseum.ac.uk/newsroom/current2003/univer sal-museums.html.

9. Geoffrey Lewis, "The Universal Museum: A Special Case?" *ICOM News* 57, no. 1 (2004): 3.

10. *United States v. An Antique Platter of Gold*, 184 K3d 131 (2nd Cir. 1999), cert, denied, 528 U.S. 1136 (2000).

11. Brief of Amici Curiae American Association of Museums, et al., In Support of the Appeal of Claimant Michael H. Steinhardt, prepared by Weil, Gotshal & Manges LLP, New York, Attorneys for Amici Curiae.

12. The country of origin of the Phiale was listed on Customs Form 3461 as "CH," the code for Switzerland.

13. Protection of Works of Artistic and Historical Interest, Law June 1, 1939, n. 1089 (law n. 1089/39).

14. Brief of Amici Curiae American Association of Museums, et al., i and ii.

15. Brief of Amici Curiae American Association of Museums, et al., i and ii.

16. Brief of Amici Curiae American Association of Museums, et al., ii.

17. Brief of Amici Curiae American Association of Museums, et al., iii.

18. Brief of Amici Curiae American Association of Museums, et al., v.

19. Brief of Amici Curiae American Association of Museums, et al., xxxiii.

20. Brief of Amici Curiae American Association of Museums, et al., xiv.

21. Brief of Amici Curiae American Association of Museums, et al., xiv.

22. Brief of Amici Curiae American Association of Museums, et al., lix. Despite the arguments of the AAM, the Second Circuit Court of Appeals affirmed the decision of the district court.

23. *United States v. Schultz*, 333 F3d 393 (2nd Cir. 2003), cert, denied, 124 S. Ct. 1041 (2004).

24. 18 U.S.C. §2315.

25. 333 F.3d at 396.

26. Schultz met Jonathan Tokeley Parry (Parry), a British national, through a mutual friend in 1992. Parry showed Schultz a photograph of an ancient sculpture of the head of Pharaoh Amenhotep III, and told Schultz that he had obtained the sculpture in Egypt earlier that year from a man who represented himself to be a building contractor. Parry had used an Egyptian middle-man named Ali Farag (Farag) to facilitate the transaction. Parry had smuggled the sculpture out of Egypt by coating it plastic so that it would look like a cheap souvenir. He removed the plastic coating once the sculpture was in England. Schultz offered Parry a substantial fee to serve as the agent for the sale of the Amenhotep sculpture. Parry and Schultz then set out to create a false provenance for the sculpture so that they

could sell it. They decided they would claim the sculpture had been brought out of Egypt in the 1920s by a relative of Parry and had been kept in an English private collection since that time. Parry and Schultz invented a fictional collection, the "Thomas Alcock Collection," and represented to potential buyers that the sculpture came from this collection. With Schultz's knowledge, Parry prepared fake labels, designed to look as though they had been printed in the 1920s and affixed the labels to the sculpture. Parry also restored the sculpture using a method popular in the 1920s. Parry later sold the sculpture to Schultz for $800,000, and Schultz sold it to a private collection in 1992 for $1.2 million. Parry and Schultz became partners in an effort to bring more Egyptian antiquities into the United States for resale, smuggling them out of Egypt disguised as cheap souvenirs, assigning a false provenance to them, and restoring them with 1920s techniques. Parry was arrested in Great Britain in 1994 and Farag was arrested in Egypt. Each was charged with dealing stolen antiquities. Although Parry was arrested, he, with Schultz, continued to obtain Egyptian antiquities. A jury found Schultz guilty, and he was sentenced to a term of thirty-three months' imprisonment. He appealed his conviction. Upon appeal, seven organizations filed amicus curiae briefs in his defense: the National Association of Dealers in Ancient, Oriental & Primitive Art, Inc., the International Association of Professional Numismatists, the Art Dealers Association of America, the Antique Tribal Art Dealers Association, the Profession Numismatists Guild, the American Society of Appraisers, and an ad hoc group called Citizens for a Balanced Policy with Regard to the Importation of Cultural Property. These groups contended in their briefs that permitting Schultz's conviction to stand would threaten the ability of legitimate American collectors and sellers of antiquities to do business. See discussion at 333 F.3d 396-8.

27. Brief of Amici Curiae Citizens for a Balanced Policy with Regard to the Importation of Cultural Property in support of the Appellant Frederick Schultz prepared by James F. Fitzgerald, Counsel, Arnold & Porter, Washington, DC, attorneys for amici curiae.

28. Brief of Amici Curiae Citizens for a Balanced Policy.

29. 19 U.S.C. § 2601 et. seq.

30. 1982 U.S.C.C.A.N (96 Stat.) 4908, 4100. See Paul M. Bator, "An Essay on the International Trade in Art," *Stanford Law Review* 34 (1982): 275-384, in which the author notes that stolen and mutilated art from the jungles of Central America had been traced into some of America's most respectable museums.

31. 1982 U.S.C.C.A.N. 4100.

32. 19 U.S.C. § 2602. The import restrictions would provide that no designated archaeological or ethnological material exported from the requesting nation can be imported into the United States unless the requesting nation has issued a certificate that the exportation was not in violation of that nation's laws. 19 U.S.C. § 2606. Any designated archaeological or ethnological material or article of cultural property that is imported into the United States is subject to seizure and forfeiture.

33. Cultural Property Procedural Reform Act, S. 1696 (December 15, 2000).

34. Council of Europe Resolution 1205, 17 (November 1999).

35. See paper by Owen C. Pell at the Spring meeting of the Section of International Law and Practice on "The Special Responsibilities of States with Regard to Holocaust Looted Art." Pell contends there is a consensus among scholars and nations that a significant amount of Holocaust-looted art remains in the hands of governments, public institutions, and museums throughout Europe and the United States and that Holocaust-looted art continues to be transferred in the art market without identification or notice of

Holocaust-related gaps in provenance. Pell notes that victims of Holocaust looting have faced special and significant factual and legal hurdles in identifying and recovering looted art.

36. The AAM has promulgated guidelines for museums concerning Holocaust-looted property. See America Association of Museums, Guidelines Concerning the Unlawful Appropriation of Objects During the Nazi Era, www.aam-us.org/nazi_guidelines.htm. The guidelines request museums to allocate the necessary funds to conduct research on items in their collection that may have changed hands during the period of 1933–1945 and encourage museums to publicize the provenance of these artifacts. Further, several U.S. museums have websites that list works in their collection with gaps in provenance for the years 1933–1945. See American Association of Museums, Nazi Era Provenance, www.aam-us.org/nazieraprov.htm.

The AAM now has established a Nazi-Era Provenance List, which is a new e-mail discussion group for World War II-era provenance research. The list was created to speed the process of identifying objects in U.S. museums that may have changed hands in Europe during the Nazi era by connecting museum professionals working directly on Nazi-era provenance questions with one another and permitting them to exchange information and share best practices. Membership in the list is limited to museum professionals working in this field.

Recently, the Virginia Museum of Fine Arts gave back the *Portrait of Jean d'Abon* by Corneille de Lyon, to art collector Julius Priester's sole heir, Karl Schlinder of Hampshire, England. Schlinder presented evidence, which included a photograph of the painting and a 1950 police report, to show the painting was stolen by the Nazis in 1944 and to prove his claim of ownership of the painting. The museum acquired the painting in 1950 from a gallery in New York. Upon learning the painting was stolen, the museum willingly returned it to Schlinder. The museum board concluded that returning the painting was "simply the correct thing to do." Schlinder's claim was handled by the New York State Banking Department's Holocaust Claims Processing Office, which, since 1997, has represented claimants seeking restitution of Holocaust-era assets at no cost. See discussion at www.vmfa.state.va.us.

In *Rosenburg v. Seattle Art Museum*, 42 F. Supp.2d 1029 (W.D.Wash. 1999), heirs of Paul Rosenburg filed a complaint against the Seattle Art Museum for return of a $1 million Matisse, which was donated to the museum by the Estate of Bloedel. The Bloedels purchased the painting from a gallery in New York in 1954. Heirs of Rosenburg, a Parisian art collector and gallery owner prior to World War II, alleged the painting was stolen by the Nazis and later possessed by the museum. Upon research into the provenance of the painting, the Seattle Art Museum agreed the Rosenburg heirs were the rightful owners of the painting and returned it to them. The museum then filed a third Party complaint against the gallery, which sold the painting to the Bloedels, for breach of title, fraud, and negligent misrepresentation. The court initially ruled the museum did not have standing to sue the gallery for defrauding the Bloedels. It noted that the law in Washington provides that transferring ownership of personal property does not transfer thereby a claim for fraud associated with the purchase of that property. However, it agreed to hear the museum's complaint after the museum obtained an assignment of the Bloedels' fraud claim from the Bloedel heirs. The case then was settled.

37. *United States v. Portrait of Wally*, 105 F. Supp. 2d 288 (S.D.N.Y. 2000) and 2002 WL 553532 (S.D.N.Y. 2002).

38. An art gallery owned by Lea Bondi Jaray was confiscated and given to Friedrich Welz. In 1939 Welz joined the Nazi party and visited Bondi at her apartment. He saw the painting hanging on a wall and "insisted" that the 1938 "arayanization" of Bondi's gallery entitled him to it. Bondi later turned over the painting and fled to London. After World War II, Welz was interned on suspicion of having committed war crimes and his possessions, including artworks, were seized by U.S. forces in Austria. See discussion at 105 F Supp. 2d 289-90.

39. See discussion at 2002 WL 553532.

40. See 2002 WL 553532.

41. *Republic of Austria v. Altmann*, 317 F.3d 954 (9th Cir. 2002) and 327 F.3d 1246 (9th Cir. 2002).

42. Maria Altmann, who resides in Los Angeles, California, filed her claim in a federal court in California in 2000. She alleged the wrongful taking of six Gustav Klimt paintings, valued at $135 million. Maria Altmann had intended to file her claim in Austria, but, because Austrian court costs are proportional to the value of the recovery sought, she could not afford the filing fee ($135,000 to $350,000). See discussion at 124 S. Ct. 2244-45.

43. 28 U.S.C. §§ 1602-1611.

44. Maria Altmann asserted jurisdiction under § 2 of the Act, 28 U.S.C. § 1605(a)(3), which expressly exempts foreign governments from immunity in certain cases involving "rights in property taken in violation of international law."

45. 317 F.3d at 965.

46. 317 F.3d at 965. The Supreme Court held that the exception to immunity under the Foreign Sovereign Immunities Act applies to conduct, like the Republic of Austria's alleged wrongdoing, that occurred prior to its enactment in 1976.

After the Supreme Court decision, the issue of restitution of the Klimt paintings to Altmann was referred to the Austrian mediation panel. In January of 2006, the panel ordered the Austrian government to return the paintings to Altmann.

The heirs of Kazimir Malevich, the Russian artist, have filed suit in the U.S. District Court in Washington, D.C., *Malevicz, et al. v. City of Amsterdam*, Civil Action No. 04-0024, against the City of Amsterdam to recover fourteen valuable Malevich artworks. The complaint sets out the history of how the City of Amsterdam, through its Stedelijk Museum, acquired the historic legacy of Kazimir Malevich. When Malevich's work was condemned by the Nazi regime as "degenerate" art, the works were hidden in the basement of the Berliner Kunstausstellung, where they had been on display and where they remained until Malevich was forced to flee Nazi Germany. After the Berlin exhibition ended, several of the pieces were loaned to the Stedelijk. Some were loaned to the Museum of Modern Art in New York and the Busch-Reisinger Museum at Harvard University. The Malevich heirs have been attempting to recover the artworks from institutions around the world. The Museum of Modern Art and the Busch-Reisinger have returned the works they had in their collections to the heirs. The City of Amsterdam, however, has refused to return any of the works in its possession to the Malevich heirs.

Recently a Restitutions Committee appointed by the Dutch government recommended that the Dutch government return more than 200 old-master paintings to the heir of Jacques Goudstikker, a Dutch Jewish dealer and collector who fled Amsterdam ahead of advancing German troops in 1940. The Dutch government announced in February of 2006 that it would return the paintings because, as Medy van der Laan, the Dutch deputy culture minister, stated, returning the works was the morally correct action. See Alan Riding, "Dutch to Return Art Seized by Nazis," *New York Times,* February 6, 2006.

47. See Pell, "The Special Responsibilities of States with Regard to Holocaust Looted Art." Pell cites *The Nurnberg Trial,* 6 P.R.D. 69, 122, 157-58 (1946).

48. 1907 Hague Convention, Article 23 at 2301-2.

49. 1919 Treaty of Versailles, Section 11, Article 238 (June 28, 1919).

50. The Nurnberg Trial, 6 FR.D. 69 (1946).

51. Pell, "The Special Responsibilities of States with Regard to Holocaust Looted Art."

52. Council of Europe Resolution 1205 (November 1999), 11.

53. Council of Europe Resolution 1205 (November 1999), 12.

54. Vilnius Forum Declaration, 1.

55. Council of Europe Resolution 1205 (November 1999), 5.

56. The United States has ratified in part the 1970 UNESCO Convention on the Means of Prohibiting and Preventing the Illicit Import, Export and Transfer of Ownership of Cultural Property. Congress enacted the Convention on Cultural Property Implementation Act, 19 U.S.C. §§ 1601-13, in 1982, effective in 1983, to implement part of the 1970 UNESCO Convention. The act provides that, when a participating nation makes a request to the United States for import restrictions on cultural property from that nation, because the requesting nation contends its cultural patrimony is in jeopardy from pillage of its cultural properties, the president may enter into a bilateral agreement with that nation to apply import restrictions on all cultural property taken from that country.

Congress enacted implementing legislation in 1980 for U.S. participation in the 1972 UNESCO Convention for the Protection of the World Cultural and Natural Heritage. 16 U.S.C. § 470a-l. The implementing legislation was part of 1980 amendments to the National Historic Preservation Act, Pub. L. No. 96-515, 1980 U.S.C.- C.A.N. (94 Stat.) 6406. Pursuant to this convention, the United States lists properties of cultural significance within the United States in a "World Heritage List."

The United States has not ratified the 1954 Hague Convention for the Protection of Cultural Property in the Event of Armed Conflict nor the 2002 UNESCO Convention for the Protection of the Underwater Cultural Heritage. (Pursuant to the 1954 Hague Convention, cultural property bears a distinctive emblem, a blue shield, during military conflict to facilitate its recognition. Cultural property being transited and bearing the blue shield is immune from seizure. Monuments bearing the blue shield are subject to special protection during a military conflict.)

57. *Nemo dat quoid non habet.* [He who hath not cannot give.] The *nemo dat* rule is set out in Article 2 of the Uniform Commercial Code at 2.403.

58. See *Menzel v. List,* 267 N.Y.S.2d 804, 819-20 (N.Y. 1966), in which a New York court stated that the "principle has been basic in the law that a thief conveys no title against the true owner."

59. *Menzel v. List,* 267 N.Y.S.2d 804, 819-20 (N.Y. 1966).

60. In *O'Keeffe v. Snyder,* 416 A.2d 862 (N.J. 1980), the Supreme Court of New Jersey commented that a possessor has the right to retain property except as against the true owner. As the court stated, the only imperfection on a bona fide purchaser's claim is the original owner's right to repossess the property. According to the New Jersey Supreme Court, once that imperfection is removed, the possessor should have good title for all purposes.

61. In *O'Keeffe v. Snyder,* 416 A.2d 862 (N.J. 1980), the New Jersey Supreme Court ruled that the statute of limitations on a suit to recover stolen paintings would begin to run

when the true owner "discovers, or by exercise of reasonable diligence and intelligence should have discovered," facts that form the basis of rights of owners whose property has been stolen to recover property even if it is in possession of a good faith purchaser.

62. In *O'Keeffe v. Snyder,* the court decided that an innocent purchaser should be protected from an owner who "sleeps on his rights." 416 A.2d at 857. Thus, the New Jersey Court would place "due diligence" requirements on the true owner. In more recent court decisions, courts have shifted the "due diligence" requirement to the purchaser of valuable cultural property. See, for example, *Autocephalous Greek- Orthodox Church of Cyprus v. Goldberg,* 917 F.2d 278, 294 (7th Cir. 1990) and *Guggenheim Found, v. Lubell,* 569 N.E.2d 426 (N.Y. 1991).

63. 569 N.E.2d 426 (N.Y. 1991).

64. *Guggenheim Found v. Lubell,* 569 N.E.2d 426 (N.Y. 1991).

65. California has adopted a three-year statutory limitation period that begins to run at "the discovery of the whereabouts of the article by the aggrieved party." Cal. Civ. Proc. Code § 338.

66. *Guggenheim Found v. Lubell,* 569 N.F.2d at 431.

67. See discussion in Robert E. Madden, "Steps to Take When Stolen Art Is Found in an Estate," *Estate Planning* 24 (1997): 459-64.

68. See discussion in *United States v. McClain,* 545 F.2d 988, 996 (5th Cir. 1977).

69. *United States v. McClain,* 545 E2d 988, 996 (5th Cir. 1977). In *Peru v. Johnson,* 720 F. Supp. 810, 814 (C.D. Cal. 1989), the court noted that restrictions on the export of certain artifacts are concerned with protection of such artifacts and that such restrictions do not imply ownership. The court commented that possession of such artifacts is allowed to remain in private ownership and that such objects may be transferred. The court characterized an export restriction as an exercise of the police power of the state. It stated that such restrictions do not create ownership in the state. See also *Jeanneret v. Mickey,* 693 F.2d 259 (2nd Cir. 1982).

The general rule that export restrictions do not prevent a possessor in another country from acquiring good title to such artifacts can be qualified by statutes or treaties. For example, in the United States, the Pre-Columbian Art Act, 19 U.S.C. 2091-2095, provides that any pre-Columbian monumental or architectural sculpture or mural imported into the United States in violation of the act is to be seized and is subject to forfeiture under the U.S. customs laws. The Convention on Cultural Implementation Act, 19 U.S.C. 2601 et. seq., provides that import restrictions will be placed on designated archaeological or ethnological material exported from a nation which requests such restrictions. If such objects are imported into the United States, they are subject to seizure and forfeiture.

70. For example, the trade in antiquities became illegal in Italy in 1939 with the enactment of the Law for the Protection of Works of Artistic and Historic Interests (law n.1089/39). Under this law, all archaeological objects belong to the state unless they were in private ownership prior to 1902. Further, only the state (or a private citizen by special permit) can conduct excavations.

As noted in *United States v. Antique Platter of Gold,* 184 F!3d 131 (2nd Cir. 1999), *cert, denied,* 528 U.S. 1136 (2000), the Egyptian government has declared ownership of all its archaeological artifacts pursuant to its Antiquities' Protection Law 117, which was adopted in 1983.

The 1932 Act with Respect to Antiquities in Greece provides that all antiquities belong to the state. Individuals cannot acquire ownership of antiquities.

In 1926 the Republic of Turkey declared in force and effect a 1906 decree that all antiquities found in or on lands in Turkey were owned by the Republic. Also, in 1926, the Republic adopted a Turkish Civil Code which remains in effect today. Article 697 of the Turkish Civil Code declares that antiquities found on Turkish land are the property of the Republic.

71. 18 U.S.C. §§ 2314-15. The NSPA provides that it is a felony knowingly to sell or receive stolen goods in interstate or foreign commerce.

72. *United States v. Schultz*, 333 F.3d 393 (2nd Cir. 2003), cert, denied, 124 S.Ct. 1041 (2004).

73. See discussion in note 56 of U.S. ratification of the international conventions.

Collections Planning
Pinning Down a Strategy

35

JAMES B. GARDNER AND ELIZABETH MERRITT

OLLECTING IS CENTRAL TO THE MISSION of most museums. Museums devote significant resources to the acquisition and maintenance of collections. It is surprising then that collections planning is among the rarest of museum activities. It is surely one of the most critically needed.

As financial and other resources become scarce and competition for them grows more intense, exerting greater control over the content and size of a museum's collection has become an issue for all institutions, large and small. All across the country, museums are discovering that they cannot afford to care for every object that they might acquire, even if it is directly related to institutional mission. As a result, some tough choices have to be made about what to collect, what not to collect, and what to remove from the collections. Even when financial resources are not a limiting factor, collecting decisions made by individuals, however knowledgeable, do not automatically result in a coherent, well-rounded collection that best serves the needs of the institution. What is needed is a carefully prepared collections plan—one that has earned the support of the director, the board, and the senior staff.

The lack of collections planning is not limited to small and mid-size museums. Even a large institution such as the Smithsonian faces the same challenges. One might assume that, as the nation's history museum, the National Museum of American History (NMAH) would have a relatively clear collecting mandate—to preserve and interpret American history and culture. But in fact, its staff acquire objects without clearly articulated institutional parameters or vision. Though the curatorial units nominally have collecting plans, these mostly are, as one staff member described them, little more than "shelf inventories." Self-directed curators build on their predecessors' interests and work, adding depth and new topics, but

James B. Gardner is senior scholar National Museum of American History, Smithsonian Institution. Elizabeth Merritt is the founding director of the Center for the Future of Museums at the American Association of Museums. "Collections Planning: Pinning Down a Strategy" is reprinted here with permission from *Museum News*, July/August 2002. Copyright 2002, the American Association of Museums. All rights reserved.

often operating in isolation from other staff and other units. As a result, while the museum's collections are exceptional in terms of their quality and depth, they are also rather idiosyncratic; the parts don't add up to a whole. There is no substitute for a serious, institutionally coordinated attempt at collections planning.

NMAH is far from alone; museums around the country face the same problem, perhaps different in scale but similar in kind. Museums often believe their collections policies constitute collecting plans, but they rarely do. Collections policies list conditions that must be met for an object to be acquired—for example, good provenance, high quality, relevant to mission—and generally outline the scope of the collection. Such "Scope of the Collection" statements draw broad boundaries—for example, geographic origin, time period, subject matter—around what might be acquired and summarize what is already in the collection. However, these statements usually provide only the most basic guidance for determining what types of items might be acquired. And the description of the collection sometimes includes material that the museum owns but does not want to retain. Policies cannot replace a current, ongoing, institutionally supported planning process.

What many institutions need is better focused and more disciplined collections planning. Planning is an inclusive effort, one that brings together staff from across departmental boundaries and may also reach out to external stakeholders. The planning process may lead board and staff to reexamine basic assumptions about the museum's mission and its role in the community. The process also may challenge assumptions about traditional staff roles and areas of authority. At NMAH, for example, a culture of autonomous curators working in relatively isolated collecting units presents a particularly daunting organizational challenge. Unless all those units buy in to a new collecting plan, it is doomed to fail. In other words, the human aspects of planning require at least as much care and thought as the physical, financial, and administrative aspects. It is one thing to write a plan; it is quite another to implement it. And the work doesn't end with implementation. Collections planning must be an ongoing process, not fossilized in a document that sits on the shelf, overlooked by the curators.

Data from AAM's Accreditation Program suggest that collections planning is a concern throughout the field. The Accreditation Program recognizes museums that are committed to the highest standards of operation and public service. Nationally about 750 museums are accredited, and about twenty-five more apply to the program each year. Each year about 100 museums are reviewed by the nine-member Accreditation Commission, either as first-time applicants for accreditation or as part of the process for subsequent accreditation. According to the Commission, a lack of collections planning is a major impediment to the success of many of the institutions that they review. These museums commit significant time and resources to achieving excellence while also submitting to a detailed, systematic review by peers. As such, they may serve as an early-warning system for issues in the field at large.

The Accreditation Commission has identified a pattern of recurring problems connected to collections stewardship and institutional planning: insufficient resources to support collections; collections unrelated to the institution's mission; and a lack of integration between planning for collections, interpretation, and facilities. These issues interfere in concrete ways with the museum's ability to succeed: the collections may suffer from poor care; limited resources may be spent on acquiring material that is unrelated to institutional mission; and the institution may perform ineffectively because its collections, exhibits, and educational activities are neither connected to each other nor supported by a financial plan. The Commission believes that these issues can be addressed through a collections-planning process that is strategic, audience-centered, visionary, tied to resource allocation, and encompasses all collections and all functional areas of the institution.

Definitions

(adapted from glossaries used by AAM's Museum Assessment and Accreditation programs):

Collecting Plan: A plan guiding the content of the collections that leads the staff in a coordinated and uniform direction over a period of years to refine and expand the value of the collections in a predetermined way. By creating a plan, a museum seeks to gain intellectual control over collections.

Collections Planning: The integrated, institution-wide process of creating a collecting plan.

Collections Management Policy or Collections Policy: A written document, accepted by the governing body, that specifies the museum's policies concerning all collections related issues including accessioning, documentation, storage, and disposition. Often includes a Scope of Collections Statement.

Scope of Collections Statement: Defines the purpose of the collection and set agreed upon limits such as subject, geographical location, and time period to which each collection must relate. The statement also may consider the uses of a collection and state the types of objects that will be acquired to fulfill the purposes of that collection. These statements tend to be very broad and often describe what is in the collection now rather than focus on plans for the future.

Recently AAM and NMAH issued a call for sample collecting plans from museums of all types, sizes, and geographic locations. These plans vary greatly in style and content, but they do have certain similarities. Although there is no field-wide "template" for a collecting plan, many museums have discovered independently that certain components are useful and necessary. After a preliminary examination, it is clear that most collecting plans:

1. **Identify the museum's audience(s) and how their needs will be served by the collections.** Selecting the "right stuff" can be done only in

the context of the intended use of the collections. A collection intended to support in-depth, scholarly research will be very different from one meant to provide the public with a general survey of a topic. This "needs assessment" also may encompass the museum's plans for exhibits and educational programs—in what ways does the collection need to grow to support those activities? In other words, an effective collecting plan must be tied to the institution's strategic planning.

2. **Review the strengths and weaknesses of the existing collections.** All curators have an understanding of their collections, but rarely put this information down on paper or share it with their colleagues throughout the museum. In an institution as large as NMAH, for example, things sometimes fall between the cracks without notice or discussion—from the little-used collections that sit unnoticed in large curatorial units to the collecting opportunities that remain unaddressed simply because they fall outside existing specializations or interests.

3. **Include a "gap analysis" contrasting the real and the ideal collection.** NMAH has taken the first step by developing a central theme—"What has it meant to be an American?"—as well as sub-themes that provide the context for assessing the existing collection and envisioning "the ideal."

4. **Set priorities for acquisition and deaccessioning based on the needs assessment and gap analysis.** This is the key to the planning process, since setting priorities can drive change and focus efforts. Prioritizing acquisitions is a way to show donors that the material you seek is key to your success. Deaccessioning is sometimes a controversial activity that museums often avoid due to concerns about bad publicity. A good collections-planning process can explain to the public that the museum is making responsible and appropriate choices about deaccessioning that will best serve its audience(s).

5. **Identify "complementary collections" held by other museums or organizations that may affect the museum's collections choices.** In a world of rapidly constricting resources, museums are turning to partnerships and cooperative agreements with other institutions. Many museums consciously choose not to collect in areas that are strongly represented in other museums, particularly if those museums serve the same audience. Some institutions have begun to cooperate by building mutually supportive, complementary collections that can be used as joint resources. Others proactively identify other museums that may be suitable recipients for donations they wish to route away from their own organizations.

6. **Take into account existing or needed resources.** A powerful collecting plan is one that ties its objectives to a concrete analysis of the financial, human, and physical resources needed to support the collection. Building a compelling vision of the future can help leverage funds and support. On the other hand, failing to plan for the necessary resources for new acquisitions can render the museum unable to fulfill its collections stewardship responsibilities.

Admittedly, NMAH's goal in partnering with AAM in this initiative is a self-serving one—the museum expects to gain not only a useful understanding of best practices but also a new collecting plan, a clearly articulated vision of how its collections should be shaped and developed. The museum takes pride in the collections that it has built, but it also recognizes that it cannot assume that its current collecting approach will meet its future responsibilities. Its staff must continue to make tough choices about what to collect. But those choices have to be better informed and made within the context of NMAH's larger role as the nation's history museum.

But there is a bonus to taking this project on: the opportunity to help AAM lead the larger museum community in a critically needed discussion about collections planning. We hope that ultimately other museums of all sizes and type, in all regions across the country, will be able to benefit from what we learn. After all, this is planning that gets at the heart of what so many of us are all about—collecting and collections.

It's Easy Being Green   36

SARAH BROPHY AND ELIZABETH WYLIE

G OING GREEN IS TOO EXPENSIVE. The payback takes too long. Green is only for new buildings or science museums. Green is a great idea, but it would look extravagant and contrived in our museum.

If you are scared off by any of these arguments about sustainable building and practices, take another look at what sustainability means, what the green-building industry is achieving across the country and how museums are becoming part of the solution to global climate change while advancing their missions.

"Most people, when they think of this topic, focus on buildings," says Patrick Kociolek, executive director and curator of the California Academy of Sciences (CAS) and an American Association of Museums (AAM) Board member. "Sustainability doesn't have to be about building a building. Sustainability should run all through operations. Should we turn off the faucet? Should we save energy?" Those energy savings speak to museums' bottom line, he says. "I would tell other institutions, 'Don't wait to get involved.'" Kociolek, his board and staff are $310 million into their $392 million capital campaign and well on their way in a comprehensive rebuilding project that will finish in late 2008.

We spoke with museum leaders across the country to learn why and how they are going green. For many, the cost savings were an early motivator. But for most the financial benefits were matched or superseded by the opportunities for education and mission fulfillment through promoting sustainability, reacting to global climate change and leading by example.

Though we tend to use "green" and "sustainable" interchangeably in this article, there is a difference. Green refers to products and behaviors that are environmentally benign, while sustainable means practices that rely on renewable/reusable materials and processes that are green or environmentally benign.

Sarah Brophy is the principal of bMuse, a sustainable museum consulting firm. Elizabeth Wylie directs business development activities for Finegold Alexander + Associates, a planning and architecture firm specializing in sustainable design. "It's Easy Being Green: Museums and the Green Movement" is reprinted here with permission from *Museum News* (September/October 2006). Copyright 2006, the American Association of Museums. All rights reserved.

The green movement, once considered fringe, now has some very mainstream advocates. Journalist and best-selling author Thomas L. Friedman told National Public Radio's *Fresh* Air that "green technology is going to be the industry of the twenty-first century." This includes green design, green building and green manufacturing. Why not green education? Why shouldn't museums—as places of learning, exploration, and demonstration, and as models of community-minded behavior—be ahead of the curve? If our job is to teach and inspire, then we are perfectly situated to model green behavior both in pursuit of our missions and in support of communities—and not just for the science, environmental and children's museums. As Betty Arenth, senior vice president at the Senator John Heinz History Center, Pittsburgh, says: "We're a history organization. Think about it: It's preservation of the environment for the future."

Whether you choose to grow a green ethic in your institution, integrate sustainable practices in your design work or improve recycling in the staff lounge, you will have opened the door to educating yourself and your colleagues about the possibilities and value of sustainable performance. You will see beyond your museum's role as collector, teacher, and town square to advancing your museum's place in whole-community thinking.

Many environmental scientists agree that the increasing severity of hurricanes—Katrina, Andrew, Rita et al.—is directly connected to global warming. The United Nations Earth Summit in 1992, the 1997 Kyoto Protocol and other international gatherings and compacts signal a clear recognition that we are all responsible for reversing the damage of non-sustainable development. The negative environmental results of non-sustainable energy use are likely climate change. In the United States alone, building construction and operation accounts for one-third of the greenhouse gas emissions and more than half of the electricity consumed annually according to the U.S. Green Building Council's website: www.usgbc.org.[1] Museums are notoriously heavy energy consumers using more than twice as much as conventional office buildings, which typically cool, heat and illuminate Monday-Friday 9 a.m. to 5 p.m. Museums often have extended hours, and collecting institutions need to maintain climate control 24/7. (Aquariums, for example, are off the map in terms of energy use.) With this degree of impact, sustainable design, construction and operation in museums can have positive global consequences.

With that growing awareness of environmental impact issues, a green buildings movement is taking hold worldwide. The World Green Building Council now counts seven national member councils and eight more under development, including one in China, where it is predicted that half of the world's construction will take place over the next ten years. In the United States, the federal government's General Services Administration requires all new and substantial renovations to federal buildings to conform to sustainable design guidelines, and a growing list of states and cities have sustainable policies in place. Colleges and universities, school systems, corporations and other property owners have also developed guidelines on sustainability.

The U.S. Green Building Council's LEED Program (Leadership in Energy & Environmental Design) developed methods to rate green building and construction practices. LEED uses a rating system with Platinum at the top, followed by Gold, Silver, Bronze and Certified—the minimum level. The rating system covers six areas: sustainable sites (from access to public transportation and light pollution control to stormwater management); water efficiency (use reduction inside and outside); energy and atmosphere (energy performance, renewable energies such as wind and solar); materials and resources (recycling of construction waste, materials with recycled and renewable content); indoor environmental quality (CO_2 monitoring, low emitting materials, thermal comfort and daylighting); and innovation and design (including providing for an educational component). Institutions undergoing a build or renewal may choose a specific LEED goal before starting. Some hope for Certified, others go for Platinum, but they choose a performance level and then they design, build and behave in ways geared toward demonstrating that level of achievement when the building is done.

In 2004 the Brooklyn Children's Museum (BCM) began construction to double the size of the museum. During the initial planning process, the building owner, the City of New York, was "looking for ways to promote environmental quality, contain future energy costs and save taxpayers money by making a special effort to pursue high-performance buildings" says Paul Pearson, vice president of programs at BCM. After completion in late 2007, the new building's high-performance features, which include a geothermal heating and cooling system, will save more than $100,000 annually in energy costs. It was a collaborative decision to go green.

"City planners were interested in the [LEED] rating structure," said Pearson. "We saw it as fitting with our interests in being leaders in our field, a chance to [invest] where our ideals around environmental stewardship reside." The measuring and quantifying that are part of the LEED rating system offer helpful guides. However, many owners pursue LEED standards without undertaking the documentation that ends in certification. Often the decision to pursue certification is based on the public relations value of the LEED brand and the value of evaluation and accountability already associated with museum culture. Reporting on project outcomes is as great motivator to do it right.

In the past decade twenty or more organizations under the museum umbrella have added green buildings or were born green. Many more follow green practices in their day-to-day operations in existing buildings. Though we can cover only a small portion here, there are many, many innovative projects that offer significant lessons.

Reduced energy costs are an important, practical driver behind the majority of museums undergoing expansion using high-performance, energy-efficient systems. Consider your own museum. Do growing utility bills compete with program allocations or even staff positions? Have you scaled back major exhibits or other projects because of expected jumps in energy costs? You are not alone. Sustainable systems, services and materials can help reduce those ever-rising utility costs. And sustainability is becoming easier and easier to implement.

When the CAS considered the sustainability of its future cafe, six providers wanted the contract—all prepared to provide guaranteed positive financial return and programmatic support that would create a seamless message of sustainability from exhibit areas to the eating area. The vendors all promised to demonstrate and interpret sustainable practices by explaining and labeling products and processes for the visitors. This can mean explaining food choices based on buying local and/ or organic produce with no to low-environmental impact from pesticides and transportation requirements. It can be eco-friendly oven-cleaning products and recycling and composting. Visitors will learn about all the practices at the museum and be able to implement them at home.

This level of vendor interest is evidence of "natural capitalism," a term popularized by Amory and L. Hunter Lovins and Paul Hawken in their 1999 book *Natural Capitalism: Creating the Next Industrial Revolution*. Without much legislation to prompt them, the world's individuals and organizations are finding ways to make their resources more productive in terms of money, time, materials and processes. Some businesses, institutions and people do it because they believe it's a moral issue, others because consumer interest demands it and the cost of going green is decreasing. If they don't do it, Hawken and the Lovinses say, "There is now sufficient evidence of change to suggest that if your corporation or institution is not paying attention to this revolution, it will lose competitive advantage."

Since the flower-power era, the sustainable technology industry has been working to perfect green processes and resources. Consumer and material choices are far better today. "It was hard to pioneer green practice when materials were scarce and technology expensive; now it is getting easier because demand is increasing," says Julie Silverman, a director at ECHO at the Leahy Center for Lake Champlain in Burlington, Vermont. ECHO is a lake aquarium and science center that in 2003, just five months after completion, became the first and only LEED-certified building in Vermont and only the third certified building in New England. Since then the number of LEED-certified buildings has dramatically increased.

"The cost to design and green will come down as demand rises," says Martin Moeller who was trained as an architect and now is senior vice president and curator at the National Building Museum in Washington, D.C. In 2003 the National Building Museum organized "Big & Green: Toward Sustainable Architecture in the 21st Century." "The Green House: New Directions in Sustainable Architecture and Design" will be up through June 3, 2007. As Wal-Mart, Home Depot, and other huge corporations are responding to the demand for green products, the cost is decreasing rapidly. Also as municipalities are changing their practices, the soft costs connected to permits, legal fees, and the like are also declining.

Choosing durable materials will reduce replacement costs and demand on the environment. Choosing sustainable materials, like fast-growing bamboo flooring and plywood, capitalizes on renewable resources, not those that take many years, or even centuries, to replace. Using carpet tiles instead of single-piece installation allows single-area replacement for stains instead of a complete re-installation, which reduces your cost and reduces the environmental demands of both manufacturing and disposal. According to ECHO's Silverman, "Making well-thought-out sustainable choices is not only good for the environment, it also makes good economic sense. With rising fuel costs, Katrina and other global issues, an efficient building can really have a significant impact on the survival of an institution when times are tough."

Those tough times may be coming sooner than we thought. Joseph C. Thompson, director of MASS MoCA in North Adams, Massachusetts, says "MASS MoCA's energy costs—always staggering—have tripled in the last three years and it's no exaggeration to say that the sustainability of this institution is linked to our success in finding radical cost savings in our utility bills." BCM's Pearson agrees, "Even now, since energy costs have risen so rapidly we see [that] our payback time will be shortened. Even since we began our project, the materials and technologies are becoming much more accessible, making green design that much more cost-effective." ECHO's energy-efficient construction—including computerized monitoring of temperature, light and airflow and an energy recovery wheel, which uses recycled energy to heat and cool—means big savings. "ECHO's annual utility bill averages $50,000 for a 28,000-square-foot building—23 percent less than if built to city code," says Executive Director Phelan Fretz.

Integrated design methods can control your project costs and help you earn your return on the investment immediately or soon after. A study of green building performance shows that the "green premium" (the cost of green choices) can be reduced or even eliminated through integrated design, a process that brings architects, engineers, lighting and landscape designers and other consultants together to work collaboratively with the owner. The team considers the project from every angle to produce a healthy and safe resource-efficient, flexible and durable building and site according to "Managing the Cost of Green Buildings," a 2002 research paper commissioned by the California State and Consumer Services Agency's Sustainable Building Task Force and the Alameda County Waste Management Authority.[2]

It's not just the consultants promoting integrated design. When asked why museums should be green, The Kresge Foundation's Sandy Ambrozy talks instead about giving incentives "for people to become informed." Rather than directing or commenting on the choices museums make, Kresge awards planning grants through its Green Building Initiative and capital grants through its core Capital Challenge Grant Program that support sustainable institutional development. It has had a fascinating result: "Integrated design means you will likely get a green building whether you meant to or not [because] integrated design is a comprehensive process that brings everyone to the table," says Ambrozy. "The outcome is a more efficient building, and that usually means green."

Kociolek at CAS says his board and staff, have a "huge" commitment to green developed after the near-destruction of their museum during a 1989 earthquake. Kociolek encouraged stakeholders to ask important questions: "What is a twenty-first-century natural history museum? What should it be? What should it look like? What should it do?" When the existing spaces proved unsuitable for the new intellectual and organizational vision, they found themselves creating a new building. Kociolek says the community and institution "had an expectation of sustainable design . . . at the highest level." For them, the way forward to the twenty-first century was sustainable building, performance, and teaching. Institutional planning was also the road to green for Fruitlands Museum in Harvard, Massachusetts. The museum cares for more than 200 acres of open space, historic structures and collections of art and artifacts. Director Maud Ayson says the process of becoming green "is about building community together and doing what's right for the twenty-first century." During the museum's 2002 public dimension assessment through AAM, the board and staff realized they wanted the community to be as proud of Fruitlands as they were. At a retreat with the project staff for the Doyle Conservation Center, a nearby green building, the Fruitlands board learned about how the center works and about how and why the Trustees of Reservations, a Massachusetts conservation organization, developed its green building. That collective learning experience finished the conversion process. Fruitlands is currently developing its sustainable site master plan.

But can you raise money for green museums? Pearson points out that BCM's project funding and momentum were significantly catalyzed by the decision to go green. "The adoption of green goals helped us obtain capital and helped us grow what was originally a cafeteria expansion into a much larger project that really met our needs," he says. "What really tipped the scale was the notion that we could use sustainable design as an expression of our mission." BCM President Carol Enseki, a former AAM board member, agrees. "It was much easier than we expected from a funding standpoint. We had tremendous enthusiasm among our stakeholders that helped carry it along. Private funders recognized that our project was more than just a building expansion, but a model project, one that demonstrated a commitment to addressing environmental issues, advancing innovation in design and increasing public awareness about sustainable design. City, state and federal legislators recognized [that] our project supported their efforts and recent legislation promoting energy conservation."

The funding situation is growing brighter as state and local government support for green initiatives increases. Burlington, Vermont's electric department provided $56,340 in energy-efficient incentives. Fourteen states have clean energy funds that provide financial incentives to encourage users to choose renewable energy from solar, wind or fuel-cell sources. The Massachusetts Technology Collaborative (MTC) in July awarded Mass MoCA, housed in an old mill building in North Adams, a $700,000 grant from the Renewable Energy Trust for a 50-kilowatt solar installation, energy-efficiency equipment and interactive exhibit to help visitors understand the value of clean energy. Thompson should see some relief for those staggering energy costs.

Of course organizations like The Kresge Foundation and the David and Lucille Packard Foundation that have recently built green headquarters are predisposed to fund green. The Kresge Foundation's core program is "to help develop better and stronger organizations through a capital-campaign process as well as a better building." It is committed to enabling a thoughtful process, not in directing the result. "We realized that the nonprofits we were supporting each year had $3 billion to $4 billion invested in projects," says Ambrozy. "[We saw] that maybe we could examine that and incentivize informed decision making." Since starting the Green Building Initiative in 2003, the foundation has awarded seventy-five planning grants totaling more than $4.7 million, including eleven grants to museums and cultural organizations plus a total of forty-two bonus grants for $7.2 million, including $900,000 in grants to six cultural organizations.

At the Heinz History Center, The Kresge Foundation and The Heinz Endowments made grants to the capital campaign and then made related bonus awards. The Heinz Endowments funded the costs of documenting and commissioning LEED certification, and The Kresge Foundation, already a supporter through green design planning, awarded a bonus grant of $150,000 when the History Center achieved LEED Silver status.

The term "environmentally advantaged" may sound a bit politically correct, but it's a powerful concept that will give institutions an edge in a competitive market for public attention and support. By integrating strategies for operational cost savings with mission objectives (both financial sustainability and environmental attainability), museums are finding a powerful voice in green that is being heard and supported.

Is saving on annual operating and facility costs connected to mission? Certainly. The Art Institute of Chicago (AIC) has long been concerned with operating energy costs and was taking steps to address them well before launching the current capital project, says Meredith Mack, vice president for finance and operations. "Energy efficiency audits done in 2005 showed specific projects we could implement to reduce our energy consumption," she said. "This interest in energy savings has intensified as energy costs have increased and will be an ongoing issue as they continue to rise."

AIC is part of the Green Museums Steering Committee, formed in June 2005 to maintain a collective effort among nine Chicago museums to promote green museum operations, exhibits and programs.[3] The consortium is supported by the city's Office of the Environment and Mayor Richard Daley, who has vowed to make Chicago the "greenest city in the country." AIC's new Modern Wing is working toward LEED Silvers, an initiative funded by the Illinois Clean Energy Foundation.

One of the world's oldest land conservation organizations, the Trustees of Reservations, operates six regional offices managing 55,000 acres of open space and historic landscapes. It also stewards four National Landmark properties and significant collections of historic structures, designed landscapes and art, artifacts and archives. President Andrew Kendall describes the decision to go green as a natural one: "What it really came down to was that, for a conservation organization launching a new building project never before undertaken in its 100-plus-year history not to go green would be a huge missed opportunity to put its money where its mouth or values are." The Trustees' Doyle Conservation Center was recently rated LEED Gold. The center's building is 60 percent more energy efficient than conventional buildings. In addition to quantifiable energy savings, the center carries a powerful message as "a showcase for responsible design and construction practices" says Kendall.

There are dozens of science and natural history museums, children's museums, zoos, aquariums, botanical gardens and conservation organizations going green. Many see this as clearly connected to their mission and are integrating green practices with community needs.

Director Carol Enseki clearly articulated this thinking when describing BCM's approach. "Children's museums have embraced it because of their heavy focus on education. For us, what clinched the decision to go green were the educational opportunities that added benefits above and beyond the operational cost savings around energy efficiency."

"Environmental education is a strong focus for us, and there has been tremendous excitement relative to our urban setting and science, education, and career preparedness," she adds. "The residents in our urban neighborhood have low representation in science fields. We see science education as a way to give kids and families access to information they can use to better their lives and advocate for change. For example, asthma rates have a direct correlation to indoor air quality; sustainable design offers solutions to this and other urban ills." Green principles also provide the institution with easy education tools. ECHO offers visitors an energy and environmental quest called E2, with special stickers and labels on LEED certification elements in the building. Staff created a scavenger hunt that shows visitors ways to conserve energy in their homes.

The Children's Museum of Pittsburgh's "Be a Green Sleuth" booklet helps visitors uncover its sustainability secrets. "Green buildings do not look different from other buildings, unless you know where to look," the booklet explains. Each section leads explorers to parts of the old building, salvaged theater seats, connections to wind and solar power, low-flow toilets, recycled wood posts and wheat-board wall panels as examples of green building and practice.

The Brooklyn Children's Museum is planning "Energy Adventures," an exhibit that will demonstrate how the building harvests and uses solar power and how water is used to heat and cool the facility through geothermal pumps. The exhibit will also cover renewable resources, such as bamboo, as well as sustainable materials such as cork, rubber and linoleum, which are all used in the museum building.

You don't have to be a science or children's museum to choose cork or bamboo—or make any other sustainable choices. Anyone in the preservation business has a huge opportunity to use sustainable design to educate audiences about the responsibilities of caring for collections in perpetuity. One art museum representative was asked why the institution's media kit on its green expansion didn't mention the LEED goal or energy efficiency or sustainable design. The response was, "It isn't our mission; we are not a science or natural history museum."

In fact, many recent and planned art museum expansions incorporate high-performance energy-efficient mechanical, ventilation and lighting systems, yet their press materials don't mention the operational cost savings and environmental advantages, and the average person is hard-pressed to know or find out about them. (The new De Young Museum, the High Museum expansion and the current construction at the Museum of Fine Arts, Boston, are just a few high-profile examples.) In part this results from the mainstreaming of sustainable design among architects, many of whom see it as simply good design. Also, perhaps art museums don't see it "as their mission." On the contrary, however, art museums would benefit from informing visitors about the dollar and environmental cost of collections care and sharing how they are responsibly managing that cost for a better bottom line and for a better environment for objects and people. This would build on the popular trend toward visible storage and sharing back-of-the-house activities.

Art museums know well the precarious balance of weather, older buildings, and their mechanical systems. Facilities managers understand the daily dance of tweaking controls for appropriate environmental conditions. AIC's expansion project includes an overhaul of the mechanical systems in the existing exhibition and storage areas to make them more energy efficient and compatible with new construction. Executive Director of Conservation Frank Zuccari and engineers tested best conditions as they designed and phased upgrades to the systems, zone by zone. He and the design team also reduced electricity use and controlled the cumulative exposure of objects to light through a new sunshade system that diffuses and redirects sunlight and works in conjunction with the artificial lighting system. Although the energy savings from an integrated approach to lighting will be significant, Zuccari doesn't necessarily see it as green; he is focused on good conservation practice: chiefly controlling light, humidity and air pollution.

If we telescope the issues from the micro-environments of exhibition and storage facilities to the macro-environment of the planet as a whole, we can see how poor environmental practices have put our shared cultural heritage at risk. Think of the collections and structures lost or damaged in Hurricane Katrina last year. In the spring 2006 issue of *Museum Practice* magazine, David Martin writes, "There is little point in preserving collections for posterity if survival of future generations is under threat or the cultural heritage is at risk from environmental catastrophes." Check UNESCO's endangered places list and you'll see that threats from energy development, sprawl, flooding, and pollution are proliferating. Athens's Acropolis amid hundreds of important sites in Rome, Venice, Mexico City, and elsewhere are being degraded by pollution, climate change, and non-sustainable development and poor land management practices.

It is an easy intellectual step—from the AIC's focus on the importance of protecting the environment of its art collection to Fruitlands' and ECHO's commitment to protecting and learning from the landscape. The argument is the same for protecting nearby historic structures and faraway world monuments. Global climate change affects them all.

Sustainability is often described as "whole-systems thinking," approaching environmental issues in an integrated fashion. "We humans are part of the place we live—not separate from it—and our decisions and choices affect the health and welfare of that place," says ECHO's Silverman.

Sustainable practices have a positive impact on the environment worldwide. They create more pleasant and attractive places to work and learn, they support preservation goals and, connected to mission advancement, they can be leveraged for support and recognition,

BCM's Enseki sees a world of opportunity in green. "As an educational institution that is going green, we have a chance to bring knowledge to the public," she says. "I can see future AAM accreditation criteria dealing with sustainability. A good aspect of planning is how to improve energy efficiency, which of course frees dollars to go towards programs and services. I would encourage museums that are going green or have already done it to get the word out."

As institutions standing at the intersection of research, education, teaching and discovery, museums are best positioned to share sustainability with the broadest audience in the most meaningful ways. In their role as a place of authority and keepers of culture, museums have unequaled power and responsibility to model and to teach the methods of preserving ourselves, our planet and our cultural resources. "[Green building] is as basic to our mission as anything," says California Academy of Sciences' Kociolek. "[Sustainable practice] is the right thing to do. Each institution will make its own decision about whether it's important to tell their audiences about sustainable practices, but we're going to shout it from the mountaintop. It's part of our mission, our ethic and values as a community."

Sustainable practice in museums serves our whole community—not just the audience inside attending lectures, visiting exhibits and participating in our town meetings, but those all around us. It is service to the whole community we inhabit, with all its members benefiting from museums even if they don't walk in our doors. It's the ultimate programmatic outreach: connecting with an expanded audience by reaching them literally where they live.

Notes

1. Data about emissions levels and energy use widely available. The U.S. Green Building Council's website is a very informative and instructive resource.

2. "Managing the Cost of Green Buildings," a research paper commissioned by the California State and Consumer Services Agency's Sustainable Building Task Force and the Alameda County Waste Management Authority, coauthors: Geof Syphers, P.E.; Arnold M. Sowell, Jr.; Ann Ludwig; Amanda Eichel. Undated (c. 2002).

3. The members of the Green Museums Steering Committee are the Adler Planetarium, Art Institute, Chicago History Museum, DuSable Museum of African American History, Field Museum of Natural History, Museum of Science and Industry, Museum of Contemporary Art, Mexican Fine Arts Museum and Shedd Aquarium.

STRATEGIC IMPLICATIONS FOR LEADERSHIP

V

I N THE END, THE COLLECTIVE VISION and leadership capacity of a museum is a significant indicator of how successful and effective that institution will be an ever-changing world and marketplace. Leadership demands are complex, requiring a sophisticated blend of reflective and informed planning supported with astute decision-making and strategies that befit the unique role of a museum. Museum directors and trustees have to stay abreast of changes in their communities, standards in the museum field and beyond, while simultaneously building new leadership competencies needed for the juggling act of managing and governing museums in contemporary times. Relevant mission statements and inspiring visions for the future cannot be a concept on paper only, rather they are essential springboards for crafting new ways of working, fostering an innovative, responsive organizational culture, and redesigning institutional infrastructures that support a museum in the twenty-first century. Vigilant fiscal and resource management embraced across an institution requires appropriate systems that strategically align resources with institutional priorities supported by ongoing assessment of the impact of achieving desired outcomes in service to the public. This in turn necessitates defining sustainable systems that balance creativity and cost efficiencies. The emergence of creative collaborations is one example of how many institutions come together for greater results—spawning institutional partnerships in some cases and mergers and strategic alliances in others. In short, the complexity of change evident in the early decades of this century require new skills and solutions and inspired, creative leaders capable of navigating turbulent times while reinventing their museums for survival.

Without a doubt, the partnership between the board of trustees and the CEO must be strong and balanced with an ongoing commitment to planning, keen fiscal management, mission-based decision-making, and the rigor to make tough, strategic adjustments to survive. An effective board is tantamount to leveraging the potential of the institution in the eyes of the director and staff, and the director's professional expertise and knowledge is critical for guiding and energizing the work of the board. This clarity of roles and interrelatedness requires board and staff to remain well informed and operate at a professional level with clearly spelled out rules of engagement that define parameters for work yet provide room for healthy collaboration. Cultivating leadership at all levels, whether trustee, director, staff, or volunteer, requires that the organizational culture reflect and translate this value into practice. In the following chapters, the selected authors each tackle a fundamental aspect of the new leadership toolkit. Refreshing and inspirational, the chapters cover emotional intelligence and leadership, new approaches to inspired governance, multicultural competencies for nonprofit organizations, twenty-first century skill sets, and, finally, the inherent challenges of leading change.

Sherene Suchy, based in Canberra, Australia, and author of the publication *Leading with Passion: Change Management in the 21ˢᵗ Century*, extracts highlights of her extensive research on museum management in the article "Emotional Intelligence, Passion, and Museum Leadership." Referencing the work *Emotional Intelligence* by Daniel Goleman and *Flow* by Mihaly Csikszentmihalyi in particular, Suchy outlines why museum practice needs an infusion of compassion, humility, and entrepreneurial spirit to increase the effectiveness of leadership.

Governance and trusteeship are the focus of the next three chapters—each tackling a different aspect on how to achieve responsible and inspired board leadership. The first piece "Governance as Leadership: Bringing New Governing Mindsets to Old Challenges" is authored by three well-known authorities on governance: Richard P. Chait, William P. Ryan, and Barbara E. Taylor. They introduce the concept of the necessary balance between three types of governance leadership: fiduciary, strategic, and generative. Acknowledging that most boards focus on fiduciary and strategic practice, essential aspects of governance, they stress the importance of emphasizing generative thinking to bring balance and deeper meaning to the work of trusteeship.

BoardSource, a recognized leader in nonprofit governance and leadership, regularly publishes a wide array of references to help boards and directors strengthen the role of trustees. In the publication entitled *The Source: Twelve Principles of Governance That Power Exceptional Boards*, a committee of national experts outline one of the most concise and valuable references created for boards in recent years. In the condensed version featured in this publication, the twelve principles address new ways of being such as embracing a culture of inquiry, ethos of transparency, and continuous learning. The amalgam of twelve principles speaks to the importance of establishing a board culture—one that is vibrant, fully engaged, strategic, and invested—for a more impactful result.

Also produced by BoardSource is a pithy article about the importance of board accountability entitled "On the Job." While the two prior articles clarify tenets of exceptional board practice, this chapter highlights the imperative of trustee oversight and financial accountability. More often than one would like to acknowledge, boards are often uninformed about institutional financial issues, cannot understand the financial reports, and are not clear about their responsibilities relating to financial stability and sustainability. This article helps clarify what practices are required and why. This is a nonnegotiable expectation of high-performing boards.

"Multicultural Organizational Development in Nonprofit Organizations: Lessons from the Cultural Competence Learning Initiative" is a welcome and practical addition to the literature about building and supporting a diverse, equitable, and open work environment. Supported by a grant by The California Endowment, Laurin Mayeno and Steve Lew created this helpful, accessible document about the challenges of establishing a sustainable multicultural organization. This should be recommended reading for museum trustees, staff and volunteers.

In response to a changing world and a commitment to fostering the next generation of leaders, The Institute of Museum and Library Services' Office of Strategic Partnerships, under the direction of Marsha Semmel, deputy director for Museum Services and director for Strategic Partnerships, undertook a project that resulted in the publication, *Museums, Libraries, and 21ˢᵗ Century Skills*. The excerpts included in this volume highlight the changes that have spurred the need for twenty-first-century skills. Not possible to reprint here but highly recommended to the reader is the very detailed and helpful self-assessment tool. The entire report should be referenced as institutions prepare for the future, create new positions, expand existing positions, and rethink organizational structures.

Dr. Robert R. Janes, author of *The Paradox of Change*, a book that chronicles the dramatic organizational change at the Glenbow Museum in the 1990s, and most recently his publication entitled *Museums in a Troubled World*, is recognized for his insightful candor. In "The Mindful Museum," Janes states that most museum practice is unsustainable given the demands of today's world. He advocates for the rise of "social, environmental and economic stewardship" as the new role for museums. Highlighting examples of innovative practice, Janes makes the case that dramatic change is required to prepare museums for a more sustainable and meaningful role.

As all of the prior chapters enumerate and imply—for museums—this is an unprecedented moment for change. It is only fitting to close out this part of the book with "Leading Change: Why Transformation Efforts Fail" written by John P. Kotter for the *Harvard Business Review*. Kotter zeros in on the challenges and pitfalls of institutional change efforts and proposes a thoughtful eight-step process for transformation. He stresses the importance of rigor and tenacity required for substantial change reminding us that a significant investment of time, patience, and resources are required for transformative change to occur and take hold.

Change comes in many forms—the hiring of a new director, the expansion of a facility, or the launch of a new initiative for a museum. These have been in our lexicon for a long time and have a certain familiarity to most museum professionals. The challenge for museums today is that many museums have been operating with an outmoded ideology, structure, and operations resulting in declining relevancy that triggers dropping attendance and contribution numbers. The change required now is transformative change in order to survive. Survival for its own sake is self-serving—but survival that aligns museums as part of the solution, part of the fabric of our communities, and a participant in improving the quality of life for people is very worthwhile. Leaders to guide and shoulder transformative change are needed more than ever. Undertaking transformative change takes time, even years, requiring sustained courage and innovation along the way.

The reinvention process referenced throughout this anthology highlights the discovery, awakening, and exploration necessary to achieve redefined, reenvisioned, and revitalized museums. The reader is encouraged to revisit the framework section to this volume where the Reinventing the Museum Tool is outlined and elements of reinvention discussed. And with the encouragement of all forty-four authors and this editor, may this volume be your reference guide for your professional and institutional journeys.

Emotional Intelligence, Passion and Museum Leadership

37

SHERENE SUCHY

Introduction

THE DIRECTOR OF THE METROPOLITAN MUSEUM of Art in New York has stated, "Passion is what sells the museum. The Development Office paves the way and the Director's charisma and passion makes the difference" (de Montebello 1996). This assertion was one of the starting points for research into the complexity of museum leadership which brought together three domains of expertise: museum management, psychology and business (Suchy 1998). In response to numerous enquiries following two papers on museum leadership presented at the 1998 ICOM Triennial congress in Melbourne, Australia, this article has been written to describe the starting points for the original research on change, challenges and complexity surrounding museum leadership. The international research on the director's role in art museum leadership has revealed, first and foremost, the critical importance of passion. A deep feeling in the heart for the work in hand sustains art museum directors on a daily basis, as well as contributing to the vision of the organisation. Passion, energy and creativity are baseline competences for leadership roles.

Charisma, that elusive characteristic which defines leaders with panache, may actually be a set of learnable skills called emotional intelligence. And passion, that sense of being deeply connected with work which is highly meaningful, is essential for all directors wishing to create a presence for their museums. The directors of over forty-five major art museums in Australia, Canada, the United States of America and the United Kingdom who participated in personal interviews for an international research project between 1996 and 1998 all shared a common strategy as they managed major change processes in the 1990s (Suchy 1998). They all spoke of the need to keep passion alive by remaining connected with some part of the job which had "heart" in it. According to the Director of the Isabella Stewart

Sherene Suchy is the director of DUO PLUS, an Australian-based consulting firm specializing in change management. "Emotional Intelligence, Passion and Museum Leadership" appeared in *Museum Management and Curatorship* (Vol. 18, No. 1, pp. 57–71) published by Taylor & Francis. It is reprinted here with permission of the publisher. All rights reserved.

Gardner Museum in Boston, this meant staying connected with one's own source of creativity.

> To keep passion alive in trying times, you have to think, read, write, and see contemporary work. Practice your own area of creative talent. Feed yourself, as only then can you feed the organisation. Do not lose your own sense of creativity. Maintain relationships with people who may be friends and colleagues who continue to inspire you. (Hawley 1996)

This observation is relevant for directors of any organisation. Although the art museum was case studied for particular reasons, outcomes from the research are applicable across a broader range of organisations. Remaining connected with some part of the job which has "heart" in it requires two things. First, increasing awareness of ways to maintain pleasure and challenge in life depends on how often we experience a phenomenon referred to as flow. Second, we need to learn how to make the connection between flow and the core competencies of emotional intelligence for leadership effectiveness. The core competencies include intentionality, creativity, resilience, interpersonal connections and managing constructive discontent (Q-metrics 1996).

Flow Theory and Executive Decision Making

Mihaly Csikszentmihalyi (1990: xi, 1993; Csikszentmihalyi and Hermanson 1995, 1999), a psychologist at the University of Chicago, has been working since 1975 with flow theory. Flow theory provides a framework and words for an experience many people have described as a "rush," "being totally in tune" or "decision making high." There are several characteristics or evidence of an individual in flow. The person is usually totally involved in the current experience and fully concentrating on the task at hand. They are enjoying themselves. They exhibit high self-esteem because their skills are well paced with the task at hand. And, they have a sense that the activities in which they are engaged are important to future goals. Writers on emotional intelligence such as Goleman (1996: 90–93) have referred to flow as a state of "self-forgetfulness" where individuals "exhibit a masterly control of what they are doing, their responses perfectly attuned to the changing demands of the task."

The research undertaken by the present author on art museum leadership "used an executive interview technique to map levels of challenge and the directors' experience of flow (Stamp 1993; Jaque and Clement 1994; Suchy 1998). When museum directors appeared to be in flow with the challenges of leadership, they appeared energised and spoke passionately about their work. It also became clear one of the keys to flow was skilled practice. This allowed the individuals to get into flow more often because they had mastered the moves of the task at hand and so there was less effort required. Mastering art museum leadership, according to the Director of the National Gallery of Canada in Ottawa, requires a "willingness to change, to grieve, learn, live and learn. It is a process of growth, making mistakes and living through them" (Thompson 1996). Certainly the director's role in any type of museum leadership is a complex job, but staying connected to some part of the job which has "heart" in it keeps passion alive. Keeping passion alive, or staying in flow, depends on five conditions. Csikszentmihalyi (1990) maintained that the five conditions are necessary for any activity in which the emotion of pleasure, a sense of achievement, and effective decision making are desired outcomes. The first condition depends on clarity around expectations, goals and interactions. In other words, the release of leadership energy involves creating and negotiating clear goals, expectations and interactions regarding tasks.

The second condition involves the perception that someone is attending to and taking a positive interest in what the director is doing. This means material resources and positive forms of moral support from trustees, staff and other stakeholders in the organisation. Leadership can be an isolating job. As the director of the Tate Gallery in London observed: "I do realise that often I am very alone. It is frightening that there are only one or two people around the world one can share one's ideas and thoughts with" (Serota 1996). This is why it is important for all museum directors to have access to and participate in professional networks where they can exchange ideas in an environment dedicated to creative leadership development. The role of the trustees or other senior management is of particular importance in maintaining the perception of support. When this support is perceived negatively, the conditions for flow are reduced. Lack of support and conflict undermines leadership confidence. According to some directors, they have often felt caught and unsupported between conflicting stakeholders such as unions, staff and trustees (Sano 1995; Parker 1995).

While the third condition involves a sense of choice and discretion in decision making, it also includes full responsibility for the outcomes. Provided that the level of organisational challenge is commensurate with the level of skill available, museum directors need to be able to exercise their judgement fully to maximise a sense of flow. This may not always be possible in an organisation where leadership roles are shared between the museum director and the board of trustees. Difficulties in this area are to be expected and require higher than average levels of skill in "emotional intelligence," such as constructive discontent and interpersonal connections. For example, the director of the Isabella Stewart Gardner Museum in Boston has noted that, "Trustees can enable a museum and they are also capable of arresting action through the demise of public and foundation funding" (Hawley 1996). The director of the Yale Center for British Art in New Haven has described situations where lack of trustee support could lead to "decision making paralysis" and dysfunctional leadership (McCaughy 1996).

The fourth condition for flow involves a sense of trust which allows total involvement with the task or activity without concern for well-being. In other words, museum directors will be most in flow when their positions are not under threat. The perception of threat can be interpreted in several ways. For some museum directors this may mean threatened loss of job or funding cuts to the organisation as a whole. Others may feel that they cannot immerse themselves in the job because of conflicts with senior management/boards, staff or industrial relation problems. Conditions which bar total involvement in the job undermine the museum director's judgement and ability to create a positive presence for the museum. For example, the director of The Fine Arts Museums of San Francisco confessed that, "I continually have to suppress my creative judgement to deal with power struggles which is frustrating and results in great anger" (Parker 1995). Finally, the fifth condition involves the need for increasingly complex challenges over time. Museum directors continue to experience pleasure in their work when the job continues to stretch their skills or capability. Too much or too little stretch or disruptions to the other four conditions reduces the sense of pleasure. For example, the director of the National Gallery of Art in Washington, D.C., observed that, "It would be nice to have a little fun again" (Powell 1996). As he reflected on changes impacting museums in the 1990s (funding cuts), it became increasingly apparent that the expectations around museum leadership had changed dramatically. Maintaining a sense of flow and a "heart" for the work in such an environment was undoubtedly presenting major challenges.

Passion, Flow and Emotional Intelligence

When conditions for flow are present and challenges are well balanced with skills, museum directors should experience a sense of well-being as well as effective decision making. In the museum context, the outcome of being in flow is a feeling of passion and meaningful work. As indicated earlier by the director of the Metropolitan Museum of Art in New York, "Passion is what sells the museum." Directors who have learned how to manage increasingly complex challenges with increasing levels of leadership skill, for example, emotional intelligence, create a strong presence for their museums internally and externally.

Researchers and writers on emotional intelligence (Gardner 1983: 237–276; 1995; Goleman 1996: xii–xiii; Cooper and Sawaf 1996; Glynn 1996; Pennar 1996) have described EQ as a combination of self-control, zeal, persistence, the ability to motivate oneself, a basic flair for living, the ability to read another's innermost feelings and handling relationships smoothly. Research suggests that IQ contributes to 20 percent of life success and EQ makes up the rest or 80 percent. First, there are emotions, then there is thought. We cannot choose the emotions we have. There is immediate perception, then reflective thought, if we have emotional intelligence. The relationship between emotional intelligence and leadership was highlighted by Gardner (1983: xxiv) over a decade ago as "capacities that cut across intelligences affect other people in ways that may be as emotional and social as they are cognitive." Gardner's (1995) research on leadership markers provided a very valuable framework for the research on the director's role in art museum leadership (Suchy 1998). The best leaders were those individuals who were able to express unspoken collective sentiments to guide their organisation toward its goals in a way that was emotionally nourishing and a pleasure to be around. Consequently, the original doctoral research undertaken by the present author on the director's role in art museum leadership has been developed into a six-week leadership program in Australia with an emphasis on what Cooper and Sawaf (1996) defined as optimal leadership performance. Optimal leadership performance uses twenty well-defined emotional intelligence skills to increase resilience under pressure, develop trusting relationships and create the future or, what one art museum director has called "that vision thing" (Kolb 1996). The program focuses on seven emotional intelligence competences which are directly related to leadership effectiveness: trust, compassion, intuition, constructive discontent, interpersonal connections, resilience and creativity. The program enables participants to use EQ to embody their leadership story in optimal leadership performance.

Creating optimal leadership performance as an art museum director while sustaining a sense of flow is a delicate balancing act. It is a subtle inner process which is not given to scientific measurement. It involves harmonising an emotional and intuitive sense of the world in creative collaboration with the rational or linear mind. The director of the National Gallery of Victoria in Melbourne described this experience as taking "pleasure in drawing together diverse experience and doing lots of things at once. To be creative is emotionally satisfying. To set frameworks is analytically satisfying" (Potts 1995). This collaboration is not always a controllable process, nor does it create a life without tension. The director of The Art Gallery of New South Wales in Sydney described it as a process of "keeping things slightly on edge . . . a slight tension keeps things creative . . . one must keep imbalances to maintain energy" (Capon 1995). The search for ways to stay in flow, as well as remaining passionate about one's work can be a potentially volatile process. This was described by the director of the Yale Center for British Art in New Haven.

> Museums tend to fragment without good direction as they are volatile organisations. You have to have people with imagination in an art museum and that has volatility. People with imagination believe in the rightness of their intuition. But passion does not equal the rational! Feelings are volatile and unstable. A successful museum depends on the interaction of the many, e.g., community, audience, staff. It is about relationships and how they are managed. (McCaughy 1996)

One of the richest outcomes from the research on the director's role in art museum leadership was the exciting connection between individual flow and cultural development. Csikszentmihalyi referred to the need for increasingly refined skills to maintain pleasure in activity or flow as a key contributor to the development of culture overall. The connection between individual flow and cultural development is found in the ways people seek to extend their skills and what they use to provide meaning in their lives. There is a strategy shared between people who are most successful at creating meaning in their lives. That strategy involves connecting with creativity and the arts in some way. This strategy underscores the critical role which museums and other types of cultural institutions play as potential sites for meaning making.

The necessity to develop increasingly refined skills to sustain enjoyment is what lies behind the evolution of culture. It is what motivates individuals and cultures to change to more complex entities. The rewards of creating order in experience provide the energy that propels evolution. . . . To create harmony in whatever one does is the last task that the flow theory presents to those who wish to attain optimal experience. It is a task that involves transforming the entirety of life into a single flow activity, with unified goals that provide constant purpose. There is much knowledge, or well-ordered information, accumulated in culture, ready for this use. Great music, architecture, art, poetry, drama, dance, philosophy, and religion are there for anyone to see as examples of how harmony can be imposed on chaos. Yet so many people ignore them, expecting to create meaning in their lives by their own devices. (Csikszentmihalyi 1990: 213 and 235)

The way directors represent the art museum as a site for "meaning making" depends on how they have mastered a range of leadership skills. When directors have mastered their emotions in a way to convey effectively their passion, the art museum's potential as a site for "meaning making" becomes readily apparent. For example, the director of The Art Gallery of New South Wales in Sydney addressed a public forum on collection development with a very emotional interpretation about art's ability to reflect values that "touch deep places in the heart" (Capon 1996), while Goleman (1996: 8) described, "knowing something is right in your heart (as) a different order of conviction or truth." Since 1996, Capon's expression of private passion in public places has engaged the hearts of others with significant increases in individual and corporate support during a decade of declining Australian government dollars. The director of the National Gallery of Canada in Ottawa described the leadership role as utterly dependent on having an emotional conviction or passion about the unique value of the arts in our personal and business lives.

Leadership depends on the willingness to change and knowing your subject well. To see that means developing a passion for some part of the arts so that it becomes an anchor in yourself. Having that anchor in what is important means you can feed and sustain yourself. Looking at art is developing non-linear thinking. That is art's greatness. Business and medicine are only just now looking at the concept of non-linear thinking. (Thompson 1996)

The forty-five-plus directors and assistant directors of art museums who were interviewed during the international research project on art museum leadership shared a range of personal passions and strategies to sustain their sense of flow. Out of their shared experiences, five key themes emerged. The five themes included: a passion for the primary product; a commitment to social principles or romanticism; building trusting relationships through education; entrepreneurism and innovation; and constructive discontent as a way of creating the future. These five themes were viewed as a significant insight into the challenges which art museum directors face. They have been subsequently developed and are used as case studies in the Australian-based six-week leadership development program for leaders in a broad range of organisations noted above. The case studies are used to illustrate the importance of emotional intelligence skills and the need to create conditions for flow so that museum directors are not swept away by the everyday demands of their jobs. Extracts from the case studies have been included in this article so as to share the art museum directors' rich insights and illustrate the relationship between passion, flow and optimal leadership performance.

A Passion for the Primary Product

A passion for the primary product, in the art museum context, has been described as love for the visual arts. The director of the Victoria and Albert Museum in London described this as a "love of objects, design, and aesthetics" (Borg 1996), while the director of the Yale Center for British Art in New Haven emphasised how important it was for the art museum director to have this "love of objects," as well as a belief in the institution or people would not support it financially.

> To do the director's job well, you have to have the desire to communicate the beauty and power of art. To communicate about context and people in different ways. To be passionate about this form of human greed which has no social drawbacks! And you have to have pleasure in what you are doing. To be a director, you have to look at lots of works of art. To love things and objects far from your own taste. You have to want to communicate about objects. You have to have ideas about objects and how they relate to one another. It is a unique area. It provides the opportunity to combine thought and action in a way like no other job. (McCaughy 1996)

According to the director of The Art Gallery of Ontario in Toronto, acting as the caretaker and interpreter for the visual artist and their creations was a "great privilege and pleasure."

> My passion? The visible pleasure of people in front of a painting. I am steward of thousands of artists, alive and dead. I feel an obligation to make their vision understood by our visitors. There are thousands of voices and visions in this gallery. . . . (Anderson 1996)

The director of the Art Gallery of Western Australia in Perth demonstrated a deep commitment to the museum as a site for spiritual renewal. Renewal involved time for "drifting" in a venue which offers new ideas and the experience of visual art as a catalyst for personal change. The director described furthermore the importance of gallery guides who shared the same passion and who could act as visual translators, creating meaningful museum experiences for the public.

> My passion is about bringing great experiences to people through great art. Bringing people in touch with the real thing. In a world without enough time for "drift," full of simulation and laminex . . . we need to see a labor of love, great beauty, evidence of great ages. This is what it's all about and it needs to be supported by an intelligent way of helping people to "see it." (Latos-Valier 1996)

The director for The Art Institute of Chicago (Wood 1996) also expressed passion and pleasure in how "art looks." He too was aware that his leadership role demanded a balance between the passionate and the rational, and he used the museum's mission statement as a way of balancing potential chaos in decision making processes.

A Passion for Social Vision or Romanticism

Leadership seems to need a sense of romanticism or social vision which motivates people to extend themselves and to reach for higher level goals. Romanticism, by definition, has an increased focus on the individual, man's fundamental irrationality and a sense of mystery. According to Spate (1980: 17), romanticism has an "emphasis on truth to individual experience" which often places the artist—whether writer, painter or social revolutionary—at a distance from others because they have a "prophetic insight into things that ordinary mortals" may not understand. Mimi Gaudieri (1996), the coordinator for the American Association of Art Museum Directors, described several directors in the United States of America and Canada as "shapers" of ideas in museum leadership based on their keen sense of social vision. Indeed, the director of the Cleveland Museum of Art described the impact of "romantic notions from the '60s" as a major influence on his approach to leadership. The 1960s in the United States was an era of social revolution and experimentation: the civil rights movement, challenges to authorities and control, a search for ways to expand consciousness, and an exploration of new forms of personal relationships.

> After fifteen years, I know organisations and communities have *genius loci*. The director's job is to recognize the inherent structure of these entities, including the museum. My job is to coax and coach genius to the surface. The first dawn of realization is my passion. My democratic spirit is based on a 1960s spirit. That spirit was based on a passion embedded in works of art that are messages about humanity over time. My passion is to reveal those messages . . . to express a democratic spirit by sharing widely. First of all, it is a difficult job and without passion, you just cannot do the director's work. You come to work for the heart of it. Like a musical conductor, to create harmony. I am a mediator, a builder of bridges, a coordinator of x and y who then get sent on their way. (Bergman 1996)

The passion for people demonstrated by the director of the Museum of Fine Arts in Houston was based on a very personal commitment to art museums as a source of social capital for the development of community life.

> The connection between my role and the mission for the museum is easy to answer. To make the art museum an institution of everyday life. To evolve into a broad based cultural center rather than a place where beautiful art is kept secure. Everyone can then think art museums are part of the environment. This can be done in a number of ways. This museum sponsors an annual run with 5,000 runners over a five-mile course. It starts and finishes in our sculpture garden. It is a big success.

> We also stage a singles night that attracts 5,000 people each year. We sponsor clay pigeon shoots. Other museum colleagues laugh at some of the things we do. I love the idea that people can come here for all sorts of things. (Marzio 1996)

Directors with a passion for romanticism are evidently shaping the art museum as a place which carries messages about humanity over time and offers life enrichment. In a leadership role, a passion for romanticism is a commitment to creating a context for personal insight based on a belief in *genius loci*. How a director creates this context depends on a range of skills, most significantly language skills. The way words and language are used is a form of leadership marker, according to Gardner (1995). They are essential tools for museum directors to translate their personal passion into leadership stories which engage the hearts of others.

A Passion for Education

Directors who are excited about interacting with people through education and discovery are building trusting relationships. Trusting relationships are evidence of essential emotional intelligence skills. Several art museum directors described their passion for enabling insight in others through education strategies. They had a clear sense of the relationship between creativity, imagination and education as a process of discovery. In this sense, a passion for education has involved a love of "drawing forth," "bringing out," "eliciting," "leading" and "developing" others. The director of the Dennos Museum Center in Traverse City, Michigan, used his enthusiasm for discovery as a major shaper for the museum's mission through the mission statement, Come Alive Inside:

> My passion is prompting people to question, how does this relate to me? It is about the act of discovery! Pure visual art has a limited appeal in the community due to the art world's focus on contemporary art and a lack of audience access to this form. The community in general does not have the visual language to understand art, particularly contemporary art. Combining a visual arts program focused on state-based artists with an international music program has been hugely successful. The center continues to offer "discovery" themes of interest to the community based on active research. For example, environmental awareness was imaginatively explored through literature, visual arts, and chamber music specifically composed for a series of performances at the center. (Jenneman 1996)

The director of the J. Paul Getty Museum in California described his representational role for the museum as a process of connections and relationships. He stressed the relationship between his role and the vision for the museum, focusing on "dreams." One of the main drivers behind the dreams was the art museum director's pleasure in teaching and an ongoing search for ways to unleash ideas in others. He described his role: "As a leader, my job is about setting goals which connect our dreams about this museum. These dreams are looked at annually and transformed into objectives and tasks" (Walsh 1995). On the other hand, the director of the Freer Gallery of Art/Arthur M. Sackler Gallery in Washington, D.C., described providing an external presence for the museum as one of the biggest recent changes around the director's role. Extending the art museum's influence depended upon the director's passionate commitment to what he saw as "the intrinsic beauty and richness of artistic and cultural expression in all its forms in the hope of transcending race, representative, interpretative, and audience barriers" (Beech 1996).

> As a college student, I never thought I would like to work in or lead a museum. I liked to teach. The opportunity to be a director, though, was ideal. Our duty here is to make the museum interesting for the family groups who come. The Freer Gallery was opened in 1923 as a walled garden for Asian art. We now have to open to the public as we have no right to be a walled garden. We need to serve well, to be accessible. Having taught for fifteen years enables me to excite others about Asia through Asian art. (Beech 1996)

According to the director of the neighbouring Hirshhorn Museum, the Smithsonian Institution's overall vision is played out through its various component parts (Demetrian 1996). The Smithsonian's vision is to achieve the greatest diffusion of knowledge possible (Bello 1993: 9). This overarching vision provided an ideal opportunity for the Hirshhorn Museum Director to focus on education as a specific aspect of the Museum's mission. The value and emphasis placed on education grew from its director's early experience in art education in secondary schools. He had a passion for expanding what he saw as a "narrow view of art."

> This job is basically fun! Some parts are more enjoyable than others. If I don't have certain kinds of information, it presents a challenge to find the what, why, and how to operate. Works of art are all different. When different pieces can be put together to create a dialogue, the art museum is then a place of ideas. (Demetrian 1996)

In this vein, the director of the National Gallery of Canada, in Ottawa, described her passion for people as a key source of leadership energy. Creative thinking, adaptability and the pleasure of working with people were fundamental aspects of the art museum director's representational role.

> A good director has to like people and the process of bringing them in touch with art. You have to like even the pompous people. You have to be excited about the work with the public. This can only be based on understanding the greatness of the art objects being worked with. (Thompson 1996)

Furthermore, the director of the Please Touch Museum in Philadelphia described her passion for children as her commitment to that museum. In this museum director's view, her passion for children and their journey of discovery had to be lived out in such a way that people around her would support her commitment through their loyalty to her and the museum. She explained how important it was to have an outlet for passion outside of the museum also in order to sustain the energy required for the leadership role. This was particularly critical because leadership involved challenges totally unrelated to the original domain of expertise.

> The director is the leader. You just can't order other people to do things. As a leader, you have to have a deep commitment to what you are doing so the staff will do what you ask them to do. They need to see your commitment. My passion is kids! But it isn't just my passion that sustains my spirit. . . . I am sustained by a gifted, talented group of people dedicated to the museum and loyal to me. This means all of my director challenges are reduced. . . . Directors who are discipline trained may sometimes find it hard to keep up confidence as so little of a director's role has to do with the training of their particular discipline. It is important to have another outlet for energy. Although my passion is kids, my outlet is actually gardening and golf. (Kolb 1996)

Art museum directors with a passion for education and the public are shaping museums based on a love of and ability to "generate ideas" in others. They use the art museum's collection both as a way of transforming what people see through the education process, and as a basis to create relationships between people both within and external to it. As a place for "discovery" and "ideas," these directors described the art museum as a social or cultural "center" rather than a site for beautiful objects. They were acutely aware that they needed to embody their commitment actively in ways which enabled others to recognise their leadership vision.

Passion for Entrepreneurship and Innovation

Entrepreneurship is one of the characteristics necessary for art museum leadership in and beyond the 1990s due to radical cuts in government funding for cultural institutions internationally. Directors who share this passion have been actively shaping and reinventing themselves as leaders of business enterprises, rather than museums. A working definition for an entrepreneur is an "individual who seizes an opportunity, takes a risk, and makes it financially successful" (Ottley 1995). Another definition concerns a state of mind in which a cause is identified and an opportunity cultivated or created which can be turned into a profit (Aberdene and Naisbitt 1994: 319-334). Typically, entrepreneurship has focused on an individual's response to an opportunity and the ability to adapt readily to change. Entrepreneurship and innovation in the museum context may be defined as "non-routine, significant, and discontinuous change" (Mezias and Glynn 1993: 78) which embodies a new idea that may not be consistent with the current concept of the organization's business. When Senge (1990) researched learning organizations, he found leaders with a passion for innovation. For museum directors to manage change successfully, innovation is critical in areas such as marketing, merchandising and customer service delivery. These were the key focal areas occupying the director of the National Gallery of Victoria in Melbourne who was creating a new presence for his museum.

> My job as director is to balance a belief in the institution and the reality of marketing. I am not reluctant to enter commercial activity but we cannot wear the

museum's mission on our sleeve in the process, e.g., to promote and understand the visual arts. We are not exactly about "entertainment and access" but about creating greater understanding so people will want to know more about the visual arts. (Potts 1995)

The director of the Isabella Stewart Gardner Museum in Boston had been recruited to lead that museum at a time when the focus was clearly on financial issues. Her sense of "entrepreneurial risk taking" was expressed as a commitment to contemporary artists and a search for profitable ways in which to engage the local community.

My passion was to work with artists and contemporary work that drives. I used that passion to look at how we were part of a neighborhood where people could walk to this museum from three neighborhood schools. We decided to work on this advantage. To do this, we engaged research through Harvard University regarding learning theory to push the museum's envelope. I got hit over the head by the Trustees for this! This introduced a whole new issue for my role as a director. (Hawley 1996)

Furthermore, the director of The Museum of Contemporary Art in Los Angeles stressed that he did not want the external presence of the museum to be based on the ideas of any one person alone, director or curator. The art museum director's passion was based on the desire to "work with artists and to be in the contemporary world where all things are open to question. To look at the fact that there is more than one way to get on a horse" (Koshalek 1996). As a result of this philosophy, The Museum of Contemporary Art creates a range of entrepreneurial activities providing an avenue for many people with a passion for the arts.

Ideas and energy are the most important characteristics a director of an art museum can have. The director has to be capable of saying "What's Next" in terms of the goals, strengths, and a concept for the museum to make it unique. This means bringing things to life constantly with artists. That is how we keep this place alive. This can be expressed in many ways. (Koshalek 1996)

In addition, the director of the Queensland Art Gallery in Brisbane had shaped the vision for museums based on a keen interest in political entrepreneurism to ensure that museum's continued success as a public institution.

You can't take yourself too seriously, you have to stay dynamic or it becomes boring. My own personal interest in politics helped me a lot. . . . As a director, you look for what can be done, not what can't. This requires skills and talent in advocacy and maintaining a position of high credibility with the mainstream of the Queensland Public Service. . . . Every institution needs to be a shaper of change. (Hall 1995)

Museum directors with a passion for entrepreneurism and innovation have used their leadership roles to focus on marketing, merchandising and investments which have "had a return on the dollar." Their passion has reflected a complex form of individual creativity as they have actively embraced "risks" and a search for "new possibilities" to enable profitable museum enterprises to be undertaken. This included a willingness to explore opportunities and learn from a range of non-traditional entrepreneurial enterprises in a museum context. Vecchio et al. (1995) identified this willingness to experiment with entrepreneurship as a prerequisite for successful leadership in the 1990s and beyond, and they have described the characteristics of entrepreneurism as the ability to adapt to, shape and create new environments.

A Passion for Constructive Discontent

A passion for constructive discontent has been described as an appreciation of diversity and difference, investigation, examination and the use of the organisation as a "site for debate" for future development. The director for the Whitney Museum of American Art in New York explained his passion for the museum as a place for "personal and community discovery":

> I learned how a museum is a social instrument for use by self and others. I saw museums as part of a community's health both socially and mentally. I learned how a museum plays a role in the lives of people from different social levels, not just the rich people which is what I originally thought. I learned that a contemporary art museum is about collecting, recording, reporting, mirroring, and is a site for delight. I fell in love with art, its power and its liability. I was prompted to live an examined life and saw the art museum as a mirror to that examination of life. It is a place for the contest of values and ideas. My job is to present the menu and if the audience likes it, they are the ones who then find their way. I learned all about passion through a project in California. I learned about people who really do "good deeds." I learned what was real, respected, and dangerous, I learned about survival [through a series of potentially life threatening accidents]. I learned that museums need people with passion, not functionaries. (Ross 1996)

The director of the Museum of Contemporary Art in Chicago described a relationship between how the leader creates an external presence to the museum and constructive discontent. His vision for the museum had been carefully constructed from the value the director placed on "contemporary culture" and the interface the public. He was excited about exploring all the known and unknown forces which make up the concept of culture, as well as ways to re-create culture for new foundations for the future.

> Sometimes, what we do is closer to journalism than history. We are investigating rather than reporting on contemporary culture. The world is one with few compass points. It is about managing ambiguity and uncertainty. (Consey 1995)

Focusing on change and change management as an ongoing interface between people creating contemporary culture, the director of The Museum of Modern Art in New York saw his leadership role in the museum as a "change agent." Change, exploration and evolution were key themes in his commitment to enabling the museum as a site for "active community engagement."

> We need to ask what to create for tomorrow. We need to use our minds and act as think tanks to think abstractly. . . . MoMA was founded with a missionary spirit and propelled over the last 65 years with that spirit. We work in a world context, forging common ground between ambitious visions of the staff and the trustees. I, as Director, am the mediator of this process. . . . Managing change is an apt description of what I do. I am part of a larger pattern of relationships. . . . My focus is on how to take the status quo toward an evolution, balancing roots and history at the same time. This involves creating team leadership with a shared goal and a common vision. (Lowry 1996)

Another leader who has thrived on change, diversity and difference is the director of The Saint Louis Art Museum and his pleasure and experience in change management has enabled him continually to reposition or reinvent his Museum within a contemporary context.

> I enjoy the interface between individuals, collections, and the role of museums in the community intersect. I enjoy the link to plural or diverse audiences. I hugely enjoy difference. I thrive on difference. The translation of this passion into the vision for The Saint Louis Art Museum has been a sixteen-year commitment to a publicly owned museum which has a global agenda like the Victoria and Albert [in London]. The founder of this museum in 1879 put no boundaries on what constituted art. He started this museum with an open-ended agenda. This came into play and got lost between 1940-60. It needed to be refound. It made a difference to re-vision the organisation with a big, open agenda. If we are able to continue to grasp the excitement of that, then we will continue to be successful. (Burke 1996)

Directors with a passion for constructive discontent have viewed their leadership roles slightly differently from other art museum directors. They have seen themselves more as "change agents," at ease with the "ambiguity" and "uncertainty" integral to contemporary culture. Their passion for "change," "diversity" and "examination" has shaped their representation of the art museum as a "social instrument." Their passion for investigation and a fascination for "the edge," or "faultlines," in cultural development has suggested that the art museum should be represented as a site for ideas rather than objects, for social debate rather than passive celebration.

Conclusion

Art museum directors who are leading with passion constitute individuals in flow and they are totally engaged with the challenges at hand. Flow theory suggests that it is possible to develop an approach which enables the experience of flow more often and more easily when the five conditions for flow are met. These conditions include clear goals, support, discretionary decision making, a sense of trust which allows total involvement in the task, and increasingly complex challenges over time. These conditions need to be present organisationally in order to create a context for current and potential leaders to demonstrate masterly control and pleasure in the job. In executive decision making, the match between level of challenge and leadership skill is essential for evidence of flow in effective decision making.

Pleasure in the job has been described in terms of a personal anchor or source of creativity which sustained art museum directors on a very personal level. When an art museum director was in flow and working from the "heart," it was most evident as contagious emotional energy. Creating and sustaining this energy is an ongoing challenge for anyone in such a leadership role. This energy was actually described by one New York–based executive search consultant as "the bottom line for 'new breed' museum directors" (Nichols 1996). Translating energy into optimal performance appears to rely increasingly on what has become known as emotional intelligence skills. With increased mastery of these skills, art museum directors can increase effectiveness under pressure, develop trusting relationships and create the museum's future or "that vision thing." In conclusion, what matters in effective art museum leadership is a passion for life, creativity and imagination. When this passionate energy is expressed through a range of executive level skills, including emotional intelligence, people respond in positive emotional and social ways.

Acknowledgment

Directors of major art museums in Australia, the United States, Canada, and the United Kingdom have given their consent—by participation in the original research—for their insights to be used in a manner that contributes to professional development in museum management.

References

Aberdene, P. and Naisbitt, J. (1994) *Mega trends for women*. Arrow. London.

Anderson, M. (1996) Interview with Max Anderson, Director of The Art Gallery of Ontario, in Toronto, 25 June 1996.

Beech, M. (1996) Interview with Milo Beech, Director of the Arthur M. Sackler Gallery and the Freer Gallery of Art, in Washington, D.C., 18 April 1996.

Bello, M. (1993) *The Smithsonian Institution, X World of Discovery: an exploration of behind-the-scenes research in the arts, sciences, and humanities*. Washington, D.C.: Smithsonian Institution.

Bergman, R. (1996) Interview with Robert Bergman, Director of the Cleveland Museum of Art, in Cleveland, 23 June 1996.

Borg, A. (1996) Interview with Alan Borg, Director of the Victoria and Albert Museum, in London, 2 May 1996.

Burke, J. (1996) Interview with James Burke, Director of The Saint Louis Art Museum, in Saint Louis, 7 June 1996.

Capon, E. (1995) Interview with Edmund Capon, Director of The Art Gallery of New South Wales, in Sydney, 13 April 1995.

————. (1996) Public presentation on fund-raising given by Edmund Capon, Director of The Art Gallery of New South Wales, in Sydney.

Consey, K. (1995) Interview with Kevin Consey, Director of the Museum of Contemporary Art, in Chicago, 12 June 1995.

Cooper, R. and Sawaf, A. (1996) *Executive EQ: emotional intelligence in leadership and organizations*. Grossett/Putnam. New York.

Csikszentmihalyi, M. (1990) *Flow: the psychology of optimal experience*. Harper and Row. New York.

————. (1993) *The evolving self: a psychology for the third millennium*. Harper Perennial. New York.

Csikszentmihalyi, M. and Hermanson, K. (1995) Intrinsic motivation in museums: what makes visitors want to learn? *Museum News*, 74, 34–62.

————. (1999) *Flow in the applied environment*. Seminar held 18 March 1999, School of Leisure and Tourism, University of Technology Sydney, Australia.

de Montebello, P. (1996) Interview with Philippe de Montebello, Director of The Metropolitan Museum of Art, in New York, 11 April 1996.

Demetrian, J. (1996) Interview with James Demetrian director of the Hirshhorn Museum and Sculpture Garden, in Washington, D.C., 16 April 1996.

Gardner, H. (1983) *Frames of mind: the theory of multiple intelligences*. Basic Books. New York (1995) *Leading minds: an anatomy of leadership*. Basic Books. New York.

Gaudieri, M. (1996) Telephone interview with Mimi Gaudieri, Coordinator for the Association of Art Museum Directors, in New York, 4 June 1996.

Glynn, M. (1996) Innovative genius: a framework for relating individual and organizational intelligences to innovation. *Academy of Management Review*, 21, 1,081–1,111.

Goleman, D. (1996) *Emotional intelligence: why it can matter more than IQ*. Bloomsbury. London.

Hall, D. (1995) Interview with Doug Hall, Director of the Queensland Art Gallery, in Brisbane, 20 February 1995.

Hawley, A. (1996) Telephone interview with Anne Hawley, Director of the Isabella Stewart Gardner Museum, in Boston, 4 April 1996.

Jaque, E. and Clement, S. (1994) *Executive leadership: a practical guide to managing complexity*. Blackwell. Cambridge, Massachusetts.

Jenneman, E. (1996) Interview with Eugene Jenneman, Director of the Dennos Museum Center, in Traverse, 13 May 1996.

Kolb, N. (1996) Telephone interview with Nancy Kolb, Director of the Please Touch Museum, in Philadelphia, 21 June 1996.

Koshalek, R. (1996) Interview with Richard Koshalek, Director of the Museum of Contemporary Art, in Los Angeles, 2 April 1996.

Latos-Valier, P. (1996) Telephone interview with Paula Latos-Valier, Director of the Art Gallery of Western Australia, in Perth, 2 September 1996.

Lowry, G. (1996) Interview with Glen Lowry, Director of the Museum of Modern Art, in New York, 12 April 1996.

Marzio, P. (1996) Telephone interview with Peter Marzio, Director of the Museum of Fine Arts, in Houston, Texas, 27 June 1996.

McCaughy, P. (1996) Interview with Patrick McCaughy, Director of the Yale Center for British Art, in New Haven, 15 April 1996.

Mezias, S. and Glynn, M. (1993) The three faces of corporate renewal: institution, revolution and evolution. *Strategic Management Journal*, 31, 235–256.

Nichols, N. (1996) Telephone interview with Nancy Nichols, Executive Recruitment Consultant with Heidrick and Struggles, in New York, 13 June 1996.

Ottley, D. (1995) Telephone interview with Dr. Dennis Ottley, senior lecturer in marketing and entrepreneurship in the Faculty of Management at the University of Western Sydney, Hawkesbury, 15 August 1995.

Parker, H. (1995) Interview with Harry Parker, Director of The Fine Arts Museums of San Francisco, in San Francisco, 14 June 1995.

Pennar, K. (1996) How many smarts do you have? *Business Week,* September 16, 52–55.

Potts, T. (1995) Interview with Tim Potts, Director of the National Gallery of Victoria, in Melbourne, 11 August 1995.

Powell, E. (1996) Interview with Earl Powell, Director of the National Gallery of Art, in Washington, D.C., 17 April 1996.

Q-metrics (1996) *EQ Map.* Trade marked product of Essi Systems and AIT in San Francisco, California.

Ross, D. (1996) Interview with David Ross, Director of the Whitney Museum of American Art, in New York, 11 April 1996.

Sano, E. (1995) Interview with Emily Sano, Director of the Asian Art Museum of San Francisco, 15 June 1995.

Senge, P. (1990) *The fifth discipline: the art and practice of the learning organization.* Doubleday. New York.

Serota, N. (1996) Interview with Nicholas Serota, Director of The Tate Gallery, in London, 30 April 1996.

Spate, V. (ed.) (1980) *French painting: the revolutionary decades 1760-1830.* Australian Gallery Directors Council Ltd., Sydney.

Stamp, G. (1993) Well-being at work: aligning purposes, people, strategies, and structures. *The International Journal of Career Management*, 5, 1–36.

Suchy, S. (1998) *An international study on the director's role in art museum leadership.* Doctoral thesis available through the library at the University of Western Sydney Nepean. Sydney, Australia.

Thompson, S. (1996) Interview with Shirley Thompson, Director of the National Gallery of Canada, in Ottawa, 25 June 1996.

Vecchio, R., Hearn, G. and Southey, G. (1995) *Organisational behavior: life at work in Australia.* Harcourt Brace. Sydney.

Walsh, J. (1995) Interview with John Walsh, Director of the J. Paul Getty Museum, in Santa Monica, 7 June 1995.

Wood, J. (1996) Interview with James Wood, Director of The Art Institute of Chicago, in Chicago, 26 June 1996.

Governance as Leadership

38

Bringing New Governing Mindsets to
Old Challenges

RICHARD P. CHAIT, WILLIAM P. RYAN, AND BARBARA E. TAYLOR

INVITED BY BOARDSOURCE TO TAKE A FRESH LOOK at the problems and potential of nonprofit boards, we decided early on to look at leadership. The transformation of leadership theory and practice in recent decades, we thought, might suggest what it would take to develop new ideas and practices for governance. But as we dug deeper, our interest in leadership shifted. In addition to looking at governance in light of leadership, we began reframing governance as leadership. We believe that the concept of governance as leadership gives boards a new way to understand governance and, more important, new practices for governing more effectively.

Governance in Light of Leadership

We found that three developments in the recent theory and practice of leadership had important implications for governance.

1. A Virtuous Circle of Theory and Practice

Why do leaders understand and practice leadership differently today than they might have fifty years ago? Partly because of a huge surge of interest in leadership that led to an abundance of new concepts and theories. Theorists and researchers in fields as varied as psychology, sociology, political science, and management all studied leaders and leadership. Leaders themselves joined in the sprawling debate about what makes for effective leadership. By studying leaders at work, the re-

Richard P. Chait is a professor at the Harvard Graduate School of Education. William P. Ryan is a consultant to foundations and nonprofit organizations and a research fellow at the Hauser Center for Nonprofit Organizations at Harvard University. Barbara E. Taylor is a senior consultant with the Academic Search Consultation Service, a nonprofit executive search firm. Reprinted with permission from the June/July 2004 edition of *BoardMember*, Vol. 13, No. 4, a publication of BoardSource, formerly the National Center for Nonprofit Boards. For more information about BoardSource, call 1-800-883-6262 or visit boardsource.org. BoardSource copyright 2011. Text may not be reproduced without written permission from BoardSource.

searchers developed new theories; the new theories, in turn, inspired new practice. This virtuous circle of theory and practice changed the field.

Governance is different. While there is urgent interest in the problems of boards, and a growing demand for more accountability, there is very little governance theory. We don't think about or debate governing; we just do it. The literature aimed at boards is mostly prescriptive, a series of dos and don'ts. It summarizes practices that are considered effective, clarifies the roles and responsibilities of boards, and, in the process, reinforces both sound practical wisdom and less valuable conventional wisdom. In short, to get new governing practices, the field will need new governing concepts.

2. Multiple Modes for Complex Organizations

Many practitioners and theorists have converged on a central insight into leadership: Effective leaders don't mobilize people and organizations because they see things in one way; they succeed because they see things in many different ways. They can look at a complex organization's most difficult problems from many vantage points, which, together, give them a better appreciation for their options. And in responding to the challenges they face, they bring different mindsets to bear, and work in multiple modes. Theorists and practitioners have identified a number of these modes, in which, for example, leaders act as politicians, icons, culture builders, coaches, enforcers, managers, bureaucrats, and so on.

In contrast, we tend to understand governance as a set of board tasks rather than a series of governing modes or mindsets. For many boards, governance is a series of routines: overseeing budgets, receiving audits, hearing reports, approving strategic plans, and so on. They might be multitaskers, but most boards are not multimodal. We simply don't have ideas and language to think about the different mindsets that boards should bring to different aspects of governing.

3. The Power of Framing

Many students of leadership have reached consensus on a second point: Leaders exercise their greatest power by framing the issues at hand. In many cases, organizations face not problems but, as Donald Schon puts it, "problematic situations," where it is clear something is wrong, but not exactly what. It's in deciding what the real problem is that leaders exercise their greatest power. Once the problem is framed, the options for solutions are set. More broadly, leaders influence their organizations by deciding what the organization should pay attention to and then providing ways of looking at it. While we are used to thinking of formal organizational processes like mission setting, strategic planning, or program development —as the source of power in organizations, effective leaders understand that framing the issues drives all of these processes.

This aspect of leadership—what we call generative thinking—raises profound questions for governance. If governance is all about setting organizational purposes and monitoring progress toward those purposes, then don't boards need to be engaged in this work? This powerful work is associated with leadership, but can boards really be governing if they do not participate in it? Those questions suggest a shift—toward governance as leadership.

Governance Reframed as Leadership

Boards could govern more effectively by taking a leadership approach to their work. Just as today's complex organizations demand leaders who work in multiple modes, they demand boards that govern in multiple modes.

We posit that there are three modes of governance that together constitute governance as leadership. Unless boards govern in these three modes, it cannot be said that they are truly governing:

- Type I, the fiduciary mode, is where boards are concerned primarily with the stewardship of tangible assets. Type I constitutes the bedrock of governance—the fiduciary work intended to ensure that nonprofit organizations are faithful to mission, accountable for performance, and compliant with relevant laws and regulations. Without Type I, governance would have no legitimacy. If a board fails as fiduciary, the organization—not to mention its donors, clients, or community—could be harmed.
- Type II, the strategic mode, is where boards develop strategy with management to set the organization's priorities and course, and to deploy resources accordingly. Without Type II, governance would have little power or influence. It would be more about staying on course than setting the course.
- Type III, the generative mode, is where boards, along with executives, frame problems and make sense of ambiguous situations—which in turn shapes the organization's strategies, plans, and decisions. Because most organizations lack frameworks and practices for this work, it's easy for boards to become bystanders to it—even though it is central to governance.

A board's effectiveness increases as the board members become more proficient in more modes. A board that excels in one mode (or two) but flounders in another one (or two) will govern far less effectively than a board that ably works in all three. To succeed in all three modes, boards need to "cross-train" so that the "muscle memory" of one mode does not dominate to the detriment of the others. When boards overemphasize one mode to the exclusion of others (a common problem), the net results are worse, not better, governance.

Many issues (although not all) will demand deliberating in all three modes. Consider the decision of the Boston Museum of Fine Arts (MFA) to loan twenty-one Monet masterpieces to the Bellagio Casino in Las Vegas. This one issue, like many others that reach boards, poses questions for Types I, II, and III governance:

- Type I Governance: Are the paintings travel worthy? What are the insurance and security arrangements? Are there any bequest-related restrictions on travel

Figure 38.1.   The governance triangle.

Generative

or venues? How long a loan period? How much will Bellagio pay? How and where will the MFA's name appear?

- Type II Governance: Will the absence of the Monets affect MFA patronage? How will association with Bellagio and Las Vegas affect the MFA's image and reputation? Should the MFA sponsor "tie-in" events in Boston or Las Vegas? What can the MFA accomplish with the income from Bellagio?
- Type III Governance: What will we do (or not do) if the price is right? Should we loan art to the highest bidder? Should we display art where the masses already are? Do MFA masterworks "belong" in neon-light, pop-culture, for-profit venues? How conservative or iconoclastic an institution do we wish to be?

To ask only about the insurance costs, or only about the patronage implications, or only about the MFA's fit with pop-culture institutions, is to govern only a little. For effective governance, boards need all three modes.

New Practices for Generative Governing

Though Types I and II governance pose many challenges, board members generally understand their responsibility to do this work, and are familiar with the practices and processes of fiduciary and strategic governance. For most, a bigger—and potentially more rewarding challenge—lies in developing new approaches to generative governing. We call it the black-box of generative thinking—the processes that leaders and groups use to frame problems and make sense of ambiguous situations—and we ask how they can be converted into systematic practices that boards can use to govern. Among the major practice challenges are

- Governing at the boundary. Generative governing requires that boards position themselves differently, moving from the seclusion of the boardroom to active learning at the organization's boundaries.

- Recruiting for generative work. Trusteeship has generally—and mistakenly—been conceived as the sum of Types I and II governing. As a result, the recruitment and development has focused on fiduciary and strategic capabilities. Generative governing requires a different appreciation for a wider array of board talents.
- New forms and norms for discourse. While fiduciary and strategy work can place a premium on consensus views, generative governing requires board members to explore multiple, sometimes conflicting views. This requires ditching Robert's Rules of Order for a different type of discourse, and adopting a norm that values frank discussion and disagreement in the boardroom.
- Focusing on the past, not just the future. Because of their role in developing or approving strategy, boards are often conditioned to plan for, and focus on, the future. But an understanding of generative thinking suggests governing requires exploring the past as well. As boards explore and reinterpret the past, they find new patterns, new ways of framing old problems, and new sources of ideas—all of which can help organizations set a different course for the future.

Although many board members might be inclined to look for more effective governance in the form of new board structures, governance as leadership suggests a different approach: bringing new governing modes and mindsets, with their related practices, to old challenges.

The Source   **39**
Twelve Principles of Governance That Power Exceptional Boards

BOARDSOURCE

EXCEPTIONAL BOARDS ADD SIGNIFICANT value to their organizations, making a discernible difference in their advance on mission. Good governance requires the board to balance its role as an oversight body with its role as a force supporting the organization. The difference between responsible and exceptional boards lies in thoughtfulness and intentionality, action and engagement, knowledge and communication. The following twelve principles offer chief executives a description of an empowered board that is a strategic asset to be leveraged. They provide board members with a vision of what is possible and way to add lasting value to the organization they lead.

Constructive Partnership[1]
Exceptional boards govern in constructive partnership with the chief executive, recognizing that the effectiveness of the board and chief executive are interdependent. They build this partnership through trust, candor, respect, and honest communication.

Mission Driven[2]
Exceptional boards shape and uphold the mission, articulate a compelling vision, and ensure the congruence between decisions and core values. They treat questions of mission, vision, and core values not as exercises to be done once, but as statements of crucial importance to be drilled down and folded into deliberations.

Strategic Thinking[3]

Exceptional boards allocate time to what matters most and continuously engage in strategic thinking to hone the organization's direction. They not only align agendas and goals with strategic priorities, but also use them for assessing the chief executive, driving meeting agendas, and shaping board recruitment.

Culture of Inquiry[4]

Exceptional boards institutionalize a culture of inquiry, mutual respect, and constructive debate that leads to sound and shared decision making. They seek more information, question assumptions, and challenge conclusions so that they may advocate for solutions based on analysis.

Independent Mindedness[5]

Exceptional boards are independent-minded. They apply rigorous conflict-of-interest procedures, and their board members put the interests of the organization above all else when making decisions. They do not allow their votes to be unduly influenced by loyalty to the chief executive or by seniority, position, or reputation of fellow board members, staff, or donors.

Ethos of Transparency[6]

Exceptional boards promote an ethos of transparency by ensuring that donors, stakeholders, and interested members of the public have access to appropriate and accurate information regarding finances, operations, and results. They also extend transparency internally, ensuring that every board member has equal access to relevant materials when making decisions.

Compliance with Integrity[7]

Exceptional boards promote strong ethical values and disciplined compliance by establishing appropriate mechanisms for active oversight. They use these mechanisms, such as independent audits, to ensure accountability and sufficient controls; to deepen their understanding of the organization; and to reduce the risk of waste, fraud, and abuse.

Sustaining Resources[8]

Exceptional boards link bold visions and ambitious plans to financial support, expertise, and networks of influence. Linking budgeting to strategic planning, they approve activities that can be realistically financed with existing or attainable resources, while ensuring that the organization has the infrastructure and internal capacity it needs.

Results Oriented[9]

Exceptional boards are results oriented. They measure the organization's progress toward mission and evaluate the performance of major programs and services. They gauge efficiency, effectiveness, and impact, while simultaneously assessing the quality of service delivery, integrating benchmarks against peers, and calculating return on investment.

Intentional Board Practices[10]

Exceptional boards purposefully structure themselves to fulfill essential governance duties and to support organizational priorities. Making governance intentional, not incidental, exceptional boards invest in structures and practices that can be thoughtfully adapted to changing circumstances.

Continuous Learning[11]

Exceptional boards embrace the qualities of a continuous learning organization, evaluating their own performance and assessing the value they add to the organization. They embed learning opportunities into routine governance work and in activities outside of the boardroom.

Revitalization[12]

Exceptional boards energize themselves through planned turnover, thoughtful recruitment, and inclusiveness. They see the correlation between mission, strategy, and board composition, and they understand the importance of fresh perspectives and the risks of closed groups. They revitalize themselves through diversity of experience and through continuous recruitment.

On the Job   **40**
For Nonprofits, Final Accountability Rests in the Board's Hands

BOARDSOURCE

LISA BATTALIA DOESN'T LIKE SURPRISES. The executive director of the Wisconsin Women's Workshop, a Racine-based nonprofit that coordinates counseling and health services for women, Battalia maps out her workday well in advance. She's got meetings to be scheduled, reports to be written, deadlines to be met. When it comes to the day-to-day operations of the organization, Battalia strives to be in the know. The last thing she wants is an unwelcome surprise to throw her off her game.

"Everyone has put a lot of trust in me to make sure the organization runs smoothly," she says. "I take that responsibility very seriously."

Battalia extends her disdain for surprises to her board as well. Even before the seven-person board meets every six months, Battalia makes sure that each member has a complete picture of the health and progress of the organization. New programs launched in the last year are described. Recent proposals are discussed. Troubled programs are evaluated. At these board meetings, there are no surprises.

"A lot of accountability rests with me, but I know that the crux of a nonprofit organization is the board," Battalia says. "The buck doesn't just stop with the board. It starts there too."

At the Women's Workshop, accountability is always on the agenda. And, like many nonprofits, its board maintains its accountability by keeping an eye on all facets of the organization—from its financial reports to its mission statement. The Workshop board has embraced a culture of responsibility, Battalia says. "Accountability is their job," she says. "There are a lot of things that a board can delegate. But accountability is not one of them."

But as accountability becomes a front page issue around the country, many nonprofit leaders worry that Battalia's group may be the exception. While few critics claim that the nonprofit world is replete with financial mismanagement and ethical abuses, many caution that boards must protect against taking their accountability for granted. "Too many boards never consider the scope of their responsibilities until they are embroiled in scandal," says Brent Longnecker, president of the Resources Connection Group, an international professional services firm based in Houston, Texas. "For those boards," Longnecker says, "it's time to brush off your mission statement and take a close look at the systems you've created to protect your organization's good name."

"There are some nonprofits that see what's happening in the corporate world and know they are vulnerable too," Longnecker says. "But most of them just don't get it. They think, 'Oh no, that's no me. That can't happen here.'"

The Top of Your List

While accountability should always be on a board's agenda, the current corporate climate has pushed the issue to the forefront. From Enron to the United Way, the public has endured a seemingly unending string of accountability scandals. "If this isn't at the top of your list right now, then it should be—soon," says Deborah House, founder of the Adare Group, a strategic consulting company in Oakbrook Terrace, Ill. And while the trials of the for-profit world differ in many ways from nonprofit problems, the subtle distinctions are often lost in the headlines. Stories of mismanaged funds and executives under fire blur in the public's mind. Someone cooked their books. Someone misrepresented donations. Someone betrayed the public trust.

"When they read about these things in the news, the public doesn't make the distinction between for-profit and nonprofit," Battalia says. "People are looking for someone to trust. When you abuse that trust, it doesn't matter if you are World-Com or the Red Cross. You are going to be lumped together as crooks."

And while questionable dealings in the for-profit world can be devastating to companies and their employees, nonprofit accountability lapses can have equally dire consequences. Nonprofits that neglect their responsibilities risk everything from their donor base to their tax-free status to, perhaps their most important resource, their good reputation. "The truth is that nonprofits are held to a higher standard," Longnecker says. "You have to answer to an entire community and, oh by the way, the IRS too."

If nonprofits aren't willing to take their accountability responsibilities seriously, numerous lawmakers are waiting to force their hand. Several pending state and federal measures would increase scrutiny and regulation of nonprofits. Some states have introduced legislation that would further limit nonprofits' lobbying activity. Others have attempted to levy different taxes on nonprofits. In Nashville, city officials recently lost their legal bid to consider a nonprofit's reputation before allowing it to raise money in the community.

In April, the Government Accounting Office (GAO) released a report that questioned whether the nonprofit sector had grown too large to fall under the IRS's purview. Instead, the report hinted that greater federal oversight might be necessary.

"Federal regulation is the last thing the nonprofit world needs," Longnecker says. "Can you imagine an SEC for nonprofits? No one wants to go down that track."

Playing the Numbers

The nonprofit world still enjoys lofty public approval ratings, despite high-profile scandals and drops in donations following September 11. A 2001 survey by Independent Sector revealed that 62 percent of the public believes that charities are more effective in providing services than they were five years ago. That's the highest degree of public confidence in the nonprofit world in fourteen years. The survey showed high confidence in nearly all charitable institutions, particularly when compared with the corporate world. Organizations like youth development groups (72 percent) and human services agencies (68 percent) were given astonishingly high degrees of trust, as opposed to major corporations (29 percent), the federal government (27 percent), and Congress (22 percent).

"Here's the message: The public likes nonprofits. They want to see you succeed," House says.

Not all the statistical news was reassuring. The same survey showed that only 62 percent of Americans believe that charities are ethical in their use of donated funds, down from 71 percent in 1990. And while nonprofits enjoy greater popularity, they also face greater public scrutiny and increasing demands of accountability. "The public knows that you are good, passionate people," House says. "But they are also saying: 'Hey, don't forget to take care of the back room.'"

But while few would downplay the importance of accountability, experts caution nonprofit boards to pay closer attention to their good reputation. "Accountability is like that joke about the weather," Longnecker says. "Everybody talks about it, but nobody does anything about it."

Board members can be unsure of the role they play in the accountability landscape, House says. To a few, board membership is still largely seen as a ceremonial position, an honor rather than a responsibility. "If you want to be on a board—whether it's a company or a nonprofit—just to have a nice appointment on your resume, then don't bother," House says. "Realize that being on a board is hard work."

Other board members may feel that the nuts-and-bolts of accountability fall outside of their job descriptions. They are happy just to know that someone else is minding the store. "Over and over, I hear people say, 'I'm sitting on this board to make a difference in the community. I don't want to have to deal with financial statements,'" Longnecker says. "It's even worse among corporate CEOs who join nonprofit boards. They invariably think, 'I do financials all day at work. I don't want to do it here too.'"

Choosing an Accountable Board
Before you agree to sit on a board, ask questions

Board membership carries heavy responsibility—both ethically and legally. In today's nonprofit climate, prospective members who merely want to add a board title to their credentials need not apply. Board members must be prepared to roll up their sleeves and get to work.

But before committing themselves to a nonprofit, prospective members must ask if the organization shares their ethics and values. "We all know that nonprofits are having more and more trouble finding people to serve on their boards," says Nancy Kiskis, a partner at the law firm of Moss & Barnett in Minneapolis. "As a board member, you are helping to set general policy for an entire organization. You are making yourself accountable. And you want to make sure that the rest of the organization is following suit."

But how can you tell if the board is as committed as you are? Before you agree to take a seat, take a look around the organization. And ask a few simple questions:

- Do you know its reputation in the community? "Does the organization have a track record of integrity?" asks Deborah House of the Adare Group. What do community leaders say about it? How about the public it serves? Talk to former board members about their experiences.
- Is the board responsive? "When you ask for information, do they give you details? Are they open about it?" says Janet Atkins, president and CEO of the Philanthropic Advisors at Goulston & Storrs law firm in Boston. "Do they admit when they don't know something—and then do they promptly research it and get back to you?"
- Is anyone home? See the environment that the staff has created. "Stop by their office space and see how it looks," House says. "It should be professional, certainly. But I get suspicious if it's too opulent."
- Are they on the job? "If possible, go to the places where they work," House says. If they build homes, go to those homes. If they maintain shelters, go to the shelters. You can learn a lot by studying documents, but seeing how the staff works with your own eyes is invaluable.
- What is the board looking for? "Pay close attention to what they say when they are interviewing you," says Brent Longnecker, of the Resources Connection Group in Houston, Texas. "Are they clearly explaining your roles and responsibilities? Do they talk to you about accountability?" Don't let them sweep that question under the rug. If you are not satisfied, ask them about their views on accountability. If it's a top priority for them, you should receive a clear answer.

More often, board members are simply baffled by the many aspects of accountability. Many are still seeking clear answers about what they are accountable for—and to whom they are accountable.

Indefinable?

No definition of accountability can apply to every nonprofit's situation. And many board members resist an absolute definition that might uncomfortably shoehorn their organization into a position they can't defend. "It's different for every organization, but most people think they know accountability when they see it," House says.

An easy answer—albeit an incomplete one—would be to lump all aspects of accountability into one word: money. Some boards feel that they have covered themselves if their numbers add up. That's a particularly tempting prospect in light of high profile cases of corporate mismanagement. "It's not your money, and the public wants you to acknowledge that," says Tom Mesaros, CEO of the Alford Group consulting firm. "You are a public steward. They want to know that you are spending the money the way they intended it to be spent."

File your 990 on time. Represent your donations accurately. Ensure that your spending is in line with donor intent. But is that enough to earn an accountability seal of approval? "Numbers. Dollars. There's no denying that there is a financial bottom line," says Danielle Baron-McPheter, director of not-for-profit services at Meaden & Moore, a regional accounting and business consulting firm in Cleveland. McPheter also serves as a member of the finance committee for the YWCA of Greater Cleveland.

"But even I have to admit that nobody gets involved with a nonprofit for the financials. It's all about the mission," she says.

As obvious as the mission-first theory sounds, it's easier to talk about than to actually put into practice. "You need to view accountability from two perspectives," says Jane Tarkerness, an associate professor of business management at Florida Atlantic University, "from a few feet off the ground and from 100,000 feet in the air. You have to see the little picture and the big. I think most of us are comfortable with the little picture, the day-to-day. But the big picture—incorporating accountability into your values and ethics and the way you do business—that can be hard to put your arms around."

The Accountable Culture

Like the corporate world, many nonprofit leaders worry that the misdeeds of a few organizations have colored the perception of the entire sector. But few are clamoring about an impending crisis of confidence in the sector as a whole. "I wouldn't panic and start scraping together bail money for your chief executive," Tarkerness says. "But it's never a bad time to take a look at where the organization is going."

While there is no one blueprint for accountability, all boards can benefit from rethinking the way they fulfill their obligations. "If you haven't gotten together to talk about the need to be more involved and to review your responsibilities, it's time to take a step back," Longnecker says.

Alford's Mesaros suggests an accountability retreat, a weekend-long meeting that focuses the board's attention on discussing how accountability fits into its strategic plans. At the very least, experts say, each nonprofit must ask itself a few questions to decide where it stands on the accountability landscape:

- Have you read your mission statement lately? "Review your bylaws and your mission statement," says Janet Atkins, president and CEO of the Philanthropic Advisors at Goulston & Storrs law firm in Boston. "Do you have clear policies regarding conflict of interest? Self-dealing? Private inurement? Do you have a code of ethics?" If you don't, Atkins suggests, ask yourself why. Many nonprofits will insist they deal with these issues on a case-by-case basis. But a solid policy foundation can support you in tough times.
- Who's keeping the books? "Are you getting regular reports from your finance committee or do you just trust that they are handling it?" YWCA's McPheter asks. Are you performing regular independent audits? It's your obligation to be aware of your overall financial situation. Ignorance is no excuse.
- Are you overusing your rubber stamp? "I hope that your board meetings are active and exciting," House says. Forget business as usual. Ask rigorous questions on all topics. Keep yourself informed. Foster a climate where there are no dumb questions.
- Does everyone know his job? "Look at your performance criteria for your CEO and your staff. And review their compensation carefully," Atkins says. Everyone should have a job description even the board members. And the board should undergo performance assessments just like chief executives and staff. If you find that the board is lagging behind on an issue, stop and plan an education session.
- Are you using your members' skills? "Make it clear to new board members that they aren't just there to contribute money. They have a skill set and you intend to take advantage of it," House says. Board members must be aware of their oversight obligations and the need to play an active role in the organization. Board service shouldn't be treated as a spectator sport.
- How transparent are you? The law requires a minimum amount of transparency. But are you taking it beyond the legal requirements? Openness breeds trust. Show that you have nothing to hide.

Danielle Baron-McPheter is used to the blank stares. The yawns don't faze her anymore. The glassy eyes? Seen them. She doesn't think anyone has actually fallen asleep during one of her presentations. But there have been enough nodding heads to suggest that it may just be a matter of time.

"I know financials are dry. It's not what people want to talk about at a board meeting," says McPheter, a member of the finance committee at the YWCA of Greater Cleveland. "But this goes with the territory. I think most boards get that."

Most, but not all. McPheter also serves as director of not-for-profit services at Meaden & Moore, a Cleveland accounting firm. While recently presenting a financial report to one nonprofit board, McPheter noticed the telltale signs of boredom. Board members drummed their fingers. They rubbed their eyes. Still, McPheter was encouraged that the board persevered through the numbers. But the first question from a board member dampened her enthusiasm.

"The member said, 'Well, that's all very interesting, but we are extremely busy,'" McPheter recalls. "He asked: 'Do we really need to know this?'"

The answer is a resounding yes. Finances may not be the driving force that inspires someone to join a board, but fiscal oversight is among the most important aspects of board accountability. Board members must be knowledgeable about where the organization's money is coming from—and where it's going. It's not just their job, McPheter notes. It's their legal obligation.

From 990s to budgets, from financial statements to donor intent, one of the many responsibilities of every board is to maintain fiscal accountability. Board members act as trustees of the organization's assets and must exercise due diligence to make sure that the nonprofit is well managed and financially sound.

Still, for many boards, money matters are relegated to a dark corner. McPheter has seen more than a few members who prefer that the finance committee add columns of numbers out of sight and mind of the full board. "As long as they think some one else is doing it, most board members don't want to think about money," McPheter says. "They assume money will take care of itself."

Some board members don't pay attention to financials until they find themselves in the midst of a fiscal crisis, warns Jane Tarkerness, an associate professor of business management at Florida Atlantic University (FAU). "In many cases, people think [the finances are] under control. When they aren't, people feel blindsided," she says. "They want to know why this didn't come up six months ago."

A careless approach to financial oversight is clearly a recipe for disaster. And while not all board members need to be math majors, they must acquire a basic working knowledge of their fiduciary responsibilities, says Janet Atkins, president and CEO of the Boston-based Philanthropic Advisors. "You don't have to be a CPA, but you have to know what's going on," Atkins says. "There should be someone on the board who understands money. Just as importantly, there needs to be someone who can translate that information to the rest of the board."

Number Block

In light of the public's impatience with recent financial scandals, "your fiduciary role may be the most important part of your job," says Nancy Kiskis, a nonprofit expert at the law firm of Moss & Barnett in Minneapolis. Board members must know their legal requirements, understand basic terminology, be able to read a financial statement, and recognize warning signs that might indicate fiscal trouble within the organization. "Pay attention. Ask questions. Be engaged," Atkins says.

Certainly, the financial aspects of an organization can be dry and intimidating. "Have you ever tried to plow through the financial statements of one of those big health care nonprofits?" says Tom Mesaros of the Alford Group consulting firm. "Their statements are an inch thick."

And not every board member walks onto the job with financial expertise. "There is a lack of education among boards about numbers," McPheter says. "It just doesn't make sense to them. They don't want to get involved in it." But even board members without financial acumen can take an interest in the money end of the organization. First, McPheter says, they have to be willing to raise their hands. "If something doesn't sound right, speak up," she says. "Believe me, if you don't understand it, chances are a whole lot of other people don't get it either."

Still, even the most engaged board members may not know the right questions to ask, notes FAU's Tarkerness. She suggests that each board member consider the following questions when faced with financial data:

- **How is this consistent with our mission?** "This should always be the first thing on your mind," Tarkerness says. "Every financial activity must be mission based. Otherwise, why are you doing it?"
- **Are our finances in line with our budget?** "You basically want to know if you are overspending," Atkins says. "What does your cash flow look like? What are your expenses? This isn't all that different from balancing your checkbook."
- **Are our expenses—including overhead and salaries—appropriate in light of our donations?** These are hardly absolutes, although Tarkerness recommends that executive compensation never exceed 7 percent of your budget while overhead costs hover at 17 percent. "Benchmark yourself against other organizations that are similar to yours," she notes. "Don't do this in a vacuum."
- **Do we have the right checks and balances in place to protect our organization against malfeasance?** Are you performing a regular independent audit to document your financial status? Does the board meet with the auditor in an executive session without staff? The external auditor plays a key role in monitoring the accounting systems and evaluating the accuracy of financial reporting.

Open Books

But beyond watching the money, the board is responsible for creating an honest fiscal culture within the organization. It's the board's job to foster an atmosphere of transparency with all of its financial dealings and information. Not only must the board be accountable for knowing how the money is spent, but it must make sure that its transactions are as open as possible. "The more forthcoming you can be, the better," Mesaros says. "When I hear about organizations that keep their money close to the vest, I wonder what they have to hide."

Likewise, an organization's integrity can be judged by the way it reacts to difficult financial situations. "When the numbers don't add up, are you fully disclosing it?" McPheter asks. "Are you going right back to your funders and telling them what happened? Or are you saying, 'We don't want anyone to know about this. We'll make up the money some other way.'"

Paying careful attention to finances is the most effective way for the board to head off potential problems. That's a lesson Mesaros learned when he served on the finance committee of the Providence Foundation of Seattle in the early 1990s. Mesaros's committee had worked feverishly to prepare a detailed budget. He presented what he believed was a first-rate report to the executive committee. But the committee announced that it was regretfully sending the budget back to finance for more work. The expenses weren't in line with the group's revenue, the board said. And they told Mesaros to fix it.

"When I stepped out of that meeting, after all the hard work we did, my assistant said to me, 'I'm so sorry. I always thought they liked you,'" Mesaros recalls. "I told her that they did like me. They just like the organization better. And that's the way it should be. That board was really on its toes. I like to think that's not a rarity."

Is the 990 enough?
A chorus of critics say that financial accountability goes beyond the IRS form

For more than thirty years, the nonprofit world has viewed the IRS Form 990 as a touchstone for accountability. All nonprofits, except for churches or those that earn less than $25,000 a year, must file the annual information form with the IRS. The 990 requires nonprofits to disclose amounts spent on programs, management, and fundraising. It also includes the salaries of the five highest paid employees and the five highest paid providers of professional services, over $50,000.

The forms, which are often cited as the most easily accessible method of ensuring nonprofit accountability, are public record. Over the last few years, Congress has expanded public access to the forms, including mandating that a nonprofit make three years worth of 990s available to anyone who asks for them. GuideStar, an online charity watchdog, has expanded public access to these forms by making them available on the Internet.

But critics are suggesting that the 990 isn't as comprehensive as the public has been led to believe. An April 2002 report by the Government Accounting Office (GAO) warned that a 990 does not give an accurate picture in regard to charity spending. It also cautioned the public not to rely on the 990 when determining a nonprofit's efficiency.

The GAO held up two aspects of the 990 for criticism: First, the document offers no means to substantiate the accuracy of the reported data. The GAO suggests that some nonprofits might misrepresent their financial information to appear more attractive to donors.

Second, the report maintains that charities exercise too much discretion in the way they categorize expenses, often misreporting the actual costs of fundraising and overhead. The report cites an Urban Institute study of more than 58,000 charities that received public donations. Of that group, 59 percent either reported zero fundraising expenses on their 990 or left the line blank.

Nonprofits can find the 990 to be an imperfect tool as well. Many contend that the form draws too much attention to employee salaries. "Some people feel that the form is preoccupied with numbers," says Harriet Bograd, a New York-based attorney. "It takes an enormous amount of effort to gather all the information needed in the form, and everyone always turns immediately to the salaries."

As a result, the BBB Wise Giving Alliance (formerly the National Charities Information Bureau) recommends greater communication and transparency between the nonprofit world and the public it serves. The group suggests that nonprofits release expanded information to the public, including annual reports containing statements of goals and accomplishments, board member information, and detailed financial records. Watchdog groups have encouraged nonprofits to disclose financial statements prepared by outside auditors. Others stress the benefits of "cyber-accountability," where nonprofits make their documents available on their websites.

Multicultural Organizational Development in Nonprofit Organizations   41
Lessons from the Cultural Competence Learning Initiative

LAURIN MAYENO AND STEVE LEW

Introduction and Context

Purpose of this Document

WHAT DOES IT TAKE TO INTEGRATE CULTURAL competence into the day-to-day operations of a community-based nonprofit organization? Once the work is started, how do you move it to the next level and sustain an ongoing process? The Cultural Competence Learning Initiative (CCLI) was initiated by CompassPoint Nonprofit Services [www.compasspoint.org] to contribute to learning and practice around these questions. Through this project, funded by The California Endowment, eleven community-based nonprofit organizations involved in improving community health outcomes received multicultural organizational development support from a CompassPoint consultant team.

This document is geared towards individual organizations, funders, or practitioners of cultural competence and multicultural organizational development. It shares lessons from the project to inform work in the field and provides practical examples of how participating organizations addressed different areas of cultural competence. Several tools and templates created as a part of this initiative can be accessed through hyperlinks provided in this document. The paper is written from the point of view of the project's lead consultants, Laurin Mayeno of Mayeno Consulting and Steve Lew of CompassPoint, and is informed by the experience and insights of participants.

Laurin Mayeno is the principal of Mayeno Consulting, a firm that assists organizations with multicultural capacity building, group facilitation, and leadership development. Steve Lew is a senior project director for CompassPoint Nonprofit Services and works with organizations in creating strategic plans, fund development plans, and board development plans. "Multicultural Organizational Development in Nonprofit Organizations: Lessons from the Cultural Competence Learning Initiative" is a 2008–2010 initiative of CompassPoint Nonprofit Services made possible by The California Endowment. It is reprinted here by permission of CompassPoint Nonprofit Services and Mayeno Consulting. All rights reserved.

Definitions of Common Terms

Cultural competence: A set of congruent behaviors, attitudes, and policies that come together In a system, agency, or among professionals to work effectively in cross-cultural situations. (Cross, T., B. J. Bazron et al., *Towards a Culturally Competent System of Care: Volume 1.* Washington, D.C.: National Technical Assistance Center for Children's Mental Health, Georgetown University Child Development Center, 1989, p. iv.)

Multicultural organizational development: A philosophy and practical approach that can help organizations to realize the potential of diversity through strategies aimed at personal, interpersonal, and organizational levels (Mayeno, L., "Multicultural Organizational Development," in *Multicultural Organizational Development: A Resource for Health Equity.* San Francisco: CompassPoint Nonprofit Services and The California Endowment, July 2007, p. 1).

Organization of the Document

In Section I, we discuss five building blocks for a sustainable process. We identified these essential elements for sustaining a process of multicultural organizational change based on our experience in the initiative. For each building block, we provide examples of work from participating organizations.

In Section II, we share five lessons learned from this project. These lessons were drawn from the experience of the consultants as well as comments and reports from participants.

In Section III, we summarize some of the impacts of multicultural development work that emerged from the initiative, including outcomes within the organization and changes in service delivery.

I. Building Blocks for a Sustainable Process

What are the key building blocks for developing and sustaining a process of multicultural development in an organization? Based on our work with participating organizations, we identified five elements that are important for a successful process. These building blocks are interconnected and each one supports development of the others.

1. Alignment and Investment of Organizational Players

A crucial aspect of the work was building individual and group investment in addressing issues of culture and difference at a deeper level. Aligning champions, leaders, and other players in the organization was identified as essential to engaging the entire organization in integrating cultural competence into its day-to-day work. Key to achieving this was surfacing and clarifying assumptions about culture and difference in a way that drew from people's personal experiences and that was

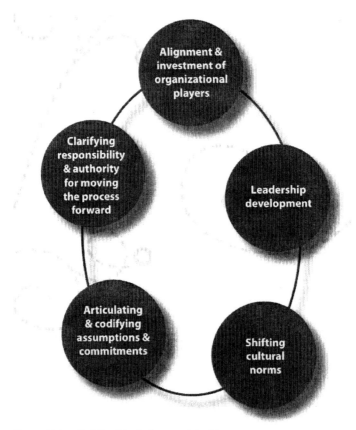

Figure 41.1.   Building blocks for a sustainable process.

relevant to their work. As a result, they could define cultural competence and multiculturalism in a way that resonated with their personal values rather than as a meaningless buzzword, obligation, or chore.

The level of organizational engagement and agreement differed depending on the agency's structure and stage of the process. For example, Women's Cancer Resource Center (WCRC) has a small staff and a large pool of volunteers, including groups focused specifically in the African American and Latino communities. WCRC engaged staff and volunteers in a series of community dialogues to develop "Principles of Cultural Humility" to guide the organization. Principles, such as "Recognize diversity within each cultural group" and "Respect my own boundaries and those of others," emerged from staff and volunteers' work with women with cancer from diverse backgrounds. By engaging constituents from different segments of its work, the organization was able to establish shared ownership, investment, and a sense of community that had not previously existed. WCRC's finalized Principles of Cultural Humility [www.compasspoint.org/cultural humility] were introduced at its annual volunteer recognition event and are being integrated into staff and volunteer orientation materials and activities. Ongoing community dialogues are also being instituted to break down silos between distinct community projects and contribute to a unified multicultural organization.

2. Leadership Development

Work on CCLI underscored the importance of cultivating and developing strong, cohesive leadership in an organization's cultural competence effort to establish a clear focus, maintain momentum, and address challenges that arise. Management's commitment was essential to assuring that multiculturalism was integrated into existing structures and practices, rather than remaining on the sidelines. Champions who were not part of the management structure also play an important leadership role in most organizations. It is generally recommended that both managers and non-managers be involved so multicultural organizational development isn't a top-down driven process; this also helps ensure that the perspectives of program and line staff, who often are closer to clients and their needs, are incorporated. In several instances in CCLI, a multicultural work group provided a structure for these formal and informal leaders to work in partnership.

The multicultural processes required that this mix of leaders stretch beyond their usual patterns of leadership in order to establish new patterns within their organizations. Requirements of leadership included:

- A commitment to do what it takes to keep cultural competence on the organizational agenda. This was particularly challenging in light of competing demands, shrinking resources, and the new level of challenge placed on leaders to sustain their organizations during the economic crisis.
- Skills and willingness to engage in "courageous conversations" that address uncomfortable or controversial topics related to multiculturalism. It was also especially powerful I when leaders modeled multicultural skills.
- A capacity to listen openly to different ideas, perspectives, and concerns. When leaders listened openly and non-defensively they gained important information and insights about what works and what could work better. Their listening and timely responses were also essential to engendering trust in the process among staff and other organizational players.

At Family Support Services of the Bay Area (FSSBA), the Senior Managers Team held responsibility for leading the organization's cultural competence work. This group took on several recommendations that emerged from an Undoing Racism workshop that staff attended. These senior managers recognized that they needed a common language and foundation to move the process forward, unify the agency, and provide leadership for the process. They spent time working with their consultant to clarify assumptions and roles, build trust, and clarify ways to respond proactively to staff recommendations.

The team of ten managers met every other month but had had difficulty maintaining forward momentum and clear direction. Although individual managers were doing the work within their departments and programs, they didn't have a clear picture of how to move it forward on an agency-wide level. The executive director, a white woman, also recognized that she had not asserted leadership to keep the process moving, because she was trying to step back to allow people of color to lead. These dynamics changed as the executive director began to provide more leadership. In addition, a subgroup of the Senior Managers Team, including the executive director, was established with responsibility for providing direction and follow up for the process as a whole.

After the Senior Managers Team worked together for several months, an agency wide training and dialogue titled Race, Power & Privilege: Interrupting the Cycle of Oppression was held and attended by all salaried staff, about sixty-five people. To encourage open dialogue, the managers made a shared commitment to the staff that there would be no negative repercussions for raising issues and concerns. As a result of their work together, the managers were able to engage throughout the day as a unified team and model open communication and courageous conversations with the rest of the staff.

3. Shifting Cultural Norms

Participating organizations established new cultural norms internally and opened up forums for courageous conversations on topics that weren't typically discussed. Most organizations worked on shifting these norms by adopting communication guidelines, modeling new communication behaviors, and building their practice through dialogues and discussion forums. Through these efforts, organizations "exercised a new muscle" to initiate and engage in courageous conversations. Questions like "Why aren't we keeping people of color in key positions?" or "What kinds of questions should we be asking clients about their culture?" began to be normalized as part of day-to-day activity.

Girls Inc. of Alameda County's Core (Cultural Competence) Team worked closely with its Senior Leadership Team to use its planning process as an opportunity to shift cultural norms. The team convened structured dialogues with defined dialogue questions [www.compasspoint.org/dialogue questions] to engage its staff of over 100 employees in the process. Joint meetings and retreats of the Core Team and Senior Leadership Team gave these leaders the opportunity to build a shared foundation to lead these dialogues throughout the organization. Discussions with staff groups were held to elicit ideas, opinions, and experiences to inform development of a plan. Staff, departmental, and program meetings were also used as forums to promote conversation. The leaders used communication guidelines [www.compasspoint.org/communication guidelines] and were intentional about setting a tone that encouraged open communication and learning.

4. Articulating and Codifying Assumptions and Commitments

Most groups were committed to addressing issues of culture and difference but didn't have a shared understanding of what that meant for their organizations. For example, in one organization some staff focused on racism and inclusion of people of color, whereas others wanted to address other "isms" like ageism or gender bias. In another organization, some wanted to talk about racism and other "isms" to build awareness and strengthen interactions. Others in that organizations believed that this type of dicussion was not relevant in the work environment. Such differences in defining and focusing the work sometimes led to conflict or lack of direction.

When people had the opportunity to talk through their assumptions and commitments, they usually reached greater investment and alignment on direction. Codifying these assumptions into written documents provided a means to communicate the ideas and institutionalize cultural competence into the fabric of the organization on an ongoing basis.

For CompassPoint, this process helped to clarify how the organization saw its role as an agent of change with nonprofits. As a result of the multicultural process, the organization made a commitment to "[s]erve as an active steward or agent of change for addressing issues of culture and power at all levels, including the nonprofit field. This includes building leadership from diverse communities and fostering dialogue and action." This perspective about the organization's role was also integrated into CompassPoint's theory of change [www.compasspoint.org/toc].

5. Clarifying Responsibility and Authority for Moving the Process Forward

For many organizations, the responsibilities related to MCOD don't fit within existing structures or job responsibilities. Often, a multicultural committee is established without a clear charge or clear linkages to decision making throughout the organization, which results in marginalizing the work.

One way to address this concern is to include administrative, operations, and program staff in the work groups. This can strengthen linkages between key organizational areas. It is also necessary to clarify organization wide responsibility and authority to decide and implement plans. Unless this happens, there may be an expectation that the work group alone is responsible for the MCOD work. Clarifying the charge of different entities helps to assure that the work is integral, rather than marginalized, within the organization [www.compasspoint.org/mcwg]. The following definitions of responsibilities and authority worked well for many groups:

- Multicultural Work Group: This group creates the organizational/project plans and monitors performance in meeting the goals and objectives of the plan. The work group provides recommendations on an ongoing basis to management, and sometimes assists with implementation.
- Directors/Senior Managers: These leaders approve the plan and then are responsible for carrying it out within the existing systems and structure. They are accountable to the Multicultural Work Group for the successful integration of this work and for managing the implementation.

- Board of Directors: The board approves the multicultural plans, holds the organization accountable to achieving important outcomes in the plan, and is accountable to the Multicultural Work Group for implementing multicultural objectives within the board.

II. Lessons Learned

In this section, we present five lessons that emerged as most common and important to participating organizations in developing and implementing their multicultural organizational development plans.

1. Pay Attention to Acknowledging and Building Upon the Organization's History with Cultural Competence

All of the participating nonprofits had some history of work in cultural competence. As a result, they carried both rich experiences to build upon and baggage to overcome. In these instances, a foundation for moving forward includes learning from past experiences, honoring and building on the work that has been done, and acknowledging the efforts and commitment of the people who were involved. It is also important to be thoughtful about how to engage the people who were involved as the organization moves ahead.

In one organization, a committee had been working to address cultural competence for several years. The committee had conducted a number of activities and developed a definition statement and communication guidelines. Some members of the committee voiced concerns that the organization had not taken its efforts seriously.

The senior leaders responsible for moving the process forward were faced with two different sets of needs. On the one hand, there was a need to establish a group of people that could take responsibility for moving cultural competence forward on an agency level. On the other hand, there was a need to ensure that the work of the previous committee would not get lost and that the people who did that work would be valued and included in the process.

These issues were addressed in the following ways: A new committee was established that included previous committee members and new members who could help engage the entire agency in the process. The consultant team conducted interviews with previous committee members and senior leaders. Members of the previous group participated in a workshop with the new group and senior leaders. Dialogues including all staff were convened. These interviews, training, and dialogues invited staff to share their thoughts and lessons learned from past experience and their perspectives on what did and didn't work. The work products of the previous committee served as a starting point for this new phase of work.

2. Balance the Internal Development and Work of the Team with the Need to Engage the Whole Staff and Maintain Transparency and Momentum

One of the biggest challenges in the process was managing multiple levels of engagement. One level was the internal work of the multicultural work group, which included capacity building and activities related to deliverables, such as guiding principles and work plans, making client space more welcoming to all groups, and creating new hiring policies. Another level was staff engagement, which involved surveys, trainings, dialogues, staff report-backs, and interfacing with the management team. Managing these different levels was particularly demanding for multicultural work group members, given that their committee work was in addition to their primary job functions.

In one organization, the multicultural work group took several meetings to clarify its role and direction. Meanwhile, staff was not informed about the process and concerns about lack of transparency began to surface. In order to address the concerns and to maintain momentum, the team identified ways for people to engage in the process, including immediate activities that could be initiated without having to wait for the plan to be completed. In one of the larger organizations, the communications manager, as a member of her organization's multicultural work group, developed internal newsletters to keep staff updated. Strong staff communication was essential to the process.

3. Acknowledge That Individuals Will Have Different Reactions and Different Levels of Receptivity to the Process

Part of being culturally competent is recognizing and allowing for people to be in different places with regards to the cultural competence process. For example, in one organization there was a difference among senior managers about whether it was appropriate to talk about racism and other "isms" in the workplace. One woman of color shared her concern that people of color, who deal with racism constantly in their daily lives, should not have to relive it in the workplace by discussing the topic. In another organization, there were several people of color who mistrusted the process based on how it had been handled in the past; they were concerned that racism wouldn't be confronted head on. And some white staff members were reluctant to engage for fear of being attacked or blamed. In all of these instances, dialogue was key to sharing and understanding different perspectives and finding common ground for moving ahead.

4. Don't Let Resisters Set the Pace for the Process

While acknowledging differences, it is important not to allow the people who are most resistant to hold the process back for everyone else. Organizations that operate by consensus can get stuck when a handful of people oppose change. When organizations faced resistance, it was important to hear the resisters and address their concerns without waiting for them to get on board before moving forward. It was possible, and often necessary, to continue advancing a multicultural change process without expecting full agreement at the outset. For example, one organization that is working to transform its culture conducted transformational trainings with different teams and programs to build a critical mass of people engaged in the change process. As others within the organization saw the changes in how these teams were functioning, interest in the process grew.

5. Courageous Conversations Offer Opportunities for Learning and Growth

In most organizations, discussions of culture, power, and difference are not a norm. Typically, these discussions are uncomfortable and even threatening for the people who raise the issues and for the people in positions of power. When we avoid these conversations we lose the opportunity to proactively address these issues, enrich our working relationships, and enhance the effectiveness of our work. When participating organizations developed the capacity to engage in courageous conversations without shaming and blaming people, tremendous learning and growth occurred for everyone involved. People learned to understand the experiences and perspectives of people who are different from themselves. They also learned to see commonality in their experiences.

In one organization, courageous conversations allowed staff to address the impact of internalized racism on interactions between staff and program participants of the same culture. In another, people were able to reflect on how their own communication styles might be perceived by others and understand each other's need for effective and productive communication.

III. Impacts of Multicultural Development Work on Clients and Community

Each of the participating groups created organizational practices that would ultimately impact its clients and the larger communities it serves. Following are examples of organizational outcomes that were realized or significant progress that was made:

1. Increased Multicultural Capacity of Staff

At New Leaf, the multicultural development process supported the recruitment of more diverse clinical interns, staff, and volunteer clinicians. This investment made a big difference in the delivery of services to diverse populations. It improved the organization's ability to fulfill client requests for therapists of color, transgender therapists, and Spanish-speaking clinicians. Over the course of the initiative, New Leaf's work group also revised the organization's "community identities" form to better facilitate matching of providers and clients based on clients' backgrounds and preferences.

Through client surveys conducted as a part of multicultural assessment, CompassPoint's multicultural work group learned that African American and Latino clients gauged the organization's services slightly less favorably than other ethnic and cultural groups. Throughout the two years of this project, staff reflected on CompassPoint's work culture, the recruitment process, and the quality of relationships with people and organizations in these communities. As a result of more focused attention to recruitment and cultivation of relationships, the organization has made significant progress in hiring from these communities.

In both examples, attention was paid to building the capacity of all staff to work effectively across differences through ongoing training and integrating multicultural practices into day-to-day work. For New Leaf, staff had difficulty discussing cultural differences in monthly agency wide case consultation and peer review; as a result of the initiative these topics were integrated into clinical trainings, through the use of diverse cultural examples, discussion, and learning opportunities that provided staff multiple options for ongoing reading and experiential learning on an individual basis. New Leaf gave staff the opportunity to "Pick Your Own Multicultural Homework" [www.compasspoint.org/mchomework] from a list of assignments with varying intensities. This list was created with the understanding that individuals have varying levels of multicultural competency and allowed staff to tailor their "homework" to their particular multicultural development needs.

2. Increased Language Capacity

Many organizations have found it difficult to increase their capacity to provide information and services in multiple languages during this period of shrinking budgets and layoffs. The multicultural planning work at Girls Inc. helped it to identify ways to prioritize language access across the organization and draw more upon internal resources. Several bilingual staff needed ongoing support to assist with interpretation services, Spanish-led groups, and material translation. These individuals are now meeting regularly as a Spanish-language group to help each other improve their written and speaking skills. Rather than limiting this group to program staff, Girls Inc. is involving staff across the organization to create a system that thoughtfully leverages the language skills of all staff.

3. Stronger Relationships with Clients and Community

Our Family Coalition promotes the civil rights and well-being of Bay Area lesbian, gay, bisexual, transgender, and queer (LGBTQ) families with children and prospective parents through education, advocacy, social networking, and grassroots community organizing. Its work through CCLI with parents of color, transgender parents, and non-LGBTQ groups based in communities of color yielded many outcomes among the board and staff that are beginning to increase the organization's impact in the community. The graphic below shows some of the major multicultural capacity-building decisions and activities the organization pursued and the resulting outcomes.

Conclusion

Our experiences with the Cultural Competence Learning Initiative affirmed that it is possible to build multiculturalism into the fabric and day-to-day functioning of an organization. It also deepened our appreciation for the tremendous complexity and challenge involved in doing this work. A multicultural organizational development approach requires strong leadership, persistence, and courage. It involves breaking out of "business as usual" to ask tough questions, create new ways of interacting, and engage many people in different ways. It requires a spirit of learning and willingness to take risks to try new things. In such an "inside out" approach, the most immediate changes occur internally to the organization. This work builds a solid foundation for developing greater capacity to serve diverse populations, improve access to services, and achieve stronger, healthier communities.

Acknowledgments

The Cultural Competence Learning Initiative was made possible through the generosity of The California Endowment. We thank TCE for its steady guidance and support on this initiative and its ongoing efforts to achieve more diverse and culturally competent health services for all Californians.

Museums and Libraries in the 21st Century 42
New Contexts and Skills Definitions

INSTITUTE OF MUSEUM AND LIBRARY SERVICES

WITHOUT QUESTION, the twenty-first century has led to profound changes in our society's economic, cultural, and educational institutions, including museums and libraries. Three significant shifts are having dramatic impacts on museums and libraries today: the economy, societal needs, and audience expectations.

Economy

The new global economy presents both opportunities and obstacles for library and museum leaders. Changes in the economy, jobs, and businesses have fundamentally altered the nature of work today. The shift in the last two decades to a globally interconnected information economy has radically expanded the types of skills necessary for individuals to succeed in work and life. For example, in 1967, the production of material goods accounted for nearly 54 percent of the country's economic output. But by 1997, the production of information products (e.g., computers, software, books) swelled, accounting for 63 percent of the country's output (Partnership for 21st Century Skills 2008). Today's economy requires the ability to perform non-routine, creative tasks, which has dramatically heightened the need for individuals to master twenty-first century skills like self-direction, creativity, critical thinking, and innovation (see figure 42.1). The dynamics of this new economy and its implications for individuals of all ages and situations have been well-documented by numerous organizations and leading thinkers.[1] And this trend is accelerating, as is shown in figure 42.1. The demand for skills that are nonroutine—e.g., critical thinking, creativity, innovation—is increasing dramatically in the twenty-first century.

The Institute of Museum and Library Services (IMLS) is a federal agency providing grants in support of the nation's museums and libraries. "Museums and Libraries in the 21st Century: New Contexts and Skills Definitions" are excerpts from *Museums, Libraries, and 21st Century Skills* produced by the IMLS Office of Strategic Partnerships under the direction of Marsha Semmel, Deputy Director of Museum Services and Director for Strategic Partnerships (July 2009). It is reprinted here by permission of the publisher. All rights reserved.

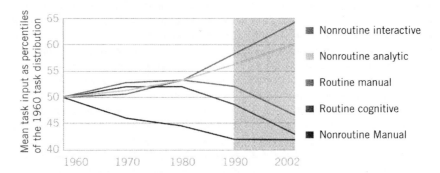

Figure 42.1.   How the demand for skills has changed. Economy-wide measures of routine and non-routine task input (United States). Source: Autor, Levy, and Murname 2003, 1279–1334.

Society and Learning
The twenty-first century has changed how, when, and where we all learn.
The lines between "formal" and "informal" learning are becoming less clear, as institutions from MIT to the University of California put their lectures and class materials online for all at no cost, and iTunes U has accelerated access to truly mobile learning. Substantive conference proceedings are documented, shared, and debated in real time via online social networks, creating meaningful dialogues and interactions among experts and interested individuals on an extraordinary scale. At no other time in history have more educational offerings been made available more widely or for so many.

Even with these changes in digital access to information and educational experiences, perhaps the most significant change is the growing interest in self-directed learning. Dr. John Falk and Dr. Lynn Dierking's pioneering work in this area has been instructive for museums and libraries in its emphasis on the importance of widely available, diverse learning environments that are accessible to everyone in a community. In *Lessons Without Limit: How Free-Choice Learning Is Transforming Education,* the authors underscore the importance not only of accessibility, but experiences that are "designed in ways that support multiple motivations, interests, skills, and knowledge levels" (Falk and Dierking 2002). Scholars in the emerging field of the learning sciences stress that learning develops across multiple timeframes and settings, and they emphasize the importance of "supporting deep links between formal schooling and the many other learning institutions available to students—libraries, science centers and history museums, after-school clubs, online activities that can be accessed from home, and even collaborations between students and working professionals" (Sawyer 2005). Indeed, a growing body of evidence points to informal learning environments as significant sources of knowledge and skill development. Dr. Dennie Palmer Wolf, Director of Opportunity and Accountability for the Annenberg Institute and a leading researcher in the area of children's out-of-school learning, notes that "goal-directed free-time activity in safe, supportive environments with responsive adults and peers make sizable contributions to learning, social skills, and mental health" (Wolf 2008).

Therefore, it is critically important to align and leverage all participants in the learning system—schools, institutions, organizations, programs, individuals, families, and neighborhoods. When such alignment happens, everyone has the potential to be a learner, educator, and collaborator, which benefits not only the individuals but entire communities as well.

An important recent contribution to the dialogue around informal learning is the National Academy of Sciences' report *Learning Science in Informal Environments: People, Places, and Pursuits*. The work offers a compelling research-based analysis of how science museums can "enrich the scientific knowledge, interest and capacity of students and the broader public" (Bell, Lewenstein, Shouse, and Feder 2009). The report emphasizes the need to view learning from an "ecological perspective" that involves "life-long," "life-wide," and "life-deep" experiences. The authors acknowledge the great degree of science learning that can occur in informal environments, building on learners' motivations and interests. They provide evidence for the types of learning that occur "across the lifespan" and describe the synergies between formal and informal learning. This richly detailed report, like much of the literature around out-of-school learning, discusses the proven benefits of designed experiences that appeal to the individual needs of learners and account for their diverse social, economic, and demographic backgrounds.

Audience Expectation

In the twenty-first century, the public has grown accustomed to personalized, customized, and on-demand experiences that are easy to access and simple to share and build upon. In physical settings and online, audiences expect higher levels of interactivity and programs tailored to individual needs. From online stores that record customer preferences for books, clothing sizes, and brands, to music collections that automatically add personalized recommendations, there are seemingly no limits to an individual's ability to access, store, re-experience, re-create, and re-imagine any number of highly personal preferences and experiences—commercial and non-commercial. In books such as Jeff Howe's *Crowdsourcing* and Clay Shirky's *Here Comes Everybody,* the expectations—and the impacts—of today's networked decision-makers are made clear. There is an undeniable trend toward collaborative, crowd-sourced decision making (e.g., online consumer reviews) and free, open source products (e.g., Google Docs). As a result, there has been a sea-change in consumer expectations: if you have something interesting to offer, you should be prepared to 1) offer it however and whenever the customer wants; 2) allow the customer to create, participate in, share, refine, save and re-use it instantly and easily; 3) make it accessible and affordable.

A recurring theme is the importance of Web 2.0-enabled ways of experiencing library and museum offerings: "Web 2.0 is democratic. Content is developed, organized, and accessed via bottom-up rather than top-down design. Instead of being a content provider, Web 2.0 is a platform provider" (Simon 2007). The "democratization" of content and the social ways in which audiences interact with content online has profoundly shifted the roles of directors, librarians, curators, and other professionals who craft designed experiences in these institutions.

The Museums, Libraries, and 21st Century Skills Task Force and IMLS Project Team observed that, increasingly, audiences expect museums and libraries to:

- Leverage their collections and content expertise to engage more effectively with increasingly diverse audiences, as well as the needs of communities in the twenty-first century;
- Act as catalysts along with other partners to enhance (in mission-appropriate ways) the learning systems across a community;
- Provide flexible, co-created, immersive experiences that connect individuals with their families and other like-minded (and sometimes not) people;
- Offer audiences multiple ways to engage in meaningful social and civic interactions;
- Focus on audience engagement and audience experience as central components of the institution's mission;
- Implement a thoughtful "architecture of participation" (O'Reilly 2005) that enables broad-based collaborative engagement among all institution audiences and stakeholders.

These three factors—the shift to the global economy, the rising importance of self-directed lifelong learning, and the expectation of customized, on-demand audience experiences—provide a compelling backdrop for museums and libraries as they position themselves as institutions of learning in the twenty-first century.

Skills Definitions

The IMLS Project Team and Task Force considered the list of skills commonly referred to as "Twenty-first Century Skills" and modified it slightly to better align with library and museum priorities.[2]

The resulting list includes the following additions: Basic Literacy, Scientific & Numerical Literacy, Visual Literacy, Cross-Disciplinary Skills, and Environmental Literacy.

Not every skill on this list will be aligned with every institution's vision and mission. Further, not every community will prioritize the same skills. Library and museum leaders should consider this list as a starting point beyond which it should be customized to fit the unique character, requirements, and priorities of the institution and its audiences.

Learning and Innovation Skills

Critical Thinking and Problem Solving

REASON EFFECTIVELY
- Use various types of reasoning (e.g., inductive, deductive, etc.) as appropriate to the situation

USE SYSTEMS THINKING
- Analyze how parts of a whole interact with each other to produce overall outcomes in complex systems

MAKE JUDGMENTS AND DECISIONS
- Effectively analyze and evaluate evidence, arguments, claims and beliefs
- Analyze and evaluate major alternative points of view
- Synthesize and make connections between information and arguments
- Interpret information and draw conclusions based on the best analysis
- Reflect critically on learning experiences and processes

SOLVE PROBLEMS
- Solve different kinds of non-familiar problems in both conventional and innovative ways
- Identify and ask significant questions that clarify various points of view and lead to better solutions

Creativity and Innovation

THINK CREATIVELY
- Use a wide range of idea-creation techniques (such as brainstorming)
- Create new and worthwhile ideas (both incremental and radical concepts)
- Elaborate, refine, analyze, and evaluate ideas in order to improve and maximize creative efforts
- Demonstrate imagination and curiosity

WORK CREATIVELY WITH OTHERS
- Develop, implement, and communicate new ideas to others effectively
- Be open and responsive to new and diverse perspectives; incorporate group input and feedback into the work
- Demonstrate originality and inventiveness in work and understand the real-world limits to adopting new ideas
- View failure as an opportunity to learn; understand that creativity and innovation is a long-term, cyclical process of small successes and frequent mistakes

IMPLEMENT INNOVATIONS
- Act on creative ideas to make a tangible and useful contribution to the field in which the innovation will occur

Communication and Collaboration

COMMUNICATE CLEARLY
- Articulate thoughts and ideas effectively using oral, written, and nonverbal communication skills in a variety of forms and contexts
- Listen effectively to decipher meaning, including knowledge, values, attitudes, and intentions
- Use communication for a range of purposes (e.g., to inform, instruct, motivate, and persuade) and in diverse environments (including multilingual)
- Utilize multiple media and technologies, and know how to judge their effectiveness a priori as well as assess their impact

COLLABORATE WITH OTHERS
- Demonstrate ability to work effectively and respectfully with diverse teams
- Exercise flexibility and willingness to be helpful in making necessary compromises to accomplish a common goal
- Assume shared responsibility for collaborative work, and value the individual contributions made by each team member

Visual Literacy
- Demonstrate the ability to interpret, recognize, appreciate, and understand information presented through visible actions, objects and symbols, natural or man-made[3]

Scientific and Numerical Literacy
- Demonstrate the ability to evaluate the quality of scientific and numerical information on the basis of its sources and the methods used to generate it
- Demonstrate the capacity to pose and evaluate scientific arguments based on evidence and to apply conclusions from such arguments appropriately
- Demonstrate ability to reason with numbers and other mathematical concepts

Cross-Disciplinary Thinking
- Apply knowledge, attitudes, behaviors, and skills across disciplines in appropriate and effective ways

Basic Literacy
- Demonstrate the ability to use language to read, write, listen, and speak

Information Literacy

ACCESS AND EVALUATE INFORMATION
- Access information efficiently (time) and effectively (sources)
- Evaluate information critically and competently

USE AND MANAGE INFORMATION
- Use information accurately and creatively for the issue or problem at hand
- Manage the flow of information from a wide variety of sources
- Apply a fundamental understanding of the ethical/ legal issues surrounding the access and use of information

Media Literacy

ANALYZE MEDIA
- Understand both how and why media messages are constructed and for what purposes
- Examine how individuals interpret messages differently, how values and points of view are included or excluded, and how media can influence beliefs and behaviors
- Apply a fundamental understanding of the ethical/legal issues surrounding the access and use of media

CREATE MEDIA PRODUCTS
- Understand and utilize the most appropriate media creation tools, characteristics, and conventions
- Understand and effectively utilize the most appropriate expressions and interpretations in diverse, multi-cultural environments

ICT (Information, Communications, and Technology) Literacy

APPLY TECHNOLOGY EFFECTIVELY
- Use technology as a tool to research, organize, evaluate, and communicate information
- Use digital technologies (e.g., computers, PDAs, media players, GPS, etc.), communication/networking tools, and social networks appropriately to access, manage, integrate, evaluate, and create information to successfully function in a knowledge economy
- Apply a fundamental understanding of the ethical/ legal issues surrounding the access and use of information technologies

Twenty-first-Century Themes

Global Awareness

- Use 21st century skills to understand and address global issues
- Learn from and work collaboratively with individuals representing diverse cultures, religions, and lifestyles in a spirit of mutual respect and open dialogue in personal, work, and community contexts
- Understand other nations and cultures, including the use of non-English languages

Financial, Economic, Business, and Entrepreneurial Literacy

- Demonstrate the ability to make appropriate personal economic choices
- Understand the role of the economy in society
- Apply entrepreneurial skills to enhance workplace productivity and career options

Civic Literacy

- Participate effectively in civic life through knowing how to stay informed and understanding governmental processes
- Exercise the rights and obligations of citizenship at local, state, national, and global levels
- Understand the local and global implications of civic decisions

Health Literacy

- Obtain, interpret, and understand basic health information and services and use such information and services in ways that enhance health
- Understand preventive physical and mental health measures, including proper diet, nutrition, exercise, risk avoidance, and stress reduction
- Use available information to make appropriate health-related decisions
- Establish and monitor personal and family health goals
- Understand national and international public health and safety issues

Environmental Literacy

- Demonstrate ecological knowledge and understanding of how natural systems work, as well as knowledge and understanding of how natural systems interface with social systems
- Demonstrate understanding of the relationship between beliefs, political systems, and environmental values of various cultures
- Demonstrate understanding of environmental issues caused as the result of human interaction with the environment, and knowledge related to alternative solutions to issues

- Demonstrate active and considered participation aimed at solving problems and resolving issues[4]

Life and Career Skills

Flexibility and Adaptability

ADAPT TO CHANGE
- Adapt to varied roles, job responsibilities, schedules, and contexts
- Work effectively in a climate of ambiguity and changing priorities

BE FLEXIBLE
- Incorporate feedback effectively
- Deal positively with praise, setbacks, and criticism
- Understand, negotiate, and balance diverse views and beliefs to reach workable solutions, particularly in multi-cultural environments

Initiative and Self-Direction

MANAGE GOALS AND TIME
- Set goals with tangible and intangible success criteria
- Balance tactical (short-term) and strategic (long-term) goals
- Utilize time and manage workload efficiently

WORK INDEPENDENTLY
- Monitor, define, prioritize, and complete tasks without direct oversight

BE SELF-DIRECTED LEARNERS
- Go beyond basic mastery of skills and/or curriculum to explore and expand one's own learning and opportunities to gain expertise
- Demonstrate initiative to advance skill levels towards a professional level
- Demonstrate commitment to learning as a lifelong process
- Reflect critically on past experiences in order to inform future progress

Social and Cross-Cultural Skills

INTERACT EFFECTIVELY WITH OTHERS
- Know when it is appropriate to listen and when to speak
- Conduct oneself in a respectable, professional manner

WORK EFFECTIVELY IN DIVERSE TEAMS
- Respect cultural differences and work effectively with people from a range of social and cultural backgrounds
- Respond open-mindedly to different ideas and values

- Leverage social and cultural differences to create new ideas and increase both innovation and quality of work

Productivity and Accountability

MANAGE PROJECTS
- Set and meet goals, even in the face of obstacles and competing pressures
- Prioritize, plan, and manage work to achieve the intended result

PRODUCE RESULTS
- Demonstrate additional attributes associated with producing high-quality products including the abilities to:
  - Work positively and ethically
  - Manage time and projects effectively
  - Multi-task
  - Participate actively, as well as be reliable and punctual
  - Present oneself professionally and with proper etiquette
  - Collaborate and cooperate effectively with teams
  - Respect and appreciate team diversity
  - Be accountable for results

Leadership and Responsibility

GUIDE AND LEAD OTHERS
- Use interpersonal and problem-solving skills to influence and guide others toward a goal
- Leverage strengths of others to accomplish a common goal
- Inspire others to reach their very best via example and selflessness
- Demonstrate integrity and ethical behavior in using influence and power

BE RESPONSIBLE TO OTHERS
- Act responsibly with the interests of the larger community in mind

Notes

1. See Partnership for 21st Century Skills, "21st Century Skills, Education and Competitiveness," "Transition Paper," as well as Richard Florida's *The Rise of the Creative Class: And How It's Transforming Work, Leisure, Community and Everyday Life*, and Daniel Pink's *A Whole New Mind*.

2. Except as otherwise noted, the skills definitions are derived from the Partnership for 21st Century Skills Framework (www.21stcenturyskills.org).

3. Derived from definition attributed to John Debes, per the International Visual Literacy Association (www.ivla.org/org_whaLvis_lit.htm).

4. Adapted from the Environmental Literacy Council Framework.

References

Autor, David H., Frank Levy, and Richard J. Murnane. 2003. The skill content of recent technological change: An empirical exploration. *Quarterly Journal of Economics* 118: 1279–1334.

Bell, P., B. Lewenstein, A. W. Shouse, and M. A. Feder. 2009. *Learning Science in Information Environments: People Places, and Pursuits.* Washington, DC: National Academies Press.

Falk, J., and L. Dierking. 2002. *Lessons Without Limit: How Free-Choice Learning Is Transforming Education.* Lanham, MD: Rowman & Littlefield.

Howe, Chris. 2008. *Crowdsourcing: Why the Power of the Crowd Is Driving the Future of Business.* New York: Random House.

Partnership for 21st Century Skills, 2008

O'Reilly 2005 (from p. 505)

Sawyer, R. K. ed. 2006. *The Cambridge Handbook of the Learning Sciences.* New York: Cambridge University Press.

Shirky, Clay. 2008. *Here Comes Everybody: The Power of Organizing Without Organizations.* New York: Penguin Press.

Simon, Nina. 2007. Discourse in the blogosphere: What museums can learn from Web 2.0. *Museums and Social Issues 2* (2): 257–274.

Wolf, Dennie P. 2008. Outside the box: How can districts and communities support informal learning? *Threshold* (Winter).

The Mindful Museum

43

ROBERT R. JANES

Introduction

ARE MUSEUMS MINDFUL OF WHAT IS GOING ON in the world around them? The planet Earth and global civilization now confront a constellation of issues that threaten the very existence of both. There is a burgeoning literature that offers dire warnings and solutions, but museums are rarely, if ever, mentioned.[1] Are not museums (with the possible exception of contemporary art museums) the self-proclaimed custodians of posterity, assuming that the responsibilities of today will be the gifts of the future? If so, there is an alarming disconnect between this belief and the trajectory that many museums are on, preoccupied as they are with the marketplace, quantitative measures of performance, and internally driven agendas devoted to collecting, exhibiting, ancillary education, and entertainment. Rethinking the role of museums as social institutions will require no less than a reinvented museum—a mindful organization that incorporates the best of enduring museum values and business methodology, with a sense of social responsibility heretofore unrecognized.

Stewardship of the highest order will also be required, demanding active engagement and shared authority with those individuals and communities that museums purport to serve.

Museums have inadvertently arrived at a metaphorical watershed where it is now imperative to ask broader questions about why they do what they do, to confront a variety of admittedly unruly issues, and to propose some new choices. This metaphorical watershed is not unlike Peter Drucker's concept of a "divide." In his words, "Within a few short decades society rearranges itself—its world view; its basic values; its social and political structure; its arts; its key institutions. Fifty years later, there is a new world" (Drucker 1994, 1).

Robert R. Janes is the editor-in-chief of the *Journal of Museum Management and Curatorship* and the past president and chief executive officer of the Glenbow Museum in Calgary, Alberta. "The Mindful Museum" appeared in *Curator: The Museum Journal* (Vol. 53, No. 3, July 2010, pp. 325–328). It is reprinted here by permission of John Wiley & Sons. All rights reserved.

To assume that existing models of museum practice can somehow fulfill the requirements of the future is to invite the scorn and alienation of future generations. As E. O. Wilson noted, "We are creating a less stable and interesting place for our descendants to inherit. They will understand and love life more than we, and they will not be inclined to honor our memory" (Wilson 2006, 81). Recognizing the possibility of this disturbing outcome, how might we envision a mindful museum?

Mindfulness and the Museum

The word "mindful" entered the museum vocabulary recently in an article titled "The Mindful Museum," by the American essayist Adam Gopnik. He wrote: "The mindful museum should first of all be mindful in being primarily about the objects it contains. Your first experience when entering the mindful museum should be of a work of art" (Gopnik 2007, 90). Although Gopnik notes that he uses "mindful" in the Buddhist sense—"of a museum that is aware of itself, conscious of its own functions, and living at this moment"—I submit that he has confused the self-absorbed behavior of museums, grounded in habit and traditional practice, with the real meaning and value of mindfulness. Ironically, the preoccupation with objects and collections is one of the primary obstacles preventing museums from becoming truly mindful. While I acknowledge that Gopnik is mainly concerned with art museums, this does not explain his use of "mindful," especially with respect to its Buddhist meaning. Now that the concept has entered the museum world, we could do with a clearer understanding of what "mindfulness" actually means.

The systematic cultivation of mindfulness has been called "the heart of Buddhist meditation." It is a particular way of paying attention, and one of its major strengths is that it is not based on any belief system or ideology. Its benefits are accessible to anyone (Kabat-Zinn 1990, 12–13). In essence, mindfulness is cultivated by purposefully paying attention to things we ordinarily ignore; it requires that we should always know what we are doing. Mindfulness actually helps us to be more aware of events in the outside world and our reactions to them (Fontana 1999, 112). Becoming more mindful is particularly important at this point in our evolution as a species, as global stresses and strains mount—all compounded by the endless distractions of the digital revolution.

Chaotic Cascades

We need only consider the dramatic changes in new technology to appreciate the new and relentless pressures of the digital age on museum work. There are computers at home and work, fax machines, cell phones, pagers, laptops, BlackBerries, high-speed connectivity, email and the Internet, all of which are convenient, efficient, and useful, but at a cost to mindfulness. Jon Kabat-Zinn, a professor of medicine and a meditation teacher, describes the consequences:

> This new way of working and living has inundated us all of a sudden with endless options, endless opportunities for interruption, distraction, highly enabled "response

ability". . . and a kind of free-floating urgency attached to even the most trivial of events. The to-do list grows ever longer, and we are always rushing through this moment to get to the next (Kabat-Zinn 2005, 148).

Added to these stresses and distractions is the chaotic thinking that marks much of our everyday lives, as our brains continue their ceaseless chatter. Much of our thinking is narrow and repetitive, and based on our personal history and our habits. Our minds are filled with anxieties about the future, how we're possibly going to get everything done that needs to be done, what people said or didn't say, are we successful, are we getting the recognition we deserve, will we ever get enough time for ourselves, about having no time, about needing more time, about having too much time, and so on and so on. Our thinking can be described as a waterfall—a continual cascade of thoughts (Kabat-Zinn 1994, 94).

Museum Chatter

Understandably, museums also suffer from unavoidable distractions, cascading thoughts, and institutional chatter. There is the continuous preoccupation with the number of visitors, the building, security, education, food, merchandise, shopping, entertainment, technology, special exhibitions, and visitor demands—just a sampling of the front-of-the-house concerns. Then there is the internal chatter, beginning with the governing authority, which may or may not be performing adequately; may have an ineffective chair; may be exercising undue or conflicting influence on the work of the museum; or may be failing to raise the necessary funding to balance the fragile operating budget. Then there is the staff, from the most senior to the most junior, who are simply human beings living out the intricacies of their lives more or less effectively—a good portion of which is done in an institutional setting. Perhaps there are also leaders and managers with twenty-five years of experience—the same year repeated twenty-five times.

Organizational stress is another perpetual distraction, and an ever-increasing feature of organizational life that has not received the attention it deserves in the museum sector. Many museum staff are understandably weary and skeptical, given the penchant for lay-offs to balance the budget, the low pay, and the fact that there will be no mythical plateau where they can pause and say "We've made it" and return to business as usual. There is no business as usual, or an idealized past, for that matter, contrary to the wishful thinking of many museum workers. The resulting stress must be seen as an inherent danger, nonetheless, and be confronted organizationally with intelligence and caring.

Negative People

Stress is also a factor in the "negative people syndrome," another source of institutional chatter and perpetual ruminations. There is always a certain amount of negativism afloat in even the most exemplary museum, and it can be salutary in counteracting complacency and providing an inadvertent source of humility for those who are paying attention. Overall, however, staff negativity is a bane, and can translate into constant complaining, hostility, and a notable lack of generosity of spirit among colleagues. It can also lead to compliance and passivity, both deadly hurdles to creativity and action. Although the negative voices are usually the loudest, it is important to acknowledge that skepticism and questioning are integral parts of a well-functioning museum. The continuous task is to determine if the negativism is self-serving or of benefit to the organization. Which leads me to the last example of unrelenting chatter the ambiguity that envelops all museums, whether or not they are mired in habit or becoming more mindful.

Ambiguity

Ambiguity should not be feared, however, contrary to the dictates of the marketplace. Marketplace disciples spend vast amounts of time and energy seeking control over their internal and external environments, in order to enhance the bottom line and profitability. Corporations, in general, succeed to the extent that they can exercise sovereignty over people's lives through marketing, hidden trade agreements, preferential government treatment, globalism and so forth, all of which provide them with ostensible public support for their corporate self-interests. The museum world is far more complex, with few privileged connections and no history of influence peddling with which to bolster one's fortunes.

Museums have no choice but to confront the ambiguity, complexities, and paradoxes which make them what they are. Paradoxical questions and imperatives abound: Is the customer always right? Are museums sustainable without significant contributions of public funding? Are there too many museums? What is the purpose of a competent museum? What role should traditional practices play in an effective museum? In light of all this ambiguity, museum boards and staff have labored long and hard to avoid surprises. Admittedly, few things disturb them more than increasing complexity (Wheatley 1992, 109–110). Questions with no ready answers are also significant management challenges in museums, and leave anxiety and discouragement in their wake.

Becoming More Mindful

The consequences of this preoccupation with complexity and control are nicely summed up by Margaret Wheatley, an organizational consultant and writer:

> We still believe that what holds a system together are point to point connections that must be laboriously woven together by us. Complexity only adds to our task, requiring us to keep track of more things, handle more pieces, make more connections. As things increase in number or detail, the span of control stretches out elastically, and, suddenly, we are snapped into unmanageability (1992, 110).

And snapped into unmindfulness, as well. All of the museum chatter discussed above, be it about governance, management morale, stress, or ambiguity, is equivalent to our cascading thoughts as individuals, and prevents museums from seeing what is actually going on in the world around them. Unlike individuals, museums are obviously incapable of mindful meditation as organizations, but asking the question "why" is a workable alternative for enhancing organizational consciousness and mindfulness.

The crucial need is for the organization to recognize that much of the incessant internal chatter can be repetitive, inaccurate, disturbing, toxic and unrelenting, and to not let it subvert vision, purpose, and the capacity of the museum to ponder the larger picture, clarify what is most important, and determine how it might be of real use in a troubled world. This could be immensely liberating and assist museums in overcoming the inertia and self-interest that define much of the status quo within the museum community. Are museums, as social institutions in the civil society, capable of expanding their consciousness and recognizing their privileged position grounded in public trust, respect and support? This does not require a radical forsaking of the values and traditions that sustain museums, since a mindful museum can exist in its own conventional consciousness, while at the same time bringing a much greater awareness to its work and its role in the broader community.

Some Characteristics of Mindfulness

Synthesis over process—Nor does increasing a museum's mindfulness require the wholesale discarding of conventional practices. In fact, museums can become more mindful in the course of their habitual activities, as long as sufficient attention is paid to the mission (Hawken et al. 2000, 310–313). The ongoing debate about the environment is a good example of the clash of dissonant voices: the free-market capitalists (rooted in conventional economics where growth is everything); the environmentalists (who see the world in terms of ecosystems and focus on depletion and damage); and the synthesizers.

All museums have the responsibility and the opportunity to become synthesizers and foster an understanding of the interconnectedness of the problems we face, both environmental and social (Hawken et al., 2000, 312). A mindful museum can empower and honor all people in the search for a sustainable and just world, by creating a mission that focuses on the interconnectedness of our world and its challenges, and promotes the integration of disparate perspectives (Janes 2008, 23).

Values—The mindful museum will also have a slate of well-considered values, but not those packaged and delivered by management consultants and branding gurus. Rather than self-serving values such as "excellence in peer recognition" and "professionalism," these values will reflect the commitment required for effective participation in the broader world. The list might include idealism, humility, interdisciplinarity, intimacy, interconnectedness, resourcefulness, transparency, durability, resilience, knowing your community and knowing your environment

Internal organization—The design of the internal organization must also reflect an increased awareness, if the promise of mindfulness is to be achieved. This will preclude the popular hierarchical organization, as it has proven categorically to restrict initiative and reward passivity. Instead, the mindful museum relies upon multifunctional work groups, not the homogeneous and silo-like departments and divisions common in museums today. These work groups will also persist through time, unlike temporary project teams, and all of them will benefit from the presence of writers, poets, artists, and performers, as well as ad hoc participants from the array of agencies and organizations that underpin the museum's role in the community. These non-traditional staff will be a key source of the emotion, imagination, intuition and reflection that are essential to catalyze and sustain the museum's mindfulness.

Rapid response groups—The organizational chart will also include one or more rapid response groups (RRG), since museums are notoriously ineffective in altering their work plans to address unanticipated issues and opportunities. The RRGs will enable the mindful museum to respond more effectively to such contingencies. Sounds idealistic? It is, but without a change in how the work gets done, there can be little hope of changing what gets done. The way a museum does its work will either permit or preclude inclusive thinking, the questioning of the status quo and heightened awareness of the external world.

More Opportunities for Consciousness

Branding—The above examples are only a glimpse of the many possibilities for enhancing mindfulness and more conscious museum work. There are many more, such as branding, which is now seen to be integral to a successful museum (Kotler et al. 2008). With few exceptions, however, most museums do not brand their values, ideas, mission or substantive contributions. Instead, they brand "stuff" (shows, dining, shops, and so on) and treat visitors and users as consumers and customers using the language of the marketplace: customer service, efficiency, entertainment, value for money, and so on (Janes and Conaty 2005, 1–17). All of this rhetoric is imported uncritically from the marketplace, even by those proponents who claim a special knowledge of museums. Perhaps most importantly, the majority of museums have failed to understand that branding is about differentiation—identifying what is unique and valuable about your museum, including what you do, why you're good at it and why you're different

Isn't it time for museums to move beyond the language of the marketplace to create civic brands around ideas and values that are based on the answers to key questions? These questions should consider why the museum exists, what changes it is trying to effect, what solutions it will generate, and what the museum's non-negotiable values are—such as collaboration, inclusiveness, diversity, consciousness, and so forth. Having answered these fundamental questions about the "why" and the "what," the task is then to develop a constellation of activities that both create and maintain the brand. Branding values and ideas is another means of heightening museum consciousness and moving beyond the reigning model of economic utility.

Collections—What about the cost of collections care? Why doesn't the global museum community have a current understanding of these costs that is analyzed and shared as a means of rationalization? They don't, and without such knowledge, it is impossible to allocate scarce resources intelligently in the face of new or competing priorities. Why are collection costs treated as fixed, when they are actually discretionary? The use of collections is still marked by little or no imagination and is hidebound by tradition. As one museum worker noted: "Museums are organisms that ingest, but do not excrete" (Keene 2005, 5).

Public programming—Moving from collections to public programming, where are the collaborative forums (including filmmakers, videographers, artists, poets, writers, storytellers, game creators, social activists, public agencies, and non-government organizations) working with museums to help them better understand the realm of experience design embedded in meaning, values, and relevance? These creative forums should involve recognized museum and non-museum innovators, thinkers and experts in an annual think tank—or preferably a "think leak," where the results of the work are widely disseminated, thus sharing the fruits of their collaborative efforts with the broader community. The typical museum conference may offer several keynote addresses from outsiders, but the overall insularity remains a pronounced liability. It has been noted that all great change in business has come from outside the firm, not from inside, and there is no reason to assume that museums are any different (Lezner and Johnson 1997, 122–128).

In Search of the Mindful Museum Practice

Although the concept of the mindful museum may suffer from a certain amount of abstraction, various museums and related organizations continue to move beyond the tyranny of the marketplace and traditional practices to demonstrate a greater awareness of their roles and responsibilities. One doesn't read or hear much about these examples in the mainstream media, or in the museum literature, for that matter, because what they do lacks the sensationalism and celebrity appeal that drive our society's preoccupation with consumption and conformity. Many of these progressive practitioners are undoubtedly too busy to make their work more widely known. The following organizational examples have replaced passivity and compliance with creativity, altruism, and originality, and are defining new ways of being for museums as mindful social institutions.

Museum Victoria—The first example of mindful museum practice is Museum Victoria in Melbourne, Australia, which actually has a "senior curator of sustainable futures" (perhaps unprecedented in the museum world) who is responsible for an ongoing project called Water Smart Home. Australia is the driest inhabited continent in the world, and yet one of the highest consumers of water per capita. A key to creating a sustainable water future is to change the way Australians think about and use water in their daily lives, and the museum's Water Smart Home is a community-based project that engages, educates, and inspires the public in how to reduce, reuse and revalue water.[2]

Heifer Village—A second example is Heifer Village, a "hands-on, global education facility" (according to its website) with interactive exhibits that introduce visitors to the possibility of a world free of hunger and poverty.[3] It also features an outdoor commons area and a state-of-the-art conference hall where academic experts, thought leaders, staff and visitors learn from each other, as well as directly from those people achieving self-sufficiency around the world. Heifer International is a non-profit organization whose mission is to end hunger and poverty while caring for the Earth. This is a powerful reversal of traditional roles: a museum in the service of global philanthropy.

The Commonwealth Association of Museums—The third example of progressive thought and action is the Commonwealth Association of Museums (CAM), a professional association and international NGO working toward the betterment of museums and their societies in the Commonwealth nations.[4] CAM is committed to fostering a strong role for museums in their societies and communities, with attention to the most urgent contemporary issues. Museums are encouraged to use their resources and their knowledge of their countries to ensure that the critical link between culture and development is used effectively for the betterment of society. CAM's areas of concern are the safeguarding of both tangible and intangible heritage, biodiversity, and environmental sustainability. A review of the online mission statements of several national museum associations (in the United Kingdom, the United States, and Canada) revealed a focus on "enhancing the value of museums" or "advancing the museum sector." The expanded awareness demonstrated by the Commonwealth Association of Museums might well serve as a model for all museum associations as global issues become increasingly prominent.

The Canadian Conservation Institute—Museum conservators might be considered an unlikely source of innovation, but significant change is actually well underway among these specialists. The Canadian Conservation Institute (CCI), one of the world's distinguished conservation laboratories and service centers, is promoting a refreshing perspective that challenges conventional wisdom.[5] Contrary to the museum community's slavish worship of environmental controls, the CCI's website notes that certain types of artifacts are much more sensitive to relative humidity fluctuation than others, and it is neither economical nor environmentally acceptable to have tightly controlled conditions if they are not necessary.

During the author's recent correspondence with CCI, one of the senior scientists referred to the time-honored mantra of 50 percent relative humidity (RH) and 22 degrees Celsius (72 degrees Fahrenheit) as the presumed museum standard, and indicated his dismay over the pretense surrounding artifact loans. He noted that nearly every loaning museum specifies impossible levels of control, which they themselves can't possibly maintain. By challenging these conventional beliefs, the CCI's conservators hope to remove some of the misinformation surrounding these issues. This willingness and ability to question time-honored assumptions are rare and laudable in the museum world, and also absolutely essential to learning, growth and change. Now it is most important that this reinterpretation be disseminated throughout the museum world so that practitioners and their museums can benefit from this rethinking.

Museum Clusters—My last example of a notable museum innovation comes from Taiwan, and is based on the cluster concept first proposed by Michael Porter, professor at the Harvard Business School (Tien 2010, 69). This concept has come to be regarded as a strategic tool for local economic development. In Taiwan, museum clusters are geographic concentrations of interconnected museums which work closely with local suppliers, tourist attractions, and public sector entities. Cluster-based development is founded on the premise that a museum can realize higher levels of competence when it looks beyond its own limited capability to address challenges and solve problems.

A case study of the Danshui museum cluster indicates that the organizational structure is flat and emphasis is placed on the sharing of resources. In addition to the director in overall charge of the museum cluster, each museum has its own manager (Tien 2010, 80). The three museums share an administration team, an education team and a day-today operations team. I'm not aware of this degree of integration and cooperation among North America's fiercely independent museums, but as funding continues to decline, the museum cluster is an obvious solution.

Fortunately, we have all of these examples of thinking and doing to demonstrate the abundance of creative possibilities. They are heartening reminders that elite boards, big budgets, and quantitative measures are not the hallmarks of meaning and worth. On the contrary, the fruits of privilege are ultimately constraining, misleading, and maladaptive, as history has proven time and again. Many museums continue to revel in marketplace success, be it high attendance, shop sales, or burgeoning tax-receipted donations, but none of these things are resilient. Instead, they are brittle embodiments of a maladaptive past.

In addition to these organizational initiatives, there is also the work of various individuals who are mindful of the present I want to mention an outstanding example. The late Stephen Weil, practitioner and scholar, was articulate in his aversion to self-serving museums, and he left a legacy of articles and books that offered alternatives.[6] His thoughts and values are best summarized in one of his typically penetrating questions: "If our museums are not being operated with the ultimate goal of improving the quality of people's lives, on what other basis might we possibly ask for public support?" (Weil 1999, 242). This question continues to reverberate, with only marginal attention being paid to its contemporary implications. As highly regarded as Weil's work is, I detect no groundswell of approbation among practitioners to ensure that his questioning is constantly held in view.

The Post-Museum Meets the Mindful Museum

Assuming that any or all of these progressive practices gain in popularity, the result will be more conscious and hence more effective museums. One organizational specialist, Margaret Wheatley, believes that some organizations are moving into the realm of increased consciousness anyway, because we inhabit "an intrinsically well-ordered universe" (Wheatley 1992, 117). Well-ordered or not—it is difficult to ignore the current human impact on the biosphere—it's too early to know if museums will commit to this path. Any progress towards increased consciousness will require decreasing hierarchy, as well as inter- and intra-organizational interaction and exchange. Perhaps when these are achieved, along with some of the other attributes described earlier, the mindful museum and the post-museum will become one. Museum theorist Eilean Hooper-Greenhill argues that it is time to move beyond the idea of the museum as a locus of authority conveyed primarily through buildings and exhibitions, and adopt a new model which she calls the post-museum (2000, 151–162).

The post-museum is fundamentally different from the traditional museum and is intended to embrace a variety of societal perspectives and values, with the traditional museum perspective being only one voice among many. Perhaps most importantly, the post-museum involves intangible heritage, along with the emotions of visitors, since the post-museum is directly linked to the concerns and ambitions of communities (Hooper-Greenhill 2000, 152). The congruence between the post-museum and the mindful museum is significant, and hopefully liberating for those who might require a theoretical construct for altering the museum's traditional agenda.

The Consequences of Inaction

The need for heightened stewardship is obvious as the warning signs of our collective vulnerability continue to accumulate: population stress; the increasing scarcity of conventional oil; the degradation of our land, water, and forests; and the structural instabilities in the global economic system; not to mention climate change and global warming. All of these complexities can be distilled into a rather simple model of what could transpire if these events continue to unfold. The economist Jeremy Rifkin notes that "our modem economy is a three-tiered system, with agriculture as the base, the industrial sector superimposed on top of it, and the service sector, in turn, perched on top of the industrial sector" (1980, 217–218). Each sector is totally dependent on more and more non-renewable energy—fossil fuels. Rifkin notes that as the availability of this energy diminishes, the public and private service areas will be the first to suffer, because services are "the least essential aspect of our survival." In short, an economy with limited energy sources will be one of necessities, not luxuries or inessentials, and will be centered on those things required to maintain life. Where do tourism, edutainment, museum shops, permanent collections, and blockbuster exhibitions fit in this looming scenario?

Although museums are unique and untapped resources in heightening societal stewardship, they are a public service, and the extent to which they will weather the future is difficult to predict. It's obvious that reducing energy consumption and avoiding large and consumptive building footprints are prerequisites, making the recent museum building boom even more bizarre. Energy-efficient buildings, however, are only one ingredient in a meaningful future. Along with the willpower required to reduce consumption is the greater need to transform the museum's public service persona and culture/industry business agenda—defined by collections, ancillary education and entertainment—into one of a locally embedded problem-solver, in tune with the challenges and aspirations of communities.

An Ecological Metaphor

An ecological metaphor is useful here, since ecology is about the relationships between organisms and their environments—dependent, independent, and inter-dependent relationships. Museums have predicated their survival on being both dependent (for all forms of support) and independent, as exemplified by commonplace comments such as "give us the money; we know what to do" or "how dare you measure our performance." In the process of overlooking the meaning of interdependence, museums have contributed greatly to their own marginalization. It is time to consider the ecology of museums and recognize that the broad web of societal relationships is essential for successful adaptation in a complex and increasingly severe world.

The lack of interdependent relationships among most museums is a growing liability, and being valued for ancillary educational offerings and often ersatz entertainment is no longer sufficient to ensure intelligent sustainability. As some of the most conservative institutions in contemporary society, many museums will be unwilling or unable to grasp the import and necessity of rethinking their current successes and failures. This is not a bad thing, for the disappearance of myopic museums may well be beneficial, as the public and private resources allocated to museums diminish. There may, in fact, be too many museums, even now. However, this is not about the survival of the fittest, but about choosing renewal over decline.

Conclusions

The meaning and value of enhanced mindfulness have yet to be tapped by the museum community at large, and its potential might well be limitless. For those boards and museum workers who are disturbed at the thought of rethinking their traditional role and responsibilities, one question remains. How is it that museums, as social institutions, may remain aloof from the litany of socio-environmental issues that confront us, when many of these issues are intimately related to the purpose, mission, and capabilities of museums as we know them? This is not a call for museums to become social welfare agencies or Greenpeace activists, but rather to heighten their awareness and deliberately coalesce their capabilities and resources to bring about change, both internally and externally. Margaret Wheatley writes: "There is no power for change greater than a community discovering what it cares about."[7] Will communities continue to care about museums in their current guise? Will museums discover what they care about? Or are museums at risk?

Acknowledgments

This article is based on *Museums in a Troubled World: Renewal, Irrelevance or Collapse?* by Robert R. Janes (2009). The author wishes to thank Matthew

Gibbons, editor for Classics, Archaeology and Museum Studies at Routledge, for permission to use this material. I am indebted to Richard Sandell, Joy Davis, James M. Bradburne and Elaine Heumann Gurian for their generous assistance and support throughout the preparation of the book on which this article is based. I also want to thank the two anonymous referees who reviewed an earlier draft of this article. Priscilla Janes also reviewed this article and provided essential editorial assistance.

Notes

1. For several powerful overviews of the world's challenges, the reader should see Homer-Dixon (2001; 2006); McKibben (2006) and E.O. Wilson (2003).

2. Museum Victoria Water Smart Program, accessed February 11, 2010 at http://museum-victoria.com.au/watersmarthome/index.aspx.

3. Heifer Village, accessed February 11, 2010 at www.heifer.org/visit/heifer-village.

4. Commonwealth Association of Museums, accessed February 11, 2010 at www.maltwood.uvic.ca/cam/about/index.html.

5. Canadian Conservation Institute, accessed February 12, 2010 at www.cci-icc.gc.ca/crc/articles/enviro/index-eng.aspx.

6. A special issue devoted to Stephen Weil, in *Curator: The Museum Journal* vol. 50, no. 2, 2007, is a result of a conference held in honor of Weil at the University of Victoria, Cultural Resource Management Program, Victoria, British Columbia, Canada, September 13–15, 2006.

7. Wheatley, M.J., quoted in Wikipedia. Accessed August 22, 2008 at http://en.wikipedia.org/wiki/Margaret_Wheatley.

References

Drucker, P. F. 1994. *Post-Capitalist Society*. New York: HarperCollins.

Fontana, D. 1999. *Meditation: An Introductory Guide to Relaxation for Mind and Body*. Shaftesbury, Dorset, UK: Element Books Limited.

Gopnik, A. 2007. The mindful museum. *The Walrus* 4 (June): 87–91.

Hawken, P., A. Lovins, and L.H. Lovins. 2000. *Natural Capitalism*. New York: Back Bay Books/Little, Brown and Company.

Homer-Dixon, T. 2001. *The Ingenuity Gap*. Toronto: Vintage Canada.

——. 2006. *The Upside of Down: Catastrophe, Creativity, and the Renewal of Civilization*. Toronto: Alfred A. Knopf.

Hooper-Greenhill, E. 2000. *Museums and the Interpretation of Visual Culture*. New York: Routledge.

Janes, R. R. 2008. Museums in a troubled world: Renewal, irrelevance or collapse? Address to the Committee on Audience Research and Evaluation (CARE), Annual Meeting of the American Association of Museums, Denver, Colorado.

——. 2009. *Museums in a Troubled World: Renewal, Irrelevance or Collapse?* New York: Routledge.

Janes, R. R., and G. T. Conaty, eds. 2005. *Looking Reality in the Eye: Museums and Social Responsibility*. Calgary: The University of Calgary Press and the Museums Association of Saskatchewan.

Kabat-Zinn, J. 1990. *Full Catastrophe Living: Using the Wisdom of Your Body and Mind to Face Stress, Pain, and Illness*. New York: Bantam, Doubleday, Dell Publishing Group, Inc.

———. 1994. *Wherever You Go, There You Are: Mindfulness Meditation in Everyday Life*. New York: Hyperion.

———. 2005. *Coming to Our Senses: Healing Ourselves and the World Through Mindfulness*. New York: Hyperion.

Keene, S. 2005. *Fragments of the World: Uses of Museum Collections*. Oxford: Elsevier, Butterworth- Heinemann.

Kotler, N. G., P. Kotler, and W. I. Kotler. 2008. *Museum Marketing and Strategy: Designing Missions, Building Audiences, Generating Revenue and Resources*. Second edition. San Francisco: Jossey-Bass.

Lezner, R., and S. S. Johnson. 1997. Seeing things as they really are: An interview with Peter F. Drucker. *Forbes* 10 (March): 122–228.

McKibben, B. 2006. *The End of Nature*. New York: Random House.

Rifkin, J. 1980. *Entropy: A New World View*. New York: Viking Press.

Tien, C. 2010. The formation and impact of museum clusters: Two case studies from Taiwan. *Museum Management and Curatorship* 25(1): 69–85.

Weil, S. 1999. From being about something to being for somebody: The ongoing transformation of the American museum. *Daedalus: Journal of the American Academy of Arts and Sciences* (128): 229–258.

Wheatley, M. J. 1992. *Leadership and the New Science: Learning about Organization from an Orderly Universe*. San Francisco: Berrett-Koehler.

Wilson, E. O. 2003. *The Future of Life*. New York: Vintage Books.

———. 2006. *Creation: An Appeal to Save Life on Earth*. New York: W.W. Norton and Company.

Leading Change

Why Transformation Efforts Fail

JOHN P. KOTTER

Harvard Business Review Editor's NOTE: GUIDING CHANGE may be the ultimate test of a leader—no business survives over the long term if it can't reinvent itself. But, human nature being what it is, fundamental change is often resisted mightily by the people it most affects: those in the trenches of the business. Thus, leading change is both absolutely essential and incredibly difficult.

Perhaps nobody understands the anatomy of organizational change better than retired Harvard Business School professor John P. Kotter. This article, originally published in the spring of 1995, previewed Kotter's 1996 book *Leading Change*. It outlines eight critical success factors—from establishing a sense of extraordinary urgency, to creating short-term wins, to changing the culture ("the way we do things around here"). It will feel familiar when you read it, in part because Kotter's vocabulary has entered the lexicon and in part because it contains the kind of home truths that we recognize, immediately, as if we'd always known them. A decade later, his work on leading change remains definitive.

OVER THE PAST DECADE, I have watched more than 100 companies try to remake themselves into significantly better competitors. They have included large organizations (Ford) and small ones (Landmark Communications), companies based in the United States (General Motors) and elsewhere (British Airways), corporations that were on their knees (Eastern Airlines), and companies that were earning good money (Bristol-Myers Squibb). These efforts have gone under many banners: total quality management, reengineering, rightsizing, restructuring, cultural change, and turnaround. But, in almost every case, the basic goal has been the same: to make fundamental changes in how business is conducted in order to help cope with a new, more challenging market environment.

John P. Kotter is the Konosuke Matsushita Professor of Leadership, Emeritus at the Harvard Business School and cofounder of Kotter International, an organization that helps company leaders develop practical skills and methodologies to lead change in complex, large-scale business environments. "Leading Change: Why Transformation Efforts Fail" is republished here with permission from Harvard Business School Publishing. Copyright 2007. All rights reserved.

Figure 44.1.   Eight Steps to Transforming Your Organization

1. Establishing a Sense of Urgency
   - Examining market and competitive realities
   - Identifying and discussing crises, potential crises, or major opportunities
2. Forming a Powerful Guiding Coalition
   - Assembling a group with enough power to lead the change effort
   - Encouraging the group to work together as a team
3. Creating a Vision
   - Creating a vision to help direct the change effort
   - Developing strategies for achieving that vision
4. Communicating the Vision
   - Using every vehicle possible to communicate the new vision and strategies
   - Teaching new behaviors by the example of the guiding coalition
5. Empowering Others to Act on the Vision
   - Getting rid of obstacles to change
   - Changing systems or structures that seriously undermine the vision
   - Encouraging risk taking and nontraditional ideas, activities, and actions
6. Planning for and Creating Short-Term Wins
   - Planning for visible performance improvements
   - Creating those improvements
   - Recognizing and rewarding employees involved in the improvements
7. Consolidating Improvements and Producing Still More Change
   - Using increased credibility to change systems, structures, and policies that don't fit the vision
   - Hiring, promoting, and developing employees who can implement the vision
   - Reinvigorating the process with new projects, themes, and change agents
8. Institutionalizing New Approaches
   - Articulating the connections between the new behaviors and corporate success
   - Developing the means to ensure leadership development and succession

A few of these corporate change efforts have been very successful. A few have been utter failures. Most fell somewhere in between, with a distinct tilt toward the lower end of the scale. The lessons that can be drawn are interesting and will probably be relevant to even more organizations in the increasingly competitive business environment of the coming decade.

The most general lesson to be learned from the more successful cases is that the change process goes through a series of phases that, in total, usually require a considerable length of time. Skipping steps creates only the illusion of speed and never produces a satisfying result. A second very general lesson is that critical mistakes in any of the phases can have a devastating impact, slowing momentum and negating hard-won gains. Perhaps because we have relatively little experience in renewing organizations, even very capable people often make at least one big error.

Error 1: Not Establishing a Great Enough Sense of Urgency

Most successful change efforts begin when some individuals or some groups start to look hard at a company's competitive situation, market position, technological trends, and financial performance. They focus on the potential revenue drop when an important patent expires, the five-year trend in declining margins in a core business, or an emerging market that everyone seems to be ignoring. They then find ways to communicate this information broadly and dramatically, especially with respect to crises, potential crises, or great opportunities that are very timely. This first step is essential because just getting a transformation program started requires the aggressive cooperation of many individuals. Without motivation, people won't help, and the effort goes nowhere.

Compared with other steps in the change process, phase one can sound easy. It is not for well over 50 percent of the companies I have watched fail in this first phase. What are the reasons for that failure? Sometimes executives underestimate how hard it can be to drive people out of their comfort zones. Sometimes they grossly overestimate how successful they have already been in increasing urgency. Sometimes they lack patience: "Enough with the preliminaries; let's get on with it." In many cases, executives become paralyzed by the downside possibilities. They worry that employees with seniority will become defensive, that morale will drop, that events will spin out of control, that short-term business results will be jeopardized, that the stock will sink, and that they will be blamed for creating a crisis.

A paralyzed senior management often comes from having too many managers and not enough leaders. Management's mandate is to minimize risk and to keep the current system operating. Change, by definition, requires creating a new system, which in turn always demands leadership. Phase one in a renewal process typically goes nowhere until enough real leaders are promoted or hired into senior-level jobs.

Transformations often begin, and begin well, when an organization has a new head who is a good leader and who sees the need for a major change. If the renewal target is the entire company, the CEO is key. If change is needed in a division, the division general manager is key. When these individuals are not new leaders, great leaders, or change champions, phase one can be a huge challenge.

Bad business results are both a blessing and a curse in the first phase. On the positive side, losing money does catch people's attention. But it also gives less maneuvering room. With good business results, the opposite is true: Convincing people of the need for change is much harder, but you have more resources to help make changes.

But whether the starting point is good performance or bad, in the more successful cases I have witnessed, an individual or a group always facilitates a frank discussion of potentially unpleasant facts about new competition, shrinking margins, decreasing market share, flat earnings, a lack of revenue growth, or other relevant indices of a declining competitive position. Because there seems to be an almost universal human tendency to shoot the bearer of bad news, especially if the head of the organization is not a change champion, executives in these companies often rely on outsiders to bring unwanted information. Wall Street analysts, customers, and consultants can all be helpful in this regard. The purpose of all this activity, in the words of one former CEO of a large European company, is "to make the status quo seem more dangerous than launching into the unknown."

In a few of the most successful cases, a group has manufactured a crisis. One CEO deliberately engineered the largest accounting loss in the company's history, creating huge pressures from Wall Street in the process. One division president commissioned first-ever customer satisfaction surveys, knowing full well that the results would be terrible. He then made these findings public. On the surface, such moves can look unduly risky. But there is also risk in playing it too safe: When the urgency rate is not pumped up enough, the transformation process cannot succeed, and the long-term future of the organization is put in jeopardy.

When is the urgency rate high enough? From what I have seen, the answer is when about 75 percent of a company's management is honestly convinced that business as usual is totally unacceptable. Anything less can produce very serious problems later on in the process.

Error 2: Not Creating a Powerful Enough Guiding Coalition

Major renewal programs often start with just one or two people. In cases of successful transformation efforts, the leadership coalition grows and grows over time. But whenever some minimum mass is not achieved early in the effort, nothing much worthwhile happens.

It is often said that major change is impossible unless the head of the organization is an active supporter. What I am talking about goes far beyond that. In successful transformations, the chairman or president or division general manager, plus another five or fifteen or fifty people, come together and develop a shared commitment to excellent performance through renewal. In my experience, this group never includes all of the company's most senior executives because some people just won't buy in, at least not at first But in the most successful cases, the coalition is always pretty powerful—in terms of titles, information and expertise, reputations, and relationships.

In both small and large organizations, a successful guiding team may consist of only three to five people during the first year of a renewal effort But in big companies, the coalition needs to grow to the twenty to fifty range before much progress can be made in phase three and beyond. Senior managers always form the core of the group. But sometimes you find board members, a representative from a key customer, or even a powerful union leader.

Because the guiding coalition includes members who are not part of senior management it tends to operate outside of the normal hierarchy by definition. This can be awkward, but it is clearly necessary. If the existing hierarchy were working well, there would be no need for a major transformation. But since the current system is not working, reform generally demands activity outside of formal boundaries, expectations, and protocol.

A high sense of urgency within the managerial ranks helps enormously in putting a guiding coalition together. But more is usually required. Someone needs to get these people together, help them develop a shared assessment of their company's problems and opportunities, and create a minimum level of trust and communication. Off-site retreats, for two or three days, are one popular vehicle for accomplishing this task. I have seen many groups of five to thirty-five executives attend a series of these retreats over a period of months.

Companies that fail in phase two usually underestimate the difficulties of producing change and thus the importance of a powerful guiding coalition. Sometimes they have no history of teamwork at the top and therefore undervalue the importance of this type of coalition. Sometimes they expect the team to be led by a staff executive from human resources, quality, or strategic planning instead of a key line manager. No matter how capable or dedicated the staff head, groups without strong line leadership never achieve the power that is required.

Efforts that don't have a powerful enough guiding coalition can make apparent progress for a while. But sooner or later, the opposition gathers itself together and stops the change.

Error 3: Lacking a Vision

In every successful transformation effort that I have seen, the guiding coalition develops a picture of the future that is relatively easy to communicate and appeals to customers, stockholders, and employees. A vision always goes beyond the numbers that are typically found in five-year plans. A vision says something that helps clarify the direction in which an organization needs to move. Sometimes the first draft comes mostly from a single individual. It is usually a bit blurry, at least initially. But after the coalition works at it for three or five or even twelve months, something much better emerges through their tough analytical thinking and a little dreaming. Eventually, a strategy for achieving that vision is also developed.

In one midsize European company, the first pass at a vision contained two-thirds of the basic ideas that were in the final product The concept of global reach was in the initial version from the beginning. So was the idea of becoming preeminent in certain businesses. But one central idea in the final version—getting out of low value-added activities—came only after a series of discussions over a period of several months.

Without a sensible vision, a transformation effort can easily dissolve into a list of confusing and incompatible projects that can take the organization in the wrong direction or nowhere at all. Without a sound vision, the reengineering project in the accounting department, the new 360-degree performance appraisal from the human resources department the plant's quality program, the cultural change project in the sales force will not add up in a meaningful way.

In failed transformations, you often find plenty of plans, directives, and programs but no vision. In one case, a company gave out four-inch-thick notebooks describing its change effort. In mind-numbing detail, the books spelled out procedures, goals, methods, and deadlines. But nowhere was there a clear and compelling statement of where all this was leading. Not surprisingly, most of the employees with whom I talked were either confused or alienated. The big, thick books did not rally them together or inspire change. In fact they probably had just the opposite effect.

In a few of the less successful cases that I have seen, management had a sense of direction, but it was too complicated or blurry to be useful. Recently, I asked an executive in a midsize company to describe his vision and received in return a barely comprehensible thirty-minute lecture. Buried in his answer were the basic elements of a sound vision. But they were buried—deeply.

A useful rule of thumb: If you can't communicate the vision to someone in five minutes or less and get a reaction that signifies both understanding and interest, you are not yet done with this phase of the transformation process.

Error 4: Undercommunicating the Vision by a Factor of Ten

I've seen three patterns with respect to communication, all very common. In the first, a group actually does develop a pretty good transformation vision and then proceeds to communicate it by holding a single meeting or sending out a single communication. Having used about 0.0001 percent of the yearly intracompany communication, the group is startled when few people seem to understand the new approach. In the second pattern, the head of the organization spends a considerable amount of time making speeches to employee groups, but most people still don't get it (not surprising, since vision captures only 0.0005 percent of the total yearly communication). In the third pattern, much more effort goes into newsletters and speeches, but some very visible senior executives still behave in ways that are antithetical to the vision. The net result is that cynicism among the troops goes up, while belief in the communication goes down.

Transformation is impossible unless hundreds or thousands of people are willing to help, often to the point of making short-term sacrifices. Employees will not make sacrifices, even if they are unhappy with the status quo, unless they believe that useful change is possible. Without credible communication, and a lot of it, the hearts and minds of the troops are never captured.

This fourth phase is particularly challenging if the short-term sacrifices include job losses. Gaining understanding and support is tough when downsizing is a part of the vision. For this reason, successful visions usually include new growth possibilities and the commitment to treat fairly anyone who is laid off.

Executives who communicate well incorporate messages into their hour-by-hour activities. In a routine discussion about a business problem, they talk about how proposed solutions fit (or don't fit) into the bigger picture. In a regular performance appraisal, they talk about how the employee's behavior helps or undermines the vision. In a review of a division's quarterly performance, they talk not only about the numbers but also about how the division's executives are contributing to the transformation. In a routine Q&A with employees at a company facility, they tie their answers back to renewal goals.

In more successful transformation efforts, executives use all existing communication channels to broadcast the vision. They turn boring, unread company newsletters into lively articles about the vision. They take ritualistic, tedious quarterly management meetings and turn them into exciting discussions of the transformation. They throw out much of the company's generic management education and replace it with courses that focus on business problems and the new vision. The guiding principle is simple: Use every possible channel, especially those that are being wasted on nonessential information.

Perhaps even more important, most of the executives I have known in successful cases of major change learn to "walk the talk." They consciously attempt to become a living symbol of the new corporate culture. This is often not easy. A sixty-year-old plant manager who has spent precious little time over forty years thinking about customers will not suddenly behave in a customer-oriented way. But I have witnessed just such a person change, and change a great deal. In that case, a high level of urgency helped. The fact that the man was a part of the guiding coalition and the vision-creation team also helped. So did all the communication, which kept reminding him of the desired behavior, and all the feedback from his peers and subordinates, which helped him see when he was not engaging in that behavior.

Communication comes in both words and deeds, and the latter are often the most powerful form. Nothing undermines change more than behavior by important individuals that is inconsistent with their words.

Error 5: Not Removing Obstacles to the New Vision

Successful transformations begin to involve large numbers of people as the process progresses. Employees are emboldened to try new approaches, to develop new ideas, and to provide leadership. The only constraint is that the actions fit within the broad parameters of the overall vision. The more people involved, the better the outcome.

To some degree, a guiding coalition empowers others to take action simply by successfully communicating the new direction. But communication is never sufficient by itself. Renewal also requires the removal of obstacles. Too often, an employee understands the new vision and wants to help make it happen, but an elephant appears to be blocking the path. In some cases, the elephant is in the person's head, and the challenge is to convince the individual that no external obstacle exists. But in most cases, the blockers are very real.

Sometimes the obstacle is the organizational structure: Narrow job categories can seriously undermine efforts to increase productivity or make it very difficult even to think about customers. Sometimes compensation or performance-appraisal systems make people choose between the new vision and their own self-interest Perhaps worst of all are bosses who refuse to change and who make demands that are inconsistent with the overall effort.

One company began its transformation process with much publicity and actually made good progress through the fourth phase. Then the change effort ground to a halt because the officer in charge of the company's largest division was allowed to undermine most of the new initiatives. He paid lip service to the process but did not change his behavior or encourage his managers to change. He did not reward the unconventional ideas called for in the vision. He allowed human resource systems to remain intact even when they were clearly inconsistent with the new ideals. I think the officer's motives were complex. To some degree, he did not believe the company needed major change. To some degree, he felt personally threatened by all the change. To some degree, he was afraid that he could not produce both change and the expected operating profit but despite the fact that they backed the renewal effort, the other officers did virtually nothing to stop the one blocker. Again, the reasons were complex. The company had no history of confronting problems like this. Some people were afraid of the officer. The CEO was concerned that he might lose a talented executive. The net result was disastrous. Lower-level managers concluded that senior management had lied to them about their commitment to renewal, cynicism grew, and the whole effort collapsed.

In the first half of a transformation, no organization has the momentum, power, or time to get rid of all obstacles. But the big ones must be confronted and removed. If the blocker is a person, it is important that he or she be treated fairly and in a way that is consistent with the new vision. Action is essential, both to empower others and to maintain the credibility of the change effort as a whole.

Error 6: Not Systematically Planning for, and Creating, Short-Term Wins

Real transformation takes time, and a renewal effort risks losing momentum if there are no short-term goals to meet and celebrate. Most people won't go on the long march unless they see compelling evidence in twelve to twenty-four months that the journey is producing expected results. Without short-term wins, too many people give up or actively join the ranks of those people who have been resisting change.

One to two years into a successful transformation effort, you find quality beginning to go up on certain indices or the decline in net income stopping. You find some successful new product introductions or an upward shift in market share. You find an impressive productivity improvement or a statistically higher customer satisfaction rating. But whatever the case, the win is unambiguous. The result is not just a judgment call that can be discounted by those opposing change.

Creating short-term wins is different from hoping for short-term wins. The latter is passive, the former active. In a successful transformation, managers actively look for ways to obtain clear performance improvements, establish goals in the yearly planning system, achieve the objectives, and reward the people involved with recognition, promotions, and even money. For example, the guiding coalition at a U.S. manufacturing company produced a highly visible and successful new product introduction about twenty months after the start of its renewal effort. The new product was selected about six months into the effort because it met multiple criteria: It could be designed and launched in a relatively short period, it could be handled by a small team of people who were devoted to the new vision, it had upside potential, and the new product-development team could operate outside the established departmental structure without practical problems. Little was left to chance, and the win boosted the credibility of the renewal process.

Managers often complain about being forced to produce short-term wins, but I've found that pressure can be a useful element in a change effort. When it becomes clear to people that major change will take a long time, urgency levels can drop. Commitments to produce short-term wins help keep the urgency level up and force detailed analytical thinking that can clarify or revise visions.

Error 7: Declaring Victory Too Soon

After a few years of hard work, managers may be tempted to declare victory with the first clear performance improvement while celebrating a win is fine; declaring the war won can be catastrophic. Until changes sink deeply into a company's culture, a process that can take five to ten years, new approaches are fragile and subject to regression.

In the recent past, I have watched a dozen change efforts operate under the reengineering theme. In all but two cases, victory was declared and the expensive consultants were paid and thanked when the first major project was completed after two to three years. Within two more years, the useful changes that had been introduced slowly disappeared. In two of the ten cases, it's hard to find any trace of the re-engineering work today.

Over the past twenty years, I've seen the same sort of thing happen to huge quality projects, organizational development efforts, and more. Typically, the problems start early in the process: The urgency level is not intense enough, the guiding coalition is not powerful enough, and the vision is not clear enough. But it is the premature victory celebration that kills momentum. And then the powerful forces associated with tradition take over.

Ironically, it is often a combination of change initiators and change resistors that creates the premature victory celebration. In their enthusiasm over a clear sign of progress, the initiators go overboard. They are then joined by resistors, who are quick to spot any opportunity to stop change. After the celebration is over, the resistors point to the victory as a sign that the war has been won and the troops should be sent home. Weary troops allow themselves to be convinced that they won. Once home, the foot soldiers are reluctant to climb back on the ships. Soon thereafter, change comes to a halt, and tradition creeps back in.

Instead of declaring victory, leaders of successful efforts use the credibility afforded by short-term wins to tackle even bigger problems. They go after systems and structures that are not consistent with the transformation vision and have not been confronted before. They pay great attention to who is promoted, who is hired, and how people are developed. They include new reengineering projects that are even bigger in scope than the initial ones. They understand that renewal efforts take not months but years. In fact, in one of the most successful transformations that I have ever seen, we quantified the amount of change that occurred each year over a seven-year period. On a scale of one (low) to ten (high), year one received a two, year two a four, year three a three, year four a seven, year five an eight, year six a four, and year seven a two. The peak came in year five, fully thirty-six months after the first set of visible wins.

Error 8: Not Anchoring Changes in the Corporation's Culture

In the final analysis, change sticks when it becomes "the way we do things around here," when it seeps into the bloodstream of the corporate body. Until new behaviors are rooted in social norms and shared values, they are subject to degradation as soon as the pressure for change is removed.

Two factors are particularly important in institutionalizing change in corporate culture. The first is a conscious attempt to show people how the new approaches, behaviors, and attitudes have helped improve performance. When people are left on their own to make the connections, they sometimes create very inaccurate links. For example, because results improved while charismatic Harry was boss; the troops link his mostly idiosyncratic style with those results instead of seeing how their own improved customer service and productivity were instrumental. Helping people see the right connections requires communication. Indeed, one company was relentless, and it paid off enormously. Time was spent at every major management meeting to discuss why performance was increasing. The company newspaper ran article after article showing how changes had boosted earnings.

The second factor is taking sufficient time to make sure that the next generation of top management really does personify the new approach. If the requirements for promotion don't change, renewal rarely lasts. One bad succession decision at the top of an organization can undermine a decade of hard work. Poor succession decisions are possible when boards of directors are not an integral part of the renewal effort. In at least three instances I have seen, the champion for change was the retiring executive, and although his successor was not a resistor, he was not a change champion. Because the boards did not understand the transformations in any detail, they could not see that their choices were not good fits. The retiring executive in one case tried unsuccessfully to talk his board into a less seasoned candidate who better personified the transformation. In the other two cases, the CEOs did not resist the boards' choices, because they felt the transformation could not be undone by their successors. They were wrong. Within two years, signs of renewal began to disappear at both companies.

There are still more mistakes that people make, but these eight are the big ones. I realize that in a short article everything is made to sound a bit too simplistic. In reality, even successful change efforts are messy and full of surprises. But just as a relatively simple vision is needed to guide people through a major change, so a vision of the change process can reduce the error rate. And fewer errors can spell the difference between success and failure.

Table 44.1. The Idea in Practice

Actions Needed	Pitfalls
• Examine market and competitive realities for potential crises and untapped opportunities. • Convince at least 75% of your managers that the status quo is more dangerous than the unknown	• Understanding the difficulty of driving people from their comfort zones. • Becoming paralyzed by risks.
• Assemble a group with shared commitment and enough power to lead the change effort. • Encourage them to work as a team outside the normal hierarchy.	• No prior experience in teamwork at the top. • Relegating team leadership to an HR, quality, or strategic-planning executive rather than a senior line manager.
• Create a vision to direct the change effort. • Develop strategies for realizing that vision.	• Presenting a vision that's too complicated or vague to be communicated in five minutes.
• Use every vehicle possible to communicate the new vision and strategies for achieving it. • Teach new behaviors by the example of the guiding coalition.	• Under communicating the vision. • Behaving in ways antithetical to the vision.
• Remove or alter systems or structures undermining the vision. • Encourage risk taking and nontraditional ideas, activities, and actions.	• Failing to remove powerful individuals who resist the change effort.
• Define and engineer visible performance improvements. • Recognize and reward employees contributing to those improvements.	• Leaving short-term successes up to chance. • Failing to score successes early enough (12–24 months into the change effort).
• Use increased credibility from early wins to change systems, structures, and policies undermining the vision. • Hire, promote, and develop employees who can implement the vision. • Reinvigorate the change process with new projects and change agents.	• Declaring victory too soon—with the first performance improvement. • Allowing resistors to convince "troops" that the war has been won.
• Articulate connections between new behaviors and corporate success. • Create leadership development and succession plans consistent with the new approach.	• Noting creating new social norms and shared values consistent with changes. • Promoting people into leadership positions who don't personify the new approach.

Select Bibliography

Articles Featured in the First Edition

The following articles were featured in the first edition of *Reinventing the Museum: Historical and Contemporary Perspectives on the Paradigm Shift* published by AltaMira Press, 2004.

Ames, Michael M. "Museums in the Age of Deconstruction." *Cannibal Tours and Glass Boxes: The Anthropology of Museums* (pp. 151–168). Vancouver: UBC Press, 1992.

Brown, Claudine. "The Museum's Role in a Multicultural Society." *Patterns in Practice* (pp. 2–8). Washington, DC: Museum Education Roundtable, 1992.

Carver, John. "Toward a New Governance." *Boards That Make A Difference: A New Design for Leadership in Nonprofit and Public Organizations* (pp.17–20). San Francisco: Jossey-Bass, 1997.

Cheit, Earl F. and Stephen E. Weil. "The Well-Managed Museum" *Rethinking The Museum* (pp. 69–72). Washington, DC: Smithsonian Institution Press, 1990.

Falk, John H. and Lynn D. Dierking. "The Contextual Model of Learning," *Learning From Museums* (Chart, pp. 12; pp. 135–140). Walnut Creek, CA: AltaMira Press.

Gaither, Edmund Barry. "'Hey! That's Mine': Thoughts on Pluralism and America." *Museums and Communities: The Politics of Public Culture* (pp. 56–64). Washington, DC: Smithsonian Institution Press, 1992.

Gurian, Elaine Heumann. "What is the Object of this Exercise?" *Daedalus* Vol. 128, No. 3, (Summer 1999): 163–183.

Hood, Marilyn. "Staying Away: Why People Choose Not to Visit Museums." *Museum News* (April 1983): 50–57.

Janes, Robert. "Persistent Paradoxes." *Museums and the Paradox of Change: A Case Study in Urgent Adaptation*. Calgary, Alberta: Glenbow Museum, 1995.

Kotler, Neil and Philip Kotler. "Can Museums Be All Things to All People?: Missions, Goals, and Marketing's Role." *Museum Management and Curatorship* Vol. 18 (2000): 271–287.

McLean, Kathleen. "Museum Exhibitions and the Dynamics of Dialogue." *Daedalus* Vol. 128, No. 3 (Summer 1999): 83–107.

Milner, Carole. "Who Cares? Conservation in a Contemporary Context." *Museum International* Vol. 51, No. 1 (1999): 22–27.

Munley, Mary Ellen. "Is There Method in our Madness? Improvisation in the Practice of Museum Education." *Presence of Mind: Museums and the Spirit of Learning* (pp. 133–139). Washington, DC: American Association of Museums, 1999.

Phillips, Will. "Institution-Wide Change in Museums." *Transforming Practice: Selections from the Journal of Museum Education* (pp. 71–77). Washington, DC: Museum Education Roundtable, 2000.

Screven, C.G. "United States: a science in the making." *Museum International* (UNESCO) Vol. XLV. No. 2 (1993).

Silverman, Lois. "Making Meaning Together: Lessons from the Field of American History." *Journal of Museum Education* Vol.18, No. 3 (Fall 1993): 7–11.

Skramstad, Harold. "An Agenda for Museums in the Twenty-First Century." *Daedalus* Vol. 128, No. 3, (Summer 1999): 109–128.

Sullivan, Robert. "Evaluating the Ethics and Consciences of Museums." *Gender Perspectives: Essays on Women in Museums.* Ed. Jane R. Glasner and Artemis A. Zenetou. Washington, DC: Smithsonian Isntutions Press, 1994.

Warren, Karen J. "A Philosophical Perspective on the Ethics and Resolution of Cultural Properties Issues." *The Ethics of Collecting Cultural Property: Whose Culture? Whose Ethics?* (pp. 1–26). Ed. Phyllis Mauch Messenger. New Mexico: University of New Mexico Press, 1999.

Weil, Stephen E. "Collecting Then, Collecting Today." *Making Museums Matter* (pp. 141–150). Washington, D.C.: Smithsonian Institute, 2002.

———. Rethinking the Museum: An Emerging New Paradigm. *Rethinking The Museum* (pp. 57–65). Washington, DC: Smithsonian Institution Press, 1990.

Wendroff, Alan L. and Kay Sprinkel Grace. *High Impact Philanthropy: How Donors, Boards, and Nonprofit Organizations Can Transform Communities.* New York, NY: Wiley & Sons, 2001.

Wittlin, Alma. "A Twelve Point Program for Museum Renewal." *In Search of a Usable Future.* (pp. 203–219). Boston, MA: The Massachusetts Institute of Technology, 1970.

Recommended References

Alexander, Edward P. *The Museum in America: Innovators and Pioneers.* Lanham, MD: AltaMira, 2008.

Alvarez, Mari-Tere and Selma Holo. *Beyond the Turnstile: Making the Case for Museums and Sustainable Values.* Lanham, MD: AltaMira Press, 2009.

American Academy of Arts and Sciences. *Daedalus: America's Museums.* Cambridge, MA: Author, 1999.

American Association of Museums. *Mastering Civic Engagement: A Challenge to Museums.* Washington, DC: American Association of Museums Press, 2002.

———. *National Standards & Best Practices for U.S. Museums.* Washington, DC: American Association of Museums Press, 2008.

———. *Museums in Motion: An Introduction to the History and Functions of Museums.* Lanham, MD: AltaMira, 1996.

———. *Museum Masters: Their Museums and Their Influence.* Lanham, MD: AltaMira, 1983.

———. *America's Museums: The Belmont Report: A Report to the Federal Council on the Arts and the Humanities.* Washington, DC: Author, 1968.

———. *Caring for Collections: Strategies for Conservation, Maintenance, and Documentation: A Report on an American Association of Museums Project.* Washington, DC: Author, 1984.

———. *Excellence and Equity: Education and the Public Dimension of Museums: A Report from the American Association of Museums.* Washington, DC: Author, 1992.

———. *Mastering Civic Engagement: A Challenge to Museums.* Washington, DC: Author, 2002.

American Association of Museums Commission on Museums for a New Century. *Museums for a New Century: A Report of the Commission on Museums for a New Century.* Washington, DC: American Association of Museums, 1984.

Ames, Kenneth L., et al., eds. *Ideas and Images: Developing Interpretive History Exhibits.* Lanham, MD: AltaMira, 1992.

Ames, Michael M. *Cannibal Tours and Glass Boxes: The Anthropology of Museums.* Vancouver, British Columbia, Canada: University of British Columbia Press, 1992.

Anderson, Gail, ed. *Museum Mission Statements: Building a Distinct Identity.* Washington, DC: American Association of Museums, Technical Information Service, 1998.

———, ed. *Reinventing the Museum: Historical and Contemporary Perspectives on the Paradigm Shift.* Lanham, MD: AltaMira Press, 2004.

Association of Art Museum Directors. *Different Voices: Social, Cultural, and Historical Framework for Change in the American Art Museum.* New York: Author, 1992.

Bell, Jeanne, Masaoka, Jan and Steve Zimmerman. *Nonprofit Sustainability: Making Strategic Decisions for Financial Viability.* San Francisco, CA: Jossey-Bass, 2010.

Bennis, Warren. *On Becoming a Leader.* Cambridge, MA: Perseus Books, 1989.

Bernoff, Josh and Charlene Li. *Groundswell: Winning in a World Transformed by Social Technologies.* Boston, MA: Harvard Business School Publishing, 2008.

Bishop, Peter and Andy Hines. *Thinking About the Future: Guidelines for Strategic Foresight.* Washington, DC: Social Technologies, LLC, 2006

BoardSource. *New BoardSource Governance Series.* Washington, DC: Author, 2002.

———. *The Source: Twelve Principles of Governance that Power Exceptional Boards.* Washington, DC: Author, 2005.

———. *Exceptional Board Practices: The Source in Action.* Washington, DC: Author, 2008.

Brophy, Sarah S. and Elizabeth Wylie. *The Green Museum: A Primer on Environmental Practice.* Lanham, MD: AltaMira Press, 2008.

Brown, Claudine K. "The Museum's Role in a Multicultural Society." *Patterns in Practice: Selections from the Journal of Museum Education.* Washington, DC, 1992.

Buck, Rebecca A. and Jean Allman Gilmore, eds. *Museum Registration Methods 5ᵗʰ Edition.* Washington, DC: American Association of Museums, 2010.

Bunch III, Lonnie G. *Call the Lost Dream Back: Essays on History, Race and Museums.* Washington, DC: The American Association of Museums Press, 2010.

Burcaw, George Ellis. *Introduction to Museum Work.* Lanham, MD: AltaMira, 1997.

Case, Mary, ed. *Registrars on Record: Essays on Museum Collections Management.* Washington, DC: Registrars Committee of the American Association of Museums, 1988.

Center for Museum Studies, Smithsonian Institution & The American Association of Museums. *Museums for the New Millennium.* Washington, DC: Authors, 1997.

Collins, Jim. *Good to Great and the Social Sector: A Monograph Accompanying Good to Great.* New York, NY: HarperCollins, 2005.

———. *Good to Great: Why Some Companies Make the Leap and Others Don't.* New York, NY: HarperCollins, 2001.

Collins, Zipporah W., ed. *Museums, Adults, and the Humanities: A Guide for Educational Programming*. Washington, DC: American Association of Museums, 1981.

Commission on Museums for a New Century. *Museums for a New Century*. Washington, DC: American Association of Museums, 1984.

Conaty, Gerald T. and Robert Janes, Eds. *Looking Reality in the Eye: Museums and Social Responsibility*. Calgary, Alberta Canada: University of Calgary Press, 2005.

Connolly, Paul M. *Navigating the Organizational Lifecycle: A Capacity-Building Guide for Non-profit Leaders*. Washington, DC: BoardSource, 2006.

Council on Museums and Education in the Visual Arts. *The Art Museum as Educator: A Collection of Studies as Guides to Practice and Policy*. Berkeley, CA: University of California Press, 1978.

Covey, Stephen M.R. *The Speed of Trust: The One Thing That Changes Everything*. New York, NY: Free Press, 2006.

Csikszentmihalyi, Mihaly. *Creativity: Flow and the Psychology of Discovery and Invention*. New York, NY: HarpersCollins Publisher, 1996.

———. *Flow: The Psychology of Optimal Experience*. New York, NY: HarperPerennial, 1991, c1990.

———. *The Meaning of Things: Domestic Symbols and the Self*. New York, NY: Cambridge University Press, 1981.

Cuno, James. *Who Owns Antiquity? Museums and the Battle Over Our Ancient Heritage*. Princeton, NJ: Princeton University Press, 2008.

Daedalus Vol. 128, No. 3 (Summer 1999).

DePree, Max. *Leadership is an Art*. New York, NY: Bantam Doubleday Dell Publishing Group, 1989.

"Designing for Conservation." *Exhibitionist* 20, No. 2 (Fall 2001).

Diamond, Judy. *Practical Evaluation Guide: Tools for Museums and Other Informal Educational Settings*. Lanham, MD: AltaMira, 1999.

Drucker, Peter F. *Managing the Non-Profit Organization: Practices and Principles*. New York, NY: HarperCollins, 1990.

Drucker, Peter F. *Innovation and Entrepreneurship: Practice and Principles*. New York, NY: Harper & Row, 1994, c1985.

Falk, John H. *Identity and the Museum Visitor Experience*. Walnut Creek, CA: Left Coast Press, 2009.

Falk, John H. and Beverly K. Sheppard. *Thriving in the Knowledge Age: New Business Models for Museums and Other Cultural Institutions*. Lanham, MD: AltaMira Press, 2006.

Falk, John H. and Lynn D. Dierking. *Learning from Museums: Visitor Experiences and the Making of Meaning*. Lanham, MD: AltaMira, 2000.

———. *The Museum Experience*. Washington, DC: Whalesback, 1992.

Fischer, Daryl K. *Museums, Trustees, and Communities: Building Reciprocal Relationships*. Washington, DC: American Association of Museums, Technical Information Service, 1997.

Fischer, Daryl, and Barbara Booker. *The Leadership Partnership*. Washington, DC: Museum Trustee Association, 2002.

———. *Building Museum Boards: Templates for Museum Trustees*. Washington, DC: Museum Trustee Association, 2002.

"Formalizing Exhibition Development." *Exhibitionist* 21, No. 1 (Spring 2002).

Gardner, Howard. *Frames of Mind: The Theory of Multiple Intelligences*. New York, NY: Basic Books, 1983.

Genoways, Hugh H. and Lynne M. Irreland. *Museum Administration: An Introduction*. Lanham, MD: AltaMira, 2003.

Genoways, Hugh, ed. *Museum Philosophy in the Twenty-First Century*. Lanham, MD: AltaMira Press, 2006.

Glaser, Jane R. and Artemis Zenetou, eds. *Gender Perspectives: Essays on Women in Museums*. Washington, DC: Smithsonian Institution, 1994.

Goleman, Daniel. *Emotional Intelligence: Why It Can Matter More Than IQ*. New York, NY: Random House, 2005, c.1995.

Grace, Kay Sprinkel. *Beyond Fundraising: New Strategies for Nonprofit Innovation and Investment*. New York, NY: Wiley & Sons, 2005.

———. *The Ultimate Board Member's Book: A 1-Hour Guide to Understanding and Fulfilling Your Role and Responsibilities*. Medfield, MA: Emerson & Church Publishers, 2007.

Greenfield, James M. *Fund-raising Fundamentals: A Guide to Annual Giving for Professionals and Volunteers*. New York, NY: Wiley & Sons, 1994.

Gurian, Elaine Heumann. *Civilizing the Museum: the Collected Writings of Elaine Heumann Gurian*. New York, NY: Routledge, 2006

———, ed. *Institutional Trauma: Major Change in Museums and Its Effect on Staff*. Washington, DC: American Association of Museums, 1995.

Harvard Business Review on Leadership. Boston, MA: Harvard Business School Publishing, 1998.

Heath, Chip and Dan Heath. *Made to Stick: Why Some Ideas Survive and Others Die*. New York, NY: Random House, 2007.

Hein, George E. *Learning in the Museum*. New York: Routledge, 1998.

Henry, Barbara and Kathleen McLean. *How Visitors Changed Our Museum: Transforming the Gallery of California Art at the Oakland Museum*, Oakland, CA: Oakland Museum of California, 2011.

Hirsch, Joanne S. and Lois Silverman. *Transforming Practice: Selections from the* Journal of Museum Education, 1992-1999. Washington, DC: Museum Education Roundtable, 2000.

Hudson, Kenneth. *Museums of Influence*. New York: Cambridge University Press, 1987.

Institute of Museum and Library Services. *Museums, Libraries, and 21st Century Skills*. Washington, DC: Author, 2009.

———. *True Needs, True Partners: Museums and Schools Transforming Education*. Washington, DC: Author, 1996.

The James Irvine Foundation. *Key Issue—The Nonprofit Business Model. In Critical Issues Facing the Arts in California: A Working Paper from the James Irvine Foundation*, 2006. Retrieved from http://www.irvine.org/publications/publications-by-topic/arts.

Janes, Robert. *Museums in a Troubled World: Renewal, Irrelevance or Collapse?* London; New York: Routledge, 2009.

Janes, Robert. *Museums and the Paradox of Change: A Case Study in Urgent Adaptation*. Calgary: University of Calgary Press and Glenbow Museum, 1997.

Janes, Robert and Richard Sandell. *Museum Management and Marketing*. Milton Park, Abingdon, Oxon; New York: Routledge, 2007.

Kanter, Beth and Alison H. Fine. *The Networked Nonprofit: Connecting with Social Media to Drive Change*. San Francisco, CA: Jossey-Bass, 2010.

Karp, Ivan, Lynn Kratz, Corinne A. Szwaja and Tomás Ybarra-Frausto. *MuseumFrictions: Public cultures/Global Transformations*. Drake University Press, 2006.

Karp, Ivan, Christine Mullen Kreamer and Steven D. Lavine, eds. *Museums and Communities: The Politics of Public Culture*. Washington, DC: Smithsonian Institution Press, 1992.

Karp, Ivan, and Steven D. Lavine, eds. *Exhibiting Cultures: The Poetics and Politics of Museum Display*. Washington, DC: Smithsonian Institution Press, 1991.

Keene, Suzanne. *Managing Conservation in Museums*. Boston, MA: Butterworth-Heinemann, 1996.

Kelley, Thomas and Jonathan Littman. *The Ten Faces of Innovation: IDEO's Strategies for Defeating the Devil's Advocate and Driving Creativity Throughout Your Organization*. New York, NY: Doubleday, a division of Random House, 2005.

King, John, King, Dave and Halee Fischer-Wright. *Tribal Leadership: Leveraging Natural Groups to Build a Thriving Organization*. New York, NY: HarperCollins, 2008.

Kotler, Neil and Philip Kotler. *Museum Strategy and Marketing: Designing Missions, Building Audiences, Generating Revenue and Resources*. San Francisco: Jossey-Bass, 1998.

Kurtz, Daniel. *Managing Conflicts of Interest*. Washington, DC: BoardSource, 2001.

Levin, Amy K., ed. *Local Museums and the Construction of History in America's Changing Communities*. Walnut Creek, CA: AltaMira, 2007.

Light, Paul C. *Sustaining Innovation: Creating Nonprofit and Government Organizations That Innovate Naturally*. San Francisco, CA: Jossey-Bass, Inc., Publishers, 1998.

Lord, Barry, and Gail Dexter Lord. *The Manual of Museum Management*. Lanham, MD: AltaMira, 1997.

——— eds. *The Manual of Museum Exhibitions*. Lanham, MD: AltaMira, 2002.

Lord, Gail Dexter and Barry Lord, eds. *The Manual of Museum Planning*, 2d ed. Walnut Creek, CA: AltaMira, 1999.

Luke, Timothy W. *Museum Politics: Power Plays at the Exhibition*. Minneapolis, MN: University of Minnesota Press, 2002.

Maher, Mary, ed. *Collective Vision: Starting and Sustaining Children's Museums*. Washington, DC: Association of Youth Museums, 1997.

Making Meaning in Exhibits. *Exhibitionist* 18, No. 2 (Fall 1999).

Malaro, Marie C. *Museum Governance: Mission, Ethics, Policy*. Washington, DC: Smithsonian Institution Press, 1994.

———. *A Legal Primer on Managing Museum Collections*. Washington, DC: Smithsonian Institution Press, 1998.

Masaoka, Jan. *The Best of the Board Café: Hands-on Solutions for Nonprofit Boards*. Saint Paul, MN: Wilder Publishing Center, 2003

Mathiasen, Karl, III. *Board Passages: Three Key Stages in a Nonprofit Board's Life Cycle*. Washington, DC: National Center for Nonprofit Boards, 1992.

McLean, Kathleen. *Planning for People in Museum Exhibitions*. Washington, DC: Association of Science-Technology Centers, 1996.

McLean, Kathleen and Wendy Pollock. *Visitor Voices in Museum Exhibitions*. Washington, DC: Association of Science-Technology Centers Inc., 2007.

Messenger, Phyllis M., ed. *The Ethics of Collecting Cultural Property: Whose Culture? Whose Ethics?* Albuquerque, NM: University of New Mexico Press, 1999.

Museum Educators of the American Association of Museums. *The Visitor and the Museum*. Berkeley, CA: University of California Press, 1977.

Newsom, Barbara Y. and Adele Z. Silver, eds. *The Art Museum as Educator*. Berkeley, CA: University of California Press, 1978.

Ross, Parry. *Museums in a Digital Age*. London, UK: Routledge, 2009.

Peniston, William A., ed. *The New Museum: Selected Writings by John Cotton Dana*. Washington, DC: American Association of Museums, 1999.

Phelan, Marilyn E. *Museum Law: A Guide for Officers, Directors, and Counsel*. Evanston, IL: Kalos Kapp, 2001.

Pink, Daniel. *Drive: The Surprising Truth About What Motivates Us*. New York, NY: Penguin Group, 2009.

Pitman, Bonnie, ed. *Presence of Mind: Museums and the Spirit of Learning*. Washington, DC: American Association of Museums, 1999.

Price, Clement Alexander. *Many Voices, Many Opportunities: Cultural Pluralism and American Arts Policy*. New York: ACA Books, Allworth Press, 1993.

Ripley, S. Dillon. *The Sacred Grove: Essays on Museums*. New York, NY: Simon & Schuster, 1969.

Roberts, Lisa C. *From Knowledge to Narrative: Educators and the Changing Museum*. Washington, DC: Smithsonian Institution Press, 1997.

Rosenbaum, Steven. *Curation Nation: Why the Future of Content is Context*. New York, NY: McGraw Hill, 2011

Rutledge, Jennifer M. *Building Board Diversity*. Washington, DC: National Center for Nonprofit Boards, 1994.

Senge, Peter. *The Fifth Discipline: The Art & Practice of The Learning Organization*. New York, NY: Random House, 2006, c1990.

Serrell, Beverly. *Exhibit Labels: An Interpretive Approach*. Lanham, MD: AltaMira, 1996.

———. *Judging Exhibitions: A Framework for Assessing Excellence*. Walnut Creek, CA: Left Coast Press, 2006.

Silverman, Lois H. *The Social Work of Museums*. London, UK; New York, NY: Routledge, 2010.

Simon, Nina. *Principles of Participation*. Santa Cruz, CA: Museum 2.0, 2010.

Skramstad, Harold and Susan Skramstad. *A Handbook for Museum Trustees*. Washington, DC: American Association of Museums, 2003.

Smithsonian Institution Task Force on Latino Issues. *Willful Neglect: The Smithsonian Institution and U.S. Latinos*. Washington, DC: Smithsonian Institution, 1994.

Suchy, Sherene. *Leading with Passion: Change Management in the 21st-Century Museum*. Lanham, MD: AltaMira, 1999.

Sullivan, Lawrence E. and Alison Edwards. *Stewards of the Sacred*. Washington, DC: American Association of Museums Press, 2004.

Tallon, Loïc and Kevin Walker (Eds.) *Digital Technologies and the Museum Experience: Handheld Guides and Other Media*. Lanham, MD: AltaMira Press, 2008.

Texas Association of Museums. *Action Plan for Multicultural Initiatives in Texas Museums*. Austin: Texas Association of Museums, 1995. Retrieved from www.io.com/~tam/multicultural/actionplan.html (accessed 26 August 2003)

Weaver, Stephanie. *Creating Great Visitor Experiences: A Guide for Museums, Parks, Zoos, Gardens, & Libraries*. Walnut Creek, CA: Left Coast Press, 2007.

Weil, Stephen E. *Beauty and the Beasts: On Museums, Art, the Law, and the Market*. Washington, DC: Smithsonian Institution Press, 1983.

———. *A Cabinet of Curiosities: Inquiries into Museums and Their Prospects.* Washington, DC: Smithsonian Institution Press, 1995.

———. *Making Museums Matter.* Washington, DC: Smithsonian Institution Press, 2002.

———. *Rethinking the Museum and Other Meditations.* Washington, DC: Smithsonian Institution Press, 1990.

——— ed. *A Deaccession Reader.* Washington DC: American Association of Museums, 1997.

Weisz, Jackie, ed. *Codes of Ethics and Practice of Interest to Museums.* Washington, DC: American Association of Museums, Technical Information Service, 2000.

Wheatley, Margaret J. *Leadership and the New Science: Discovering Order in a Chaotic World.* San Francisco, CA: Berrett-Koehler Publishers, 1999.

Wolf, Thomas. *Managing a Nonprofit Organization in the Twenty-first Century.* New York: Simon & Schuster, 1999.

Journals for Contemporary Scholarship

American Archivist. Chicago, IL: The Society of American Archivists.

BoardMember. Washington, DC: BoardSource.

Collections: A Journal for Museum and Archives Professionals. Lanham, MD: AltaMira Press.

Common Ground: Preserving Our Nation's Heritage. The National Park Service.

Cultural Resources Management: The Journal of Heritage Stewardship. The National Park Service.

Curator: The Museum Journal. New York, NY: Wiley-Blackwell Publishers.

Dimensions. Association of Science-Technology Centers (ASTC).

History News. Nashville, TN: American Association for State and Local History (AASLH).

ICOM News. International Council of Museums (ICOM).

Journal of Museum Education: A Publication of the Museum Education Roundtable. Walnut Creek, CA: Left Coast Press.

Muse. Ottawa ON, Canada: Canadian Museum Association.

Museum (formerly *Museum News*). Washington, DC: American Association of Museums.

Museum History Journal. Walnut Creek, CA: Left Coast Press.

Museum Management and Curatorship. London, UK; New York, NY: Routledge.

Museums & Social Issues: A Journal of Reflective Discourse. Walnut Creek, CA: Left Coast Press.

About the Editor

Gail Anderson has been active in the museum field for thirty-five years. Today, as president of the museum management consulting firm, Gail Anderson & Associates (GA&A), Anderson focuses on helping museum leaders position their institutions for greater relevancy and success in today's complex world. Anderson's practice includes institutional planning, governance, and leadership development; organizational transformation; institutional capacity building; community and civic engagement; and professional development. Prior to beginning her own consulting business, Anderson was deputy director of The Mexican Museum; vice president of Museum Management Consultants; chair of the Graduate Department of Museum Studies at JFK University in Berkeley, California; assistant director at the Southwest Museum in Los Angeles; and museum educator at the Museum of Northern Arizona in Flagstaff.

Throughout her career, Anderson has been active in professional organizations as a board member of the American Association of Museums (AAM), an invited member of the AAM committee that produced *Excellence & Equity: Education and the Public Dimension of Museums,* and longtime board member and past president of the Western Museums Association Board of Directors. In 1997, she received the Director's Chair award for distinguished service and leadership from the Western Museums Association. She is a member of the national group of consultants, The Museum Group. Anderson is the author and editor of the AAM publication, *Museum Mission Statements: Building A Distinct Identity.* This volume is the second edition of the 2004 AltaMira Press publication, *Reinventing the Museum: Historical and Contemporary Perspectives on the Paradigm Shift.* Anderson continues her commitment to advancing the field through frequent speaking engagements, writing, and teaching. She is writing her next book, the companion book to *Reinventing the Museum,* with the working title of *A Framework for Revitalizing Museums.*